ESSENTIALS IN
CHURCH HISTORY

✶

A History of the Church from the Birth of Joseph Smith
to the Present Time, with Introductory Chapters
on the Antiquity of the Gospel and
the "Falling Away"

✶ ✶

Twenty-seventh Edition

1974
✶ ✶ ✶

BY JOSEPH FIELDING SMITH

✶ ✶ ✶ ✶

PUBLISHED BY
THE DESERET BOOK COMPANY
FOR
THE CHURCH OF JESUS CHRIST
OF LATTER-DAY SAINTS
1974

Library of Congress No. 67-21351
ISBN No. 0-87747-081-2

Copyright, 1950
GEORGE ALBERT SMITH
Trustee-in-Trust for the Church of Jesus Christ
of Latter-day Saints

Dear Lowell + Chris,

We love you with all of our hearts and feel priviledged to have been a part of the great event that has taken place in your lives. We know what choice special people you are and we treasure your friendship. We know that our friendship is an eternal one and always has been. Brother + Sister, thank you so much for sharing so much with us. We love you and want you to know that our prayers are with you and even though miles may someday separate us we are always with you in spirit.

Love ya,
Sister Moore
Sister Diehl

PREFACE

The need of a history of the Church in one volume that can be used for general reading, and at the same time meet the requirements of a textbook in the priesthood quorums, Church schools and auxiliary organizations, for a long time has been recognized. In the preparation of this volume, all these requirements have been given thoughtful consideration. As the title of the book, *Essentials in Church History*, implies, the vital and essential points of history and doctrine have been selected, and as far as possible, arranged in chronological order. The doctrines and revelations given to the Prophet Joseph Smith have been interwoven with the main story of the history in a manner, it is hoped, that will prove to be both interesting and instructive to the casual reader, as well as to the careful student. Moreover, the work has been prepared with the desire that the arrangement of the material will stimulate in the reader a zeal for further research and study of other and more extensive histories, particularly the *Documentary History of the Church*, in six volumes, which covers the period of the life of the Prophet Joseph Smith.

It is impossible to give, in one volume, in detail, all the important incidents in the history of the Church. However, this volume is sent forth on its mission with the hope that it will answer fully the purpose for which it was written.

Grateful appreciation is hereby acknowledged for invaluable assistance given by Dr. John A. Widtsoe, of the Council of the Twelve, in the preparation of the manuscript. I also desire to express sincere thanks to Elders Edward H. Anderson, J. M. Sjodahl, Andrew Jenson, August William Lund and others, who have so willingly and cheerfully assisted in the preparation of the work.

JOSEPH FIELDING SMITH

Table of Contents

PART ONE

INTRODUCTORY: THE GOSPEL IN ANCIENT AND MEDIAEVAL TIMES.

1.	Antiquity of the Gospel	1
2.	The Falling Away	6
3.	The Protestant Revolution	13

PART TWO

OPENING OF THE DISPENSATION OF THE FULNESS OF TIMES.

4.	Necessity for a Restoration	19
5.	The Ancestry of Joseph Smith	22
6.	Boyhood of Joseph Smith	28
7.	The Vision	36
8.	The Visitation of Moroni	43
9.	Joseph Smith Receives the Record—The Priesthood Restored	51
10.	The Witnesses of the Book of Mormon	61
11.	Revelation on Doctrine and Church Government	72
12.	Organization of the Church	78
13.	Beginning of the Public Ministry of the Church	81
14.	The Public Ministry of the Church (2)	92

PART THREE

THE OHIO AND MISSOURI PERIOD.

15.	Removal of the Church in New York to Ohio	100
16.	The Land of Zion	108
17.	The Book of Commandments—The Vision of the Glories—The Hiram Mobbing	115
18.	Organization of the First Presidency	124

CONTENTS

19. Expulsion from Jackson County 131
20. The Patriarchal Priesthood—Zion's Camp 141
21. Choosing of the Twelve and Seventy—Dedication of the Kirtland Temple 150
22. Clay County Rejects the Saints—Apostasy and Sorrow 162
23. The Presidency Move to Missouri 172
24. Difficulties in Missouri 181
25. Persecutions of the Saints 194
26. The Expulsion from Missouri 208

PART FOUR

THE NAUVOO PERIOD.

27. The Founding of Nauvoo 218
28. Foreign Missionary Labors 227
29. Appeal to Washington for Redress—Further Missouri Persecutions 238
30. The Nauvoo Temple and Ordinances Therein 250
31. Joseph Smith Accused as Accessory to Assault on Boggs 264
32. Doctrinal Development and Prophecy 275
33. Missouri's Third Attempt to Capture Joseph Smith 283
34. Joseph Smith's Candidacy for President—Nauvoo Conspiracy 291
35. The Martyrdom 303
36. The Succession of the Twelve Apostles — Preparation to Leave Nauvoo 318

PART FIVE

THE SETTLEMENT IN THE ROCKY MOUNTAINS.

37. The Exodus from Nauvoo 331
38. The Mormon Battalion 347
39. The Pioneers 356
40. The Land of Promise 371
41. Organization of the Presidency — Church Activities 1847-1849 380
42. Church Activities — 1850-1857 391
43. "The Utah War" 405
44. The Mountain Meadows Massacre 418
45. The Army in Utah 423
46. A Period of Strife and Bitterness 432
47. The Mission of Governor Shaffer and Judge McKean 448
48. Church Colonization and Progress 460

PART SIX

RECENT DEVELOPMENT.

49. The Second Period of Apostolic Presidency 468
50. The Administration of President John Taylor 478
51. The Administration of President Wilford Woodruff 491
52. The Administration of President Lorenzo Snow 501
53. The Administration of President Joseph F. Smith 507

CONTENTS

54.	The Administration of President Heber J. Grant	519
55.	The Administration of President George Albert Smith	532
56.	The Administration of President David O. McKay	537
57.	The Administration of President Joseph Fielding Smith	546
58.	The Administration of President Harold B. Lee	555
59.	The Administration of President Spencer W. Kimball	561
	The Auxiliary Organizations of the Church	567
	General Authorities of the Church	580
	Stakes of Zion	619
	Stakes of Zion—New Names	641
	Missions	650
	Church Publications	659
	Index	665

ILLUSTRATIONS

Birthplace of Joseph Smith, Sr.	24
Joseph Smith, the Prophet	28
Hyrum Smith, the Patriarch	30
Birthplace of Joseph Smith, the Prophet	31
The Sacred Grove	38
The Hill Cumorah	47
Circular Containing Characters from the Plates	53
The Susquehanna River	59
Oliver Cowdery	62
David Whitmer	63
Martin Harris	64
Book of Mormon Printing Press	68
Title Page of Book of Mormon	69
Sidney Rigdon	97
Title Page of Evening and Morning Star	117
Frederick G. Williams	127
Title Page of Doctrine and Covenants	156
The Kirtland Temple	160
Vauxhall Chapel, Preston, England	170
Lyman Wight's House, near Adam-ondi-Ahman	177
City of Nauvoo	222
Nauvoo Temple	255
Orson Hyde	258
Mount of Olives	259
The Mansion House, Nauvoo, Ill.	288
Proclamation Issued by Joseph Smith, Mayor of Nauvoo	306
Letter Written by Joseph Smith in Carthage Jail to his Wife	312
Brigham Young	320
Council Bluffs Ferry	337
Daniel H. Wells	345
Elkhorn River Crossing	358
Pioneer Camp at Wood River	359
Chimney Rock	363
Fort Laramie	364

CONTENTS

Orson Pratt 368
Erastus Snow 369
Salt Lake Valley in 1847 372
The Old Fort 376
Heber C. Kimball 381
Willard Richards 382
Kanesville 383
Deseret News Press 394
Hand-Cart Company on the Plains 398
Jedediah M. Grant 403
George A. Smith 440
St. George Temple 458
Brigham Young 459
John Taylor 469
The Endowment House 472
George Q. Cannon 480
Logan Temple 481
Wilford Woodruff 491
Manti Temple 492
Salt Lake Temple 492
Lorenzo Snow 501
Joseph F. Smith 507
John R. Winder 508
Anthon H. Lund 509
John Henry Smith 515
Charles W. Penrose 516
Heber J. Grant 519
Hawaiian Temple 520
Anthony W. Ivins 521
George Albert Smith 532
David O. McKay 537
Joseph Fielding Smith 546
Harold Bingham Lee 555
Spencer W. Kimball 561

MAPS

The New England States 32
New York and Pennsylvania 83
Ohio 102
Upper Missouri 199
Northern Illinois 292
The Mormon Battalion 349
The Pioneer Route 362

ESSENTIALS IN CHURCH HISTORY

PART ONE

Introductory: The Gospel in Ancient and Mediaeval Times

CHAPTER 1
ANTIQUITY OF THE GOSPEL

The Gospel Older than the Law.—From the time of the exodus from Egypt until the advent of Jesus Christ the Israelites were subject to the laws given to Moses. The belief is held by many that when the Savior supplanted these laws with the Gospel it was the first appearance among men of that great plan of salvation. The Gospel is much older than the law of Moses; it existed before the foundation of the world. Its principles are eternal, and were made known to the spirits of men in that antemortal day when Jesus Christ was chosen to be the "Lamb slain from the foundation of the world." All necessary preparations were made in the spirit life for the peopling of this earth in a mortal existence. It was there decided that Adam should come to this earth and stand as the progenitor of the race.

The Fall of Man and His Redemption.—That Adam and his posterity might gain the experience that can only be obtained in mortality, it was necessary that he should break the law by which he was governed in the Garden of Eden, and thereby subject himself and his posterity to death. To gain an exaltation man must have experience and must exercise his free will. Then, knowing both good and evil, by obeying the will of the Father he will receive a reward for the good deeds done while in the flesh. The fall of man brought temptation, sin and death. It was therefore essential that a Redeemer be provided through whose atonement for the fall, all men, without regard to their belief, race, or color, are entitled to come forth in the resurrection of the dead, to be judged according to their works. "For since by man came death, by man came also the resurrection of the dead. For as in Adam all die, even so in Christ shall all be made alive" (1 Cor. 15:21-22).

Individual Salvation Taught to Adam.—Individual salvation requires that a man must repent and accept the fulness of the Gospel if he would be exalted in the kingdom of God. This plan of salvation was taught to Adam after his expulsion from the Garden of Eden. He was baptized in water for the remission of his sins, in the name of the only Begotten of the Father, and received the Holy Ghost. He and his wife, Eve, were commanded to teach their children the Gospel, that they also "might be sanctified from all sin, and enjoy the words of eternal life in this world, and eternal life in the world to come, even immortal glory" (Moses ch. 6).

In obedience to this commandment Adam and Eve made all these things known to their sons and daughters. Thus the Gospel was taught in the beginning and was declared from generation to generation. Adam received the Holy Priesthood, which was also conferred upon the patriarchs who followed after him. They were "preachers of righteousness, and spake and prophesied, and called upon all men, everywhere, to repent, and faith was taught unto the children of men" (Moses 6:23).

The Gospel Rejected in Days of Noah.—In the days of Noah the Gospel was universally rejected, save by Noah and his immediate family—in all eight souls. Noah had labored diligently and long to bring mankind to repentance, but without avail, "for all flesh had corrupted his way upon the earth" (Moses 8:29). After the destruction of the wicked in the flood, the Gospel continued to be taught by Noah and the later patriarchs, but quite generally it was not received. Melchizedek, king of Salem, through his faithfulness, became a great high priest, and the people of the Church in his day honored him by calling the "Holy Priesthood after the order of the Son of God," by his name, "out of respect or reverence to the name of the Supreme Being" (Doc. and Cov. 107:4). From Melchizedek, Abraham received the Priesthood, and to Melchizedek, as the properly authorized servant of the Lord, Abraham paid tithes of all he possessed (Gen. 14:20).

The Covenant with Abraham.—Unto Abraham also was the Gospel preached and the Lord made covenant with him that through him and his posterity should all nations of the earth be blessed (Gen. 22:18). This same Gospel was also declared to the children of Israel in its simple truth; but they proved unworthy to receive it in its fulness, due to their long sojourn in Egypt, where they had partaken of the customs, traditions and theology of the Egyptians, and therefore "the word preached did not profit them, not being mixed with faith in them that heard it" (Heb. 4:2). The Lord endeavored to establish the fulness of his Gospel and authority among them, which Moses plainly taught, and he sought to sanctify the people, "that they might behold the face of God; but they hardened their hearts and could not endure his presence, therefore the Lord in his wrath (for his anger was kindled against them) swore that they should not enter into his rest while in the wilderness, which rest is the fulness of his glory" (Doc. and Cov. 84:23-24).

The Higher Priesthood and the Carnal Law.—It became necessary, therefore, for the Lord to take Moses and the Higher Priesthood out of their midst, but the Lesser Priesthood, which holds the keys of the ministering of angels and the preparatory Gospel—faith, repentance and baptism for the remission of sins—he permitted to remain. To this he added the carnal law, known as the law of Moses, which was added, so Paul informs us, as a schoolmaster to prepare them to receive the fulness of the Gospel when restored by Jesus Christ.

The Israelites, from the time they entered the promised land, to the coming of the Son of God, were living under the law of Moses, which laid upon them severe and exacting restrictions because of their refusal to receive the fulness of the Gospel when it was offered in the wilderness. When the Savior came, it was to complete and fulfil the ends of this law, of which he said not one jot or tittle should pass until all was fulfilled.

Dispensation of the Meridian of Time.—In the Dispensation of the Meridian of Time, when the Savior ministered among the Jews, he restored the Gospel with the Higher Priesthood. He called and ordained Twelve Apostles and gave them power, before his ascension into heaven, to complete the church organization, and commissioned them to carry the message of divine salvation into all the world. In restoring that which had been taken away, he annulled the carnal law, which had been added in the place of the higher law, for it had filled the measure of its creation.

Commission of the Apostles.—Under the commission Jesus gave the apostles to carry the Gospel message into all the world and preach it to every creature, they commenced their active ministry on the day of Pentecost, preaching in power to the convincing of many souls. As the work of the ministry grew, and the assistance of other laborers was required to carry on the work, men were divinely called and ordained to specific offices in the Church. The Lord, himself, had called and ordained, besides the twelve, seventies, and sent them forth throughout Judea bearing the message of truth. When they returned from that missionary journey, it was with much rejoicing because even the devils were subject unto them. What other officers the Lord ordained and set apart, the scriptures do not reveal. That the Twelve Apostles were empowered to set in order all things pertaining to the Church, is, nevertheless, beyond dispute. We learn that under their direction and ministry, as branches were formed and the work of the ministry required it, high priests, evangelists, (patriarchs), elders, bishops, deacons, priests, pastors and teachers were called into the service of the Church. The organization was in this manner effected during the days of the apostles. The Church was also blessed with the divine gifts and blessings of the Spirit of the Lord in those early days, just as it was during the Savior's ministry. There were in the Church many prophets who uttered, by the gift of the Holy Ghost, many remarkable predictions.

Essential Offices in the Church.—All of these offices in the Church are essential to the advancement of the members and cannot be discarded with impunity. Paul said, the Lord "gave some apostles; and some prophets; and some evangelists; and some pastors and teachers; for the perfecting of the saints, for the work of the ministry, for the edifying of the body of Christ." These were not merely to remain in the Church during the formative period, or for a brief season in order to start the work, and then to be replaced by other officers of another kind. Men were ordained to these callings "for the edifying of the body of Christ, till we all come to the unity of the faith, and of the knowledge of the Son of God, unto a perfect man, unto the measure of the stature of the fulness of Christ" (Eph. 4:12-13). Evidently, then, as long as there is imperfection in the Church among the members, in doctrine, knowledge, or love, they fall short of "the stature of the fulness of Christ."

These officers are all needed and cannot justly be removed, for the Lord never so intended. The writer of the epistle to the Ephesians also further compares all these officers to the various parts of the human body and says: "From whom the whole body fitly joined together and compacted by that which every joint supplieth, according to the effectual working in the measure of every part, maketh increase of the body unto the edifying of itself in love." This same apostle also likens the spiritual gifts to the physical body, declaring each to be essential in the Church, just as the parts of the body are each necessary and one part cannot say to another, "I have no need of you," for all are necessary that all men may "profit withal."

CHAPTER 2

THE FALLING AWAY

The Body of the Church Destroyed.—Notwithstanding that the early officers of the Church were endowed with the Holy Priesthood and exercised the spiritual gifts, which were to remain until all came "unto a perfect man unto the stature of the fulness of Christ," there came a great and terrible change, absolutely destroying the perfect body of the Church. In its place arose a strange organization which eventually gained dominion over the earth and ruled the destinies of men, not in love unfeigned, but in blood and carnage most appalling, and with an iron hand.

The Falling Away Predicted.—The rise of this power had been predicted by many of the prophets of old and by the apostles of our Lord. Even the Savior, when instructing his disciples regarding the signs of the times, intimated that this would occur. Isaiah, seven centuries before the birth of Christ, predicted that the time would come when the earth would be defiled under its inhabitants because of the transgression of the law, the changing of ordinances and the breaking of the new and everlasting covenant. It is evident that this was to occur in the latter days, and not in the days of Israel's subjection to the law, for the law of Moses was not an everlasting covenant. This prophecy was to receive its consummation in the day when the earth, defiled by the wickedness and corruption of its inhabitants, should be cleansed by fire and few men left (Isaiah 24:1-6).

The Prophecies of Isaiah and Amos.—Speaking of this event Isaiah says: "For the Lord hath poured out upon you the spirit of deep sleep, and hath closed your eyes: the prophets and your rulers, the seers hath he covered." Shortly before this time, Amos also predicted that the time would come when the Lord would send a famine in the land, "not a famine of bread," said he, "nor a thirst for water, but of hearing the words of the Lord."

The Vision of Daniel.—Daniel saw in the vision the overthrow of the Church established by the Savior in the meridian of time. In his vision of the four beasts, representing the kingdoms seen by Nebuchadnezzar in his dream, he saw one horn, or power, come up among the ten that succeeded the Roman Empire, "more stout than his fellows." This horn had eyes and a mouth that spake very great words against the Most High, and three other kingdoms were subdued by this great horn. The same power "made war with the saints and prevailed against them," and through continued conflict and exrcise of might was able to "wear out the saints of the Most High" and thought to "change times and laws." This blasphemous power was to rule until the coming of the Ancient of Days, when the Kingdom and dominion was to be "given to the people of the saints of the Most High whose kingdom is an everlasting kingdom."

Apostasy Commenced in Days of Apostles.—The falling away from the faith commenced before the close of the ministry of the apostles. Paul, when at Miletus taking his final departure from the elders of Ephesus who had come to meet him, earnestly entreated them to take heed to feed the Church of God, for, said he, "I know this, that after my departing shall grievous wolves enter in among you, not sparing the flock, and of yourselves shall men arise, speaking perverse things to draw away disciples after them." He also took occasion to warn the Saints at Thessalonica not to be deceived regarding the ushering in of the second advent of the Son of God, "for that day," he wrote to them, "shall not come, except there come a falling away first, and that man of sin be revealed, the son of perdition; who opposeth and exalteth himself above all that is called God, or that is worshiped; so that he as God sitteth in the temple of God, showing himself that he is God."

The Predictions of Paul.—The Saints at Galatia commenced very early to depart from the faith. Timothy was warned by Paul, and instructed that in the last days perilous times would come and men would be "lovers of their ownselves, covetous, boasters, proud, blasphemers, disobedient to parents, unthankful, unholy, without natural affection, truce breakers, false accusers, incontinent, fierce, despisers of those that are good, traitors, heady, highminded, lovers of pleasures more than lovers of God; having a form of godliness but denying the power thereof." Moreover, he said the time would come, "when they will not endure sound doctrine; but after their own lusts shall they heap to themselves teachers, having itching ears; and they shall turn away their ears from the truth, and shall be turned unto fables."

Prophecy of Peter.—Peter, likewise, by the spirit of prophecy, bore record of the departure from the faith when he wrote to the Saints saying: "But there were false prophets also among the people, even as there shall be false teachers among you, who privily shall bring in damnable heresies, even denying the Lord that bought them, and bring upon themselves swift destruction. And many shall follow their pernicious ways; by reason of whom the way of truth shall be evil spoken of." Then he sought to impress upon the minds of the Saints the fact that the prophets before him had also predicted these direful events, saying: "That ye may be mindful of the words which were spoken before by the holy prophets, and of the commandment of us the apostles of the Lord and Savior; knowing this first, that there shall come in the last days scoffers, walking after their own lusts, and saying: Where is the promise of his coming? for since the fathers fell asleep, all things continue as they were from the beginning of the creation."

The Mystery of Iniquity.—As already stated, Paul declared to the Thessalonians that the "mystery of iniquity" was already at work, and to Timothy he said: "All they which are in Asia be turned away from me." He had, we are led to believe, had some dispute with Asiatic converts, for he wrote to Timothy in great sorrow because some of his companions had forsaken him and were advocating doctrines contrary to the Gospel of Jesus Christ. In trying to correct these evils he was left to contend alone, for he adds: "At my first answer no man stood with me, but all men forsook me."

Decline of Spiritual Gifts.—It was not long after the departure of the apostles that spiritual gifts ceased to be manifest in the Church. The decline of these blessings, which are inseparably connected with the Church of Christ, led to the belief, so prevalent even in this day, that they were not to be continued, having been instituted in the incipiency of the Church, merely as a means of aiding in its establishment, after which they were no longer needed.

Revelation and heavenly communication also came to an end. There was no more vision, for the people had closed their eyes. This condition also led to the universal belief, which the world holds even now, that the canon of scripture is full and there is to be no more scripture, notwithstanding the Lord has revealed through his servants that revelation is to continue.

Changes in Church Government.—The offices in the Priesthood were also changed because those unto whom the Gospel was preached would not endure sound doctrine, but after their own lusts heaped to themselves teachers having itching ears and were "men of corrupt minds, reprobate concerning the faith."

The Church Taken from Among Men.—Instead of apostles and prophets there came, as time went on, a very different ecclesiastical order from that instituted by the Lord. The Church established by the Redeemer was taken from the earth because of continued persecution and apostasy, until there was but a dead form of the true Church left. The great ecclesiastical organization that arose and claimed to be the Church of Christ was of gradual growth. The change from truth to error was not made all in one day. It commenced in the first century and continued during the immediate centuries that followed, until the Church established in the days of the apostles was no more to be found among men. Without the direction of inspired men, who could communicate with God, the change was a natural one.

Rise of the Church of Rome.—In the beginning of the fourth century this great religious power, under the Emperor Constantine became the state religion of the Roman Empire. From that time forth its dominion spread and before many years had passed away it became the ruling power in religion in the so-called civilized world. By it "times and laws" were changed. The simple principles of the Christian faith were embellished almost beyond recognition with pomp and mystic rites borrowed from pagan worship. The priests and potentates, who officiated in these ceremonies, no longer followed the simple customs of the humble fishermen of Galilee, but dressed in splendid and costly robes, with mitres on their heads, they performed their various parts in pride and with mystifying ceremonies that over-awed and bewildered the humble people.

Changes in the Doctrines of the Church.—The correct doctrine regarding the Godhead taught by Jesus Christ, was changed into a mystery. The ordinance of baptism was changed from burial in the water for remission of sins, to sprinkling of a little water on the head. Sprinkling of infants, miscalled baptism, a custom which "is mockery before God, denying the mercies of Christ, and the power of the Holy Spirit," became a fixed and universal custom. Changes in the administration of the sacrament of the Lord's supper were also introduced, and the doctrine advanced that the bread and wine became the flesh and blood of our crucified Redeemer, by transubstantiation. Those who entered the ministry were forbidden to marry, and many other changes, which need not be mentioned here, were made in the principles of the Gospel, in the functions of the Priesthood and the worship of the Lord.

Temporal Power of the Pope.—Rome became the capital of this ecclesiastical power and the bishop or pope, as he was called, its head. As its power grew it claimed dominion not only in matter religious, but in civil affairs as well. During the acme of its glory it ruled practically the known world. By it kings were made and by it they were dethroned. Unless they bowed before the papal power in abject submission they were made to feel the weight of its mighty hand.

Frederick Seebohm, in his *Era of the Protestant Revolution*, says: "Kings were not secure on their thrones till they had the sanction of the Church. On the other hand the clergy claimed to be free from prosecution under the criminal laws of the land they lived in. They struggled to keep their own ecclesiastical laws and their own ecclesiastical courts, receiving authority direct from Rome, and with final appeal, not to the crown, but to the pope."

"To establish an accusation against a bishop," writes Motley, in his *Rise of the Dutch Republic*, "seventy-two witnesses were necessary; against a deacon, twenty-seven; against an inferior dignitary, seven; while two were sufficient to convict a layman" (Vol. 1, p. 60).

Power of the Clergy.—Few outside of the clergy were educated enough to read and write; therefore priests became the lawyers, diplomats, ambassadors, instructors and prime ministers in the nations. All learned men talked and wrote in Latin, which was the language of Rome. It is said that for centuries a man convicted of a crime in England, by showing that he could read or write, could claim the benefits of a trial in the ecclesiastical court, which, "by long abuse came to mean exemption from the punishment of the criminal law of the land."

Not only did the priests fill these important offices where they were enabled to wield great power and to control, very largely, the destinies of nations, but many of them became extremely avaricious and "divined for money." Jean Valdez, brother of the secretary to King Charles V, wrote of the times as follows: "I see that we can scarcely get anything from Christ's ministers but for money; at baptism money, at bishoping money, at marriage money, for confession money—no, not extreme unction without money! They will ring no bells without money, no burial in Church without money; so that it seemeth that Paradise is shut up from them that have no money. The rich is buried in the Church, the poor in the church-yard. The rich may marry with his nearest kin, but the poor not so, albeit he be ready to die for love of her. The rich may eat flesh in Lent, but the poor may not, albeit fish perhaps be much dearer. The rich man may readily get large indulgences, but the poor none, because he wanteth money to pay for them" (*Era of the Protestant Revolution,*" p. 60).

In addition to all this they taxed the people in various ways, receiving a tithing from all produce of the farms, a tenth of the land and of the wages of the working man. Writes Motley: "Not content, moreover, with their territories and their tithings, the churchmen perpetually devised new burdens upon the peasantry. Plows, sickles, horses, oxen, all implements of husbandry were taxed for the benefit of those who toiled not, but who gathered into barns."

Sale of Indulgences.—Some of these ecclesiastical rulers became so avaricious and filled with the spirit of greed that they advanced the blasphemous doctrine of forgiving sins by the sale of indulgences. It is claimed by the church of Rome that these evils were the sins of individuals who perverted the doctrine of the church in relation to penance and forgiveness of sin. The indulgence was, according to their teaching, "a pardon usually granted by the pope, through which the contrite sinner escaped a part, or all, of the punishment which remained even after he had been absolved. The pardon did not therefore forgive the guilt of the sinner, for that had necessarily to be removed before the indulgence was granted; it only removed or mitigated the penalties which even the forgiven sinner would, without the indulgence, have expected to undergo in purgatory."[a]

However, the sale of indulgences in various parts of Europe, was a means of creating large fortunes for those who sanctioned it. There was no crime in the category for which the power of forgiveness was not offered if the party seeking it could pay the price. The various countries were districted and farmed for the collection of these revenues, according to John Lathrop Motley, the historian, who writes:

"The price current of the wares offered for sale was published in every town and village [in the Netherlands]. God's pardon for crimes already committed, or about to be committed, was advertised according to a graded tariff. Thus poisoning, for example, was absolved for eleven ducats, six livres tournois. Absolution for incest was afforded at thirty-six livres, three ducats. Perjury came to seven livres and three carlines. Pardon for murder, if not by poison, was cheaper. Even a parricide could buy forgiveness at God's tribunal at one ducat, four livres, eight carlines. Henry de Mountfort, in the year 1448, purchased absolution for that crime at that price. Was it strange that a century or so of this kind of work should produce a

---

[a]"History of Western Europe," p. 39, James Harvey Robinson.

Luther? Was it unnatural that plain people, who loved the ancient Church, should rather desire to see her purged of such blasphemous abuses than to hear of St. Peter's dome rising a little nearer to the clouds on these proceeds of commuted crime? * * * The Netherlands, like other countries, are districted and farmed for the collection of this papal revenue. Much of the money thus raised remains in the hands of the vile collectors. Sincere Catholics, who love and honor the ancient religion, shrink with horror at the spectacle offered on every side. Criminals buying paradise for money, monks spending the money thus paid in gaming houses, taverns, and brothels; this seems to those who have studied their Testaments a different scheme of salvation from the one promulgated by Christ. There has evidently been a departure from the system of earlier apostles. Innocent conservative souls are much perplexed; but at last all these infamies arouse a giant to do battle with the giant wrong."[b]

Thus were the prophecies of the scriptures fulfilled; the laws transgressed by a power that exalted itself "above all that is called God" and in his sacred name speaking "great words against the Most High."

---

[b]"The Rise of the Dutch Republic," Vol. 1, pp. 63-66, Motley.

CHAPTER 3

THE PROTESTANT REVOLUTION

The "Dark Ages."—Not content with absolute dominion over the spiritual and temporal affairs of the people, this papal kingdom attempted the exercise of authority also over the consciences of men. Especially was this so during the dark ages, when this power was at the zenith of its glory. This exercise of authority extended also far into the day when the light of religious freedom commenced to break forth, during the period known as the revival of learning. Previous to this revival, as we have seen, the language of learning was the Latin tongue. The people were helplessly dependent upon their priests for all instruction in scientific as well as religious thought. The few copies of the Bible extant were guarded by the clergy, and the scriptures were not accessible to the common people, and since they could neither read nor write, and in very few instances understood Latin, they would have been helpless even with the Bible in their hands. Under these conditions it is not to be wondered at that the poor people of those benighted countries of Europe, credulous and filled with superstitious fear, were ready to accept almost anything that was made known to them, in doctrine or deed, by unscrupulous priests.

The Revival of Learning.—Neither is it to be wondered at that priests attempted to use force and coercion during the revival of learning to check the opportunities of the people in obtaining light and truth. It was due to the exercise of greater knowledge on the part of the priests and their performance of mystic ceremonies, that over-awed the people and enabled the clergy to keep them shackled by the chains of ignorance and superstition. Ignorance was a ready tool in the hands of the priests by which they shaped and moulded the masses into vessels to their liking. The increase of learning among the people, aided by the discoveries and inventions of the times, would change all this; for the people would not be so ready to accept every wind of doctrine without some mental cogitation and desire to have a reason given why things were thus and so. Moreover, the revival of learning meant the end of many practices and blasphemous doctrines advanced in the name of Jesus Christ, such as the exercise of force over the consciences of men and the sale of indulgences for the pardon of sin—if not the end, at least a wonderful modification of such an evil system.

Early Translations of the Bible.—Evidently this ruling ecclesiastical power realized that enlightened conditions would bring rebellion against its authority. For that reason stringent laws were framed to enforce the edicts and regulations of the church of Rome: During the "Reformation" and before, there were several translations of the Bible made in the languages which the common people understood. Wycliffe's Bible appeared in 1380 and was followed by translations at a later date, both in English and other tongues. At first there was an attempt to destroy these copies which were prepared without authority or sanction from the Catholic Church. With the invention of printing in the fifteenth century, however, the cause of religious freedom received a wonderful impetus, and Bibles were distributed all over Europe. Before the time of printing, a Bible cost five hundred crowns, and such copies as were in existence were in the keeping of the clergy, who guarded them with the utmost zeal. Through the aid of printing, the price of Bibles was reduced to five crowns, which made it possible for the people not only to have the privilege of hearing the scriptures read in their own tongue, but also to acquire the understanding by which they could read them for themselves.

Scripture-Reading Forbidden.—An English chronicler, Henry Kneighton, many years before the "Reformation" expressed the prevailing notion about the reading of the scriptures when he denounced the general reading of the Bible, lamenting "lest the jewel of the Church, hitherto the exclusive property of the clergy and divines, should be made common to the laity." Archbishop Arundel in England had issued an enactment that "no part of the scriptures in English should be read, either in public or in private, or be thereafter translated, under pain of the greater excommunication." The New Testament translation of Erasmus was forbidden at Cambridge, and the Vicar of Croyden said from his pulpit: "We must root out printing, or printing will root us out." In the reign of Henry VIII the reading of the Bible by the common people, or those who were not of the privileged class, had been prohibited by act of Parliament, and men were burned at the stake in England as well as in the Netherlands and other parts of Europe for having even fragments of the scriptures in their hands.

For those who were considered derelict in church duties or heretical in doctrine, edicts were declared, forbidding them to gather in private assemblies for devotion, in various parts of Europe. All reading of the scriptures; all discussion within one's own doors concerning faith, the sacraments, the papal authority, or other religious matter, was forbidden "under penalty of death. The edicts were no dead letter. The fires were kept constantly supplied with human fuel by monks who knew the act of burning reformers better than of arguing with them. The scaffold was the most conclusive of syllogisms, and used upon all occasions" (*The Rise of the Dutch Republic,* Motley).

The Inquisition.—Continuing this woeful account of conditions in the rebellious Netherlands and other countries under Spanish rule, the author of *The Rise of the Dutch Republic* says: "Charles V introduced and organized a papal institution, side by side with those horrible 'Placards' of his invention, which constituted a masked inquisition even more cruel than that of Spain. * * * The execution of the system was never permitted to languish. The number of Netherlanders who were burned, strangled, beheaded, or buried alive, in obedience to his edicts, and for the offense of reading the scriptures, of looking askance at a graven image, or of ridiculing the actual presence of the body and blood of Christ in a wafer, have been placed as high as one hundred thousand by distinguished authorities, and have never been put at a lower mark than fifty thousand."

Dawning of a Better Day.—Conditions like these could not go on forever. The dawn of a better day began to break over the nations. The Spirit of the Lord was striving with men and preparations commenced for the introduction into the world of the re-established Gospel at a later day. It was necessary that the shackles of superstitious fear and illiteracy, which bound the world so completely, should be broken, that men might exercise their right of free agency before the fulness of Gospel light should break forth. Not only was advancement made in the art of printing, but there came a revival of learning and research in all directions and in all parts of Europe. It was not confined to one land or to one people, but the whole of

Europe took on a new life. The discovery of the telescope, the law of gravitation, the invention of gunpowder and many other wonderful things were revolutionizing the thoughts of men.

The Mission of Columbus.—With the discovery of the mariner's compass navigators became more bold and daring, and gradually extended their explorations until they discovered the way to India around the Cape of Good Hope. Near the close of the fifteenth century the belief prevailed that the earth was flat and inhabited only on the upper side. Beyond the shores of lands then known it was thought there hung a pall of fog and darkness. The sea was referred to as the "Sea of Darkness" beyond the boundaries known to man. Far off in or beyond the ocean it was believed great dragons had their lair, and if any man should be so unfortunate as to drift among them he would return no more. Mariners had been afraid to traverse the seas far beyond the sight of land. Shortly before the end of this century there came one navigator more daring than his fellows, who proposed to cross the sea. After many pleading and attempts to interest some one with means in the venture, he finally succeeded and the remarkable feat was done. In accomplishing this he made discoveries that the Lord, in his wisdom, had kept hid from the nations of the east all down through the ages, until in his own due time, he desired them to be revealed. Columbus was moved upon by the Spirit of the Lord and crossed the waters in fulfilment of predictions made by a prophet, who lived on this continent, five hundred years before the birth of Christ.

The "Reformation."—All these things played an important part in the establishment of individual and religious freedom. The most important agency of all in this great work was doubtless the so-called "Reformation," which was in fact a revolution from the bondage of the church of Rome. Great men of intellectual power began to undermine the thraldom of the religious world. This rebellion against the dominion of Rome was almost simultaneous in the various lands. In England, Scandinavia, France, Switzerland, the Netherlands and Germany, many "reformers" arose near the end of the fifteenth and during the sixteenth century. They were of varying degrees of enthusiasm and opposition to the teachings of that time. In the beginning their only desire was to correct evils within the Catholic Church, but failing in this many of them openly rebelled and set up independent churches of their own.

Martin Luther.—The greatest of these "reformers" was Martin Luther in Germany, who did more than any other individual in casting off the yoke of bondage placed upon the people by the papacy. Powerful princes came to his aid, but there was not in Germany at that time the cohesion of the people, or the centralization of power, that existed in England under Henry VIII, or in Sweden, where Gustavus Vasa reigned. Luther's task, therefore, was a heavy one, but he nobly carried it through to the bitter end.

The Protestant Revolution a Preparatory Work.—Their mission was not, however, to set up the Church of Christ, for the time was not ripe, and that important event was reserved for another generation. They were called to be forerunners of that eventful day, and did much to prepare the world for the ushering in of the Dispensation of the Fulness of Times. The Lord did not call them to their great work by an opening of the heavens; by visitation of angels or direct communication, as in times of old; neither did any of them claim that in this manner they had been called. Nevertheless it was the Spirit of the Lord which rested upon them and inspired them to fight against the abominations and practices of their times committed in the name of religion. Such, at least, was the case with most of them. The motive of Henry VIII of England, was a selfish one; yet the Lord brought good out of it in behalf of religious freedom. At first Henry opposed the rebellion of Luther and others most vigorously, even writing in defense of the pope of Rome, for which service he received the benediction of the pope and the title of "Defender of the Faith." Afterwards, when his own interests were in conflict with the policy of the Catholic Church and in no wise he could prevail, he became rebellious, with the result that he was excommunicated by the pope. In defense he established an independent church, known today as the Church of England, of which he became the head. Parliament and the people were back of him and thus the great state church of England was brought into being.

Disagreement Among "Reformers."—The pity of it all is that these "reformers" when they established their religious freedom, could not agree among themselves. They were constantly in turmoil, contending one with another on points of doctrine, which led to considerable bitterness and the establishing of various and conflicting sects. Moreover, they had not learned the lesson themselves, through all the persecutions they were forced to suffer, that toleration was a fundamental principle of freedom. Because this great lesson had not been learned the persecuted became the persecutors in many cases, and were just as intolerant where they had the power with those who disagreed with them as their enemies had been with them.

America a Land of Freedom.—Nevertheless the seeds of toleration had been sown, but they were of slow growth. Toleration was a matter of education and therefore came by degrees and could not burst forth in full fruition at once. Not until there had been much shedding of blood in Europe, and more particularly in America during the war for independence, were the people fully awakened to this truth. It required a planting in new soil in a choice land above all other lands. Here in America freedom and religious toleration became a fundamental part of our great government. Our land became a land of refuge for the afflicted, the downtrodden, and the oppressed of other nations, who found in the United States a haven of rest; for this land had been dedicated to liberty by the shedding of blood.

Praise be to the great souls who conducted the Protestant Revolution. They helped to make it possible for the establishment of The Church of Jesus Christ of Latter-day Saints in the early part of the nineteenth century, preparatory to the second coming of the Son of God. For all the good they did we honor them, and they shall receive their reward which shall be great. They were not restorers, but were sent to prepare the way for one who was yet to come with a mission of restoration and everlasting power.

PART TWO

Opening of the Dispensation of the Fulness of Times

CHAPTER 4

NECESSITY FOR A RESTORATION

The Marvelous Work.—The work of the Protestant revolution having been accomplished, and the land of America having been prepared by the sowing of the seed of religious freedom, the time for the restoration of the Gospel had arrived. The promise made by the Savior that the Gospel of the kingdom should be preached in all the world for a witness, was about to be fulfilled, and the Church of Jesus Christ was again to be established in the earth. The "marvelous work and a wonder," which Isaiah predicted should come forth in the latter days, was about to make its appearance, to the confounding of the wisdom of the worldly wise.

Reasonable and Scriptural to Expect a Restoration.—It is reasonable as well as scriptural, to believe that the Lord, before he shall come in judgment and to commence his reign of a thousand years, will send a messenger to prepare the way before him. In justice the people should be warned and given the privilege of repentance and remission of sins, through the preaching of the Gospel, and have an opportunity for membership in the Church of Christ. "Surely the Lord God will do nothing," said Amos, "until he revealeth the secret unto his servants the prophets."[a]

Ancient Predictions to be Fulfilled.—Many of the ancient prophets had spoken of the opening of the heavens and revealing anew to man, the everlasting Gospel, before the second coming of the Lord. The visitation of heavenly messengers, and the pouring out of the Spirit of the Lord, in which the sons and daughters of Israel should prophesy, old men dream dreams, and the young men see visions, were also foretold as events for the latter days.

Daniel Saw Our Day.—Daniel, in vision, while an exile at the court of Babylon's great king, saw our day and the work of setting up the kingdom which should be given to the Saints of the Most High, who should possess it "even forever and forever." The same event he confirmed in the interpretation of Nebuchadnezzar's dream of the wonderfully constructed image. It was to be in the last days at a time when the kingdoms represented by the toes of the image should bear rule. In that day the God of heaven will "set up a kingdom which shall never be destroyed, or left to other people."

Vision of John.—John also saw the time when the Gospel should be declared by an angel flying in the midst of heaven "having the everlasting Gospel to preach unto them that dwell on the earth, and to every nation, and kindred, and tongue, and people, saying with a loud voice, Fear God, and give glory to him; for the hour of his judgment is come; and worship him that made heaven, and earth, and the sea, and the fountains of waters." This also was to be in the last day, when the people were departed from the teachings of the Lord, and needed a call unto repentance, for this angel was to be followed by another who should say: "Babylon is fallen, is fallen," and before Babylon should fall, she was to be warned and given a chance of repentance.

Joseph Smith Divinely Called.—It was necessary, therefore, that one should be chosen and clothed with power from the Father to re-establish the Church of Jesus Christ on the earth.[b] In choosing a

---

[a]Amos 3:7. The Prophet Joseph Smith's revision.
[b]The erroneous idea which prevails in the world in relation to the Church, is set forth in Smith's Bible Dictionary, Article—Church, Vol. 1, p. 458, as follows: "We have seen that according to the scriptural view the Church is a holy kingdom, established by God on earth, of which Christ is the invisible king—it is a divinely organized body, the members of which are knit together amongst themselves, and joined to Christ their Head, by the Holy Spirit, who dwells in and animates it; it is a spiritual but visible society of men united by constant succession to those who were personally united to the Apostles, holding the same faith that the Apostles held, administering the same sacraments, and like them forming separate, but only locally separate, assemblies, for the public worship of God. This is the Church according to the Divine intention. But as God permits

NECESSITY FOR A RESTORATION

representative to stand at the head of this "great and marvelous work about to come forth unto the children of men," the Lord did not select one who was versed in the learning and traditions of the world. His ways are not the ways of man, neither are his thoughts like the thoughts of men. One taught in the learning of the world would have had too much to unlearn of the traditions and philosophy of men. In his great wisdom the Lord chose an unsophisticated child—a boy fourteen years of age. Unto this youth the Lord revealed the fulness of the gospel, which the world would not receive because of unbelief. Through years of heavenly guidance—for he was instructed by messengers from the presence of the Lord—this young man, Joseph Smith, was prepared to direct the work of the restoration of the Gospel and the building of the Kingdom of God.

---

men to mar the perfection of his designs in their behalf, and as men have both corrupted the doctrines and broken the unity of the Church, we must not expect to see the Church of Holy Scripture actually existing in its perfection on earth. It is not to be found, thus perfect, either in the collected fragments of Christendom, or still less in any one of these fragments; though it is possible that one of those fragments more than another may approach the scriptural and Apostolic ideas which existed only until sin, heresy, and schism, had time sufficiently to develop themselves to do their work."

CHAPTER 5

THE ANCESTRY OF JOSEPH SMITH

1638-1805

Ancestry of Joseph Smith.—Joseph Smith was born in Sharon, Windsor County, Vermont, December 23, 1805. He was the third son and fourth child of Joseph and Lucy Mack Smith, who had a family of ten children. His parents were of sturdy New England stock, honest, godfearing, industrious, but poor in worldly substance. Joseph Smith had descended on his paternal side from Robert Smith, who emigrated from England in the year 1638. Robert Smith was born August 6, 1626, in Sutterton, Lincolnshire, England. His father was also named Robert Smith, born in 1589 in Sutterton, Lincolnshire, England. His mother, Margaret, was born about 1593 in Frampton, Lincolnshire, England. He had two brothers, Edward and the other also by the name of Robert, and one sister, Margaret. In his early youth he went to Boston, Lincolnshire, and then to London, where he took ship for America. He landed in Boston, Massachusetts, and moved to that part of Rowley, in Essex County, which afterwards became the township of Boxford. Here, later, he purchased two hundred eight acres of land, a portion of which was in Topsfield township. He married Miss Mary French. They were the parents of ten children. Robert was known among his neighbors as a quiet, unassuming man, devoted to the welfare of the settlement. Through his industry he was able to provide some comforts for his family, who were reared in the prevailing religious teachings of that day, but strictly in the knowledge of the scriptures.

Patriotic Service of Samuel Smith.—Samuel, son of Robert and Mary, was born January 26, 1666. He married Rebecca, daughter of

THE ANCESTRY OF JOSEPH SMITH 23

John Curtis, a prominent citizen of the town of Topsfield. After his father's death, Samuel moved to Topsfield, where he became an influential member of that community and was honored by the citizens with several offices of trust. He was the father of nine children. His son Samuel, born January 26, 1714, was one of the most prominent citizens of Topsfield. The greater part of his life was spent in the service of the people. He passed through the stormy days of the American Revolution and bore arms in defense of the liberties of the people. Among the many positions he held are the following;—He was grand juryman in 1760; in 1770, road supervisor; in 1779, 1780, 1783, 1784 and 1785, on the committee of safety; from 1771 to 1777 and in 1781 and 1782, assessor and selectman in Topsfield, declining the honor in 1783; he was moderator in 1758-60, 1762, 1764, 1766-73, 1777-80, and 1782-83; representative to the General Court (House of Representatives) in 1764-70, 1772, 1777-78, and 1781; town clerk in 1774, 1776 and 1777; delegate to the Provincial Congress at Concord, October 11, 1774, and again January 19, 1775, and on the tea committee, from Topsfield and acted as chairman, in 1773.

He was known as Captain Samuel Smith, receiving his military title during service in the militia of Massachusetts. He married Priscilla, daughter of Zacheus Gould of Topsfield. They had five children, two sons and three daughters. The mother died shortly after the birth of her youngest child, and Samuel married a cousin of his first wife who bore the same name. He died November 14, 1785, leaving an estate valued at more than 544 pounds sterling. The Salem Gazette of November 22, 1785, made mention of him in the following words:

"Died.—At Topsfield, on Monday, the 14th instant, Samuel Smith, Esq. So amiable and worthy a character as he evidently appeared, both in public and private, will render the memory of him ever precious. For a number of years he represented the town in the General Court, where he was esteemed a man of integrity and uprightness. His usefulness among those with whom he was more immediately conversant was eminent. He was a sincere friend to the liberties of his country, and a strenuous advocate for the doctrine of Christianity."

"The memory of the Just be blessed."

Asael Smith, Grandfather of Joseph Smith.—Asael Smith was the second son and youngest child of (2) Samuel. He was born in Topsfield, March 7, 1744. His mother died, as already noted, shortly after his birth. His early life was spent in Topsfield. February 12, 1767, he took to wife, Mary Duty, of Windham, New Hampshire, and later moved to that place. From there he went to Dunbarton and then to

Derryfield, now the city of Manchester. During the Revolution he followed the example of his illustrious father and served with the Colonial forces. After the death of his father in 1785, he returned to Topsfield and made his home on the family estate. He lived in the old

Birthplace of Joseph Smith, Sr.

home, about one mile north of the town, where a number of his children were born, notably Joseph, father of the Prophet Joseph Smith.

Asael was a man of very liberal views, far in advance of his time. Some of his children were members of the Congregational Church, but in his religious views he leaned toward the teachings of the Universalists. However, he held aloof from all sects, because he could not reconcile his understanding of the scriptures with their many conflicting creeds. He advocated the truth very strongly, that all men should have free and equal religious liberty. In his opinions he was frank and explicit, expressing himself without fear of the prevailing opinions of his neighbors. He was somewhat gifted with the pen and wrote some worthy sentiments which have been preserved and are still in possession of members of the family. Many years before his death he wrote a charge to his family in which the advice given could be followed with great profit by parents and children even in our day. An excerpt from this document will give an insight into the character of this man and depict his remarkable faith in Jesus Christ:

Advice of Asael Smith to His Family.—"And first to you, my dear wife," he wrote, "I do with all the strength and power that is in me, thank you for your kindness and faithfulness to me, beseeching God who is the husband of the widow, to take care of you and not to leave you nor forsake you, or suffer you to leave nor forsake him, nor his ways. Put your whole trust solely in him, he never did nor never will forsake any that trust in him. * * * And now my dear children, let me pour out my heart to you and speak first of immortality in your souls. Trifle not in this point; the soul is immortal; you have to deal with an infinite Majesty; you go upon life and death, therefore in this point be serious. Do all to God in a serious manner; when you think of him, speak of him, pray to him, or in any way make your addresses to his great majesty, be in good earnest. Trifle not with his name or with his attributes, nor call him to witness to any thing but is absolute truth, nor then, but when sound reason or serious consideration requires it. And as to religion, I would not wish to point out any particular way for you; but first I would wish you to search the scriptures and consult sound reason and see if they (which I take to be two witnesses that stand by the God of the whole earth) are not sufficient to evince to you that religion is a necessary theme * * *.

"For the public.—Bless God that you live in a land of liberty and bear yourselves dutifully and conscionably towards the authority under which you live. See God's providence in the appointment of the Federal Constitution and hold union and order precious jewels."

Prediction of Asael Smith.—In the spring of 1791 he moved from Topsfield to Tunbridge, Vermont, where he made his home for several years. As old age came on and his health impaired, he removed to Stockholm, St. Lawrence County, New York, and made his home with his son Silas. Here he died, October 31, 1830, at the advanced age of more than 86 years. In stature he was tall, his body was well proportioned and possessed of unusual strength. At times the spirit of inspiration rested upon him. On one occasion he said: "It has been borne in upon my soul that one of my descendants will promulgate a work to revolutionize the world of religious faith." Perhaps he did not expect to live to see that day, but such proved to be the case. The first summer after the organization of the Church, his son Joseph and grandson, Don Carlos Smith, paid him a visit and presented him with a copy of the Book of Mormon. At the time he was in feeble health, but he diligently read the book, or most of it, and said he was convinced that the work of his grandson, Joseph Smith, was of divine origin. He was not baptized, due to his weakened physical condition, and died shortly after this visit. His wife, Mary Duty Smith, later moved to Kirtland, where she died in 1836, firm in the faith of the restored gospel.

John Mack of Connecticut.—On his maternal side, Joseph Smith was descended from John Mack, who was born in Inverness, Scotland, March 6, 1653. John Mack came to America about 1669, and resided, first in Salisbury, Massachusetts. He married Sarah, daughter of Orlando and Sarah Bagley, and moved to Lyme, Connecticut, where eight or more of their twelve children were born. He was the founder of the Mack family of Connecticut. He died Feb. 24, 1721.

Ebenezer, son of John Mack, was born in Lyme, Conn., Dec. 8, 1697. He was a man of thrift and was well respected by the people of Lyme, where he served for many years as minister of the Second Congregational Church. He married Hannah, daughter of Aaron Huntly, an honored citizen of Lyme. At one time, Ebenezer Mack possessed considerable property and "lived in good style, commanding all the attention and respect which are ever shown to those who live in fine circumstances and habits of strict morality."[a] Reverses came, however, and he was reduced, in his declining years, to poverty. He was the father of nine children.

Maternal Grandparents of Joseph Smith.—Solomon, son of Ebenezer Mack, was born in Lyme, Conn., Sept. 26, 1735. At the age of twenty-one years he enlisted in the services of his country under the command of Captain Henry, and the regiment of Col. Whiting. He was engaged in the king's service with two teams carrying supplies to Fort Edwards. In 1748 he enlisted under Major Spenser and was engaged in several bloody engagements in which his life was spared miraculously. He served until the spring of 1759, when he received his honorable discharge at Crown Point. That same year he met a young schoolteacher, Lydia Gates, daughter of Nathan Gates, a wealthy citizen of East Haddam, Connecticut. The friendship of these young people ripened and they were married after a short acquaintance. In 1761 Solomon and his young wife moved to Marlow where they took up their residence in a wilderness. Only four other families resided within forty miles of them. It was while here he learned to fully appreciate the excellent virtues of his wife, "For," he writes, "as our children were deprived of schools she assumed charge of their education, and performed the duties of instructress as none, save a mother, is capable of. Precepts, accompanied with examples such as theirs, were calculated to make impressions on the minds of the young, never to be forgotten. She, besides instructing them in the various branches of an ordinary education, was in the habit of calling them together both morning and evening, and teaching them to pray, meanwhile urging

---

[a]"History of the Prophet Joseph," by Lucy Mack Smith.

them the necessity of love towards each other as well as devotional feelings towards Him who made them."

In this manner their children became confirmed in the virtues and were established in faith in their Redeemer.

Patriotic Service of Solomon Mack.—In 1776, Solomon Mack enlisted in the American army. For some time he served in the land forces and later was transferred to the navy. With his two sons, Jason and Stephen, he was engaged in a privateering expedition commanded by Captain Havens. In this service they passed through some thrilling experiences, but escaped without great harm. His service in the war covered a period of about four years. After his discharge he went to Gilsum, New Hampshire, to make his home. Owing to the rigorous campaigns through two wars, he became broken in health and suffered considerably in his declining years. His son Stephen moved to Vermont and later to Detroit, where he engaged in mercantile pursuits and was one of the founders of Detroit. During the war of 1812 Stephen again entered the service of his country. He held the commission of a captain at the time of the siege of Detroit and was ordered by his superior officer to surrender, which he boldly refused to do. Breaking his sword across his knee he threw the parts into the lake and said he would not submit to such a disgraceful compromise while the blood of an American ran in his veins.

Such is the character of the forbears of Joseph Smith.

CHAPTER 6

BOYHOOD OF JOSEPH SMITH

1805-1820

The Birth of Joseph Smith, the Prophet.—Joseph Smith, son of Asael, was born in Topsfield, July 12, 1771. Near the close of the eighteenth century he was residing in Tunbridge, Vermont, where he owned a good farm and engaged in tilling the soil. It was here he met Lucy Mack, daughter of Solomon Mack, of Gilsum, who later became his wife. She was visiting in Tunbridge with her brother Stephen, who at that time was a resident of Tunbridge. Joseph Smith, after his marriage continued to reside in Tunbridge for about six years. In 1802 he rented his farm and moved to Randolph, to engage in the mercantile business. Later he sold his farm in Tunbridge and moved to Royalton, then to Sharon, Windsor County, where their son Joseph was born, December 23, 1805. In 1811 the Smith family moved from Vermont to Lebanon, New Hampshire, just over the border line where they intended to settle down "and began to contemplate with joy and satisfaction" the prosperity which had attended their exertions. They were desirous, as most parents are, to provide comfortably for their children and give them the advantages of an education. Of this desire the mother writes:

Joseph Smith

Early Struggles of the Smiths.—"As our children had, in a great measure, been debarred from the privilege of schools, we began to make every arrangement to attend to this important duty. We established our second son, Hyrum, in an academy at Hanover; and the rest, that were of sufficient age, we were sending to a common school that was quite convenient; meanwhile myself and companion were doing all that our abilities would admit of for the future welfare and advantage of the family; and were greatly blessed in our labors."

These desires, however, were rudely shattered, for an epidemic of typhus fever passed over the land and all the Smith children were sorely afflicted. The oldest daughter, Sophronia, lay for a long time nigh unto death, and was saved only by Divine providence in answer to prayer. Joseph recovered from the fever after an illness of two weeks, but was left suffering with extreme pain in his shoulder which was first treated as the result of a sprain, but later developments proved it to be from another cause. A bag of pus had formed which had to be lanced. The description of his suffering is very vividly told by his mother in the following words:

Serious Affliction of Joseph Smith.—"As soon as the sore had discharged itself, the pain left it, and shot like lightning (using his own terms) down his side into the marrow of the bone of his leg, and soon became very severe. My poor boy, at this, was almost in despair, and he cried out, 'Oh, father, the pain is so severe, how can I bear it!'

"His leg soon began to swell, and he continued to suffer the greatest agony for the space of two weeks longer. During this period I carried him much of the time in my arms in order to mitigate his suffering as much as possible; in consequence of which I was taken very ill myself. The anxiety of mind that I experienced, together with physical over-exertion, was too much for my constitution, and my nature sank under it.

Tenderness of Hyrum Smith.—"Hyrum, who was rather remarkable for his tenderness and sympathy, now desired that he might take my place; as he was a good, trusty boy we let him do so; and, in order to make the task as easy for him as possible, we laid Joseph upon a low bed, and Hyrum sat beside him, almost day and night, for some considerable length of time, holding the affected part of

Hyrum Smith

his leg in his hands, and pressing it between them so that his afflicted brother might be enabled to endure the pain, which was so excruciating that he was scarcely able to bear it.

Surgical Aid Sought.—"At the end of three weeks, we thought it advisable to send again for the surgeon. When he came, he made an incision of eight inches on the front side of the leg, between the knee and ankle. This relieved the pain in a great measure, and the patient was quite comfortable until the wound began to heal, when the pain became as violent as ever.

"The surgeon was called again, and he this time enlarged the wound, cutting the leg even to the bone. It commenced healing the second time, and as soon as it began to heal, it also began to swell again, which swelling continued to rise till we deemed it wisdom to call a council of surgeons; and when they met in consultation, they decided that amputation was the only remedy.

A Council Held.—"Soon after coming to this conclusion, they rode up to the door, and were invited into a room, apart from the one in which Joseph lay. They being seated, I addressed them thus: 'Gentlemen, what can you do to save my boy's leg?' They answered, 'We can do nothing; we have cut it open to the bone, and find it so affected that we consider his leg incurable, and that amputation is absolutely necessary in order to save his life.'

"This was like a thunderbolt to me. I appealed to the principal surgeon, saying, 'Dr. Stone, can you not make another trial? Can you not, by cutting around the bone, take out the diseased part, and perhaps that which is sound will heal over, and by this means you will save his leg? You will not, you must not, take off his leg until you try once more. I will not consent to let you enter his room until you make me this promise.'

Birthplace of the Prophet Joseph Smith

"After consulting a short time with each other, they agreed to do as I had requested, then went to see my suffering son. One of the doctors, on approaching his bed, said 'My poor boy, we have come again.' 'Yes,' said Joseph, 'I see you have; but you have not come to take off my leg, have you sir?' 'No,' replied the surgeon, 'It is your mother's request that we make one more effort, and that is what we have now come for.'

"The principal surgeon, after a moment's conversation, ordered cords to be brought to bind Joseph fast to the bedstead; but to this Joseph objected. The doctor, however, insisted that he must be confined, upon which Joseph said very decidedly, 'No, doctor, I will not be bound, for I can bear the operation much better if I have my liberty.' 'Then,' said Dr. Stone, 'will you drink some brandy?'

" 'No,' said Joseph, 'not one drop.'

" 'Will you take some wine?' rejoined the doctor. 'You must take something, or you can never endure the severe operation to which you must be subjected.'

"'No,' exclaimed Joseph, 'I will not touch one particle of liquor, neither will I be tied down; but I will tell you what I will do—I will have my father sit on the bed and hold me in his arms, and then I

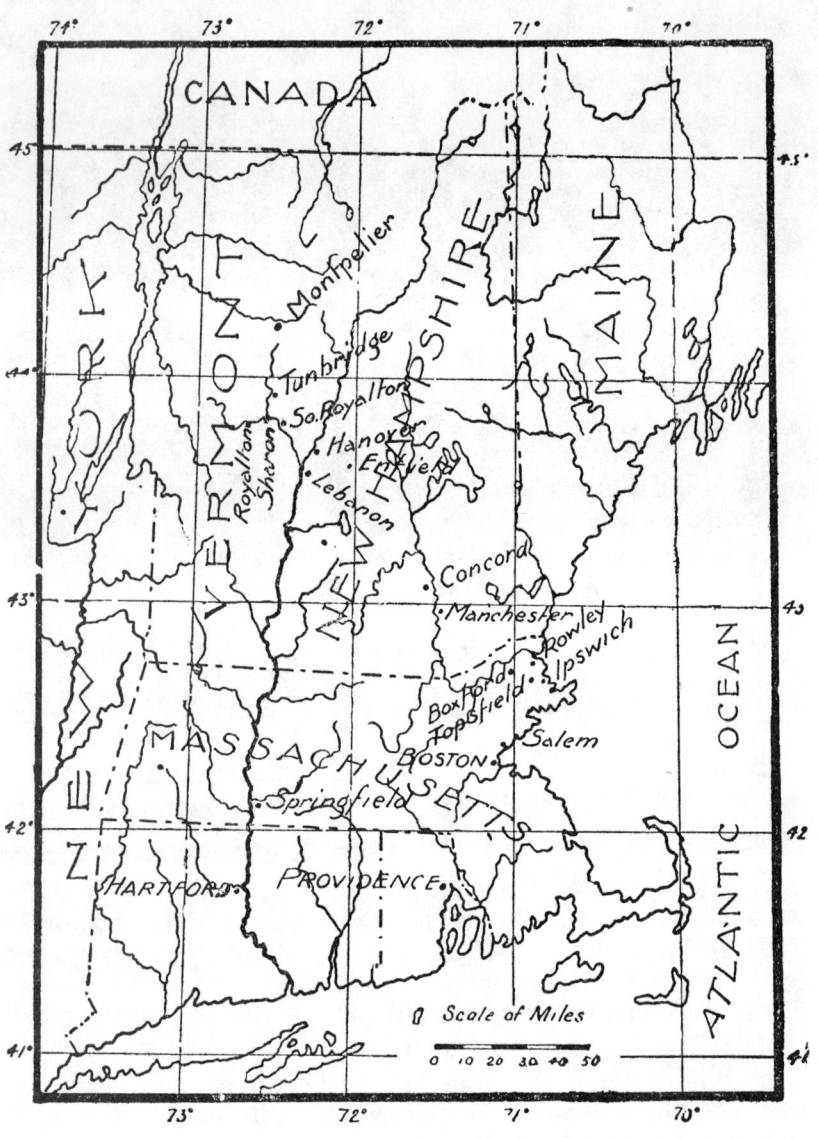

Map of New England States

will do whatever is necessary in order to have the bone taken out.' Looking at me, he said, 'Mother, I want you to leave the room, for I know you cannot bear to see me suffer so; father can stand it, but you have carried me so much, and watched over me so long, you are almost worn out.' Then looking up into my face, his eyes swimming in tears, he continued, 'Now, mother, promise me that you will not stay, will you? The Lord will help me, and I shall get through with it.'

"To this request I consented, and getting a number of folded sheets, and laying them under his leg, I retired, going several hundred yards from the house in order to be out of hearing.

The Operation.—"The surgeons commenced operating by boring into the bone of his leg, first on one side of the bone where it was affected, then on the other side, after which they broke it off with a pair of forceps or pincers. They thus took away large pieces of the bone. When they broke off the first piece, Joseph screamed out so loudly, that I could not forbear running to him. On my entering the room, he cried out, 'Oh, mother, go back, go back; I do not want you to come in—I will try to tough it out, if you will go away.' * * *

"I was immediately forced from the room, and detained until the operation was complete; but when the act was accomplished, Joseph put upon a clean bed, the room cleaned of every appearance of blood, and the instruments which were used in the operation removed, I was permitted again to enter.

He is Healed.—"Joseph immediately commenced getting better, and from this onward continued to mend until he became strong and healthy. When he had so far recovered as to be able to travel, he went with his uncle Jesse Smith, to Salem, for the benefit of his health, hoping the sea breezes would be of service to him, and in this he was not disappointed."

Removal to New York.—Continued sickness pursued the family for a year; this, together with three successive years of crop failure, placed the family in rather straitened circumstances. So discouraged did they become that the decision was reached to move to the milder climate and more fertile region of western New York, where there would be a better opportunity to retrieve their fortunes.

As soon as arrangements could be made and obligations settled, Joseph Smith and family moved to Palmyra, New York, a distance of about three hundred miles from their home in New Hampshire. The members of the family now counseled together relative to the course they should adopt. It was finally decided to purchase about one hundred acres of land, situated about two miles south of Palmyra on the border of Manchester township. It should be remembered that western New York, at that time, was sparsely settled. Ohio, Michigan and Illinois were still largely in a state of wilderness, and beyond the great "Father of Waters" lay a vast country scarcely known. More than ten years later Missouri was spoken of by the Lord to Joseph Smith, in a revelation as being on the "borders of the Lamanites."[a]

The Purchase of a Home.—At the time of the removal to Palmyra, two of the boys, Alvin and Hyrum, were able to be of material assistance in making their new home. With their father they set to work clearing the newly acquired land from a heavy growth of timber, a condition which generally prevailed in that country one hundred years ago. During the first year they cleared about thirty acres,—no small task in itself—besides engaging in a day's labor now and again, as opportunity afforded, in order to raise means to meet their obligations. Thus, during the first year, they were able to meet most of their first payment on the land, which during that year was not in a condition to be farmed. The mother, through her untiring industry, took upon herself the task to provide the household necessities, which she did through the sale of hand-painted oil-cloth table covers, a work in which she was quite skilled, and in which she met with fair success.

Removal to Manchester.—About four years after the arrival of the Smith family in Palmyra, they moved to the farm where they built a four-room log house, which was later increased by the addition of sleeping rooms on the rear. It was while living in this house that Joseph received his glorious visions. The building of a more commodious home was contemplated under the direction of Alvin, the oldest son, who much desired to see his parents comfortably located. "I am going to have," he said, "a nice, pleasant room for father and mother to sit in, and everything arranged for their comfort, and they shall not work any more as they have done." This was indeed a noble thought and desire, for his parents had toiled and labored much in the midst of trials and tribulations that had reduced them to a state of poverty.

Death of Alvin Smith.—Alvin did not live to realize the blessings thus contemplated and to see the fulfilment of his dream. The frame of the new house was raised and the necessary material procured to complete the structure in the fall of 1823; but in November of that year Alvin was stricken. He died on the 19th day of that month

---

[a]Doc. and Cov. 54:8.

in the twenty-seventh year of his age. He lived to know of the visitation of the Father and the Son, and of the coming of Moroni, and was convinced that these things were true. He died with a prayer on his lips for his younger brother Joseph, and admonished him to be true to the great work entrusted to his care. Alvin is spoken of as a "youth of singular goodness and disposition, kind and amiable."

The Hand of Providence.—While hard to bear, the many misfortunes of the Smiths were all overruled by the providence of the Lord, for their good. Had they remained in Vermont, or New Hampshire, the purposes of the Lord could not as well have been accomplished. He had a great work for the youthful Joseph to perform, and it was necessary that the family should move to the field of his activities. Therefore, through the valley of tribulation they were led by the hand of the Lord to the place he had prepared for them.

CHAPTER 7

THE VISION

1820

Joseph Smith's Own Story.—Never has the story of the wonderful vision of the Father and the Son to Joseph Smith been told so effectively and clearly as by Joseph Smith, himself, as he related it in complete simplicity. Therefore, it is repeated here:

"Some time in the second year after our removal to Manchester, there was in the place where we lived an unusual excitement on the subject of religion. It commenced with the Methodists, but soon became general among all the sects in that region of country. Indeed, the whole district of country seemed affected by it, and great multitudes united themselves to the different religious parties, which created no small stir and division amongst the people, some crying, 'Lo, here!' and others, 'Lo, there!' Some were contending for the Methodist faith, some for the Presbyterian, and some for the Baptist. For notwithstanding the great love which the converts to these different faiths expressed at the time of their conversion, and the great zeal manifested by the respective clergy, who were active in getting up and promoting this extraordinary scene of religious feeling, in order to have everybody converted as they were pleased to call it, let them join what sect they pleased—yet when the converts began to file off, some to one party and some to another, it was seen that the seemingly good feelings of both the priests and the converts were more pretended than real, for a scene of great confusion and bad feeling ensued; priest contending against priest, and convert against convert; so that all their good feelings one for another, if they ever had any, were entirely lost in a strife of words and a contest about opinions.

"I was at this time in my fifteenth year. My father's family was proselyted to the Presbyterian faith, and four of them joined that church, namely—my mother Lucy; my brothers Hyrum and Samuel Harrison; and my sister, Sophronia.

A Time of Religious Excitement.—"During this time of great excitement, my mind was called up to serious reflection and great uneasiness; but though my feelings were deep and often poignant, still I kept myself aloof from all these parties, though I attended their several meetings as often as occasion would permit. In process of time my mind became somewhat partial to the Methodist sect, and I felt some desire to be united with them; but so great were the confusion and strife among the different denominations, that it was impossible for a person young as I was, and so unacquainted with men and things, to come to any certain conclusion who was right and who was wrong. My mind at times was greatly excited, the cry and tumult were so great and incessant. The Presbyterians were most decided against the Baptists and Methodists, and used all the powers of either reason or sophistry to prove their errors, or, at least to make people think they were in error. On the other hand, the Baptists and Methodists in their turn were equally zealous in endeavoring to establish their own tenets and disprove all others.

The Promise of James Tested.—"In the midst of this war of words and tumult of opinions, I often said to myself, What is to be done? Who of all these parties are right; or, are they all wrong together? If any one of them be right, which is it, and how shall I know it? While I was laboring under the extreme difficulties caused by the contests of these parties of religionists, I was one day reading the Epistle of James, first chapter, and fifth verse, which reads: *If any of you lack wisdom, let him ask of God; that giveth to all men liberally, and upbraideth not; and it shall be given him.*

"Never did any passage of scripture come with more power to the heart of man than this did at this time to mine. It seemed to enter with great force into every feeling of my heart. I reflected on it again and again, knowing that if any person needed wisdom from God I did; for how to act I did not know, and unless I could get more wisdom than I then had, I would never know; for the teachers of religion of the different sects understood the same passages of scripture so differently as to destroy all confidence in settling the question by an appeal to the Bible. At length I came to the conclusion that I must either remain in darkness and confusion, or else I must do as James directs, that is, ask of God. I at length came to the determination to 'ask of God' concluding that if he gave wisdom to them that lacked wisdom, and would give liberally and not upbraid, I might venture. So, in accordance with this my determination to ask of God, I retired to the woods to make the attempt. It was on the morning of a beautiful clear day, early in the spring of eighteen hundred and twenty. It was the first time in my life that I had made such an attempt, for amidst all my anxieties I had never as yet made the attempt to pray vocally.

The Sacred Grove

The Vision.—"After I had retired to the place where I had previously designed to go, having looked around me, and finding myself alone, I kneeled down and began to offer up the desires of my heart to God. I had scarcely done so, when immediately I was seized upon by some power which entirely overcame me, and had such an astonishing influence over me as to bind my tongue so that I could not speak. Thick darkness gathered around me, and it seemed to me for a time as if I were doomed to sudden destruction.

"But, exerting all my powers to call upon God to deliver me out of the power of this enemy which had seized upon me, and at the very moment when I was ready to sink into despair and abandon myself to destruction—not to an imaginary ruin, but to the power of some actual being from the unseen world, who had such marvelous power as I had never before felt in any being—just at this moment of great alarm, I saw a pillar of light exactly over my head, above the brightness of the sun, which descended gradually until it fell upon me.

"It no sooner appeared than I found myself delivered from the enemy which held me bound. When the light rested upon me I saw two personages, whose brightness and glory defy all description, standing above me in the air. One of them spake unto me, calling me by name, and said, pointing to the other—*This is my beloved Son, hear Him!*

"My object in going to inquire of the Lord was to know which of all the sects was right, that I might know which to join. No sooner, therefore, did I get possession of myself, so as to be able to speak, than I asked the personages who stood above me in the light, which of all the sects was right—and which I should join. I was answered that I must join none of them, for they were all wrong; and the personage who addressed me said that all their creeds were an abomination in his sight; that those professors were all corrupt; that 'they draw near to me with their lips, but their hearts are far from me; they teach for doctrines the commandments of men, having a form of godliness but they deny the power thereof.' He again forbade me to join with any of them; and many other things did he say unto me, which I cannot write at this time. When I came to myself again I found myself lying on my back, looking up into heaven.

"When the light had departed, I had no strength; but soon recovering in some degree, I went home. And as I leaned up to the fireplace, mother enquired what the matter was. I replied, 'Never mind, all is well—I am well enough off.' I then said to my mother, 'I have learned for myself that Presbyterianism is not true.'

Sectarian Opposition.—"It seems as though the adversary was aware, at a very early period of my life, that I was destined to prove a disturber and an annoyer of his kingdom; else why should the powers of darkness combine against me? Why the opposition and persecution that arose against me almost in my infancy?

"Some few days after I had this vision, I happened to be in company with one of the Methodist preachers, who was very active in the before-mentioned religious excitement; and, conversing with him on the subject of religion, I took occasion to give him an account of the vision which I had had. I was greatly surprised at his behavior; he treated my communication not only lightly, but with great contempt, saying it was all of the devil, that there were no such things as visions or revelations in these days; that all such things had ceased with the apostles, and that there would never be any more of them.

"I soon found, however, that my telling the story had excited a great deal of prejudice against me among professors of religion, and was the cause of great persecution, which continued to increase; and though I was an obscure boy, only between fourteen and fifteen years of age, and my circumstances in life such as to make a boy of no consequence in the world, yet men of high standing would take notice sufficient to excite the public mind against me, and create a bitter persecution; and this was common among all the sects—all united to persecute me.

Joseph Smith's Reflections.—"It caused me serious reflection then, and often has since, how very strange it was that an obscure boy, a little over fourteen years of age and one, too, who was doomed to the necessity of obtaining a scanty maintenance by his daily labor, should be thought a character of sufficient importance to attract the attention of the great ones of the most popular sects of the day, and in a manner to create in them a spirit of the most bitter persecution and reviling. But strange or not, so it was, and it was often the cause of great sorrow to myself. However, it was nevertheless a fact that I had beheld a vision. I have thought since, that I felt much like Paul, when he made his defense before King Agrippa, and related the account of the vision he had when he saw a light and heard a voice; but still there were but few who believed him; some said he was dishonest, others said he was mad; and he was ridiculed and reviled. But all this did not destroy the reality of his vision. He had seen a vision, he knew he had, and all the persecution under heaven could not make it otherwise; and though they should persecute him unto death, yet he knew, and would know to his latest breath, that he had both seen a light and heard a voice speaking unto him, and all the world could not make him think or believe otherwise.

"So it was with me. I had actually seen a light, and in the midst of that light I saw two personages, and they did in reality speak to me and though I was hated and persecuted for saying I had seen a vision, yet it was true; and while they were persecuting me, reviling me, and speaking all manner of evil against me falsely for so saying, I was led to say in my heart: Why persecute me for telling the truth? I have actually seen a vision, and who am I that I can withstand God, or why does the world think to make me deny what I have actually seen? For I had seen a vision; I knew it, and I knew that God knew it, and I could not deny it, neither dared I do it, at least I knew that by so doing I would offend God, and come under condemnation.

"I had now got my mind satisfied so far as the sectarian world was concerned; that it was not my duty to join with any of them, but to continue as I was until further directed. I had found the testimony of James to be true, that a man who lacked wisdom might ask of God, and obtain, and not be upbraided."

Joseph Smith's Great Honor.—There is no account in history or revelation extant, where ever before both the Father and the Son appeared in the presence of mortal man in glory. Most wonderful was the honor bestowed upon this unsophisticated boy. Great was his faith—so great that he was able, like the brother of Jared, to penetrate the veil and behold the glory of these holy Beings, whose glory rested upon him. Without this power overshadowing him, he could not have endured their presence, for their brightness was far greater than the brightness of the noonday sun. It was not, therefore, with the power of the natural eye that this great Vision was beheld, but by the aid of the eye of the spirit. The natural man, without the saving grace of the power of the Lord, could not behold his presence in this manner, for he would be consumed. Joseph Smith, through the power of the Lord, was able to behold the presence of the Great Creator and his Glorified Son, for they deigned to honor him, with their presence and converse with him.

The Heavens No Longer Sealed.—No longer were the heavens as brass. No more would man be forced to stumble and grope in darkness. Salvation was made known and the glad tidings were to sound forth, as with the blast of a mighty trumpet, to the ends of the earth. Satan's reign was nearing its end, and the message of eternal peace was shortly to be proclaimed to every nation, and kindred, and tongue and people.

The Vision Rejected by the World.—No wonder Joseph Smith rejoiced, he now possessed greater knowledge than all the professors and divines in all the world! Naturally he desired that others should share his joy and partake of his wonderful information. He would proclaim it to them with gladness, surely they would be pleased to receive it and would rejoice with him! But great disappointment awaited him, for with one accord his message was rejected. Only the members of his household would believe. He was treated with scorn by great men of learning, although he was but a boy. He was mocked and shamed. Instead of the spirit of love and gratefulness following him for revealing this glorious message of truth, it was the spirit of contempt and hatred with which he had to contend. In sorrow he learned to hold his peace and wait—wait for further light and inspiration which he had been promised. Though all the world would mock and former friends deride, he knew he had beheld the vision. There was one Friend to whom he now could go and pour out his soul in humble hope of encouragement and succor. What did it matter though the whole world should laugh, if the Son of God would hearken to his humble pleadings?

Not Strange that the Message should be Rejected.—Yet, when we stop to reflect, it is not strange that this message of light and truth should be rejected by the world, for the Lord had said long years before, "Men love darkness rather than light, because their deeds are evil." As for the priests, was not their craft in danger? The message left with the youthful seer by the God of heaven was most drastic. It had been declared in language that could be clearly understood, that the creeds of men were not in accord with his Gospel. This was not a message to please the religious teachers of the day. Moreover, the vision had shattered the traditions of the times. The doctrines taught in the churches were emphatically contradicted and disproved. The world was teaching and believing that the canon of scripture was full; that there was not to be and could not be, more revelation; that the visitation of angels had ceased with the early Christian fathers, and such things as these had passed away forever. Again, the doctrine was taught that the Father, Son and Holy Ghost were incomprehensible, without body, parts and passions. A revelation of the Father and the Son as separate persons, each with a body tangible and in the form of the body of man, was destructive of this doctrine, as revelation was of the doctrine of the closed heavens. The world had held that perfection in religion and the organization of the Church of Christ was not to be expected, but that men were led by their own human reason to interpret the word of the Lord as set forth in the scriptures.

A Bold Denunciation of False Doctrine.—A bold denunciation of all such false teachings and traditions, although told in confiding simplicity by a humble youth, fourteen years of age, was not likely to bring rejoicing and peace of mind to those who thus believed and loved their old traditions dearly. Nevertheless the story must be told; for in the world were thousands of honest souls who were likewise praying that the light of the everlasting Gospel would be restored, and the message of salvation again be proclaimed as a witness before the end of unrighteousness should come.

CHAPTER 8

THE VISITATION OF MORONI

1823-1827

Life of Joseph Smith Between 1820-23.—"I continued to pursue my common vocations in life until the twenty-first of September, one thousand eight hundred and twenty-three, all the time suffering severe persecution at the hands of all classes of men, both religious and irreligious, because I continued to affirm that I had seen a vision.

"During the space of time which intervened between the time I had the vision and the year eighteen hundred and twenty-three—having been forbidden to join any of the religious sects of the day, and being of very tender years, and persecuted by those who ought to have been my friends and to have treated me kindly, and if they supposed me to be deluded to have endeavored in a proper and affectionate manner to have reclaimed me,—I was left to all kinds of temptations; and, mingling with all kinds of society, I frequently fell into many foolish errors, and displayed the weakness of youth and the foibles of human nature; which I am sorry to say, led me into divers temptations, offensive in the sight of God. In making this confession, no one need suppose me guilty of any great or malignant sins. A disposition to commit such was never in my nature. But I was guilty of levity, and sometimes associated with jovial company, etc., not consistent with that character which ought to be maintained by one who was called of God as I had been. But this will not seem very strange to any one who recollects my youth, and is acquainted with my native cheery temperament.

"In consequence of these things, I often felt condemned for my weakness and imperfections; when on the evening of the above-mentioned twenty-first of September, after I had retired to my bed for the night, I betook myself to prayer and supplication to Almighty God for forgiveness of all my sins and follies, and also for a manifestation to me, that I might know of my state and standing before him; for I had full confidence in obtaining a divine manifestation, as I previously had one.

The Appearing of Moroni.—"While I was thus in the act of calling upon God, I discovered a light appearing in my room, which continued to increase until the room was lighter than at noonday, when immediately a personage appeared at my bedside, standing in the air, for his feet did not touch the floor. He had on a loose robe of most exquisite whiteness. It was a whiteness beyond anything earthly I had ever seen; nor do I believe that any earthly thing could be made to appear so exceedingly white and brilliant. His hands were naked, and his arms also, a little above the wrists; so, also, were his feet naked, as were his legs, a little above the ankles. His head and neck were also bare. I could discover that he had no other clothing on but his robe, as it was open, so that I could see into his bosom. Not only was his robe exceedingly white, but his whole person was glorious beyond description, and his countenance truly like lightning. The room was exceedingly light, but not so very bright as immediately around his person. When I first looked upon him, I was afraid; but the fear soon left me.

The Book of Mormon Revealed.—"He called me by name, and said unto me that he was a messenger sent from the presence of God to me, and that his name was Moroni; that God had a work for me to do; and that my name should be had for good and evil among all nations, kindreds, and tongues, or that it should be both good and evil spoken of among all people. He said there was a book deposited, written upon gold plates, giving an account of the former inhabitants of this continent, and the source from whence they sprang. He also said that the fulness of the everlasting Gospel was contained in it, as delivered by the Savior to the ancient inhabitants; also, that there were two stones in silver bows—and these stones, fastened to a breastplate, constituted what is called the Urim and Thummim—deposited with the plates; and the possession and use of these stones were what constituted seers in ancient or former times; and that God had prepared them for the purpose of translating the book.

Moroni Quotes Ancient Prophets.—"After telling me these things, he commenced quoting the prophecies of the Old Testament. He first quoted part of the third chapter of Malachi, and he quoted also the fourth or last chapter of the same prophecy, though with a little variation from the way it reads in our Bibles. Instead of quoting the first verse as it reads in our books, he quoted thus:

"*For behold, the day cometh that shall burn as an oven and all the proud, yea, and all that do wickedly, shall burn as stubble; for they that come shall burn them, saith the Lord of Hosts, that it shall leave them neither root nor branch.*

"And again, he quoted the fifth verse thus: *Behold, I will reveal unto you the Priesthood, by the hand of Elijah the prophet, before the coming of the great and dreadful day of the Lord.*

"He also quoted the next verse differently: *And he shall plant in the hearts of the children the promises made to the fathers; and the hearts of the children shall turn to their fathers; if it were not so, the whole earth would be utterly wasted at his coming.*

"In addition to these, he quoted the eleventh chapter of Isaiah, saying that it was about to fulfilled. He quoted also the third chapter of Acts, twenty-second and twenty-third verses, precisely as they stand in our New Testament. He said that that prophet was Christ; but the day had not yet come when they who would not hear his voice should be cut off from among the people, but soon would come. He also quoted the second chapter of Joel, from the twenty-eighth verse to the last. He also said that this was not yet fulfilled, but was soon to be. And he further stated that the fulness of the Gentiles was soon to come in. He quoted many other passages of scripture, and offered many explanations which cannot be mentioned here.

Moroni's Admonition.—"Again, he told me, that when I got those plates of which he had spoken—for the time that they should be obtained was not yet fulfilled—I should not show them to any person; neither the breastplate with the Urim and Thummim; only to those to whom I should be commanded to show them; if I did I should be destroyed. While he was conversing with me about the plates, the vision was opened to my mind that I could see the place where the plates were deposited, and that so clearly and distinctly that I knew the place again when I visited it.

"After this communication, I saw the light in the room begin to gather immediately around the person of him who had been speaking to me, and it continued to do so, until the room was again left dark, except just around him, when instantly I saw, as it were, a conduit open right up into heaven, and he ascended till he entirely disappeared, and the room was left as it had been before this heavenly light had made its appearance.

The Second Appearance of Moroni.—"I lay musing on the singularity of the scene, and marveling greatly at what had been told me by this extraordinary messenger; when, in the midst of my meditation, I suddenly discovered that my room was again beginning to be lighted, and in an instant, as it were, the same heavenly messenger was again by my bedside.

"He commenced, and again related the very same things which he had done at his first visit, without the least variation; which, having done, he informed me of great judgments which were coming upon the earth, with great desolations by famine, sword and pestilence; and that these grievous judgments would come on the earth in this generation. Having related these things, he again ascended as he had done before.

The Third Appearance of Moroni.—"By this time, so deep were the impressions on my mind, that sleep had fled from my eyes, and I lay overwhelmed in astonishment at what I had both seen and heard. But what was my surprise when again I beheld the same messenger at my bedside, and heard him rehearse or repeat over again to me the same things as before; and added a caution to me, telling me that Satan would try to tempt me (in consequence of the indigent circumstances of my father's family), to get the plates for the purpose of getting rich. This he forbade me, saying that I must have no other object in view in getting the plates but to glorify God, and must not be influenced by any other motive than that of building His kingdom; otherwise I could not get them. After this third visit, he again ascended into heaven as before, and I was again left to ponder on the strangeness of what I had just experienced; when almost immediately after the heavenly messenger had ascended from me the third time, the cock crowed, and I found the day approaching, so that our interviews must have occupied the whole of that night.

The Fourth Appearance of Moroni.—"I shortly after arose from my bed, and, as usual, went to the necessary labors of the day, but, in attempting to work as at other times, I found my strength so exhausted as to render me entirely unable. My father, who was laboring along with me discovered something to be wrong with me, and told me to go home. I started with the intention of going to the house; but, in attempting to cross the fence out of the field where we were, my strength entirely failed me, and I fell helpless on the ground, and for a time was quite unconscious of anything. The first thing that I can recollect was a voice speaking unto me, calling me by name. I looked up, and beheld the same messenger standing over my head, surrounded by light as before. He then again related unto me all that he had related to me the previous night, and commanded me to go to my father and tell him of the vision and commandments which I had received. I obeyed; I returned to my father in the field and rehearsed the whole matter to him. He replied to me that it was of God, and told me to go and do as commanded by the messenger. I left the field, and went to the place where the messenger had told me the plates were deposited; and owing to the distinctness of the vision which I had concerning it, I knew the place the instant that I arrived there.

The Hill Cumorah.—"Convenient to the village of Manchester, Ontario county, New York, stands a hill of considerable size, and the most elevated of any in the neighborhood. On the west side of the hill, not far from the top, under a stone of considerable size,

Hill Cumorah

lay the plates, deposited in a stone box. This stone was thick and rounding in the middle on the upper side, and thinner towards the edges, so that the middle part of it was visible above the ground, but the edge all around was covered with earth.

"Having removed the earth, I obtained a lever, which I got fixed under the edge of the stone, and with a little exertion raised it up.

I looked in, and there indeed did I behold the plates, the Urim and Thummim, and the breastplate, as stated by the messenger. The box in which they lay was formed by laying stones together in some kind of cement. In the bottom of the box were laid two stones crossways of the box, and on these stones lay the plates and other things with them.

"I made an attempt to take them out, but was forbidden by the messenger, and was again informed that the time for bringing them forth had not yet arrived, neither would it, until four years from that time; but he told me that I should come to that place precisely in one year from that time, and that he would there meet with me, and that I should continue to do so until the time should come for obtaining the plates.

The Four Annual Visits to the Hill.—"Accordingly as I had been commanded, I went at the end of each year, and at each time I found the same messenger there, and received instruction and intelligence from him at each of our interviews, respecting what the Lord was going to do, and how and in what manner His kingdom was to be conducted in the last days.

"As my father's worldly circumstances were very limited, we were under the necessity of laboring with our hands, hiring out by day's work and otherwise, as we could get opportunity. Sometimes we were at home and sometimes abroad, and by continued labor, were enabled to get a comfortable maintenance."

Temptation of Joseph Smith.—As Joseph Smith journeyed to the Hill Cumorah on that memorable first visit, he was beset by many conflicting emotions. His father's family were poor and in financial distress. Creditors had been bearing down heavily upon them. The adversary of all righteousness took advantage of these conditions to sorely tempt the youth with all his power. The plates of the book were made of gold and were of great intrinsic value. Could they not be used to relieve the financial embarrassment of the family? Or was there not something else deposited with the plates that might be used for such purpose? Such were the thoughts Satan put into his heart as he approached the hill, and the admonition of the angel was temporarily forgotten.

He had no difficulty in locating the spot where the records were hidden.[a] It was a matter of but a moment to scrape away the

---

[a]The following description of Cumorah is from the pen of Oliver Cowdery.

You are acquainted with the mail road from Palmyra, Wayne County, to Canandaigua, Ontario County, New York, and also, as you pass from the former to the latter place, before arriving at the little village of Manchester, say from three

grass and dirt and with a lever pry loose the stone which served as a covering to the box containing the sacred treasure. There before him, lying on two stones which were crossways of the box, he beheld the record. With it were the Urim and Thummim, two transparent stones set in bows of silver and attached to the breastplate—all as the angel had described. He was enraptured. Putting forth his hand he attempted to remove the plates, but received a shock, which in a measure deprived him of his strength. After a moment's hesitation he made a second attempt, but received a greater shock than at first. The cause of this was unknown to him, for he supposed that physical strength and exertion were all that were necessary for him to obtain the record. The third time he stretched forth his hand to take the plates and again received a shock with considerable violence, which sapped his strength and made him powerless. In his great excitement and without meditation he exclaimed: "Why cannot I obtain the book?" "Because you have not kept the commandments of the Lord," answered a voice near by him. Looking up he was astonished to behold the heavenly messenger of his former visits.

Powers of Good and Evil Shown.—In humble repentance he sought the Lord in prayer. His vision was opened and the glory of the Lord shone around about him, and he was made to feel the sweet influence of the power of righteousness. While he was beholding this vision the angel said, "Look!" Joseph beheld the prince of darkness surrounded by his innumerable train of associates in all their diabolical fury. As the visions of evil passed before him, the angel said: "All this is shown, the good and the evil, the holy and impure, the glory of God and the power of darkness, that you may know, hereafter, the two powers and never be influenced or overcome by that wicked one. Behold, whatever entices and leads to good and to do good is of God, and whatever does not is of that wicked one. It is he who fills the hearts of men with evil, to walk in darkness and

---

to four, or about four miles from Palmyra, you pass a large hill on the east side of the road. Why I say large, is because it is as large, perhaps as any in that country. To a person acquainted with this road a description would be unnecessary, as it is the largest and rises the highest of any on that route. The north end rises quite sudden until it assumes a level with the more southerly extremity, and I think I may say an elevation higher than at the south a short distance, say half or three-fourths of a mile. As you pass toward Canandaigua it lessens gradually until the surface assumes its common level, or is broken by other smaller hills or ridges, water courses and ravines. I think I am justified in saying that this is the highest hill for some distance around and I am certain that its appearance, as it rises so suddenly from a plain on the north, must attract the notice of the traveler as he passes by.—*Messenger and Advocate*, 1834, page 158.

blaspheme God; and you may learn from henceforth, that his ways are to destruction; but the way of holiness is peace and rest."[b]

Joseph was further informed that the records had been deposited for the sake of the glory of the Lord, for they contained the fulness of the Gospel as it was given to the ancient inhabitants of this American continent, and was to be brought forth by the power of God; and moreover that the translation would go forth to the Gentiles, many of whom would believe—afterwards it should go to the house of Israel many of whom should also be brought into the Church of Christ.

Value of the Prophet's Lesson.—The lesson taught to Joseph Smith on this occasion was one of lasting benefit to him. Henceforth he understood the power of the evil one and was prepared to resist temptation. Years afterwards, when speaking of this event he said, "Ever afterwards I was willing to keep the commandments of God." Had the lesson not been taught in this manner, at a later day he might have fallen into temptation when off his guard, with results that would have brought disaster.

The Interval of Four Years.—During the interval of four years, from 1823 to 1827, Joseph Smith was under the necessity of aiding his father's family in paying their debts and procuring a living. At times he found employment at home and at times abroad, as opportunity afforded. The death of his oldest brother Alvin, in 1823, made it all the more needful that he exert himself for the benefit of the family. In October, 1825, he entered the employ of an aged gentleman named Josiah Stowel. Mr. Stowel had heard of some old Spanish silver mines in Harmony, Pennsylvania, and employed his hired help in searching for the hidden treasure. Joseph, after about one month of fruitless search, persuaded this kindly gentleman to forsake the foolish venture. From this employment came the cry that Joseph Smith, the "Mormon" Prophet, was a "money-digger."

The Prophet's Marriage.—While residing in Harmony and in the employment of Mr. Stowel, Joseph boarded at the home of Mr. Isaac Hale. It was here, and under these conditions, that he met Miss Emma Hale, daughter of Isaac Hale. The friendship of these young people ripened into love, and they were married about one year and three months later, January 18, 1827, by Squire Tarbill, in South Bainbridge, New York.

---

[b]See Improvement Era, Vol. 2, p. 807.

CHAPTER 9

JOSEPH SMITH RECEIVES THE RECORD—
THE PRIESTHOOD RESTORED

1827-1829

Joseph Receives the Record.—Each year, on the twenty-second day of September, between the years 1823 and 1827, Joseph went to the Hill Cumorah, as the angel had instructed him, where he was taught in matters pertaining to his sacred duties. At last the time arrived for the delivery of the plates, the Urim and Thummim, and the breastplate. It was the 22nd day of September, 1827. The Prophet went to the hill to keep the final appointment with Moroni, before the record should be given into his hands. Once more the angel instructed him in his duties and impressed upon his mind the great responsibility now to be placed upon him, saying:

"Now you have got the record into your own hands, and you are but a man, therefore you will have to be watchful and faithful to your trust or you will be overpowered by wicked men; for they will lay every plan and scheme that is possible to get it away from you, and if you do not take heed continually, they will succeed. While it was in my hands, I could keep it, and no man had power to take it away, but now I give it up to you. Beware, and look well to your ways, and you shall have power to retain it."[a]

Moreover, he was told, if he let the record go out of his hands or neglected his duty, he should be cut off, but through faithfulness

---

[a]"History of the Prophet Joseph," p. 106, Lucy Smith.

and perseverance he should be protected until the angel should come for the record and again take it into his keeping.

Designs of the Wicked Frustrated.—Joseph soon found that the warning of the angel was all too true concerning the powers of darkness arrayed against him, and the desire of evil-disposed persons to destroy him and obtain the plates. Scarcely was the record in his possession before strenuous exertions were made by wicked persons to get it out of his hands. Every scheme and invention which the powers of darkness could devise, were used. Conjurors, diviners with peepstones and other means were employed. Mobs gathered and searched the premises of the Smith home, even breaking into the house and ransacking it. Under pretext of law searches were made. At times it became necessary to hide the records in strange places. Once they were hidden in a hollow log in the woods; again, under the hearthstone in the house, and under the floor in a nearby shop. When the Prophet departed for Pennsylvania he hid them in a barrel of beans, and when a search was made they were not discovered. The Lord was with him in his labor and the powers of darkness were overcome and of no avail.

Martin Harris.—So intense and bitter became the opposition in Manchester that the Prophet sought a place of refuge in another locality. Having received an invitation from his wife's parents to come to their home in Harmony, Pennsylvania, he accepted the invitation and prepared to go. Being very poor he experienced some difficulty in procuring the necessary means to meet his obligations and make the journey. In this hour of distress, and in the midst of persecution, he found a friend in Martin Harris, of Palmyra, New York. Joseph, with his wife's brother, Alva Hale, had gone to Palmyra to transact some business, and while there he was approached by Martin Harris, who said to him: "How do you do, Mr. Smith? Here are fifty dollars. I give this to you to do the Lord's work with; no, I give it to the Lord for His own work." Joseph offered to take the money and give his note which Alva Hale also agreed to sign, but Martin Harris refused to take the note. This money enabled the Prophet to make the journey to Harmony where he found a haven of rest.

Removal to Pennsylvania.—Shortly after this event Joseph moved to Harmony, Susquehanna County, Pennsylvania, to the home of Isaac Hale. Later he purchased from Mr. Hale a small farm, to which he removed. Here in comparative peace he commenced to make a copy of the characters on the plates, which consisted of the learning of the Jews and the language, in hieroglyphics, of the Egyptians. He also, by Urim and Thummim, made a translation of some of them. This was done between December, 1827, and the February following. In the month of February, 1828, Martin Harris came to Harmony to visit with Joseph Smith. He had been much impressed with the Prophet's story and desired to know more concerning the work.

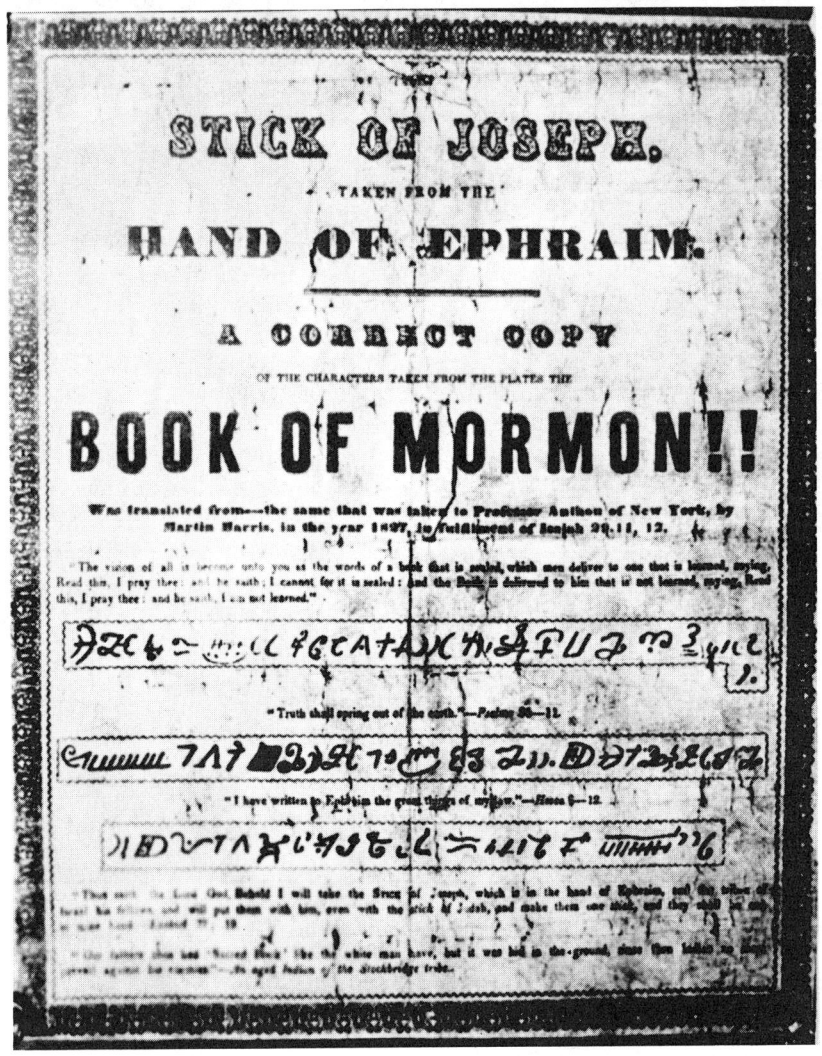

Circular Depicting Characters from the Plates

The Prophecy of Isaiah Fulfilled.—Martin Harris took the transcript that had been made together with the partial translation, and departed for New York. Just what his object was, and what he had in mind, is not made clear. That he was led to do so by inspiration was later shown. He first submitted the characters to Professor Charles Anthon of Columbia College with the request that he examine them. He then took them to Dr. Samuel L. Mitchell, also of New York. When Martin returned he made the following report:

"I went to the city of New York and presented the characters which had been translated, with the translation thereof, to Professor Charles Anthon, a gentleman celebrated for his literary attainments. Professor Anthon stated that the translation was correct, more so than any he had before seen translated from the Egyptian. I then showed him those which were not yet translated, and he said that they were Egyptian, Chaldaic, Assyrian and Arabic; and he said they were true characters. He gave me a certificate, certifying to the people of Palmyra that they were true characters, and that the translation of such of them as had been translated was also correct. I took the certificate and put it into my pocket, and was just leaving the house, when Mr. Anthon called me back, and asked me how the young man found out that there were gold plates in the place where he found them. I answered that an angel of God had revealed it unto him.

"He then said to me, 'Let me see that certificate.' I accordingly took it out of my pocket and gave it to him, when he took it and tore it to pieces, saying that there was no such thing now as ministering of angels, and that if I would bring the plates to him, he would translate them. I informed him that part of the plates were sealed, and that I was forbidden to bring them. He replied, 'I cannot read a sealed book.' I left him and went to Mr. Mitchell, who sanctioned what Professor Anthon had said, respecting both the characters and the translation."

A number of years later, when he discovered the use to which his testimony had been given, Professor Anthon denied the statement of Martin Harris, although he did confess that such a person called to see him with such characters, but he treated it as a hoax. There may be some slight errors in the account of Martin Harris, but in the main his story must be true for it is the fulfillment of an ancient prophecy of Isaiah[b] almost word for word. It is not likely that Martin

---

[b]Isaiah's prophecy is as follows: "And the vision of all is become unto you as the words of a book that is sealed, which men deliver to one that is learned, saying, Read this, I pray thee: and he saith, I cannot; for it is sealed: And the book is delivered to him that is not learned, saying, Read this, I pray thee: and

Harris was familiar with the prophecy of Isaiah at that time and without question Professor Anthon had no intention of fulfilling prophecy in making his answer, but nevertheless such proved to be the case.

The Lost Manuscript.—The impression made on the mind of Martin Harris by this interview, resulted in his removal to Harmony to give further aid to Joseph Smith. He arrived about the 12th of April, 1828, and immediately commenced to write as the Prophet dictated his translation of the record. Martin continued in this work until the 14th of June, at which time one hundred and sixteen pages of manuscript on foolscap paper had been prepared. Some time after Martin Harris commenced to write he importuned the Prophet for the privilege of taking the manuscript home and showing it to some skeptical friends, who had sorely criticized him for the part he was taking in the work. He was desirous of convincing them; and they had, without doubt, pleaded with him to do this thing. Especially had his wife implored him for a look at the manuscript.

The Prophet inquired by Urim and Thummim, and the request of Martin was denied. However, he was not satisfied and importuned and pleaded with Joseph again to inquire of the Lord. This he did, but the answer was the same as before. Still Martin implored, and so insistent and prolonged were his pleadings that Joseph Smith again, the third time, inquired of the Lord. This time the answer was favorable. The request was granted on certain positive conditions. Martin was to show the manuscript to his brother, Preserved Harris, his wife, his father and mother and his wife's sister, Mrs. Cobb. No other person was to see the writings. In a most solemn covenant Martin bound himself to this agreement. When he arrived home, and pressure was brought to bear upon him, he forgot his solemn oath and permitted others to view the manuscript, with the result that by stratagem it passed out of his hands.

The Lord was displeased with Joseph Smith for his constant importuning, and took from him the Urim and Thummim after the departure of Martin Harris with the partial translation from the plates. When the fact was known that Martin had lost the manuscript,

---

he saith, I am not learned. Wherefore the Lord said, Forasmuch as this people draw near me with their mouth, and with their lips do honour me, but have removed their heart far from me, and their fear toward me is taught by the precept of men: Therefore, behold, I will proceed to do a marvellous work among this people, even a marvellous work and a wonder: for the wisdom of their wise men shall perish, and the understanding of their prudent men shall be hid" (Isa. 29:11-14).

For a discussion of this point see the "History of the Mormon Church," by B. H. Roberts, chapter 8. Also "Orson Pratt's Works." Chapter 6, and the Book of Mormon, 2 Nephi, 27 chapter.

the Prophet suffered the torments of the damned. He found no rest; there was no peace of conscience. In the bitterness of his soul he feared to approach the Lord. This condition continued for some time until one day the angel appeared to him, and returned the Urim and Thummim, that he might through them receive a revelation from the Lord (Doc. and Cov. Sec. 3). In this revelation it was made known that the purposes of the Lord were not frustrated, but the designs of men. Joseph was soundly rebuked and warned against yielding to temptation. Nevertheless the mercy of the Lord was extended to him because of his severe punishment and sore repentance. After the revelation was received, both the Urim and Thummim and the plates were taken from him, but in a few days were restored again. This was the most bitter lesson Joseph Smith ever received. It seemed necessary to prepare him for the great responsibilities yet before him.

In May of 1829 Joseph received another revelation (Doc. and Cov. Sec. 10) in which he was forbidden again to translate the portion of the record which had been lost. Satan had put it into the hearts of wicked men, the revelation declared, to alter the writings of the manuscript and then, if Joseph Smith should translate again, they would say that he could not do it twice alike, and thus they would catch him in his words which he had pretended to translate.

What the Lost Record Contained.—The lost manuscript contained the abridgment made by Mormon of the record of Nephi, from the time Lehi left Jerusalem down to the reign of King Benjamin, or to the words of Mormon, in the Book of Mormon. When Mormon made his abridgment of the records of the Nephites, the Lord directed him to attach also the small plates of Nephi, which contained the record of the people covering the same period of time as the abridgment down to the reign of King Benjamin. In this manner there were two accounts of that history, the abridgment and the original. Now the translation of the abridgment was lost; but the better account could still be translated, and the designs of Satan be defeated. Thus the "wise purpose" of the Lord, in directing Mormon to include Nephi's plates, was made known to Joseph Smith.

The Coming of Oliver Cowdery.—Martin Harris was never permitted to act as scribe again. For a time the Prophet was without assistance. For several months he was under the necessity of "laboring with his hands" on his small farm in Harmony and otherwise seeking employment. The work of the Lord was lagging. He must be about his mission. He prayed to the Lord for help. On the 5th of

JOSEPH RECEIVES THE RECORD

April, 1829, a young school teacher, Oliver Cowdery, came to Harmony to inquire of Joseph Smith regarding his work. Oliver Cowdery had been teaching school near the home of the Smiths in Manchester, and part of the time boarded with that family. From them he learned of the Prophet's vision, the coming of Moroni, and of the plates. He had a feeling that these stories were true and desired to investigate at close quarters. He was convinced of the truth of Joseph's story, and two days after his arrival in Harmony, commenced to write as the Prophet translated from the record. Later in the month of April the Lord gave to Oliver a revelation through Joseph Smith in which he was called to the work. In that revelation things were revealed that only Oliver Cowdery knew. From that time forth he continued to act as the amanuensis for Joseph Smith, until the Book of Mormon was finished.

Restoration of the Aaronic Priesthood.—While translating, Joseph Smith and Oliver Cowdery discovered that the question of baptism for the remission of sins was mentioned several times in the record. This caused them to marvel, for the doctrine of baptism was misunderstood in the world. They concluded to inquire of the Lord for light. On the 15th day of May, 1829, they retired to the woods and prayed for instruction on this question. While thus engaged in prayer a heavenly messenger descended in a cloud of light and said that he was John, known as John the Baptist in the New Testament. He said he acted under the direction of Peter, James and John, who held the keys of the Melchizedek Priesthood, and had been sent to confer on Joseph and Oliver the Aaronic Priesthood, which holds the keys of the temporal Gospel. He laid his hands upon their heads and said:

"Upon you my fellow servants, in the name of Messiah, I confer the Priesthood of Aaron, which holds the keys of the ministering of angels, and of the Gospel of repentance, and of baptism by immersion for the remission of sins; and this shall never be taken again from the earth, until the sons of Levi do offer again an offering unto the Lord in righteousness."

He stated that the Melchizedek Priesthood would soon be conferred upon them and that Joseph Smith should be called the first and Oliver Cowdery the second elder of the Church.

Joseph and Oliver Baptized.—This messenger, after conferring the Priesthood, instructed Joseph and Oliver to go down into the water and baptize each other. After which they were to lay hands upon each other and re-confer the Priesthood which he had bestowed upon them. There are two reasons why they should be commanded to do this thing. First, to confer the Priesthood before baptism, is contrary to the order of the organized Church, therefore they were commanded to confer the Priesthood upon each other in the regular way; after they were baptized. Second, the angel did for them that which they could not do for themselves. There was no one living in mortality who held the keys of this Priesthood, therefore it was necessary that this messenger, who held the keys of the Aaronic Priesthood in the Dispensation of the Meridian of Time, should be sent to confer this power. It is contrary to the order of heaven for those who have passed beyond the veil to officiate and labor for the living on the earth, only wherein mortal man cannot act, and thereby it becomes necessary for those who have passed through the resurrection to act for them. Otherwise John would have followed the regular order, which is practiced in the Church, and would have first baptized Joseph Smith and Oliver Cowdery and then conferred upon them the Aaronic Priesthood.

As the angel had commanded them, they repaired to the water where Joseph first baptized Oliver and then Oliver baptized Joseph. Immediately after coming out of the water they experienced great and glorious blessings, and being filled with the Holy Spirit, began to prophesy of the coming forth of the Church and the establishment of the great work of the Lord in the latter days. Their minds were now enlightened and the scriptures were opened to their understandings. For the first time in many centuries there now stood on the earth men with power to officiate in baptism for the remission of sin.

The fear of opposition compelled them to keep secret the matter of their ordination and baptism, except where they revealed it to a few personal friends, whom they could trust.

Restoration of the Melchizedek Priesthood.—In course of time, and very shortly after the coming of John the Baptist, Joseph and Oliver received the Melchizedek Priesthood from Peter, James and John. The date when this Priesthood was conferred is unknown, but it was only a few days after the first ordination. In a revelation given in 1842 (Doc. and Cov. Sec. 128) we are informed that it was between Harmony, Pennsylvania, and Colesville, New York, on the Susquehanna River, where it was conferred. In another revelation given in September, 1830, we are informed that the restoration was under the hands of Peter, James and John, "whom I have sent unto you, by whom I have ordained you and confirmed you to be apostles, and special witnesses of my name" (Doc. and Cov. Sec. 27).

Susquehanna River

Help from Joseph Knight.—While the work of translating was going on the Lord sent a friend in time of need to give material assistance to Joseph Smith and Oliver Cowdery. This was Joseph Knight, Sen., of Colesville, Broome County, New York. Having heard of the manner in which Joseph and Oliver were occupying their time, Mr. Knight brought them provisions from time to time, a distance of some thirty miles, and thus enabled them to continue their labor without interruption, which otherwise would have delayed the work.

Joseph and Oliver Remove to Fayette.—It was not destined that the work of translation should go on in Harmony, without interruption. Opposition finally made itself manifest and became so strong that even Isaac Hale—a man who believed in justice, law and order, but who did not express much faith in the mission of Joseph Smith— became somewhat bitter in his feelings. The necessity of a change of residence was apparent. Oliver Cowdery wrote to a young friend, David Whitmer of Fayette, New York, with whom he had previously corresponded regarding the coming forth of the Book of Mormon, desiring that he would come and take Joseph and himself to the Whitmer home in Fayette. This David Whitmer consented to do, and the removal was made in June, 1829.

When David was on the journey to Harmony on this mission, he was met some distance from the town of Harmony by Joseph and Oliver. In referring to this circumstance some years later, David Whitmer wrote: "Oliver told me that Joseph had informed him when I started from home, where I stopped the first night, how I read the sign at the tavern, where I stopped the next night, etc., and that I would be there that day for dinner, and this is why they had come out to meet me. All of which was exactly as Joseph had told Oliver, at which I was greatly astonished" (*Millennial Star*, Vol. 40, pp. 769-774).

At the Whitmer Home.—When they arrived in Fayette, they found Mr. Peter Whitmer, father of David, ready to receive them and anxious to know more concerning the work. Joseph and Oliver received their board free at the Whitmer home, and other timely assistance was also given them by members of the Whitmer family. David, John and Peter Whitmer, Jr., became very zealous in the work. The Lord spoke to each of them by revelation, calling them to cry repentance to their generation. The people of Seneca County, in which Fayette was situated, were friendly, and many houses were opened by those desiring to know more of the Prophet's message. Many were convinced and showed a willingness to obey the Gospel. Hyrum Smith, who had come to Fayette, David Whitmer and Peter Whitmer, Jr., were baptized, Hyrum and David by the Prophet, and Peter by Oliver Cowdery. Samuel H. Smith, younger brother of the Prophet, had been baptized while the Prophet and Oliver were in Harmony, Pennsylvania. He was the third person baptized in this dispensation, receiving the remission of his sins on the twenty-fifth day of May, 1829, just ten days after the appearing of John the Baptist; Oliver Cowdery baptized him. Samuel had accompanied Oliver from Manchester to Harmony early in April when Oliver came to inquire concerning the Prophet and the record he claimed to have, and remained with his brother Joseph during the spring. Samuel Smith had not taken to the Prophet's story as readily as other members of the family, and was rather hard to convince that Joseph and Oliver had been ordained and baptized. After much inquiry and explanation by Joseph and Oliver, Samuel retired alone to the woods, and in secret prayer obtained a revelation for himself. Now convinced, he was anxious to be baptized and to engage in the work of establishing "the cause of Zion."

CHAPTER 10

THE WITNESSES OF THE BOOK OF MORMON
1829-1830

The Witnesses Called.—In due time, in June, 1829, the Book of Mormon translation was finished. Three special witnesses must now be chosen who should behold the plates through divine favor and bear record to the world. This was according to the predictions of the ancient prophets who had kept the records of the Nephites. Nephi, son of Lehi, had prophesied: "Wherefore at that day when the book shall be delivered unto the man of whom I have spoken, the book shall be hid from the eyes of the world, that the eyes of none shall behold it save it be that three witnesses shall behold it, by the power of God, besides him to whom the book shall be delivered; and they shall testify to the truth of the book and the things therein. And there is none other which shall view it, save it be a few according to the will of God, to bear testimony of his word unto the children of men; for the Lord God hath said that the words of the faithful speak as if it were from the dead."[a]

In a revelation given at the request of Martin Harris (after his repentance, in March, 1829 (Doc. and Cov. Sec. 5), this statement is reiterated, and Martin was told he might be granted this great privilege of being one of the witnesses, if he would humble himself sufficiently and overcome his pride in mighty prayer and sincerity of heart, and acknowledge the things he had done which were wrong.

---

[a] 2 Nephi 27:12-13. Ether 5:2-4. Compare John 8:16-18.

It was natural for Oliver Cowdery, the Prophet's scribe, and David Whitmer, to desire to be the two other witnesses of the special three.

When the translation was finished, Joseph wrote to his parents requesting them to come to him. This information they conveyed to Martin Harris at Palmyra, who desired to accompany them. The next day after the word was received they started on the journey. The evening of their arrival at the Whitmer home was spent in reading the manuscript of the Book of Mormon, which caused them all to rejoice exceedingly. They had not previously realized the magnitude of the work of translation, nor had they received a clear understanding of what the book contained.

Oliver Cowdery

When the time arrived for the manifestation of the power of the Lord to the witnesses, as was the custom, early in the morning the little group at the Whitmer home engaged in singing and prayer. At the close of these services Joseph Smith arose and approaching Martin Harris said: "Martin Harris, you have got to humble yourself before God this day, that you may obtain a forgiveness of your sins, if you do, it is the will of God that you should look upon the plates, in company with Oliver Cowdery and David Whitmer." Lucy Smith, the Prophet's mother, who was present, said this was spoken, "with the solemnity that thrills through and through my veins to this day, when it occurs to my recollection."

These three men earnestly sought for the privilege of being the special witnesses, Joseph laid the matter before the Lord and received a revelation by Urim and Thummim granting their petition. The revelation is as follows:

Revelation to the Witnesses.—"Behold, I say unto you, that you must rely upon my word, which if you do with full purpose of heart, you shall have a view of the plates, and also of the breastplate, the sword of Laban, the Urim and Thummim, which were given to the brother of Jared upon the mount, when he talked with the Lord face to face, and the miraculous directors which were given to Lehi while in the wilderness, on the borders of the Red Sea.

"And it is by your faith that you shall obtain a view of them, even by that faith which was had by the prophets of old.

"And after that you have obtained faith, and have seen them with your eyes, you shall testify of them, by the power of God;

"And this you shall do that my servant Joseph Smith, Jun., may not be destroyed, that I may bring about my righteous purposes unto the children of men in this work.

"And ye shall testify that you have seen them, even as my servant Joseph Smith, Jun., has seen them, for it is by my power that he has seen them, and it is because he had faith.

"And he has translated the book, even that part which I have commanded him, and as your Lord and your God liveth it is true.

"Wherefore you have received the same power, and the same faith, and the same gift like unto him;

David Whitmer

"And if you do these last commandments of mine, which I have given you, the gates of hell shall not prevail against you; for my grace is sufficient for you, and you shall be lifted up at the last day.

"And I, Jesus Christ, your Lord and your God, have spoken it unto you, that I might bring about my righteous purposes unto the children of men. Amen." (Doc. and Cov. Sec. 17).

The Witnesses Behold the Plates.—A short time after this revelation was given, these four, Joseph Smith, Oliver Cowdery, David Whitmer and Martin Harris, retired to the woods and engaged in humble prayer. They asked the Lord to bestow upon them the blessing of the promise. Each prayed in turn, according to previous agreement. Joseph prayed first and after each had prayed and no answer of divine favor was obtained, they again observed the same order of prayer, but without result. Feeling it was because of his transgressions that no answer was received, Martin Harris suggested that he would withdraw from the others. After consultation this was agreed to, and Martin withdrew. Again the three knelt in prayer. Presently they beheld above them a light of great brilliancy, and an angel descended and stood before them. In his hand he held the plates, and before them were the other records and sacred things spoken of in the revelation. The angel took the golden book and turning leaf by leaf exhibited to the witnesses, the engravings thereon. He then turned to David and said, "David, blessed is the Lord, and he that keeps his commandments." Immediately after this they heard a voice in the bright light which shone above them saying: "These plates have been revealed by the power of God, and they have been translated by the power of God. The translation of them which you have seen is correct, and I command you to bear record of what you now see and hear."

Martin Harris

Joseph Smith now left Oliver and David and went in search of Martin Harris. He found him at a considerable distance fervently petitioning the Lord in prayer. With earnestness he pleaded with Joseph to join him that he too might be blessed with a vision of the plates. Joseph readily consented, and before they had prayed very long the same vision burst upon their presence and they beheld the same messenger. The angel again turned the leaves one by one and the same scene was enacted. Martin Harris was overjoyed and cried out: "'Tis enough; 'tis enough; mine eyes have beheld; mine eyes have beheld!" Jumping up he shouted hosannah and praised the Lord.

When they returned from this interview it was between three and four o'clock in the afternoon. The incident is related by the Prophet's mother in the following words:

"On coming in, Joseph threw himself down beside me, and exclaimed, 'Father, mother, you do not know how happy I am: the Lord has now caused the plates to be shown to three more besides myself. They have seen an angel, who has testified to them, and they will have to bear witness to the truth of what I have said for now they know for themselves, that I do not go about to deceive the people and I feel as if I was relieved of a burden which was almost too heavy for me to bear; and it rejoices my soul, that I am not any longer to be entirely alone in the world.' Upon this Martin Harris came in; he seemed almost overcome with joy, and testified boldly to what he had both seen and heard. And so did David and Oliver, adding, that no tongue could express the joy in their hearts, and the greatness of the things which they had both seen and heard."[b]

Testimony of the Three Witnesses.—In accord with the instruction they received in the revelation and by direct command from the voice of the Lord when they viewed the plates, the three witnesses gave to the world their united testimony in writing. This testimony, together with the testimony of eight other witnesses who also beheld the plates, has been published in every copy of the Book of Mormon as a witness to the unbelieving world. Their testimony is as follows:

"Be it known unto all nations, kindreds, tongues, and people, unto whom this work shall come: That we, through the grace of God the Father, and our Lord Jesus Christ, have seen the plates which contain this record, which is a record of the people of Nephi, and also of the Lamanites, their brethren, and also of the people of Jared, who came from the tower of which hath been spoken. And we also know that they have been translated by the gift and power of God, for his voice hath declared it unto us; wherefore we know of a surety that the work is true. And we also testify that we have seen the engravings which are upon the plates; and they have been shown unto us by the power of God, and not of man. And we declare with words of soberness, that an angel of God came down from heaven, and he brought and laid before our eyes, that we beheld and saw the plates, and the engravings thereon; and we know that it is by the grace of God the Father, and our Lord Jesus Christ, that we beheld and bear record that these things are true. And it is marvelous in our eyes. Nevertheless, the voice of the Lord commanded us that we should bear record of it; wherefore, to be obedient unto the commandments of God, we bear testimony of these things. And we know that if we are faithful in Christ, we shall rid our garments of the blood of all men, and be found spotless before the judgment seat of Christ, and shall dwell with him eternally in the heavens. And

---

[b]"History of the Prophet Joseph," p. 139, Lucy Smith.

the honor be to the Father, and to the Son, and to the Holy Ghost, which is one God. Amen.

>   Oliver Cowdery,
>   David Whitmer,
>   Martin Harris."

Testimony of the Eight Witnesses.—In addition to the testimony of the three witnesses, eight other witnesses were called to view the plates and to give testimony to the world, and became the "few according to the will of God, to bear testimony of his word unto the children of men." These eight men did not obtain the same privilege as the three special witnesses, for it was in the presence of an angel that they beheld the record, but they were shown the plates by Joseph Smith by command of the Lord. Their testimony is as follows:

"Be it known unto all nations, kindreds, tongues, and people, unto whom this work shall come: That Joseph Smith, Jun., the translator of this work, has shown unto us the plates of which hath been spoken, which have the appearance of gold; and as many of the leaves as the said Smith has translated we did handle with our hands; and we also saw the engravings thereon, all of which has the appearance of ancient work, and of curious workmanship. And this we bear record with words of soberness, that the said Smith has shown unto us, for we have seen and hefted, and know of a surety that the said Smith has got the plates of which we have spoken. And we give our names unto the world, to witness unto the world that which we have seen. And we lie not, God bearing witness of it.

Christian Whitmer,	John Whitmer,	Hyrum Smith,
Jacob Whitmer,	Hiram Page,	Samuel H. Smith."
Peter Whitmer, Jun.,	Joseph Smith, Sen.,	

Necessity of the Testimonies.—In all ages of the world when the Lord has had a work to be performed he has raised up witnesses. In this manner his works are attested so that those who reject them will be left without an excuse. The justice of the Lord demands that this shall be done. The Lord commanded Moses, when in the wilderness, that no man should be condemned except it be on the testimony of two or three witnesses. "One witness shall not rise up against a man for any iniquity, or for any sin in any sin that he sinneth; at the mouth of two witnesses or at the mouth of three witnesses, shall the matter be established" (Deut. 19:15.) The Savior himself bore witness to the justice and validity of this law when he contended with the Jews. Said he: "It is also written in your law, that the testimony of two men is true. I am one that beareth witness of myself, and the Father that sent me beareth witness of me." In this manner he condemned them for rejecting his testimony, which was attested by the scriptures and had the approval of his Father.

If Joseph Smith had given no other testimony, but his own, then he might justly have been condemned, for his testimony would not have been in keeping with the word of the Lord, but the testimony of three other men should be sufficient. Reinforced as that testimony is by the testimony of the eleven others, and by the witness which the book itself affords, the testimony given by Joseph Smith becomes binding on the world. All who reject it, the Lord said, shall be condemned, for the "testimony of two men is true," provided they are truthful witnesses. The Book of Mormon declares that in "the mouth of three witnesses shall these things be established; and the testimony of three, and this work, in the which shall be shown forth the power of God and also his word, of which the Father and the Son, and the Holy Ghost bear record—and all this shall stand as a testimony against the world at the last day" (Ether 5:4).

Validity of the Testimonies.—The witnesses of the Book of Mormon were true and faithful to their testimony throughout their lives. The time came, however, when all three of the special witnesses became estranged from Joseph Smith and departed from the Church because of their spirit of rebellion against the Prophet and the work. They were dealt with for their fellowship and excommunicated from the Church. While the Prophet lived, they retained their bitterness of spirit and remained aloof, but during all those years, and to the end of life, all three were steadfast in their testimony as found in the Book of Mormon. In the year 1848, after the Church had been driven from Nauvoo, Oliver Cowdery returned to the Church at Kanesville and humbly begged to be re-admitted as a member. Martin Harris also sought again a place and standing in the Church, and in the year 1870 he came to Utah to make his home. He was re-baptized Sept. 17, 1870, by Elder Edward Stevenson in the Endowment House and confirmed by Orson Pratt. He died in 1875, at Clarkston, Utah at the age of 92 years. David Whitmer never came back to the Church, but shortly before his death, in refutation of the statements that had gone forth that he had denied his testimony, he published it again to the world, in which he said: "It is recorded in the American Cyclopedia and the Encyclopedia Britannica, that I, David Whitmer, have denied my testimony as one of the Three Witnesses to the divinity of the Book of Mormon; and that the other two witnesses, Oliver Cowdery and Martin Harris, denied their testimony of that book. I will say once more to all mankind, that I have never at any time denied that testimony or any part thereof. I also testify to the world, that neither Oliver Cowdery nor Martin Harris ever at any time denied their testimony. They both died reaffirming the truth of the divine authenticity of the Book of Mormon."*c*

Impossibility of Collusion.—If there had been collusion between Joseph Smith and the witnesses, then of necessity they would have had to hold together and tell the same story. A disagreement on the part of any, or all of them, would have meant destruction to their plan, if it were not true. The boldness with which Joseph Smith and the Church met the situation, when these men rebelled, and took action against them and severed them from the Church, would never have been done if there had been fraud and collusion. The Prophet and the high council would not have dared to do it. This fact together with the other fact that after they were severed from the Church and had become estranged, that all three bore the same testimony, and all told the same story which they told when in the Church, precludes even the remotest possibility that they had planned together to deceive. These truths, together with much more evidence which cannot be mentioned here, is strong presumptive evidence of the authenticity of the solemn message given by these witnesses to the world.

Press on Which the Book of Mormon was Printed

The Angel Receives the Plates. —After the completion of the translation of the Book of Mormon in 1829, the angel again appeared to Joseph Smith and received back the plates into his keeping. Of this circumstance the Prophet wrote in 1838: "By the wisdom of God, they [the plates] remained safe in my hands, until I had accomplished by them what was required at my hand. When, according to arrangement, the messenger called for them, I delivered them up to him, and he has them in his charge until this day."

The Book of Mormon Printed. —The question of printing the

---

c"An Address to All Believers in Christ," David Whitmer. Compare "Millennial Star," 43:301.

THE
BOOK OF MORMON:

AN ACCOUNT WRITTEN BY THE HAND OF MORMON, UPON PLATES TAKEN FROM THE PLATES OF NEPHI.

Wherefore it is an abridgment of the Record of the People of Nephi; and also of the Lamanites; written to the Lamanites, which are a remnant of the House of Israel; and also to Jew and Gentile; written by way of commandment, and also by the spirit of Prophesy and of Revelation. Written, and sealed up, and hid up unto the LORD, that they might not be destroyed; to come forth by the gift and power of GOD, unto the interpretation thereof; sealed by the hand of Moroni, and hid up unto the LORD, to come forth in due time by the way of Gentile; the interpretation thereof by the gift of GOD; an abridgment taken from the Book of Ether.

Also, which is a Record of the People of Jared, which were scattered at the time the LORD confounded the language of the people when they were building a tower to get to Heaven: which is to shew unto the remnant of the House of Israel how great things the LORD hath done for their fathers; and that they may know the covenants of the LORD, that they are not cast off forever; and also to the convincing of the Jew and Gentile that JESUS is the CHRIST, the ETERNAL GOD, manifesting Himself unto all nations. And now if there be fault, it be the mistake of men; wherefore condemn not the things of GOD, that ye may be found spotless at the judgment seat of CHRIST.

BY JOSEPH SMITH, JUNIOR,
AUTHOR AND PROPRIETOR.

PALMYRA:
PRINTED BY E. B. GRANDIN, FOR THE AUTHOR.
1830.

Title Page of Book of Mormon

manuscript now confronted Joseph Smith. Not only was he without the necessary means, but printers were scarce and those who were approached were either prejudiced through bigotry, or unwilling for fear of the opposition of customers. Martin Harris, who possessed the means, came to the rescue with a promise to pay for the printing of the book. Finally a contract was entered into with Mr. Egbert B. Grandin, of Palmyra, who consented to print five thousand copies of the Book of Mormon for three thousand dollars. In the meantime the copyright to the book had been secured. The appearance of the words "Author and Proprietor," which appear on the title page of the first edition of the Book of Mormon, have caused some ridicule by enemies of Joseph Smith. This expression was printed in the book in accord with the law governing copyrights, and in no way detracts from the validity of the story of the translation of the record.

Soon after the completion of the translation and the securing of the copyright, the Lord commanded that Oliver Cowdery should transcribe the entire manuscript, and that in furnishing copy to the printer, the second copy should be used, and that only sheet by sheet, as the type should be set up. It was further provided that in going to and from the printing office, there should always be a guard to protect the manuscript, and that a guard should be placed at the home constantly to watch and protect the translation from evil disposed persons. These precautions were necessary because of the malicious opposition which prevailed in and about Palmyra, where the work was done. At times attempts were made to get the manuscript from the possession of Joseph and those who, with him, had the work in charge.

One man, named Cole, more cunning than the others who opposed the work, devised the plan of anticipating the publication of the book. Cole, an ex-justice of the peace, was printing a paper which he called *The Reflector*. The publisher was listed as Obediah Dogberry, who stated, "This paper will be published every week, at our Bower on Wintergreen Hill." He had announced to his subscribers that he would furnish them weekly installments of the Book of Mormon in his paper. Having access to the Grandin printing office, he commenced his publication by working on Sundays when the office was closed. In this manner he was able to publish a number of issues containing extracts from the printed sheets of the Book of Mormon. As the copyright was secured, he was warned and finally stopped from this method of stealing. The work of printing the book continued, but not without interruption, for great pressure was brought to bear upon the printer who was threatened by enemies of the latter-day work with a withdrawal of trade that would ruin his business. This came near breaking the contract. However, after some delays, the book was finished some time in the spring of 1830, and made ready to go forth, as the Nephite prophets had foretold, to the Gentiles and then to the house of Israel as a voice speaking out of the dust.

CHAPTER 11

REVELATION ON DOCTRINE AND CHURCH GOVERNMENT

1829-1830

Revelation to the Witnesses.—Before the Church could be organized it was essential that there be revealed such matters as pertained to the organization of the Church. This was done between the time the witnesses viewed the plates of the ancient record and the sixth of April, 1830. The first of these (Doc. and Cov. Sec. 18) was given to Joseph Smith, Oliver Cowdery and David Whitmer, at Fayette. It made known the calling of the Twelve Apostles who should be chosen in this dispensation, although it was about six years before they were called. It gave instructions "relative to the building up of the Church of Christ according to the fulness of the Gospel." It was also stated that the Book of Mormon contained "all things written concerning the foundation" of the Church and the Gospel. The Church, when organized, should be built upon the foundation of the Gospel and "the gates of hell shall not prevail" against it. Moreover, it was declared that "the world is ripened in iniquity, and it must needs be that the children of men are stirred up unto repentance both the Gentiles and also the house of Israel." To Oliver Cowdery and David Whitmer, the Lord said that all men were now called on to repent, for the Priesthood was restored and the opportunity given for the remission of sins. These men had been called as special witnesses, and therefore were under obligation to warn the world. Until this time men had not been privileged to be baptized, for there had been no authority on earth to officiate in Gospel ordinances. The

Lord said the worth of souls was great, for Christ had suffered "the pains of all men that all might repent and come unto him." As many as would repent and be baptized in the name of Jesus Christ and endure to the end should be saved. It was made clear in this revelation that all men must take upon them the name of Jesus Christ, for in his name should "they be called in the last day." Otherwise they "cannot have a place in the kingdom" of the Father.

The Twelve Apostles.—Not only were Joseph Smith and the witnesses to the Book of Mormon to be called to testify, but there were to be twelve other witnesses, who should be appointed to declare the Gospel to both Gentile and Jew. The three witnesses of the Book of Mormon were designated to search out these Twelve Apostles, who were to have charge of the preaching of the Gospel in all the world.

Revelation Given to Martin Harris.—The next great commandment (Doc. and Cov. Sec. 19) was given to Martin Harris, in March, 1830, as one of the special three witnesses. Martin was admonished and warned against his weaknesses, and was commanded to teach the first principles of the Gospel and declare "glad tidings" upon the mountains, and "every high place, and among the people," unto the end of his life. If he should fail, then misery should he receive. He was further instructed to keep his contract with the printer, and impart of his substance for the printing of the Book of Mormon, which "contains the truth and the word of God."

The Atonement and Eternal Punishment Explained.—The most important teaching in this revelation was the doctrine of the atonement and the explanation of the expression "eternal punishment." "I am Alpha and Omega," said the Lord, "yea, even I am he, the beginning and the end, the Redeemer of the world. I, having accomplished and finished the will of him whose I am, even the Father, concerning me—having done this that I might subdue all things unto myself. Retaining all power, even to the destroying of Satan and his works at the end of the world, and the last great day of judgment, which I shall pass upon the inhabitants thereof, judging every man according to his works and the deeds which he hath done.

"And surely every man must repent or suffer, for I, God, am endless. Wherefore, I revoke not the judgments which I shall pass, but woes shall go forth, weeping, wailing and gnashing of teeth, yea, to those who are found on my left hand. Nevertheless, it is not written that there shall be no end to this torment, but it is written endless torment. Again it is written eternal damnation; wherefore it is more express than other scriptures, that it might work upon the hearts of the children of men, altogether for my name's glory. Wherefore, I shall explain unto you this mystery for it is meet unto you to know even as mine apostles. * * *

"For, behold, the mystery of godliness, how great is it! For, behold, I am endless, and the punishment which is given from my hand, is endless punishment, for Endless is my name. Wherefore—

Eternal punishment is God's punishment.

Endless punishment is God's punishment."

Then follows the statement that Jesus Christ "suffered the pains of all that they might not suffer if they would repent." These sufferings were most exquisite and sore, which caused him "the greatest of all, to tremble because of pain, and bleed at every pore, and to suffer both body and spirit," and would that he "might not drink the bitter cup and shrink." Nevertheless he partook of that cup and finished his work, and this that men might not suffer if they will repent; but if they will not repent then they must suffer even as he.

Revelation on Church Government.—In April, 1830, just before the organization of the Church, another very important revelation (Doc. and Cov. Sec. 20) was received on Church government. In it the date for the organization of the Church was designated as April 6. The Church was to be regularly "organized and established agreeable to the laws of our country" by the will and commandment of the Lord. These commandments were given to Joseph Smith and Oliver Cowdery, who had been called and ordained to be apostles, or special witnesses for Christ. Joseph Smith was to be the first elder of the Church and Oliver Cowdery the second elder, and they were to ordain each other to these callings, according to the grace of Jesus Christ. Other matters of great importance revealed are as follows:

Mention is made of the matter of translation of the Book of Mormon, which is said to contain the record of a fallen people, and the fulness of the Gospel to the Gentiles and also the Jews. By the opening of the heavens, and the inspiration given to men who are called to his holy work, the Lord has shown that "he is the same God yesterday, today, and forever," and does inspire men and call them to his work in this age and generation, as well as in generations of old.

By these great witnesses the world shall be judged, "even as many as shall come to a knowledge of the work." Those who receive it in righteousness shall receive a crown of eternal life, while those who reject it shall be condemned. It is declared that the Lord has spoken, and the elders of the Church have heard and bear witness so that through their testimony man may know there is a God in heaven, who is infinite and eternal, from everlasting to everlasting, the same unchangeable Framer of heaven and earth and all things which are in them. Man is created in the image of God, male and female, and is commanded to love and serve him. Through transgression of his laws, man became fallen, wherefore the Only Begotten Son was sent into the world to suffer temptations—but gave no heed to them—was crucified, died, and rose the third day and ascended into heaven to reign in power. All who believe on him and are baptized and endure to the end, shall be saved, no matter when they lived on the earth. Men everywhere must repent and believe in Christ, worshiping the Father in the name of the Son and enduring in faith, or they cannot be saved. Justification through grace is true, as also is sanctification, to all who love the Father with all their might, mind and strength. The dangers of falling away from grace are pointed out, with a warning to the members of the Church to "take heed and pray lest they fall into temptation."

Manner of Baptism Explained.—By way of commandment to the Church the manner of Baptism is set forth as follows: "All those who humble themselves before God, and desire to be baptized and come forth with broken hearts and contrite spirits, and witness before the Church that they have truly repented of all their sins, and are willing to take upon them the name of Jesus Christ, having a determination to serve him to the end, and truly manifest by their works that they have received of the Spirit of Christ unto the remission of their sins, shall be received into his church." No person can be received into the Church unless he has arrived unto the years of accountability, which is eight years, for he must be capable of repentance, which infants are not. Baptism is to be administered in the following manner unto all who repent:

How Baptism is Performed.—"The person who is called of God, and has authority from Jesus Christ to baptize, shall go down into the water with the person who has presented him or herself for baptism, and shall say, calling him or her by name,—Having been commissioned of Jesus Christ, I baptize you in the name of the Father, and of the Son, and of the Holy Ghost. Amen. Then shall he immerse him or her in the water, and come forth again out of the water."

Duties of Elders, Priests, Teachers, Deacons and Members.—An apostle is said to be an elder. His calling is to baptize and ordain other officers in the Church. It should here be explained that at the organization of the Church and for some time thereafter, the officers mentioned here were all that were needed. As the Church expanded the Lord revealed the duties of other officers in their time. Elders are to baptize, confirm members, preach, expound the scriptures, administer the sacrament and take charge of meetings which are to be conducted "as they," the elders, "are led by the Holy Ghost, according to the commandments and revelations."

The priest is to teach, expound, baptize, and administer the sacrament. He may ordain other priests, teachers and deacons, but cannot lay on hands for the gift of the Holy Ghost. He may take the lead of meetings in the absence of higher authority. It is his duty to visit the home of the members and exhort them to pray vocally and in secret and to attend to all family duties. When called upon he is to assist the elder in his duties.

The teacher is to be the guardian of the Church. He is to see that there is no iniquity in the Church, neither lying, backbiting, or evil speaking among the members, and to see that the Church meet together often and that the members perform their duties. He is to take the lead of meetings if there is no elder or priest present and may assist them in their duties. He cannot baptize, confirm, or administer the sacrament.

The deacon is to assist the teacher and other officers in the Church, but he cannot baptize, confirm, or administer the sacrament.

Conferences of the Church.—The elders of the Church are instructed to meet in conference once in three months, or from time to time as they may determine, to transact such business as may come before them. All who are ordained are to receive certificates of ordination, and shall be accepted as officers in the Church by the vote of the members.

Duties of Church Members.—All members shall be received by baptism after they have repented of their sins. They shall have sufficient time to be taught the Gospel and church government before they are confirmed and partake of the sacrament. Children are to be brought to the elders of the Church, who shall bless them. The members must meet together often to partake of the sacrament in remembrance of the Lord Jesus Christ. The elder or priest who shall administer "shall kneel with the Church and call upon the Father in solemn prayer," repeating the words which the Lord himself has given.

Transgressors.—Any member of the Church transgressing the commandments of the Lord, or the rules of the Church, shall be dealt with as the scriptures direct. If any are expelled their names shall be "blotted out" and not kept on the records of the Church.

Recommendations of Members.—Records of members are to be kept in a book, and the members moving from one branch to another shall take a letter of recommendation, or certificate, stating that they are in standing in the Church. This shall be presented to the presiding officer in the branch with which they desire to unite.

Summary.—These commandments and instructions were given through Joseph Smith, shortly before the organization of the Church, to guide him and his companions in Church government. They are all important because they deal with the fundamental principles of the Gospel and doctrines of the Church. They set forth clearly many things which were familiarly known in the primitive Church, but which were either lost or perverted during the ages of apostasy and departure from the standards set by the Savior and his disciples. Again they are restored in their simplicity, freed from all mysticism and error, for the salvation of mankind.

CHAPTER 12

ORGANIZATION OF THE CHURCH
1830

The Church Organized.—It was made known shortly after the bestowal of the Melchizedek Priesthood, that the Church of Jesus Christ was to be organized. It was after Joseph Smith and his companions had engaged in solemn prayer that the word of the Lord came to them in the home of Father Peter Whitmer, "commanding us," the Prophet writes, "that I should ordain Oliver Cowdery to be an elder in the Church of Jesus Christ; and that he also should ordain me to the same office; and then to ordain others, as it should be made known unto us from time to time. We were, however, commanded to defer this our ordination until such time as it should be practicable to have our brethren, who had been and who should be baptized, assembled together, when we must have their sanction to our thus proceeding to ordain each other, and have them decide by vote whether they were willing to accept us as spiritual teachers or not; when also we were commanded to bless bread and break it with them, and to take wine, bless it and drink it with them; afterward proceed to ordain each other according to commandment; then call out such men as the Spirit should dictate, and ordain them; and then attend to the laying on of hands for the gift of the Holy Ghost, upon all those whom we had previously baptized, doing all things in the name of the Lord."

Fulfilment of the Promise.—On the sixth day of April 1830, the time for the fulfilment of this promise arrived, Joseph and a few of those who had been baptized met in the house of Peter Whitmer,

Sen., and proceeded, as the Lord had instructed them, to organize the Church. It was on a Tuesday, and there were six in number, namely, Joseph Smith, Oliver Cowdery, Hyrum Smith, Peter Whitmer Jr., David Whitmer and Samuel H. Smith. The small, but momentous meeting, was opened by solemn prayer. Those present then proceeded to express their willingness, as instructed by divine commandment, to accept Joseph Smith and Oliver Cowdery as their teachers in the things of the kingdom of God. Then they were called upon to declare whether or not they were willing to proceed to organize the Church of Jesus Christ. To both propositions they consented with unanimous voice. "I then laid my hands upon Oliver Cowdery," says the Prophet, " and ordained him an elder of the Church of Jesus Christ of Latter-day Saints; after which he ordained me also to the office of elder of said Church. We then took bread, blessed it, and brake it with them; and also wine, blessed, and drank it with them. We then laid our hands on each individual member of the Church present, that they might receive the gift of the Holy Ghost, and be confirmed members of the Church of Christ. The Holy Ghost was poured out upon us to a very marked degree, some prophesied, whilst we all praised the Lord, and rejoiced exceedingly."

All six of these young men—Hyrum Smith, the oldest, was but 31 years of age—had been baptized previously to the organization. They were all again baptized on that memorable day, April 6, 1830.

A Record to be Kept.—While they were still in session in this meeting of organization, a revelation (Doc. and Cov. Sec. 21) was given to the Church in which they were instructed to keep a record. In this record, Joseph Smith was to be called "a seer, a translator, a prophet, an apostle of Jesus Christ, and elder of the Church through the will of God the Father, and the grace of your Lord Jesus Christ." The Church was also commanded to give heed unto all his words and commandments, "as he receiveth them, as if from mine own mouth, in all patience and faith," said the Lord. By doing this "the gates of hell" should not prevail against them, for the Lord would dispel the powers of darkness. The Prophet would no longer have to mourn for Zion, for he should have inspiration to move the cause of Zion in mighty power, for the days of her rejoicing were at hand. Oliver Cowdery was appointed "the first preacher of the Church, unto the Church, and before the world, yea, before the Gentiles and * * * to the Jews also."

Destiny of the Church.—In the manner here described, there came into the world a power, destined to grow and expand until it shall fill the earth, for it is the "kingdom which shall never be destroyed * * * and it shall stand forever." At the time of the organization, however, its influence and power appeared to be insignificant; yet it caused, even then, consternation and fear in the hearts of the wicked, and strenuous efforts were launched to bring it to destruction.

Others Called to the Ministry.—Before the meeting closed Joseph and Oliver called out others and ordained them to different offices in the Priesthood, as the Spirit manifested unto them, presumably to the offices in the Aaronic Priesthood. The Spirit of the Lord was poured out upon them in abundance, and after a happy time spent in testimony and witnessing to each other the blessings of the Lord, they dismissed the meeting, feeling that they were now individually members of The Church of Jesus Christ, and acknowledged as such of God. There were others present besides the six who performed the organization of the Church. Six persons were required by law to properly form a society or organization of the kind. Others who were present also received of the Spirit of the Lord in the meeting and being convinced of the truth came forward and desired to be united with the Church. Shortly afterwards they were also baptized. Among these were the Prophet's parents, Joseph Smith, Sen. and Lucy Mack Smith; also Martin Harris and Orrin Porter Rockwell.

Baptism a New and Everlasting Covenant.—As stated, all six of the original members of the Church were again baptized on the day of the organization. This action was due, in part at least, to the fact that baptism is the doorway into the Church as well as for the remission of sins. There had been a few others baptized before the sixth of April. (See Ch. 9.) Some of those previously baptized raised the question as to why they should again be baptized. In consequence of their desire to unite with the Church without re-baptism, the Prophet inquired of the Lord in relation to the matter and received the following revelation:

"Behold, I say unto you, that all old covenants have I caused to be done away in this thing; and this is a new and an everlasting covenant, even that which was from the beginning.

"Wherefore, although a man should be baptized an hundred times it availeth him nothing, for you cannot enter in at the strait gate by the law of Moses, neither by your dead works.

"For it is because of your dead works that I have caused this last covenant and this church to be built up unto me, even as in days of old.

"Wherefore, enter ye in at the gate, as I have commanded, and seek not to counsel your God. Amen" (Doc. and Cov. Sec. 22).

CHAPTER 13

BEGINNING OF THE PUBLIC MINISTRY OF THE CHURCH
1830

The First Public Discourse.—On Sunday, April 11, 1830, the work of proselyting was publicly launched. The first discourse was preached by Oliver Cowdery. The meeting was held by appointment at the home of "Father" Peter Whitmer, where the meeting of organization had been held the Tuesday preceding. A goodly number of members and investigators were present. The impression made on the minds of those assembled was favorable, and the same day Hiram Page, Katherine Page, Christian Whitmer, Anne Whitmer, Jacob Whitmer and Elizabeth Whitmer, were baptized. One week later (April 18) Peter Whitmer, Sen., Mary Whitmer, William Jolly, Elizabeth Jolly, Vincent Jolly, Richard B. Preston and Elizabeth Ann Whitmer, were added to the Church.

The Ministry of Joseph Smith in Colesville.—Later in the month of April Joseph Smith paid a visit to the Knight family in Colesville, Broome County, N.Y. He had been on very friendly terms with Joseph Knight, Sen., and had been materially assisted by that gentleman from time to time, while translating the plates. Mr. Knight and his family were Universalists, with broad, liberal views. They were willing to reason in a friendly spirit with Joseph Smith on the scriptures. Several public meetings were held in Colesville which were attended by many friends and strangers. Newel Knight, son of Joseph Knight, Sen., was a regular attendant at these meetings, and seemed to be deeply impressed. He and the Prophet held many conversations on scriptural subjects and the plan of salvation, in which a favorable impression was made on the mind of Newel. He promised to assist Joseph in one of these meetings by offering vocal prayer, but when the time came his courage failed him. Later he expressed a desire to go out in the woods by himself and there, where he could be alone, offer vocal prayer, a thing to which he evidently was not accustomed. The following morning, in fulfilment of his promise, he retired into the woods alone, with a troubled conscience because of his failure to keep his promise on the previous occasion. Kneeling in a secluded spot he attempted to offer vocal prayer, but his lips were sealed. He could not pray. He began to feel uneasy and became troubled in both mind and body. When he arrived home his wife was greatly alarmed at his strange appearance. He requested her to send for Joseph, which was done. When he came he found Newel suffering very much; his visage was distorted, and his limbs were twisted out of shape in a frightful manner. Presently he was caught up from the floor and tossed about the room. The strange scene and excitement brought many of the neighbors to the house, who witnessed his peculiar malady.

The First Miracle.—After some difficulty Joseph succeeded in taking Newel by the hand, and with great earnestness Newel pleaded with him to cast the devil out of him, for he knew he was possessed. The Prophet said, "If you know that I can, it shall be done." Then, almost unconsciously, he rebuked the evil spirit in the name of Jesus Christ and commanded him to depart. Immediately Newel spoke, saying he saw the evil spirit leave him and vanish from his sight. This was the first miracle performed in this dispensation. As soon as the devil departed Newel became normal again, his distortions of body ceased, and the Spirit of the Lord opened his vision to a glorious manifestation of the heavens.

Those who were present were greatly astonished when they saw the casting out of the devil, and the witness of the Spirit of the Lord. Nearly all of those who were present later became members of the Church.

The First Conference of the Church.—Shortly after this event, Joseph returned to Fayette. Newel Knight followed him and was baptized during the last week in May, by David Whitmer. On the 9th of June the first conference of the Church was held in Fayette. The Church at that time numbered twenty-seven souls. There were many others present at the meetings, some of whom were friendly and some who believed. At this conference the sacrament was administered and those recently baptized were confirmed. Others were sustained by the members to receive the Priesthood, and were ordained. The officers at the commencement of the Conference were, Joseph Smith, Oliver Cowdery, David Whitmer, Peter Whitmer and Ziba Peterson, each of whom held the office of elder in the Church. During this conference Samuel H. Smith was ordained to the office of

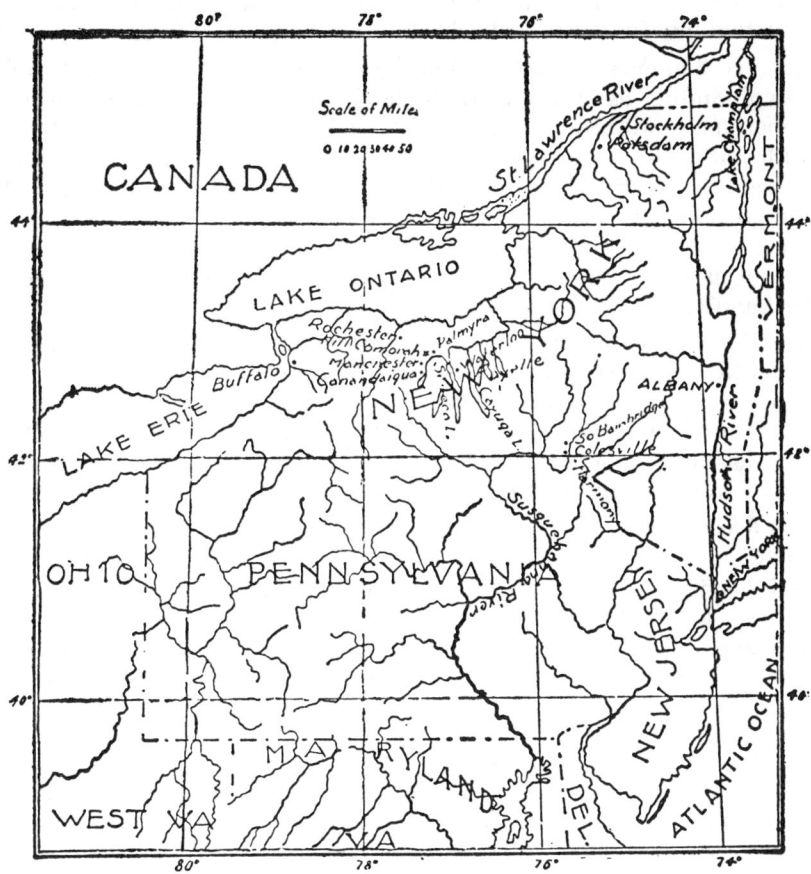

Map of New York and Pennsylvania

an elder, Joseph Smith, Sen., Hyrum Smith and Martin Harris were ordained priests, and Hiram Page and Christian Whitmer were ordained teachers. At the close of this conference there were in the Church seven ordained elders, three priests and two teachers. Oliver Cowdery was appointed to keep the record of the Church and minutes of meetings until the next conference. The Holy Spirit was poured out upon them. Many of this little band composing the Church were given the spirit of prophecy, while others beheld visions and remarkable manifestations from the heavens. Newel Knight saw in vision the great work which would yet be accomplished through the preaching of the Gospel and the organization of the Church. He beheld the Redeemer and received the assurance that he would be admitted into his presence to dwell in his kingdom forever.

"To find ourselves engaged in the very same order of things," said Joseph Smtih, "as observed by the holy apostles of old; to realize the importance and solemnity of such proceedings; and to witness and feel with our own natural sense, the like glorious manifestations of the powers of the Priesthood, the gift and blessing of the Holy Ghost, and the goodness and condescension of a merciful God unto such as obey the everlasting Gospel of our Lord Jesus Christ, combined to create within us sensations of rapturous gratitude, and inspire us with fresh zeal and energy in the cause of truth."

Eleven other converts were baptized at the close of this conference, by David Whitmer, in Seneca Lake, where most of the other baptisms were performed. Those added to the Church at this time were: John Poorman, John Jolly, Julia Ann Jolly, Harriet Jolly, Jerusha Smith (the wife of Hyrum Smith), William, Catherine and Don Carlos Smith; and Peter, Caroline and Electa Rockwell.

Second Visit to Colesville.—Joseph Smith again paid a visit to Colesville a short time after this conference. Oliver Cowdery, John and David Whitmer accompanied him. They found a number of persons anxiously awaiting them and desiring baptism. A meeting was appointed for the Sabbath; on Saturday a dam was constructed across a stream in preparation for the ordinance on the following day. During the night the dam was maliciously destroyed. It was later learned that this was the work of a mob, at the instigation of sectarian priests. On Sunday the meeting was held as contemplated. Oliver Cowdery was the principal speaker, but others also spoke. The first principles of the Gospel were presented and witness to the divine message of the Book of Mormon was borne. In the meeting were many who had helped to form the mob, who, at the close, endeavored to destroy the influence of the meeting, but were unsuccessful. Extreme bitterness was manifested on the part of those who opposed. The sister of Newel Knight's wife was violently treated because she was kindly disposed, and against her will was forced by a Rev. Shearer, to return to her father's home, some distance from her sister's where she was stopping. This man, a Presbyterian minister, on false pretenses, obtained from the father a power of attorney, by which

BEGINNING OF THE PUBLIC MINISTRY

he dragged her off. His labor was all in vain, for she also was baptized.

Early Monday morning the dam was replaced and thirteen persons were baptized by Oliver Cowdery. They were: Emma, wife of Joseph Smith; Hezekiah Peck and wife, Joseph Knight, Sen., and wife, William Stringham and wife, Joseph Knight, Jr., Aaron Culver and wife, Levi Hale, Polly Knight and Julia Stringham.

Arrest of Joseph Smith.—Before they were through with the ordinance the mob began to gather. They surrounded the house of Joseph Knight, Sen., prepared to do violence, but through the blessings of the Lord the Saints were protected, but were subjected to numerous insults and threatenings. A meeting was called for that evening for the purpose of attending to the confirmation of those baptized in the morning. When they met at the appointed hour, they were all surprised at the appearance of a constable, who with a warrant, arrested Joseph on the charge of being "a disorderly person, setting the country in an uproar by preaching the Book of Mormon." The constable frankly informed him that the arrest was for the purpose of getting him into the hands of a mob, then lying in ambush for him, but he would save him from their hands as he, the constable, had discovered that Joseph was not the sort of person he had been led to believe. As Joseph accompanied the constable in a wagon, they encountered the mob, not far from the home of Joseph Knight. The mobbers waited for the prearranged signal from the constable, but he, whipping up his horse, obtained a lead. The mobbers followed as best they could. In the flight one of the wagon wheels came off, and before it could be replaced the mobbers were again in sight. However, the wheel was replaced in time and with renewed energy Joseph was able to escape.

The constable took Joseph to South Bainbridge, Chenango County, and lodged him in a tavern, where he kept guard all night. The following day a court convened to investigate the charges. Great excitement prevailed because of falsehoods which had been circulated freely among the people. Joseph Knight, Sen., engaged the services of two respectable farmers who were versed in the law, namely, James Davidson and John Reid, and brought them to South Bainbridge to defend the Prophet.

The Trial at South Bainbridge.—The enemies of Joseph Smith scoured the country for witnesses who would testify against him. The justice of the peace who heard the case, Joseph Chamberlain, was a man of fair mind and a lover of justice. Many witnesses were heard, but among those who testified were Josiah Stowel, Jonathan Thompson and the two daughters of Mr. Stowel, all of whom gave evidence of his good character. Other testimony was proved to be false. The trial lasted from ten o'clock in the morning until midnight, when a verdict of "not guilty" was rendered.

The Second Arrest.—No sooner was Joseph freed by the court than he was again arrested on a second warrant from Broome County, a distance of about fifteen miles. The constable who came for him forced him to leave that night without permitting him to eat, although he had been in the court room all day without nourishment. He took him to Colesville and lodged him in a tavern. Then, calling in a number of rowdies, he began to abuse his prisoner with the assistance of his rabble. Spitting upon him and pointing their fingers at him they cried in fiendish glee, "Prophesy! prophesy!" Being near his home, Joseph requested the constable to take him there for the remainder of the night, but this was denied him. He asked for something to eat and was given some crusts of bread and water.

The Trial at Colesville.—The next day the trial began before three justices. The most able help had been secured to prosecute the case while the defense was again represented by Esquires Reid and Davidson. Many witnesses were called who bore false and contradictory testimony. Newel Knight was placed upon the stand and questioned in ridicule by one of the lawyers, named Seymour, in relation to the casting out of a devil from his person, but the testimony turned to the discomfiture of the prosecution.

At the close of the testimony the court deliberated for about thirty minutes, although it was then nearly two o'clock a.m. and they had been in session since the morning of the previous day. The prisoner was brought before the court and the presiding justice said: "Mr. Smith, we have had your case under consideration, examined the testimony and find nothing to condemn you, and therefore you are discharged." The judges then proceeded to reprimand him severely, "Not because anything derogatory to his character in any shape had been proved against him by the host of witnesses that had testified during the trial," said Mr. Reid, "but merely to please those fiends in human shape who were engaged in the unhallowed persecution of an innocent man, sheerly on account of his religious opinions."

Statement of Mr. Reid.—Several years later, Mr. Reid visited Nauvoo, and in the course of an address said, speaking of these trials:

"But, alas! the devil, not satisfied with his defeat (at the first trial) stirred up a man not unlike himself, who was more fit to dwell among the fiends of hell than to belong to the human family, to go to Colesville and get another writ, and take him to Broome County for another trial. They were sure they could send that boy to hell, or to Texas, they did not care which; and in half an hour after he was discharged by the court he was arrested again, and on the way to Colesville for another trial. I was again called upon by his friends to defend him against his malignant persecutors, and clear him from the false charges they had preferred against him. I made every reasonable excuse I could, as I was nearly worn down through fatigue and want of sleep, as I had been engaged in law suits for two days, and nearly the whole of two nights. But I saw the persecution was great against him; and here, let me say, Mr. Chairman, singular as it may seem, while Mr. Knight was pleading with me to go, a peculiar impression, or thought struck my mind, that I must go and defend him, for he was the Lord's anointed. I did not know what it meant, but thought I must go and clear the Lord's anointed. I said I would go, and started with as much faith as the apostles had when they could remove mountains, accompanied by Father Knight, who was like the old patriarchs that followed the ark of God to the city of David. * * * We got him away that night from the midst of three hundred people without his receiving any injury; but I am well aware that we were assisted by some higher power than man; for to look back on the scene, I cannot tell how we succeeded in getting him away. I take no glory to myself; it was the Lord's work and marvelous in our eyes" (*Times and Seasons* 5:549-552).

Inspiration of the Attorneys.—At the trial the Prophet's lawyers, who were not members of the Church, spoke with an inspiration that caused their enemies to quake before them. So powerful were their words that many of the assembled multitude were pricked in their hearts. The constable who had been so vicious came forward and apologized for his ill-treatment and misbehavior, and revealed the plans of the mob who were then prepared to tar and feather the Prophet and ride him on a rail. By the aid of the constable, Joseph was able to escape and make his way in safety to his sister's home, where he found his wife awaiting him.

The Mob Threatens Joseph and Oliver.—A few days later Joseph Smith and Oliver Cowdery returned to Colesville to confirm those whom they had been forced to leave, at the time of Joseph's arrest. Their presence was the signal for the mobbers to again assemble. So sinister were their movements that Joseph and Oliver departed from the town without waiting for refreshments. Their enemies pursued them but through extreme diligence they were able to make their escape. All night they traveled, except for a short period when they sought some rest in sleep, each taking turn in watching. The next day they arrived home, footsore and weary.

The spirit of opposition which took such decided form, was the result of agitation on the part of professors of religion. The Rev. Shearer, Cyrus McMaster, Dr. Boyington and a Mr. Benton, pillars in the Presbyterian Church, incited the mobbers to do their work. Benton was the man who signed the first warrant for Joseph Smith's arrest as a "disorderly person" for preaching the Book of Mormon. In this manner Satan stirred up the hearts of the people to try and overthrow the work.

Missionary Journey of Samuel H. Smith.—In the month of June, 1830, Samuel Harrison Smith was set apart by the Prophet to take a missionary journey to the east. This may be termed the first missionary journey in the Church. Taking with him several copies of the Book of Mormon, he started on his way. The first day he traveled twenty-five miles, and on the way attempted to sell copies of the book, but without success. When night came on he went to an inn, faint and hungry; approaching the proprietor he asked him if he did not want to buy a book which contained the history of the Indians.

"I do not know," the man replied, "how did you get hold of it?"

"It was translated by my brother, from some plates of gold, that he found buried in the earth," was Samuel's reply.

"You liar!" said the landlord, "get out of my house, you shan't stay one minute with your books."

Samuel Smith was discouraged but continued his journey, sleeping under an apple tree. In the morning he called at the home of Rev. John P. Greene, a Methodist minister, who was just leaving on a preaching tour. Like the others, whom he had approached, he was not interested in the book. However, he manifested a friendly spirit, and at the earnest solicitation of Samuel consented to take a subscription paper and try to sell copies of the book. Samuel left him a copy of the Book of Mormon with the promise to call again in about two weeks. At his return Samuel was disappointed to learn that there had been no sale. On his way to the home of Mr. Greene, Samuel again passed the tavern and found the tavern keeper had died of smallpox. He returned home after his labors were finished, feeling that his work had proved to be fruitless. More out of curiosity than desire, both Mr. Greene and his wife read the book and were deeply impressed. Samuel sold a copy to Phineas Howe Young and this copy was read by his brother, Brigham Young. The copy left with John P. Greene and the one sold to Phineas Howe Young brought the first direct information of the restoration of the gospel to the Young family and some of their friends, including **Heber C. Kimball.**

Joseph Smith, Sen., Visits Potsdam.—About this time Joseph Smith, Sen., and his youngest son, Don Carlos, departed on a similar journey to Potsdam, New York. Potsdam was the home of Asael Smith, father of Joseph Smith, Sen., and several of his children. Joseph was more successful on this trip than his son Samuel apparently had been, for his father Asael accepted the truth of the everlasting Gospel, as also did most of his children. Jesse, the oldest son of Asael, rejected the message of his brother Joseph and manifested a very bitter spirit against the Gospel all his life.

Book of Moses Revealed.—During the summer of 1830, the Lord revealed to the Church a number of important revelations. In June, the Prophet received the words of the Lord to Moses, at a time when Moses was caught up into a high mountain where he talked with the Lord face to face. This revelation was augmented later by more of the writings of Moses, which are found in the Pearl of Great Price. Some of the important knowledge imparted in this revelation is as follows: The works of the Lord are without end. No man can behold all the works of the Father without partaking of his glory, and that cannot be given in mortal life. Moses was created in the similitude, or likeness, of the Only Begotten Son. The generations of men passed before his view and he saw from the beginning to the end—all through the spiritual eye, for the natural eye cannot behold the glory of the Lord. After this vision had passed, Moses was left unto himself and it was several hours before he gained his natural strength. Then Satan came, tempting him and commanding him to worship him, but Moses said: "Who art thou? For behold, I am a son of God, in the similitude of his Only Begotten Son; and where is thy glory, that I should worship thee? For behold, I could not look upon God, except his glory should come upon me, and I were strengthened before him. But I can look upon thee in the natural man." Moreover, Moses said: "I will not cease to call upon God, I have other things to inquire of him; for his glory has been upon me, wherefore I can judge between him and thee. Depart hence, Satan." When Moses had said this Satan cried with a loud voice saying he was the Only Begotten. Then Moses feared exceedingly but did not cease to call upon the Lord and there was opened to his vision the bitterness of hell, and in the strength of his power Moses again rebuked Satan, who with trembling and gnashing of teeth, departed from him. Moses bore record of all these things, but because of the wickedness of men it is not had among them.

The Work and Glory of the Lord.—After this trying scene the Lord again spoke with Moses who was commissioned to deliver the people of Israel from bondage. His eyes were opened and he beheld many lands and their inhabitants without number. The Lord taught him, and explained that there were many heavens and many earths like this on which we stand. They are innumerable to man, yet the Lord knows them all and they are numbered unto him. These earths were peopled by his children, for his work and his glory are to bring to pass the immortality and eternal life of man. Therefore, as one earth and its accompanying heaven shall pass away, having filled the measure of its creation, so shall others come. There is no end to the works and the words of the Father, for in this there is eternal progression. However, our knowledge, in the wisdom of the Lord, is, of necessity, limited to the earth on which we dwell.

Other Important Revelations.—The information contained in this ancient scripture caused the hearts of the brethren to rejoice. The Lord continued to pour out knowledge upon them, here a little, and there a little, as they were able to receive it. Early in July (1830) another revelation was given to Joseph Smith and Oliver Cowdery, in Harmony, Pennsylvania. They were commanded to return to the Saints in Colesville, Manchester and Fayette, and the members would support them. They should expound the scriptures and devote their time exclusively to the cause of Zion, and if the members should not support them in these labors, then would the Lord withdraw his blessings. "Be patient in afflictions," said the Lord, "for thou shalt have many: but endure them, for lo, I am with thee, even unto the end of thy days." The afflictions surely came, for Joseph Smith was called on to suffer, as few men have had to suffer. He was to attend to his calling, for the Lord would withhold his power in temporal things that he should not have strength.

Oliver Cowdery was also commanded to continue in the ministry and not suppose that he could say enough in the cause, and if he would be faithful the Lord would open his mouth and he should have strength such as is not known among men. This promise was fufilled, for the Lord blessed Oliver in preaching to that extent that those who heard him were caused to quake and tremble.[a] Power was given to these men to bless or curse; those who received them they were to bless, and from those who rejected them they were to withhold their blessing and to wash their feet against them as a testimony. Should any lay violent hands upon them, they should command them to be smitten, and the Lord would smite them in his own due time. They

---

[a]Statement of President Wilford Woodruff, "Deseret News," March 3, 1889.

were to take neither purse nor scrip, neither two coats, as they went forth to prune the vineyard, with a mighty pruning, "even for the last time."

Emma Smith to Select Hymns.—In the same month (July, 1830) the Lord gave a revelation to Emma Smith, the wife of Joseph Smith, in which she was commanded not to murmur because of the things which she had not seen. As many other wives have thought, she could not understand why her husband should withhold from her a view of sacred things. The Lord assured her that it was for a wise purpose, in him, that these things were withheld, except from the few who were called to be witnesses to the world. She was called "an elect lady" whose duty it was to expound scripture, and exhort the Church, as she was directed by the Spirit; but more especially was she called to assist her husband in writing and to be his scribe, that Oliver Cowdery might be relieved to attend to other duties. She was also chosen to make a selection of sacred hymns for the Church, "for," said the Lord, "my soul delighteth in the song of the heart, yea, the song of the righteous is a prayer unto me, and it shall be answered with a blessing upon their heads." If she would continue in meekness, and beware of pride, and keep the commandments of the Lord, she should receive a crown of righteousness; except she did this, where the Lord was she should not come, which truth applied to all.

CHAPTER 14

THE PUBLIC MINISTRY OF THE CHURCH (2)
1830

Oliver Cowdery's Error.—Another revelation given in July, 1830, instructed Joseph Smith, Oliver Cowdery and John Whitmer, to devote their time to the study of the scriptures, to preaching and confirming the Church in Colesville, and performing such labors as should be required of them, until after they should go to the west to hold conference. All things were to be done in the Church by common consent, in prayer and faith. Oliver Cowdery returned to Fayette and Joseph began to arrange the revelations ready for recording. In this work he was assisted by John Whitmer. While they were thus engaged a letter was received from Oliver Cowdery commanding Joseph "in the name of God to erase" certain words from one of the revelations, "that no priestcraft be amongst us." Joseph immediately answered by letter that he could not alter the revelations of the Lord. It became necessary, however, for him to make a trip to Fayette to correct the error in Oliver's mind, for the latter had convinced several others that the revelation was wrong. After some difficulty and earnest prayer, they were all convinced that the words of the revelation were right and peace again prevailed.

Instructions on the Sacrament.—In the month of August, Newel Knight and his wife came to Harmony on a visit. As the wives of Newel Knight and Joseph Smith had neither of them been confirmed, that matter was attended to at this time. A meeting was held in which the four and John Whitmer participated, and desiring to partake of the sacrament, Joseph set out to purchase some wine. He had

THE PUBLIC MINISTRY OF THE CHURCH

not proceeded far from his door when he was met by an angel who gave him the following commandment:

"Listen to the voice of Jesus Christ, your Lord, your God, and your Redeemer, whose word is quick and powerful. For, behold, I say unto you, that it mattereth not what ye shall eat or what ye shall drink when ye partake of the sacrament, if it so be that ye do it with an eye single to my glory—remembering unto the Father my body which was laid down for you, and my blood which was shed for the remission of your sins. Wherefore, a commandment I give unto you, that you shall not purchase wine neither strong drink of your enemies; Wherefore, you shall partake of none except it is made new among you; yea, in this my Father's kingdom which shall be built up on the earth."

This is one of the many important revelations (Doc. and Cov. Sec. 27) given to the Church. The knowledge that it matters not what we eat or drink, if we partake of the sacrament in the Spirit of the Lord and by divine authority, is the foundation for the present practice in the Church of using water instead of wine, for so the Lord has commanded.

In September the Lord added to this revelation stating that the time would come when he would "drink of the fruit of the vine" on the earth with the ancient prophets and apostles, from Michael, or Adam, the "ancient of days," down to our own day, including all the faithful whom the Father has given him out of the world.

In obedience to the above commandment, they prepared wine of their own making and partook of the sacrament, confirming the two sisters as members of the Church.

Joseph Moves to Fayette.—The spirit of persecution became so strong in Harmony, that Joseph Smith was forced to leave and take up his residence in Fayette. Even his father-in-law, Isaac Hale, turned against him because of the falsehoods which were circulated and the prejudice existing in the neighborhood. This bitterness he retained throughout his life. In August, Joseph and Hyrum Smith, with John and David Whitmer, went to Colesville and visited the members of the Church residing there. They prayed that the eyes of their enemies might be blinded, for the enmity in Colesville was extreme. Their prayers were answered, and though they passed by a number of the most bitter of the mobocrats, who looked intently upon them, yet they were not recognized. In the evening of the day of their arrival—a meeting was held and those who had been previously baptized were all confirmed. They partook of the sacrament, sang and praised the Lord in testimony without molestation. The next morning the brethren took leave of the Saints in peace and in due time arrived home in safety.

Spurious Revelations of Hiram Page.—Shortly after Joseph Smith made his home in Fayette, Satan commenced a subtle attack upon the work within the Church. Hiram Page, one of the eight witnesses, obtained a stone with which he was receiving revelations purporting to be for the guidance of the Church; but these revelations were at variance with those given to Joseph Smith, and also with the teachings of the Savior and his apostles, as contained in the New Testament. Oliver Cowdery and members of the Whitmer family were deceived. Through the Prophet the Lord gave a revelation to Oliver Cowdery in which the order of heaven, in regard to revelation, was pointed out for the guidance of the Church. "Behold, verily, verily, I say unto thee," said the Lord, " no one shall be appointed to receive commandments and revelations in this Church, excepting my servant Joseph Smith, Jun., for he receiveth them even as Moses; and thou shalt be obedient unto the things which I shall give unto him, even as Aaron, to declare faithfully the commandments and the revelations, with power and authority in the Church." It was further stated that there should be none other appointed to receive revelations, until the Lord should appoint another in his stead, for he held the keys of this power. Oliver was instructed to take Hiram Page, alone, and tell him that the revelations he had received were not from the Lord, but were given through the power of Satan, who had deceived him. Oliver was also instructed that he was to write by wisdom, but he was not to command him who was at the head.

The Mission to the Lamanites.—The Lord, in this revelation, appointed Oliver Cowdery to take a mission to the Lamanites in the west, "and inasmuch as they receive thy teachings," it read, "thou shalt cause my Church to be established among them." There were other reasons for this mission, which were not fully revealed. It is probable that in the spurious revelations of Hiram Page some reference was made to the building of the city Zion. In any case, the Lord explained that it was not revealed, and no man knew, where the city Zion shall be built, "but it shall be given hereafter. Behold, I say unto you, that it shall be on the borders of the Lamanites." This mission was not to be taken until after the conference which had been appointed for the 26th of September. Oliver was also first to settle the difficulty with Hiram Page, who was to be taught that he had not been appointed to receive revelations for the Church.

The Doctrine of Gathering—Destruction of the Wicked.—Again the heavens were opened and the Lord made known many of his

THE PUBLIC MINISTRY OF THE CHURCH

purposes and decrees which were for these latter days. A revelation (Doc. and Cov. Sec 29) was given shortly before the second conference of the Church, containing instruction which was helpful for the guidance of the elders at that conference. They were taught the doctrine of the gathering of the Saints. The decree had gone forth from the mansions of the Father, that the Saints should be gathered into one place, for they were chosen out of the world, and they were to prepare their hearts against the day when tribulation and desolation would be sent forth upon the wicked. The hour is nigh, the Lord declared, when the earth should be ripe for destruction, for wickedness shall cease.

Because of the wickedness of the world, for the inhabitants thereof will not repent, the Lord should send forth terrible plagues to torment mankind. Great hailstorms should destroy the crops of the earth; flies shall "take hold of the inhabitants" and eat their flesh; their tongues shall be staid, and their flesh fall from their bones and their eyes from their sockets. The beasts of the forests, and the fowls of the air shall eat their bodies, and the great and abominable church, which shall endure until the end of unrighteousness on the earth, shall be cast down by devouring fire, as Ezekiel had said, for abomination must not reign.

All these things were predicted by the apostles and must be fulfilled; and the twelve who were with the Savior in his ministry shall come in glory to judge the house of Israel who have been faithful, "and none else." The trump shall sound, the righteous dead will rise and Christ reign on the earth with his Saints for a thousand years. After the thousand years are ended, and men begin again to forsake the Lord, the earth shall be spared but a little season. The final resurrection shall come; and the righteous received into eternal life and the wicked banished to partake of the second death with the devil and his angels. The second death is the same death which was first pronounced on Adam—banishment from the presence of the Lord. Those who partake of it cannot return, for they have no power. Then shall come the redemption of the earth, for old things shall pass away and all things become new, yet not "one hair, neither mote, shall be lost" for it is the workmanship of the hands of the Lord.

The Second Conference of the Church.—According to appointment, on the 26th of September, the Church met in conference at Fayette. There were present eight elders, four priests and two teachers when the conference convened. Thirty-five persons had joined the Church, making a total of sixty-two in all. Joseph Smith opened the meeting with prayer and then read the fifth chapter of Isaiah, which speaks of the gathering, and made comments thereon. The matter of Hiram Page's "peepstone" was discussed and after considerable investigation, Hiram Page and all who were present, renounced the stone, and there was mutual satisfaction and happiness again. At this conference, which continued for three days, the Spirit of the Lord was manifest; much business was attended to, and those previously baptized were confirmed. Special prayer was offered in behalf of Oliver Cowdery and Peter Whitmer, Jr., who were called to go to the Lamanites. Peter Whitmer, Jr., was called by revelation at this conference to that mission. When the conference adjourned it was to meet January 1, 1831, and David Whitmer was appointed to keep the record. There were some baptisms during the conference and a number of the brethren were ordained.

The Call to Ziba Peterson and Parley P. Pratt.—A great desire being made manifest on the part of others to accompany Oliver Cowdery and Peter Whitmer, Jr., to the Lamanites, it was made a matter of inquiry before the Lord. The result was that Ziba Peterson and Parley P. Pratt were also appointed to go. Ziba Peterson was among the first baptized and was an elder at the first conference of the Church. Parley P. Pratt was a resident of the wilderness of Ohio not far from the city of Cleveland. While on a missionary tour for the "Disciples" or "Campbellites," as they are called, and a visit to his former home in Columbia County, New York, he first heard of the Book of Mormon through a Baptist preacher by the name of Hamlin, who placed a copy in his hands. After reading it partly through Parley changed his plans and went to Manchester in search of the Prophet Joseph Smith. There he met Hyrum Smith who taught him the Gospel and presented him with a copy of the Book of Mormon which he again very carefully read. Late in August, with Hyrum Smith, he journeyed to Fayette, where he was baptized by Oliver Cowdery about the first of September. Shortly afterwards he was ordained an elder and then continued on his journey to his father's home. There he preached the Gospel to his parents and many of his boyhood friends. His younger brother, Orson, a youth of 19 years of age, readily accepted his message, and became a member of the Church. Returning to Fayette, Parley P. Pratt was appointed by revelation to take the missionary journey with Oliver Cowdery to the borders of Missouri, among the Lamanites.

The Missionaries Depart.—In the fall of 1830, these four missionaries started on their journey to the west. On their way they preached the Gospel among the people as opportunity would permit. Near Buffalo, New York, they visited the Catteraugus Indians and left two copies of the Book of Mormon with members of the tribe who could read, and then continued on their journey. When they came to Kirtland, Ohio, near the home of Elder Pratt, they tarried for some time. Parley P. Pratt was acquainted with Mr. Sidney Rigdon, one of the leaders of the "Disciples," who with Alexander Campbell and Walter Scott, had been instrumental in the founding of that sect. They believed in the doctrines of faith, repentance and baptism for the remission of sins; but accepted the Bible as the only guide unto salvation. Convinced that the religious world had gone astray, these men had formed this organization with sincere desire to follow closely the teachings of the early disciples of the Lord. Through his preaching Sidney Rigdon had converted many souls unto this faith.

Parley P. Pratt, believing that many of the "Disciples" would readily receive the truth, had persuaded his fellow missionaries to spend some time among them in Ohio where they were located on what was called the "Western Reserve."

Sidney Rigdon.—T h e first house at which they called, in Mentor, was the home of Sidney Rigdon. After the usual greetings, they presented Mr. Rigdon with a copy of the Book of Mormon, stating that it contained the record of the ancient people of America, and that the Lord had again established his Church in the earth with the authority of the Holy Priesthood. This was the first time Sidney Rigdon had heard of the Book of Mormon and of Joseph Smith. Replying to their statements, he said he had the Bible, which he believed to be the word of God; as for the Book of Mormon, he had considerable doubt of its divinity. He refused to argue with them, but promised to read the book. At their earnest solicitation Sidney Rigdon allowed the elders to hold meetings in his chapel. A large congregation assembled and gave close attention to the remarks of the elders. At the conclusion of the services Sidney Rigdon instructed the people to consider carefully the remarkable things they had heard, lest it should prove to be the

Sidney Rigdon

truth. With deep and earnest study, he read the contents of the Book of Mormon, praying for divine guidance, and in the course of about two weeks, he received a manifestation so that he could say, "Flesh and blood hath not revealed it unto me, but my Father, which is in heaven." He and his wife were then baptized and also many of his congregation.

In Kirtland the elders were also successful. The people besieged the missionaries both day and night, until they had very little time for rest. The greater number heard the tidings gladly, but some there were, who came to dispute and oppose the work of the Lord. In a very short time branches of the Church were established numbering in all about one thousand souls.

The Journey Continued.—The missionary elders continued on their journey after a stay of two or three weeks in Kirtland, leaving a number of new converts to continue with the work. Sidney Rigdon, Frederick G. Williams, Isaac Morley, John Murdock, Lyman Wight and Edward Partridge later became members of the Church and were ordained to the Priesthood.

Having accomplished this great work, and leaving watchmen for the tender flock, the missionaries took Dr. Frederick G. Williams with them. About fifty miles west of Kirtland, they passed through the country where Parley P. Pratt first made settlement in the western country. Here, again, they made a stop and preached the Gospel. The people were all excited over the things they had heard, for the knowledge of the labors of the brethren had preceded them. Other converts were made, including Simeon Carter, and although some opposition and bitterness was manifest, in the course of a short time a branch was raised up numbering about sixty souls. Arriving near the border of Ohio, the missionaries spent some days among the Wyandots, who received them kindly and rejoiced in the story of their fathers as they learned it from the Book of Mormon. In the city of Cincinnati they spent several days, and being disappointed in not being able to take boat, continued on their journey afoot to St. Louis. In the midst of winter weather, and suffering great hardships in a country little traveled by man, they pursued their journey till they arrived at Independence, Jackson County, Missouri, at that time scarcely more than a trading post on the borders of the United States. They reached Independence early in the year 1831; their journey had taken them a distance of nearly fifteen hundred miles, through a wilderness, in the most inclement season of the year. Four months had they been upon the journey, but during that time they had preached the Gospel to many thousands of white people and two nations of Indians. Churches had been built up and the work advanced along the route of their travels. This was the first missionary journey west of the state of New York, and its results were to be of incalculable benefit to the Church in years to come.

The Book of Mormon Taken to the Lamanites.—In the land of the Lamanites, the elders preached the Gospel to the Delawares, presenting them with the Book of Mormon which they received with rejoicing. Oliver Cowdery explained to them in detail the coming forth of the Book of Mormon. A Mr. Pool, who believed the testimony of these elders, became their interpreter. Several of the Indians could read, and to them they gave copies of the Book of Mormon. The Indians answered them by saying: "We feel thankful to our white friends who have come so far, and been at such pains to tell us good news, and especially this new news concerning the book of our forefathers; it makes us glad in here," and the speaker of the tribe placed his hand on his heart. This good labor, however, was not to last, for the excitement reached the settlements in Missouri, and due to the efforts of sectarian priests the Indian agents ordered the missionaries out of the Indian country as disturbers of the peace, threatening to use military force in case of non-compliance. With disappointment they withdrew and thus ended the first mission to the Lamanites. From this time on they devoted their labors to the white people in Jackson County. However, they had declared the message of salvation to three great tribes, the Catteraugus, in New York; the Wyandots of Ohio, and the Delawares west of Missouri.

It was now decided that Parley P. Pratt should return to Kirtland, and perhaps to New York to report their labors, visit the branches they had organized on their journey, and procure more books. In February he started on his journey, alone. In Kirtland he met the Prophet, who had come to that place and to him he made a report.

PART THREE

The Ohio and Missouri Period

CHAPTER 15

REMOVAL OF THE CHURCH IN NEW YORK TO OHIO

1830-1831

"A Crooked Generation."—In October, 1830, Ezra Thayre and Northrop Sweet were called by revelation, as they had sought the will of the Lord, to preach the Gospel unto "a crooked and perverse generation." "My vineyard," declared the Lord, "has become corrupt every whit; and there is none which doth good save it be a few; and they err in many instances because of priestcrafts; all having corrupt minds. And verily, verily, I say unto you, that this Church have I established and called forth out of the wilderness: and even so will I gather mine elect from the four quarters of the earth, even as many as will believe in me, and hearken unto my voice."

Call of Edward Partridge and Orson Pratt.—In November Orson Pratt, the younger brother of Parley P. Pratt, who had been baptized by his brother Parley a few weeks earlier in Canaan, Columbia County, N. Y., came to Fayette to learn the will of the Lord concerning himself. In the following December Sidney Rigdon came from Ohio on a similar visit, bringing with him a young man named Edward Partridge, who was not a member of the Church. Edward

Partridge, the day after his arrival, satisfied with what he had seen and heard, was baptized by Joseph Smith and later was confirmed by Sidney Rigdon. Both of these young men, Orson Pratt and Edward Partridge, were called to labor in the ministry and received the commendation and blessing of the Lord for their faith and desire to serve him. "And this commandment," said the Lord, "shall be given unto the elders of my Church, that every man which will embrace it with singleness of heart, may be ordained and sent forth, even as I have spoken."

Sidney Rigdon to Write.—Sidney Rigdon was commanded to be a companion to Joseph Smith and to "forsake him not"; moreover, he was to write for him, "and the scriptures shall be given, even as they are in mine own bosom, to the salvation of mine elect," was the word of the Lord to him.

Lost Scriptures Restored.—By commandment of the Lord, a revision of the scriptures by inspiration had already commenced. Much conjecture frequently occurred among the Saints regarding scripture mentioned in the Bible that could not be found. They had learned in the reading of the Book of Mormon, "that many plain and precious things" had been taken away from the Bible as it went forth among the Gentiles. Many of these the Lord promised to restore. From time to time, as their labors would permit, the Prophet received by revelation these scriptures which had been lost, and Sidney Rigdon wrote for him. Shortly after the coming of Sidney Rigdon to Fayette, the Lord revealed the writings of Enoch, spoken of by Jude, which caused much rejoicing among the Saints. These revelations now form a part of the Book of Moses, in the Pearl of Great Price.

Command to Go to Ohio.—Soon after the restoration of the words of Enoch, the Lord commanded that the correction of the scriptures should cease until Joseph Smith and companions could remove to Ohio. Such a step was necessary, the Lord declared, "because of the enemy and for your sakes." However, they were not to go in haste, but first to strengthen the several branches of the Church in New York; especially that at Colesville, where the members exercised much faith. Not only were Joseph and the brethren with him to go to Ohio, but the Lord instructed all the Saints in New York also to journey there "against the time" when Oliver Cowdery should return from the Lamanites.

Conference of January, 1831.—In January, 1831, a conference was held in Fayette. Ordinary business was transacted and a revelation given in which the Lord made known the reason for the removal of the Church to the West. (Doc. and Cov. Sec. 38.) "All

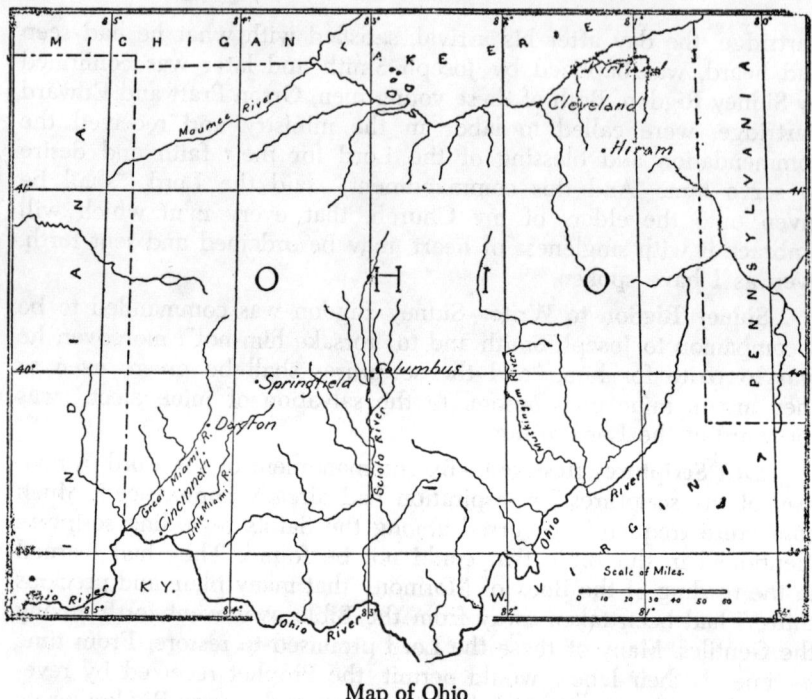

Map of Ohio

eternity is pained," the revelation read, "and the angels are waiting the great command to reap down the earth, to gather the tares that they may be burned." This was because "all flesh is corrupted" and the powers of darkness prevail. The Lord revealed that the wicked were plotting in secret chambers the destruction of Joseph Smith and the Church. However, he would lead the Saints to a land of promise, and they and their children after them should possess it forever, if they would seek it with all their hearts as an inheritance. This reference was to Zion, the location of which the Lord had not yet revealed. They were commanded to assemble in Ohio, and there he would give unto them his law and these things should be made known. They were to dispose of their property as best they could; farms that could not be sold should be rented, and men of wisdom were to be appointed to look after the interests of the poor and needy and send them forth to the place the Lord commanded them.

In the latter part of January, Joseph Smith and his wife, accompanied by Sidney Rigdon and Edward Partridge, moved to Kirtland. They were welcomed there by Newel K. Whitney, and Joseph and his wife remained in the Whitney home for several weeks receiving every kindness and attention which could be shown in Christian love.

The Branch in Kirtland.—The branch of the Church in Kirtland had been living according to a plan called "common stock" or the holding of all property in common. This arrangement had been in practice before they joined the Church, but false spirits crept in among them causing them to receive strange notions in variance with the Gospel plan. With a little caution and exercise of wisdom, the Prophet persuaded them to abandon this plan and their difficulties were removed.

The Law Given to Govern the Church.—On the fourth of February, the Lord gave direction by revelation that the elders of the Church should assemble together to agree on his word; for he would give them his law by which the Church was to be governed. Instructions were also given that Joseph Smith should have a house built wherein he could live and translate, and receive the ancient scriptures from the Lord. Edward Partridge was to receive the office of bishop in the Church and to spend all his time in that ministry, leaving his merchandise, to labor in the interests of the members of the Church.

At Kirtland, on the 9th of February, in the presence of twelve elders, the Lord revealed his law by which the Church was to be governed, according to the promise given in Fayette. This important revelation (Doc. and Cov. Sec. 42) may be termed a code of laws for the government and guidance of the members of the Church. Their attitude towards the law of the land as well as the moral law was clearly established. As members of the Church they were to keep the Church covenants and articles, and the Lord would reveal unto them, from time to time, other covenants sufficient to establish them in Ohio and later in the New Jerusalem, or city of Zion, the site of which would presently be revealed. The duties of the bishop and other officers of the Church were defined. Idlers were condemned; for, said the Lord, "the idler shall not eat the bread nor wear the garments of the laborer." The Bible and the Book of Mormon were to be the standards on doctrine, and they who have not the Spirit were not to teach. The manner of administering to the sick was explained, and the Saints instructed to live together in love. This is one of the very important revelations given to the Church.

A Woman's "Revelation."—Soon after this revelation was given a woman named Hubble came among the people pretending to have revelations, and professing to be a prophetess of the Lord. By declaring that the Book of Mormon was the word of the Lord, and appearing to be very righteous, she deceived some of the Saints.

For the benefit of the members a revelation was received by Joseph Smith in which the Church was instructed to hearken to him, for there was none other appointed to receive revelations for the Church, and none other should be appointed while he lived, if he remained true to his trust. This commandment had previously been given, when Hiram Page was led into error; but it seemed the Lord must speak again on this point before the Saints could understand. The members of the Church were instructed to purge themselves from all iniquity, and the Lord would give them knowledge, even the mysteries of his kingdom would be revealed, if they would sustain and assist Joseph Smith. The elders were instructed to go forth and preach the Gospel, laboring in the vineyard for the last time, for the Lord would shortly come upon the earth in judgment.

Important Revelations to The Church.—During the spring and summer of 1831, a number of important revelations were received. On March 7, the Lord made known many things (Doc. and Cov. Sec. 45) pertaining to his second coming and the signs of the times. After revealing in clearness the teachings given to his disciples in Jerusalem, relative to the destruction of the temple, the scattering of the Jews, and the signs which should precede his second coming, he made known many things which should take place in the day in which we live. He spoke of the signs and wonders; of the gathering of the Jews; the darkening of the sun and the bathing of the moon in blood; of his second coming and his judgments upon the nations; the redemption of the Jews, who shall look upon him whom they have pierced; the binding of Satan; the millennial reign; and the redemption of heathen nations and those who knew no law.

Zion a Place of Refuge.—Zion, the New Jerusalem, shall be built, and then the righteous shall come to Zion from among all nations, singing songs of everlasting joy. They will be the only people who will not be at war, and every man who will not take up his sword against his neighbor, must flee to Zion for safety. Such is to be the condition of the world before the coming of the Lord.

John Whitmer, Historian.—In another revelation John Whitmer was appointed to keep the records of the Church, and assist Joseph Smith in transcribing all things given for the history.

"For," said the revelation, "Oliver Cowdery I have appointed to another office. Wherefore it shall be given him (Whitmer) inasmuch as he is faithful, by the Comforter, to write these things."

REMOVAL OF THE CHURCH TO OHIO 105

The Purchase of Lands.—As the Saints in New York had been commanded to settle in Ohio, the residents in that place were instructed to impart of their lands, as they were able to do, for the benefit of their brethren from the east, for it was needful that they should remain in Ohio for a time. Eventually, however, it was expected that they would move farther westward, and the members of the Church were to save their money for the purpose of buying lands for an inheritance in the city Zion, when the location of that place should be revealed. This information should be made known when the brethren arrived from the east, for to them it was to be revealed. "And they shall be appointed to purchase the lands, and to make a commencement to lay the foundation of the city, and then shall you begin to be gathered with your families, every man according to his family—as is appointed to him by the presidency and the bishop of the Church."

Equality Among the Families.—In the month of May the Saints from New York commenced to arrive in Ohio, and it fell to the lot of Bishop Partridge to assign to them their lands. They were to be made equal according to their families and their needs. The head of each family was to receive a certificate to secure him and his portion and inheritance in the Church. Should a man transgress, after receiving his portion and standing, he was not to have power to claim that portion which had been consecrated to the bishop for the use of the poor and needy of the Church; but he could retain that portion which was deeded to him. A storehouse was to be provided and the substance of the people, more than needful for individual use, was to be placed therein, for the wants of the people, to be kept by the bishop, who was to distribute it as the necessities of the people should demand. In this manner the doctrine of consecration was partially put into practice, as a preparatory step before the members of the Church should go to Zion—for in Zion the law of the united order, or consecration of properties, was the law upon which that city should be built. "And thus I grant unto this people," the Lord declared, with reference to the New York Saints, "a privilege of organizing themselves according to my laws; and I consecrate unto them this land for a little season, until I, the Lord, shall provide for them otherwise, and command them to go hence."

The Important Conference of June, 1831.—In the month of February the Lord had commanded that word be sent out to the elders of the Church calling them from the east and from the west; from the north and from the south; to meet in conference and receive instruction. Accordingly, a conference was set for June 3, which convened at Kirtland and continued until the sixth. The Spirit of the

Lord was displayed in a marvelous way, and the power of the evil one, which was made manifest in opposition to the work, was successfully rebuked.

The First High Priests Ordained.—At this conference the first high priests in this dispensation were ordained. Lyman Wight, John Murdock, Reynolds Cahoon, Harvey Whitlock and Hyrum Smith, were ordained to the office of high priest, by Joseph Smith the Prophet; Joseph Smith, Sen., Joseph Smith the Prophet, Parley P. Pratt, Thomas B. Marsh, Isaac Morley, Edward Partridge, Joseph Wakefield, Martin Harris, Ezra Thayre, Ezra Booth, John Corrill, Samuel H. Smith, John Whitmer and Sidney Rigdon, were ordained to the office of high priest, under the hands of Lyman Wight. Edward Partridge, the bishop of the Church then blessed those who had been ordained. John Corrill and Isaac Morley were then sustained and ordained as assistants, or counselors, to Bishop Partridge, under the hands of Lyman Wight. All this was done by commandment from the Lord.

The Mission of John.—During the conference, Joseph Smith the Prophet was led to say, "that John the Revelator was then among the ten tribes of Israel who had been led away by Shalmaneser, king of Assyria, to prepare them for their return from their long dispersion."

The Elders Called to Missouri.—The spirit of prophecy was abundantly manifest and during the sessions of this conference a number of revelations were received. Many of the elders were called to take their journey through the western country, going two by two, preaching the Gospel, and were to assemble again in Jackson County, Missouri, where the next conference was to be held. The Lord said to them: "And thus, even as I have said if ye are faithful, ye shall assemble yourselves together to rejoice upon the land of Missouri, which is the land of your inheritance, which is now the land of your enemies. But, behold, I the Lord, will hasten the city in its time, and will crown the faithful with joy and rejoicing."

The Thompson Branch.—The members of the Church from Colesville, New York, on their arrival in Ohio, were located at a place called Thompson, about sixteen miles northeast of Kirtland. Here, as we have learned, they were directed to live according to the Lord's law, that is, the order of stewardship and consecration of properties. Among these people there resided a man named Leman Copley, who was a member of the "Shaking Quakers" before he joined the Church. He owned a large tract of land which he agreed to turn over to the Colesville branch to occupy in this manner of stewardship, agreeable with the revelation they had received.

It appears that Copley had not been fully converted to the Gospel and he, with some others, later rebelled and broke the covenant of consecration. This caused confusion among the Colesville Saints and placed them at the mercy of their enemies, as well as in jeopardy before the Lord. In their distress they sent Newel Knight, who was in charge of the branch at Thompson, to the Prophet to learn what they should do. The Lord spoke unto them saying that their covenant had been broken and therefore was of no effect, and it would have been better for the one who was responsible for the offense, "had he been drowned in the depth of the sea." The members of the branch were now commanded to journey to Missouri, "unto the borders of the Lamanites," and there they were to seek "a living like unto men," until the Lord might prepare a place for them. Almost immediately they took their departure under the guidance of Newel Knight, for Missouri.

A Letter from Missouri.—A few days following the conference a letter was received from Oliver Cowdery, dated May 7, giving an account of the labors of himself and companions in Missouri. He spoke of their labors among the Lamanites, and of the tribe of "Navashoes" farther to the west, near Santa Fe. Almost the whole country where he and his fellow laborers were located, he declared, consisted of "Universalists, Atheists, Presbyterians, Methodists, Baptists, and other professing Christians, priests and people; with all the devils from the infernal pit, united and foaming out their shame," against the elders of the Church. Then he adds: "God forbid that I should bring a railing accusation against them, for vengeance belongs to him who is able to pay." His expressed opinion of these inhabitants of the border land was all too true, as events immediately to follow will attest.

The Mission to the West.—About the middle of June (1831) the elders who were appointed at the conference, commenced their journey westward, traveling two by two. Ezra Thayre, the companion chosen for Thomas B. Marsh, failed to go. Selah J. Griffin was appointed to go in his stead. On the 19th of June, Joseph Smith, Sidney Rigdon, Martin Harris, Edward Partridge, William W. Phelps, Joseph Coe, and Algernon Sidney Gilbert, took up their journey to Missouri. All these missionaries, and others not here mentioned, commenced their travels with great anticipation of what the result would be. Their destination was the "land of their inheritance," where Zion—the New Jerusalem—should be built. The Lord had promised that the site for this holy city should be revealed to them at their journey's end.

CHAPTER 16

THE LAND OF ZION—ITS DEDICATION

1831

Character of Inhabitants—About the middle of July, 1831, the missionaries commenced to arrive in western Missouri, and were met with tears of joy by their brethren there. Here, on the borders of the United States, had gathered renegades from the east; lawless and vile outcasts, who had been forced to flee to the west for safety. "How natural it was," wrote the Prophet, "to observe the degradation, leanness of intellect, ferocity, and jealousy, of a people that were nearly a century behind the times."

First Sabbath in Zion.—The first Sabbath (July 17, 1831), the elders spent in Jackson County. William W. Phelps preached a public discourse. His congregation was composed of "specimens of all the families of the earth." After this meeting two persons, who had previously believed, were baptized.

Arrival of the Colesville Branch.—A few days later the members of the Colesville branch, from Thompson, Ohio, arrived in Missouri and were located on lands in Kaw township, where a portion of Kansas City is now built.

Assignment of Labors.—The duty devolved on the Prophet to assign the labors to the several elders who were to remain in the Land. Some of them were called by revelation to make their permanent settlement in Missouri, while others were instructed to return to the eastern lands, after their mission in the west was finished. William W. Phelps, who joined the Church at the time the little band of missionaries were leaving Ohio for Missouri, had previously been instructed by the Lord (Doc. and Cov. Sec. 55) to engage with Oliver Cowdery, in the work of printing and selecting and writing books for schools in the Church, that "little children also may receive instruction" which would be pleasing to the Lord. Upon his arrival in Jackson County, this commandment was repeated.

Algernon Sidney Gilbert was appointed to act as agent for the Church in receiving moneys and buying lands on which the Saints might locate. Edward Partridge was to act in his calling as bishop of the Church. His great duty was to divide the inheritances of the members, severally, according to their needs. In this manner duties were assigned to each of those expected to remain as a nucleus for the building up of Zion. (Doc. and Cov. Sections 57-58).

Location of the City Revealed.—As the Lord had promised, he now fulfilled. In answer to the questions: "When will the wilderness blossom as the rose? When will Zion be built up in her glory, and where will thy temple stand, unto which all nations shall come in the last days?" the Lord gave the following:

'Hearken, O ye elders of my church, saith the Lord your God, who have assembled yourselves together, according to my commandments, in this land, which is the land of Missouri, which is the land which I have appointed and consecrated for the gathering of the saints. Wherefore this is the land of promise, and the place for the city of Zion. And thus saith the Lord your God, if you will receive wisdom here is wisdom. Behold, the place which is now called Independence, is the center place; and a spot for the temple is lying westward, upon a lot which is not far from the court house. Wherefore, it is wisdom that the land should be purchased by the saints, and also every tract lying westward, even unto the line running directly between Jew and Gentile; And also every tract bordering by the prairies, inasmuch as my disciples are enabled to buy lands. Behold, this is wisdom, that they may obtain it for an everlasting inheritance" (Doc. and Cov. Sec. 57).

The Saints to Keep the Law.—In another revelation (Doc. and Cov. Sec. 58) given at this time, the members of the Church were commanded to keep the law the Lord had given them, as well as to observe the laws of the land. "Let no man think he is ruler," it read, "but let God rule him that judgeth, according to the counsel of his own will; or, in other words, him that counseleth or sitteth upon the judgment seat. Let no man break the laws of the land, for he that keepeth the laws of God hath no need to break the laws of the land; wherefore, be subject to the powers that be, until he reigns whose right it is to reign, and subdues all enemies under his feet."

After Much Tribulation, the Blessings.—That Zion was to be established and the city built at once, was evidently the idea possessed by some of the Saints; moreover, that they were at liberty to establish their own laws, independent of all else. Hence the instructions as here given by the Lord regarding the keeping of the law. The Lord had warned them previously and given instruction in regard to their duties and requirements in that land. That the city was not to be built at that time is indicated in his word: "Ye cannot behold with your natural eyes, for the present time, the design of your God concerning those things which shall come hereafter, and the glory which shall follow after much tribulation. For after much tribulation come the blessings. Wherefore the day cometh that ye shall be crowned with much glory; the hour is not yet, but is nigh at hand. Remember this, which I tell you before, that you may lay it to heart, and receive that which shall follow. Behold, verily I say unto you, for this cause I have sent you—that you might be obedient, and that your hearts might be prepared to bear testimony of the things which are to come; And also that you might be honored in laying the foundation, and in bearing record of the land upon which Zion of God shall stand"; (Doc. and Cov. Sec. 58).

From this we see that the glory and greatness of the city Zion was reserved for the future; although in the scriptural sense, the time "is nigh at hand." These early settlers were to lay the foundation, and prepare the way for the Saints, who were yet to come, after the preaching of the Gospel "to the uttermost parts of the earth," for the elders were to "push the people together from the ends of the earth." It was a great honor conferred upon the first laborers in the vineyard, if they would be faithful to every command.

Dedication of the Land.—The Colesville Saints were located in Kaw township. The Prophet assisted them in laying the first log, "for a house, as a foundation of Zion" in that place. The log was carried by twelve men representing the twelve tribes of Israel. At the same time it was made manifest through prayer that the land should be consecrated and dedicated by Sidney Rigdon. "It was a season of joy," the Prophet said, "to those present, and afforded a glimpse of the future, which time will yet unfold to the satisfaction of the faithful." All this took place on the second day of August, 1831.

Sidney Rigdon, according to his appointment, stood up and asked:

"Do you receive this land for the land of your inheritance, with thankful hearts, from the Lord?"

"We do."

"Do you pledge yourselves to keep the law of God on this land, which you never have kept in your own lands?"

"We do."

"Do you pledge yourselves to see that others of your brethren who shall come hither do keep the laws of God?"

"We do."

After prayer, Elder Rigdon arose and said: "I now pronounce this land consecrated and dedicated unto the Lord for a possession and inheritance for the Saints, and for all the faithful servants of the Lord, to the uttermost ages of time, in the name of Jesus Christ, having authority from him. Amen" (*Documentary History of the Church*, Vol. 1, p. 196).

Description of the Land.—In addition to the appointment to dedicate the land, Sidney Rigdon was also called by revelation to write a description of it, to be sent "unto all the churches." One object of this description was to stir up the Saints to donate for the purchase of the lands, by placing in the hands of the bishop money for that purpose. Those who would do this should be given an inheritance, for Zion was to be built by purchase; otherwise they could not obtain it except by the shedding of blood, which was forbidden. The first description written was rejected by the Lord, and Sidney Rigdon was commanded to write another.

The Future Glory of Zion.—Many of the ancient prophets spoke of Zion and her glory. Isaiah declared that in the latter days "out of Zion shall go forth the law, and the word of the Lord from Jerusalem," in that day when swords will be made into plowshares, and spears into pruning-hooks.[a] Moreover, again he prophesied, saying:

"For the nation and kingdom that will not serve thee shall perish; yea, those nations shall be utterly wasted. The glory of Lebanon shall come unto thee, the fir tree, the pine tree, and the box together, to beautify the place of my sanctuary; and I will make the place of my feet glorious. The sons also of them that afflicted thee shall come bending unto thee; and all they that despised thee shall bow themselves down at the soles of thy feet; and they shall call thee, The city of the Lord, The Zion of the Holy One of Israel. Whereas thou hast been forsaken and hated, so that no man went through thee, I will make thee an eternal excellency, a joy of many generations. * * * For brass I will bring gold, and for iron I will

---
[a]Isaiah 2:1-4.

bring silver, and for wood brass, and for stones iron: I will also make thy officers peace, and thine exactors righteousness. Violence shall no more be heard in thy land, wasting nor destruction within thy borders; but thou shalt call thy walls Salvation, and thy gates Praise. The sun shall be no more thy light by day; neither for brightness shall the moon give light unto thee; but the Lord shall be unto thee an everlasting light, and thy God thy glory. Thy sun shall no more go down; neither shall thy moon withdraw itself: for the Lord shall be thine everlasting light, and the days of thy mourning shall be ended. Thy people also shall be all righteous: they shall inherit the land forever, the branch of my planting, the work of my hands, that I may be glorified. A little one shall become a thousand, and a small one a strong nation: I the Lord will hasten it in his time."*b*

Dedication of the Temple Site.—On the 3rd day of August, Joseph Smith, Oliver Cowdery, Sidney Rigdon, Edward Partridge, William W. Phelps, Martin Harris and Joseph Coe, met on a spot a little west of the Independence court house, and there they dedicated the site for the great temple of the latter days. The 87th Psalm was read, and the scene was most impressive; for here the house of the Lord was to be reared in the holy city Zion, which had been spoken of by ancient seers, from whence should go forth the law to the ends of the earth.

---

*b*Isaiah 60:12-22.

The following reference to Zion, or the New Jerusalem, is from the prophecy of Ether; Book of Mormon, Ether, 13th chapter:

"Behold Ether saw the days of Christ, and he spake concerning a New Jerusalem upon this land. And he spake also concerning the house of Israel, and the Jerusalem from whence Lehi should come—after it should be destroyed it should be built up again, a holy city unto the Lord; wherefore, it could not be a new Jerusalem for it had been in a time of old; but it should be built up again, and become a holy city of the Lord; and it should be built unto the house of Israel. And that a New Jerusalem should be built up upon this land, unto the remnant of the seed of Joseph, for which things there has been a type. For as Joseph brought his father down into the land of Egypt, even so he died there; wherefore, the Lord brought a remnant of the seed of Joseph out of the land of Jerusalem, that he might be merciful unto the seed of Joseph that they should perish not, even as he was merciful unto the father of Joseph that he should perish not. Wherefore the remnant of the house of Joseph shall be built upon this land; and it shall be a land of their inheritance; and they shall build up a holy city unto the Lord, like unto the Jerusalem of old; and they shall no more be confounded, until the end come when the earth shall pass away. And there shall be a new heaven and a new earth; and they shall be like unto the old save the old have passed away, and all things have become new. And then cometh the New Jerusalem; and blessed are they who dwell therein, for it is they whose garments are white through the blood of the Lamb; and they are they who are numbered among the remnant of the seed of Joseph, who were of the house of Israel."

First Conference in Zion.—On the 4th day of August (1831) the first conference in that land was held at the home of Joshua Lewis, in Kaw township. The members of the Colesville branch formed the greater part of the congregation—a total of thirty-one souls. The Spirit of the Lord was with them and they rejoiced. Sidney Rigdon preached and exhorted the Saints "to obedience to the requisition of heaven," that they might be planted in their inheritances in Zion. Ziba Peterson, who had been silenced for wrongdoing, humbled himself and made confession; by unanimous vote he was reinstated. Joseph Smith addressed the conference and admonished the people to be true to their covenants that they might receive the blessings.

A Commandment and a Promised Blessing.—On the 7th, Polly Knight, wife of Joseph Knight, Sen., died; she had been in failing health while on the westward journey. The same day the Prophet received a revelation of commandment and blessing to the Saints, in which they were admonished again to keep the commandments of the Lord. Their course of action was pointed out for them with a statement that all who had come up to the land to keep the commandments should be blessed; if they lived they should inherit the earth; if they died they should rest in the mansions of the Father. On the Lord's day they were to rest from all labor and assemble in the house of prayer to partake of the sacrament and confess their sins. (Doc. and Cov. Sec. 59).

The Return to Kirtland.—On the 9th day of August Joseph Smith and the elders who were to return, started on their journey back to Kirtland. They traveled down the Missouri River towards St. Louis. On the third day out they encountered some of the dangers common on these waters. At a place called McIlwaine's Bend, William W. Phelps, in open vision, saw the destroyer in his power, riding upon the waters. The next morning the Prophet Joseph received a revelation in confirmation of the vision of Elder Phelps.

Dangers on the Waters.—The Lord revealed (Doc. and Cov. Sec. 61) to Joseph Smith the great dangers that would be upon the waters in these latter days. "Behold, I the Lord, in the beginning blessed the waters, but in the last days, by the mouth of my servant John, I cursed the waters. Wherefore, the days will come that no flesh shall be safe upon the waters. * * * I, the Lord, have decreed, and the destroyer rideth upon the face thereof, and I revoke not the decree." It was further stated that the time would come when none would dare go upon the waters but those who were pure in heart, and the elders were counseled to travel by other means than by the rivers, that their faith fail not.

Object of the Mission to Zion.—On the 27th day of August Joseph Smith, Oliver Cowdery and Sidney Rigdon arrived in Kirtland; others of the elders had previously arrived. Their mission had been fulfilled. They had gone to Missouri for the purpose of receiving definite knowledge concerning the location of the land and site for the future city of Zion; to dedicate the land as the "inheritance of the Saints," also to choose and dedicate a spot for the building of the temple. Those who were to remain were instructed in their duties and given commandments by which they were to be governed in that land and upon which their inheritances, and those of the Saints who should follow after, might be made secure.

CHAPTER 17

**THE BOOK OF COMMANDMENTS—THE VISION OF THE
GLORIES—THE HIRAM MOBBING**

1831-1832

Desire of the Saints for Knowledge of Zion.—August 28, the day after the return of the brethren from Missouri, fell on Sunday. An inspirational meeting was held at which the brethren reported their labors. Among the business transacted was the ordination of Oliver Cowdery to the office of high priest "by the voice of the Church and the command of God, under the hand of Sidney Rigdon," says the record. Oliver Cowdery was in Missouri when the conference in June was held, at which the first high priests were ordained.

As the Saints were very anxious to know more in relation to Zion, the purchasing of lands there and their inheritances, the Prophet inquired of the Lord, and received a revelation (Doc. and Cov. Sec. 63) in which the difficulties and persecutions of the Saints in that land were fore-shadowed. Again the people were cautioned and reproved wherein they had not kept the commandments of the Lord. Among other things the Lord declared the following:

"And now, verily I say unto you, that as I said that I would make known my will unto you, behold I will make it known unto you, not by the way of commandment, for there are many who observe not to keep my commandments. But unto him that keepeth my commandments I will give the mysteries of my kingdom, and the same shall be in him a well of living water, springing up unto everlasting life. And now, behold, this is the will of the Lord your

God concerning his saints, that they should assemble themselves together unto the land of Zion, not in haste, lest there should be confusion, which bringeth pestilence. Behold, the land of Zion—I, the Lord, hold it in mine own hands; nevertheless, I, the Lord, render unto Caesar the things which are Caesar's. Wherefore, I the Lord will that you should purchase the lands, that you may have advantage of the world, that you may have claim on the world, that they may not be stirred up unto anger. For Satan putteth it into their hearts to anger against you, and to the shedding of blood. Wherefore, the land of Zion shall not be obtained but by purchase or by blood, otherwise there is none inheritance for you. And if by purchase, behold you are blessed; and if by blood, as you are forbidden to shed blood, lo, your enemies are upon you, and ye shall be scourged from city to city, and from synagogue to synagogue, and but few shall stand to receive an inheritance. I, the Lord, am angry with the wicked; I am holding my Spirit from the inhabitants of the earth."

Apostasy of Ezra Booth.—In September Joseph Smith moved his family to Hiram, in Portage County, Ohio, about thirty miles southeast of Kirtland, and commenced living at the home of John Johnson. About this time Ezra Booth left the Church. He had been ordained a high priest, and had taken the trip to Missouri, but had been rebellious. Before coming into the Church he was a Methodist priest; but through the performance of a miracle he was baptized, and from that time he desired to make men believe by the performance of miracles, even by smiting them, or with forcible means. After leaving the Church he wrote a number of articles against the truth which were afterwards published in an anti-"Mormon" book.

Purchase of a Printing Press.—As Oliver Cowdery and William W. Phelps had been called to print and publish books and writings for the Church, it was necessary that a printing press be purchased. William W. Phelps was instructed, therefore, to call at Cincinnati on his return to Missouri and purchase a press for this purpose. This press was to be taken to Independence, where they were to print a monthly paper to be called the *Evening and Morning Star*. This was the first publication in the Church.

Revision of the Bible.—While residing at Hiram, Joseph Smith was engaged in the revision of the Bible, which work was commenced in Fayette, but had been delayed by command of the Lord until this time because of other duties. Sidney Rigdon, who also had located in Hiram, continued to write for him. In course of time the Prophet went through the Bible, topic by topic, revising as he was led by revelation. The work was never fully completed, for he had

The Evening and Morning Star

intended, while at Nauvoo, a number of years later, to finish the work, but was cut off by his enemies. Nevertheless, many plain and precious things were revealed which throw great light upon many subjects.

Special Conference of November.—As Oliver Cowdery and John Whitmer were appointed to go to Missouri to attend to duties there, which had been assigned to them, a special conference was called for November 1, 1831, to consider such matters as might need attention before their departure.

Preparation for Publication of Commandments.—At this special conference, which was held at Hiram, the matter of publishing the revelations and commandments given through Joseph Smith, was considered. This was the will of the Lord, for during that conference he gave the revelation—one of the most important in the Doctrine and Covenants—which he called "my preface unto the book of my commandments, which I have given them to publish unto you, O inhabitants of the earth" (Doc. and Cov. Sec. 1). These inhabitants were commanded, as well as were the Saints, to "search these commandments, for they are true and faithful, and the prophecies and promises which are in them shall be fulfilled." The Lord was willing, "to make these things known unto all flesh, for I am no respecter of persons," he said, "and will that all men shall know that the day speedily cometh; the hour is not yet, but is nigh at hand, when peace shall be taken from the earth, and the devil shall have power over his own dominion; and also the Lord shall have power over his Saints, and shall reign in their midst, and shall come down in judgment upon Idumea, or the world."

Endorsement of the Revelations.—It was decided that an edition of ten thousand copies of the Book of Commandments should be published. However, at a later date (May 1, 1832) this was changed to three thousand copies. Joseph Smith addressed the elders and said, inasmuch as the Lord had bestowed a great blessing upon them in giving commandments and revelations, he would ask the conference what testimony they were willing to give regarding these commandments which should shortly be sent to the world. After the reading of the Lord's preface, a number of the brethren arose and bore witness to the truth of the revelations, which were to be published in the Book of Commandments. The conference lasted two days and much other business was transacted.

Criticism of the Revelations.—Not all of those present at the conference fully endorsed these revelations; there was one at least, who questioned their language. This was William E. McLellin, who had but recently joined the Church. The Prophet, thereupon received a commandment from the Lord (Doc. and Cov. Sec. 67) in which he was directed to invite the "most wise among you" to choose out of the revelations the least, and attempt to make one like unto it;

THE BOOK OF COMMANDMENTS

and if this "wise" individual could duplicate the least of the revelations, then the elders might be justified in saying they did not "know that they are true." If this proved to be a failure, then they would be "under condemnation" if they did not bear record that they are true.

William E. McLellin's Folly.—William E. McLellin, as the wisest man, accepted the challenge from the Lord. His attempt was a humiliating failure, to the convincing of the elders present, who unitedly signified their willingness to bear testimony to all the world, of the truth of the revelations given to Joseph Smith.

Other Important Revelations.—At the conclusion of this conference the Lord gave another commandment (Doc. and Cov. Sec. 68) for the benefit of Orson Hyde, Luke Johnson, Lyman E. Johnson and William E. McLellin, who had inquired concerning themselves. In addition to the advice and commandments given to these men there was much counsel and commandment for the inhabitants in Zion, for there were idlers among them, the Lord declared, and they were to keep the Sabbath day, to remember their prayers, to teach their children the principles of the Gospel and have them baptized when eight years old, for these things they were failing to do; therefore the Lord was not pleased with them. Instructions were also given regarding the Priesthood and its powers, for the guidance of the Church. This information Oliver Cowdery was to carry on his return to Zion.

On the 3rd of November, the Lord gave the great revelation known as the Appendix, to the Book of Commandments, which appears as Section 133 in the book of Doctrine and Covenants.

Arrangement of the Revelations.—It was decided that Oliver Cowdery should carry the revelations to Missouri, where they should be printed. Joseph Smith was therefore kept busy during the days intervening, as Oliver expected to leave about the 15th of November. The Prophet writes: "My time was occupied closely in reviewing the commandments and sitting in conference, for nearly two weeks; for from the first to the twelfth of November, we held four special conferences."

Worth of the Revelations.—At the last of these conferences, held in Hiram, at the home of John Johnson, the members voted, after deliberate consideration of the revelations, "that they prize the revelations to be worth to the Church the riches of the whole earth, speaking temporally." The benefits to the Church and to the world, which come from the Book of Mormon and the revelations to Joseph Smith, were also considered, and the expression of the conference was to the effect that the infinite wisdom of the Lord, in granting for their salvation and the salvation of the world, these sacred things, should be fully appreciated.

Commandments Dedicated.—It was voted that Joseph Smith be appointed to dedicate and consecrate these brethren, Oliver Cowdery and John Whitmer, and the sacred writings entrusted to their care, to the Lord. Moreover, it was also voted that, in consequence of Joseph Smith, Oliver Cowdery, John Whitmer and Sidney Rigdon, "in bringing to light, by the grace of God, these sacred things, they be appointed to manage them according to the laws of the Church, and that their families as well as the families of Hyrum Smith, Christian Whitmer, Peter Whitmer, Jacob Whitmer, Hiram Page and David Whitmer, also Samuel H. Smith, William Smith and Don Carlos Smith be remembered to the bishop of Zion as worthy of inheritances in the land of Zion. In accord with this motion regarding the dedication of the revelations and those who should carry them, this action was taken at this time by Joseph Smith. Shortly after this conference, Oliver Cowdery and John Whitmer departed on their journey.

Labors Among the Enemy.—On the 1st of December, Joseph Smith and Sidney Rigdon were commanded to take "a mission for a season" and call upon the inhabitants of the earth, and, said the Lord, "confound your enemies; call upon them to meet you, both in public and in private; and inasmuch as ye are faithful, their shame will be made manifest. Wherefore let them bring forth their strong reason against the Lord." The reason for this commandment was due to the activities of the apostate Ezra Booth, who was publishing in Ravenna, Ohio, many falsehoods against the Church. According to this call Joseph Smith and Sidney Rigdon left on the 3rd of December for Kirtland, to fulfil this revelation. For some time they spoke in Kirtland, Shalersville, Ravenna, and other places, vindicating the cause and confounding their enemies. They were blessed with the Spirit of the Lord, and witnessed the fulfilment of the promises made to them; for they were able to allay much of the excitement and change false impressions which had grown out of the scandalous articles in the *"Ohio Star"* at Ravenna.

The Amherst Conference.—On the 25th day of January, 1832, a conference was held at Amherst, Lorain County, Ohio. At this conference much business was transacted in harmony and in the spirit of fellowship. Joseph Smith was sustained as President of the High Priesthood. The revelation known as Section 75 in the Doctrine and Covenants was also given in which a number of elders were

THE BOOK OF COMMANDMENTS 121

called to take missions, two by two, in several directions throughout the land.

The Visions of the Glories.—At the close of this conference, Joseph Smith and Sidney Rigdon again took up their work of revising the scriptures. While doing so, "it appeared self-evident," they declared, "from what truths were left, that if God rewarded every one according to the deeds done in the body, the term 'Heaven' as intended for the Saints' eternal home, must include more kingdoms than one." Accordingly on the 16th of February, 1832, while revising St. John's Gospel, and in answer to their prayer, they saw the heavens opened and beheld the Father and the Son. The account of this vision, as it is given in Section 76 of the Doctrine and Covenants, is one of the choicest bits of literature, and one of the greatest revelations ever given to man. It throws a flood of light upon eternity and the destiny of the human race and teaches the mercy of a loving Father, who saves all the workmanship of his hands, save it be the sons of perdition, who sin against the light and crucify their Redeemer again unto themselves. That every man shall be rewarded according to his works, and that a place has been prepared for each individual somewhere in the mansion of the Father, after he is purged from sin, is a glorious and merciful provision in the plan of salvation, which this vision declares, was provided before the world began. It would be folly to attempt to comment on this most wonderful revelation of the power and loving kindness of the Lord, which the words of man cannot adequately express.

The Prophet's View on the Vision.—The words of Joseph Smith pertaining to this opening of the heavens, are well expressed. "Nothing," he has written, "could be more pleasing to the Saints upon the order of the kingdom of the Lord, than the light which burst upon the world through the foregoing vision. Every law, every commandment, every promise, every truth, and every point touching the destiny of man, from Genesis to Revelations, where the purity of the scriptures remains unsullied by the folly of men, go to show the perfection of the theory [of different degrees of glory in the future life] and witness the fact that that document is a transcript from the records of the eternal world. The sublimity of the ideas; the purity of the language; the scope for action; the continued duration for completion, in order that the heirs of salvation may confess the Lord and bow the knee; the rewards for faithfulness, and the punishments for sins, are so much beyond the narrow-mindedness of men, that every honest man is constrained to exclaim: 'It came from God!'" Joseph Smith or any other man guided by the inspiration of man's power could not have written it.

Mob Violence in Hiram.—Before going to Hiram, Ohio, to live, Joseph Smith and his wife adopted two children (twins) of Elder John Murdock's. Their mother died at their birth, and Emma Smith, having lost twins of her own which were born the same day took the Murdock twins to raise. In March, 1832, when these children were about eleven months old, they took the measles, and their care caused both the Prophet and his wife to lose much rest. On the night of the 24th, after the family had retired, a mob surrounded the house, broke open the door and dragged the Prophet into the open. On the way he managed to get one foot loose with which he kicked one of the ruffians and knocked him down. At this, with blasphemous oath, the fiends swore they would kill the Prophet if he made further resistance. They then choked him until he was unconscious. When he came to, he discovered Sidney Rigdon, whom they had also taken from his home and dragged by his heels so that his head struck at every step on the frozen earth. He was unconscious on the ground. About sixty rods from the house the mob held a council to decide what further action they might take. Some were ready to kill the Prophet, but returning to him they attemped to force a vial of acid in his mouth, but the vial was broken against his teeth. An attempt was also made to fill his mouth with tar; failing in this they tore from him his clothes, and applied the tar with feathers to his body. After shamefully beating him they left him helpless on the ground. Joseph attempted to rise, but fell to the ground again. After a while he began to recover his strength, and made his way with difficulty to his home.

Sidney received similar treatment, which left him delirious for several days. The Prophet's friends spent the night cleaning the tar from his body, and the following day, it being the Sabbath, he met with the people at the regular hour, and addressed them. Several of the members of the mob were present, including Simonds Ryder, an apostate, and leader of the mob; a Mr. McClentic and Felatiah Allen, who had provided the mob with a barrel of whiskey to raise their spirits and make them "brave" to do the deed. During the mobbing one of the twins became exposed, contracted a severe cold, and a few days later, died.

Second Visit to Missouri.—The first of April, Joseph Smith, with Newel K. Whitney and Jesse Gause, left for Missouri to fulfil the provisions of a revelation (Doc. and Cov. Sec. 78) in respect to regulating and establishing the affairs of the storehouse for the poor, and the consecration of properties. They were later joined by Sidney Rigdon. On the way they purchased paper, at Wheeling, Virginia, for the press in Zion, and arrived at Independence on the 24th of April.

Two days later at a general council of the Church, Joseph Smith was acknowledged by the Saints in Zion as President of the High Priesthood, ratifying the action of the Amherst conference, held January 25, 1832.

Zion and Her Stakes.—During this conference a revelation was given commanding the elders to bind themselves in a covenant of consecration, which could not be broken. Kirtland was to become a "stake of Zion."[a] "For I have consecrated the land of Shinehah (Kirtland), in mine own due time," said the Lord, "for the benefit of the Saints of the Most High, and for a stake of Zion. For Zion must increase in beauty, and in holiness; her borders must be enlarged; her stakes must be strengthened; yea, verily I say unto you, Zion must arise and put on her beautiful garments. Therefore I give unto you this commandment, that ye bind yourselves by this covenant, and it shall be done according to the laws of the Lord."

Return to Kirtland.—Joseph and the brethren visited the Colesville Saints in Kaw township, who rejoiced greatly to see them. It was agreed in a council held on the first of May to print but three thousand copies of the Book of Commandments, and that the revelations should be reviewed and prepared by Oliver Cowdery, William W. Phelps and John Whitmer; and that the hymns selected by Emma Smith be prepared for printing. After the transaction of other necessary business, Joseph Smith and his companions, Rigdon and Whitney, returned to Kirtland. On this journey Joseph was poisoned and Bishop Whitney met with an accident breaking his leg and foot in several places; both were healed by the power of the Lord.

---

[a]The term "Stake of Zion," which was first used in a revelation given in November, 1831 (Sec. 68) is a comparison to the stakes which bind a tent. Isaiah says: "Look upon Zion, the city of our solemnities: thine eyes shall see Jerusalem a quiet habitation, a tabernacle that shall not be taken down; not one of the stakes thereof shall ever be removed, neither shall any of the cords thereof be broken" (Ch. 33:20). Again: "Enlarge the place of thy tent and let them stretch forth the curtains of thine habitations: spare not, lengthen thy cords, and strengthen thy stakes" (Ch. 54:2).

Zion is the tent, the settlements surrounding her, are the cords and stakes. It is as improper to speak of Zion in Missouri as the "center stake of Zion," as it would be to call a tent a stake.

CHAPTER 18

ORGANIZATION OF THE FIRST PRESIDENCY—
IMPORTANT REVELATIONS
1832–1833

Important Revelations.—In the fall of 1832 and continuing through the winter and spring of 1833, a number of remarkable revelations were given for the edification and guidance of the Church. Great principles of science and philosophy, as well as of doctrine and spiritual truth, were revealed.

On the 22nd and 23rd of September, at the inquiry of a number of elders of the Church, the history and power of the Priesthood were revealed (Doc. and Cov. Sec. 84); the responsibilities taken by those who are ordained, were explained; the promises made to those who are faithful that they shall receive the fulness of the blessings of the Father's kingdom—for he had declared it "with an oath and covenant, which belongeth to the Priesthood," with the penalty attached that "whoso breaketh this covenant * * * and altogether turneth therefrom, shall not have forgiveness of sins in this world, nor in the world to come"—were clearly defined; the place of the great temple, and when it shall be built, and many other things dealing with the gathering of the Saints, the building of Zion and its redemption, were set forth.

November 27 the Lord stated that he would send one mighty and strong to arrange the inheritances of the Saints in Zion. (Doc. and Cov. Sec. 85.) December 6, the parable of the wheat and the tares was explained. (Doc. and Cov. Sec. 86.) On Christmas day the prophecy on war, which has so far been fulfilled, was given.

(Doc. and Cov. Sec. 87.) Two days later the remarkable revelation on scientific and doctrinal truth, known as the "Olive Leaf" (Doc. and Cov. Sec. 88), was presented to the Church. In this wonderful communication from the heavens the following eternal principles, among many others, were revealed:

The light of Christ is the light of truth and is the light of the sun, the planets, the stars, and the power by which they were made; it is the light which quickeneth the intelligence of man; it is the life and light of all things, and is the law by which they are governed; it fills the immensity of space; to every kingdom there is given laws which have their bounds and conditions; there is no space in which there is no kingdom, great or small; the worlds in space are peopled with the children of our Father; the earth on which we dwell is a living body and shall die, but shall be raised again a celestial body and shall become the abode of celestial beings; the inhabitants of the earth who are unfaithful must inherit another kingdom in eternity; he who cannot abide the law of the celestial kingdom, cannot abide a celestial glory; every man in the resurrection is quickened by the glory of the kingdom to which he has attained: the spirit and the body is the soul of man, and the redemption of the soul is through the death and resurrection of Jesus Christ; after the testimonies of the elders will come the testimonies of judgments; the order of the signs preceding the coming of the Savior, are made known; the redemption of the just; the destruction of the "great and abominable church;" and the fate of the wicked, are declared among the great truths contained in this revelation.

In February, 1833, the Lord gave to Joseph Smith the "Word of Wisdom" (Doc. and Cov. Sec. 89), for the temporal salvation of mankind. March 15, 1833, the doctrines of the eternity of matter; the glory of God is Intelligence; the innocence of man in the beginning; and many other things were received. (Doc. and Cov. Sec. 93.)

The School of the Prophets.—In the revelation of December 27, 1832 (Doc. and Cov. Sec. 88), the elders of the Church were also commanded to "teach one another the doctrines of the kingdom." They were to be instructed "more perfectly in theory, in principle, in doctrine, in the law of the Gospel in all things that pertain unto the kingdom of God," that were expedient for them to understand. They were to tarry in Kirtland for this instruction, before they should "go forth, among the Gentiles for the last time, as many as the mouth of the Lord shall name, to bind up the law and seal up the testimony, and to prepare the Saints for the hour of judgment which is to come." They were to seek diligently out of the best books, words of wisdom and learning "even by study and also by faith." That this should be accomplished, they were to prepare a house of prayer, learning and faith, even a house of glory—a house of God. In it they were to call their solemn assemblies; one should be appointed as teacher, and not all speak at once. While one speaks, all others should give attention. In this manner there was to be perfect order in the School of the Prophets—for so it should be called. Moreover, the Lord declared: "And this shall be the order of the house of the presidency of the school: He that is appointed to be president, or teacher, shall be found standing in his place, in the house which shall be prepared for him. Therefore, he shall be first in the house of God, in a place that the congregation in the house may hear his words carefully and distinctly, not with loud speech." Those who were entitled to attend should be the officers of the Church who are called to the ministry, "beginning at the high priests, even down to the deacons." They were to greet each other in fellowship with proper salutations. They should be men who were clean from the blood of this generation, soberminded and full of faith. Further, the Lord stated: "And ye are called to do this by prayer and thanksgiving as the Spirit shall give utterance in all your doings in the house of the Lord, in the School of the Prophets, that it may become a sanctuary, a tabernacle of the Holy Spirit to your edification."

The Coming of Brigham Young and Others.—September 10, George Albert Smith, son of John Smith and cousin to the Prophet, was baptized in Potsdam, New York. He was a youth fifteen years of age, who in later years was to play an important part in the work of these latter days. About the 8th of November, Joseph Young, Brigham Young, Heber C. Kimball and John P. Greene, came from Mendon, Monroe County, New York. This was the first meeting of Joseph Smith and these brethren. They remained in Kirtland for a number of days and were privileged to meet with the Prophet on several occasions. In one of their meetings, Brigham Young and John P. Greene spoke in tongues, as did also the Prophet Joseph Smith. These brethren had received the Gospel in Mendon. It had first been brought to their attention in the spring of 1830, through the labors of Samuel H. Smith, who had left a copy of the Book of Mormon with John P. Greene and also a copy with Phineas Howe Young, brother of Brigham Young. Later, through the preaching of Elders Alpheus Gifford, Elial Strong and others, they were persuaded to receive the truth. Brigham Young was baptized by Elder Eleazer Miller, April 14, 1832; was ordained an elder and at once entered the ministry and assisted in raising up several branches in the vicinity of Mendon, New York.

The Prophet's Labors in Kirtland.—The winter of 1832-3 was spent by Joseph Smith in revision of the scriptures; in the School

THE FIRST PRESIDENCY

of the Prophets, which had just been organized by commandment (Doc. and Cov. Sec. 88); and in the holding of conferences from time to time. In January a number of meetings of the elders were held, in which the ordinances of washing of feet, as spoken of in the 13th chapter of John, was attended to, as commanded by the Lord. (Doc. and Cov. Sec. 88.) On the 2nd of February the Prophet finished the revision of the New Testament, as far as he was directed to revise it at that time, and sealed it up not to be opened until it arrived in Zion. Several epistles were written to the Saints, and much correspondence passed between the elders in Zion and those in Kirtland in relation to their work.

Organization of the First Presidency.—March 18, 1833, the First Presidency of the Church was organized, with Joseph Smith, president, and Sidney Rigdon and Frederick G. Williams, counselors. This was in fulfilment of the commandment given in a revelation (Doc. and Cov. Sec. 90) on the 8th of that month, wherein the Lord said to Joseph Smith: "And again, verily I say unto thy brethren, Sidney Rigdon and Frederick G. Williams, their sins are forgiven them also, and they are accounted as equal with thee in holding the keys of the kingdom." One year before, in March, 1832, the Lord had called Frederick G. Williams to this position by revelation (Doc. and Cov. Sec. 81), and to hold "the keys of the kingdom, which belongeth always unto the Presidency of the High Priesthood." Joseph Smith laid his hands on the heads of each of these men and ordained them to take part with him in this great responsibility. Thus another step in the organization of the Church was completed.

Frederick G. Williams

Kirtland a Stake of Zion. —March 23, 1833, a council of the elders was called for the purpose of appointing a committee to purchase lands in Kirtland, upon which the Saints might build a stake of Zion. After some deliberations a committee was appointed consisting of Ezra Thayre and Joseph Coe. Later the property was purchased for this purpose, and many of the elders commenced to labor in various ways for the building of a city for the Saints at Kirtland.

First Gathering of the Mob in Zion.—In April, 1833, the first gathering of the mob in Jackson County took place. About three hundred men came together to decide upon a plan of campaign for the removal of the members of the Church in Jackson County. At the same time the elders in Jackson County met in solemn prayer and petitioned the Lord that the efforts of their enemies might fail. They had reason to meet and pray, for the wickedness of their enemies was extreme. Nor were the Saints free from guilt before the Lord. They had failed to keep strictly the commandments of the Lord which had been given them for the building up of Zion. Jealousies had arisen and murmurings were heard; even the Prophet, as well as others of the leading brethren, had been criticized. Some of the members had failed to observe the law of consecration, which had been given for the building of Zion, and their humility, in some respects, had been forgotten. However, on this occasion the deliberations of their enemies came to nothing. The Lord had heard the prayers of the Saints.

A House of the Lord in Kirtland.—At a conference of high priests held May 4, 1833, a committee was appointed to obtain subscriptions for the building of a house for a school, in compliance with the revelations of December 27, 1832, and March 8, 1833, where the elders might receive instructions before going out to warn the world. Hyrum Smith, Jared Carter and Reynolds Cahoon, were appointed as that committee. May 6, Joseph Smith received another revelation in which the Church was commanded to "commence a work of laying out and preparing a beginning and foundation of a stake of Zion," in Kirtland. A house was also to be built for the work of printing, translating, and "all things whatsoever the Lord should command them." The committee immediately went to work to gather means by subscriptions for this purpose. They had previously been commanded to build a house unto the Lord, to be a house of prayer and fasting, to be a temple unto His name.

Commencement of the Kirtland Temple.—By the first of June the preparations for the building of the Kirtland Temple were under way. A circular letter was sent out by the building committee to the various branches of the Church. June 1, the Prophet received the word of the Lord in relation to the building of the temple, in which the Saints were commanded to hasten the work, and the necessity for such a building was made known. "Ye have sinned against me a very grievous sin, in that ye have not considered the great commandment in all things, that I have given unto you concerning the building of mine house," said the Lord. Then he states the reason, in part—for the full purpose for such a house was not at that time made known—to be as follows: "For the preparation wherewith I design to prepare mine apostles to prune my vineyard for the last time, that I may bring to pass my strange act, that I may pour out my Spirit upon all flesh. * * * Yet, verily I say unto you, I give you a commandment that you should build an house, in the which I design to endow those whom I have chosen, with power from on high. For this is the promise of the Father unto you, therefore I command you to tarry, even as mine apostles at Jerusalem."

From this it is discovered that there were certain endowments and blessings to be given to the elders, before they could go forth fully prepared to preach the Gospel in the world, which could only be obtained in the temple of the Lord. For this cause the Lord commanded that the temple be built at once, for the preaching of the Gospel was urgent, and the laborers were few. The Saints therefore, went to work diligently in the midst of many difficulties, both within as well as without, the Church, to build the house of the Lord.

The First Work on the Temple.—On the 5th of June, George A. Smith hauled the first load of stone, and Hyrum Smith and Reynolds Cahoon, two of the building committee, commenced to dig the trench for the foundation, which they later finished with their own hands. Others also volunteered, and by these means the work progressed.

The Case of "Doctor" Hurlburt.—On the 3rd of June a charge was preferred against Philastus Hurlburt, who was accused of unchristian conduct while on a mission to the east. On investigation his elder's license was taken from him. On the 21st he appealed his case and on making confession of his improper conduct and a seeming show of repentance, he was reinstated. Two days later, however, his sincerity was called in question, and on the testimony of witnesses who had heard him say that he had not repented and had deceived "Joseph Smith's God," he was excommunicated from the Church. He later manifested a bitter spirit and in April, 1834, was bound by the court to keep the peace, "with good and sufficient security in the sum of two hundred dollars," for threats against the life of Joseph Smith.[a]

---

[a]Any reference to "Dr." Hurlburt might be considered insignificant but for one thing which developed after his apostasy and excommunication, which may be mentioned briefly here. He was not a doctor, but was so called because he was the seventh son. He had been a Methodist, but had been expelled from that body for immoral conduct, before he joined the Church. While engaged in

missionary work in Pennsylvania he heard of a manuscript that had been written by one Solomon Spaulding, which dealt with the subject of the American Indian. Hurlburt had an evil thought. If he could make it appear that the Book of Mormon was taken, or plagiarized, from the Spaulding Manuscript, it would prove to be an irreparable injury to "Mormonism." Others became interested in the scheme and a book was produced by E. D. Howe, entitled "Mormonism Unveiled." Of course the Spaulding story was lost so that no comparison was possible. For many years the publication of E. D. Howe was made to do mighty service against the Book of Mormon. As time went on, however, the manuscript of Mr. Spaulding was found, and is now in the archives of Oberlin College, in Ohio. A comparison with the Book of Mormon proved that the two products were no more alike than the Bible is like the story of Gulliver's Travels. Since that day the Hurlburt-Howe theory of the origin of the Book of Mormon has been dead.

For a thorough account of this question the reader is referred to "The Myth of the Manuscript Found," by Elder George Reynolds; and " New Witnesses For God," Vol. 3; Page 354, by Elder B. H. Roberts.

CHAPTER 19

THE EXPULSION FROM JACKSON COUNTY
1833

The Prophet's Warning.—The impending storm about to break over the heads of the Saints in Missouri was foreseen by the Prophet Joseph Smith. In January, 1833, he wrote to William W. Phelps as follows: "The Lord will have a place whence his word will go forth in these last days in purity; for if Zion will not purify herself so as to be approved of in all things in his sight, he will seek another people; for his work will go on until Israel is gathered, and they who will not hear his voice must expect to feel his wrath. * * * Our hearts are greatly grieved at the spirit which is breathed both in your letter and that of Brother Gilbert's, the very spirit which is wasting the strength of Zion like a pestilence; and if it is not detected and driven from you, it will ripen Zion for the threatened judgments of God. * * * This from your brother who trembles for Zion, and for the wrath of heaven, which awaits her if she repent not." These fears were also expressed in an epistle written the same day from a conference of high priests in Kirtland to their brethren in Zion. "We feel more like weeping for Zion than we do like rejoicing over her, for we know that the judgments of God hang over her, and will fall upon her except she repent," was their message.

Rise of Mob Force in Jackson.—Almost as soon as the members of the Church commenced settling in Jackson County, opposition began to show itself. The settlers were incited to violence by their ministers, who started a campaign of abuse and falsehood. They received ready aid from others of the citizens, which ultimately resulted in the expulsion of the Latter-day Saints from the State. The Rev. Finis Ewing publicly distributed the report that "the 'Mormons' were the common enemies of mankind," while the Rev. Pixley circulated falsehoods among the religious papers of the east, and used his influence among both the Indians and the whites for the destruction of the Church in Jackson County.

Nearly all the Latter-day Saints were from the Eastern States, while the Missourians were from the South. The Missourians feared that the "Mormons" would increase and take from them their political domination. The question of slavery, even in that day, was quite keen, and the Missourians were determined to keep the state within the control of the slave holders. Above all else, however, was their extreme hatred for the "Mormons" because of their industry and belief. Some of the latter had also failed to show the proper discretion and wisdom, for they openly stated that the Lord had given them the land for their eternal inheritance, and although they were to purchase the lands, yet in time there the city Zion would be built unto which none but the faithful would be privileged to come. Such expressions aroused the Missourians to fever heat, for they naturally hated the doctrines of the Church, and to be informed that the lands would ultimately be taken from them, was adding fuel to the flame.

As early as the spring of 1833, the mob resorted to violence. In the still hours of the night, windows in many of the houses of the Saints were broken, and other damage done by their enemies, who naturally performed their deeds in the dark; but this was only the beginning of sorrow.

The Mob Council.—July 20, 1833, a council of all Missourians who were opposed to the Latter-day Saints was called to meet in the Independence Court house. Between four and five hundred men assembled and chose Richard Simpson, chairman, and Samuel D. Lucas and J. H. Flournoy, secretaries. They then proceeded to discuss means for the ejection of the members of the Church from Jackson County, "peaceably if we can," they said, "forcibly if we must." After deliberating for some time, they concluded that "the arm of the civil law does not afford a guarantee," or at least a sufficient one, against the "evils" which were inflicted upon them. These "evils" were such that "no one could have foreseen," and "therefore, unprovided for by the laws;" and the "delays incident to legislation would put the mischief beyond remedy." They must because of this take into their own hands the matter of expulsion of hundreds of citizens from their homes.

Some of the "evils" of the "Mormons" were stated to be as follows: The declaration that miracles have been performed and supernatural cures achieved among the sick; a belief in heavenly manifestations and that they have held converse with God and his angels; possession and exercise of the gifts of divination and unknown tongues; and "fired with the prospect of obtaining inheritance without money and without price." Yet they were well aware that the "Mormons" had never made the attempt to obtain lands except by purchase, as the Lord had commanded them. Nevertheless all these "crimes" must be punished; for against such evils "self preservation, good society and public morals," made demands that the "Mormons" should be expelled. The following articles were drawn up and unanimously approved, to be submitted to the elders of the Church.

Declaration of the Mob.—(1). "That no Mormon shall in future move and settle in this county.

(2). "That those now here, who shall give a definite pledge of their intention within reasonable time to remove out of the county, shall be allowed to remain unmolested until they have sufficient time to sell their property, and close their business, without any material sacrifice.

(3). "That the editor of the *Star* be required forthwith to close his office and discontinue the business of printing in this county; and as to all other stores and shops belonging to the sect, their owners must in every case strictly comply with the terms of the second article of this declaration; and upon failure, prompt and efficient measures will be taken to close the same.

(4). "That the Mormon leaders here are required to use their influence in preventing any further emigration of their distant brethren to this county, and to counsel and advise their brethren here to comply with the above requisitions.

(5). "That those who fail to comply with these requisitions be referred to those of their brethren who have the gifts of divination, and of unknown tongues, to inform them of the lot that awaits them."

This address was read and after approval a committee consisting of twelve men was appointed to wait upon the presiding elders of the Church. They were instructed to "see that the foregoing requisitions are strictly complied with by tHem; and upon their refusal, that said committee do, as the organ of this county, inform them that it is our unwavering purpose and fixed determination, after the fullest consideration of all the consequences and responsibilities under which we act, to use such means as shall insure full and complete adoption." Such was the ungodly manifesto of the mob.

The Enemy's Demands.—A recess was taken for two hours in which the committee was to carry this message of unrighteous demands to the elders of the Church and then make report. Naturally these brethren desired time to consider these drastic terms. They had come into the land by command of the Lord, to receive their inheritance; it was here the great city of the New Jerusalem was to be built; they had hoped for a peaceful possession of their property, and as they had not interfered with the privileges of others they justly felt that they were entitled to maintain their rights. They asked for three months for consideration of these evil terms; but were denied. They then asked for ten days; but were informed that fifteen minutes was time enough. If immediate answer was not forthcoming an unfavorable report would be returned, with consequences of serious character speedily to follow. A refusal of these demands was evidently the desire of the unlawful gathering at the court house, which sought a pretext to vent their anger upon the Saints violently.

The Committee's Report.—The committee returned and made their report. "Whereupon," their minutes read, "it was unanimously resolved by the meeting, that the *Star* printing office should be razed to the ground; the type and press secured." With the understanding that they would meet again three days later, the horde of wretches started forth on their mission of destruction. They did not overlook the opportunity to advertise their deliberations "that the Mormon brethren may know at a distance that the gates of Zion are closed against them—that their interests will be best promoted by remaining among those who know and appreciate their merits."

Vengeance of the Mob.—With the utmost fury these human fiends proceeded to the office of the *Evening and Morning Star* and razed it to the ground. The office was a part of the dwelling occupied by William W. Phelps. Mrs. Phelps and her children including a sick infant, were thrown out of doors amidst the furniture which was destroyed. They then proceeded to the store of Gilbert, Whitney and Co., bent on further destruction; but Elder Gilbert assuring them that the goods would be packed by the 23rd of that month, and no more would be sold, they left him and the store and turned their attention to personal violence. They took Bishop Edward Partridge and Charles Allen, stripped them and applied a coat of tar which had been mixed with acid which burned into their flesh, and then coated them with feathers. Others of the brethren were scourged, amidst horrid yells and blasphemous oaths, while others in the excitement, for all their captors were intent upon the "sport," were able to make their escape from similar treatment by the mob.

EXPULSION FROM JACKSON COUNTY

Second Gathering of the Mob.—On the morning of July 23, 1833, the mob, to the number of about five hundred, again approached Independence, carrying a red flag—the emblem of lawlessness—and armed with all manner of weapons of war. They rode through the streets, giving vent to hideous yells and blasphemous oaths, searching for the presiding elders of the Church. They threatened to whip any "Mormon" whom they captured, with from fifty to five hundred lashes each, demolish their dwellings, and turn negroes loose to destroy their fields.

Offer of Ransom for the Church.—Elders John Corrill, John Whitmer, William W. Phelps, Algernon S. Gilbert, Edward Partridge and Isaac Morley, the leading elders, made no resistance, but offered themselves a ransom for the Church. They were willing to be scourged and even die, if that would appease the wrath of the mob. The Missourians, with blasphemous oaths, assured them that every man, woman and child would be whipped and scourged even to death if they did not leave Jackson County. "The Mormons," said the mobbers, "must leave the county, or they or the Mormons must die." The brethren mentioned, knowing that resistance was useless and to save the Saints and avoid the shedding of blood, entered into an agreement with the mob to leave the county within a reasonable time.

The Forced Agreement of the Mob.—The terms forced by the mob upon the Saints were as follows: Oliver Cowdery, William W. Phelps, William E. McLellin, Edward Partridge, Lyman Wight, Simeon Carter, Harvey Whitlock and the two Whitmers, Peter and John, were to remove their families from the county on or before the first day of January, 1834; they were to use all their influence to induce all other members of the Church to remove as soon as possible, one half by January first, and the rest by the first of April following; and to do all in their power to stop others of their brethren from moving into Jackson County; John Corrill and Algernon S. Gilbert were allowed to remain as general agents to wind up the business, Gilbert to sell the merchandise on hand but to buy no more; the *Star* was not to be published nor a press set up; Edward Partridge and William W. Phelps were to remove their families, but they would be permitted to come and go to wind up the affairs of the Church. The mob pledged themselves to use no violence so long as the brethren complied with the terms presented. To this the names of the elders and the members of the second committee appointed by the mob were subscribed.

The Contract Broken by the Mob.—Since there is no honor among knaves, the mob failed to keep their agreement. Constantly they sallied forth, breaking windows in the homes of the members of the Church and offering abuse when occasion afforded. These attacks, however, did not pass unnoticed by the better class of citizens in the state. The *Western Monitor,* a paper published in Fayette, Missouri, first showed a friendly spirit toward the mob, but later censured them for their conduct and advised the "Mormons" to seek redress for their wrongs. Other papers adopted a similar view, whereupon the members of the mob declared that if any "Mormon" attempted "to seek redress by law or otherwise, for character, person, or property, they should die."

Appeal to Governor Dunklin.—When hostilities broke out the brethren in Missouri sent Oliver Cowdery to Kirtland to make report and consult the First Presidency in respect to future action. In sorrow for the afflicted members in Missouri the presidency sent Orson Hyde and John Gould with instructions for their brethren in that land. Shortly after their arrival, necessary preparations having been made, Elders William W. Phelps and Orson Hyde, were sent to Jefferson City with a petition, under date of September 28, 1833, to Governor Daniel Dunklin. In their petition the wrongs of the Latter-day Saints were clearly set forth, and it was signed by nearly all the members of the Church in Missouri.

The Governor's Reply.—On the 19th of October, Governor Dunklin made reply to the memorial of the members of the Church, and advised them to take their grievances before the courts, for, said he: "No citizen, nor number of citizens, have a right to take the redress of their grievances, whether real or imaginary, into their own hands. Such conduct strikes at the very existence of society, and subverts the foundation on which it is based. * * * The judge of your circuit is a conservator of the peace: if an affidavit is made before him by any of you, that your lives are threatened, and you believe them in danger, it would be his duty to have the offenders apprehended, and bind them to keep the peace." He could not "permit himself to doubt that the courts were open to" the Saints.

Futility of the Advice.—Under ordinary circumstances the governor's advice might have been of some worth. The conditions, however, were of no ordinary nature. The leaders of the mob were Samuel D. Lucas, judge of the county court; Samuel C. Owens, county clerk; John Smith, justice of the peace; Samuel Weston, justice of the peace; William Brown, constable; Thomas Pitcher, deputy constable; James H. Flournoy, postmaster, and Lilburn W. Boggs, lieutenant governor of the state, the latter, however, keeping in the background and aiding and abetting the others in their evil work. For the "Mormon" people to accept the governor's advice, would mean their trial

EXPULSION FROM JACKSON COUNTY

would be conducted before their avowed and open enemies, if they were permitted a trial at all.

Counsel Employed by the Saints.—Nevertheless, accepting the governor's advice, attorneys were engaged to fight the case. They were William T. Wood, Amos Reese, Alexander W. Doniphan and David R. Atchison, who agreed to plan suits and carry them through for one thousand dollars. Notes for that amount were given by William W. Phelps and Bishop Partridge and endorsed by Gilbert, Whitney and Co. However, very little benefit was ever derived by the members of the Church from this action.

Continued Activities of the Mob.—As soon as it was known that the "Mormons" would appeal to the courts, the mobbers began to prepare for war. On the night of October 31, a band of about fifty marauders proceeded against a branch of the Church west of the Big Blue River, not far from Independence. There they unroofed and partly demolished a number of houses, whipped in a savage manner several men and frightened the women and children, who were forced to flee for safety. On the first of November, another attack was made on a branch on the prairie, fourteen miles from Independence. The same night another party raided the homes of the Saints in Independence, where a number of houses were demolished and the goods in the store of Gilbert, Whitney and Co., were scattered in the street. One Richard McCarty was caught in the act of breaking into the store and demolishing property and was taken before Samuel Weston, justice of the peace, where a complaint was made against him; Judge Weston, however, refused to consider the complaint, and turned McCarty loose. The next day McCarty caused the arrest of the witnesses who had captured him in this unlawful act, and had them tried for false imprisonment. The same justice, on the testimony of this fellow alone, found the witnesses, Gilbert, Morley and Corrill, guilty and committed them to jail. "Although we could not obtain a warrant against him for breaking open the store," said John Corrill, "yet he had gotten one for us for catching him at it."

The Battle of the Blue.—These attacks upon the Saints were repeatedly continued; attempts were made to obtain peace warrants, but no justice would issue them for fear of the mob. Monday, November 4, 1833, a band of mobbers gathered at the Big Blue River and commenced to destroy property. Nineteen men, members of the Church, gathered in defense, but discovering the superior number of the mob, turned back. Their enemies, learning of this attempt, immediately went in pursuit of the "Mormons" who fled in various directions for safety. About thirty more of the brethren from the prairie armed with seventeen guns approached and a battle commenced. The mobbers soon fled leaving two of their number, Hugh L. Brazeale and Thomas Linville, dead on the ground. Among the "Mormons" Andrew Barber received a mortal wound and died the following day. Philo Dibble also received a severe wound, but was almost instantly healed by the laying on of hands by Elder Newel Knight.

The Mob Militia.—Following the battle of the Blue, excitement ran high. November 5, 1833, at the instigation of Lieutenant Governor Lilburn W. Boggs, the militia was called out under command of Colonel Thomas Pitcher, one of the leaders of the mob of July 23. It was stated that the militia had been called for the protection of the Saints, but it had every appearance of a mob and in its ranks were many of the most bitter enemies of the Church. Colonel Pitcher demanded that the Saints surrender their arms. This they refused to do unless their enemies should also be disarmed. Colonel Pitcher readily agreed to this proposition to which Lieutenant Governor Boggs also pledged his honor. Another demand was that certain brethren who had been engaged in the battle the day before were to be surrendered and tried for murder. Both of these demands were complied with by the Saints.

Misplaced Confidence.—Having confidence in the pledge of the lieutenant governor, the Saints returned to their homes feeling somewhat secure from further attacks. Their confidence, however, had been misplaced, for it was a cunning scheme of this state official, and the other leaders of the mob, to place the members of the Church in a defenseless position and then drive them from the county; which, forthwith, they proceeded to do. The arms were never taken from the members of the mob, but those taken from the Saints were distributed among their enemies to be used against them.[a] The following day gangs of men, numbering sixty or more, went from house to house whipping the men, driving the women and children from their homes at the muzzles of their guns, and setting fire to their houses, to make sure their owners would not return. More than two hundred houses were destroyed in the several raids of the mob. The men who surrendered themselves under the charge of murder, were detained for one day and a night and sorely abused; then they were taken out into a cornfield by this same Colonel

---

[a]In the spring of 1834, Governor Dunklin issued a requisition to Colonel S. D. Lucas to return the arms of the "Mormons" which were taken from them in November, 1833; but Lucas had resigned his commission and moved to Lexington, Missouri. A second requisition to Colonel Pitcher was contemptuously ignored. The arms were distributed among the mob and they boasted that they would not return them, notwithstanding the order of the governor of the state; and the arms were never returned.

Pitcher and told to "clear!" meaning they were to leave immediately for parts unknown.

The Saints in Exile.—These attacks continued for several days and among those directing the forces of the mob were several "reverend" gentlemen who took pleasure in these wicked deeds. By the 7th of November, the banks of the Missouri River were lined with refugees who had gathered in the utmost confusion, so hasty had been their flight. Twelve hundred souls were thus forced to seek shelter, the best they could, in the dead of winter, and in the midst of storms. Many died from exposure and the abuse otherwise heaped upon them and the fleeing multitude left, in the frozen stubble, a trail of blood from their lacerated feet. The exiled Saints sought refuge in the neighboring counties, but from some of these they were again forced to flee before the inhospitable inhabitants among whom they found themselves. In Clay County, just across the river north of Jackson, they were received temporarily with some degree of kindness.

An Attempt to Seek Redress.—Through their attorneys, and by direct petition to Governor Daniel Dunklin, the Saints sought to repossess their property in Jackson County. The governor acknowledged the justice of their claims and expressed a willingness to furnish an "adequate force" to effect that object; but he declared he had no power to protect them after they were once returned to their lands. He was also willing, so it was declared by Attorney General R. W. Wells, to organize them in companies of militia that they might aid in their restoration. The Saints knew that such a thing would only arouse their enemies to greater fury, and as no protection was guaranteed them when once restored, such an offer could not be accepted.

Farcical Effort to Enforce the Law.—It may have been the intention of the state officials, at the first, to restore the exiles to their lands, but they evidently lacked the courage to cope with the lawless, but determined, enemies of the Saints. A number of leading elders were subpoenaed in behalf of the state to appear at the February (1834) term of court to be held at Independence. On the 23rd of that month, under the protection of Captain Atchison's company of "Liberty Blues"—nearly fifty rank and file—these witnesses crossed the Missouri River bound for Independence. That night they camped in the woods. Captain Atchison, becoming alarmed at the appearance of the enemy, sent an express to Colonel Allen for two hundred drafted militia, and to Liberty for more ammunition. Early the next morning this company marched to Independence, and after breakfast they were visited by District Attorney Amos Reese and Attorney General R. W. Wells, who informed the witnesses that all hopes of criminal prosecution were at an end. Mr. Wells had been sent by the governor to investigate the Jackson County outrages, but the bold front of the mob evidently intimidated the state officials who were willing to appease the wrath of the mob rather than to maintain the majesty of the law.

As soon as Captain Atchison was informed that his services were no longer needed, he took his witnesses and marched them out of town, to the tune of Yankee Doodle, quick time, and soon returned to camp. One of the witnesses, Elder William W. Phelps, wrote of this farcical proceeding as follows: "This order was issued by the court, apparently on the speedy gathering of the old mob, or citizens of Jackson County, and their assuming such a boisterous and mobocratic appearance. Much credit is due to Captain Atchison for his gallantry and hospitality, and I think I can say of the officers and company, that their conduct as soldiers and men, is highly reputable; so much the more, knowing as I do, the fatal results of the trial had the militia come or not come. * * * Thus ended all hopes of redress, even with a guard ordered by the governor for the protection of the court and witnesses."

CHAPTER 20

THE PATRIARCHAL PRIESTHOOD—
ZION'S CAMP

1833-1834

The Patriarchal Priesthood.—December 18, 1833, a number of elders assembled in the printing office in Kirtland and dedicated the printing press, with all that pertained thereunto, unto the service of the Lord. The first sheets of the re-printed *Evening and Morning Star* were struck off, it having been decided to continue that periodical in Kirtland until the press could be restored in Independence.*a* While the elders were assembled in the printing office on this occasion the Prophet gave the first patriarchal blessings in this dispensation. It was his privilege to do this, for he held the keys of all the authority in the Church, and was spoken of as the first patriarch in the Church because of this fact, in the minutes which were kept at that time. Those who received blessings under his hand on this occasion were: Oliver Cowdery, the father and mother of the Prophet, and three of his brothers, Hyrum, Samuel and William Smith. Oliver Cowdery, who held the keys of Priesthood with the Prophet, also gave a number

---

*a*At a meeting held in Kirtland Sept. 11, 1833, it was decided that a press should be established in that place and a paper published to be called the "Messenger and Advocate," and that the "Evening and Morning Star," formerly published in Independence, be continued in Kirtland until it could again be published in Zion, which the brethren thought would be but a short time. All the numbers of the Star published in Independence were republished in quarto size. The first number of the Star was issued in June, 1832, and the last in July, 1833, the month the press was destroyed by the mob. In December, 1833, the first number in Kirtland (No. 15) was issued, it continued until September, 1834, when it was succeeded by the "Messenger and Advocate."

of patriarchal blessings. Joseph Smith, Sen., was ordained to the Patriarchal Priesthood, to hold the keys of blessing on the heads of all the members of the Church, the Lord revealing that it was his right to hold this authority. He was also set apart as an assistant counselor to the Prophet Joseph in the presidency, and at a later day Hyrum Smith, the Prophet's brother, and John Smith, his uncle, were set apart to this same calling.

Organization of the First High Council.—The first high council in this dispensation was organized at the home of Joseph Smith in Kirtland, February 17, 1834. The First Presidency presided in this council and the following brethren were chosen as its members: Joseph Smith, Sen., John Smith, Joseph Coe, John Johnson, Martin Harris, John S. Carter, Jared Carter, Oliver Cowdery, Samuel H. Smith, Orson Hyde, Sylvester Smith and Luke S. Johnson.[b] Several days before this action was taken the Prophet had explained the manner in which councils should be conducted. "No man," said he, "is capable of judging a matter in council unless his own heart is pure." Ancient councils were conducted with strict propriety; no one was permitted to whisper, leave the room, or think of anything but the matter before them for consideration. If the presiding officer could stay, others were expected to do the same, until the Spirit was obtained and a righteous decision was reached.

There were a number of cases awaiting the action of the high council as soon as it was organized, and within a day or two several trials were held and matters of discipline passed upon. One question considered was as follows: "Whether disobedience to the word of wisdom was a transgression sufficient to deprive an official member from holding office in the Church, after having it sufficiently taught him?" After a free and full discussion Joseph Smith, who presided, gave his decision as follows: "No official member in this Church is worthy to hold an office after having the word of wisdom properly taught him; and he, the official member, neglecting to comply with or obey it." This decision was confirmed by unanimous vote.

Zion Shall Not be Removed.—A revelation was given to Joseph Smith December 16, 1833, giving the reason for the expulsion of the members of the Church from Jackson County. (Doc. and Cov. Sec. 101.) Nevertheless the Lord declared that Zion should "not be moved out of her place, notwithstanding her children are scattered." In his own due time he would redeem Zion, and let fall the sword of his indignation in behalf of his people. The cup of his wrath was to be

---

[b]See Doc. and Cov. Sec. 102, for procedure in High Councils and minutes of this organization.

poured out without measure upon all nations, when the cup of their iniquity is full. The Saints were instructed to "Importune for redress and redemption" before the judge and if he should fail, then before the governor, and if they could not obtain redress from him they were to importune the president of the United States, and if he heeded them not, then the Lord would "vex the nation." The Church was instructed to purchase lands in Jackson and neighboring counties, for inheritances for the Saints. Moreover, they were instructed in a parable to gather together the strength of the Lord's house, "My young men and they that are middle aged also among all my servants, who are the strength of mine house, save those only whom I have appointed to tarry," said the Lord, "and go straightway unto the land of my vineyard, and redeem my vineyard, for it is mine, I have bought it with money." February 24, 1834, the Lord further declared that if his Saints would, from that time forth, repent and keep his commandments, they should "begin to prevail" against his enemies from that very hour; but if they polluted their inheritances they were to be thrown down, for he would not spare them if they polluted their inheritances. "The redemption of Zion must needs come by power," he declared, therefore the Saints were to collect money and purchase lands, as they had been commanded, and the young and middle aged were to gather to Zion and seek its redemption.

Zion's Camp.—According to this instruction, a call went forth asking for volunteers to go to Zion. Five hundred men were wanted; yet, said the Lord: "If you cannot obtain five hundred, seek diligently that peradventure ye may obtain one hundred;" for with less than one hundred they were not to go. The first of May (1834) a part of these volunteers left Kirtland, and on the fifth Joseph Smith and the remainder took up their journey. At West Portage, about fifty miles west of Kirtland, they met and were organized in companies for their journey. Each company was divided as follows: a captain, two cooks, two firemen, two tent-men, two water-men, one runner, two wagoners and horsemen, and one commissary, twelve men in all. Every night before retiring, at the sound of the bugle they bowed before the Lord in prayer in their several tents, and every morning, at the trumpet's call about four o'clock, every man again knelt in prayer, imploring the blessings of the Lord for the day. As they traveled they endeavored to keep their identity unknown so as not to arouse opposition in the country through which they passed. As it was they were followed by enemies and spies, and delegations approached them from time to time to learn the meaning of their journey. The following questions were frequently put and answered in this manner:

"Where are you from?"

"From the East."

"Where are you going?"

"To the West."

"What for?"

"To see where we can get land cheapest and best."

"Who leads the camp?"

"Sometimes one and sometimes another."

Their journey took them through Dayton, Indianapolis, Springfield and Jacksonville, Illinois, and across the Mississippi River into Missouri. It was near the banks of the Illinois River, west of Jacksonville, where the bones of Zelph[c] the white Lamanite, were dug up and mounds, or ancient altars, were discovered. This was about the first of June, and on the third, while still camped on the banks of the river refreshing themselves, the Prophet Joseph got up on a wagon and uttered this prophecy: "I said the Lord had revealed to me that scourge would come upon the camp in consequence of the fractious and unruly spirits that appeared among them, and they should die like sheep with the rot; still, if they would repent and humble themselves before the Lord, the scourge in great measure might be turned away; but as the Lord lives, the members of this camp will suffer for giving way to their unruly temper." Even this warning did not prevent some of the members of the camp from murmuring and finding fault against their brethren.

Message to Governor Dunklin.—Acting on the commandment in the revelations the brethren in Missouri did not cease to importune the judge and the governor of the state, May 29, 1834, and again, June 5, the Saints in Clay County petitioned the governor, and on the 6th, he wrote to Colonel J. Thornton acknowledging the just cause of the Saints in this demand of him, stating:

"Uncommitted as I am to either party, I shall feel no embarassment in doing my duty—though it may be done with the most extreme regret. My duty in the relation which I now stand to the parties, is plain and straight forward. * * * A more clear and indisputable right does not exist than that of the Mormon people, who were expelled from their homes in Jackson County, to return and live on their lands; and if they cannot be persuaded, as a matter of policy, to give up that right, or to qualify it, my course as the chief executive of the State, is a plain one. The constitution of the United States declares

---

[c]See Documentary History of the Church, Vol. 2:79, for this interesting incident.

that, 'The citizens of each state shall be entitled to all the privileges and immunities of citizens in the several states.'"

He then suggested to Colonel Thornton, which proposition he also presented to the Saints, that they sell out and move from their possessions; or, to attempt to peaceably settle their difficulties, and he would attempt to get the citizens to "rescind their illegal resolves" against the "Mormons" and agree to conform to the laws. If all this should fail, and they could not agree to divide their lands, then he would have to conform his action to that end, indicating that in justice he would be bound to assist the exiles to regain their property.

All such expressions led the members of the Church to hope for redress. Acting on this thought, about the 8th of June, a delegation from Zion's Camp was sent to Jefferson City to ascertain from the Governor if he was ready to reinstate the Latter-day Saints on their lands in Jackson County, and leave them there to defend themselves, as he had previously indicated that he would. If so, they were ready, by command of the Lord, to take that course.

In the meantime the camp continued on its journey. To accept the governor's proposition to sell their lands, was out of the question; as soon would they expect to sell their children, for the Lord had commanded them to retain their possessions, or inheritances in that land. On the 15th of June, 1834, Orson Hyde and Parley P. Pratt, the delegates, returned from Jefferson City and reported that the governor refused to fulfill his promise. For some reason, which is not explained but which may be guessed, he had received a change of heart, although his reason was stated to be on the ground of "impracticability." Such a lamentable failure on the part of the governor to do his duty, was a severe blow to the Saints.

Threats of the Mob.—On the morning of June 19, 1834, as the camp was passing through Richmond, Missouri, they were informed by a friendly farmer who entertained them and gave them refreshments, that they had many enemies about, and that a mob from Jackson and other counties was intending to intercept them before they could reach their brethren in Clay County. This was later confirmed. Their progress, by act of divine providence, was impeded which forced them to camp between the Little and Big Fishing rivers that night. As they were making camp five men rode up and told them they would "see hell before morning." They stated that an armed force from Ray and Clay counties was to join a Jackson County force at the Fishing River ford bent on the utter destruction of the camp. While these five men were in the camp, cursing and swearing vengeance, signs of an approaching storm were seen. No sooner had these men left the camp than the storm burst in all its fury. Hailstones so large that they cut limbs from the trees fell all around the camp, while the trees were twisted from their roots by the force of the wind. The earth trembled and quaked, the streams became raging torrents, and the mobbers dispersed seeking shelter that could not be found. One mobber was killed by lightning and another had his hand torn off by a fractious horse, and in fear they dispersed, saying, if that was the way God fought for the "Mormons" they would go about their business. On the morning of June 21, Colonel Sconce with two companions visited the camp to learn what the intention of the members were. He said: "I see there is an almighty power that protects this people, for I started from Richmond, Ray County, with a company of armed men, having fixed determination to destroy you, but was kept back by the storm." The Prophet related to these men the sufferings of the Saints, and they left the camp offering to use their influence to allay the excitement which prevailed. During all this storm the members of the camp were protected from its fury.

Judge Ryland's Proposition.—Evidently with the best of intentions, Judge John F. Ryland, on the 10th of June, 1834, wrote to Algernon S. Gilbert offering to call a meeting in Liberty on the 16th, for the purpose of allaying the "disturbances between the Mormons and the citizens of Jackson County." A similar communication was sent to prominent citizens of Jackson County. In their answer Elders John Corrill and A. S. Gilbert expressed a willingness to meet, but declared that under no condition would the Saints sell their property in Jackson County. On the 16th, the proposed meeting was held. A deputation from Jackson County was present and made a proposition to this effect: They would buy all the lands that the "Mormons" own in Jackson County, and also all improvements, the value of said land to be determined by three disinterested parties; twelve of the "Mormons" would be permitted to go into Jackson County, to show their lands and improvements; the purchase was to be made within thirty days after the decision was reached, and one hundred per cent would be added to the appraisement. On the other hand, the "Mormons" were offered all the lands of the citizens of Jackson on the same terms. This proposition was signed by ten men who stated they were authorized to take this action.

After the reading of the proposition Samuel C. Owens, one of the Jackson committee, made a war speech and was followed by Rev. Riley who declared that "the Mormons have lived long enough in Clay County; and they must clear out, or be cleared out." The moderator of the meeting, Mr. Turnham, replied: "Let us be republicans; let us honor our country, and not disgrace it like Jackson County; don't disfranchise or drive away the Mormons. They are better citizens than many of the old inhabitants." General A. W. Doniphan arose and said: "That's a fact, and as the Mormons have armed themselves, if they don't fight they are cowards. I love to hear that they have brethren coming to their assistance. Greater love can no man show, than he who lays down his life for his brethren." At this instant pistols and knives were drawn and the cry was raised at the door that a man was stabbed. The mass instantly rushed out to see what had happened, and the meeting broke up in confusion.

Unfairness of the Proposition.—Reflecting on the proposition offered by the mob committee from Jackson, the Prophet Joseph writes: "It may be thought, at first view, that the mob committee made a fair proposition to the Saints, in offering to buy their lands at a price fixed by disinterested arbitrators, and one hundred per centum added thereto, payment to be made in thirty days, and offering theirs on the same terms; but when it is understood that the mob held possession of a much larger quantity of land than the Saints, and that they only offered thirty days for the payment, having previously robbed the Saints of nearly everything, it will be readily seen that they were only making a sham to cover their previous unlawful conduct." To meet this proposition, which was not made in sincerity, the Saints would have been under the necessity of raising in thirty days approximately six hundred thousand dollars, a thing out of reason, which the mobbers knew. Moreover, they were well aware of the fact that the Saints would not sell although ten times the value of the land were offered, for the Lord had commanded them to hold to their inheritances.

Counter Proposition of the Saints.—Some time later a counter proposition was made by the Saints to the Missourians. They offered to buy out all those who were unwilling to dwell in Jackson County with them in peace, on such terms as had been offered except that the payment would be made in one year. A committee of twelve, six from each side, were to determine the value of the lands. It is needless to say that the proposition was not received very kindly by these hypocrites and deceivers.

Word of the Lord at Fishing River.—While the camp was on Fishing River the word of the Lord came to Joseph Smith (Doc. and Cov. Sec. 105) stating that it was not required of the camp to continue the journey for the redemption of Zion. The camp had been brought to the borders of Jackson County, "for a trial of their faith." However, if it had not been for transgression of the people, the Lord declared, "they might have been redeemed even now. But behold, they have not learned to be obedient to the things which I require at their hands, but are full of all manner of evil, and do not impart of their substance, as becometh saints, to the poor and afflicted among them, and are not united according to the union required by the law of the celestial kingdom. And Zion cannot be built up unless it is by the principles of the law of the celestial kingdom, otherwise I cannot receive her unto myself; and my people must needs be chastened until they learn obedience, if it must needs be by the things which they suffer. I speak not concerning those who are permitted to lead my people, who are the first elders of my church, for they are not all under this condemnation; but I speak concerning my churches abroad—there are many who will say, Where is their God? Behold, he will deliver them in time of trouble, otherwise we will not go up unto Zion, and will keep our moneys. Therefore, in consequence of the transgression of my people, it is expedient in me that mine elders should wait for a little season for the redemption of Zion."[d] The elders were to be endowed with power from on high in the house of the Lord at Kirtland, and be taught more perfectly in doctrine and have experience and a better knowledge of their duties, before Zion could be redeemed. This was one reason for the building of the temple in Kirtland.

Disbanding of the Camp.—On the 23rd of June (1834), the camp continued its march and the next day arrived near the home of Algernon Sidney Gilbert on Rush Creek, where, on the morning of the 25th, in compliance with the revelation of the 22nd, the camp was separated into small groups to quiet the feelings of the people, and dispersed among the brethren who were residing in Clay County.

The Prophecy Fulfilled.—As soon as the camp arrived on Rush Creek, the cholera broke out among the members and continued for several days. The victims were seized suddenly and so powerful was the disease that within a few minutes some of the brethren were dead. About sixty-eight members were attacked and fourteen died. Among the number who succumbed was Algernon Sidney Gilbert, keeper of the Lord's storehouse in Zion, and one of the stalwart

---

[d]In a letter to the high council in Zion the Prophet said: "Now my beloved brethren, you will learn by this we have a great work to do, and but little time to do it in; and if we do not exert ourselves to the utmost in gathering up the strength of the Lord's house that this thing may be accomplished, behold there remaineth a scourge for the Church, even that they shall be driven from city to city, and but few shall remain to receive an inheritance." This had reference to preparations "against the time" when the Lord should call them again to the redemption of Zion.

leaders who had stood in defense of the liberty and lives of the Saints in Jackson County.

Organization of the High Council in Missouri.—The day after the revelation was given regarding the endowments (Doc. and Cov. Sec. 105), a council of high priests met and called a number of individuals to receive these blessings in the house of the Lord; and on the 3rd of July, 1834, the high priests assembled and a high council for the Church in Missouri was organized agreeable to the revelation and pattern given in Kirtland. Six days later the Prophet started back for Kirtland with a number of the brethren.

What the Camp Accomplished.—While the object for which Zion's Camp was organized and for which they made the journey, as understood by the members, was not attained, yet without question they did accomplish all that the Lord expected of them. So he stated in the Fishing River revelation. Their faith was tried; experience had been gained by which men were to be chosen for responsible positions in the Church in days to come, and the work of the Lord advanced; but in addition to all this the Lord was preparing men through this experience for the responsibility of moving the entire people, of Latter-day Saints in the great exodus to the West, which was later to come. The purposes of the Lord do not fail and all things are turned to his advantage.

CHAPTER 21

CHOOSING OF THE TWELVE AND SEVENTY—
DEDICATION OF THE KIRTLAND TEMPLE

1834-1836

Charges Against the Prophet.—As already stated, there was some dissension in Zion's Camp on the way to Missouri. One of the chief offenders on that trip was Sylvester Smith, and when he returned to Kirtland he repeated many of his grievances against the Prophet Joseph Smith. This resulted in a trial before the Bishop, Newel K. Whitney, and the high priests, and after a full investigation, the Prophet was vindicated and Sylvester Smith after much persuasion made confession of his wrongdoing, and repented of his sin.

The Law of Tithing.—Up to this time the Saints had donated of their means according to their disposition for the support of the Church. In Zion and Kirtland the law of consecration had been given; but it had not been generally practiced. and since the driving of the Saints from their homes, they were compelled to seek a living individually after the manner of the world. In the fall of 1834, Joseph Smith and Oliver Cowdery set an example for the Church by covenanting with the Lord that they would give one-tenth of all he should give them, to be bestowed upon the poor, as Jacob had covenanted centuries before. This was nearly four years before the law of tithing was given to the Church. (Doc. and Cov. Sec. 119.)

Oliver Cowdery Assistant President.—December 5, 1834, Oliver Cowdery was ordained by Joseph Smith by the command of the Lord, an Assistant President of the High Priesthood, to hold the keys of presidency with Joseph Smith in this ministry. This was in harmony with the ordinations he received under the hands of John the Baptist and other holy messengers in 1829.[a]

Temporary Peace.—Notwithstanding the Saints in Missouri were not permitted to return to their possessions, the spirit of opposition began to subside for a season, and the elders commenced going forth two by two, preaching the Gospel throughout the land, and many were added to the Church daily. The year 1834 came to a close with the Saints laboring diligently to build the house of the Lord in Kirtland, and in preparing for the School of the Elders which was to be held during the winter months. In January, 1835, the School of the Elders commenced. Lectures on theology were given and the study of the scriptures and other subjects were considered for the benefit of the members of the Church, in keeping with the revelations of the Lord.

Twelve Apostles Chosen.—On the 8th of February, 1835, Brigham Young and his brother Joseph came to the house of President Joseph Smith and sang for him. While they were visiting with the Prophet on this occasion he told them that he desired to call together all those who were members of Zion's Camp, for he had a blessing for them. At this meeting he conversed with these two brethren on the scenes of their memorable journey and said: "Brethren, I have seen those men who died of the cholera in our camp; and the Lord knows, if I get a mansion as bright as theirs, I ask no more." At this he wept and could not speak for some time. He then said the Lord had called Brigham Young to be one of the twelve special witnesses, and Joseph Young to be a president of the seventies.

A meeting was called for the 14th of February, and on that day all the members of Zion's Camp that could be called together assembled to receive such blessings as the Lord had promised them. Presi-

---

[a]The record which gives an account of this ordination has this to say: "The office of Assistant President is to assist in presiding over the whole Church, and to officiate in the absence of the President, according to his rank and appointment, viz.; President Cowdery, first; President Rigdon, second, and President Williams, third, as they were severally called. The office of this priesthood is also to act as spokesman, taking Aaron for an example. The virtue of the above Priesthood is to hold the keys of the kingdom of heaven or the Church militant" (MS. History of the Church Book A, Chapter 1).

The account of Oliver's ordination is given in the same record as follows: "After addressing the throne of mercy, President Smith laid hands upon High Counselor Cowdery, and ordained him to the Presidency of the High Priesthood in the Church, saying: 'Brother, in the name of Jesus Christ of Nazareth, who was crucified for the sins of the world, that we through the virtue of his blood might come to the Father, I lay my hands upon thy head, and ordain thee a President of the High and Holy Priesthood, to assist in presiding over the Church, and bearing the keys of this kingdom—which Priesthood is after the order of Melchizedek—which is after the order of the Son of God.'"

dent Joseph Smith then stated that the object of the meeting was to choose men for important positions in the ministry to go forth and prune the vineyard for the last time. He had been commanded by the Lord to prepare for the calling of Twelve Apostles, in fulfilment of the revelation given before the organization of the Church. (Doc. and Cov. Sec. 18.) These twelve men were to be chosen from among those who went up in Zion's Camp, and the three special witnesses to the Book of Mormon were to select and ordain them. After the usual opening exercises and appropriate instructions a recess was taken for one hour. When the meeting was later called to order the three witnesses were blessed by the laying on of hands by the presidency; they then united in prayer and proceeded to make choice of the Twelve Apostles. Their names in the order in which they were chosen are as follows:[b]

1. Lyman E. Johnson,
2. Brigham Young,
3. Heber C. Kimball,
4. Orson Hyde,
5. David W. Patten,
6. Luke S. Johnson,
7. William E. McLellin,
8. John F. Boynton,
9. Orson Pratt,
10. William Smith,
11. Thomas B. Marsh,
12. Parley P. Pratt.

The witnesses then proceeded to ordain these brethren, and the first three were ordained at that meeting. The following day all the others except Parley P. Pratt, who was absent, Thomas B. Marsh and Orson Pratt, who were on a mission, were ordained. Parley P. Pratt was ordained February 21; Thomas B. Marsh on April 25 and Orson Pratt the following day.

A charge was given to these brethren by President Oliver Cowdery, and items of valuable instruction were imparted by President Joseph Smith. In this way another important step in the development of the Priesthood and the organization of the Church was accomplished.

The Seventy.—On the 28th of February, 1835, another meeting was called and selection was made from those who went to Missouri in Zion's Camp to create the first quorum of seventy. Hazen Aldrich, Joseph Young, Levi W. Hancock, Leonard Rich, Zebedee Coltrin, Lyman Sherman and Sylvester Smith were called to the office of

---

[b]Later they were arranged in order of precedence according to age as follows:
1. Thomas B. Marsh,
2. David W. Patten,
3. Brigham Young,
4. Heber C. Kimball,
5. Orson Hyde,
6. William E. McLellin,
7. Parley P. Pratt,
8. Luke S. Johnson,
9. William Smith,
10. Orson Pratt,
11. John F. Boynton,
12. Lyman E. Johnson

CHOOSING OF THE TWELVE 153

presidents of this quorum of seventy. These brethren and those appointed to form the quorum[c] were ordained under the hands of the First Presidency. This was another step toward the completion of the ministry and perfect development of the latter day work. Each step came in its turn, and in like manner the doctrines of the kingdom were unfolded, here a little and there a little, until the perfect organization was established on the earth.

Blessings of Those Who Built the Temple.—Another conference was called March 7, for the purpose of blessing those who had assisted, by labor or other means, in the building of the Kirtland Temple, which was nearing completion. This conference continued during the 8th, and all those who were available were blessed with special blessings who had assisted in this necessary work preparatory to the receiving of the promised endowment.

The Great Revelation on Priesthood.—The Twelve Apostles met in council, March 12, 1835, and were appointed by the presidency to a mission through the Eastern States, visiting the branches and regulating the affairs of the Church therein. March 28, as they were about ready to depart, they sought the Prophet for a blessing by revelation from the Lord. "We have unitedly asked God our heavenly Father to grant unto us," they said, "through his seer a revelation of his mind and will concerning our duty the coming season, even a great revelation, that will enlarge our hearts, comfort us in adversity, and brighten our hopes amidst the powers of darkness." They were not disappointed, for the Lord gave unto them a great revelation on Priesthood (Doc. and Cov. Sec. 107) in which the various offices, and powers pertaining thereto, were fully defined. It was explained that there are two Priesthoods in the Church, "namely, the Melchizedek and the Aaronic, including the Levitical Priesthood. Why the first is called the Melchizedek Priesthood, is because Melchizedek was such a great High Priest. Before his day it was called *The Holy Priesthood after the Order of the Son of God;* but out of respect or reverence to the name of the Supreme Being, to avoid the too frequent repetition of his name, they, the Church in ancient days, called that Priesthood after Melchizedek, or the Melchizedek Priesthood. All other authorities or offices in the Church are appendages to this Priesthood."[d] Immediately following the giving of this revelation

---

[c]For the names of those who formed this quorum of seventy see the Documentary History of the Church, Vol. 2:203; and for the names of the members of Zion's Camp see the same volume, pages 183-5.

[d]This important revelation should receive careful study, for few revelations have been given containing greater instruction for the Church.

which sets forth the duties of the twelve, the apostles started on their first missionary journey as they had been appointed.

The Book of Abraham.—On the 3rd of July, 1835, Michael H. Chandler, came to Kirtland exhibiting four mummies and some rolls of papyrus covered with hieroglyphic figures. Mr. Chandler had been directed to the Prophet Joseph Smith as one who could translate the characters for him. At his request Joseph Smith gave a translation of a few of them which Mr. Chandler stated agreed with the decipherings of learned men who had examined them. He gave the Prophet a certificate to this effect. Shortly after this interview some of the Saints in Kirtland purchased the mummies and the manuscripts, and, with Oliver Cowdery and Wm. W. Phelps as scribes, the Prophet commenced to translate these records. To their great joy they discovered that one of these rolls contained writings of Abraham, or instructions given to him in Egypt from the Lord. The other contained writings of Joseph, son of Jacob. During the summer the Prophet prepared for complete translation of the Book of Abraham, as it is called, which now appears in the Pearl of Great Price,[e] one of the accepted standard works of the Church.

The Doctrine and Covenants.—A general assembly of the Church was held in Kirtland, August 17, 1835, to consider the labors of a committee appointed by a general assembly of the Church, September 24, 1834, for the purpose of arranging the items of doctrine and the revelations for publication. This committee was composed of the following: Joseph Smith, Oliver Cowdery, Sidney Rigdon and Frederick G. Williams. The committee having finished their work they called a general assembly on the above date to consider their labors. It should be understood that the printing of the revelations according to the actions of the conference of the Church, on a previous date in 1831, had miscarried, due to the destruction of the printing press in Independence in July, 1833, and the destruction of most of the forms which had been issued up to that time. At this general assembly Oliver Cowdery and Sidney Rigdon, of the presidency, were in charge; the Prophet and Frederick G. Williams were at the time on a visit in Michigan. All the quorums of the Priesthood were arranged in order; Thomas Burdick, Warren Parrish and Sylvester Smith were appointed clerks. The usual procedure at conferences of the Church

---

[e]This Book of Abraham, like the Book of Moses, which also appears in the Pearl of Great Price, is another addition to our collection of lost scripture which the Lord, through his wisdom, has restored. These records contain many important revelations, and should be carefully read. The history of the discovery of these rolls of papyrus, and the guiding hand of the Lord which placed them in the hands of Joseph Smith, is set forth in the Documentary History of the Church, Vol. 2:348-51. See also "Messenger and Advocate." Dec., 1835.

was followed, and the morning session was devoted to ordinations and the transaction of other important business. In the afternoon Oliver Cowdery introduced the "Book of Doctrine and Covenants of the Church" in behalf of the committee. Sidney Rigdon followed with instructions pertaining to the manner of voting, by which they intended to obtain the voice of the assembly for or against the book. Each of the councils and quorums of the Priesthood then by separate vote acknowledged the revelations which had been selected for a place in the book, as from the Lord, and the doctrine and covenants of their faith. A written acknowledgment from the Twelve Apostles, which had evidently been prepared before their departure, for their mission, was read. It is as follows:

TESTIMONY OF THE TWELVE APOSTLES TO THE TRUTH OF THE BOOK OF DOCTRINE AND COVENANTS

"*The testimony of the Witnesses to the Book of the Lord's Commandments, which commandments he gave to his Church through Joseph Smith, Jr., who was appointed by the voice of the Church, for this purpose.*

"We therefore feel willing to bear testimony to all the world of mankind, to every creature upon the face of all the earth, that the Lord has borne record to our souls, through the Holy Ghost shed forth upon us, that these commandments were given by inspiration of God, and are profitable for all men, and are verily true. We give this testimony unto the world, the Lord being our helper; and it is through the grace of God the Father, and His Son Jesus Christ, that we are permitted to have this privilege of bearing this testimony unto the world, in which we rejoice exceedingly, praying the Lord always that the children of men may be profited thereby.

THOMAS B. MARSH,	PARLEY P. PRATT,
DAVID W. PATTEN,	LUKE S. JOHNSON,
BRIGHAM YOUNG,	WILLIAM SMITH,
HEBER C. KIMBALL,	ORSON PRATT,
ORSON HYDE,	JOHN F. BOYNTON,
WILLIAM E. MCLELLIN,	LYMAN E. JOHNSON."

To the revelations were added by vote of this assembly, the Lectures on Faith, which had been given in the School of the Elders (Prophets) earlier in the year, and an article on Government and Laws in General; also one on Marriage. These lectures and the two articles mentioned were not received, however, as doctrine and binding

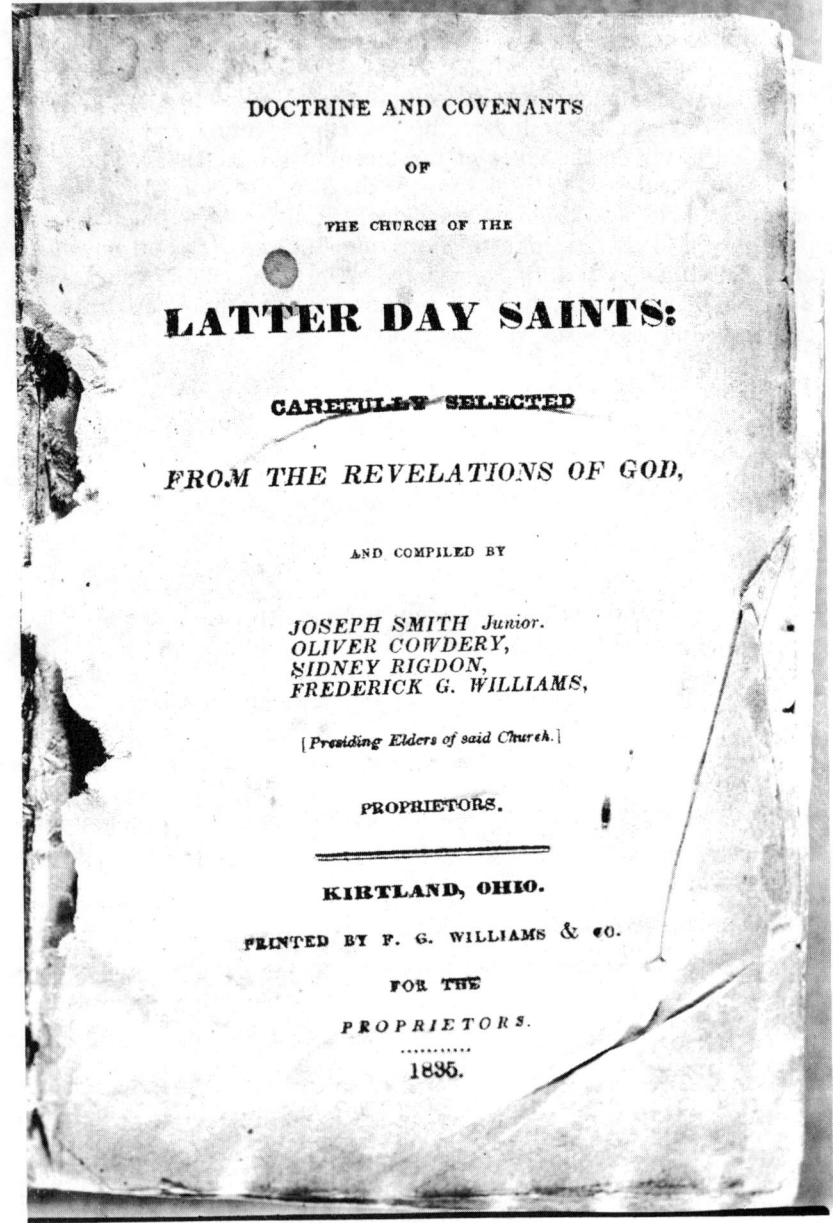

Title Page of the First Edition of the Doctrine and Covenants

on the Church, as were the revelations. The minutes of this gathering were signed by Oliver Cowdery and Sidney Rigdon as Presidents, and by the three clerks. They were published in the book when printed, with a preface signed by the presidency, with date of February 17, 1835.

Close of the Year 1835.—The close of the year 1835 found the Prophet busy working on the Book of Abraham, which, among other great truths, revealed principles pertaining to astronomy as taught to Abraham. Many council meetings were held, and the twelve were instructed that they were to take their families and move to Missouri the following summer with the presidency, after the endowment in the temple was received. The School of the Elders was continued, and the study of grammar and Hebrew, under a competent instructor, became an important part of their work. The elders were preparing for the solemn assembly which was soon to convene in the Kirtland Temple, now nearly completed. Peace and tranquility prevailed, which permitted the Prophet and the Saints to accomplish many things essential to the welfare of the Church. The one thing that marred the peace which was granted for a season was the rebellious spirit manifested by William Smith against the Prophet, which nearly cost William his standing in the Church. Charges were made against him before the high council, but on his show of repentance he was forgiven. Christian Whitmer, one of the eight witnesses to the Book of Mormon, died in Clay County, Missouri, November 27, 1835, firm in the faith. He was one of the members of the high council in Missouri.

Anointing and Blessings in the Temple.—Much time was spent in January and February, 1836, in council meetings and the filling of vacancies in the various organizations of the Priesthood. Professor Seixas, a thorough Hebrew scholar, was employed to teach the Hebrew language, in the stead of Dr. Piexotto, who had failed to live up to his contract. Thursday, January 21, the first of a number of meetings in the temple was held. These gatherings continued through several days, in which the faithful elders of the Church received blessings by the laying on of hands and anointing with oil.

At this first meeting the presidency met, and Father Joseph Smith, the patriarch, was anointed and blessed. He then anointed and blessed each of the brethren of the presidency, beginning with the oldest, pronouncing such blessings upon them as the Spirit of the Lord revealed, and many prophecies were uttered by each of them.

A Vision.—While thus engaged the heavens were opened and the Prophet received the following vision:

"I beheld the celestial kingdom of God, and the glory thereof, whether in the body or out I cannot tell. I saw the transcendent beauty of the gate through which the heirs of that kingdom will enter, which was like unto circling flames of fire; also the blazing throne of God, whereon was seated the Father and the Son. I saw the beautiful streets of that kingdom, which had the appearance of being paved with gold. I saw Fathers Adam and Abraham, and my father and mother, my brother, Alvin, that has long since slept, and marveled how it was that he had obtained an inheritance in the kingdom, seeing that he had departed this life before the Lord had set his hand to gather Israel the second time and had not been baptized for the remission of sins.

"Thus came the voice of the Lord to me, saying—

"'All who have died without a knowledge of this Gospel, who would have received it if they had been permitted to tarry, shall be heirs of the celestial kingdom of God; also all that shall die henceforth without a knowledge of it, who would have received it with all their hearts, shall be heirs of that kingdom, for I, the Lord, will judge all men according to their works; according to the desire of their hearts.'

"And I also beheld that all children who die before they arrive at the years of accountability are saved in the celestial kingdom of heaven."

Many other wonderful manifestations they beheld, and angels ministered to them; the power of the Lord rested upon them and the house was filled with the glory of God. The Prophet's scribe, Warren Parrish, saw the armies of heaven, and visions of the redemption of Zion.

At this and succeeding meetings the various councils and presiding officers in the several quorums, each in turn, received blessings by the anointing of oil and laying on of hands, such as the patriarch and presidency had received, and the visions of heaven were opened to their view with wonderful manifestations of the glory and power of God, and they shouted, "Hosanna to God and the Lamb."

The Solemn Assembly.—In the city of Kirtland on Sunday, March 27, 1836, the members of the Church realized their hopes, long anticipated, when they gathered in the temple in solemn assembly. As early as 1832, the Lord had given commandment for the building of a house to his name, for such a place was not to be found on the earth; nor had there been for many centuries. The ground was broken for this building, June 5, 1833; the corner stones were laid on the 23rd of the following month—the same day the Saints in

CHOOSING OF THE TWELVE

Jackson County were forced by mob violence from their homes. Now the house was finished; a monument to the faith and industry of the little band of Latter-day Saints who had constructed it in their poverty, amidst the threatened violence of enemies. It is a building of no mean proportions; built of stone; eighty feet in length, sixty in width, fifty feet to the square, with a tower one hundred ten feet from the ground. The 27th of March, 1836, was a solemn and momentous occasion. Long before the appointed hour the building was thronged with eager and interested people, many were turned away for lack of room. At nine o'clock the session was called to order by President Sidney Rigdon, who in the midst of breathless silence, read the 96th and the 24th psalms. The choir then sang: "Ere long the veil will rend in twain,"—which declaration was to be fulfilled earlier than the congregation realized. After prayer and another song appropriate remarks were made, and then the various officers of the Church were sustained by separate vote, which procedure was interspersed with singing.

The Prayer of Dedication.—The prayer of dedication which had been given by revelation (Doc. & Cov. Sec. 109) was offered and the house was presented to the Lord.[f] Following the prayer, the congregation sang the hymn "Hosanna"[g] which had been written for this occasion, and then shouted "Hosanna, hosanna, hosanna, to God and the Lamb," sealing it with "Amen, Amen, and Amen." Angels were present and the Holy Spirit, like the sound of a mighty rushing wind, filled the house and rested upon the assembly. The people of the neighborhood came running together hearing a strange sound and seeing a bright light resting on the temple. The house had been accepted by the Lord.

Endowments Given.—As soon as the Temple was dedicated, ordinance work for the elders was commenced. The ordinance of washing of feet—which the Prophet said was never intended but for the official members of the Church[h]—was attended to in behalf of the leading quorums, and other ordinances were performed. The Savior appeared to several of the brethren and angels ministered to others in these meetings. It was indeed a time of Pentecost to the Saints.

The Coming of Moses, Elias and Elijah.—After the administering of the Sacrament, in the temple at the meeting held Sunday, April 3, 1836, Joseph Smith and Oliver Cowdery retired to the pulpit, the

---

[f]These ceremonies were repeated for the benefit of those who could not gain admittance at the first session.
[g]"The Spirit of God like a fire is burning."
[h]Documentary History of the Church. Vol. 2:309.

The Kirtland Temple

veils[i] being dropped, and there bowed in silent prayer. After rising from their knees the Savior appeared to them standing on the breastwork of the pulpit and blessed them, accepting the building in his name. After this vision closed, the heavens were again opened, and

---

[i]There were four veils in the temple arranged crosswise, so that they could be lowered and divide the assembly room into four parts.

Moses appeared committing to them the keys of the gathering of Israel; Elias, who lived in the days of Abraham, then appeared, and committed to them the keys of the dispensation of the Gospel of Abraham. Then another glorious vision burst upon them and Elijah appeared and committed to them the keys, in fulfilment of the prediction of Malachi, of the turning of the hearts of the fathers to the children, and the hearts of the children to the fathers, which was to be done before the coming of the great and dreadful day of the Lord.[j]

The Elders Prepared to Teach.—In the revelation given on Fishing River (Doc. and Cov. Sec. 105) the Lord had said the elders must be endowed with power from on high before they would be fully prepared to go forth to build up the Church and "prune" his vineyard. This endowment having now been received, and the various keys of different dispensations having now been restored, the elders were prepared for their ministry among the nations of the earth. Following these blessings they began to go forth, spreading abroad in all parts of the land, preaching the word in power as they had never experienced it before, and many received their testimony and were numbered among the people of the Lord.

---

[j]See Doc. and Cov. Sec. 110, for an account of these visions.

CHAPTER 22

CLAY COUNTY REJECTS THE SAINTS—APOSTASY AND SORROW

1836-1837

Dishonorable Action of Governor Dunklin.—Governor Daniel Dunklin, of Missouri, who showed some sense of honor and willingness to enforce the law at the beginning of the trouble in Jackson County, later manifested a spirit of fellowship with the stronger side, against right and justice—a trait common with many politicians. In a communication to William W. Phelps and others, bearing date of July 18, 1836, he cravenly insinuated that the mobbings and expulsion of the Latter-day Saints from Jackson County, was due to faults of their own; the people would not have united against them, without some reason, and while they had some friends at first even these had forsaken them. Whether his conclusion was right or wrong, he maintained it to be the duty of the Saints to convince their enemies of their innocence and worthiness. "If you cannot do this," he wrote, "all I can say to you is that in this Republic the vox populi is the vox Dei." Such was the contemptible answer of the governor of a sovereign state, to an innocent people, driven from their homes and smitten by their enemies, because of their faith in the Gospel of our Redeemer.

Clay County Rejects the Saints.—When the exiled Saints were driven from Jackson County, they found a place of refuge in Clay County, just over the Missouri River to the north. Here the people were hospitable and kindly disposed. The Saints had no intention of remaining in Clay County, for they fully expected to be restored to their former homes. After exhausting every source of redress, even to an appeal to the President of the United States, they prepared to make permanent settlement by purchasing lands. As time passed and the indication pointed to the gathering of the Latter-day Saints in that county, the citizens became alarmed. The people from Jackson were constantly menacing the Saints, even though they were peacefully minding their business in their new homes, but wrong begets wrong, and the deep-seated hatred of these mobbers had no end. Finally the citizens of Clay County decided to do the wrong thing, to their everlasting injury, and rid themselves, once and for all, from the danger which they felt confronted them by harboring the "Mormons" in their midst. That there was danger of conflict there can be no question, with the menacing influence on the south, and growing hatred, because of association of the mobbers with many of the residents of the county to the north. However, these Clay County citizens preferred to expel the Saints in a gentle way if it could be done. A mass meeting was held June 29, 1836, for the purpose of presenting, with united front, a petition to the undesirable exiles, kindly requesting them to move to some part of the country where they could be entirely by themselves. The new country of Wisconsin was suggested as a suitable place. A report of conditions as they understood them and resolutions embodying their request, were unanimously approved. They did not fail to call attention to their great hospitality and kindness in 1833, when they received the exiles among them; and endeavored to impress upon the Saints the thought that they were devoid of "one spark of gratitude" if they refused to accept the suggestions offered to depart in peace to a more congenial locality. Yet they frankly admitted, "we do not contend that we have the least right to expel them by force," but if they would not go they were sure it would lead to civil war, "bearing ruin, woe, and desolation, in its course."

Some of the reasons why the "Mormons" had become "objects of the deepest hatred and detestation" to many of the citizens were declared in the petition to be as follows:

"They are eastern men, whose manners, habits, customs, and even dialect, are essentially different from our own. They are non-slave-holders, and opposed to slavery, which in this peculiar period, when Abolitionism has reared its deformed and haggard visage in our land, is well calculated to excite deep and abiding prejudices in any community where slavery is tolerated and protected.

"In addition to all this, they are charged, as they have hitherto been, with keeping up a constant communication with our Indian tribes on our frontiers, with declaring, even from the pulpit, that the

Indians are a part of God's chosen people and are destined by heaven to inherit this land, in common with themselves. We do not vouch for the correctness of these statements; but whether they are true or false, their effect has been the same in exciting our community. In times of greater tranquility, such ridiculous remarks might well be regarded as the offspring of frenzied fanaticism; but at this time, our defenseless situation on the frontier, the bloody disasters of our fellow citizens in Florida, and other parts of the South, all tend to make a portion of our citizens regard such sentiments with horror if not alarm. These and many other causes have combined to raise a prejudice against them; and a feeling of hostility, that the first spark may, and we deeply fear will, ignite into all the horrors and desolations of a civil war, the worst evil that can befall any country."

For these real and fancied "wrongs" this people must move again, for their presence was obnoxious. These foolish citizens, acting as they thought in their own best interests, rejected the everlasting Gospel against themselves, as well as the people who proclaimed it.

The Saints' Reply.—Three days later (July 1, 1836), the Saints met in council and formulated their reply. They accepted the requisitions of the citizens of Clay County, notwithstanding the added loss of property that would be entailed. They also thanked these citizens for their hospitality during the period of the sojourn among them, which covered a period of more than two and one half years. Let it be said that many of these citizens sympathized with the "Mormons" and proffered material help to aid them in the removal from the county; but in this drastic action they were acting, as they sincerely thought, in the best interests of their communities.

When the First Presidency heard of this ultimatum they fully endorsed the action taken by the Missouri Saints, and in a communication to the Clay County committee notified them of the fact. They also took occasion to inform the committee of many other things, in humility, which should have appealed to their sense of justice and touched their hearts.[a]

Caldwell County Organized.—In pursuance of this action the Saints began to move from Clay County as soon as circumstances would permit, and located on Shoal Creek, in an uninhabited section in the north part of Ray County. The property of the few settlers in that part, they purchased, and commenced to build their homes. By December, 1836, a goodly number had taken up their residence

---

[a]The minutes of these meetings and the communications involved in the question of the removal of the Saints are found in full in the Documentary History of the Church, Vol. 2:448-462.

there and a petition was sent to the governor asking for a county organization. This petition was granted about the middle of that month. This organization, and the prospect of a peaceful habitation, gave impetus to the growth of the "Mormon" colonies, and the County of Caldwell, as it was called "grew like Jonah's gourd."[b]

The Kirtland Safety Society.—Affairs in Kirtland had been progressing smoothly for some time, and many blessings were bestowed upon the people. Such a condition, however, was not to last. On the 2nd of November, 1836, articles of agreement were prepared for the organization of the "Kirtland Safety Society Bank," the State of Ohio, through prejudice, refused to grant a charter, so the matter rested until January, 1837, when a society was organized within the provisions of the law. Stock was subscribed for and the business commenced. During this year (1837) speculation was at high ebb throughout the entire nation. The Latter-day Saints in Kirtland partook of that spirit; several business ventures had failed to come up to expectations, and many of the members of the Church were financially involved. The authorities of the Church, with others of the leading brethren who had subscribed for stock in the Kirtland Safety Society, pledged themselves to be responsible for the redemption of all the notes of the institution, in proportion to the amount of stock subscribed. Since they had no charter, other banking institutions refused their notes. The cashier of this society, at one time the Prophet's clerk and a faithful elder in the Church, was found guilty of immoral conduct. He was forgiven on a show of repentance and confession, and retained his standing in the Church; but he never regained the spirit and shortly after became disaffected. He misappropriated the funds of the society to the extent of over twenty-five thousand dollars, which placed the institution in a precarious condition. Seeing how matters were being conducted the Prophet gave a warning which was not heeded; therefore, early in the summer of 1837, he withdrew from the concern, resigned his office and disposed of all his interests therein, stating that he was satisfied after five months' experience, "that no institution of the kind, established upon just and righteous principles for a blessing not only to the Church, but to the whole nation, would be suffered to continue its operations in such an age of darkness, speculation and wickedness."

The Financial Panic of 1837.—At this time the panic of 1837 swept over the United States. During the months of March and April, the failures in the City of New York amounted to over

---

[b]The Missourians were willing—feeling that the section chosen by the "Mormons" was of little value.

$100,000,000 and hundreds of institutions were driven to the wall. It was only natural that the Kirtland Safety Society, so improperly managed, should share in the general condition of failure.

Other Causes of Embarrassment.—Other causes for the financial stress among the Saints, which also weighed heavily upon the heads of the Church, were the afflictions undergone at the hands of enemies, and the expenses attached to the erection of the Kirtland Temple. Moreover, the poor, destitute and needy, who had received the Gospel came to Kirtland seeking assistance and necessary homes. Large contracts for land were entered into for the benefit of these poor, that they might obtain homes to call their own; but those concerned were not always prompt in the payment of their dues—a common failure of mankind.

Apostasy and Sorrow.—As the fruit of this condition, an apostasy followed rapidly, and it seemed, said the Prophet, "as though all the powers of earth and hell were combining their influence in an especial manner to overthrow the Church at once, and make a final end." Enemies abroad, aided by apostates within, united in various schemes to overthrow the Prophet as if he had been the sole cause of the evils, not only in the communities of the Church, but throughout the entire land. Most of this evil which befell the Church might have been avoided if the Prophet's counsel had been accepted by the Saints. Apostasy developed within all the councils of the Church, and many of the leading brethren, who previously had been true and faithful, were involved.

The Pure in Heart Able to Withstand.—It is strange to think of this dire condition, when just one brief year before, the glorious manifestations in the temple had been given to many of these men, who now possessed such bitterness of spirit. They seemed to have forgotten their many blessings, and the wonderful visions, and the great promises made them by the Lord, if they would be true and faithful in their ministry. The spirit of speculation and desire for wealth, during the brief spell of peace and harmony, had beclouded the minds of many, and their souls were filled with deadly hatred against their former brethren. Joseph Smith was called a fallen prophet by those whom he had cherished and loved, and whose love for him had been pronounced. Some, in their bitterness and darkness of mind, sought his life. Those who sought his welfare and spoke in his defense, were ridiculed and treated with great contempt. It was a time when the souls of men were tested, and only those who kept themselves pure and unspotted from the sins of the world, were able to withstand the trial. Every influence was brought to bear upon the members of the Church to get them to renounce the Prophet. Many good men were dragged into the net; others barely escaped, and only through their deep humility and great repentance, were they spared the awful fate which carried so many to destruction. It was during this time of disaffection that Brigham Young, Heber C. Kimball, Wilford Woodruff, and others, including John Taylor and Willard Richards, who had but recently joined the Church, stood nobly in defense of the Prophet Joseph, in the face of a murderous spirit of opposition.

The Prophet's Visit to Missouri.—In September, 1837, Presidents Joseph Smith and Sidney Rigdon went to Missouri to assist the Saints in that land in establishing places of gathering. Other brethren from Kirtland accompanied them. They arrived about the first of November in Caldwell County and immediately went into council with the elders there, regarding locations for the Saints. Those who met in council were Joseph Smith, Sidney Rigdon, Hyrum Smith, Thomas B. Marsh, William E. McLellin, Lyman E. Johnson and William Smith from Ohio, and the high council of the Church in Far West, with William W. Phelps at their head. It was decided that there was room in that land to make it desirable to invite the Saints from other parts to locate there. The city Far West, which had been laid out and incorporated, was chosen as a central gathering place. It was decided to postpone the building of the Lord's house in Far West, which had been decided on, until the Lord should reveal his will to have it commenced.

Death of Jerusha Smith.—A sad event occurred, while Hyrum Smith was engaged in Far West assisting the Saints to locate, in the death of his wife Jerusha Barden Smith, October 3, 1837. "Tell your father when he comes that the Lord has taken your mother home and left you for him to take care of," was her dying statement to her five little children.

Attempt to Depose the Prophet.—Presidents Smith and Rigdon returned to Kirtland from Missouri, on the 10th of December. They discovered that during their absence, Warren Parrish, John F. Boynton, Luke S. Johnson, Joseph Coe, Sylvester Smith, and others of the leading councils had united to overthrow the Church. Some of these men had earlier in the year shown a spirit of opposition, but on a show of repentance had been reinstated; but the evils were not fully eradicated from their minds. Warren Parrish was a seventy, who a few short months before shared the Prophet's fullest confidence, as one of his closest and dearest friends. Now, through transgression, he became one of the Prophet's bitterest enemies and the leader of a movement to depose him and install David Whitmer in his stead. Meetings had been held by this clique in the temple, which they claimed as their own, and they resorted to violence to maintain their contention. In this manner the Kirtland Temple, so recently accepted by the Lord, was desecrated and defiled so that it ceased to be a sacred edifice to his holy name.

The British Mission.—During these sad days of trial and tribulation, the word of the Lord came to Joseph Smith stating that something must be done for the salvation of the Church. The solution was the carrying of the Gospel to Great Britain. On Sunday, the 4th day of June, the Prophet approached Elder Heber C. Kimball in the Kirtland Temple and whispered to him, saying: "Brother Heber, the Spirit of the Lord has whispered to me: 'Let my servant Heber go to England and proclaim my Gospel, and open the door of salvation to that nation.'" Brother Kimball, feeling his weakness, asked if Elder Brigham Young could not go with him. The Prophet answered that the Lord had something else for Brigham Young to do. Following this conversation Elder Kimball was set apart for this great work in the British Isles, which was to be the first foreign mission of the Church. While the First Presidency were setting Elder Kimball apart, Orson Hyde, of the council of the twelve came in, and listening to the blessing being given to his fellow laborer asked that he also might have the privilege of assisting in that work. Elder Hyde had been among those disturbed because of speculation. His heart melted within him and he now acknowledged his faults, and sought a blessing. His offering was accepted and he was set apart for the British labor.

The Work in Canada.—The movement to send elders to Great Britain was the outgrowth of the work in Canada. Several of the elders had taken trips to Canada and had preached the Gospel there. Elder Orson Pratt was the first to carry the message into Canada in the year 1833. In the fall of that same year the Prophet and Sidney Rigdon went on a brief mission to Upper Canada and made a number of converts. In 1836, Elder Parley P. Pratt went to the City of Toronto and surrounding country and preached with wonderful success. It was here at this time that Elder John Taylor, afterwards of the council of the twelve and later President of the Church, received the Gospel. It was also here, and due to the preaching of Elder Pratt, that Joseph Fielding and his two sisters, Mary—who a few months later became the wife of Hyrum Smith—and Mercy R., were baptized. Others who received the Gospel in Canada were John Goodson, John Snyder and Isaac Russell. All of these people were in correspondence with relatives and friends in Great Britain, whom they informed of the rise and progress of the Church, thus preparing them for events to come.

Departure for Great Britain.—Elder Willard Richards, having requested the privilege of going to Great Britain, was set apart by Sidney Rigdon and Hyrum Smith, on the 12th of June, 1837. The following day Elders Heber C. Kimball, Orson Hyde, Willard Richards, and Joseph Fielding, a priest, who came from Honeydon, England, left Kirtland on their mission to the British Isles. They were accompanied on their journey as far as Fairport by Elder Brigham Young and others. This little band of missionaries was later augmented by the addition of Isaac Russell, John Goodson and John Snyder, and on the 23rd of June, 1837, they engaged passage on the merchant ship "Garrick," for Liverpool. On the morning of the 20th of July, the "Garrick" anchored in the River Mersey. As soon as these brethren landed they went to Preston, about thirty miles from Liverpool. It was election day for members of Parliament, and Queen Victoria, who had recently come to the throne, was about to organize her cabinet. As the missionaries alighted from their coach, they saw in letters of gold on a banner above their heads an inscription, "Truth will prevail," which they accepted as a favorable omen.

Elder Joseph Fielding had a brother Rev. James Fielding, who resided in Preston, and the brethren went to hear him preach on Sunday, July 23, 1837. At the service Rev. Fielding unexpectedly announced that there were present some ministers from America and they would occupy his pulpit in the afternoon. The invitation was joyfully accepted and President Kimball gave a brief address followed by Elder Hyde. That evening Mr. Fielding again offered his pulpit to the brethren and Elder Goodson and Brother Fielding preached. This was the opening of the door for the Gospel in England.[c]

The following Wednesday (July 26, 1837) another meeting was held in Rev. James Fielding's chapel. Elders Hyde and Richards preached and much interest was manifested by the congregation, many were convinced and sought baptism. Fearing that he would lose his entire flock the Rev. Fielding closed the doors of his chapel against the elders and from that time opposed the work with all his power. However, the work was started, a foothold had been gained, and the brethren received many invitations to preach in private

---

[c]The inspiration of the Prophet Joseph to send elders to Great Britain for the salvation of the Church, was fully attested, for members were baptized by the thousands in the course of a few months following. Many of them emigrated and became stalwarts in the Church, and branches of great magnitude were raised up in various parts of England.

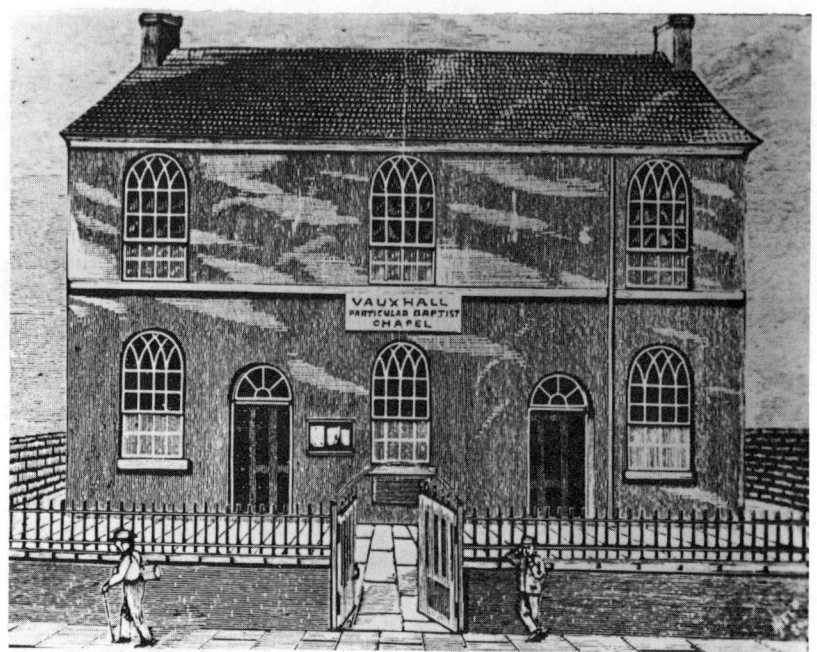
Vauxhall Chapel, Rev. James Fielding's Church, Preston, England

homes. The work spread rapidly throughout the nation, many branches were organized and many souls sought salvation through the remission of their sins.

Revelation to the Twelve.—The same day that the Gospel was first preached in England (July 23, 1837) the Lord gave a revelation through Joseph Smith to Thomas B. Marsh and the twelve. They were commanded to gird up their loins, take up their cross and follow the Savior and feed his sheep. "Exalt not yourselves," said the Lord, "rebel not against my servant Joseph, for verily I say unto you, I am with him, and my hand shall be over him; and the keys which I have given unto him, and also to youward, shall not be taken from him till I come."

This was a timely warning, for even then some of the members of that council were in secret collusion with enemies of the Church. Their actions later developed, and before the close of the year they were in open rebellion as previously indicated.

Frederick G. Williams Removed.—A conference of the elders held in Far West, November 7, 1837, refused to sustain Frederick G. Williams as a counselor to President Joseph Smith, and Hyrum Smith was appointed in his place. President Williams, Lyman E. Johnson, Parley P. Pratt and Warren Parrish had previously been cited to appear before a council of the Church, charges having been preferred against them, but the council being improperly organized, no action was taken at that time. President Williams became disaffected with many others, due to speculations and financial troubles in the fore part of the year 1837, and permitted himself to become estranged from the work.

Flight of Brigham Young.—The feeling of opposition against the Prophet became so intense near the close of the year 1837, that it was with danger that anyone in Kirtland could speak in his defense. On the morning of December 22, 1837, Elder Brigham Young left Kirtland because of the fury of the enemies of the Church. Apostates had threatened to destroy him because he continued to proclaim publicly that Joseph Smith was a prophet of the Most High and had not transgressed and fallen, as the apostates declared.

This was the condition of affairs in Kirtland at the close of the year 1837.

CHAPTER 23

THE PRESIDENCY MOVE TO MISSOURI—EXCOMMUNICATION OF OLIVER COWDERY AND OTHERS

1838

Lowering Clouds.—Threatening and sinister were the clouds which hung over the Church at the beginning of the year 1838. Apostasy had broken into the ranks, and many of the former faithful defenders of the truth had fallen by the wayside. Satan rejoiced, and the enemies of the Saints gained great power, which was later to be made manifest with extreme bitterness.

Flight of Joseph Smith and Sidney Rigdon.—So bitter became the spirit of opposition in Kirtland that Joseph Smith and Sidney Rigdon were forced to seek safety in flight. They departed from that place January 12, 1838, on horseback, and journeyed towards Far West. Unjust and vexatious law suits had been planted against them by their enemies. Several times Joseph had been cited to appear before the courts on trivial charges, from which he was cleared, which action did not tend to lessen the ugly feelings of his enemies. Some sixty miles west of Kirtland they tarried at Norton, where they were joined by their families. On the 16th, the journey was resumed, Elder Brigham Young accompanying them. At Dublin, in Indiana, the Prophet sought employment, cutting and sawing wood, to relieve his necessities. Here, through the aid of Elder Young, a Brother Tomlinson sold some property, and gave the Prophet three hundred dollars to help him on his way.

The weather was extremely cold and the fleeing brethren were forced because of enemies, to secrete themselves in their wagons without sufficient means to keep warm. Their adversaries followed them for more than two hundred miles from Kirtland, with guns and knives, seeking their lives. "They," wrote the Prophet, "frequently crossed our track; twice they were in the houses where we stopped, and once we tarried all night in the same house with them, with only a partition between us and them; and we heard their oaths and imprecations, and threats concerning us, if they could catch us; and late in the evening they came into our room and examined us, but decided we were not the men. At other times we passed them in the streets, and gazed on them, and they on us, but they knew us not." About two hundred and twenty miles from Far West a number of brethren met the Prophet, and assisted him with teams to that place, where he arrived, March 14, 1838. He was welcomed by the Saints with open arms. President Rigdon did not arrive in Far West until the 4th of April, having been detained by sickness in his family.

Rejection of the Missouri Presidency.—The spirit of darkness spread from Kirtland to Missouri, and some of the leading brethren became affected. Martin Harris was dropped from the high council in Kirtland, with three others, September 3, 1837, and Oliver Cowdery, who had been in transgression, was retained in his calling on condition that he would repent; and should he fail to repent, the Prophet said, "the Church will soon be under the necessity of raising their hands against him; therefore pray for him." These men, and others in Kirtland, influenced some of the brethren in Missouri, and the spirit of disaffection in Caldwell County commenced to grow. A general assembly of the Saints was held in Far West, February 4, 1838, and the members withdrew the hand of fellowship from their presiding officers, David Whitmer, William W. Phelps and John Whitmer. Similar action was taken on the succeeding days in Carter's settlement, Durphy's home, and Haun's Mill.

The charges against two of them, William W. Phelps and John Whitmer, were that they had sold their possessions in Jackson County, contrary to the revelations of the Lord, which was paramount to a denial of the faith; and for the misappropriation of funds borrowed for the use of the Church. The Lord, in a revelation, had rebuked these men for their transgression and warned them, but they did not heed the warning. David Whitmer was likewise charged with improper conduct and neglect of duty, and with the violation of the word of wisdom, in the persistent use of tea, coffee and tobacco, and the Church had gone on record by vote that they would not sustain any officer who indulged in such things. Thomas B. Marsh and David W.

Patten were sustained as presiding officers in Missouri, until the coming of Presidents Joseph Smith and Sidney Rigdon. The three accused men persisted in showing contempt for the decision of these conferences of the Church, in which action they were joined by Oliver and Marcellus F. Cowdery; therefore they were cited to appear before the high council, March 10, 1838, and William W. Phelps and John Whitmer were excommunicated. Marcellus F. Cowdery was disfellowshiped and the case of David Whitmer and Oliver Cowdery was held over for future investigation.

Political Motto of the Church.—Shortly after the arrival of Presidents Smith and Rigdon in Far West the following political motto was adopted:

"The Constitution of our country formed by the fathers of liberty. Peace and good order in society. Love to God, and good will to man. All good and wholesome laws, virtue and truth above all things, and aristarchy, live forever! But woe to tyrants, mobs, aristocracy, anarchy, and toryism, and all those who invent or seek out unrighteous and vexatious law suits, under the pretext and color of law, or office, either religious or political. Exalt the standard of democracy; down with that of priestcraft, and let all the people say, Amen! that the blood of our fathers may not cry from the ground against us. Sacred is the memory of the blood which bought for us our liberty."

First General Conference at Far West.—April 6, 1838, the first general conference of the Church in Missouri was held at Far West. John Corrill and Elias Higbee were chosen historians and George W. Robinson general church recorder and clerk of the First Presidency. Thomas B. Marsh, David W. Patten and Brigham Young were sustained as the presidency of the Church in Zion. The following day, David W. Patten, in reporting the labors of the council of the twelve, said he could not recommend William E. McLellin, Luke S. Johnson, Lyman E. Johnson, John F. Boynton, and was doubtful of William Smith. The other brethren were faithfully discharging their duties.

John Whitmer Withholds the Church Record.—A demand by letter was made, by sanction of the conference, of John Whitmer, the former historian, calling for the record of the Church in his keeping. This he refused to deliver and retained it until the day of his death. A copy of it is now in the archives of the Church.

Oliver Cowdery, David Whitmer and Others Excommunicated. —Wednesday, April 11, 1838, Seymour Brunson preferred nine charges against Oliver Cowdery who was cited to appear for trial the following day. Oliver refused to appear, but sent a letter, written in a very bitter spirit, and defiant attitude, in which he boasted of his "personal liberty," and with injured demeanor denied the right of any church tribunal to control him in his temporal interests, which was contrary to his constitutional privileges. Therefore he would voluntarily "withdraw from a society assuming they have such right." Two of the charges when presented to the council were rejected and one was withdrawn, the other six were sustained. There was no other course for the council to take than to excommunicate the rebellious Assistant President of the Church, who had turned so bitter in his feelings against his former associates.

On the 9th, five charges were also preferred against David Whitmer, who was cited to appear for trial on the 13th. David also replied by letter, in which he refused to recognize the authority of the general assemblies of the Church and the action taken against him; nor would he recognize the authority of the present council which had been called to try his case. And, since the council would pursue its "unlawful course at all hazards," he preferred to withdraw from their "fellowship and communion—choosing to seek a place among the meek and humble, where the revelations of heaven will be observed, and the rights of men regarded." Action was therefore taken against David Whitmer and thus another of the special witnesses, was cut off from the Church.[a]

Lyman E. Johnson and William E. McLellin.—The same day charges were preferred against Lyman E. Johnson; these were sustained, and he was cut off from the Church. One month later, May 11, 1838, William E. McLellin was handled for his fellowship, and he also lost his standing in the Church. About this time Jacob Whitmer and Hiram Page also left the Church having partaken of the spirit of apostasy.

A Day of Sadness.—This was a day of sadness for Joseph Smith. To see the witnesses who were associated with him in the incipiency of the Church fall by the wayside, touched his heart. Yet right must prevail, and righteousness triumph, even though it should cause wounds which could not be healed. To their credit, be it said, that none of the witnesses who had beheld angels and the plates from which the Book of Mormon was translated, ever denied his testimony concerning these things, notwithstanding the extreme bitterness of heart manifested against Joseph Smith the Prophet.[b]

---

[a]For full account of these trials see Documentary History of the Church, Vol. 3:16-20.

[b]During these days of darkness all three of the special witnesses of the Book of Mormon left the Church. So did also three of the eight witnesses, viz. Jacob Whitmer, John Whitmer and Hiram Page. Christian Whitmer died in full fellowship and with a strong conviction of the truth, in Missouri, Nov. 27, 1835, and his brother Peter Whitmer Jr., died September 22, 1836, also firm in the faith

Return of Elders Kimball and Hyde.—April 1, 1838, a conference of the Church was held in Preston, England, in Temperance Hall (the "Cock Pit"), for the purpose of setting in order the branches in that mission. Joseph Fielding was sustained as President of the British Mission, to succeed Heber C. Kimball, and Willard Richards and William Clayton, an English convert, were chosen as his counselors. These men were ordained high priests. On the 20th of April, 1838, Elders Kimball and Hyde sailed from Liverpool for the United States, in the same ship which had carried them to England, the "Garrick." They arrived in Kirtland, May 21, 1838, and immediately notified the Prophet, at Far West, of their good feeling and firmness in the faith.

Far West—The House of the Lord.—In a revelation given April 26, 1838, the Lord accepted Far West as a central gathering place for the Saints in Missouri, and a place of refuge, which should be holy and consecrated to him. There a house was to be built to his name, and the beginning should be made on the 4th of July following, then the Saints were to continue their labors diligently until the house was finished. However, the presidency, Joseph Smith, Sidney Rigdon and Hyrum Smith, the latter having taken the place of Frederick G. Williams, were not to get into debt. Other settlements in the region round about, besides Far West, were to be selected as gathering places for the Saints, and stakes of Zion were to be established.

Stakes of Zion.—In accordance with the revelation, about the middle of May, 1838, Presidents Joseph Smith and Sidney Rigdon with a number of other elders, including David W. Patten and Bishop Edward Partridge, took a trip in the wilderness north of Far West for the purpose of locating sites for settlements and the laying off of stakes of Zion. They pursued their course up Grand River, some twenty-five miles to a place they called Tower Hill, because they found ruins of an old Nephite tower there. Here Elder Lyman Wight had his home, and here they camped May 20, which was the Sabbath day. In the afternoon Presidents Smith and Rigdon, with their clerk, George W. Robinson, went up the river about one half mile, to Wight's ferry, for the purpose of selecting and laying claim to a city plat. This was in Daviess County, township 60, ranges 27 and 28, which the brethren called "Spring Hill," but by the mouth of the Lord, the record states, "it was named Adam-ondi-Ahman, because, said he, it is the place where Adam shall come to visit his

---

and fellowship of the Saints. Later Oliver Cowdery and Martin Harris returned to the Church and died in full fellowship, also Luke S. Johnson and many others who became disaffected during these days of tribulation.

people, or the Ancient of Days shall sit, as spoken of by Daniel the Prophet."[c] We are also informed that this is the place where Adam assembled his posterity three years before his death, and there be-

Lyman Wight's House, Near Adam-ondi-Ahman

stowed upon them his blessing. On that occasion the Lord appeared to them, and the posterity of Adam rose up and blessed him, and called him Michael, the Prince, the Arch-angel; and the Lord administered comfort to Adam, and said unto him: "I have set thee to be at the head—a multitude of nations shall come of thee, and thou art a prince over them forever."[d] The name of this place was first revealed as early as March, 1832, but it is evident that the Saints did not know where Adam-ondi-Ahman was until this visit of these brethren. Adam-ondi-Ahman is located on the north side of Grand River, in Daviess County, Missouri, about twenty-five miles north of Far West. It is situated on an elevation, which, said the Prophet, "renders the place as healthful as any part of the United States." It overlooks the river in a wonderfully beautiful location.

Other Sites Chosen.—Other territory, which was unoccupied, was also selected for the gathering of the Saints, as the Lord had

---

[c]Doc. and Cov. Sec. 116, Daniel 7th Chapter.
[d]Doc. and Cov. Sec. 107:53-55.

commanded by revelation. The history gives the following account of the selection of these lands:

"Monday 21.—This morning, after making some locations in this place, which is in township 61, ranges 27 and 28, we returned to Robinson's Grove, about two miles, to secure some land near Grand River, which we passed the day previous; and finding a mistake in the former survey, I sent the surveyor south five or six miles to obtain a correct line, while some of us tarried to obtain water for the camp. In the evening I called a council of the brethren to know whether it was wisdom to go immediately into the north country, or tarry here and hereabouts, to secure land on Grand River. The brethren spoke their minds freely on the subject, when I stated to the council that I felt impressed to tarry and secure all the land near by, that is not secured between this and Far West, especially on Grand River. President Rigdon concurred, and the council voted unanimously to secure the land on Grand River, and between this and Far West."

For many days following, the brethren spent their time surveying, selecting sites for settlements, building houses and preparing for the gathering of the Saints who were rapidly coming to these parts. In their travels they, at times, came across antiquities in the form of mounds, which were erected by the ancestors of the Indians.

Independence Day at Far West.—July 4, 1838, was spent by the Saints in celebrating Independence Day. A declaration of Independence from all mobs and persecutors was declared, and after a parade the people assembled at the excavation made for the building of the Lord's house, and the corner stones of the proposed temple were laid, agreeable with the commandment of April 26, 1838.[e] The southeast corner stone was laid by Bishop Edward Partridge, assisted by twelve men and the northeast corner stone was laid by the teachers, assisted by twelve men. The building was to be one hundred and ten feet long and eighty feet wide.

Sidney Rigdon was the orator of the day, and at the close of these services, the assembly shouted hosanna, and after singing they adjourned.

The Law of Tithing.—The law of tithing, which was given as a substitute law for consecration, and to act as a "school-master" to train the Saints, was given July 8, 1838, at Far West, by revelation. Earlier, as we have discovered, Joseph Smith and Oliver Cowdery made a covenant that they would give one tenth of all they received, for the support of the poor. Now the Prophet inquired of the Lord to know what course should be taken by the Saints, and received the following revelation:

---

[e]Doc. and Cov. Sec. 115.

"Verily, thus saith the Lord, I require all their surplus property to be put into the hands of the bishop of my church in Zion, For the building of mine house, and for the laying of the foundation of Zion and for the priesthood, and for the debts of the Presidency of my Church. And this shall be the beginning of the tithing of my people. And after that, those who have thus been tithed shall pay one-tenth of all their interest annually; and this shall be a standing law unto them forever, for my holy priesthood, saith the Lord.

"Verily, I say unto you, it shall come to pass that all those who gather unto the land of Zion shall be tithed of their surplus properties, and shall observe this law, or they shall not be found worthy to abide among you.

"And I say unto you, if my people observe not this law, to keep it holy, and by this law sanctify the land of Zion unto me, that my statutes and my judgments may be kept thereon, that it may be most holy, behold, verily I say unto you, it shall not be a land of Zion unto you. And this shall be an ensample unto all the stakes of Zion. Even so. Amen."

It was also made known that the tithing should be disposed of by a council composed of the First Presidency, Twelve Apostles and Presiding Bishopric.[f]

The Mission of the Twelve.—On the same day the revelation on tithing was received the Lord also gave a revelation to the council of the apostles, calling them to the foreign field in Europe. They were to take their departure from the Saints in Far West on the 26th day of April, 1839, from the building spot of the Lord's house. How this revelation was fulfilled at that date, in the midst of murderous opposition will later be shown. John Taylor, John E. Page, Wilford Woodruff and Willard Richards, the latter at the time acting as one of the presidency of the British Mission, were called to the apostleship, to take the places of William E. McLellin, Luke S. Johnson, John F. Boynton and Lyman E. Johnson, who had fallen.

Elders Heber C. Kimball and Orson Hyde, who had recently returned from England, spoke at the meeting in Far West, Sunday, July 29, 1838, relating their remarkable experiences in that foreign field. On the 5th of August, at a meeting, Frederick G. Williams was re-confirmed a member of the Church, he having been recently rebaptized. He had partaken of the spirit of bitterness and opposition in Kirtland and through it lost his place as one of the First Presidency, but had come to Far West seeking fellowship in the Church.

The Kirtland Camp.—A meeting of all the seventies in Kirtland was held in the temple, March 6, 1838, to consider the removal of

---

[f]See Doc. and Cov. Sec. 119 and 120.

the Saints to Missouri. The matter was left in the hands of the presidents and a meeting called for the 10th instant. At this meeting the presidents reported; they stated that it was doubtful that the journey could be taken in a body because of the extreme poverty of the people. The effort of the high council and high priests to get means and remove the Saints had failed, and they, the seventies, felt that perhaps it would be better for the journey to be taken as individuals. However, while they were in this meeting the Spirit of the Lord rested upon them, and it was made known that they should journey as a body to Zion, according to the commandments and revelations, pitching their tents by the way, and by doing this they should not want for any necessity while on their travels.

This action having been decided, a constitution for their government on the journey was drawn up under the supervision of President Hyrum Smith, and adopted. They were to travel under the direction of the seven presidents, but organized in companies and divisions, for their guidance and convenience. On the 6th day of July, 1838, the journey was commenced. There were in the camp 529 souls, 256 males, and 273 females, consisting of 105 families. A few others joined them on the way. In this manner one of the most remarkable migrations covering a distance of approximately nine hundred miles was undertaken by these afflicted Saints. The Lord blessed them abundantly on their way. Their provisions, like the widow's meal and cruse of oil, were not diminished, and they were fed miraculously during their journey. As might be expected, there were among them some who complained, and a few were expelled from the camp to travel alone because of the infraction of the rules; but the great majority traveled in humility and obedience. A few died, which brought sorrow to the camp; some obtained employment among the people of the various settlements through which they passed, and in this way means were obtained to help them on the way. After enduring various trials and afflictions, incident to a journey of this proportion, they arrived at their destination, Far West, October 2, 1838. There they received a joyful salutation from their brethren. On the 3rd, they continued their march to Ambrosial Creek and on the 4th near sunset pitched their tents at the public square of Adam-ondi-Ahman. Thus the Saints from Kirtland and those scattered abroad began to gather to the settlements in Missouri; but their peace and happiness were not to remain undisturbed, for the threatening clouds of mobocracy were already gathering.

CHAPTER 24

DIFFICULTIES IN MISSOURI—GOVERNOR
BOGGS' ORDER OF EXTERMINATION
1838

Election Day at Gallatin.—At the election held at Gallatin, Daviess County, Missouri, August 6, 1838, hostilities between the Missourians and the "Mormons" broke out. This was the kindling of the flame which was to result in the expulsion of the Latter-day Saints from that state. The Saints had been warned two weeks before by Judge Morin, candidate for the state senate, that an attempt would be made to prevent them from voting; however, they paid little attention to the warning, hoping for better things. On that day, as a number of the brethren approached the polls, Col. William P. Peniston, who had led a mob against the Saints in Clay County, mounted a barrel and harangued the crowd, which he had gathered for the purpose, against the "Mormons." He accused their leaders of various vicious crimes and called the members "dupes, and not too good to take a false oath * * * they would steal, and he did not consider property safe where they were; that he opposed their settling in Daviess County, and if they suffered the 'Mormons' to vote, the people would soon lose their suffrage." Peniston was a candidate for the legislature, and knowing the brethren would not vote for him, he was determined to prevent them forcibly from casting their ballots.

The result was that a premeditated attack was made upon the little band of voters. These "Mormons," about twelve in number, held their ground against a force of over one hundred. Many heads were broken in the conflict. Elder John L. Butler, filled with righteous rage, seized a club and knocked men down right and left. The mobbers dispersed swearing vengeance and threatening to get fire arms and return. The brethren were persuaded by the election officials to depart to save further conflict, since this was a prearranged attack, and their enemies came fully intending to create trouble. The brethren returned to their homes, collected their families and concealed them in the thickets, while they stood guard over their homes during the night.

The Prophet's Investigation.—The next day the report having reached Far West that two or three of the brethren had been killed and the Missourians would not permit their bodies to be removed, or interred, Joseph Smith and about fifteen others armed themselves and started for Gallatin. At Colonel Lyman Wight's home they learned the correct status of the affair. On the 8th, some of the brethren called at the home of Adam Black, justice of the peace and judge elect for Daviess County, and had some conversation with him in which they asked him if he was their friend or enemy. While he said some very bitter things against the "Mormons," he assured them he was not in sympathy with the mob, and would not aid them. He was asked if he would make such a statement in writing, and willingly did so in the following unique document:

"I, Adam Black, a justice of the Peace of Daviess County do hereby Sertify to the people coled Mormin, that he is bound to support the Constitution of this State and of the United States and he is not attached to any mob, or will he attach himself to any such people, and so long as they will not molest me, I will not molest them. This the 8th day of August, 1838.

"Adam Black."

Peniston's Affidavit.—Two days after the interview with Adam Black, William P. Peniston, William Bowman and others made affidavit before Judge Austin A. King, stating that the "Mormons," to the number of about five hundred men, were armed and collected in Daviess County, for the purpose, they verily believed, of committing great violence to the citizens, and to take vengeance for some injuries, or imaginary injuries, done to some of their friends, and to intimidate and drive from the country, all the old citizens, and possess themselves of their lands, or to force such as do not leave, to come into their measures and submit to their dictation. They also stated that about one hundred and twenty men did commit violence on Adam Black, "by surrounding his house and taking him in a violent manner, and subjecting him to great indignities, by forcing him, under threats of immediate death, to sign a paper writing of a very disgraceful character."

DIFFICULTIES IN MISSOURI

Adam Black made affidavit of similar nature on August 28, 1838,[a] in this manner maliciously falsifying and breaking his promise made to the brethren.

Effect of These Falsehoods.—These emissaries of evil knew the effect of their falsehoods would be to stir the Missourians, who needed very little provocation, to acts of violence against the "Mormons." They also hoped, with apparent reason, to win the sympathy of the officers of the state, especially Governor Lilburn W. Boggs. In fact it is not so clear that the governor was not secretly aiding them. He had been elected to the highest office in the state since the disgraceful expulsion of the Saints from Jackson County, in which he took a very prominent part.

Mob Gatherings.—These evil reports soon spread through other counties, and the people were informed by many rumors that the "Mormons" were preparing to commit acts of violence against the older citizens, in other parts of the state. Every conceivable plan was adopted to provoke the members of the Church to acts of violence. Their enemies captured prisoners and punished them; then circulated the report in the "Mormon" settlements that these prisoners had been tortured to death. Thus they hoped to stir the Saints up to anger, trusting they would seek revenge that occasion might be found against them as their aggressors; but the Lord revealed the evil intent of their adversaries.

Arrest of Joseph Smith and Lyman Wight.—Based on these falsehoods of Peniston, Black, et al., charges were preferred against Joseph Smith and Lyman Wight. At first they objected to being tried in Daviess County, where the writ was issued, because of the enmity of the citizens there. After consulting with their attorneys, Atchison and Doniphan, they volunteered to be tried in Daviess County, before Judge Austin A. King. When the trial was held, Adam Black was the only witness who appeared against them, and William P. Peniston was the prosecutor. Several witnesses, both non-members and members of the Church, testified in their defense. However, the judge, who manifested a bitter spirit, bound them over in the sum of five hundred dollars. At the close of the trial he admitted to some of the witnesses that there was no evidence to warrant his action, but the people demanded it.

Proclamation of Governor Boggs.—These rumors and false affidavits reached the governor, as their authors intended they should. On the pretext that the "Mormons" had entered into an alliance with

---

[a]For the Prophet's reply to these charges see Documentary History of the Church, Vol. 3:70.

the Indians and were in rebellion, Governor Boggs issued an order, through Adjutant General B. M. Lisle, to General Atchison and six other commanders of the militia, that as a "precautionary measure," an effective force of the militia be held in readiness to meet either contingency (i. e. the rising of the Indians or the "Mormons"). This force was to consist of four hundred men from each of seven divisions, mounted, armed, and equipped as infantry or riflemen, and formed into companies according to law, thus making a force of 2,800 men.

During all this excitement armed forces of the mob were collecting at various points and making threats against the Saints. Under the direction of the civil authorities, some of the brethren who were members of the state militia, intercepted a wagon load of arms and ammunition on the way to a camp of mobbers. These brethren from Far West took the guns and supplies, arrested three men who appeared to be in charge, and carried them to Far West. Here the men were examined before Albert Petty, justice of the peace, and held in bail to appear at the next term of the circuit court. Judge King was informed of the action taken and he replied that the prisoners should be turned loose and treated kindly. What disposition to make of the guns he did not seem to know, but said they belonged to the militia. Because of this statement, the brethren kept the guns and distributed them; but later, on the order of General Doniphan, they were gathered and delivered up to him.

Austin's Mob Force at Diahman.—False accusations continued to spread and great excitement was manifest on every hand. The militia, according to the order of Governor Boggs, was mustered into service. In their ranks were many of the most bitter enemies of the Saints. Near Diahman a large mob force had gathered under the command of Dr. Austin, armed and in a threatening mood. General Doniphan, with an equal force of militia ordered them to disperse. They claimed that they had gathered in self-defense, yet they were besieging the small settlement of "Mormons" at Diahman. Lyman Wight, who was a colonel in the state militia, had gathered such force as he could to protect the Saints. At the request of Doniphan he showed a willingness to disperse, but demanded that the force under Austin do the same. This, however, the force under Austin refused to do. General Doniphan took up a position between the mob and the people at Diahman, hoping that in a few days they would all disband.

Siege of De Witt.—When Austin saw that his purpose to destroy Diahman was foiled he moved his force to De Witt, in Carroll County, with the determination of expelling the "Mormons" from that place. The citizens here attempted to defend themselves the best they could, and Austin thereupon laid siege to the town, firing upon the inhabitants from time to time, and threatening their extermination or removal from the state. In the meantime both Atchison and Doniphan, as well as a committee of citizens from Chariton County, who had come to investigate the situation, reported to the governor that the "Mormons" were very much alarmed and entirely on the defensive in this unequal conflict. General Atchison writing to the governor said: "Things are not so bad in that county as represented by rumor, and in fact, from affidavits I have no doubt your Excellency has been deceived by the exaggerated statements of designing or half crazy men. I have found there is no cause of alarm on account of the 'Mormons;' they are not to be feared; they are very much alarmed." When the governor received these reports he seemed very much elated, and replied: "The quarrel is between the 'Mormons' and the mob, and they can fight it out." Nevertheless, when he discovered that the "Mormons" were determined to fight it out and maintain their legal and constitutional rights against such overwhelming odds, he was much incensed, which later events will show.

Defense of De Witt.—The forces of the Saints at De Witt, under Lieutenant Colonel George M. Hinkle, who held a commission in the state militia, prepared to defend themselves against their foes, who had come upon them without warrant or provocation. The mob forces under Dr. Austin first threatened De Witt, September 21, 1838, in defiance of all law, and ordered the inhabitants to leave the country by October first. If they were not gone by that time they were to be exterminated, "without regard to age or sex." The following day the citizens of the town petitioned Governor Boggs for relief against the mob. The governor turned a deaf ear to all appeals from the Saints, and seemingly failed to heed the expressions of any but their enemies. The siege of De Witt continued until the 11th of October, in the presence of state troops, under General Parks and Captain Bogart, a Methodist preacher, who looked on, but made no effort to interfere.

The Prophet Visits De Witt.—When Joseph Smith learned of the distress of his brethren in De Witt, he paid a visit to that place. Although the town was under siege by the mob, he risked his life and slipped past the guards. He found the poor Saints in dire distress; their provisions were gone, and they had no prospect of obtaining more; their cattle had been driven off and consumed by their enemies. Again an appeal was made to the governor through the services of a number of gentlemen, not members of the Church, but who understood the situation. This appeal was unheeded. On the 11th of October the Saints accepted the proposition of the mob, to vacate

De Witt, with the understanding that they were to be recompensed for the loss of their property. That afternoon they started for Far West, destitute, hungry and cold. They were emaciated by their long siege; many had died from this abuse; several more died on the march to Far West, a distance of fifty miles. That they failed to receive compensation as they were promised, need hardly be mentioned.

Other Attacks by the Mob.—Very much elated over their success at De Witt, the mobbers sought other fields of conquest. The Rev. Sashiel Woods, a Presbyterian, called the mob together and informed them that the land sales were coming on, and if they could get the "Mormons" driven out, they could get all the lands entitled to pre-emptions, and to hasten to Daviess County in order to accomplish their object. Moreover, that the lands purchased by the "Mormons" would again come into their hands, and they could have both the lands and the money the "Mormons" had paid for them. Cornelius Gilliam was also busy in Platte and Clinton Counties raising a mob to aid Woods in this wicked scheme. These mobbers commenced to burn the houses of the Saints and drive them from their doors, in the midst of a snow storm on the 17th and 18th of October, 1838. Among those who were deprived of shelter, was Agnes M. Smith, wife of Don Carlos Smith who was in the mission field. She was forced to wade Grand River carrying two small children in the midst of inclement winter weather.

General Doniphan Orders a Defense.—General Doniphan ordered out an officer with a force to march to the scene of trouble at Adam-ondi-Ahman, but these troops were in sympathy with the mob, and so were sent back by Doniphan, who said they were "damned rotten hearted." He then commanded Lieutenant Colonel George M. Hinkle, to organize a force at Far West, and march them to Diahman, while he would raise a force in Clay and other counties for the same purpose. At the same time General Parks commanded Col. Lyman Wight, who held a commission in the 59th regiment, under Parks, to collect his force at Diahman, which was done. When the mobbers learned of the action of these troops, they broke their camp and fled. What they could not accomplish by force, they now hoped to gain by stratagem; therefore they moved the goods from several of their log huts at Millport and Gallatin and set them on fire. Then they spread the report in the country round about that the "Mormons" had "riz" and were burning all before them.[b] This action had the

---

[b]These houses really belonged to the Latter-day Saints who had purchased them but had not taken possession.

desired effect, and mob forces commenced to gather in various parts of upper Missouri, and prepared for war. This evil action was augmented by the cunning falsehoods of Samuel Bogart, Col. William P. Peniston, Dr. Samuel Venable, and many others who circulated affidavits of an inflammatory nature, accusing the "Mormons" of all the wicked deeds committed by the mob. Because of this the Saints in the various settlements were forced to flee to Far West, seeking protection.

Battle of Crooked River.—Captain Bogart, although a member of the state militia, continued his depredations against the Saints. On the night of the 24th of October, 1838, this reverend captain with his force went to the home of Nathan Pinkham and took him and two other brethren prisoners, together with some horses and arms. The word reached Far West, and Judge Elias Higbee, the first judge of the County of Caldwell, ordered Lieutenant Colonel Hinkle, the highest officer in the militia at Far West, to send out a company to disperse the mobbers and release the prisoners. The trumpet sounded in the public square about midnight and the brethren assembled. Captain David W. Patten was given command of a company and ordered to go on horseback to the scene of the difficulty. The history of what occurred is given as follows:

"Fifteen of the company were detached from the main body while sixty continued their march till they arrived near the ford of Crooked River, where they dismounted, tied their horses and leaving four or five men to guard them, proceeded towards the ford, not knowing the location of the encampment. It was just at the dawning of light in the east, when they were marching quietly along the road, and near the top of the hill which descends to the river, that the report of a gun was heard, and young Patrick O'Banion reeled out of the ranks and fell mortally wounded. Thus the work of death commenced, when Captain Patten ordered a charge and rushed down the hill on a fast trot, and when within about fifty yards of the camp formed a line. The mob formed a line under the bank of the river, below their tents. It was yet so dark that little could be seen by looking at the west, while the mob looking towards the dawning light, could see Patten and his men, when they fired a broadside, and three or four of the brethren fell. Captain Patten ordered the fire returned, which was instantly obeyed, to great disadvantage in the darkness which yet continued. The fire was repeated by the mob, and returned by Captain Patten's company, who gave the watchword, 'God and Liberty.' Captain Patten then ordered a charge, which was instantly obeyed. The parties immediately came in contact, with their swords, and the mob were soon put to flight, crossing the river at the ford, and such places as they could get a chance. In the pursuit, one of the mob fled from behind a tree, wheeled and shot Captain Patten who instantly fell, mortally wounded, having received a large ball in his bowels.

"The ground was soon cleared, and the brethren gathered up a wagon or two, and making beds therein of tents, etc., took their wounded and retreated towards Far West. Three brethren were wounded in the bowels, one in the neck, one in the shoulder, one through the hips, one through both thighs, one in the arm, all by musket shot. One had his arm broken by a sword. Brother Gideon Carter was shot in the head, and left dead on the ground so defaced that the brethren did not know him. Bogart reported that he had lost one man. The three prisoners were released and returned with the brethren to Far West. Captain Patten was carried some of the way in a litter, but it caused so much distress that he begged to be left by the wayside. He was carried into Brother Winchester's, three miles from the city of Far West, where he died that night. Patrick O'Banion died soon after, and Brother Carter's body was also brought from Crooked River, when it was discovered who he was."[c]

The result of this conflict brought sorrow to the Church at Far West. Joseph and Hyrum Smith and Lyman Wight met the brethren on their return, at Log Creek, where they did all that could be done for Captain Patten before his death. "Brother Patten," said the Prophet "was a very worthy man, beloved by all good men who knew him. He was one of the Twelve Apostles, and died as he had lived, a man of God, and strong in the faith of a glorious resurrection, in a world where mobs will have no power or place. One of his last expressions to his wife was—'whatever you do else, O do not deny the faith.' How different his fate to that of the apostate, Thomas B. Marsh, who this day vented all the lying spleen and malice of his heart towards the work of God, in a letter to Brother and Sister Abbot, to which was annexed an addendum by Orson Hyde." The funeral of Brothers Patten and O'Banion was held at Far West, Saturday, October 27, 1838. On that occasion the Prophet said of Elder Patten: "There lies a man that has done just as he said he would—he has laid down his life for his friends."

Apostasy of Thomas B. Marsh.—Thomas B. Marsh, President of the council of the Twelve Apostles, suddenly left Far West in October, 1838, and went to Richmond in an ugly mood. He had been offended over a trivial matter and thereupon left the Church and made false accusations against his former brethren. Orson Hyde, in the same spirit, followed him on the 18th of October. On the 24th, Marsh went before Henry Jacobs, justice of the peace at Richmond, and made an affidavit the gist of which is as follows:

---

[c]Documentary History of the Church, Vol. 3, pp. 170-1.

"They have among them a company, considered true 'Mormons,' called the Danites, who have taken an oath to support the heads of the Church in all things that they say or do, whether right or wrong. Many, however, of this band are much dissatisfied with this oath, as being against moral and religious principles. On Saturday last, I am informed by the 'Mormons,' that they had a meeting at Far West at which they appointed a company of twelve, by the name of the 'Destruction Company,' for the purpose of burning and destroying, and that if the people of Buncombe came to do mischief upon the people of Caldwell, and committed depredations upon the 'Mormons,' they were to burn Buncombe; and if the people of Clay and Ray made any movement against them, this destroying company were to burn Liberty and Richmond. * * * The Prophet inculcates the notion, and it is believed by every true 'Mormon,' that Smith's prophecies are superior to the laws of the land. I have heard the Prophet say that he would yet tread down his enemies, and walk over their dead bodies; and if he was not let alone, he would be a second Mohammed to this generation, and that he would make it one gore of blood from the Rocky Mountains to the Atlantic Ocean; that like Mohammed, whose motto in treating for peace was, 'the Alcoran or the Sword;' so should it be eventually with us, 'Joseph Smith or the Sword.' These last statements were made during the last summer. The number of armed men at Adam-ondi-Ahman was between three and four hundred.

"THOMAS B. MARSH."

"Sworn to and subscribed before me, the day herein written.
"HENRY JACOBS, J. P.,
"Ray County, Missouri."

"Richmond, Missouri, October 24, 1838."

"Affidavit of Orson Hyde"

"The most of the statements in the foregoing disclosure I know to be true; the remainder I believe to be true.   "ORSON HYDE."

"Richmond, October 24, 1838."

"Sworn to and subscribed before me, on the day above written.
"HENRY JACOBS, J. P."[d]

---

[d]Orson Hyde returned to the body of the Church in June, 1839, at Commerce (Nauvoo) Illinois, and on the 27th of that month was reinstated in the council of the twelve. He was repentant and in tears of humility begged forgiveness from his brethren for the unfortunate part he had taken in this lying report with Thomas B. Marsh. He had been overcome by the spirit of darkness and had borne false witness against his brethren while under that influence. After his return to the Church, he faithfully performed his part to the end. It was Orson Hyde, who, in the life time of Joseph Smith, was intrusted with the important mission of dedicating the land of Palestine for the return of the Jews. The

General Atchison's Report to Boggs.—After the expulsion of the Saints from De Witt, General Atchison reported the condition to Governor Boggs. He informed him that the mob was on the way to Daviess County to continue their ravages, "where it is thought," said the general in his communication, "the same lawless game is to be played over, and the 'Mormons' to be driven from that county, and probably from Caldwell County. Nothing, in my opinion, but the strongest measures within the power of the executive, will put down this spirit of mobocracy." Again, showing the spirit of disapproval of the course taken by the officials in the state, he wrote the governor and said: "I do not feel disposed to disgrace myself, or permit the troops under my command to disgrace the state and themselves by acting the part of a mob. If the 'Mormons' are to be driven from their homes, let it be done without any color of law, and in open defiance thereof; let it be done by volunteers acting upon their own responsibilities!" This was evidently intended as a rebuke, but it and other reports of like character were entirely ignored by Governor Boggs, who remained true to his colors as the advocate of mob rule.

Evil Reports.—Governor Boggs preferred to believe—or more correctly, accepted contrary to his knowledge—the evil reports which flooded his office from the enemies of the Saints. In reporting to the governor the siege of De Witt, General Samuel D. Lucas, referred to the Saints as "base and degraded beings," who would be exter-

---

consciousness of his guilt in this unfortunate act in Missouri, preyed upon his mind all his life, and many were the days he shed bitter tears because that chapter in his history could not be blotted out.

Thomas B. Marsh, at a later day (1857), also returned to the Church. On the 4th of September, 1857, he arrived in Salt Lake City with the immigrants of William Walker's company. He had crossed the plains from Harrison County, Mo. Two days after his arrival he addressed a congregation in the tabernacle and in his remarks said: "I can say, in reference to the quorum of the twelve, to which I belonged that I did not consider myself a whit behind any of them and I suppose that others had the same opinion; but let no one feel too secure; for before you think of it, your steps will slide. You will not then think nor feel for a moment as you did before you lost the Spirit of Christ; for when men apostatize, they are left to grovel in the dark. * * * But let me tell you, my brethren and friends, if you do not want to suffer in body and mind, as I have done; if there are any of you that have the seeds of apostasy in you, do not let them make their appearance, but nip that spirit in the bud; for it is misery and affliction in this world, and destruction in the world to come." (Deseret News, Sept. 16, 1857). He was a broken man in health and spirit, and showed that the hand of affliction had been over him. "If you want to see the fruits of apostasy," he would say, "look at me!" He was later ordained a high priest.

The shadow of color for the report made by Thomas B. Marsh and Orson Hyde was in the fact that a Dr. Sampson Avard, who had shortly before joined the Church, did organize a band which he called "Danites." These Danites did subscribe to some oath of vengeance on their enemies. However, as soon as Joseph Smith discovered what was going on, he put a stop to it and Avard was excommunicated.

minated if they dared to kill one of the mobbers besieging them; for such was the hatred of the people. Lucas was one of the most bitter of the enemies of the Church. Reverend Sashiel Woods and Joseph Dickson, October 24, 1838, reported to the governor that "Captain Bogart and all his company, amounting to between fifty and sixty men, were massacred by the 'Mormons' at Buncombe, twelve miles north of Richmond, except three." This false report was made about the time of the battle of Crooked River; and they added that it might be relied on as being true that the "Mormons" expected to lay Richmond in ashes that very morning. Their fiendish appeal ended with these words: "We know not the hour or minute we will be laid in ashes—our country is ruined—for God's sake give us assistance as quick as possible!" This was sent from Carrolton. Similar reports were sent by Amos Reese, formerly attorney for the Church in the Jackson trouble, and Wiley C. Williams, mobocrat, in a communication to Judge Ryland. Judge Ryland answered and said:

"Since Mr. Morehead left Richmond, one of the company (Bogart's) has come in and reported that there were ten of his comrades killed, and the remainder were taken prisoners, after many of them had been severely wounded; he stated further that Richmond would be sacked and burned by the 'Mormon' banditti tonight. Nothing can exceed the consternation which this news gave rise to. The women and children are flying from Richmond in every direction. * * * My impression, is that you had better send one of your number to Howard, Cooper and Boone counties in order that volunteers may be getting ready. * * * They must make haste and put a stop to the devastation which is menaced by these infuriated fanatics, and they must go prepared and with the full determination to exterminate or expel them from the state *en masse*. Nothing but this can give tranquility to the public mind, and re-establish the supremacy of the laws. There must be no further delaying with this question anywhere. The 'Mormons' must leave the state, or we will, one and all, and to this complexion it must come at last." (*Documentary History of the Church*, Vol. 3:172).

The Saints had no thought of making any attack on Richmond or any other place. This Judge Ryland must have known; but he evidently had become drunken with the bitter spirit of the times. His very letter refutes the falsehoods contained therein.

Atchison's False Report.—Even General David R. Atchison, who previously had shown a spirit of justice and fair play, was overcome by the lying spirits abroad in the land. He permitted himself, under date of October 28, 1838, after the battle of Crooked River, to join that evil genius, Samuel D. Lucas, in a false report to Governor Boggs, as follows:

"Sir:—From late outrages committed by the 'Mormons,' civil war is inevitable. They have set the laws of the country at defiance, and are in open rebellion. We have about two thousand men under arms to keep them in check. The presence of the commander-in-chief is deemed absolutely necessary, and we most respectfully urge that your excellency be at the seat of war as soon as possible."

"Your most obedient servants,"

"DAVID R. ATCHISON, M. G. 3rd Div."
"SAMUEL D. LUCAS, M. G. 4th Div."

The surprising thing is that General Atchison would permit his name to be attached to such a document as this, which both these officers knew perfectly well was not true. But good men are at times overcome. Apparently he could not stand the pressure of the consolidated effort against the Saints, who were seeking merely to defend themselves and their rights against the aggressions of mobocracy. Nevertheless it appeared to be a capital offense for a weak and pratically defenseless people to resist such invasion. For doing so they were guilty of causing a state of civil war!

General Atchison's conscience must have troubled him for thus yielding to the mob spirit, for, later, because he manifested a spirit of fairness towards the Saints, he was "dismounted" by the governor, and relieved of his command.

Boggs' Order to Clark.—October 25, 1838, the Governor issued orders to General John B. Clark to raise sufficient troops to reinstate the inhabitants of Daviess County on their possessions, for said he: "they [the "Mormons"] have burnt to ashes the town of Gallatin and Millport in said county; the former being the county seat of said county, and including the clerk's office and all the public records of the county, and that there is not now a civil officer within said county." Two thousand men were to be raised, in addition to those already under arms, to "restore" these people, who had not been molested, in these towns.

The Order of Extermination.—This first order to General Clark was followed by another the following day, the report of the battle of Crooked River having reached the ear of the governor. When he discovered that the "Mormons" were attempting to "fight it out," he had a great change of heart and issued his disgraceful "exterminating order," the greatest blot on the escutcheon of the state of Missouri. Others among the mob, and even officers of lesser dignity, had hinted at such a thing, but it remained for Lilburn W. Boggs, governor of the state of Missouri, without provocation or due investigation, to issue by authority of the great office which he held, to the militia of that commonwealth, an order to exterminate or drive from Missouri twelve thousand defenseless citizens who had done no wrong. And the execution of this shameful and wicked order was to be carried out in the dead of winter, which would bring to pass exposure and death of delicate women and innocent children, against whom there could have been no charge.[e]

A Match to the Flame.—The Governor's order soon became generally known and the mobbers looked upon it, as well they might, as an approval of their unlawful course. Great excitement prevailed, and mobs assembled on every side. Marauders sallied forth, burning houses, driving off cattle, destroying property, ravishing women and threatening with death any who dared resist their fiendish deeds.

---

[e]The exterminating order of Governor Boggs to General Clark is as follows:

"Sir:—Since the order of the morning to you, directing you to cause four hundred mounted men to be raised within your division, I have received by Amos Reese, Esq., and Wiley C. Williams, Esq., one of my aids, information of the most appalling character, which changes the whole face of things, and places the Mormons in the attitude of open and avowed defiance of the laws, and of having made open war upon the people of this state. Your orders are, therefore, to hasten your operations and endeavor to reach Richmond, in Ray County, with all possible speed. The Mormons must be treated as enemies and must be exterminated or driven from the state, if necessary for the public good. Their outrages are beyond all description. If you can increase your force, you are authorized to do so, to any extent you may think necessary. I have just issued orders to Major-General Wallock, of Marion County, to raise five hundred men, and to march them to the northern part of Daviess and there to unite with General Doniphan, of Clay, who has been ordered with five hundred men to proceed to the same point for the purpose of intercepting the retreat of the Mormons to the north. They have been directed to communicate with you by express; and you can also communicate with them if you find it necessary. Instead, therefore, of proceeding as at first directed, to reinstate the citizens of Daviess in their homes, you will proceed immediately to Richmond, and there operate against the Mormons. Brigadier-General Parks, of Ray, has been ordered to have four hundred men of his brigade in readiness to join you at Richmond. The whole force will be placed under your command.

"L. W. BOGGS,"
"Governor and Commander-in-Chief."

"To General Clark."

CHAPTER 25

PERSECUTION OF THE SAINTS
1838

Clark's Fitness for His Job.—General John B. Clark was a resident of Jackson County. So was General Samuel D. Lucas. Both assisted in driving the "Mormons" from that county in 1833. Governor Lilburn W. Boggs was also from Jackson, and aided in that expulsion. At that time he was lieutenant governor, and worked secretly. These three men hated the Latter-day Saints with a mortal hate. General Clark was not the ranking officer in the state militia in 1838, but Boggs knew, from former experiences, whom to depend upon to execute his dastardly job. Few of the other generals, though several of them disliked the "Mormons," could debase themselves enough to reach the level required to execute the governor's inhuman decree. Clark, who received the command, and Lucas who assisted him, were the two most fitted to carry out the order of extermination.

The Haun's Mill Massacre.—There were a great many petty officers, and some sectarian priests, who could descend to any level. Human butchery, if "Mormons" were the victims, was to them but a recreation. Such a man was Col. William O. Jennings, of the state militia. Another was Captain Nehemiah Comstock, who served under Jennings. These "brave" men with an armed force of characters like themselves—all from the state troops—were assembled, at the close of the month of October, 1838, near a small settlement of the Saints at Haun's Mill, on Shoal Creek, about twelve miles due east of Far West. On the 28th day of that month, a Sunday, Jennings approached the settlement and proposed a treaty of peace. The members of the Church located there, who were quietly minding their own business, knew not, when they were at peace, why they should be called on to enter into such an agreement. However, knowing the status of affairs throughout upper Missouri, they gladly entered into such a treaty, and continued with their domestic affairs, feeling perfectly secure. In the meantime Col. Ashley had informed Col. Jennings of the governor's order of extermination. Thereupon Jennings and Nehemiah Comstock gathered their forces, about two hundred and forty men, and immediately started for Haun's Mill.

Monday, October 29, 1838, passed in peace and quiet. Tuesday the 30th was clear and pleasant, an Indian summer day. In the afternoon, the Saints were engaged in their daily pursuits, the men in the fields and the shops; the women attending to domestic duties, and the children playing on the banks of the creek. Suddenly Jennings and his force approached at full speed, riding upon the settlement. David Evans, perceiving their evil intentions, raised his hands as a sign of peace; but they heeded him not. Continuing their advance, they commenced to fire. The stricken people fled, seeking shelter and endeavoring to escape. Some fled into the thickets near their homes, and by this means escaped. For lack of time and want of a better protection, several of the men and boys rushed into the blacksmith shop. The cracks between the logs of the shop were so wide that the fiends on the outside could see their victims within. Surrounding the place, they poured volley after volley through the cracks with deadly effect. Several intended victims rushed from the shop amidst the fire of the mob; some escaped to the thicket; others were shot. Miss Mary Steadwell, while fleeing, was shot in the hand and fainted; falling over a log she remained protected by it. After the work of destruction was over, more than twenty musket balls were discovered in the log. Yet the executioners were principally seeking for the men, and let most of the women escape.

After completing all the execution possible on the outside of the shop, the ruffians pushed through the door and finished their bloody work. The terrible scene enacted there was one of the utmost brutality. It is told in the "History of Caldwell County," Missouri, with such excuses for the attacks as the writers of such a history could employ. Nevertheless the diabolical deeds of these members of the state militia, are partly related as follows:

"Esq. Thomas McBride was an old soldier of the Revolution. He was lying wounded and helpless, his gun by his side. A militiaman named Rogers came up to him and demanded it. 'Take it,' said McBride. Rogers picked up the weapon, and finding that it was loaded, deliberately discharged it into the old man's breast. He then cut and hacked the old veteran's body with a rude sword, or corn knife, until it was frightfully mangled. Wm. Reynolds, a Livingston County man, killed the little boy Sardius Smith, 10 years of age. The lad had run into the blacksmith shop and crawled under the bellows for safety. Upon entering the shop the cruel militiaman discovered the cowering trembling little fellow, and without even demanding his surrender, fired upon and killed him, and afterwards boasted of the atrocious deed to Charles R. Ross and others. He described, with fiendish glee, how the poor boy struggled in his dying agony, and justified his savage and inhuman conduct in killing a mere child by saying, 'Nits will make lice, and if he had lived he would have been a Mormon.'"

The names of those killed are as follows: Thomas McBride, Levi N. Merrick, Elias Benner, Josiah Fuller, Benjamin Lewis, Alexander Campbell, Warren Smith, George S. Richards, William Napier, Austin Hammer, Simeon Cox, Hiram Abbott, John York, John Lee, John Byers, Sardius Smith and Charles Merrick. Some of these were mere children. Many others were severely wounded but managed to escape with their lives, among them a boy, Alma Smith, who had the flesh of his hip shot away. He had the presence of mind to lie perfectly still and the fiends thought he was dead. Alma was miraculously healed through prayer and faith.

After this terrible work the murderers proceeded to rob the houses, wagons and tents, and left the widows and children who escaped destitute of the necessities of life. They even stripped the bodies of the slain, and carried off their booty, shouting in fiendish glee and boasting of their deeds of blood, as though they were deeds of valor, worthy of the greatest praise and honor.

Gathering of the Mob-Militia.—The same day of the massacre at Haun's Mill, General Samuel D. Lucas, in command of two thousaid men, arrived at Far West. With him were Brigadier Generals Doniphan, Parks, Graham and Wilson, the latter another ruffian. General Clark was at Chariton, under a forced march, with the governor's exterminating order and a force of about one thousand men.

As the troops approached Far West towards the evening of that day, they formed in double file about one half mile from the city. With a flag of truce they sent messengers to the city. They were met by Captain Morley, with a few other individuals, who desired to know what the gathering of the large armed force could mean, for as yet the "Mormon" people had not learned of the Boggs exterminating order. To their horror they were told that the body of troops were state militia, ordered there by the governor, to exterminate the people and burn the place. They demanded three persons in Far West, Adam Lightner, a non-"Mormon," John Cleminson, who had lost the faith, and his wife, to be brought to them. When these three came out, the messengers told them to leave Far West at once and save their lives, for they would be protected. The determination of the force of militia was to destroy Far West and kill the inhabitants. All three nobly said if the people were to be dsetroyed they would return and die with them. The officers immediately returned to the camp.

Charles C. Rich was then dispatched with a flag of truce toward the camp of militia to have an interview with Generals Atchison and Doniphan, who in the past had shown some sympathy for the "Mormons." On his way he was fired at by Captain Bogart. Nevertheless, he continued on his way and was granted the interview with Doniphan, who informed him that General Atchison had been "dismounted" a few miles back, by order of the governor, for being too merciful to the "Mormons." He then plead with Doniphan to use his influence to protect the city from an attack, at least until the following morning. Doniphan replied that the governor had ordered the extermination of the "Mormons," but his order had not arrived, and until it did there would be no attack upon the Saints. However, he could not vouch for the action of Cornelius Gilliam's company, which had just arrived, painted and decorated as Indians; their commander styling himself the "Delaware Chief." These savages spent the night in making hideous yells and other disturbances. When Charles C. Rich returned to Far West and reported, Col. George M. Hinkle, who commanded the forces at Far West, sent another messenger to the mob-militia to plead for the lives of the people. He returned without a satisfactory answer and reported that he had learned that several members of the Church had been captured by some of the troops, and had been brutally murdered, with no one to raise a voice in protest.

During the night the Saints made such temporary fortifications as they were able and with grim determination prepared to fight the best they could to the last, being outnumbered more than five to one. Recruits were hourly joining the forces of their enemies. Among these came Col. Jennings and his band, fresh from the great "victory" at Haun's Mill. The Saints spent an anxious night in solemn supplication to the Lord. The women gathered such few loose articles as might be carried, and prepared for flight if the chance was offered them. Lyman Wight, with a small force, came from

Adam-ondi-Ahman and succeeded in gaining Far West during the night.

The Siege of Far West.—Early on the morning of the 31st, Col. Hinkle sent another messenger to General Doniphan. When he returned he stated that Doniphan had said that the governor's order had arrived and Lucas was preparing to carry it out. "He would be damned, if he would obey the order," was the report, "but Lucas could do as he pleased."

The army, while encamped, permitted no person to go out or come in the city. Those who attempted it were shot at. Corn fields were destroyed and cattle, sheep and hogs wantonly killed by members of the mob-militia.

Colonel Hinkle's Treachery.—About eight o'clock Col. Hinkle sought another interview, this time with General Lucas, to learn if some compromise could not be arranged to avoid a battle. Lucas promised to meet him with a flag of truce at two o'clock. At the time appointed the interview was held. Hinkle, John Corrill, who had within the past few weeks become disaffected, William W. Phelps and a Captain Morrison, met with Lucas and his aids when the following propositions were presented to Col. Hinkle for acceptance in behalf of the "Mormons:"

1. "To give up their leaders to be tried and punished.

2. "To make an appropriation of their property, all who had taken up arms, to the payment of their debts and indemnity for damage done by them.

3. "That the balance should leave the state, and be protected out by the militia, but to be permitted to remain under protection until further orders were received from the Commander-in-Chief.

4. "To give up the arms of every description, to be receipted for."

At least, these were the terms according to the report Lucas made to Governor Boggs. What else he may have said is not on record. To these terms Col. Hinkle agreed, but asked to be given until the next day to comply with them. Lucas consented to this on the condition that Joseph Smith, Sidney Rigdon, Lyman Wight, Parley P. Pratt and George W. Robinson be turned over to the camp of the militia as hostages. If in the morning Hinkle failed to comply with the terms, these men would be returned to Far West, and the attack should commence on the city. If he did comply, then these brethren, among others, should be retained as prisoners to be tried. Hinkle returned to Far West and reported to Joseph Smith that the officers of the state militia desired an interview with the brethren

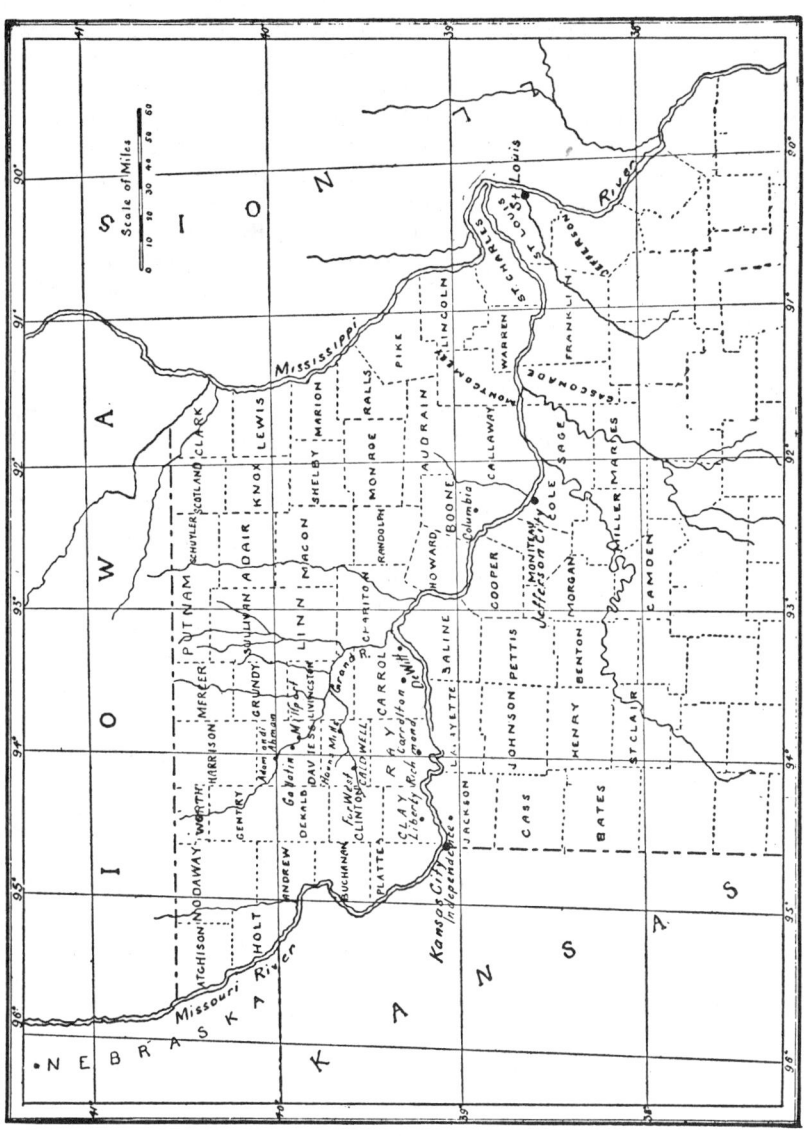

Map of Upper Missouri

mentioned, hoping that the difficulties might be settled without carrying out the exterminating order. Said Parley P. Pratt: "We had no confidence in the word of a murderer and robber; but there was no alternative, but to put ourselves into the hands of such monsters, or to have the city sacked, and men, women and children massacred. We therefore commended ourselves to the Lord, and voluntarily surrendered." As they approached the camp in compliance with this order, General Lucas, with a guard of several hundred men, rode up, and with a haughty air ordered his men to surround the brethren. Colonel Hinkle was heard to say: "General, these are the prisoners I agreed to deliver up." The prisoners were then marched into the camp surrounded by several thousand savage looking soldiers. "These all set up a constant yell," says Brother Pratt, "like so many bloodhounds let loose upon their prey. * * * If the vision of the infernal regions could suddenly be opened to the mind, with thousands of malicious fiends, all clamoring, exulting, deriding, blaspheming, mocking, railing, raging and foaming like a troubled sea, then could some idea be formed of the hell which we had entered."

The prisoners were placed under a strong guard and forced to remain without shelter during the night in inclement winter weather. The guard blasphemed; mocked the Savior; demanded miracles and said: "Come, Smith, show us an angel; give us one of your revelations; show us a miracle; come, there is one of your brethren in camp whom we took prisoner yesterday in his own house, and knocked his brains out with his own rifle, which we found hanging over his fireplace; he lies speechless and dying;[a] speak the word and heal him, and then we will all believe; or, if you are apostles or men of God, deliver yourselves, and then we will be "Mormons."[b]

Condemned to be Shot.—Thursday morning, November 1, 1838, Hyrum Smith and Amasa Lyman were brought to Col. Hinkle into the camp. That night a court martial was held, at which, besides the commanding officers of the mob-militia, Col. Hinkle, Judge Austin A. King, District Attorney Birch, and the Reverends Sashiel Woods, Bogart and several other priests, played a part. The prisoners were sentenced to be shot in the public square in Far West, Friday morning at 9 o'clock. This was, let it be said to their honor, over the protest of Generals Doniphan and Graham, and perhaps a few others. General Doniphan was given the order to carry out the execution. It was a

---

[a]This was a brother named Carey, who had been beaten over the head until his brains oozed out. He died shortly afterwards, having been exposed in that condition without shelter, all afternoon and night.
[b]Autobiography of Parley P. Pratt, p. 204.

most fortunate thing that he was selected, for he refused to obey the command. The order given him was as follows:

"Brigadier General Doniphan.

"*Sir*:—You will take Joseph Smith and the other prisoners into the public square of Far West, and shoot them at 9 o'clock tomorrow morning."

"Samuel D. Lucas,"
"Major General Commanding."

General Doniphan replied to this order by saying to his superior:

"It is cold blooded murder. I will not obey your order. My brigade shall march for Liberty tomorrow morning at 8 o'clock; and if you execute these men, I will hold you responsible before an earthly tribunal, so help me God."

"A. W. Doniphan,"
"Brigadier General."

Although this was an act of insubordination, it frightened the criminal general and his willing aids. No charge was ever made against Doniphan, for they dared not make one.

Plundering of the Militia.—Col. Hinkle, according to his agreement, marched the militia companies at Far West out of the city and grounded their arms, which were the private property of the men who held them. Then the mob force was let loose. They entered the city without restraint, on pretext of searching the homes for additional arms. They tore up floors; ruined furniture; destroyed property; whipped the men and forced them to sign deeds to their property at the point of the bayonet; and violated the chastity of women, until their victims died. About eighty men were taken prisoners and the people were ordered to leave the state, and were forbidden, under threat of death, to assemble more than three in a place. Notwithstanding all this, General Lucas reported to the governor how orderly and decorous were his troops.

Prisoners Taken to Independence.—The prisoners after an earnest appeal, were permitted to visit their homes, under a strong guard, to obtain a change of clothing. They were, however, given strict command not to speak, or enter into conversation with the members of their families. When the Prophet visited his home the children clung to his garments. He requested the privilege of a private interview with his family, which was denied him. Hyrum Smith, whose wife less than two weeks later was confined,[c] drew attention to the condition in his home; but received in answer only gibes and insults. Parley P. Pratt underwent a similar scene, and in the anguish of his soul appealed to General Moses Wilson, who answered him with an exultant laugh, and a taunting reproach.

After these painful scenes the prisoners were started for Independence under a strong guard commanded by Generals Lucas and Wilson. On the way orders came from General Clark to have the prisoners sent to him, but this General Lucas was not willing to do. Clark, without question, wanted the honor of putting the prisoners to death. Through his vanity, Lucas wanted to exhibit them before their enemies in Jackson County, and pose as a great hero in triumph. Between the rivalry of the two, not forgetting the hand of the Lord which was over them, their lives were spared.[d]

Prisoners in Richmond.—On the 3rd of November, 1838, the prisoners arrived in Jackson County and the next day were taken by order of General Lucas, to Independence. General Clark, however, would not permit them to stay, desiring to gain possession of them himself. Therefore, he sent Col. Sterling Price with instructions to have them removed immediately to Richmond, Ray County. They arrived in Richmond on the 9th, and were imprisoned in a vacant house. On their way they met General Clark, and asked him why they had been carried from their homes and what the charges were against them. Clark said he was not then able to determine, but would be prepared to tell in a short time. When they were confined Clark sent Price with two chains and padlocks and had the prisoners fastened together. The windows were then nailed down; the prisoners were searched and the only weapons they had (their pocket knives) were taken away. While this was going on armed guards stood with cocked guns pointed at them. Here the brethren were kept many days awaiting trial.

---

[c]During these trying scenes, November 13, 1838, while Hyrum Smith, with the Prophet and the other prisoners, were incarcerated, Joseph Fielding Smith, who afterwards became President of the Church of Jesus Christ of Latter-day Saints, was born at Far West. When he was but a few days old, members of this mob-militia entered the home, ransacked it, and turned the bedding, on which the infant lay, upside down, smothering him until his life was apparently gone when he was discovered.

[d]Parley P. Pratt declared that General Wilson made the following statement: "It was repeatedly insinuated, by the other officers and troops, that we should hang you prisoners on the first tree we came to on the way to Independence. But I'll be d——d if anybody shall hurt you. We just intend to exhibit you in Independence, and let the people look at you, and see what a d————d set of fine fellows you are. And, more particularly, to keep you from that old bigot of a general, Clark, and his troops, from down county, who are so stuffed with lies and prejudice, that they would shoot you down in a moment."

Rebuking the Guards.—While incarcerated in this prison, the brethren were guarded by some of the vilest wretches that could be found, who spent their time in the presence of their prisoners relating their horrible deeds of wickedness. This thing continued for some time, when the Prophet, unable to stand it any longer, arose and rebuked them. The occurrence is graphically related by Elder Parley P. Pratt in the following words:

"During this time Elder Rigdon was taken very sick, from hardship and exposure, and finally lost his reason; but still he was kept in a miserable, noisy and cold room, and compelled to sleep on the floor with a chain and padlock round his ankle, and fastened to six others. Here he endured the constant noise and confusion of an unruly guard, the officer of which was Colonel Sterling Price, since governor of the State.

"These guards were composed generally of the most noisy, foul-mouthed, vulgar, disgraceful rabble that ever defiled the earth. * * * Mrs. Robinson, a young and delicate female, with her infant, came down to see her husband [George W. Robinson], and to comfort and take care of her father [Sidney Rigdon] in his sickness. When she first entered the room, amid the clank of chains and the rattle of weapons, and cast her eyes on her sick and dejected parent and sorrow-worn husband, she was speechless and only gave vent to her feelings in a flood of tears. This faithful lady, with her little infant, continued by the side of her father till he recovered from his sickness, and till his fevered and disordered mind resumed its wonted powers.

"In one of those tedious nights we had lain as if in sleep till the hour of midnight had passed, and our ears and hearts had been pained, while we had listened for hours to the obscene jests, the horrid oaths, the dreadful blasphemies and filthy language of our guards, Colonel Price at their head, as they recounted to each other their deeds of rapine, murder, robbery, etc., which they had committed among the 'Mormons' while at Far West and vicinity. They even boasted of defiling by force wives, daughters, and virgins, and of shooting or dashing out the brains of men, women and children.

"I had listened till I became so disgusted, shocked, horrified, and so filled with the spirit of indignant justice that I could scarcely refrain from rising upon my feet and rebuking the guards; but had said nothing to Joseph, or any one else, although I lay next to him and knew he was awake. On a sudden he arose to his feet, and spoke in a voice of thunder, or as the roaring lion, uttering, as near as I can recollect, the following words:

"SILENCE, ye fiends of the infernal pit. In the name of Jesus Christ I rebuke you, and command you to be still. I will not live another minute and hear such language. Cease such talk, or you or I die THIS INSTANT!"

Majesty in Chains.—"He ceased to speak. He stood erect in terrible majesty. Chained, and without a weapon; calm, unruffled and dignified as an angel, he looked upon the quailing guards; whose weapons were lowered or dropped to the ground, whose knees smote together, and who, shrinking into a corner, or crouching at his feet, begged his pardon, and remained quiet till a change of guards.

"I have seen the ministers of justice, clothed in magisterial robes, and criminals arraigned before them, while life was suspended on a breath, in the courts of England; I have witnessed a Congress in solemn session to give laws to nations; I have tried to conceive of kings, of royal courts, of thrones and crowns; and of emperors assembled to decide the fate of kingdoms; but dignity and majesty have I seen but once, as it stood in chains, at midnight, in a dungeon in an obscure village of Missouri."[e]

General Clark at Far West.—In the meantime (November 4), General Clark arrived at Far West with 1600 men, and 500 more on the outskirts of the city. He ordered General Lucas to send to Adam-ondi-Ahman and there take all the "Mormon" men prisoners and secure their property, till the best means could be adopted for paying damages due to the mob troubles. On the 5th, Clark ordered all the men at Far West to form in line, when the names of fifty-six were called and they were made prisoners to await trial for something which was not defined. On the 6th, he again gathered the male portion of the population and read to them a written address which he had prepared.

His Harangue.—Feeling safe in the presence of so many helpless men, and flanked by his troops, he made bold to impress upon the brethren the enormity of their crimes. He read to them a number of stipulations to which they must comply. The first, second and third, to the effect that they must surrender their leading men, deliver their arms, and sign over their properties to defray expenses of the "war." This, he said, they had done. The fourth is here repeated:

"Another article yet remains for you to comply with, and that is, that you leave the state forthwith; and whatever may be your feelings concerning this, or whatever your innocence, it is nothing to me; General Lucas, who is equal in authority with me, has made

---

[e]Autobiography of Parley P. Pratt. Pages 228-9.

this treaty with you—I approve of it—I should have done the same had I been here. I am therefore determined to see it fulfilled. The character of this state has suffered almost beyond redemption, from the character, conduct and influence that you have exerted, and we deem it an act of justice to restore her character to its former standing among the states, by every proper means.

"The orders of the governor to me were that you should be exterminated, and not allowed to remain in the state, and had your leaders not been given up, and the terms of the treaty complied with, before this, you and your families would have been destroyed and your houses in ashes.

"There is a discretionary power vested in my hands which I shall exercise in your favor for a season; for this lenity you are indebted to my clemency. I do not say that you shall go now, but you must not think of staying here another season or of putting in crops, for the moment you do this the citizens will be upon you. If I am called here again, in case of a non-compliance of a treaty made, do not think that I shall act any more as I have done—you need not expect any mercy, but extermination, for I am determined the governor's order shall be executed. As for your leaders, do not once think—do not imagine for a moment—do not let it enter your mind that they will be delivered, or that you will see their faces again, for their *fate is fixed—their die is cast—their doom is sealed."*

He then very graciously pleaded with them, and invoked the "Great Spirit, the unknown God," to make them sufficiently intelligent to break the chains of superstition, that they no longer worship man, and never again organize with bishops, presidents, etc., but to become like other men.

Trial in Daviess County.—About this time Governor Boggs wrote General Clark to hold a military court in Daviess County, and try those "guilty of the late outrages, committed towards the inhabitants of said county." He was desirous of having the whole matter "settled completely, if possible" before the forces should be disbanded. "If the 'Mormons' are disposed," said Boggs, "voluntarily to leave the state, of course it would be advisable in you to promote that object, in any way deemed proper. The ringleaders of this rebellion, though, ought by no means to be permitted to escape the punishment they merit." General Robert Wilson was detailed to Daviess County to take possession of the prisoners. All the men in the town of Adam-ondi-Ahman were placed under arrest, and a court of inquiry instituted with the mobber Adam Black on the bench. Notwithstanding this, after three days of examination, Black acquitted them all. No one knew better than he of their innocence.

The Charges Against Joseph Smith and Companions.—General Clark spent some time searching the laws to find some authority by which the Prophet and companions could be tried for treason by court martial. He even sent to Fort Leavenworth seeking such information, which could not be found. It caused him extreme annoyance that no law could be invoked to try private citizens by military code when there was no war. He knew some charges would have to be preferred against the accused, so he wrote the governor saying he had, on November 10, 1838, made out charges against the prisoners and had called Judge Austin A. King to try them as a committing court. He also suggested that they be tried by court martial, especially, said he, should Joseph Smith be so tried, but he could not discover authority for such procedure, and requested the opinion of the attorney general on that point. "There being no civil officers in Caldwell," he said, "I have to use the military to get witnesses from there, which I do without reserve." The civil officers in Caldwell, being "Mormons" had all been cast into jail, and of course were not available. He closed his epistle by saying the accused brethren were guilty of "treason, murder, arson, burglary, robbery, larceny, and perjury." The reply he received was to turn the prisoners over to the civil law, which order hurt him very much, for he hoped to have the pleasure of attending to their execution, after a military trial. In fact, he and Lucas had on several occasions set the date of execution, but the hand of the Lord was always over the afflicted brethren.

The Trial.—Monday, November 12, 1838, Judge King sent out armed men to obtain witnesses, some of whom came and testified willingly to falsehoods; others came reluctantly. Among the witnesses who testified against the brethren were: Dr. Sampson Avard, originator of the "Danites," who, later, was excommunicated from the Church for the offense; John Corrill, George M. Hinkle, Reed Peck, John Cleminson, Burr Riggs, William W. Phelps, John Whitmer, and others who formerly belonged to the Church. The testimony of the prosecution continued until the 18th. Then the court called for witnesses for the defense; forty or more names were given, and the Reverend-Captain Bogart was dispatched with a company of militia to get them. He got them and brought them, not to the court, but to prison, and confined them there. During the week, the judge taunted the brethren because no witnesses appeared in their defense. Other names were given, and the same reverend-captain was sent for them. He did not find many, for the witnesses, learning what had happened to their fellows, could not be found. The few he did discover he also brought and cast behind the bars. In this manner the mock trial proceeded from day to day. On the 24th, twenty-three of the defendants were released, and by the 28th all the others were acquitted or admitted to bail, excepting the following: Joseph Smith, Sidney Rigdon, Hyrum Smith, Lyman Wight, Caleb Baldwin and Alexander McRae, who were ordered to be taken to Liberty, Clay County, and there committed to stand trial on the various charges named; Parley P. Pratt, Morris Phelps, Luman Gibbs, Darwin Chase and Norman Shearer, who were taken to Richmond Jail, there also to await trial for the same "crimes."

Nature of the Testimony.—Some of the witnesses testified that the Church was a temporal kingdom, which would, according to the teachings of its leaders, eventually "fill the whole earth and subdue all other kingdoms." The seventh chapter of Daniel was referred to several times. The brethren were asked by the judge if they believed in Daniel's prophecy and when they answered in the affirmative, Judge King turning to his clerk said: "Write that down; it is a strong point for treason." The defendants' attorneys, Doniphan and Reese, protested saying, "Judge you had better make the Bible treason." These attorneys advised their clients not to make any defense or attempt to furnish other witnesses, for it was useless. Doniphan observed that if a cohort of angels were to come down, and declare the prisoners innocent, it would all be the same, for Judge King had determined from the beginning to cast them into prison.

Malinda Porter, Delia F. Pine, Nancy Rigdon, Jonathan W. Barlow, Thoret Parson, Ezra Chipman and Arza Judd, Jr., volunteered to testify for the defense, but were prevented from giving testimony favorable to the accused at the point of the bayonet.

November 29, 1838, Joseph Smith and fellow prisoners were committed to the keeping of the sheriff of Clay County, who took them to Liberty and cast them in prison. Parley P. Pratt and fellows were likewise retained in Richmond, and thus ended this "trial" before Judge King.

CHAPTER 26

THE EXPULSION FROM MISSOURI

1838-1839

The Case Before the Legislature.—In December, 1838, the Legislature of Missouri met. Governor Boggs laid before that body the information in his hands relative to the difficulty with the Latter-day Saints. This information was woefully lacking in the matter of the petitions and documents sent to him in defense of the Saints. On the 10th of that month Brigham Young, Heber C. Kimball, John Taylor and other brethren petitioned the legislature, setting forth their side of the case. This petition was presented to David R. Atchison and others, December 17. The following day Mr. Turner, from a joint committee, presented before the senate a report of findings, based on the governor's information. This report stated that the evidence was "not authenticated," and was confined chiefly to investigation of criminal charges against individuals under arrest; the evidence was *ex parte;* and without aid of further evidence, the committee could not form a satisfactory opinion in relation to the material points. For these reasons, and because "it would be a direct interference with the administration of justice, the committee reported that this document ought not to be published, with the sanction of the legislature." December 19, the petition of the brethren was presented by John Corrill, who had but recently departed from the Church. It was read in profound silence, but at the close of the reading, the house was in an uproar. A Mr. Childs, of Jackson County, denounced the petition saying there was not a word of truth in it. Mr. Ashley, of Livingstone County, denounced the "Mormons" as did also Mr.

Young, of Lafayette. Ashley was one of the murderers at Haun's Mill, and even boasted of that slaughter before the house. Mr. Redman, of Howard County, and Mr. Gyer, of St. Louis, and a few other members, demanded a full investigation, for they believed there was truth in the petition, and the actions of those members in opposing an investigation was because they feared their evil deeds might be brought to light. The result of it all was that the petition was laid on the table, "until the 4th day of July next,"—Independence day. January 16, 1839, Mr. Turner introduced in the senate a bill "to provide for the investigation of the late disturbances in this state." The bill passed the senate, but when it came to the house (Feb. 4) it followed the petition and was laid on the table, also to be taken up on Independence day. Many considered this an approval of the wrongs committed on the "Mormons" in Missouri. David R. Atchison and a few others vigorously protested against such criminal action, but found themselves in the minority, for the motion prevailed by a majority of eleven votes.

Legislative Appropriations.—In December, the legislature of Missouri appropriated two thousand dollars "to be distributed among the people of Daviess and Caldwell Counties." The "good" people of Daviess were very "generous" and felt that they could do without the portion of this appropriation, and let it be given to the people of Caldwell. They could well afford to do such a thing, for they had robbed the "Mormon" people of nearly all they possessed. They had ransacked their homes and carried off their household furniture and goods, and otherwise enriched themselves at the expense of the Saints who had dwelt among them. This sum, so it was pretended, was distributed among the people in Caldwell. Judge Cameron and others attended to the "distribution." The way they did it was to drive off the hogs belonging to the "Mormons" and shoot them, and without further bleeding, cut them up and deliver them to the Saints, at four or five cents a pound. They also "gave them a few calicos," and the "sweepings of an old store," charging them an extra price for the goods, and thus was the "munificent" sum of two thousand dollars distributed among the "Mormons." Later the same legislature appropriated two hundred thousand dollars to pay the troops for their work in driving the "Mormons" from the state. In this manner were law and justice administered in Missouri in the years 1838 and 1839.

Extent of "Mormon" Losses.—The total value of the property destroyed in Missouri, which belonged to the Saints, is beyond our knowledge. It was estimated to be not less than two million dollars, from the time they first settled in that state until their expulsion. About twelve hundred members of the Church were driven from

Jackson County in 1833, and all their property was lost to them. When again they were forced to leave Clay County, though they went peaceably at the request of the other citizens, they left behind them a vast amount of property for which no remuneration was ever received. When they were expelled from the state in the winter of 1838-9, the Saints numbered between twelve and fifteen thousand souls. All their property, except the little they were able to gather hastily and carry with them, was either destroyed or stolen by their enemies. In the appeal made to Congress and the President of the United States, in 1839, the amount of their losses was estimated at two million dollars. Claims against Missouri for the losses were presented to Congress in the sum of $1,381,044.00, and this represented only 491 individuals; many others who lost property, entered no claims for damages against that state.

In addition to this loss of property, the Prophet Joseph paid in lawyer's fees, for the defense of the people and himself, against the unhallowed persecutions of their enemies, about fifty thousand dollars; with very little benefit in return. And for all this, the generous state of Missouri, for a show before the world of their charity and kindness toward the people they had robbed, could afford to appropriate the magnificent sum of two thousand dollars! And what of the blood of men, women and children which had been shed by these human fiends?

In Liberty Prison.—After the mock trial in Richmond, Joseph Smith and his five companions were imprisoned in Liberty, Clay County, for a period of six months. Here they suffered, during that time, many untold hardships. Much of the time they were bound in chains. Their food was often not fit to eat, and never wholesome or prepared with the thought of proper nourishment. Several times poison was administered to them in their food, which made them sick nigh unto death, and only the promised blessings of the Lord saved them. Their bed was on the floor, or on the flat side of a hewn white oak log, and in this manner they were forced to suffer. Is it any wonder that they cried in the anguish of their souls unto the Lord, for relief from such inhuman treatment?

Epistles From Prison.—The Lord did not forsake them. While they were confined, the brethren wrote a number of communications to the Saints. Occasionally their friends were privileged to visit them, but always in the presence of a strong and heavily armed guard. Letters with words of comfort were occasionally received, and in this way their spirits were buoyed up, which enabled them to stand their trials. On March 25, 1839, an epistle of special import was written from the prison to the Saints scattered abroad, and to the bishop, Edward Partridge, in particular. This epistle portrayed many of their grievances and expressed their love and fellowship for the Saints. Above all this, however, they poured out their souls to the Lord asking for relief, and wondering why they were so severely punished. The Lord gave them answer which comforted them and built them up in hope. They also received encouragement, and assurance of their delivery from bonds, which was soon to come to pass.[a]

Release of Sidney Rigdon.—The Prophet wrote in his Journal that January 1, 1839, "dawned upon us as prisoners of hope, but not as sons of liberty. O Columbia, Columbia! How thou art fallen! 'The land of the free, the home of the brave!' 'The asylum of the oppressed'—oppressing thy noblest sons, in a loathsome dungeon, without any provocation, only that they have claimed to worship the God of their fathers according to his own word, and the dictates of their own consciences." Elder Parley P. Pratt and his companions in tribulation were still held in bondage in their doleful prison in Richmond. The brethren appealed to the supreme court in Missouri for a writ of habeas corpus. Twice their petition was denied. They also petitioned the judges of the county for like privileges, and sent a memorial to the legislature asking that they be granted a fair and impartial trial before an unprejudiced judge in some other circuit, where they might have hope of justice, which could not be obtained from Judge King. Finally, in the latter part of February, 1839, they prevailed on Judge Turnham, one of the county judges, who granted their request after some reluctance. The judge was afraid of the mob, for the threats were made by the members of the banditti, that if any judge, jury or court of any kind, should free the prisoners they would be killed. Great threatenings were made at the time of this trial, and the brethren would have been liberated, only for the blundering, wilfully or ignorantly, of their lawyers. Sidney Rigdon, who had suffered terribly because of exposure and the ill-treatment he had received, he being much older and less able to endure than the other brethren, was released by the action of the judge, at this time. Through a kindness on the part of the sheriff, Samuel Hadley, and the jailer, Samuel Tillery, he was let out of prison in the night, for fear of the mob, and told to make his way out of the state as soon as he could. Even as it was, he was pursued by a body of armed men; but having a good start made his way to Quincy, Illinois.

Departure for Daviess.—The refusal on the part of the courts and officials to grant a final trial—for it should be remembered the

---

[a]The prayer and the answer the Lord gave the Prophet are found in sections 121, 122, 123, of the Doctrine and Covenants.

brethren were being held on a preliminary hearing all these months—and the threatenings of numerous enemies caused the brethren to determine on making their escape if possible. Once they tried and failed. Again the opportunity presented itself, and the Lord indicated to them that if they were united they could gain their freedom, but the stubbornness of Lyman Wight defeated their purpose. The latter part of March, Elders Heber C. Kimball and Theodore Turley went to Jefferson City with necessary papers, to see the governor, but he was absent. However, they saw the secretary of state, who appeared astonished at the action of Judge King, and who wrote the judge a letter. They also saw the supreme court judges, but due to the blundering of their attorney, Doniphan, they were unable to obtain a writ of habeas corpus. They returned to Liberty on the 30th of March. April 4, they had an interview with Judge Austin A. King, who was angry to think they had been to see the governor. King said he could have done all that they desired, and would have signed their petition if he had been approached, for all the prisoners, but Joseph Smith, "and he was not fit to live." Fearing that the brethren might obtain a change of venue, Judge King hurried off with them, April 6, 1839, to Daviess County, where he hoped to continue his persecution. Perhaps he hoped they would be murdered, for a band of fifty men in Daviess County, on learning that the prisoners were coming, took an oath that they would neither eat nor drink until they had murdered the Prophet. The prisoners arrived at Gallatin, April 8, and the following day the examination of witnesses commenced before the grand jury, over which Judge King acted as the presiding judge. Judge Birch, the county judge, who previously assisted in the persecution of the brethren, was associated with him. Both judges and jury were drunk while the case proceeded, and the men of the jury were members of the raiding party of Haun's Mill. They served on the jury during the day and as guards at night, and in their drunken debauchery boasted of their many crimes. On the 11th of April, they brought in a "true bill" against the prisoners for "murder, treason, burglary, arson, larceny, theft and stealing."

A Change of Venue.—On April 15, 1839, the brethren obtained from Judge Birch a change of venue from Daviess to Boone County, and a mittimus was made out by him without date, name or place. The prisoners were fitted out with a two-horse wagon, necessary horses, and four men besides the sheriff, to guard them to Boone County. The prisoners numbered five, as follows: Joseph Smith, Hyrum Smith, Lyman Wight, Caleb Baldwin, and Alexander McRae. They started from Gallatin in the afternoon and went as far as Diahman, where they camped for the night at Judge Morin's. The next day they went about twenty miles where a jug of whiskey was procured, and all of the guards, save one, got drunk and went to bed. The sheriff showed the prisoners the mittimus and said to them that Judge Birch told him never to carry them to Boone County, and never to show the mittimus, and, the sheriff said: "I shall take a good drink of whiskey and go to bed, and you may do as you are a mind to."

The Escape.—The prisoners bought from the guards two of the horses, paying for one with clothing, and giving their note for the other. After four of the guards had retired and were asleep in drunken slumber, the fifth helped them to saddle the horses and started them on their way. Two of the brethren mounted and three went on foot, changing places from time to time. Said Hyrum Smith, "we took our change of venue for the state of Illinois, and in the course of nine or ten days arrived at Quincy, Adams County." They found their families in good health, but in a state of poverty due to their persecutions and expulsion from Missouri's soil.

A "Concocted Plan."—Samuel Tillery, the jailer at Liberty, told the prisoners that the persecutions against the Saints was a "concocted plan," framed by the various officers who took part in it, from the governor down. It was first planned in the fore part of the year 1838, but was not fully carried out until the militia was sent down against the Saints in Caldwell and Daviess Counties. "But," said Tillery, shortly before the removal of the brethren to Daviess County from Liberty Prison, "you need not be concerned, for the governor has laid a plan for your release." He also said that the governor was now ashamed enough of the whole transaction, and would be glad to set the prisoners at liberty, if he dared to do it. Without question the conspirators became alarmed. They did not plan the escape of the Prophet and associates because of any repentance, or remorse of conscience, but because of the fear of public sentiment, without as well as within the state. Knowledge of the dastardly actions of the officers of Missouri, who were pledged by oath to uphold and honor their constitution, which grants liberty to all citizens[b] in their religious

---

[b]The Constitution of Missouri read as follows:

Article 4. That all men have a natural and indefeasible right to worship Almighty God according to the dictates of their own consciences; and that no man can be compelled to erect, support, or attend any place of worship, or to maintain any minister of the Gospel, or teacher of religion; that no human authority can control or interfere with the rights of conscience; that no person can ever be hurt, molested, or restrained in his religious professions, or sentiments, if he do not disturb others in their religious worship.

Article 5. That no person, on account of his religious opinions, can be rendered ineligible to any office of trust or profit under this state; that no preference can ever be given by law, to any sect or mode of worship.

worship, spread abroad into other commonwealths. The citizens of western Illinois received the exiled Saints with open arms, and invited them to make their homes among them. The governor of Iowa, Robert Lucas, wrote and spoke in a vehement manner in opposition to the treatment the "Mormon" people received in Missouri. He invited the Saints to make their homes within the borders of the territory of Iowa. All these things had their effect on the assassins in Missouri, and caused them to fear and tremble. Governor Boggs, himself, became sick of the reproach brought upon the state, and reached the point where he would have gladly released Joseph Smith and his fellow prisoners, but feared that such an action would properly be interpreted as an acknowledgment of his unlawful course. He preferred to have it so arranged that they could escape and appear before the world as fugitives from justice.

Escape of Parley P. Pratt.—At the time Joseph Smith and his companions were sent to Liberty, Elders Parley P. Pratt, Morris Phelps, Luman Gibbs, Norman Shearer and Darwin Chase, were sent to Richmond, to await trial on the same charges. Here they suffered many untold hardships and deprivations in their dungeon, until April 24, 1839, a period of six months, when they were taken before the grand jury in Ray County, for a hearing of their case. The same notorious Judge Austin A. King presided at the deliberations of this body. Norman Shearer and Darwin Chase, who were only boys, were released, and King Follett, an aged man, was added to the list of prisoners. A change of venue having been granted them, the brethren were taken to Columbia, Boone County, and again cast into prison. In the meantime Luman Gibbs apostatized, hoping to gain his liberty, but the crafty officers, although they treated him with improved consideration, still kept him in prison to act as a spy on his former brethren. July 4, 1839, Elders Pratt, Phelps and Follett, assisted on the outside by Orson Pratt and a young man named John W. Clark, a brother-in-law of Elder Phelps, escaped in a very thrilling and novel manner. Elder Follett was re-captured, but the other two made their way, after many hardships and difficulties, to Illinois and the presence of their families. Elder Follett was again cast into prison and bound in chains, but in course of a month or two was dismissed, no charge having been proved against him.

Departure of the Exiles.—With all three members of the First Presidency in prison, the burden of removing the Saints from Missouri was placed on the shoulders of President Brigham Young, of the council of the apostles. A public meeting was held at Far West, January 26, 1839, and a committee composed of the following brethren was selected to draft resolutions and consider means for the removal

THE EXPULSION FROM MISSOURI

of the Saints from Missouri: Brigham Young, Heber C. Kimball, John Taylor, Alanson Ripley, Theodore Turley, John Smith and Don Carlos Smith. This committee went to work gathering such means as could be obtained, and devising plans for the removal of the poor. Later a committee on removal was appointed with the following members: William Huntington, chairman; Charles Bird, Alanson Ripley, Theodore Turley, Daniel Shearer, Shadrach Roundy and Jonathan H. Hale. During the winter months the exodus began, and many of the Saints gathered at Quincy, Illinois, where they received a kindly welcome. Due to their extreme poverty—for they had been robbed and plundered—many of the members of the Church were unable to get away before the spring of 1839. April arrived and the vicious mobocrats met in council on the 6th, and determined that all the "Mormons" should be out of Caldwell County by the 12th of that month. All available teams were secured, and help was solicited from the members of the Church who were already in Illinois, and the remaining Saints at Far West began their journey from Missouri. Thirty families were removed into Tenney's Grove, twenty-five miles from Far West, by the 14th of April, on their way to Quincy. Most of the committee remained at Far West until the last. President Brigham Young was forced to leave about the middle of February, to save his life from the angry Missourians who sought it. From the Illinois side he directed the location of the Saints.

Thursday, April 18, 1839, Elder Heber C. Kimball notified the members of the committee on removal to wind up their affairs at once, and be off, for their lives were in grave danger. An armed force went to the home of Theodore Turley to shoot him; similar action was taken against other members of the committee, and a number of mobbers tried to kill Heber C. Kimball in the streets of Far West. The members of the Church had now departed; many went by way of Richmond and the Missouri River to Quincy. The members of the committee who still remained, were given one hour to get out of the place. Hurriedly gathering up such articles as they could take with them, they departed. The mobbers then commenced to loot the homes, which had not already been looted of all they contained.

Governor Boggs and his aides had gained a great victory; the Latter-day Saints had either been exterminated, or driven from the borders of Missouri, according to his order. Only those remained who were incarcerated, and the day for their deliverance was near at hand.

Fulfilment of Prophecy.—A revelation was given July 8, 1838, calling John Taylor, John E. Page, Wilford Woodruff and Willard

Richards to the apostleship. John Taylor and John E. Page were ordained under the hands of Brigham Young and Heber C. Kimball at a meeting held in Far West, December 19, 1838. In this revelation (Doc. and Cov., Sec. 118) the apostles were commanded to take their leave of the Saints from the temple lot in Far West on the 26th day of April, 1839. April had arrived and the Saints were scattered, likewise the members of the council of the apostles. On the 5th day of April, Samuel Bogart, the mobber, with John Whitmer and a few other apostates, came to the room occupied by the committee on removal and read this revelation to Theodore Turley. With much laughter and assurance that it could not be fulfilled, they called on him to renounce Joseph Smith, which now he must do as a rational man. The apostates said: "The twelve are now scattered all over creation; let them come here if they dare; if they do, they will be murdered. As that revelation cannot be fulfilled, you will now give up your faith." Turley jumped up and said: "In the name of God that revelation will be fulfilled." They laughed him to scorn. John Whitmer hung his head in shame. In the course of the conversation Turley asked John Whitmer if his testimony regarding the Book of Mormon was true, and Whitmer answered: "I now say, I handled those plates; there were fine engravings on both sides. I handled them;" and he then described how they were hung, and then he said, "They were shown to me by a supernatural power."

The 26th day of April arrived, and so also did the apostles at the temple lot in Far West. Early that morning, these brethren and a few of the Saints assembled at the temple lot, and proceeded to transact the business of their mission as they were commanded, according to the following minutes:

"At a conference held at Far West by the twelve, high priests, elders, and priests, on the 26th day of April, 1839, the following resolution was adopted:

"Resolved: That the following persons be no more fellowshiped in the Church of Jesus Christ of Latter-day Saints, but excommunicated from the same, viz.: Isaac Russell, Mary Russell, John Goodson and wife, Jacob Scott, Sen., and wife, Isaac Scott, Jacob Scott, Jun., Ann Scott, Sister Walton, Robert Walton, Sister Cavanaugh, Ann Wanless, William Dawson, Jun., William Dawson, Sen., and wife, George Nelson, Joseph Nelson, and wife, and mother, William Warnock and wife, Jonathan Maynard, Nelson Maynard, George Miller, John Griggs and wife, Luman Gibbs, Simeon Gardner, and Freeborn Gardner.[c]

[c]At a conference held in Quincy, Illinois, March 17, 1839, George M. Hinckle, Sampson Avard, John Corrill, Reed Peck, Frederick G. Williams, Thomas B. Marsh, Burr Riggs and several others were excommunicated from the Church.

"The council then proceeded to the building spot of the Lord's House; when the following business was transacted: Part of a hymn was sung, on the mission of the twelve.

"Elder Alpheus Cutler, the master workman of the house, then recommenced laying the foundation of the Lord's House; agreeably to the revelation, by rolling up a large stone near the southeast corner.

"The following of the twelve were present: Brigham Young, Heber C. Kimball, Orson Pratt, John E. Page, and John Taylor, who proceeded to ordain Wilford Woodruff and George A. Smith, who had been previously nominated by the First Presidency, accepted by the twelve, and acknowledged by the Church, to the office of apostles and members of the quorum of the twelve, to fill the places of those who had fallen. Darwin Chase and Norman Shearer, who had just been liberated from Richmond prison, where they had been confined for the cause of Jesus Christ, were then ordained to the office of the seventies."

After vocal prayer by each of the members of the council of the twelve, and singing, the apostles took their leave of the Saints there assembled, and departed for Illinois, and later for their mission to Great Britain. And thus closed the history of the Latter-day Saints in Missouri until some future day.

PART FOUR

The Nauvoo Period

CHAPTER 27

THE FOUNDING OF NAUVOO
1839–1840

Seeking a New Home.—In January, 1839, the threats of the mob, and their violence, became so severe that the Saints at Far West were forced to flee from Missouri. In November, 1838, those members of the Church residing at Adam-ondi-Ahman had been driven from their homes, and General Clark, in his abusive harangue at Far West, told the people they must not think of remaining another season. Should they attempt to put in crops he would extend no mercy, and extermination at his hands would be their doom.

The exodus was carried on as rapidly as circumstances would permit. Even in the inclement weather of the winter months the vanguard made their way eastward as far as Quincy, Illinois. Here they were met with a kindly welcome by the citizens of that place. Just where the Saints would locate was an indefinite problem, and the Prophet, still held in prison, could give them very little help. He advised them to locate in some friendly territory between Far West and Kirtland, where they might dwell in peace. It is likely that many of the refugees from Missouri, who started on their eastward journey expected to work their way back to the former settlements of the Saints in Ohio; but the hospitable treatment they received and the suggestions from the people of western Illinois, caused them to stop at Quincy. In fact, they could do little else in their stricken condition, and a kind word and a hand outstretched with relief were most welcome. In Quincy an organization known as the Democratic Association extended every kindness to the exiles, and proffered to help them in their distress. Several meetings of this society were held, in which other citizens of Quincy took a part, in February and March of 1839. Sympathy was expressed for the "Mormons" and steps were taken to allay the prejudice of the misguided residents of Quincy, who felt an opposition to the Saints. At one of these meetings the "Mormons" were invited to attend, and Sidney Rigdon and others related the persecutions in Missouri, which account fell on sympathetic ears. Through this organization material assistance was given the Saints, and employment for many was provided. The organization voiced its disapproval of the evil treatment accorded the exiles while in Missouri, in the following resolutions:

"Resolved, that we regard the rights of conscience as natural and inalienable, and the most sacred guaranteed by the Constitution of our free government.

"Resolved, that we regard the acts of all mobs as flagrant violations of law; and those who compose them, individually responsible, both to the laws of God and man, for every depredation committed upon the property, rights, or life of any citizen.

"Resolved, that the inhabitants upon the western frontier of the state of Missouri, in their late persecutions of the class of people denominated 'Mormons,' have violated the sacred rights of conscience, and every law of justice and humanity.

"Resolved, that the governor of Missouri, in refusing protection to this class of people, when pressed upon by a heartless mob, and turning upon them a band of unprincipled militia, with orders encouraging their extermination, has brought a lasting disgrace upon the state over which he presides."

The Saints also were kindly received by Governor Thomas Carlin and United States Senator Richard M. Young, and many other prominent citizens of western Illinois.

In a communication to the Quincy *Argus,* Elder John Taylor expressed the gratitude of the "Mormon" people, and said they felt under peculiar obligations to the citizens of Quincy; but he warned them against imposition on the part of any who may pretend to belong to the community of Latter-day Saints, but who were not— either those who never belonged to the Church, or those who, for cause, had been expelled.

While the sympathies of these good people were, without question, given in sincerity, nevertheless there was more or less selfishness connected with their action. It is quite evident, from events to follow, that they expected to obtain some political and business advantages, out of the kindness extended to these destitute and stricken refugees, who sought a haven of peace and rest within the borders of the state. The expulsion from Missouri occurred shortly before one of the most intense presidential elections, and a residence within the State of Illinois for six months gave the citizens a right to vote. The politicians on both sides lost no opportunity to seek the advantage which the "Mormon" vote would bring; and the "Mormons," too heavily engaged with thoughts of recent persecutions, and hopes of building communities where they could dwell in perfect peace, failed to comprehend the situation in which they were being placed. By siding with one faction, it was bound to alienate the other, and thus cause bitterness of feeling which might not be overcome. In course of time such proved to be the case.

Committee to Locate Lands.—While the Saints were gathering at Quincy, committees were appointed to seek out suitable places for permanent settlement. A meeting was held in February, 1839, to consider the proposition of purchasing about twenty thousand acres, at two dollars an acre, between the Des Moines and Missouri Rivers, on what were called half-breed lands. Other sites were also considered from time to time, but no definite action was taken until the arrival of Joseph Smith at Quincy, from his long confinement in Liberty prison. Elder Israel Barlow, on his flight from Missouri, made his way to the northeast and arrived in a destitute condition near the mouth of the Des Moines River. There he was kindly received and related the sad experiences of the Latter-day Saints. He made the acquaintance of Dr. Isaac Galland, who owned considerable property both in Iowa and Illinois, a short distance farther north. Mr. Galland resided at a place called Commerce, in Hancock County, Illinois, about fifty miles up the Mississippi from Quincy and lying on the bank of the river.

Commerce.—Mr. Galland in a communication to David W. Rogers, suggested that the Saints locate in Iowa, which was a territory; for he thought they would be more likely to receive protection from mobs under the jurisdiction of the United States, than they would be in a state of the Union, "where murder, rapine and robbery are admirable(!) traits in the character of a demagogue; and where the greatest villains often reach the highest offices." He also wrote to Governor Robert Lucas of Iowa, who had known the "Mormon" people in Ohio, and who spoke very highly of them as good citizens.

However, when the Prophet arrived at Quincy in April, he purchased from Hugh White a farm of one hundred and thirty-five acres, for the sum of five thousand dollars; also another farm from Dr. Isaac Galland lying west of the White purchase, for nine thousand dollars. This property, which was located in the vicinity of Commerce was secured on long time notes. To these farms the destitute Saints commenced to gather, also to the little town of Montrose on the Iowa side of the river.

Joseph Smith Moves to Commerce.—Friday, May 10, 1839, President Joseph Smith took up his residence in a small log house on the bank of the Mississippi, on the White purchase, one mile south of Commerce. The first house built by any of the Saints in that part was raised by Theodore Turley, in June, 1839. When the purchase was made of the White and Galland property, Commerce consisted of one stone house, three frame and two block houses, three of which were log cabins. Between Commerce and David Hibbard's place on the south front of the river there were four houses, three of which were log cabins, and into one of these the Prophet moved. The place was virtually a wilderness. The land was covered with trees and bushes, and much of it, in the lower parts near the river, was so wet that travel by team was impossible, and on foot, most difficult. Notwithstanding the unhealthful condition, the Prophet felt that by draining the land, and through the blessing of the Lord, the place could be made a pleasant habitation for the Saints, and he decided to build there. There was inspiration in this decision, for this was an excellent site for the building of a city, when the unfavorable conditions of the lowlands were removed. The Mississippi makes a half circle around the place, giving three fronts on the river. The ground gradually rises from the river front for a distance of about one mile to the common level of the prairie lands which extend beyond. A more beautiful site could not be imagined.

The City of Nauvoo.—The name "Commerce" was soon changed to the City of "Nauvoo." This word is of Hebrew origin, and "signifies a beautiful situation, or place," says the Prophet, "carrying with it, also, the idea of rest; and is truly descriptive of the most delightful location. It is situated on the east bank of the Mississippi River, at the head of the Des Moines Rapids, in Hancock County, bounded on the east by an extensive prairie of surpassing beauty, and on the north, west and south, by the Mississippi." Nauvoo is about one hundred and ninety miles up the river from St. Louis, and nearly the same distance from Chicago, towards the west.

City of Nauvoo

Other Sites Chosen.—Other lands were also purchased, for the gathering of the Saints, all on easy terms. Additional property adjoining that obtained from White and Galland was obtained from David Hibbard, Daniel H. Wells, Hiram Kimball, Horace R. Hotchkiss and others, which later became a portion of the city of Nauvoo. Across the river on the Iowa side, extensive holdings also were obtained. The village of Nashville, in Lee County, with twenty thousand acres adjoining, was purchased; also other lands opposite Nauvoo. Here the Prophet instructed the Saints that a city should be built, to be called Zarahemla. A number of members of the Church had located here when the Saints were driven from Missouri, and it appeared to be a suitable location for a permanent settlement of the people.

Stakes of Zion Organized.—At the general conference held at Commerce, October 5-7, 1839, two stakes of Zion were organized, one at Commerce, with William Marks as president, and one in Iowa, with John Smith as president. Later a number of other stakes were organized in Quincy, Lima, Columbus and Geneva, Illinois, but they did not continue very long.[a] The idea seemed to be that the Latter-day Saints should spread out over considerable territory and form organizations in various parts of the country, but this plan was abandoned,

---

[a]See table of stakes in appendix.

and the Saints scattered abroad were commanded by revelation in January, 1841, to gather to Hancock County, Illinois, and to Lee County, Iowa, and to build up the settlements in these parts occupied by the members of the Church. This was, the presidency wrote, "agreeable to the order of heaven." Consequently, the Saints began to immigrate to Nauvoo, and the city grew rapidly by such additions. About one year after the location of the site, Nauvoo had a population of over three thousand souls, and six years later, at the time of the great western exodus, about twenty thousand. The stake at Zarahemla was later discontinued, but John Smith remained there to preside over the Saints in Iowa.

Miraculous Healing of the Sick.—Due to the unhealthful condition of the place when the people first arrived at Commerce, many were taken sick with malaria fever, and were nigh unto death. Some of the refugees were sheltered only by tents and wagon covers, for there had been little time, and less means, by which houses, even of logs, could be built. On the morning of July 22, 1839, the Prophet arose from his own bed of sickness and being filled with the Spirit of the Lord, he went forth along the river bank healing all who were afflicted. Among the number were Henry G. Sherwood and Benjamin Brown, who appeared in a dying condition. He later crossed over the river to Montrose and healed Brigham Young and a number of other brethren of the twelve, and took them along with him to assist him in this ministry. What took place in Iowa is thus related by Elder Wilford Woodruff:

"After healing all the sick upon the bank of the river as far as the stone house, he called upon Elder Kimball and some others to accompany him across the river to visit the sick at Montrose. Many of the Saints were living at the old military barracks. Among the number were several of the twelve. On his arrival, the first house he visited was that occupied by Elder Brigham Young, the president of the quorum of the twelve, who lay sick. Joseph healed him, then he arose and accompanied the Prophet on his visit to others who were in the same condition. They visited Elder W. Woodruff, also Elders Orson Pratt and John Taylor, all of whom were living in Montrose. They also accompanied him. The next place they visited was the home of Elijah Fordham, who was supposed to be about breathing his last. When the company entered the room the Prophet of God walked up to the dying man, and took hold of his right hand and spoke to him; but Brother Fordham was unable to speak, his eyes were set in his head like glass, and he seemed entirely unconscious of all around him. Joseph held his hand and looked into his eyes in silence for a length of time. A change in the countenance of Brother Fordham was soon perceptible to all present. His sight returned, and upon Joseph asking him if he knew him, he, in a low whisper, answered, 'Yes.' Joseph asked him if he had faith to be healed. He answered, 'I fear it is too late; if you had come sooner I think I would have been healed.' The Prophet said, 'Do you believe in Jesus Christ?' He answered in a feeble voice, 'I do.' Joseph then stood erect, still holding his hand in silence several moments; then he spoke in a very loud voice, saying: 'Brother Fordham, I command you in the name of Jesus Christ to arise from this bed and be made whole.' His voice was like the voice of God, and not of man. It seemed as though the house shook to its very foundations. Brother Fordham arose from his bed and was immediately made whole. His feet were bound in poultices, which he kicked off, then putting on his clothes, he ate a bowl of bread and milk, and followed the Prophet into the street."

In this manner the Prophet and the brethren passed from house to house, healing the sick and recalling them from the mouth of the tomb. It was on this occasion that a man, not a member of the Church, seeing the mighty miracles which were performed, begged the Prophet to go with him and heal two of his children who were very sick. The Prophet could not go, but said he would send some one to heal them. Taking from his pocket a silk handkerchief he handed it to Elder Wilford Woodruff and requested him to go and heal the children. He told Elder Woodruff to wipe the faces of the children with the handkerchief, and they should be healed. This he did and they were healed. "As long as you keep that handkerchief," said Joseph to Brother Woodruff, as he sent him on his way, "it shall remain a league between you and me."

Incorporation of the City of Nauvoo.—Nauvoo was incorporated in December, 1840. On the 16th day of that month Governor Thomas Carlin signed the bill. Stephen A. Douglas was secretary of state; and Abraham Lincoln, a member of the legislature, had favored the bill. The boundaries of the city were defined, with ample provision for expansion. The city council was to consist of a mayor, four aldermen and nine councilors. The election was to take place on the first Monday in February, 1841.

A Liberal Charter.—The charter of the city was one of most liberal powers. It was all—yes, even more—than the Saints, so long harassed by mobs, had hoped to receive. It contained twenty-eight sections and was bounded in its limitations only by the Constitution of the United States and that of the state of Illinois. All the powers "conferred on the city council of the city of Springfield" were granted to the city of Nauvoo. The Mayor and Aldermen were given all the powers of justices of the peace, both in civil and criminal cases, arising under the laws of the state. A municipal court was provided composed of the mayor as chief justice, and the aldermen as associates. This court had power to grant writs of habeas corpus under all cases arising under the ordinances of the city council, and trial by jury was guaranteed before twelve men.

The University of Nauvoo.—The city council was authorized to establish and organize the "University of the City of Nauvoo," for "the teaching of the arts, sciences and learned professions." This institution was to be under the management of a board of trustees, consisting of a chancellor, registrar and twenty-three regents. These trustees were to be appointed by the city council, and they were empowered with all the "privileges for the advancement of the cause of education which appertain to the trustees of any other college or university of this state."

The Nauvoo Legion.—Another provision granted the city council the power to "organize the inhabitants of said city, subject to military duty, into a body of independent military men, to be called the 'Nauvoo Legion,' the court martial of which shall be composed of the commissioned officers of said legion, and constitute the lawmaking department, with full power and authority to make, ordain, establish, and execute all such laws and ordinances as may be considered necessary for the benefit, government, and regulation of said legion; provided said court-martial shall pass no law or act, repugnant to, or inconsistent with the Constitution of the United States, or of this State; and provided also that the officers of the legion shall be commissioned by the Governor of the State." This legion was to perform the same amount of military duty as other bodies of the regular militia, and to be subject to the call of the mayor in executing the laws and ordinances of the city, and the governor for public defense.

Election of Municipal Officers.—On the day appointed the election was held and John C. Bennett, who had taken a most active part in the securing of the charter, was elected mayor. The aldermen were William Marks, president of the stake, Samuel H. Smith, Newel K. Whitney and Daniel H. Wells, the latter at that time, not a member of the Church. The councilors were Joseph Smith, Hyrum Smith, Sidney Rigdon, Charles C. Rich, John T. Barnett, Wilson Law, John P. Greene, Don Carlos Smith, and Vinson Knight. The council appointed Henry G. Sherwood, marshal; James Sloan, recorder; Robert B. Thompson, treasurer; James Robinson, assessor; and Austin Cowles, supervisor of streets. When the Nauvoo Legion was organized, Joseph Smith was elected lieutenant general, which position he held until his death.

Character of the Mayor.—John C. Bennett, the first mayor of Nauvoo, came to that place near the close of the year 1840. He was born in Massachusetts in 1804; practiced medicine in Ohio and later in Illinois. He first heard of the Latter-day Saints during their persecutions in Missouri, and in the summer of 1840 corresponded with the Prophet, expressing great sympathy for the Saints, and disapproval of the evil treatment they had received. At the time of his writing he was quartermaster-general of the state of Illinois, and had previously served as "brigadier general of the Invincible Dragoons," in the state militia. After coming to Nauvoo he joined the Church and was the most active agent in securing the city charter. He was a man of some ability, with many human weaknesses, and was bombastic and self-important. We must give him credit for sincerity of purpose in joining the Church although, without question, he was seeking worldly fame; but through later immoral conduct he became most bitter in his feelings, and an arch-traitor to the cause. His inaugural address, delivered February 3, 1841, contains many worthy sentiments, but expressed in a spirit of pedantry which spoiled much of the good effect.

Freedom for All.—The first act passed by the city council of Nauvoo, was a resolution presented by Joseph Smith thanking the governor, the council of revision and the legislature of the state of Illinois, "for their unparalleled liberality" for the powers which the charter conferred. Later, but among the first ordinances introduced, was one assuring protection to Catholics, Presbyterians, Methodists, Baptists, Latter-day Saints, and all other religious organizations. As the ordinance read, they were to have, "free toleration and equal privileges in this city, and should any person be guilty of ridiculing and abusing, or otherwise deprecating another, in consequence of his religion, or of disturbing or interrupting any religious meeting within the limits of this city, he shall, on conviction before the mayor or municipal court, be considered a disturber of the public peace, and fined in any sum not to exceed five hundred dollars, or imprisonment not exceeding six months." In various other ways were the liberties and personal rights of the citizens safeguarded against the acts of rowdies, mobbers, and disturbers of the peace.

CHAPTER 28

FOREIGN MISSIONARY LABORS

1839–1841

The Foreign Mission of the Twelve.—On the 26th day of April, 1839, a majority of the apostles took their leave of the Saints at Far West—then a hostile land—to go forth and declare the everlasting Gospel "over the great waters" as they had been commanded. The families of these brave men had been recently and ruthlessly banished from their homes, and were on their journey seeking shelter and a friendly habitation. It required the greatest courage and the highest quality of faith for men to go forth across the ocean to a foreign country to preach the Gospel without purse or scrip, leaving their families in poverty, homeless, destitute, and ill. Yet this was the test to which these brethren were put at this time. They did not fail, but manfully and nobly took up their cross and started on their missions. Other brethren, of the seventies, just as faithful, accompanied them on their journey to the foreign field.

No sooner was the main body of the Saints located in Iowa and Illinois, out of the reach of mobs, than most of the members of the council of the twelve started on their way to the British Isles. On the 2nd day of July, 1839, the presidency met with the apostles, and some others who were to accompany them, and gave them instructions pertaining to their labors. On this occasion many important items on doctrine, the Priesthood, and the deportment of missionaries in the field were discussed. In the course of his instructions President Joseph Smith taught them to beware of self-sufficiency, and to observe charity and wisdom and to exercise the principle of mercy; for if we forgive our brother, or even an enemy, before he repent or ask forgiveness, our heavenly Father will be equally merciful unto us. He further instructed them that they were not sent out to be taught, but to teach, and to be honest, open and frank in all intercourse with mankind. He closed his instructions with the following words:

"I will give you one of the keys of the mysteries of the kingdom. It is an eternal principle, that has existed with God from all eternity: That man who rises up to condemn others, finding fault with the Church, saying they are out of the way, while he himself is righteous, then know assuredly, that that man is in the high road to apostasy and if he does not repent he will apostatize, as God lives. The principle is as correct as the one that Jesus put forth in saying that he who seeketh a sign is an adulterous person; and that principle is eternal, undeviating, and firm as the pillars of heaven; for whenever you see a man seeking after a sign, you may set it down that he is an adulterous man."

Items on Priesthood.—About this time he also instructed the brethren on various matters of Priesthood, from which the following excerpts are taken:

"The Priesthood was first given to Adam; he obtained the First Presidency, and held the keys of it from generation to generation. He obtained it in the creation, before the world was formed. * * * He is Michael, the Archangel, spoken of in the scriptures. Then to Noah, who is Gabriel, he stands next in authority to Adam in the Priesthood, he was called of God to this office, and was the father of all living in his day, and to him was given the dominion. These men held keys first on earth, and then in heaven.

"The Priesthood is an everlasting principle, and existed with God from eternity, and will to eternity, without beginning of days or end of years. The keys have to be brought from heaven whenever the Gospel is sent. When they are revealed from heaven, it is by Adam's authority.

"Daniel in his seventh chapter speaks of the Ancient of Days; he means the oldest man, our father, Adam, Michael; he will call his children together and hold a council with them to prepare them for the coming of the Son of Man. He (Adam) is the father of the human family, and presides over the spirits of all men and all that have had the keys must stand before him in this grand council. This may take place before some of us leave this stage of action. The Son of Man stands before him, and there is given him glory and dominion. Adam delivers up his stewardship to Christ, that which was delivered to him as holding the keys of the universe, but retains his standing as head of the human family. * * *

"The keys were first given to him and by him to others. He will have to give an account of his stewardship, and they to him.

"The Priesthood is everlasting. The Savior, Moses, and Elias, gave the keys to Peter, James and John, on the mount, when they were transfigured before him. * * *

"Christ is the Great High Priest, Adam next."[a]

Epistle of the Twelve.—After receiving their charge from the First Presidency, before their departure for their fields of labor, the members of the council of the twelve wrote an epistle to the elders of the Church, the churches scattered abroad, and all the Saints, giving them instruction and encouragement in their afflictions. To the Saints they said:

"We wish to stimulate all the brethren to faithfulness; you have been tried, you are now being tried; and those trials, if you are not watchful, will corrode the minds, and produce unpleasant feelings; but recollect that now is the time of trial; soon the victory will be ours. Now may be a day of lamentation—then will be a day of rejoicing. Now may be a day of sorrow—but by and by we shall see the Lord; our sorrow will be turned into joy, and our joy no man taketh from us."

To the elders they said:

"God has called you to an important office. He has laid upon you an onerous duty. He has called you to an holy calling, even to be the priests of the Most High God, messengers to the nations of the earth; and upon your diligence, your perseverance and faithfulness, the soundness of the doctrines which you preach, the moral precepts that you advance and practice, and upon the sound principles that you inculcate, while you hold that Priesthood, hang the destinies of the human family. You are the men that God has called to spread forth his kingdom. He has committed the care of souls to your charge, and when you received this Priesthood, you become the legates of heaven; and the Great God demands it of you, that you should be faithful; and inasmuch as you are not, you will not be chosen; but it will be said unto you, 'Stand by and let a more honorable man than thou art take thy place and receive thy crown.' "

The Missionaries Depart.—At a meeting held in Commerce, Sunday, July 7, 1839, Elders Brigham Young, John Taylor, John E. Page, Wilford Woodruff and Orson Hyde, made their farewell remarks before their departure on their foreign mission. The following day Elders Taylor and Woodruff took up their journey toward their field of labor. Sunday, July 28, Elder Parley P. Pratt, who had arrived

---

[a]Documentary History of the Church, Vol. 3:385-8.

in Commerce on the 10th from his long confinement in Missouri prisons, made his farewell talk; so also did his brother Orson, who had assisted Parley in his escape. August 29, Elders Parley P. Pratt, Orson Pratt and Hiram Clark left Commerce on their missionary journey and they were followed September 18, by President Brigham Young and Elder Heber C. Kimball. Elders George A. Smith, Reuben Hedlock and Theodore Turley, left three days later. William Smith, of the council of the twelve, failed to go. Willard Richards, not yet ordained an apostle, was in England where he had remained since the opening of the mission. Elders Orson Hyde and John E. Page were shortly afterwards set apart for a mission to Palestine to dedicate the land for the return of the Jews, and there was one vacancy in the council caused by the death of David W. Patten, which was not filled until April, 1841, when Lyman Wight was chosen.

Circumstances under which these brethren departed were extremely distressing, as may be well imagined. Elder Heber C. Kimball thus reports the departure of President Brigham Young and himself on their missionary journey:

"September 14, President Brigham Young left his home at Montrose to start on the mission to England. He was so sick that he was unable to go to the Mississippi, a distance of thirty rods, without assistance. After he had crossed the river he rode behind Israel Barlow on his horse to my house, where he continued sick until the 18th. He left his wife sick with a babe only three weeks old, and all his other children were sick and unable to wait upon each other. Not one soul of them was able to go to the well for a pail of water, and they were without a second suit to their backs, for the mob in Missouri had taken nearly all he had. On the 17th Sister Mary Ann Young got a boy to carry her up in his wagon to my house, that she might nurse and comfort Brother Brigham to the hour of starting.

"September 18, Charles Hubbard sent his boy with a wagon and a span of horses to my house; our trunks were put into the wagon by some brethren; I went to my bed and shook hands with my wife who was then shaking with a chill, having two children lying sick by her side; I embraced her and my children, and bade them farewell. My only well child was little Heber P., and it was with difficulty he could carry a couple of quarts of water at a time, to assist in quenching their thirst.

"It was with difficulty we got into the wagon, and started down the hill about ten rods; it appeared to me as though my very inmost parts would melt within me at leaving my family in such a condition, as it were almost in the arms of death. I felt as though I could not endure it. I asked the teamster to stop, and said to Brother Brigham, 'This is pretty tough, isn't it; let's rise up and give them a cheer.'

We arose, and swinging our hats three times over our heads, shouted: 'Hurrah, Hurrah for Israel.' Vilate, hearing the noise, arose from her bed and came to the door. She had a smile on her face. Vilate and Mary Ann Young cried out to us: 'Good-by, God bless you.' We returned the compliment, and then told the driver to go ahead. After this I felt a spirit of joy and gratitude, having had the satisfaction of seeing my wife standing upon her feet, instead of leaving her in bed, knowing well that I should not see them again for two or three years" (*Life of Heber C. Kimball*, p. 275).

The conditions of some of the other brethren were little better. Elders George A. Smith and companions upset their wagons in the soft ground before they got out of sight of the village of Commerce, and Elders Smith and Turley were so weak they could not get up and Brother Hedlock had to lift them into the wagon again. Soon after, as they were on their way, some gentlemen passing them asked who had been robbing the burying ground; so miserable did they appear.[b] After passing through many hardships, traveling without purse or scrip, the Lord coming to their assistance many times in a miraculous way, these brethren finally reached their destination. Elders John Taylor, Wilford Woodruff and Theodore Turley arrived in Liverpool, January 11, 1840, and were followed by President

---

[b]Another incident worthy to relate is the following statement by Elder Wilford Woodruff:

"Inasmuch as the devil had been thwarted in a measure by the twelve going to Far West and returning without harm, it seemed as though the destroyer was determined to make some other attempt upon us to hinder us from performing our missions; for as soon as any one of the apostles began to prepare for starting he was smitten with chills and fever, or sickness of some kind. * * *

"On the 25th of July, I was attacked with chills and fever, for the first time in my life; this I had every other day, and whenever attacked I was laid prostrate. My wife, Phoebe, was also taken down with the chills and fever, as were quite a number of the twelve. * * *

"Although feeble, I walked to the banks of the Mississippi River; there President Young took me in a canoe and paddled me across the river. When we landed, I lay down on a side of sole leather, by the postoffice, to rest. Brother Joseph, the Prophet of God, came along and looked at me. 'Well, Brother Woodruff,' said he, 'you have started upon your mission.' 'Yes,' said I, 'but I feel and look more like a subject for the dissecting room than a missionary.' Joseph replied: 'What did you say that for? Get up, and go along; all will be right with you. * * *'

"Soon a brother came along with a wagon, and took us (Elders Taylor and Woodruff) in. As we were driving through the place, we came to Parley P. Pratt, who was stripped to his shirt and pants, with his head and feet bare. He was hewing a log, preparatory to building a cabin. He said: 'Brother Woodruff, I have no money, but I have an empty purse, which I will give you.' He brought it to me, and I thanked him for it. We went a few rods and met Brother Heber C. Kimball, in the same condition, also hewing a log to build a cabin. He said: 'As Parley has given you a purse, I have got a dollar I will give you to put in it. He gave me both a dollar and a blessing" ("Wilford Woodruff—His Life and Labors" p. 108).

Brigham Young, Heber C. Kimball, Parley P. Pratt, Orson Pratt, George A. Smith and Reuben Hedlock, who arrived April 6, after a stormy passage of twenty-eight days. At the time of sailing, President Young and Elder Kimball were still in poor health, and Elder George A. Smith was suffering extremely with ague. It was impossible for the brethren journeying on this mission to go together in a body, and inadvisable. Due to sickness they were detained many days, yet they pursued their course as rapidly as circumstances would permit. As President Young and party left the New York harbor, the shore resounded by the voices of the assembled Saints who had come to bid them farewell on their journey. They unitedly sang: "The Gallant Ship is under Weigh," composed by Elder William W. Phelps.

Ordination of Willard Richards.—The first council meeting of the apostles on foreign soil was held in Preston, England, April 14, 1840, at the house of Elder Willard Richards, who on this occasion was ordained to the apostleship by President Brigham Young, and under the hands of all the brethren of the council who were present. Other business was transacted and the brethren assigned to fields of labor. On this occasion Brigham Young was also unanimously sustained by the brethren of the twelve as the president of that council. There were present: President Brigham Young, Heber C. Kimball, Parley P. Pratt, Orson Pratt, John Taylor, Wilford Woodruff, George A. Smith and Willard Richards.

The Millennial Star.—A general conference of all the Saints in the British Isles was held in Preston the following day, April 15, 1840, at which there were present, or represented, the following: elders, 36; priests, 45; teachers, 36; deacons, 11; members, 1686; all contained in 34 branches, which had been raised up since the opening of that mission by Elder Kimball and companions in 1837. At this conference it was decided to publish a hymn book, and a monthly periodical under the direction and superintendency of the twelve, for the benefit and information of the members of the Church. The next day, in a council meeting of the apostles, Parley P. Pratt was chosen to edit the monthly periodical which was to be called *The Latter-day Saints Millennial Star*, which soon made its appearance and has been issued continuously ever since. The committee selected to prepare for printing a book of hymns was Brigham Young, Parley P. Pratt and John Taylor.

British Copyright of the Book of Mormon.—It was also decided, agreeable to the counsel of the First Presidency previously obtained, that copyright of the Book of Mormon and of the Doctrine and Covenants be secured in England; and that editions of these books

FOREIGN MISSIONARY LABORS 233

be printed. The first number of the *Millennial Star* was issued in Manchester, in pamphlet form of twenty-four pages, Wednesday, May 27, 1840. Later the place of publication was transferred to Liverpool, which became the headquarters for most of the publications of the Church, until comparatively recent years.

The First Patriarch in England.—Under the labors of the twelve and their missionary companions, branches of the Church had sprung up in various parts of England, and the population of the Church was now growing rapidly. At another council meeting of the twelve, held April 16, 1840, it was decided that a patriarch be ordained, and the honor fell to the lot of Elder Peter Melling, a most worthy man, who was ordained in Preston the following day. Early in 1841, John Albiston was also ordained to this sacred calling.

Individual Labors of the Twelve.—Elders John Taylor, Wilford Woodruff and Theodore Turley, the first of the missionaries to arrive in England, met in a special council Friday, January 17, 1840, with Joseph Fielding and Willard Richards of the presidency of the British Mission, and decided on their fields of labor. It was agreed that Elders Taylor and Fielding should go to Liverpool; Elder Hiram Clark, to Manchester, with Elder William Clayton; and Brother Richards to labor where the Spirit should direct. In Liverpool Elders Taylor and Fielding raised up a branch of about thirty members before the arrival from America of the other brethren of the twelve. This number rapidly increased and at the beginning of the year 1841, numbered more than two hundred souls. In March, 1842, the headquarters of the mission were transferred to Liverpool.

In Herefordshire.—In the Potteries of Staffordshire, Elders Woodruff and Turley found a fruitful field. Elder Woodruff labored in Burslem, Hanley, Stoke, Lane End and the Potteries from the 22nd of January, 1840, to the 2nd of March, preaching every night in the week, and two or three times on the Sabbath day, and the people flocked to hear his words and many were baptized. While preaching on the Sabbath, March 1, which was the anniversary of his birth, the Lord manifested to him that he was to leave that part of the country and go to the south. Acting on the impression from the Spirit, he left on the 3rd of March and continued his journey to the farming communities of Herefordshire and stopped at the home of Mr. John Benbow, at Castle Frome, Ledbury. Mr. Benbow was a wealthy farmer, cultivating some three hundred acres of land. Elder Woodruff presented himself to this gentleman as a missionary from America and an elder of The Church of Jesus Christ of Latter-day Saints, who had been sent to preach the Gospel to him and his household and all the inhabitants of the land. Mr. Benbow rejoiced in the statements of Elder Woodruff, and informed him that there were in that place six hundred persons and more, who had broken off from the Methodists and had taken the name of "United Brethren." They had forty-five preachers and a number of meeting houses that were duly licensed according to the law of the land. They were searching for light and truth. Losing no time, on the morning of the 5th, Brother Woodruff stated he would like to begin his labors by preaching to the people. There was a large hall in the mansion of Mr. Benbow, which was available for that purpose, and the people were invited to come and hear the new message, from the new world across the sea. The people of the neighborhood deserted their ministers and came to hear this strange preacher, who, in the course of a short time, baptized over six hundred persons in that place. At the meeting held on March 8, a constable, sent through complaint of the parish rector, came to arrest him for "preaching to the people." Elder Woodruff said he had a license to preach as well as the rector, and if the constable would take a chair and sit beside him until the close of the meeting he would be at his service. He then launched forth on a discourse treating the first principles of the Gospel, and at the close of the meeting opened the door for baptism, and several came forward to be baptized; among the number were four preachers and the constable, who said, "Mr. Woodruff, I would like to be baptized." The constable went to the rector and told him that if he wanted Mr. Woodruff arrested, he must go himself and serve the writ, for he had heard him preach the only true Gospel sermon he had ever heard. The rector then sent two clerks of the Church of England as spies, and they were both baptized. The ministers and rectors of the Church of England then sent a petition to the Archbishop of Canterbury, to request Parliament to pass a law prohibiting the "Mormons" from preaching in the British nation, stating that they had baptized fifteen hundred persons, many of whom were members of the Church of England. But the Archbishop, knowing well that the laws of England permitted religious freedom, replied that the petitioners, if they had the worth of souls at heart as much as they valued ground where hares, foxes and hounds ran, they would not lose so many of their flock.

The other brethren also met with remarkable success. The field was ripe, ready for the harvest, and thousands of the House of Israel were soon gathered into the fold. At a conference of the Church in the British Isles held in October, 1840, there was reported a Church membership of about 4,000 souls, and in the meantime a number had emigrated to the United States.

The First Emigration to the United States.—In June, 1840, a company of forty Saints sailed in the ship *Britannia* from Liverpool for New York, being the first Saints to leave England for Zion.

The Mission to Palestine.—At the general conference of the Church held in Nauvoo, Hancock County, April 6-8, 1840, Elder Orson Hyde, who had not departed for England with the other apostles, was appointed to take a mission to Palestine to dedicate there the land for the gathering of the Jews. Elder John E. Page, who had also tarried at home, was called to accompany him. While addressing the congregation on the 6th, Elder Hyde remarked that it had been prophesied, some years before, that he had a great work to perform among the Jews; and that he had recently been moved by the Spirit of the Lord to visit that people, and gather all the information he could find respecting their movements, hopes and aspirations, and communicate them to the Church. He expressed the desire to visit the Jews in New York, London and Amsterdam, on his way to the field of his appointment. It was moved and carried that he proceed at once on his mission and that Elder John E. Page be given proper credentials and accompany him. On the 15th of April, Elder Hyde left Nauvoo for Jerusalem. Working his way across the country to New York, he sailed, after some delays, for Liverpool, on his way to Palestine, Saturday, February 13, 1841. He traveled alone, as Elder John E. Page had failed to make the journey.

Other Missionary Appointments.—Other missionary appointments to foreign fields were made in these early days. In July, 1840, William Barrett, a boy seventeen years of age, was ordained an elder by Elders George A. Smith and Alfred Cordon, in Hanley, Staffordshire, England, and set apart to take a mission to Australia, to be the first missionary to that country. In August, following, Elder William Donaldson, of the British army, having been assigned to the field in India, was also blessed and set apart to labor for the Church in that land. The following year, at the conference of the Church, Elder Harrison Sagers was called to go to Jamaica; Elder Joseph Ball, to South America; Elder Simeon Carter to Germany; and Elder Arza Adams to Canada, where the Gospel had previously been preached.

The Return of the Apostles.—On the 20th day of April, 1841, President Brigham Young and Elders Heber C. Kimball, Orson Pratt, John Taylor, Wilford Woodruff, George A. Smith, and Willard Richards, with a company of Saints left Liverpool on the ship *Rochester*, for New York. Parley P. Pratt continued in England to edit the *Millennial Star* and preside over the mission. After a period of one month upon the water they arrived safely in New York, and continuing their journey arrived in Nauvoo, July 1, 1841. Some eighteen or twenty months before, these brethren had left Nauvoo, poverty-stricken, afflicted and sorrowful of heart. Now they returned rejoicing and with gladness of heart, bearing the fruit of their labors. They started on their way without money, and returned with none. Yet, during their labors abroad, they had published an edition of five thousand copies of the Book of Mormon; and an edition of three thousand copies of the Hymn Book; over fifty thousand tracts and pamphlets; had established a permanent magazine, the *Millennial Star*, organized an emigration agency for the gathering of the Saints to Zion, and had been instrumental in the hands of the Lord in bringing thousands of the children of the House of Israel to a knowledge of the everlasting Gospel. Truly it was a marvelous work, worthy of all commendation.

The Prophet's Comments.—Commenting on the labors of these members of the council of the apostles, the Prophet said:

"All the quorum of the Twelve Apostles who were expected here this season, with the exception of Elders Willard Richards and Wilford Woodruff, have arrived. We have listened to the accounts which they give of their success, and the prosperity of the work of the Lord in Great Britain with pleasure. They certainly have been the instruments in the hands of God of accomplishing much, and must have the satisfaction of knowing that they have done their duty. Perhaps no men ever undertook such an important mission under such peculiarly distressing and unpropitious circumstances. Most of them when they left this place, nearly two years ago, were worn down with sickness and disease, or were taken sick on the road. Several of their families were also afflicted and needed their aid and support. But, knowing that they had been called by the God of Heaven to preach the Gospel to other nations, they conferred not with flesh and blood, but obedient to the heavenly mandate, without purse or scrip, they commenced a journey of five thousand miles entirely dependent on the providence of that God who had called them to such a holy calling. While journeying to the seaboard they were brought into many trying circumstances; after a short recovery from severe sickness, they would be taken with a relapse, and have to stop among strangers, without money and without friends. Their lives were several times despaired of, and they have taken each other by the hand, expecting it would be the last time they should behold one another in the flesh. However, notwithstanding their afflictions and trials, the Lord always interposed in their behalf, and did not suffer them to sink in the arms of death. Some way or other was made for their escape—friends rose up when they most needed them and relieved their necessities; and thus they were enabled to pursue their journey and rejoice in the Holy One of Israel. They truly 'went forth weeping, bearing precious seed,' but have returned with rejoicing, bearing their sheaves with them" (*Documentary History of the Church,* Vol. 4:390).

CHAPTER 29

APPEAL TO WASHINGTON FOR REDRESS—
FURTHER MISSOURI PERSECUTIONS

1839—1840

Importuning for Redress.—Having appealed in vain to the courts, the governor and the legislature of Missouri, the Saints now determined to "importune for redress and redemption at the feet of the President." This course the Lord commanded them to take. It was his will that the national government should have the privilege of correcting the wrongs of the Latter-day Saints, or share in the responsibility of their persecutions, should they also turn a deaf ear to the appeal of thousands of citizens, who had been banished from their homes.[a] The Constitution guarantees that "the citizens of each state shall be entitled to all the privileges and immunities of citizens of the several states." This great privilege had been denied the Latter-day Saints by the officers of the state of Missouri.

President Sidney Rigdon arrived in Quincy, Illinois, after his release from prison, in March, 1839, and was at that time very zealous for the punishment of Missouri for the violation of the constitutional rights of the Saints while in that state. He devised a plan, on an elaborate scale, for the impeachment of Missouri before the other states and the general government. He proposed to have the governors of the several states present before their legislative bodies the matter of Missouri's abdication of republican government, and at the same time have presented to the President of the United States and

---

[a]Doc. and Cov. 101:76-89.

Congress a petition for redress of the wrongs inflicted upon the Saints. Governor Carlin of Illinois encouraged him in this desire and promised to aid in the work. Governor Robert Lucas of Iowa also lent some assistance to the plan. The latter issued letters of introduction to President Martin Van Buren and Governor Shannon of Ohio, conveying the information that President Rigdon expected to visit Washington as the representative of the "Mormon" people to seek an investigation into the causes for the expulsion of the Saints from Missouri. However, nothing came of this rather impractical plan.

The Prophet's Appeal to the People.—About this same time (April, 1839) the Prophet made an appeal to the citizens of the United States in the following language:

"I ask the citizens of this Republic whether such a state of things is to be suffered to pass unnoticed, and the hearts of widows, orphans, and patriots to be broken, and their wrongs left without redress? No! I invoke the genius of our Constitution. I appeal to the patriotism of Americans to stop this unlawful and unholy procedure; and pray that God may defend this nation from the dreadful effects of such outrages.

"Is there no virtue in the body politic? Will not the people rise up in their majesty, and with that promptitude and zeal which are so characteristic of them, discountenance such proceedings, by bringing the offenders to that punishment which they so richly deserve, and save the nation from that disgrace and ultimate ruin, which otherwise must inevitably fall upon it?"[b]

A Delegation Appointed to Visit Washington.—At a conference of the Church held in Quincy in May, 1839, President Rigdon was formally appointed to carry the message of grievances to Washington, and Elder Lyman Wight was appointed to collect the necessary affidavits from those injured, to be presented at Washington. President Rigdon made no great effort to get away on this mission, and as time passed his ardor cooled and his desire to fill his appointment lessened. At the October Conference, held at Commerce, President Joseph Smith, who had arrived in Illinois during the summer, and Judge Elias Higbee were also chosen to go to Washington as well as Sidney Rigdon, to importune for redress. On the 29th of October, these three delegates left Commerce in a carriage driven by Orrin Porter Rockwell, with the intention of laying before Congress the grievances of the Saints while in Missouri. At Quincy they were joined by Dr. Robert D. Foster who accompanied them on their

---

[b]Documentary History of the Church. Vol. 3, p. 332.

way to administer to Sidney Rigdon, who was ill. At Springfield Judge James Adams took the Prophet to his home and treated him with every consideration as though he had been his own son. After an eventful journey the Prophet and Judge Higbee arrived in Washington, November 28, 1839. They did considerable preaching on the way and were forced to leave Sidney Rigdon in Ohio because of his sickness; Orrin P. Rockwell and Dr. Robert D. Foster remained with him.

Interview with the President.—The first step taken by the Prophet and Judge Higbee after securing a boarding place was to call on the President of the United States, Martin Van Buren. This was the following day, November 29. They proceeded to the house of the President, which they state they found to be a very large and splendid palace, decorated with all the fineries and elegance of this world. After some preliminary arrangements they were ushered into the presence of Mr. Van Buren. They handed him some of their letters of introduction which stated the object of their visit and as soon as the President read one of them, he looked up with a frown and said: "What can I do? I can do nothing for you! If I do anything, I shall come in contact with the whole state of Missouri." The delegates were not to be denied a hearing without some effort, so they pressed the matter of their case with considerable vigor. The result was that President Van Buren promised to reconsider what he had said, and expressed deep sympathy with the Saints on account of their suffering.

The Petition before Congress.—Following the interview with the President the brethren spent some time hunting up senators and representatives with whom they might converse and receive a hearing. They found the delegation from Illinois friendly, and were able to make a number of friends among the honorable gentlemen in Washington. A meeting was held with the congressional delegation from Illinois, for the purpose of considering the best means for getting their business before Congress. Mr. Robinson, of the delegation, offered some opposition against the Saints presenting any claims against Missouri to be liquidated by the United States, on the ground that the Saints should make their appeal to the judiciary of Missouri and the state officials, where the wrongs were committed. The Prophet opposed such a stand with great vigor, explaining that every effort had already been made to get the governor of Missouri and the courts to consider their claims, but without result. Mr. Robinson then said this was his first impression of the matter, but he would take it under consideration. The following day another meeting was held and it was decided that a petition should be drawn up to be presented to Congress, and Senator Richard M. Young, of Illinois, promised to present it in the United States Senate. They were advised that all facts presented should be authenticated by affidavits, so word was sent to the Saints in Illinois to prepare immediately such necessary information as would be required.*c* The petition was duly presented to the judiciary committee. It covered the outrages against the members of the Church from the expulsion from Jackson County, in 1833, to the banishment from the state in 1838-39. The dastardly course of Governor Boggs in aiding the enemies of the Saints and his exterminating order received proper consideration. The concluding paragraphs of this petition are as follows:

"For these wrongs, the 'Mormons' ought to have some redress: yet how and where shall they seek and obtain it? Your constitution guarantees to every citizen, even the humblest, the enjoyment of life, liberty, and property. It promises to all, religious freedom, the right to all to worship God beneath their own vine and fig tree, according to the dictates of their conscience. It guarantees to all the citizens of the several states the right to become citizens of any one of the states, and to enjoy all the rights and immunities of the citizens of the state of his adoption. Yet of all these rights have the 'Mormons' been deprived. They have, without a cause, without a trial, been deprived of life, liberty and property. They have been persecuted for their religious opinions. They have been driven from the state of Missouri, at the point of the bayonet, and prevented from enjoying and exercising the rights of citizens of the state of Missouri. It is the theory of our laws, that for the protection of every legal right, there is provided a legal remedy. What then, we would respectfully ask, is the remedy of the 'Mormons?' Shall they apply to the legislature of the state of Missouri for redress? They have done so. They have petitioned, and these petitions have been treated with silence and contempt. Shall they apply to the federal courts? They were, at the time of the injury, citizens of the state of Missouri. Shall they apply to the court of the state of Missouri? Whom shall they sue? The order for their destruction, then extermination, was granted by the executive of the state of Missouri. Is not this a plea of justification for the loss of individuals, done in pursuance of that order? If not, before whom shall the 'Mormons' institute a trial? Shall they summon a jury of the individuals who composed the mob? An appeal to them

*c*The Saints' petition to Congress is found on pages 24-38 of the Documentary History of the Church, Vol. 4. The affidavits are also found in the same volume pages 52-73. These should be carefully considered.

were in vain. They dare not go to Missouri to institute a suit; their lives would be in danger.

"For ourselves we see no redress, unless it is awarded by the Congress of the United States. And here we make our appeal as *American Citizens,* as *Christians,* and as *Men*—believing that the high sense of justice which exists in your honorable body, will not allow such oppression to be practiced upon any portion of the citizens of this vast republic with impunity; but that some measures which your wisdom may dictate, may be taken, so that the great body of people who have been thus abused, may have redress for the wrongs which they have suffered. And to your decision they look with confidence; hoping it may be such as shall tend to dry up the tears of the widow and orphan, and again place in situations of peace, those who have been driven from their homes, and have had to wade through scenes of sorrow and distress.

"And your Memorialists, as in duty bound, will ever pray."

The Prophet's Interview with President Van Buren.—While the Prophet was waiting for the action of Congress, he visited several branches of the Church in Pennsylvania, New Jersey and other parts, returning to Washington the fore part of February. During this time he had another interview with President Martin Van Buren and one with John C. Calhoun, and he records the following in his journal:

"During my stay I had an interview with Martin Van Buren, the President, who treated me very insolently, and it was with great reluctance he listened to our message, which, when he had heard, he said: 'Gentlemen, your cause is just, but I can do nothing for you;' and 'If I take up for you I shall lose the vote of Missouri.' His whole course went to show that he was an office-seeker, that self-aggrandizement was his ruling passion, and that justice and righteousness were no part of his composition. I found him such a man as I could not conscientiously support at the head of our noble Republic. I also had an interview with Mr. John C. Calhoun, whose conduct towards me very ill became his station. I became satisfied there was little use for me to tarry, to press the just claims of the Saints on the consideration of the President and Congress, and stayed but a few days, taking passage in company with Porter Rockwell and Dr. Foster on the railroad and stages back to Dayton, Ohio" (*Documentary History of the Church,* Vol. 4:80).

The Action of Congress.—Judge Elias Higbee remained in Washington during the time the petition was before Congress. He met on several occasions with the judiciary committee, which had the matter in hand. The members from Missouri offered considerable opposition as naturally might be supposed, to the charges made against the officials of that state. They did all in their power to prevent any consideration of the petition. Many false statements and charges were made which Judge Higbee was able to refute. On the 26th of February, he wrote the Prophet as follows: "I am just informed by General Wall (the chairman of the committee), before whom, or to whom, our business is referred, that the decision is against us, or in other words unfavorable, that they believe redress can only be had in Missouri, the courts and the legislature." On the 4th of March, 1840, President Joseph Smith arrived in Nauvoo. The same day the senate committee made its report. After setting forth some of the items in the petition the committee said:

"The petition is drawn up at great length, and sets forth, with feeling and eloquence, the wrongs of which they complain; justifies their own conduct, and aggravates that of those whom they call their persecutors, and concludes by saying they see no redress, unless it be obtained of the Congress of the United States, to whom they make their solemn, last appeal, as American citizens, as Christians, and as men; to which decision they say they will submit.

"The committee have examined the case presented by the petition, and heard the views urged by their agent, with care and attention; and after full examination and consideration, unanimously concur in the opinion—

"That the case presented for their investigation is not such a one as will justify or authorize any interposition by this government.

"The wrongs complained of are not alleged to be committed by any of the officers of the United States, or under the authority of its government in any manner whatever. The allegations in the petition relate to the acts of its citizens, and inhabitants and authorities of the State of Missouri, of which state the petitioners were at the time citizens, or inhabitants.

"The grievances complained of in the petition are alleged to have been done within the territory of the State of Missouri. The committee, under these circumstances, have not considered themselves justified in inquiring into the truth or falsehood of the facts charged in the petition. If they are true, the petitioners must seek relief in the courts of judication of the State of Missouri, or of the United States, which has the appropriate jurisdiction to administer full and adequate redress for the wrongs complained of and doubtless will do so fairly and impartially; or the petitioners may, if they see proper, apply to the justice and magnanimity of the State of Missouri—an appeal which the committee feel justified in believing will never be made in vain by the injured or oppressed.

"It can never be presumed that a state either wants the power or lacks the disposition to redress the wrongs of its own citizens, committed within her own territory, whether they proceed from the lawless acts of her officers or of any other persons. The committee therefore report that they recommend the passage of the following resolution:

"*Resolved,* That the committee on the judiciary be discharged from further consideration of the memorial in this case; and that the memorialists have leave to withdraw the papers which accompany their memorial" (*Documentary History of the Church,* Vol. 4:90-2).

Compliance with the Word of the Lord.—The Senate, of course, adopted this resolution, and this brought to an end the appeal of the Latter-day Saints for redress of their wrongs while in Missouri.[d] The Saints had the satisfaction of knowing they had complied with the command of the Lord, wherein he instructed them to appeal for redress, first at the feet of the judge, then the governor and then the President of the United States. The matter was now to be left in the hand of the Great Judge who had promised, under the circumstances as they had developed, to "come forth out of his hiding place, and in his fury vex the nations" (Doc. and Cov. 101:89).

The Resolutions of the April Conference.—At the general conference of the Church held April 6-8, 1840, a set of resolutions were adopted approving of the labors of the Church committee who visited Washington, and condemning the action of the senate in the rejection of the consideration of the wrongs of the Saints. Some of the items in which the resolutions disagree with the action of Congress are as follows: The failure to consider the petition was subversive to the rights of a free people, and justly called for the disapprobation of all the supporters and lovers of good government. The judiciary committee stated in their report, "that our memorial aggravates the case of our oppressors," and at the same time they said they had "not examined into the truth or falsehood of the facts mentioned." This was deemed by the petitioners a great insult to their "good sense, better judgment and intelligence," when numerous affidavits were laid before the committee to prove that the Saints could go into the State of

---

[d]For the reason why the Saints did not accept the advice of the committee and appeal to the Federal Courts, see article by Elder B. H. Roberts, in the introduction to the Documentary History of the Church, Vol. 4, under the caption: "The Appeal of the Church to the National Government for Redress of Wrongs Suffered in Missouri."

Missouri only in opposition to the exterminating order of the governor, and at the risk of their lives. Moreover, that exterminating order was before the committee for consideration, it was a direct infraction of the Constitution of the United States. The failure of the committee to investigate the actions of the governor and other officers of Missouri, was "turning a deaf ear to the cries of widows, orphans, and innocent blood, which had been shed," and was "no less than seconding the proceedings of that murderous clan, whose deeds are recorded in heaven, and justly call down upon their heads the righteous judgment of an offended God." The thanks of the Saints were extended to Governors Lucas of Iowa, and Carlin of Illinois, for their sympathy and aid, also to the citizens of Illinois for their kind, liberal and generous conduct. The delegates were instructed to continue their endeavors to obtain redress, and the resolutions closed with the following appeal: "And if all hopes of obtaining satisfaction for the injuries done us be entirely blasted, that they (the delegates) then appeal our case to the Court of Heaven, believing that the Great Jehovah, who rules over the destiny of nations, and who notices the falling sparrows, will undoubtedly redress our wrongs, and ere long avenge us of our adversaries."[e]

Return of the Prodigals.—At the general conference held in April, 1840, Frederick G. Williams, who had been excommunicated by the action of the conference of the Church at Quincy, March 17, 1839, along with Thomas B. Marsh, George M. Hinkle and others, presented himself on the stand, and humbly asked forgiveness for his conduct while in Missouri. He expressed his determination to do the will of the Lord in the future, for he had a knowledge of the divinity of the work. His case was presented to the people by President Hyrum Smith, and he was received back into fellowship by the unanimous vote of the conference. From this time on he remained true to the Church and his brethren, until his death in Quincy, October 10, 1842.

In the following June William W. Phelps wrote to the Prophet from Dayton, Ohio, confessing his sins and begging for reinstatement in the Church. "I am," said he, "as the prodigal son, though I never doubt or disbelieve the fulness of the Gospel. I have been greatly abused and humbled, and I blessed the God of Israel when I lately read your prophetic blessing on my head, as follows: 'The Lord will chasten him because he taketh honor to himself, and when his soul

---

[e]The day of retribution came, at least in part, during the Civil War. For this account see the Introduction of Documentary History of the Church, Vol. 3, under the caption, "Retribution," by B. H. Roberts.

is greatly humbled he will forsake the evil. Then shall the light of the Lord break forth upon him as at noonday and in him shall be no darkness.' I have seen the folly of my way, and I tremble at the gulf I have passed. So it is, and why I know not. I prayed, and God answered; but what could I do? Says I, 'I will repent and live and ask my old brethren to forgive me, and though they chasten me to death, yet I will die with them, for their God is my God. * * * I have not walked with my friends according to my holy anointing. I ask forgiveness in the name of Jesus Christ of all the Saints, for I will do right, God helping me.'"

The Prophet answered him saying his case had been presented to the Saints and an expression of their feelings was unanimously given that he should be received back into the Church.

Death of Bishop Partridge.—Bishop Edward Partridge died Wednesday, May 27, 1840, in Nauvoo, in the forty-sixth year of his age. He was the first bishop of the Church, having been called to that position by revelation in 1831. He was born in Berkshire County, Massachusetts, August 27, 1793. His daughter Harriet Pamela, aged nineteen years, preceded her father to the grave by eleven days. They were victims of the Missouri persecutions, and were among those who suffered privations and exposure in the mobbings and expulsion in the winter of 1838-9. Others who likewise laid down their lives about this time were John Young, father of President Brigham Young, Seymour Brunson and James Mulholland, the Prophet's secretary. Each of these brethren died shortly after the settlement of the Saints in Illinois. John Young was a veteran of the Revolution. He had been driven from his home in Missouri and died in his seventy-seventh year, a martyr to his religion, for his death was caused by his sufferings in the cruel persecution. Seymour Brunson, died August 10, 1840. He was a man of strong character, and had taken an active part in the Church almost from the beginning, serving in various councils. He it was who entered charges against Oliver Cowdery and David Whitmer at the time of their excommunication. He died in his forty-first year and was at the time a member of the high council in the Nauvoo Stake. James Mulholland died in November, 1839, aged thirty-five years. He was a man of excellent education and was a faithful elder in the Church.

Death of Patriarch Joseph Smith.—Another victim of Missouri persecution was the Patriarch Joseph Smith, who died in Nauvoo, September 14, 1840. He was the first person who received the Prophet's testimony after the appearance of the angel, and was always true to the mission of his son. He moved to Kirtland in 1831, where he was ordained patriarch and an assistant counselor to the Prophet in the Presidency of the High Priesthood, December 18, 1833. He served as a member of the first high council in 1834. During the persecutions in Kirtland, in 1837, he was made a prisoner by the apostate enemies of the Church, but gained his liberty and made his way to Far West in 1838. From here he was again driven by enemies under the exterminating order of the infamous Lilburn W. Boggs. In midwinter he made his way to Quincy, and later in the spring of 1839, to Commerce, where he made his home. He was six feet two inches tall, and well proportioned. His ordinary weight was about two hundred pounds. He was a very strong, active man, but the exposure he suffered during the expulsion from Missouri, brought on consumption, from which he died. His funeral services were held September 15, 1840, Elder Robert B. Thompson delivering the discourse.

More Trouble from Missouri.—The action of Congress and the President of the United States, in refusing to consider the complaint, had its effect for evil on the Missourians. Their hatred, great as it was against the Latter-day Saints, was augmented by the presentation of the petition of the Saints to the general government. They seemed to chafe under the exposures to the world of their evil deeds. The action of Congress also made them bold in their desire to continue their persecutions of the Saints. If the President of the United States could refuse to give ear to the appeal of the thousands who had been so wilfully and maliciously wronged; and if Congress could advise that the proper place for redress was back in Missouri, and that, too, at the hands of the very officials who had so wickedly and unconstitutionally expelled, robbed, and murdered the Saints, what was there for Missourians to fear? Was not this evidence that the "Mormons," everywhere hated, were the common prey of their mortal enemies? It is true they had driven the Saints to the confines of another state, but it was a matter of little moment to cross that border and drag them back again for further abuse. Especially so, if they could enter into collusion with the officers of the other states which they hoped to do, and which they did.

Kidnapping of Alanson Brown and Others.—On the 7th day of July, 1840, Alanson Brown, Benjamin Boyce, Noah Rogers and James Allred, were surrounded by an armed force of mobbers in Hancock County, Illinois, who asked them if they were "Mormons." When they said they were, the mobbers with many vile oaths declared that they were sworn to kill "all the damned 'Mormons' that they could find." The brethren were forced across the river to a small town in

Lewis County, Missouri, called Tully, where they were kept under guard until about eleven o'clock at night. Then Alanson Brown and Benjamin Boyce were taken out to the woods with ropes around their necks. Boyce inquired what they intended to do and was answered by the mobbers that they were going to kill them and "make catfish bait" of them. The two brethren were then separated. Boyce was stripped and tied to a tree and whipped with gads until his body was mangled from his shoulders to his knees. In the meantime Brown had been hung by the neck until life appeared to be gone, then the ruffians cut him down, revived him, and returned to Tully with them both. They then placed ropes on the necks of Allred and Rogers and took them out to the woods, where they stripped them of their clothing and made many threats against their lives. Rogers was badly beaten, as Boyce had been, but for some reason the fiends refrained from whipping Allred. These brethren were then returned to Tully and confined in the same room with the other two brethren. Brown and Allred were liberated some days later, but Boyce and Rogers were confined in irons until the 21st day of August, when, through the blessings of the Lord, they made their escape.

Memorial to Governor Carlin.—A mass meeting of the citizens of Nauvoo was held July 13, 1840, at which the committee consisting of Isaac Galland, Robert B. Thompson, Sidney Rigdon and Daniel H. Wells, drew up resolutions of protest against the treatment accorded the four men who were kidnaped, which were adopted. The citizens then memorialized Governor Carlin, petitioning him to take steps to have released the four men who were then held prisoners in Missouri, and have punished the perpetrators of the crime. Daniel H. Wells and George Miller waited upon the governor and laid the case before him. As they recited the story of the cruelties, the governor's wife, who was present, was moved to tears, and the governor promised to take the matter in hand. However, his friendship for the Saints had greatly cooled and no action was ever taken by Governor Carlin to release the prisoners, or to bring to justice the perpetrators of the crime.

Missouri's Requisition for the Prophet.—The next move on the part of Missouri was a requisition made on Governor Carlin of Illinois, by Governor Lilburn W. Boggs, of Missouri, in September, 1840, for Joseph Smith, Sidney Rigdon, Lyman Wight, Parley P. Pratt, Caleb Baldwin and Alanson Brown, as fugitives from justice. This came after a silence of nearly two years, and was the outgrowth of the action taken by Congress. Governor Carlin complied with this unnatural, illegal and absurd request. When the sheriff came to serve his papers none of the brethren were found at home. Thus matters rested until the summer of 1841. On the 4th day of June, 1841, the Prophet called at the residence of Governor Carlin and had an interview with him and was treated very kindly. A few hours after his departure the governor sent the sheriff of Adams County, Thomas King, with a posse, and an officer from Missouri, to arrest him and deliver him up to the authorities of Missouri. They found the Prophet about twenty-eight miles south of Nauvoo. Some of the posse, on discovering the spirit of the officer from Missouri, returned to their homes in disgust. The party returned to Quincy where the Prophet obtained a writ of habeas corpus, and Judge Stephen A. Douglas, who providentially happened to be in Quincy, promised to give a hearing at Monmouth, Warren County, the following week. The news of the Prophet's arrest soon spread and a rescuing party was formed to prevent the Prophet being carried to Missouri, if that attempt should be made. He returned to Nauvoo in the custody of the sheriff, whom he entertained at his own house and waited on him, the sheriff being sick. June 7, Sheriff King and the Prophet, accompanied by a number of citizens from Nauvoo, left for Monmouth, seventy-five miles distant, where the trial commenced on the 9th, and concluded the following day. Attorney O. H. Browning, of the defense, made an eloquent plea closing his remarks in the following words:

"Yes, my eyes have beheld the blood-stained traces of innocent women and children, in the dreary winter, who had traveled hundreds of miles barefoot, through frost and snow, to seek a refuge from their savage pursuers. 'Twas a scene of horror sufficient to enlist sympathy from an adamantine heart. And shall this unfortunate man, whom their fury has seen proper to select for sacrifice, be driven into such a savage land and none dare to enlist in the cause of justice? If there was no other voice under heaven ever to be heard in this cause, gladly would I stand alone, and proudly spend my last breath in defense of an oppressed American citizen."

The Decision of Judge Douglas.—Judge Douglas gave the following decision: That the writ, being once returned to the executive by the sheriff of Hancock County, was dead, and stood in the same relationship as any other writ which might issue from the circuit court, and consequently the defendant could not be held in custody on that writ. On the question whether or not evidence was admissible, he would not pass, but would take under advisement, but on the other point, the defendant must be dismissed. Once again the Prophet Joseph had been freed from the clutches of the inhuman officials of Missouri.

CHAPTER 30

THE NAUVOO TEMPLE AND ORDINANCES THEREIN—IMPORTANT EVENTS

1840–1842

The House of the Lord.—In the various gathering places of the Saints from the days of Kirtland the Lord commanded that temples to his name should be built. In Jackson County and Far West, they were prevented from building temples by their enemies, who drove them from their homes. At the conference of the Church held in October, 1840, President Joseph Smith spoke of the necessity of building a "house of the Lord" in Nauvoo. Reynolds Cahoon, Elias Higbee and Alpheus Cutler were appointed a committee to build such a house. On motion it was also resolved that a commencement be made ten days from that date (Oct. 3, 1840) "and that every tenth day be appropriated for the building of the temple." Early in January, 1841, the First Presidency issued a proclamation to the Saints scattered abroad, in which they stated that "the temple of the Lord is in progress of erection here, where the Saints will come to worship the God of their fathers, according to the order of his house and the powers of the Holy Priesthood, and will be so constructed as to enable all the functions of the Priesthood to be duly exercised, and where instructions from the Most High will be received."

The Revelation of January 19, 1841.—A very important revelation was received January 19, 1841, dealing with various subjects, but particularly with the building of the temple and the ordinances to be performed therein. The Lord declared that the prayers of the Prophet were acceptable to him, and he was called upon to make a solemn proclamation of the Gospel to "all the kings of the world, to the four corners thereof; to the honorable President-elect, and the high-minded governors of the nation * * * and to all the nations of the earth." It was to be written in the spirit of meekness, yet of warning, for he was "about to call on them to give heed to the light and glory of Zion, for the set time has come to favor her." The Lord would visit the mighty and the rulers of the earth in the day of his visitation. Therefore, said he, "Awake, O kings of the earth! Come ye, O, come ye, with your gold and your silver to the help of my people, to the house of the daughters of Zion."

The Saints to Come from Afar.—The Saints were also commanded to come from afar. Messengers were to be chosen and sent unto them saying: "Come ye, with all your gold, and your silver, and your precious stones, and with all your antiquities; and with all who have knowledge of antiquities, that will come, may come, and bring the box tree, and the fir tree, and the pine tree, together with all the precious trees of the earth; and with iron, with copper, and with brass, and with zinc, and your precious things of the earth, and build a house to my name for the Most High to dwell therein."

Fulness of the Priesthood.—"For there is not a place," said the Lord, "found on earth where he may come and restore again that which was lost unto you, or which he hath taken away, even the fulness of the Priesthood," which fulness can only be obtained in the house of the Lord.

The Kirtland Temple and its Mission.—This declaration from the Lord would indicate that the purpose for which the Kirtland Temple was erected was now fulfilled, and its mission completed; and this was indeed the case. The Kirtland Temple served temporarily only. It was built because a house was necessary where the Lord could come and restore the various keys of former dispensations, that the Dispensation of the Fulness of Times might be made complete. In the Kirtland Temple the Lord gave a partial endowment, but not in the fulness, that the apostles and others might be endowed with necessary power to go forth "to prune the vineyard for the last time." But the great object was the restoration of the keys of former dispensations. When these were bestowed, then greater light was revealed, and the full purpose of temples and ordinance work therein was made known. It then became necessary that a house of the Lord should be built that would be perfect in all its parts, which was not the case in the structure of the Kirtland Temple. That edifice, although one of the most important ever erected by the Church, was not a complete structure as temples are understood through increased revelation. In it there were no provisions for the salvation of the dead; it had not a baptismal font—a fundamental part of the perfect temple—and therefore, since it had filled the measure of its creation, the Lord declared in the revelation of January, 1841, that there was not a house on the earth where he could come to bestow the fulness of the Priesthood and introduce the essential ordinances for the salvation of both the living and the dead. Moroni, John the Baptist, Peter, James and John, all came before there was a temple; but their coming was necessary that the foundation might be laid and the Church established. The Lord has made provision that in the sacred grove, the forest, and on the mountain top, such keys may be bestowed, when there is no temple erected to his name, and in the poverty of the people. Otherwise such keys are to be received only in the temple reared to his holy name.

Baptism for the Dead.—The doctrine of baptism for the dead was first made known to the Saints in a discourse by the Prophet at the funeral of Elder Seymour Brunson, August 10, 1840. This doctrine was not understood by him until after the restoration of the keys and the Priesthood of Elijah in the Kirtland Temple, although it had been referred to since the night of the first appearance of Moroni. In this revelation of January, 1841, the Lord revealed greater light regarding this wonderful principle. It was here made known that this ordinance was to be performed in the temple of the Lord. A baptismal font for this purpose was to be placed in the basement of the temple, "as a simile of the grave, and was commanded to be in a place underneath where the living are wont to assemble, to show forth the living and the dead; and that all things may have their likeness, and that they may accord one with another; that which is earthly conforming to that which is heavenly" (Doc. and Cov. Sec. 128:13).

In an epistle to the Twelve Apostles, who were at the time in Europe, President Joseph Smith, October 19, 1840, made the following statement:

"I presume the doctrine of 'baptism for the dead' has ere this reached your ears, and may have raised some inquiries in your minds respecting the same. I cannot in this letter give you all the information you may desire on the subject; but aside from knowledge independent of the Bible, I would say that it was certainly practiced by the ancient churches; and St. Paul endeavors to prove the doctrine of the resurrection from the same, and says, 'Else what shall they do which are baptized for the dead, if the dead rise not at all? Why are they then baptized for the dead?'

"I first mentioned the doctrine in public when preaching the funeral sermon of Brother Seymour Brunson; and have since then given general instructions in the Church on the subject. The Saints have the privilege of being baptized for those of their relatives who are dead, whom they believe would have embraced the Gospel, if they had been privileged with hearing it, and who have received the Gospel in the spirit, through the instrumentality of those who have been commissioned to preach to them while in prison."

The Rite Performed in the River.—After this doctrine was revealed the Lord granted the Saints the privilege of performing the ordinance of baptism for the dead in the Mississippi River, until such time as a font could be prepared in the basement of the temple. When a temporary font was prepared, and long before the temple was completed, this privilege of baptizing for the dead in any other place than the temple was discontinued by commandment of the Lord. So important was this work in behalf of the salvation of the worthy dead, that the Lord declared that the living could not be made perfect without them, and, when the opportunity presented itself, should the members of the Church fail to perform the ordinance for their dead, the Lord said he would reject them, for the dead were to be saved by the same principles which would save the living.

Things Hid from the Foundation of the World.—Not only was the ordinance of baptism for the dead to be performed in the temple, but the Lord promised to reveal many things "which have been kept hid from before the foundation of the world, things that pertain to the Dispensation of the Fulness of Times." Here the keys of the Holy Priesthood were to be received, for such were ordained to be obtained in temples that the Saints may receive honor and glory, both the living and, by proxy, the dead, even those blessings by which they should be crowned with honor, immortality and eternal life.

The Nauvoo House.—Another house was also to be built in Nauvoo. This was the Nauvoo House, a place for the boarding of strangers. Joseph Smith, Sidney Rigdon, Hyrum Smith, and many others were called upon to "pay stock" for themselves and their seed after them "from generation to generation," in this house. It was to be a place where the "weary traveler may find health and safety while he shall contemplate the word of the Lord; and the corner stone [stake] I have appointed for Zion," said the Lord. Those who took stock were not to pay less than fifty dollars, and not more than fifteen thousand dollars for any one man.

The Calling of Hyrum Smith.—Another important commandment in this revelation was the appointment of Hyrum Smith, to act as patriarch in the office which had been held by his father, and also his ordination to be a "prophet, seer and revelator" unto the Church, as well as Joseph Smith. The Lord had pointed out several years before, when Joseph Smith, Sen., was called to be the patriarch of the Church, that this office was his by right of lineage, and descended from father to son and was the right based on faithfulness of the first born. At the time of Hyrum Smith's call, he was serving as second counselor in the First Presidency, a place he was called to occupy after the transgression of Frederick G. Williams. The revelation relating to this appointment reads as follows:

"And again, verily I say unto you, let my servant William [Law] be appointed, ordained, and anointed, as a counselor unto my servant Joseph [Smith] in the room of my servant Hyrum, that my servant Hyrum may take the office of Priesthood and Patriarch, which was appointed unto him by his father, by blessing and also by right.

"That from henceforth he shall hold the keys of the patriarchal blessing upon the heads of all my people;

"That whoever he blesses shall be blessed, and whoever he curses shall be cursed; that whatsoever he shall bind on earth shall be bound in heaven; and whatsoever he shall loose on earth shall be loosed in heaven.

"And from this time forth I appoint unto him that he may be a prophet, and a seer and a revelator unto my Church, as well as my servant Joseph.

"That he may act in concert also with my servant Joseph, and that he shall receive counsel from my servant Joseph, who shall show unto him the keys whereby he may ask and receive, and be crowned with the same blessing, and glory, and honor, and Priesthood, and gifts of the Priesthood, that once were put upon him that was my servant Oliver Cowdery;

"That my servant Hyrum may bear record of the things which I shall show unto him, that his name may be had in honorable remembrance from generation to generation, forever and ever."

Oliver Cowdery's Blessings Transferred to Hyrum Smith.—Oliver Cowdery, as we have learned, stood with the Prophet Joseph Smith in holding the keys of the kingdom. He was associated with Joseph Smith in all his ordinations and in the bestowal of keys from the heavens from the beginning. It was Oliver Cowdery, not Sidney Rigdon or Frederick G. Williams, who knelt with the Prophet Joseph at the altar in the Kirtland Temple, April 3, 1836, when the Savior, Moses, Elias, Elijah, and perhaps other ancient prophets, came and conferred with them, bestowing keys, Priesthood and authority of

Nauvoo Temple

former dispensations that all things might be complete and perfect in the Dispensation of the Fulness of Times. All these blessings Oliver Cowdery would have held throughout eternity if he had remained faithful and true to his calling; but he fell away, and therefore the Lord bestowed these gifts, blessings and powers of presidency, upon the head of Hyrum Smith, the faithful brother of the Prophet Joseph of whom the Lord also said in this revelation: "And again, verily I say unto you, blessed is my servant Hyrum Smith, for I, the Lord, love him because of the integrity of his heart, and because he loveth that which is right before me."

Sunday, January 24, 1841, Hyrum Smith received the ordination to these holy callings under the hands of President Joseph Smith. On the same occasion George Miller was ordained a bishop in the place of Edward Partridge, deceased.

Laying Corner Stones of the Temple.—April 6, 1841, which was the eleventh anniversary of the organization of the Church, the corner stones of the Nauvoo Temple were laid. Early in the morning fourteen companies of the Nauvoo Legion, and two military companies from across the river in Iowa, assembled and were conducted to the grounds assigned for the general review. During the forenoon, various military maneuvers were conducted. It was an impressive scene. At twelve o'clock the procession arrived at the temple grounds and the ceremonies of laying the corner stones were commenced. President Sidney Rigdon addressed the assembly at some length after which the architects, under the direction of the First Presidency, lowered the south-east corner stone to its place, and the Prophet said:

"This principal corner stone in representation of the First Presidency, is now duly laid in honor of the Great God; and may it there remain until the whole fabric is completed; and may the same be accomplished speedily; that the Saints may have a place to worship God, and the Son of Man have where to lay his head."

Adjournment was taken for one hour and after the people reassembled the three other corner stones were laid in the following order; the south-west, the north-west and the north-east, after which the services were closed.

Order of Temple Building.—The Prophet later gave instructions pertaining to the order of the laying of corner stones of temples as follows:

"If the strict order of the Priesthood were carried out in the building of Temples, the first stone would be laid at the south-east corner, by the First Presidency of the Church. The south-west corner should be laid next; the third, or north-west corner, next; and the fourth, or north-east corner, last. The First Presidency should lay the south-east corner stone and dictate who are the proper persons to lay the other corner stones.

"If a temple is built at a distance, and the First Presidency are not present, then the quorum of the Twelve Apostles are the persons to dictate the order for that temple; and in the absence of the Twelve Apostles, then the presidency of the stake will lay the south-east corner stone; the Melchizedek Priesthood laying the corner stones on the east side of the temple, and the Lesser Priesthood those on the west side."

Baptisms in the River Discontinued.—At the conference of the Church held in Nauvoo, October 2nd to 5th, 1841, the Prophet made this announcement: "There shall be no more baptisms for the dead, until the ordinance can be attended to in the Lord's House; and the Church shall not hold another General Conference, until they can meet in said house. *For thus saith the Lord!*" The reason for this announcement was that the temple had progressed so far that the font in the basement had been prepared for this ordinance, therefore, baptisms for the dead could no longer be performed in the river.

Dedication of the Font in the Temple.—One month later, November 8, 1841, the baptismal font in the temple was dedicated. President Brigham Young was spokesman. The font is described as being situated in the center of the basement room, under the main hall of the temple. It was constructed of pine timber, and put together of staves tongued and grooved, oval shaped, sixteen feet long east and west, and twelve feet wide seven feet high from the foundation, the basin four feet deep, the moulding of the cap and base were formed of beautiful carved work. It stood upon twelve oxen four on each side, and two at each end, their heads, shoulders, and fore legs projecting out from under the font. The oxen and ornamental mouldings were carved by Elder Elijah Fordham, which took him eight months to finish. This font was replaced later by a permanent font which was more durable.

First Baptisms in the Temple.—Sunday, November 21, 1841, the twelve met in council at President Brigham Young's house, and at four o'clock they repaired to the baptismal font in the temple, where President Brigham Young, Elders Heber C. Kimball and John Taylor baptized about forty persons for their dead. Elders Willard Richards, Wilford Woodruff and George A. Smith, confirmed them. These were the first baptisms for the dead in the font in the Lord's House. From this time forth, as long as the Saints remained in Nauvoo, baptisms for the dead were performed in the temple.

Death of Don Carlos Smith.—Sunday, August 7, 1841, Don Carlos Smith, the youngest brother of the Prophet, died in Nauvoo. He was only twenty-six years of age, and was one of the first to receive the testimony of the Prophet. He received the Priesthood when but fourteen years of age, and in 1836 was made president of the high priests' quorum. He was on a mission in Tennessee and Kentucky in 1838. During his absence in the midst of winter his wife was driven from her home which was burned, and she was forced to wade Grand River with her two little children. In Kirtland he labored in the office of Oliver Cowdery and learned the art of printing. In the flight of his father's family from Missouri in the winter of 1839, he took charge, and saw them removed to Quincy, Illinois. In June, 1839, he commenced making preparations for printing the *Times and Seasons,* a periodical published in Nauvoo. The press and type had been rescued by Elias Smith, Hiram Clark and others, from Dawson's yard in Far West, where it had been buried the night that place was besieged by the mob-militia under General Lucas. The *Times and Seasons* was issued by Don Carlos Smith and Ebenezer Robinson, the first number appearing in November, 1839. At the time of his death the editors were Don Carlos Smith and Robert B. Thompson. Don Carlos was six feet four inches tall, was very straight, strong and active. The Prophet said of him: "I never knew any fault in him; I never saw the first immoral act, or the first irreligious or ignoble disposition in the child from the time he was born until the time of his death. He was a lovely, a good-natured, a kind-hearted, and a virtuous and faithful, upright child; and where his soul goes let mine go also."

Death of Robert B. Thompson.—Three weeks later, Robert Brashel Thompson, general Church recorder, died at his residence in Nauvoo, in the thirtieth year of his age. As already stated, he was associate editor of the *Times and Seasons,* and had been engaged in writing for the Prophet and for the Church, and was a colonel in the Nauvoo Legion. In 1837, he married Mercy Rachel Fielding, sister of Mary Fielding Smith, wife of the Patriarch Hyrum Smith. He and his associate Don Carlos Smith, both fell victims to the unhealthful conditions which prevailed in Nauvoo at the time of its settlement.

Dedication of Palestine.—Early Sunday morning, October 24, 1841, Elder Orson Hyde, of the council of the twelve, ascended the Mount of Olives and dedicated by prayer the land of Palestine for the gathering of the Jews. He was appointed to this mission at the April conference in 1840. Elder John E. Page was also appointed to go with him, but lost the spirit of his mission before he reached the eastern border of the United States, and failed to cross the water, leaving Elder Hyde to make the journey alone. After passing through many difficulties and privations Elder Hyde arrived in Jerusalem in October, 1841. He prayed "for the gathering together of Judah's scattered remnants," according to the predictions of the holy prophets; for the building of Jerusalem again after it has been trodden down by the Gentiles so long; and for rearing a temple to the name of the Lord. "Grant, therefore," he prayed "O Lord, in the name of thy well-beloved Son, Jesus Christ, to remove the barrenness and sterility of this land, and let springs of living water break forth to water its thirsty soil. Let the vine and olive produce in their strength, and the fig tree bloom and flourish. Let the land become abundantly fruitful and possessed by its rightful heirs; let it again flow with plenty to feed the returning prodigals who come home with a spirit of grace and supplication. Upon it let the clouds distil virtue and richness, and let the fields smile with plenty. Let the flocks and the herds greatly increase and multiply upon the mountains and the hills; and let thy great kindness conquer and subdue the unbelief of thy people. Do thou take from them their stony heart, and give them a heart of flesh; and may the sun of thy favor dispel the cold mists of darkness which have beclouded their atmosphere. Incline them to gather in

Orson Hyde

THE NAUVOO TEMPLE

upon this land according to thy word. Let them come like clouds and like doves to their windows. Let the large ships of the nations bring them from the distant isles; and let kings become their nursing fathers, and queens with motherly fondness wipe the tear of sorrow from their eye."

In this manner Elder Hyde prayed upon the Mount of Olives, dedicating the land for the return of the remnant of Judah from the four corners of the earth. He also erected a pile of stones as a witness according to the ancient custom, on the top of the Mount of Olives, and another on the top of Mount Moriah, where the ancient temple stood.

Orson Hyde of the House of Judah.—Elder Orson Hyde was of the house of Judah. It was therefore very proper that he, as one of the apostles of the Lord in this last dispensation, should be sent to bless the land for the gathering of the Jews. At one time, nearly ten years before, the following blessing was pronounced upon him: "In due time thou shalt go to Jerusalem, the land of thy fathers, and be a watchman unto the house of Israel; and by thy hand shall the

Mount of Olives

Most High do a work, which shall prepare the way and greatly facilitate the gathering of that people."ᵃ

ᵃThe evidence of the divine power accompanying the dedication of the land of Palestine is seen in the wonderful changes which have come over that land in recent years, and also in the changed attitude of the Jews, in relation to their return and also their belief in Jesus Christ. Nephi prophesied as follows regarding the restoration of the Jews: "And it shall come to pass that the Jews which are scattered also shall begin to believe in Christ; and they shall begin to gather in upon the face of the land; and as many as shall believe in Christ shall also become a delightsome people" (2 Nephi 30:7). The Savior also referred to this in his instruction to the Nephites: "And I will remember the covenant which I have made with my people; and I have covenanted with them that I would gather them together in mine own due time, that I would give unto them again the land of their fathers for their inheritance, which is the land of Jerusalem, which is the promised land unto them forever, saith the Father. And it shall come to pass that the time cometh, when the fulness of my gospel shall be preached unto them; and they shall believe in me, that I am Jesus Christ, the Son of God, and shall pray unto the Father in my name" (3 Nephi 20:29-30).

At the time of the dedication of Palestine the feeling expressed by the Jews towards Jesus Christ was most bitter. This condition is stated by Dr. Isadore Singer, as follows: "When I was a boy, had my father who was a very pious man, heard the name of Jesus uttered from the pulpit of our synagogue he and every other man in the congregation would have left the building and the rabbi would have been dismissed at once.

"Now it is not strange in many synagogues to hear sermons preached eulogistic of this Jesus, and nobody thinks of protesting—in fact we are glad to claim Jesus as one of our people." Compare the letter of Rabbi Landau, Documentary History of the Church, Vol. 3:356.

In 1891, Baron Maurice de Hirsch founded the Jewish Colonization Association. The "Lovers of Zion" Associated was commenced about 1878, and was supported by Baron Edmund de Rothschild. The Zionist Federation was organized in 1896, and was strongly promulgated by Theodore Herzl of Vienna, Baron de Rothschild and many other renowned Jews. All of these organizations were formed to aid in the colonization of the Jews in Palestine. The first congress of the Zionist Federation was held in Basel, Switzerland, in 1897, where the old nationalistic sentiment was revived and organizations were established for the gathering of the Jews.

At the Zionist Congress held in London in 1901, Professor R. Gothell, president of the federation, said: "It is time the nations understood our motives. Our purpose is gradually to colonize Palestine. We political Zionists desire a charter from the Sultan authorizing us to settle in our Holy Land, and we ask the powers to approve and protect this charter."

A few years ago the firm of Funk and Wagnalls published an edition of Dr. George Croley's work: "Tarry Thou Till I Come," and in the introduction Dr. Funk said: "It has been believed by many from the earliest ages of the Christian era that among the signs of Christ's coming would be the recognition of him by the Jews as one sent of the Father; and that they would then be restored to the Father's favor." Dr. Funk also collected a number of expressions from leading Jews, their belief in regard to the Savior, which were published in Dr. Croley's work. Some of them are as follows:

Rabbi Henry Berkowits: "This Jew, Jesus, is the greatest, noblest rabbi of them all."

Morris Jastrow: "From the historic point of view, Jesus is to be regarded as a direct successor of the Hebrew prophets. His teachings are synonymous with the highest spiritual aspirations of the human race."

Jacob H. Schiff: "We Jews honor and revere Jesus of Nazareth as we do our own prophets who preceded him."

The Book of Abraham.—During the month of March the Prophet prepared for publication his translation of the Book of Abraham, which he commenced to translate while residing at Kirtland. Due to the persecutions and drivings of the Saints this matter could not be attended to before this time, but the manuscript had been carefully preserved, and was now published for the benefit of the Church and all the world. This work together with the Book of Moses, has since been received among the standard works of the Church.

The Wentworth Letter.—At the request of Mr. John Wentworth, editor of the Chicago Democrat, the Prophet prepared an article for publication giving a brief history of the Church. This history was published in the *Times and Seasons*, March 1, 1842. Mr. Wentworth stated that he wished to furnish the information to a Mr. Bastow who was writing a history of New Hampshire. This article is one of the earliest documents giving a consecutive account of the history of the Church. It is concise and comprehensive, yet covers only a few pages. The most important feature in this paper is the publication therein, for the first time, of the Articles of Faith. These articles, thirteen in number, were given by inspiration, and form a simple, comprehensive declaration of many doctrines of the Church, which have since been accepted by the vote of the Church as a standard epitome of belief. They are as follows:

"We believe in God the Eternal Father, and in His Son Jesus Christ, and in the Holy Ghost.

"We believe that men will be punished for their own sins, and not for Adam's transgression.

"We believe that through the atonement of Christ all mankind may be saved by obedience to the laws and ordinances of the gospel.

"We believe that these ordinances are 1st: Faith in the Lord Jesus Christ; 2nd: Repentance; 3rd: Baptism by immersion for the remission of sins; 4th: Laying on of hands for the gift of the Holy Ghost.

The Savior said to his disciples in relation to the destruction of Jerusalem: "And they shall fall by the edge of the sword, and shall be led away captive into all nations: and Jerusalem shall be trodden down of the Gentiles until the times of the Gentiles be fulfilled" (Luke 21:24). The indication that this time of restitution is at hand is seen in the results coming out of the capture of Palestine by General Allenby in December, 1917, during the Great War. Since that time the Holy Land has been under the control of the British nation, and Dr. Herbert Samuel, an orthodox Jew, has been sent there as governor of the land. This is the first time since before the fall of Jerusalem (70 A. D.) which was predicted by the Savior, that a ruler from the house of Judah has presided in that land. It is an event of great significance.

"We believe that a man must be called of God by prophecy and by the laying on of hands by those who are in authority, to preach the gospel and administer in the ordinances thereof.

"We believe in the same organization that existed in the primitive church, namely, Apostles, Prophets, Pastors, Teachers, Evangelists, etc.

"We believe in the gift of tongues, prophecy, revelation, visions, healing, interpretations of tongues, etc.

"We believe the Bible to be the word of God as far as it is translated correctly; we also believe the Book of Mormon to be the word of God.

"We believe all that God has revealed, all that He does now reveal, and we believe that He will yet reveal many great and important things pertaining to the kingdom of God.

"We believe in the literal gathering of Israel and in the restoration of the Ten Tribes; that Zion will be built upon this continent; that Christ will reign personally upon the earth; and that the earth will be renewed and receive its paradisiacal glory.

"We claim the privilege of worshiping Almighty God according to the dictates of our own conscience, and allow all men the same privilege, let them worship how, where or what they may.

"We believe in being subject to kings, presidents, rulers and magistrates, in obeying, honoring and sustaining the law.

"We believe in being honest, true, chaste, benevolent, virtuous, and in doing good to all men; indeed we may say that we follow the admonition of Paul, 'We believe all things, we hope all things,' we have endured many things, and hope to be able to endure all things. If there is anything virtuous, lovely or of good report, or praiseworthy, we seek after these things."

Organization of the Relief Society.—March 17, 1842, "The Female Relief Society of Nauvoo" was organized by the Prophet Joseph Smith. Emma Smith was chosen president with Elizabeth Ann Whitney and Sarah M. Cleveland, as counselors. The purpose of the society is to furnish the sisters of the Church an organization through which they may actively foster the welfare of the members. The duty of the society was stated to be to aid the poor, nurse the sick and afflicted, and in a general way, under the direction and guidance of the bishop, to engage in true charitable work in behalf of all whose necessities require assistance. This was the first organization of women in the world, so far as history records. It is in keeping with the genius of the Gospel, for the Lord provides duties and labors for all the members of the Church, both men and women, wherein service may be rendered for the temporal as well as the spiritual salvation of mankind.

Inauguration of Endowments.—In the revelation of January 19, 1841, the Lord promised to reveal to Joseph Smith all things pertaining to the temple and the Priesthood thereof, which revelation and knowledge were necessary before the temple was erected. Wednesday, May 4, 1842, the Prophet met with his brother, Patriarch Hyrum Smith, President Brigham Young, Elders Heber C. Kimball, Willard Richards, James Adams of Springfield, Bishops Newel K. Whitney and George Miller, and instructed them in the principles and orders of the Priesthood that belong to the temple of the Lord. He made known to them the doctrines of washings and anointings and communications spoken of in the revelation. In this council, which was held in the upper room over his store, Joseph Smith also instructed these brethren in "all those plans and principles by which any one is enabled to secure the fulness of those blessings which have been prepared for the Church of the Firstborn." These same blessings, the Prophet stated would in due time be given in the temple to all the Saints who were worthy to receive them. This was the introduction of the temple ceremonies in their fulness in this dispensation, as they apply to the living and to the dead. From time to time after this, these instructions (*Documentary History of the Church*, Vol. 5:1-2) were repeated and the other members of the council of the twelve and their wives, and a few others, received their endowments under the direction of the Prophet Joseph Smith, as he was commanded to make these things known. The members of the Church at large, however, were required to wait until such time as these ordinances could be performed in the temple, the place designated by the Lord for such instructions and ordinance work to be given.

CHAPTER 31

JOSEPH SMITH ACCUSED AS ACCESSORY TO ASSAULT ON BOGGS

1842

Perfidy of John C. Bennett.—Doctor John C. Bennett came to Nauvoo in August, 1840, and joined the Church. Through his zealous activity in assisting to procure the Nauvoo Charter, he was honored by the citizens in the first election, by being chosen mayor of Nauvoo. He also rose to prominence in the councils of the Church, and appeared to be a firm believer in the Gospel, and a staunch friend to President Joseph Smith. Not many months later, however, through immoral conduct, he lost the spirit of the Gospel, and likewise his love for President Joseph Smith. His case is an illustration of the truth, that the Spirit of the Lord will not dwell in an unholy tabernacle. When men transgress, the Holy Spirit withdraws, and the light in them turns to darkness. The first intimation that all was not well with Dr. Bennett was made manifest to the Prophet May 7, 1842, after a drill and sham battle by the Nauvoo Legion. This event had been under preparation since the previous January, and it was the intention of all to make it a grand success. In the forenoon of that day there was a parade of the legion, some twenty-six companies, comprising about two thousand troops. Judge Stephen A. Douglas, who was holding court at Carthage, adjourned, and with some leading attorneys, went to Nauvoo to witness the military maneuvers of the legion. While there he was the guest of President Joseph Smith. The day passed harmoniously without confusion. A large company of spectators and distinguished strangers had assembled to witness the sham battle.

Dr. Bennett who was major general of the legion requested President Smith as lieutenant general to take command of the first cohort during the sham battle. But this the Prophet declined to do. Bennett next requested him to take his station in the rear of the cavalry without his staff, while the engagement was going on; but Captain Albert P. Rockwood of the Prophet's body guard would not consent, and kept close by his leader's side, who chose his own position. The Spirit of the Lord whispered to Joseph Smith that all was not well, and after the day's celebration was over he said, "If General Bennett's true feelings toward me are not made manifest to the world in a very short time, then it may be possible that the gentle breathings of that Spirit which whispered to me on parade, that there was mischief concealed in that sham battle, were false; a short time will determine the point. Let John C. Bennett answer at the day of judgment: Why did you request me to command one of the cohorts, and also to take my position without my staff, during the sham battle, on the 7th of May, 1842, where my life might have been the forfeit, and no man have known who did the deed?"

Bennett's Resignation.—Ten days later, Dr. Bennett resigned his office as mayor of Nauvoo having been accused of immorality. The same day he went before Alderman Daniel H. Wells, who was not a member of the Church, and made affidavit to the effect that he had never been taught anything in the least contrary to the principles of the Gospel, and the strictest morality in both word and deed, by Joseph Smith. On the 19th, the city council met and elected Joseph Smith to fill Bennett's unexpired term as mayor of Nauvoo. Before the council on this occasion, Bennett was accused with having said Joseph Smith taught him to practice immorality. He replied that "those who made such a statement were infernal liars," for Joseph Smith had always taught him to be virtuous. He then plead to be forgiven of his wrongdoing, and said he hoped yet to prove by repentance his worthiness to fellowship in the Church. For the sake of his mother, he prayed that his evil practices might not be exposed. In this apparently repentant spirit he appeared before nearly one hundred brethren and cried like a child, stating, "that he was worthy of the severest chastisement." The brethren thought him sincere and the Prophet in mercy plead in his behalf. In a very short time, it was discovered that not only had Bennett been guilty of immoral practices, but he had taught others to be like himself, placing the responsibility for such teachings on the shoulders of the Prophet. The result was that others had to be handled for their fellowship. For this cause, and a defiant spirit, Chauncey L. Higbee, was excommunicated. Others, on confession of their wrongdoing, and repentance, were forgiven.

J. C. Bennett Leaves Nauvoo.—Notwithstanding the mercy extended to Bennett by the brethren some time during the month of June, he left Nauvoo, breathing out threatenings against the Prophet and the Church. He made the statement "that he had withdrawn from the fellowship of the Saints because they were not worthy of his society." He then entered into correspondence with the enemies of Joseph Smith in Missouri, endeavoring to stir them up to continue their persecutions against him. This made it necessary that a public statement be made in regard to the immoral practices of Dr. Bennett. This document which was signed by the Prophet contained a supporting affidavit, bearing the signatures of the aldermen and councilors of the city of Nauvoo. Bennett later published a book, *The History of the Saints*, which represented to be an exposé of "Mormonism." The work was so filled with corrupt expressions, such as would naturally come from so vile a source, that it only created a spirit of disgust in those who read it, and it proved to be a failure.

Shooting of Ex-Governor Boggs.—On the 6th day of May, 1842, ex-Governor Lilburn W. Boggs was shot while sitting alone in a room of his residence in Independence. He was badly wounded and for several days his life was in the balance, but he soon recovered.

President Smith Accused as an Accessory.—July 20, 1842, Boggs went before Samuel Weston, justice of the peace in Independence, and made affidavit that Orrin Porter Rockwell, a resident of Illinois, had done the shooting. He applied to Governor Carlin in his affidavit, for the surrender of Rockwell "according to law." Subsequently he made another affidavit in which he said he had "good reason to believe, from evidence and information now in his possession, that Joseph Smith, commonly called 'the "Mormon" Prophet,' was accessory before the fact of the intended murder, and that the said Joseph Smith is a citizen or resident of the state of Illinois." He applied to Governor Thomas Reynolds of Missouri, for a demand on Governor Carlin of Illinois, to deliver up Joseph Smith, to be dealt with according to law. Governor Reynolds very willingly granted the request, and appointed Edward R. Ford agent to receive the Prophet. In the requisition, Governor Reynolds stated "Joseph Smith is a fugitive from justice, charged with being accessory before the fact, to an assault with the intent to kill, made by one O. P. Rockwell, on Lilburn W. Boggs, in this state (Missouri) and is represented to the executive department of this state as having fled to the state of Illinois." He therefore demanded the surrender of the Prophet on these grounds. Boggs had not accused Joseph Smith of being a fugitive, or with fleeing from Missouri; this charge was added by Reynolds. No doubt his reason was that he knew Missouri could have no claim upon Joseph Smith without making it appear that he had committed the alleged crime within Missouri and fled from her borders.

The foundation for this accusation was perhaps based on the rumor circulated at the time, and printed in the *Quincy Whig*, that Joseph Smith had prophesied that Boggs would die a violent death. As soon as the Prophet heard of this rumor he took occasion to deny it publicly, saying that he had made no such statement. Nevertheless, it gave occasion for an accusation, and it appears evident that Boggs and his fellow conspirators thought it an opportunity, and an excuse, to get the Prophet within their clutches, where they might kill him "according to law."

Governor Carlin's Action.—Governor Carlin of Illinois appeared to be a party to this conspiracy. He had, at least, become embittered against President Joseph Smith, and was very willing to accede to the demand from Missouri. He was thoroughly acquainted with the law and knew perfectly well that the Prophet was in Nauvoo on the 6th day of May, 1842, consequently was not subject to the requisition of Governor Reynolds of Missouri. He knew that President Smith was not a fugitive from justice; and, even if the false and malicious charge had been true, he knew the Prophet was entitled to a fair and legal trial in Illinois, not Missouri. Yet he would yield to this unlawful and unrighteous demand against his knowledge of these facts.

The Rocky Mountain Prophecy.—On Saturday, August 6, 1842, President Joseph Smith passed over the river to Montrose, in company with General James Adams, Colonel Brewer, Hyrum Smith and a number of others, and witnessed the installation of the officers of the Rising Sun Lodge of Masons, by General Adams, deputy grand master of Illinois. While General Adams was giving instructions to the master-elect, Joseph Smith had a conversation with a number of the brethren who were resting in the shade of the building. His topic was the persecutions of the Saints in Missouri, and the constant annoyance which had followed them since coming to Illinois and Iowa. In the course of his conversation the Prophet uttered a prophecy which he recorded in his journal as follows:

"I prophesied that the Saints would continue to suffer much affliction and would be driven to the Rocky Mountains, many would apostatize, others would be put to death by our persecutors, or lose their lives in consequence of exposure or disease, and some of them would live to go and assist in making settlements and build cities and see the Saints become a mighty people in the midst of the Rocky Mountains."

Arrest of President Smith.—The governor of Illinois honored the demand of the Missourians, and on the 8th day of August, 1842, President Joseph Smith and Orrin P. Rockwell were both taken into custody by the deputy sheriff of Adams County, on a warrant issued by the governor. The prisoners demanded the right of habeas corpus, and the court of Nauvoo issued a writ demanding that the bodies of the two accused men be brought before that court. The deputy sheriff and his aids refused to recognize the jurisdiction of the court, and returned to Governor Carlin for further instructions, leaving the Prophet and Rockwell in the hands of the marshal of Nauvoo. The marshal had no papers by which they could be held, so permitted them to go about their business.

The Prophet's Comments on His Arrest.—Commenting on his arrest, the Prophet said:

"I have yet to learn by what rule of right I was arrested to be transported to Missouri for a trial of the kind stated. 'An accessory to an assault with intent to kill,' does not come under the provision of the fugitive act, when the person charged has not been out of Illinois. An accessory before the fact to manslaughter is something of an anomaly. The isolated affidavit of ex-Governor Boggs is no more than any other man's, and the constitution says, that no person shall be liable to be transported out of the state for an offense committed within the same. The whole is another Missouri farce."

Expecting the return of the deputy sheriff, President Smith secured a writ of habeas corpus from the master in chancery for the district of Illinois, fearing that the court of Nauvoo might be deemed without jurisdiction or authority. Two days later when the officers returned, President Smith and Rockwell were not at home. The deputy sheriff made many threats and tried to intimidate the brethren at Nauvoo, but failing in this, when questioned, he admitted that the course the governor had taken was unjustifiable and illegal.

President Joseph Smith in Retirement.—Because of the excitement which prevailed and the fear that they would be unlawfully dragged to Missouri, Joseph and O. P. Rockwell retired to seclusion. While in retirement the Prophet kept in touch with affairs in Nauvoo and wrote to the Saints from time to time. It was while thus confined that he wrote the important letters which now appear as sections 127 and 128 in the Doctrine and Covenants, on baptism for the dead.

Threats of Mob Vengeance.—When the officers failed to find President Smith and Orrin Porter Rockwell, they were enraged and threatened to return with a sufficient force to search every house in Nauvoo. Ford, the officer from Missouri, declared that he would come with a mob from Missouri and take the Prophet by force. Hearing of these reports, President Smith wrote to Wilson Law, major general of the Nauvoo Legion, advising him to take necessary steps to protect the citizens of Nauvoo against any such attack. In his communication he said he had come to the conclusion that he would never suffer himself to fall into the hands of the Missourians alive, if he could help it. To surrender to the officers of Illinois meant the same thing, for Governor Carlin had joined hands with Missouri, taking unlawful steps to send him to that state. "I am determined, therefore," the Prophet said, "to keep out of their hands, and thwart their designs, if possible."

Emma Smith Appeals to Governor Carlin.—August 17, 1842, Emma Smith wrote a pathetic appeal to Governor Carlin pleading the cause of her husband and the Latter-day Saints, and requesting that he rescind his order to turn President Smith over to his enemies in Missouri. She set forth in a clear, logical manner the fact that the decision to deliver him to the authorities in Missouri was contrary to law. That if he had been guilty of any crime it must have been committed in Illinois, and the pursuit of President Smith was a continuation of the old mob spirit and persecution which had followed the Saints during all the years of their sojourn in Missouri. Others also appealed to the governor, reminding him of the many threats that were made against the citizens of Nauvoo, by John C. Bennett, Edward R. Ford and others. His reply to all of these was that he could not conceive of an attack by violence upon the citizens, and there was "no excitement anywhere but in Nauvoo, amongst the Mormons themselves." There was no apprehension of trouble in other places, so far as he was able to ascertain. At the same time he confessed in conversation, that "persons were offering their services every day, either in person or by letter, and held themselves in readiness to go against the Mormons" whenever he should call upon them. Judge Ralston, who was present when the governor read Emma Smith's letter, asked him how he thought Mr. Smith could go through the midst of his enemies, without violence being used towards him; and, if acquitted, how was he to get back? The governor was unable to make satisfactory reply.

Answering Emma Smith's letter, the governor said he had been "prompted by a strict sense of duty," and in discharge of that duty, had "studiously pursued that course least likely to produce excitement and alarm." He hoped that Joseph Smith would submit to the laws and that justice might be done. At the same time he said the Constitution and the laws of the United States, required him to take the course he did regarding Joseph Smith as a fugitive from justice. Yet he was perfectly aware that President Smith was not a fugitive in any sense of the term. He further suggested that if "he is innocent of any crime, and the proceedings are illegal, it would be the more easy for him to procure an acquittal," and he felt that Missouri would grant the "utmost latitude" in his defense. It was clear that he had no friendly disposition towards the President of the Church.

A Ruse to Capture President Smith.—In the meantime President Joseph Smith returned to Nauvoo and in a meeting of a special conference August 29, addressed the Saints. Some of the Saints thought he had gone to Washington, others that he had gone to Europe, however, he had been in Nauvoo most of the time. Sunday, October 2, 1842, word came from Quincy, that Governor Carlin had offered a reward of two hundred dollars for the capture of Joseph Smith and the same amount for O. P. Rockwell. The *Quincy Whig* also stated that Governor Reynolds of Missouri, had offered a reward of three hundred dollars for each of the brethren. President Sidney Rigdon, who had been in conversation at Carthage with Judge Stephen A. Douglas, concerning Governor Carlin's proceedings, informed William Clayton that he had learned that the governor had purposely issued an illegal writ, expecting President Joseph Smith would be drawn by it to Carthage to be acquitted before Judge Douglas on habeas corpus proceedings. As soon as that was done a legal writ would be served and he would be carried away to Missouri. Elder Elias Higbee confirmed President Rigdon's report, adding thereto that many Missourians were coming to unite with the militia of Illinois, voluntarily, at their own expense. If President Smith should fail to go to Carthage they would come in force to Nauvoo and search the city. Receiving this knowledge, the Prophet concluded again to leave home for a season, and thus defeat the plans of Governor Carlin and his aids.

Justin Butterfield's Legal Opinion.—While all these trials and tribulations were going on, the case of President Joseph Smith had been presented to United States District Attorney Justin Butterfield, of Chicago, by the master in chancery, Major Warren. Mr. Butterfield wrote to Sidney Rigdon, October 10, 1842, an elaborate opinion on the case. The salient points in his opinion are as follows: If it could be proved that Joseph Smith had not *fled* from Missouri since the commission of the crime of which he was accused, and that he was not in the state at that time, then the governor of Illinois had no power to surrender him to Missouri. According to the Constitution, a man to be a fugitive, "must be a person who shall flee from justice and be found in another state." The defendant has the right to show the process upon which he was arrested was obtained by false pretense, that it is untrue that he fled from Missouri to evade being brought to justice there, for the crime of which he is charged. The affidavit of Boggs is not conclusive and may be rebutted; the defendant has the right to show the affidavit false. The affidavit of Boggs "on its face was not sufficient to authorize the arrest of Smith." The opinion concluded with the following advice:

"I would advise that Mr. Smith procure respectable and sufficient affidavits to prove beyond all question, that he was in the state (Illinois) and not in Missouri, at the time the crime with which he is charged was committed, and upon these affidavits, apply to the governor to countermand the warrant he has issued for his arrest.

"If he should refuse to do so, I am clearly of the opinion that, upon the above state of facts, the supreme court will discharge him upon habeas corpus."

Governor Carlin's attitude being unfavorable, no further action was taken until December, when the term of Carlin expired. On the 8th of that month Thomas Ford was inaugurated as the chief executive of Illinois. Immediately affidavits were obtained to prove beyond controversy that President Joseph Smith was in the state of Illinois on the 6th day of May, 1842, the day of the shooting of ex-Governor Boggs, but Governor Ford refused to interfere with the action of his predecessor. The supreme court being in session, he passed the case with all the papers up to them for a decision. The judges held that the writ was illegal, but were divided as to whether or not Ford should interfere. The governor thereupon addressed President Joseph Smith, December 17, 1842, stating that he had submitted the case to the supreme court of Illinois. The governor then said:

"I can only advise that you submit to the laws and have a judicial investigation of your rights. If it should become necessary, for this purpose, to repair to Springfield, I do not believe that there will be a disposition to use illegal violence towards you; and I would feel it my duty in your case, as in the case of any other person, to protect you with any necessary amount of force from mob violence whilst asserting your rights before the courts, going to and returning."

The Prophet Receives Advice.—Justin Butterfield, in a letter from Springfield of the same date, advised the Prophet to accept the suggestion of Governor Ford. He said the judges of the supreme court were unanimous in the opinion that he would be entitled to a discharge under a habeas corpus writ. Therefore he advised President Smith to go to Springfield without delay, for he had the right to bring the case before the United States court, which was then in session. "I will stand by you," he said, "and see you safely delivered from your arrest."

Another letter was received from Judge James Adams, who greatly loved the Prophet. He said:

"My Son:—It is useless for me to detail facts that the bearer can tell. But I will say that it appears to my judgment that you had best make no delay in coming before the court at this place for a discharge under a habeas corpus."

Joseph Smith Surrenders for Trial.—Acting on this advice, President Smith prepared to go to Springfield. December 26, he was arrested by General Wilson Law on the proclamation of Governor Carlin. The next day in the custody of William Law and a number of his closest friends, he commenced his journey. On the way they obtained a writ of habeas corpus from the master in chancery at Carthage. On the 30th, he arrived at the home of Judge James Adams, in Springfield. The next day, to save delay, and possible legal complications, Governor Ford was petitioned for another writ that the case might be tried thereon and it was issued. At half-past eleven President Smith went before Judge Pope, where Mr. Butterfield presented all the papers in the case and asked for habeas corpus, because the accusation was false, which was granted. The Prophet was then placed under bail in the sum of four thousand dollars. Judge Adams and Wilson Law went bail for him, and his case was set for Monday morning, January 2, 1843.

The Trial.—A postponement of the trial was taken until the following Wednesday. When the case came before the court, the attorney general, Josiah Lamborn, moved to dismiss the proceedings, objecting to the jurisdiction of the court. He was overruled and the trial proceeded. On the 5th day of January, 1843, Judge Pope rendered a lengthy decision,[a] discharging the Prophet on the grounds that he was entitled to his discharge for defect in the affidavit on which the demand for his surrender to Missouri was made. "To authorize the arrest in this case," the opinion said, "the affidavit should have stated distinctly—1st, that Smith had committed a crime; 2nd, that

---

[a]For the full decision, which should be read see Documentary History of the Church, Vol. 5:223-231. See also pages 233-244 for papers on the trial.

he committed it in Missouri. It must appear that he fled from Missouri to authorize the governor of Missouri to demand him, as none other than the governor of the state from which he fled can make the demand. He could not have fled from justice unless he committed a crime, which does not appear. It must appear that the crime was committed in Missouri, to warrant the governor of Illinois in ordering him to be sent to Missouri for trial."

On these grounds an order was entered discharging the prisoner from arrest. Once again Missouri, persecutor of saints and prophets, was defeated; but her thirst for their blood was not satisfied.

Bennett's Letter to Sidney Rigdon and Orson Pratt.—January 10, 1843, John C. Bennett sent a communication from Springfield to Sidney Rigdon, and addressed to Rigdon and Orson Pratt, in which he states that he was leaving for Missouri to confer with the messenger charged with the arrest of Joseph Smith, Hyrum Smith, Lyman Wight, and others, who would be demanded in a few days on the old charge of "murder, burglary, treason, etc." This was on the new indictments found by the grand jury and based on the original evidence. He said: "We shall try Smith on the Boggs case, when we get him into Missouri. The war goes bravely on; and although Smith thinks he is now safe, the enemy is near, even at the door." Moreover, he stated that they had the assurance that the governor of Illinois would acknowledge the new demand. "There is but one opinion on the case," he wrote, "and that is, nothing can save Joe on a new requisition and demand predicated on the old charges on the institution of new writs. He must go to Missouri; but he shall not be harmed if he is not guilty; but he is a murderer, and must suffer the penalty of the law." A postscript requested that Sidney Rigdon hand the letter to Orson Pratt. After reading it, Sidney Rigdon did as he was requested, but Orson Pratt immediately took the letter to President Joseph Smith and informed him that he was not in league with such a character as Bennett. Bennett wrote to these men knowing that at the time they were both lukewarm towards the work, and that Orson Pratt, for disobedience, had been handled for his fellowship. Following this episode, Orson Pratt was received back in the fellowship of the Church. For some time previous to this incident, Sidney Rigdon had failed to magnify his calling and had gone contrary to counsel. When confronted with the letter from Bennett he denied having had any correspondence with him.

Rejoicing in Nauvoo.—When President Smith returned to Nauvoo, from his trial, there was great rejoicing. Tuesday, January 17,

1843, was set apart by the apostles as a "day of humiliation, fasting, praise, prayer and thanksgiving" before the Lord. Many public meetings were held throughout the city. One public gathering of this kind was held at the home of President Joseph Smith. The following day a party of invited guests assembled at his home to celebrate his deliverance from his enemies. The day passed very pleasantly; many interesting anecdotes were related, and what added interest to the occasion was the fact that it was the fifteenth anniversary of the Prophet's wedding day.

CHAPTER 32

DOCTRINAL DEVELOPMENT AND PROPHECY

1843

A Brief Period of Peace.—At the beginning of the year 1843, peace reigned in Nauvoo; for a time the Saints remained undisturbed, and the Prophet had a breathing spell of freedom. Yet there were ripples on the surface of the water. President Joseph Smith had been delivered from his enemies in Missouri. The persecutors of the Church had been defeated; but were still determined to pursue their evil course. The Missourians were in league with the enemies of the Prophet in Illinois, with a relentless determination to bring him to his death.

This brief period of peace gave the Prophet an opportunity to instruct the Saints in various duties and doctrines and more fully to establish the order and authority of the Priesthood. The building of the temple progressed; increased light was thrown on the subject of salvation for the dead, and the Saints were impressed with the wonderful importance and responsibility connected with their obligations in relation to their fathers. Important revelations were received. The number of inhabitants in Nauvoo rapidly increased, and there was a time of prosperity and general rejoicing. But such a condition was not destined to continue very long. The clouds of malicious hatred were to be seen in the distance, and soon the storm of bitter persecution was to break forth once again in redoubled fury. Traitors within, and enemies without, were to join hands for the destruction of the Prophet.

President Joseph Smith's Intimation of Death.—President Smith evidently understood that this spell of peace and prosperity would not last. With constant pleading he urged the Saints to increase their labors on the temple, and they responded with hearty good will. In his prophecy, August 6, 1842, he declared to his brethren that he was not destined to go with them to the Rocky Mountains; yet they failed to comprehend his meaning. On several occasions he intimated in his remarks that his enemies would not be satisfied with anything short of his life, and then they would pursue others. He spoke to the Saints at a meeting in the unfinished temple, January 22, 1843, taking for his text, "The Setting up of the Kingdom of God." In the course of his discourse he said: "I shall not be sacrificed until my time comes; then I shall be offered freely. All flesh is as grass, and a governor is no better than other men; when he dies he is a bag of dust. I thank God for preserving me from my enemies. I have no enemies but for the truth's sake. I have no desire but to do all men good. I feel to pray for all men. We don't ask any people to throw away any good they have got; we only ask them to come and get more. They would then see eye to eye, and the blessings of God would be poured out upon the people, which is the desire of my whole soul. Amen."

Doctrinal Development.—Early in January, 1843, in discoursing on the kingdom of God, the Prophet said. "Some say the kingdom of God was not set up on the earth until the day of Pentecost, and John the Baptist did not preach the baptism for repentance for the remission of sins. But I say, in the name of the Lord, that the kingdom of God was set up on the earth from the days of Adam to the present time. * * * Where there is no kingdom of God, there is no salvation. What constitutes the kingdom of God? Where there is a prophet, a priest, or a righteous man unto whom God gives his oracles, there is the kingdom of God; and where the oracles of God are not, there the kingdom of God is not." In relation to the Gospel and baptism preached by John, he said: "John came preaching the Gospel for the remission of sins. He had his authority from God, and the oracles of God were with him." Speaking of the sign of the Holy Ghost, he stated: "The Holy Ghost is a personage, and in the form of a personage. It does not confine itself to the form of a dove, but in the sign of a dove. The Holy Ghost cannot be transformed into the form of a dove; but the sign of a dove was given to John to signify the truth of the deed [baptism of Christ], as the dove is an emblem or token of truth and innocence." In February he received a revelation embodying the following principle: There are two kinds of beings in heaven; angels, who are resurrected personages, having bodies of flesh and bones; and spirits of just men made perfect who are not yet resurrected, but inherit the same glory. In April, 1843, he gave instructions at Ramus, as follows: "When the Savior shall appear, we shall see him as he is. We shall see that he is a man like ourselves and that same sociality which exists among us here will exist among us there, only it will be coupled with eternal glory, which glory we do not now enjoy." The reckoning of God's, time, angel's time and man's time is according to the planet on which they reside. All angels who minister on this earth, have belonged to it. Angels reside in the presence of God on a globe like a sea of glass and fire, where all things for their glory are manifest. The place where God dwells is a great Urim and Thummim. This earth, in its sanctified and immortal state, will be like unto crystal and will be a Urim and Thummim to the inhabitants who dwell thereon, whereby all things pertaining to an inferior kingdom, or all kingdoms of a lower order, will be manifest to those who dwell on it. The white stone mentioned in Revelations 2:17 will become a Urim and Thummim to each individual who receives one, through which things of a higher order will be made known. Again, he taught that all principles of intelligence we attain unto in this life, will rise with us in the resurrection. The Father has a body of flesh and bones as has the Son, Jesus Christ, also, but the Holy Ghost is a personage of Spirit. During the time of the trial at Springfield, in answer to questions, he said: "Christ and the resurrected Saints will reign over the earth during the thousand years. They will not probably dwell upon the earth, but will visit it when they please, or when it is necessary to govern it. There will be wicked men on the earth during the thousand years. The heathen nations who will not come up to worship will be visited with the judgments of God." In this manner, in conversations, discourses and writings, the Prophet taught the people.

Attempt to Repeal the Nauvoo Charter.—When Governor Thomas Ford delivered his inaugural address in December, 1842, he recommended modification of the Nauvoo charter, on the grounds that many objections had been raised because of exceptional powers, which had been granted. Yet these powers had proved beneficial to the Saints, and where righteous government was administered, as it was in Nauvoo, such a charter proved to be a blessing. In the hands of despots such privileges might have been abused. When the charter was granted, the Prophet said: "The city charter of Nauvoo is of my own plan and device. I concocted it for the salvation of the Church, and on principles so broad, that every honest man might dwell secure under its protective influence without distinction of sect or party." A bill was presented in the legislature to repeal certain sections of the charter shortly after that body convened. The enemies of the Saints endeavored to repeal much more than had at first been contemplated, and take from the charter many provisions like those found in the charters of the other cities in Illinois. This attempt was made purposely to hurt the "Mormons," by restricting their rights. The bill passed the house in March with a vote of 58 to 33. When it reached the senate it was tabled. The time for the repeal had not arrived.

A General Missionary Call.—At the conference of the Church in April, 1843, a general missionary movement was contemplated. President Joseph Smith, in the course of his remarks, advised that the elders when they went forth as missionaries, should preach repentance and the things they were sent to preach. "Declare the first principles," he said, "and let mysteries alone, lest you be overthrown. Never meddle with the visions of beasts and subjects you do not understand." Following the general conference a special conference convened April 10, and continued through the 12th, presided over by the apostles. At this conference elders were chosen and their appointments given for various mission fields in Canada and the several states, excepting blighted Missouri. On the 11th of May, following, Addison Pratt, Noah Rogers, Benjamin B. Grouard and Knowlton F. Hanks, were selected to go on missions to the Pacific isles; Dan Jones, to Wales; James Sloan, to Ireland; John Cairnes and Samuel James to England, with Reuben Hedlock, who was appointed to preside in Great Britain with Hiram Clark and Thomas Ward, who were in England, as his assistants.

Eternity of the Marriage Covenant.—While at Ramus, May 16 and 17, 1843, the Prophet made the following declaration:

"In the celestial glory there are three heavens or degrees; and in order to obtain the highest, a man must enter in to this order of the Priesthood (meaning the new and everlasting covenant of marriage); and if he does not, he cannot obtain it.

"He may enter into the other, but that is the end of his kingdom; he cannot have an increase.

"Salvation means a man's being placed beyond the power of all his enemies.

"The more sure word of prophecy (mentioned by Peter) means a man's knowing that he is sealed up unto eternal life, by revelation and the spirit of prophecy, through the power of the Holy Priesthood.

"It is impossible for a man to be saved in ignorance.

"There is no such thing as immaterial matter. All spirit is matter, but it is more fine or pure, and can only be discerned by purer eyes.

"We cannot see it; but when our bodies are purified we shall see that it is all matter."

The New and Everlasting Covenant.—A revelation dealing with the subject of marriage for eternity, or celestial marriage as it is known, was reduced to writing July 12, 1843 (Doc. and Cov. 132.) It had been revealed to the Prophet a long time before this date, but had not been recorded or publicly announced. In it the Lord defines the "new and everlasting covenant." In a number of revelations previously given the new and everlasting covenant is mentioned, and various principles of the Gospel are spoken of as new and everlasting covenants. Thus, in the Lord's Preface to the Book of Doctrine and Covenants, he says he gave commandments to Joseph Smith, that his "everlasting covenant might be established; that the fulness of the Gospel might be proclaimed." Immediately after the organization of the Church, he declared that baptism is a "new and an everlasting covenant, even that which was from the beginning," and in a revelation given October 25, 1831 (Doc. and Cov. Sec. 66), the everlasting covenant is defined as the fulness of the Gospel, "sent forth unto the children of men, that they might have life and be made partakers of the glories which are to be revealed." But the full meaning and significance of the "new and everlasting covenant," was not revealed until the Prophet received this revelation (Doc. and Cov. Sec. 132), in which it is defined as follows:

"For behold, I reveal unto you a new and an everlasting covenant; and if ye abide not that covenant, then are ye damned; for no one can reject this covenant, and be permitted to enter into my glory. For all who will have a blessing at my hands shall abide the law which was appointed for that blessing, and the conditions thereof, as were instituted from before the foundation of the world."

This reference has bearing on the new covenant of celestial marriage, or marriage for eternity, spoken of by President Joseph Smith at Ramus in May, 1843. Then the Lord defines the law of the new and everlasting covenant, which embraces all other covenants and principles belonging to the Gospel:

"And as pertaining to the new and everlasting covenant, it was instituted for the fulness of my glory; and he that receiveth a fulness thereof must and shall abide the law, or he shall be damned, saith the Lord God.

"And verily I say unto you, that the conditions of this law are these: All covenants, contracts, bonds, obligations, oaths, vows, performances, connections, associations, or expectations, that are not made and entered into and sealed by the Holy Spirit of promise, of him who is anointed, both as well for time and for all eternity, and that too most holy, by revelation and commandment through the medium of mine anointed, whom I have appointed on the earth to hold this power (and I have appointed unto my servant Joseph to hold this power in the last days, and there is never but one on the earth at a time, on whom this power and the keys of this Priesthood are conferred), are of no efficacy, virtue, or force in and after the resurrection from the dead; for all contracts that are not made unto this end have an end when men are dead."

Conversely, then, all contracts entered into in this life, and sealed by this authority, are binding and of force after the resurrection, as the revelation further on declares:

"Behold, mine house is a house of order, saith the Lord, God, and not a house of confusion. Will I accept of an offering, saith the Lord, that is not made in my name? Or will I receive at your hands that which I have not appointed? And will I appoint unto you, saith the Lord, except it be by law, even as I and my Father ordained unto you, before the world was? I am the Lord thy God; and I give unto you this commandment—that no man shall come unto the Father but by me or by my word, which is my law, saith the Lord. And everything that is in the world, whether it be ordained of men, by thrones, or principalities, or powers, or things of name, whatsoever they may be, that are not by me or by my word, saith the Lord, shall be thrown down, and shall not remain after men are dead, neither in nor after the resurrection, saith the Lord your God. For whatsoever things remain are by me; and whatsoever things are not by me shall be shaken and destroyed."

Revealed by Elijah.—The keys of this wonderful and impressive doctrine were restored when Elijah conferred his Priesthood. The mission of Elijah in this dispensation, as prophesied of by Malachi, was to restore the sealing, or binding power, through which covenants and contracts, as here described by the Lord, are approved and ratified in the heavens. Referring to this subject, President Joseph Smith remarked in one of his discourses:

"Elijah was the last prophet that held the keys of the Priesthood, * * * It is true that the Savior had authority and power to bestow this blessing; but the sons of Levi were too prejudiced. 'And I will send Elijah the Prophet before the great and terrible day of the Lord,' etc. Why send Elijah? Because he holds the keys of the authority to administer in all the ordinances of the Priesthood; and without the authority is given, the ordinances could not be administered in righteousness."

Again:

"The spirit, power, and calling of Elijah is, that ye have power to hold the key of the revelation, ordinances, oracles, powers and endowments of the fulness of the Melchizedek Priesthood and of the kingdom of God on the earth; and to receive, obtain and perform all the ordinances belonging to the kingdom of God, even unto the turning of the hearts of the fathers unto the children, and the hearts of the children unto the fathers, even those who are in heaven. * * * What is this office and work of Elijah? It is one of the greatest and most important subjects that God has revealed. He should send Elijah to seal the children to the fathers, and the fathers to the children."

In the Temple these Blessings are Obtained.—In the temple of the Lord these sealing blessings may be obtained. Only in the days of poverty, when there is no temple, can they be received elsewhere. The Prophet added further instruction to this subject in a discourse, Sunday, June 11, 1843, wherein he said:

"One of the ordinances of the house of the Lord is baptism for the dead. God decreed before the foundation of the world that that ordinance should be administered in a font prepared for that purpose in the house of the Lord.

"If a man gets a fulness of the Priesthood of God, he has to get it in the same way that Jesus Christ obtained it, and that was by keeping all the commandments and obeying all the ordinances of the house of the Lord. * * *

"All men who become heirs of God and joint-heirs with Jesus Christ, will have to receive the fulness of the ordinances of his kingdom; and those who will not receive all the ordinances will come short of the fulness of that glory, if they do not lose the whole" (*Documentary History of the Church*, Vol. 5: p. 423).

Plural Marriage.—This revelation, dated July 12, 1843, also contains the doctrine of plural wives. This doctrine was made known to the Prophet as early as the summer of 1831, and by him was taught to a few others, but it was not practiced until the Lord commanded it. Secrecy was imposed by the Lord until such time as he saw fit for its introduction. When the Prophet was commanded to practice this principle, he hesitated and deferred taking action for some time. To do so was one of the greatest trials of his life. He knew the doctrine was in conflict with the traditions and teachings of the world and would arouse increased persecution; moreover, his own prejudices were in opposition to the doctrine. However, the Lord had commanded and he must act.

In Nauvoo the doctrine was revealed to many of the leading brethren, and wives were sealed to some of them by President Joseph Smith, and to others, under his direction. However, it was not until 1852, after the Saints had come to Utah that the revelation was published to the world.

The Douglas Prophecy.—On the return from Ramus where the doctrine of the eternity of marriage was taught to a number of brethren, President Joseph Smith and his scribe, William Clayton, paid a visit to Judge Stephen A. Douglas, at Carthage, where he was holding court. On invitation they dined with Judge Douglas, and after dinner he requested President Smith to relate the history of the persecutions of the Saints while in Missouri. This he did in some detail, covering a period of about three hours. He also gave an account of his visit to Washington, with Judge Elias Higbee and Sidney Rigdon, in 1839, and their treatment by President Martin Van Buren, Henry Clay, John C. Calhoun and others. Judge Douglas listened with the closest attention and deprecated the conduct of Governor Boggs and his aids in Missouri. He said that any people who would do as the Missourians had done to the Latter-day Saints ought to be brought to judgment and punished.

President Smith, in concluding the conversation, uttered the following prophecy which was recorded in the journal of his secretary, William Clayton, under date of the event, May 18, 1843:

"Judge, you will aspire to the presidency of the United States; and if ever you turn your hand against me or the Latter-day Saints, you will feel the weight of the hand of the Almighty upon you; and you will live to see and know that I have testified the truth to you; for the conversation of this day will stick to you through life."[a]

---

[a]Stephen A. Douglas lived to see the fulfillment of this prophecy. He did aspire to the presidency of the United States. He did raise his voice against the Latter-day Saints in a speech delivered in Springfield, Illinois, June 12, 1857. The speech was published in the "Missouri Republican." While Mr. Douglas had more reason to expect to be elected than any other candidate, he was overwhelmingly defeated, and Abraham Lincoln was elected President of the United States.

For full particulars in relation to this subject, the reader is referred to the "History of the Mormon Church," chapter 46, by Elder B. H. Roberts.

CHAPTER 33

MISSOURI'S THIRD ATTEMPT TO CAPTURE JOSEPH SMITH

1843

Conspiracy Against Joseph Smith.—When John C. Bennett wrote to Sidney Rigdon and Orson Pratt, saying he was on his way to Missouri to obtain a new requisition for Joseph Smith and others, it was not an idle threat. Not many weeks had passed before reports reached Nauvoo that new indictments had been found against President Smith, based on the old Missouri charges, and that John C. Bennett was making desperate threats. Moreover, Bennett must have some definite information which caused him to say that Governor Ford would acknowledge the new requisition. A conspiracy, evidently, was on foot, in which the governors of the two states were to play their parts. Further evidence that Governor Ford was a party to the conspiracy is discovered in a communication dated June 10, 1843, from Sam C. Owens of Independence, to the governor of Illinois. Owens, one of the bitterest persecutors of the Saints in Missouri, stated in his letter that John C. Bennett had authorized him to write Governor Ford, "without hesitation" in regard to the charges against Joseph Smith. "At the last term of the circuit court of Daviess County," he wrote, "an indictment was found by the grand jury against Joseph Smith for treason against the state," and necessary papers were on the way to Governor Thomas Reynolds, who, on receipt thereof, would issue a requisition, and Mr. Joseph H. Reynolds would be sent as a special agent "to attend to the business." Owens also said that "Dr. Bennett further writes that he has made an agreement with Harmon T. Wilson, of Hancock County (Carthage seat of justice), in whose hands he wishes the writ that shall be issued by you to be put. From the tenor of his letter I am induced to believe that he has made the same suggestion to you."

A Warrant for His Arrest.—June 13, 1843, Governor Reynolds issued the requisition and Joseph H. Reynolds was dispatched to Illinois. Governor Ford lost no time in issuing a warrant for the arrest and placed it in the hands of Harmon T. Wilson, who, with Reynolds, immediately started for their prisoner. The night before the warrant was issued Governor Ford incidentally remarked to Judge James Adams that the next day he would issue such a writ. Judge Adams sent an express at once to Nauvoo to warn the Prophet of impending danger. His message arrived in the evening of Sunday, June 18, but President Smith was not at home. On the 13th, he and his family had gone north to visit with Mrs. Wasson, sister of Emma Smith, who resided near Dixon, Lee County, Illinois. Hyrum Smith sent William Clayton and Stephen Markham on horseback with all speed to warn his brother Joseph. They arrived at Wasson's on the afternoon of Wednesday, June 21, a distance of two hundred and twelve miles. Hearing their report, Joseph said: "I have no fear. I shall not leave here; I shall find friends, and Missourians cannot hurt me, I tell you in the name of the Lord." He cancelled an appointment to preach in Dixon, and concluded to remain with the Wassons, fearing that if he started for home he might fall into the hands of his enemies where he had no friends.

His Arrest by Reynolds and Wilson.—From some source Reynolds and Wilson learned that Joseph was at Dixon and thither they went with haste. On the way to Wasson's they passed William Clayton, who had been sent to spy out the land, but as they were disguised, Clayton did not know them. Arriving at their destination the sheriffs represented themselves to be "Mormon" elders and were directed to the Wasson home. President Smith was in the yard when they arrived. Springing upon him like fiends, and without showing any papers for his arrest, they pointed cocked pistols at his head and with many vile oaths, threatened to shoot him if he stirred. They repeatedly jabbed the muzzles of their pistols in his ribs, and were for hurrying him off to Dixon without giving him a chance to say farewell to his family or friends, or obtain his hat and coat. Stephen Markham grabbed the horses by the bits and held them saying: "There is no law on earth that requires a sheriff to take a prisoner without his clothes." They threatened to shoot him, but he paid no heed to their threats, and Emma Smith brought her husband his hat and coat.

As the wagon rolled away, Joseph called to Markham to go to Dixon and secure a writ of habeas corpus. On the way the officers repeatedly thrust their pistols in the Prophet's sides with accompanying oaths of blasphemy, and did not desist until shortly before reaching Dixon, when Markham, who had overtaken them, upbraided them for their cowardice and brutal treatment of their prisoner, who was defenseless.

Arriving at Dixon, the officers placed their prisoner in a room of the tavern, and ordered fresh horses to be ready in five minutes. Joseph asked them if he could interview counsel, but was cruelly treated for his request. A man passed the window and the Prophet shouted to him to secure him a lawyer, for he was falsely imprisoned. Attorney Edward Southwick came to the door, but it was shut in his face, with a threat. Shepherd G. Patrick, another attorney, also came and was insulted in like manner. The neighborhood was soon aroused, and Mr. Dixon, owner of the house, with some friends surrounded the door and threatened violence to the inhuman sheriffs if they did not alter their brutal course. This had a sobering effect upon them, and lawyers Southwick and Patrick came into the room. President Smith showed them his bruised sides, and asked them to obtain a writ of habeas corpus. A messenger was sent by Mr. Dixon to Mr. Chamberlain, master in chancery, who lived some six miles away, and another messenger was sent for Attorney Cyrus Walker, who happened to be campaigning near that place. Walker, Whig candidate for Congress, said he would come provided Joseph Smith would promise to vote for him, which the latter said he would do. This promise, Walker thought, would give him the united vote of the "Mormon" people, which would insure his election. About eight o'clock the master in chancery arrived and issued a writ of habeas corpus returnable before Judge John D. Caton, of the ninth judicial district, at Ottawa, which was served on Reynolds and Wilson. The same day William Clayton was sent by the Prophet to notify his brother Hyrum, and get assistance.

Reynolds and Wilson Under Arrest.—Stephen Markham went before a justice of the peace and obtained a warrant for Reynolds and Wilson for threatening his life. He later obtained other warrants from the circuit court of Lee County against them for threatening the life of Joseph Smith, and for false imprisonment, claiming ten thousand dollars damages, on the ground that the writ issued by Governor Ford was a void writ in law. As they could not obtain bondsmen outside of Missouri, they were taken into custody by Sheriff Campbell of Lee County. They also obtained a writ of habeas corpus and under these circumstances the entire party, including the lawyers and Mr. Dixon, started for Ottawa.

President Joseph Smith's Discourse at Pawpaw Grove.—Saturday night, June 24, they arrived at Pawpaw Grove, thirty-two miles distant from Dixon, and the following morning the people assembled at the hotel and requested that the Prophet preach. To this Reynolds objected, saying that Joseph Smith was his prisoner, and the people must disperse. They had witnessed his abuse of his prisoner, and Mr. David Town, an aged gentleman, who was lame, advanced and gave Reynolds to understand that he could not interrupt gentlemen. Bringing his heavy walking stick down with a thud, he said:

"You——Infernal puke, we'll learn you to come here and interrupt gentlemen. Sit down there (pointing to a very low chair), and sit still. Don't open your head till General Smith gets through talking. If you never learned manners in Missouri, we'll teach you that gentlemen are not to be imposed upon by a nigger-driver. You cannot kidnap men here, if you do in Missouri; and if you attempt it here, there's a committee in this grove that will sit on your case; and sir, it is the highest tribunal in the United States, as *from its decision there is no appeal!*"

Reynolds very meekly and in fear took the seat while President Smith addressed the people for one hour and a half.

The Issuing of New Writs.—It was learned that Judge Caton was in New York, so they all returned to Dixon, where new writs were obtained, made returnable before the nearest tribunal in the fifth judicial district, at Markham's request. Provision was now made to go to Quincy, where Judge Stephen A. Douglas was holding court. Twice on the way Reynolds and Wilson engaged in plots to raise mobs and carry Joseph Smith to the mouth of Rock River where there was a company from Missouri waiting to receive him; but each time the plans were discovered and foiled.

On the way Joseph convinced Sheriff Campbell and the attorneys that the court of Nauvoo was nearer than that of Quincy, and had full power to try his case, and hither they bent their way. Reynolds and Wilson endeavored to get Sheriff Campbell, who had them in custody, to go by way of Rock River, to Quincy, not knowing that their plots were discovered, saying that they would never go through Nauvoo alive. Joseph pledged his word of honor that they would not be molested, and the journey was resumed by land in the direction of Nauvoo.

A Party to the Rescue.—William Clayton arrived in Nauvoo on Sunday, June 25, 1843, and at the afternoon meeting in the temple Hyrum Smith requested to see all the brethren. He informed them of his brother Joseph's arrest, and called for volunteers to go to his assistance. That evening a company of about one hundred and seventy-five men left on horseback. Wilson Law refused to go unless his expenses could be met, whereupon President Brigham Young went to work and raised seven hundred dollars by subscription. About seventy-five men on board the *Maid of Iowa,* under Captain Dan Jones, went down the Mississippi to the mouth of the Illinois River, thence up that river toward Peoria, to examine the steamboats, suspecting the Prophet might be forced on one of them to be carried down the river to Missouri.

Shortly after the party with the Prophet left Geneseo on the 27th, the advance guard of the brethren, nine in all, from Nauvoo came up, and Reynolds and Wilson began to tremble fearing for their lives. Reynolds asked if "Jim" Flack was in the crowd. When he was informed that he would be present the next day, the criminal sheriff replied: "Then I am a dead man; for I know him of old." When Stephen Markham, who had gone to locate the brethren from Nauvoo rode up, Reynolds said, "Do I meet you as a friend? I expected to be a dead man when I met you again," but he was assured that he would not be hurt. Thursday, June 29, James Flack with others of the brethren met the company a short distance south of Monmouth. President Joseph Smith took Flack to one side and charged him not to harm Reynolds, for he had given his word of honor that he would not be injured. This Flack promised to do although he had cause for vengeance.

Arrival at Nauvoo.—Other bodies of men from Nauvoo joined the company from time to time and when they reached that place there were about one hundred and forty riding on horseback. who were joined by the populace in procession and thus they marched into the town. President Smith was greeted with cheers and the firing of cannon. He was still a prisoner in the hands of Reynolds and Wilson, and they in turn were prisoners in the hands of Sheriff Campbell. The Prophet took them to his house and placed Reynolds and Wilson at the head of the table, where about fifty persons were served. This was a very different reception from the one he had received from these men when they took him prisoner in Lee County, at the Wasson home.

The Trial Before the Municipal Court.—The same day they arrived in Nauvoo the municipal court convened, and a requisition was made on Reynolds to return the writ, but he refused to recognize the summons, whereupon the Prophet petitioned the court for a writ of habeas corpus to be directed to Reynolds, commanding him to bring his prisoner before the court. The summons was issued and Reynolds complied with the attachment and delivered the Prophet into the hands of the marshal of the city. That afternoon President Smith addressed the people at great length, declaring that

The Mansion House

he would not peacefully submit again to such ill-treatment. While he was speaking Reynolds and Wilson with a lawyer named Davis, of Carthage, left for that place threatening to raise the militia and come again and take President Smith out of Nauvoo.

Saturday, July 1, 1843, the court convened to examine the writ of habeas corpus. Messrs. Cyrus Walker, Shepherd G. Patrick, Edward Southwick and a Mr. Backman, defended Joseph Smith while Attorney Mason was counselor for Reynolds. Witnesses were examined and the case tried on its merits, Hyrum Smith, Parley P. Pratt, Brigham Young, George W. Pitkin, Lyman Wight and Sidney Rigdon giving testimony, at the conclusion of which the prisoner was discharged.

The Citizens of Lee County Thanked.—July 1, 1843, a mass meeting of the citizens of Nauvoo was held in the assembly hall and it was "unanimously resolved that Messrs. Sager and Dixon, of the town of Dixon, and the citizens of Dixon, Pawpaw Grove, and Lee County, receive the warmest thanks for the firm patriotism, bold and decided stand taken against lawless outrage and the spirit of mobocracy, as manifested in the arrest or capture of General Joseph Smith, while on a visit to his friends in that district of country."

Reynold's Further Attempt to Obtain Joseph Smith.—The proceedings of the municipal court of Nauvoo in this case were promptly forwarded to Governor Ford, with affidavits from the attorneys and others bearing upon the case and the kindly treatment Reynolds and Wilson had received in Nauvoo. Judge James Adams came from Carthage with the information that Reynolds and Wilson were exciting the people there to mobocracy, and petitioning the governor for a posse forcibly to take Joseph Smith, on the grounds that he had been unlawfully taken out of their hands. A remonstrance against the Carthage proceedings was prepared and forwarded to Carthage by Messrs. Southwick and Patrick, and a petition was sent to Governor Ford praying him not to issue any more writs.

Governor Ford refused to comply with the request of Sheriff Reynolds, and subsequently, when Governor Reynolds of Missouri requested him to call out the militia—a method they had of doing in Missouri—to retake Joseph Smith, Governor Ford replied that Joseph Smith had been tried before the municipal court of Nauvoo on a writ of habeas corpus, and discharged from arrest. He, as governor, had fully executed the duty which the laws imposed, and had not "been resisted either in the writ issued for the arrest of Smith or in the person of the officer appointed to apprehend him," and the constitution would not permit him to take such action as the Missouri official proposed.

The Case of O. P. Rockwell.—Orrin Porter Rockwell, who was accused as the principal in the shooting of ex-Governor Boggs, went into retirement with the Prophet when Governor Ford issued papers for his extradition. He traveled east as far as New Jersey where he remained for some time. Following the discharge of President Joseph Smith by Judge Pope, Rockwell concluded to return to Nauvoo, evidently by way of the Ohio and Mississippi Rivers. In St. Louis he was recognized by Elias Parker who had placed him under arrest, March 4, 1843. They carried him to Independence in chains, where he was placed under bonds in the sum of five thousand dollars, which they knew he could not raise, as no person outside of Missouri would be accepted by the court as bondsman. In the custody of the notorious Joseph H. Reynolds, sheriff of Jackson County, he was cast into prison bound hand and foot. Here he remained a prisoner for eight months.

March 15, 1843, the Prophet wrote: "I prophesied in the name of the Lord Jesus Christ, that Orrin Porter Rockwell would get away honorably from the Missourians."

On Christmas evening, 1843—the last Christmas day Joseph and Hyrum Smith celebrated on earth—a large party assembled at the Prophet's home, and spent the time in music, dancing and a social visit. During the festivities, a man with long shaggy hair, apparently drunk, came in and acted like a Missourian. A scuffle ensued and the Prophet had an opportunity to see the stranger's face. To his great surprise and joy he discovered his "long-tried, warm, but cruelly persecuted friend, Orrin Porter Rockwell." The party came to order while Rockwell related in detail his experiences and sufferings while in Missouri.

Orrin P. Rockwell's Story.—The story is too long to tell in full at this point. It is sufficient to relate the following incidents. When he arrived in Independence a large crowd had gathered and suggested hanging him at once, but he was placed in jail. In two or three days he underwent a mock trial, where false witnesses testified against him. The magistrate said he found no evidence against him, but placed him in prison for safe keeping, where Sheriff Reynolds chained him hand and foot. One time he was able to escape, but was recaptured and only by the providence of the Lord was saved from being hanged. About the time that President Smith was demanded by the governor of Missouri, Reynolds, the sheriff, came to Rockwell and said that he had discovered from letters that Joseph Smith had unlimited confidence in Rockwell, and if Rockwell would only "tote him out by riding or any other way," so that the Missourians might apprehend him, Rockwell might please himself whether he stayed in Illinois or returned to Missouri, they would protect him, and any pile that he would name the citizens of Jackson County, would club together and raise. "You only deliver Joe Smith into our hands, and name your pile." Rockwell replied: "I will see you all damned first, and then I won't."

The time of further trial was continually delayed, but on the 13th of December, he was taken before the court and tried—not on the charge of shooting Boggs, but for breaking jail! He was found guilty and sentenced to "five minutes' imprisonment in the county jail," but was kept there five hours, while his enemies tried to think of some other charge to make against him. He was finally released and with great difficulty made his way to Nauvoo, where he arrived that Christmas night.

CHAPTER 34

JOSEPH'S SMITH CANDIDACY FOR PRESIDENT —NAUVOO CONSPIRACY

1843–1844

Threats of the Mob.—Following the unsuccessful attempt to carry President Joseph Smith into Missouri, the hatred of his enemies became intense. Lying accusations were published in anti-"Mormon" papers and circulated against the Saints. Threats were made, both in Missouri and Illinois, of mob attacks and the legion was kept in readiness to withstand any mob assault. The governor was apprised of these conditions from time to time, and petitioned for protection, but refused to give credence to the rumors, or take any measures to repel any proposed invasion. This attitude increased the boldness of the enemies of the Saints, who declared, in reference to the governor, should he attempt to protect the "Mormons" in their rights: "If he opens his head we will punch a hole through him! He dare not speak! We will serve him the same sauce we will the 'Mormons!'"

Growth of Nauvoo.— Through the gathering of converts from Great Britain as well as from various parts of the United States, Nauvoo had become the foremost city of Illinois. It had risen from a swamp and wilderness in 1839, to a commonwealth of some twenty thousand souls. The people were frugal, industrious and law abiding. Many factories had been established, and measures were on foot, at the suggestion of President Smith, to dam the Mississippi for water power purposes. He also suggested that Congress be petitioned to build a

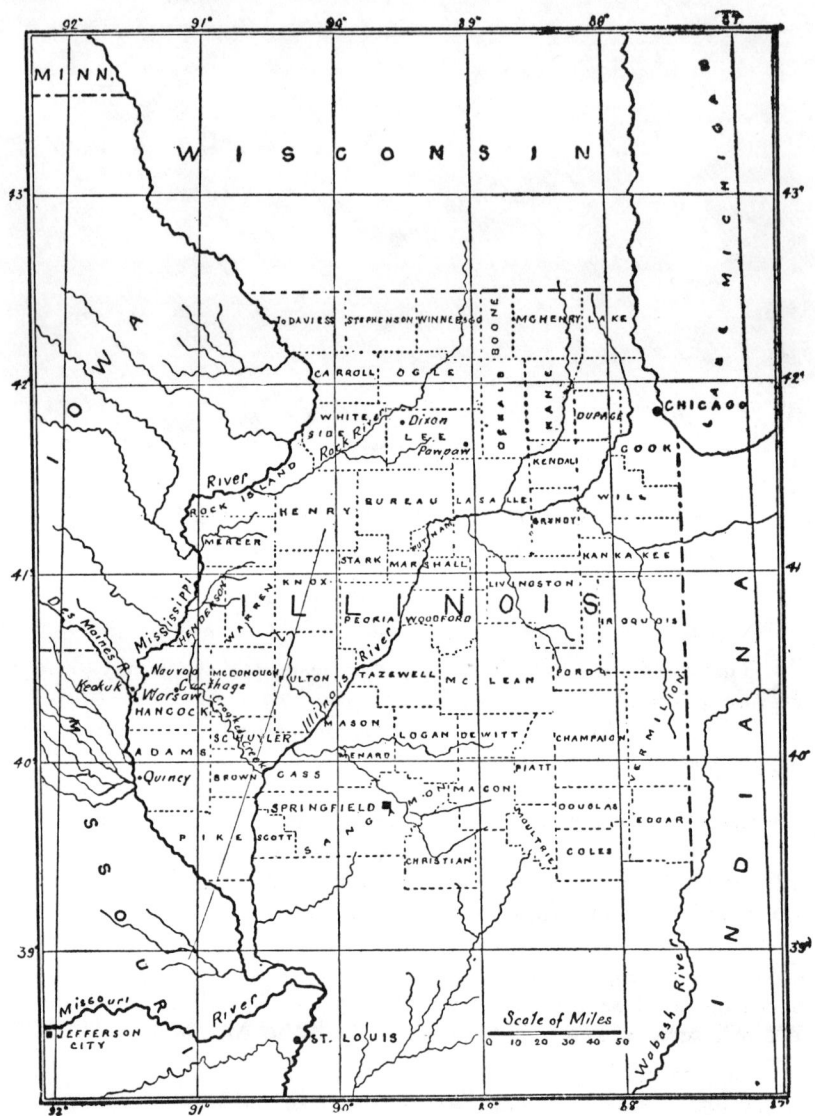

Map of Northern Illinois

canal around the Des Moines rapids to admit the passage of boats for commercial purposes.[a] He instructed the Saints to be producers and

---

[a]Such a canal was built, and completed in 1877, at a cost to the government of more than four million dollars.

to manufacture from the raw materials, rather than to be consumers only, and under his direction and inspiration the city prospered.

Jealousy of Other Towns.—All this augmented the jealousy and hatred of the neighboring towns, where thrift and unity were lacking. Another thing that increased the opposition, especially of the politicians, was the fact that the Saints usually voted as a unit. It was this tendency which caused Cyrus Walker to seek the favor of Joseph Smith in the summer of 1843. However, the voting of the "Mormons" in this manner was not due to instruction from the leading councils of the Church, but from necessity and for self-preservation. Both the Whig and the Democratic office-seekers sought the support of the Saints, and when it was not forthcoming, hatred filled their breasts, and vengeance was threatened. The constant arrival of immigrants, who were instructed to gather at Nauvoo, was also looked upon as an attempt to lay plans to control the state. So strong were the Latter-day Saints that they held the balance of power in the elections and naturally threw their support to those most friendly to them, which aroused the animosities of their opponents to a murderous degree.

In the August (1843) election Robert D. Foster and George W. Thatcher were elected to county offices. They went to Carthage to give bonds and take their oaths and were threatened by Harmon T. Wilson and some fifteen or twenty others, who were armed with knives and pistols. The bonds, however, were accepted, and the mob gave notice of a meeting of anti-"Mormons" to consider the question of the "Mormons" holding office. At their meeting they made all manner of accusations and threats, stating that they "pledge themselves in the most determined manner" to aid Missouri should another demand be made for Joseph Smith, which gave encouragement to the enemies of the Saints within that state.

Near the close of the year 1843, they openly resorted to mob violence. Daniel Avery and his son Philander, were kidnaped and delivered to the Missourians. On false accusations they were imprisoned and brutally treated for some time. The son finally made his escape and the father was later released on habeas corpus proceedings.

Joseph Smith and the Presidency of the United States.—From the time of the organization of the Church the Saints had suffered most cruelly at the hands of enemies. Governors and lesser state dignitaries, had aided in the persecutions. No redress, even from the government of the United States, could be obtained. Mobs still menaced them, and their chances for protection by lawful means were not the best for the governor of Illinois was intimidated by mob threats. It was agreed, therefore, to inquire of the various candidates for the presidency of the United States what their feelings would be, if elected, towards the Latter-day Saints, and their course of action in relation to the cruel oppression the Saints had suffered. Accordingly letters were sent to the leading candidates. Only two, Henry Clay and John C. Calhoun, deigned to make reply. Their answers were so unsatisfactory that the "Mormon" people decided they could vote for neither of them. Clay replied that if he ever entered that high office he must go into it free and unfettered, with no guarantees but such as were to be drawn from his whole life, character and conduct, although he had sympathized with the Saints in their sufferings under injustice. Calhoun was more frank, stating that the case of the Saints in Missouri, candor compelled him to say, "did not come within the jurisdiction of the Federal Government, which is one of limited and specific powers."

Under these conditions the citizens of Nauvoo felt that the only consistent step they could take was to place their own candidate in the field. Consequently, at a political convention held in Nauvoo, January 29, 1844, Joseph Smith was nominated as a candidate for the presidency of the United States, and on May 17, a state convention was held in Nauvoo where his nomination was sustained. There was no thought on the part of President Joseph Smith or the Saints that he would be elected, but it gave to them an opportunity to express their feelings, and to sustain a candidate who would advocate their rights against oppression. In the *Times and Seasons* (Feb. 15) an editorial was published entitled: "Who Shall Be Our Next President?" in which the reasons for selecting their own candidate were clearly and emphatically stated by the editor (John Taylor) in behalf of the Latter-day Saints.

James Arlington Bennett, of New York, was asked to become their candidate for the vice-presidency, but as he was born in Ireland, was not eligible. Sidney Rigdon, who had moved from Nauvoo to Pittsburgh—contrary to revelation and to the feelings of the Prophet—was selected for that place.

Views on the Powers and Policy of the Government.—In February, 1844, Joseph Smith published to the world his "Views on the Powers and Policy of the Government of the United States." After speaking of the greatness and glory of the United States under the early presidents he says that "'since the fathers have fallen asleep,' wicked and designing men have unrobed the government of its glory." He advocated the reduction of the number of congressmen by two-thirds; the pardoning of prisoners in state prisons; the making of laws to provide for useful employment of prisoners on roads, public works or elsewhere, where they may be taught more wisdom and more virtue, and only murderers should be confined or put to death. He would turn the prisons into seminaries of learning; and petition the inhabitants of the slave states to abolish slavery by 1850, or before, "and save the abolitionist from reproach and ruin, infamy and shame." This should be done by Congress paying every man a reasonable price for his slaves out of the revenue from the sale of public lands, and deducted pay from members of Congress, that liberty may be granted to all men. He would abolish the practice of trying men by court martial for desertion, and if a man deserts send him his pay with instructions that his country will never trust him more and that he has forfeited his honor. Make honor the standard with all men; render good for evil, "and the whole nation, like a kingdom of kings and priests, will rise up in righteousness." He advocated more economy; less taxes; greater equality, and less distinction among the people. Also the establishment of a national bank, with branches in each state and territory, the net revenue therefrom to be applied to government interests. The president should have full power to send an army to suppress mobs, and there should be a repeal of the requirement for governors to petition the president for troops in cases of invasion or rebellion. A governor himself may be a mobber and power should be given the president to protect citizens in such an event. Oregon, by right, and with the consent of the Indian should belong to the United States, and he would invite Texas, Canada, Mexico, to join the sons of liberty, and let the Union spread.

Such, in brief, is the platform of Joseph Smith, and when it was circulated throughout the United States, it created much commotion and favorable comment for its direct and fearless advocacy of principles which other candidates, for policy's sake, dared not express.

The Contemplated Expedition to the West.—The rising tide of persecution portended a repetition of the cruel Missouri scenes. President Joseph Smith knew full well, even in the face of continued urging of the Saints to build Nauvoo and make her towers glorious, that the time would come when they would have to seek a new home in the wilderness. The prophecy of August 6, 1842, had stamped this fact upon the minds of others, and the Prophet had referred to it from time to time. He records in his history under date of February 20, 1844, the following:

"I instructed the Twelve Apostles to send out a delegation and investigate the locations of California and Oregon, and hunt out a good location, where we can remove to after the temple is completed, and where we can build a city in a day, and have a government of our own, get up into the mountains, where the devil cannot dig us out, and live in a healthful climate, where we can live as old as we have a mind to."

The next day another meeting was held in the mayor's office, in Nauvoo, most of the twelve were present, and Jonathan Dunham, Phineas H. Young, David D. Yearsley, and David Fullmer, volunteered to go. Alphonzo Young, James Emmett, George D. Watt and Daniel Spencer were requested to go, and another meeting was called to meet on February 23, to further discuss matters pertaining to this expedition. On that date President Smith and the twelve met again. Patriarch Hyrum Smith and Sidney Rigdon were also present. The Prophet instructed them saying he wanted an exploration of all the mountain country. Perhaps it would be best for them to go by way of Santa Fe. "Send twenty-five men," he said, "let them preach the Gospel wherever they go. Let that man go that can raise $500, a good horse and mule, a double-barrel gun, one barrel rifle and the other smooth bore, a saddle and bridle, a pair of revolving pistols, bowie-knife, and a good sabre. Appoint a leader and let them beat up for volunteers. I want every man that goes to be a king and a priest. When he gets on the mountains he may want to talk with his God; when with the savage nations, have power to govern. If we don't get volunteers, wait till after the election." On this occasion, Samuel Bent, Joseph A. Kelting, Samuel Rolf, Daniel Avery and Samuel W. Richards were added to the expedition and others joined from time to time. Sunday, February 25, the Prophet predicted that within five years the Saints would be out of the power of their old enemies, whether they were apostate or of the world, and commanded the brethren to write it down "that when it comes to pass they need not say they had forgotten the saying."

Memorial to Congress.—March 26, 1844, a memorial was prepared by President Joseph Smith asking Congress to pass an ordinance for the protection of citizens of the United States emigrating to the territories and that indefinite country known as California and Oregon. He asked for authorization to raise a company of one hundred thousand volunteers, at such times and places as he might find necessary for this purpose. At this time Oregon was a disputed territory, unsettled, and held by the United States and Great Britain jointly by treaty. Texas was asking for admission into the United States, but had been denied. Orson Pratt and John E. Page and later Orson Hyde, were sent to Washington to urge the consideration of the scheme. Most of the Illinois delegation favored it. For political reasons no official action was ever taken, but the general sentiment of the politicians, who were afraid to act openly, was in favor of the proposition.

Traitors From Within.—It was not so much from Missouri and among the mobocrats of Illinois, that the Prophet had cause to fear, but from traitors within the councils of the Church. In the highest quorums, men were found who secretly plotted against his life. He remarked in a discourse in October of 1843: "This generation is as corrupt as the generation of the Jews that crucified Christ; and if he were here today, and should preach the same doctrine he did to them they would put him to death. I defy all the world to destroy the work of God; and I prophesy they never will have power to kill me *till my work is accomplished, and I am ready to die.*" In January, 1844, it became necessary to increase the police force for the protection of the city. Joseph Smith, as mayor, addressed these newly appointed officers of the peace, and instructed them in their duties. In the course of his remarks he said:

"I am exposed to far greater danger from traitors among ourselves than from enemies without, although my life has been sought for many years by the civil and military authorities, priests, and people of Missouri; and if I can escape from the ungrateful treachery of assassins, I can live as Caesar might have lived, were it not for a right-hand Brutus. I have had pretended friends betray me. All the enemies upon the face of the earth may roar and exert all their power to bring about my death, but they can accomplish nothing, unless some who are among us and enjoy our society, have been with us in our councils, participated in our confidence, taken us by the hand, called us brother, saluted us with a kiss, join with our enemies, turn our virtues into faults, and, by falsehood and deceit, stir up their wrath and indignation against us, and bring their united vengeance upon our heads. All the hue-and-cry of the chief priests and elders against the Savior, could not bring down the wrath of the Jewish nation upon his head, and thereby cause the crucifixion of the Son of God, until Judas said unto them, 'Whomsoever I shall kiss, he is the man; hold him fast.' Judas was one of the Twelve Apostles, even their treasurer, and dipt with their Master in the dish, and through his treachery, the crucifixion was brought about; and *we have a Judas in our midst.*"

"The Wicked Flee."—These remarks gave offense to William and Wilson Law, William Marks, Leonard Soby, Dr. Foster and others. William Law was the Prophet's second counselor, and his brother had been honored with the position of major general of the Nauvoo Legion, and was also prominent in the Church. William Marks was president of the Nauvoo Stake of Zion. Commenting on their fears, President Joseph Smith stated: "What can be the matter with these men? Is it that the wicked flee when no man pursueth * * * or that Presidents Law and Marks are absolutely traitors to the Church, that my remarks should produce such excitement in their minds? Can it be possible that the traitor whom Porter Rockwell reports to me as being in correspondence with my Missouri enemies is one of my quorum?[b] The people in the town are astonished, almost every man saying to his neighbor, 'Is it possible that Brother Law or Marks is a traitor, and would deliver Brother Joseph into the hands of his enemies in Missouri?' If not what can be the meaning of all this? The righteous are bold as a lion."

Councils of Apostates.—It soon developed that some of these men were secretly plotting the death of the Prophet and the destruction of the Church, claiming that he had fallen from his high and holy calling. Among them were those who had been tinctured by the wickedness of John C. Bennett, from which they did not recover. Others had been guilty of immoral conduct within more recent months and had been exposed. Their vengeance was directed against President Joseph Smith towards whom they now entertained a murderous spirit.

Experience of Scott and Harris.—In the spring of 1844, a number of secret meetings were held by these conspirators, to which all whom they could trust among the disaffected spirits, were invited. Two young men, Denison L. Harris and Robert Scott, the latter living with the family of William Law, were invited to attend. Young Harris was also asked to invite his father, Emer Harris. The boys pondered over the invitation and then consulted with Emer Harris, who concluded to lay the matter before President Joseph Smith. After hearing the story the Prophet advised the father to stay away, but said he would like to have the boys attend, but they must first receive some advice from him. As they were instructed, they attended the first two meetings and each time made their report to the Prophet. These gatherings were given over to abuse and falsehood affecting President Smith, and the discussion of future plans. When the young men reported the second time Joseph was in doubt whether they should go again and asked them to visit him for further instructions just before the third meeting, which, like the others, was to be held on the Sabbath day. When the time came he said to them: "This will be the last time that they will admit you into their councils. They will come to some determination, but be sure that you make no covenant, nor enter into any obligations whatever with them." Arriving at the place of meeting the young men were astonished to see it guarded by men with muskets, and after due scrutiny they were admitted. In the meeting the Prophet and his brother Hyrum and others were accused of the most wicked acts. Joseph was

---

[b]It was later discovered that William Law was in league with the Missourians.

called a fallen prophet, and his death was said to be necessary to save the Church. An oath had been prepared which each member present was required to take. The candidate would step forward to the table, where Francis M. Higbee, a justice of the peace, was stationed, and he would ask: "Are you ready?" Receiving a favorable reply he administered the following oath:

"You solemnly swear, before God and all holy angels, and these your brethren by whom you are surrounded that you will give your life, your liberty, your influence, your all, for the destruction of Joseph Smith and his party, so help you God!"

The person being sworn would say "I do," after which he would lay down the Bible on which the oath was taken, and sign his name to a written copy of the oath in a book, which would then be acknowledged by the justice of the peace.

The boys sat in amazement wondering how these men, formerly faithful in the councils of the twelve, could fall so low. In this manner the oath was administered to about two hundred, among whom were three women, heavily veiled.

Their Lives Threatened.—Presently the turn for the two youths came to take the pledge, and they both manfully refused, stating that Joseph Smith had done them no harm and they were too young to understand these things. This aroused the anger of the conspirators, and when coaxing and argument failed, they threatened them with death. "Come boys," they said, "do as we have done. You are young, and will not have anything to do in the affair, but we want you should keep it a secret, and act with us; that's all." "No," they replied, "we cannot take an oath like that against any man who has never done us any injury." They tried to pass out, but one of the band stopped them saying: "No, not by a ——! You know all our plans and arrangements, and we don't propose that you should leave in that style. You've got to take the oath, or you'll never leave here alive." The boys were surrounded by these evil conspirators, who with drawn swords and knives, were determined to take their lives. The leaders, no less determined, concluded that the deed of blood could not be committed there, as the house was too near the street. So the young men were taken to the cellar and preparations were made for their murder. At this point, however, as if by an act of Providence, someone spoke up and said it was evidently known by the parents of these boys that they were there, and if they did not return a search would be put on foot that might prove to be very dangerous to the plotters. The result was that after some consultation they were released, with a strict injunction, and many threats, not to reveal to any one what they had heard, or they would be killed, and under a guard they were permitted to depart. They immediately took their course towards the river in the opposite direction from their homes, conveying the impression to their enemies by word and act, that they would keep their secret. On the river bank they met the Prophet and an elder brother of Robert Scott, and to them they told their story. (*Contributor,* Vol. 5:25.)

On the 27th day of March, 1844, Abiathar B. Williams and M. G. Eaton, each made affidavit before Daniel H. Wells, justice of the peace, confirming the story of these young men, and implicating Chauncey L. Higbee, Robert D. Foster, Joseph H. Jackson and Wilson and William Law, as the leaders among the plotters. Shortly afterwards (April 18, 1844) the two Laws and Robert D. Foster, were excommunicated from the Church. Others prominent in this conspiracy were Austin Cowles, Francis M. Higbee, Charles Ivins and Charles A. Foster.

Apostates Attempt to Organize a Church.—An attempt was made by these apostates to organize a church of their own, patterned after the Church of Christ, with William Law at the head. Their following was small and the attempt was a failure. They soon joined hands openly with the most bitter enemies of the Saints and aided them in all their anti-"Mormon" persecutions. They advocated the repeal of the Nauvoo Charter; insulted the officers of the city and maliciously violated the ordinances, endeavoring to bring the city into ill-repute. Their evil deeds they laid at the door of others and with lying tongues made brutal accusations against the innocent, and threatened the life of the Prophet.

Plot to Kill Joseph Smith.—May 25, 1844, William Law, Robert D. Foster and Joseph H. Jackson, had Joseph Smith indicted at Carthage on the charge of polygamy and perjury. Two days later Joseph left for Carthage, accompanied by a number of his friends, and voluntarily gave himself up for trial. He secured legal assistance and endeavored to have his case tried, but the opposition insisted on the case going over until the next term of court. On the way to Carthage, Charles A. Foster overtook the Prophet and his company, and had some conversation. When they reached their destination Foster called Joseph Smith aside and informed him of a conspiracy against his life. His brother Robert D., with tears in his eyes, also said there were persons there who had planned to kill the Prophet before he left that town. The spark of repentance kindled in their breasts, however, soon died out, and these two men again banded with the conspirators in Nauvoo, to bring to pass the death of Joseph and Hyrum Smith.

The "Nauvoo Expositor."—To better advance their malicious course, the conspirators of Nauvoo procured a press and proposed the publishing of a paper to be called the *Nauvoo Expositor*. The object of the paper, as set forth in the prospectus was, to advocate *"the unconditional repeal of the Nauvoo City Charter,* to restrain and correct the abuses of the *unit power,* to ward off the iron rod which is held over the devoted heads of the citizens of Nauvoo * * * * to advocate an *unmitigated disobedience to political revelations,* and to censure and decry gross moral imperfections wherever found, either in plebeian, patrician or *self-constituted Monarch*—to advocate the pure principles of morality." In plain words to attack the Church and destroy the protection of the Saints guaranteed by the Charter of Nauvoo.

The first and only number of the *Expositor* appeared June 7, 1844, filled with vile and malicious slanders against the Prophet and the leading citizens of Nauvoo. In attacking the charter, these wicked conspirators knew they were taking a course which would gain them the sympathy and aid of all the enemies of the Church, as nothing else could do. The charter, with its liberal provisions, had aroused the hatred of anti-"Mormons" because it prevented their sinister and diabolical designs. These same evil actors had lived under the charter from the beginning, and had been loud in its praise and defense, until Satan entered their hearts and their minds became darkened. They knew that the Latter-day Saints, without the charter would be a prey to their enemies, and at the mercy of their apostate persecutors, the small minority of population, who could wreak vengeance upon their former brethren without restraint.

The circulation of the first number of this paper filled the hearts of the people with righteous indignation. Their liberty was attacked, their lives threatened, and the prospect, from the circulation of falsehoods within their city, and bitter hatred without, was another expulsion from their homes. Were they to submit peaceably to such attacks?

The "Expositor" Declared a Nuisance.—At a meeting of the city council held June 10, after full consideration, the *Expositor* was declared a public nuisance and was ordered to be abated. The city marshal John P. Greene was instructed to proceed to the printing office and carry out the order of the council. Taking with him a few men he proceeded to inform the proprietors of his mission and demanded entrance into the building which was denied. With little effort he opened the door, pied the type, carried out the press and burned the printed papers that were found. He then reported to the mayor who immediately forwarded an account of the proceedings to the governor of Illinois.

In a rage the conspirators set fire to the building and hastened to Carthage, stating that their lives were in danger and they had been driven from their homes. The fire was discovered and extinguished before any damage had been done, but the falsehoods circulated aroused the people of Carthage and other towns. Indignation meetings were held and mobs began to gather under arms.

CHAPTER 35

THE MARTYRDOM
1844

Charge of Francis M. Higbee.—June 11, 1844, Francis M. Higbee made complaint before Thomas Morrison, a justice of the peace at Carthage, charging Joseph Smith and the members of the Nauvoo city council with riot committed in destroying the press of the *Expositor*. The warrant was served by Constable David Bettisworth the following day. It required that the accused should go before the justice issuing the warrant, "or some other justice of the peace, for trial." The Prophet expressed his willingness to go before some other justice, as he had lawful right to do, but was not willing to be taken to Carthage to be tried before his mobocratic enemies. Bettisworth, in anger, declared that he would take him to Carthage. His attention was called to the nature of the warrant and that his actions were contrary to law, and with righteous indignation, Joseph Smith obtained a writ of habeas corpus and was legally tried before the municipal court of Nauvoo and discharged. Each of the members of the city council did the same, and were likewise discharged.

Anger of the Mob.—When Bettisworth returned to Carthage without his prisoners, the disappointment of the mobocrats was intense, and they threatened to go against Nauvoo in force. Indignation meetings were held in Warsaw and in Carthage, and inflammatory speeches were made against the Saints. The assembled mobbers in each place adopted resolutions in which they said, "We hold ourselves at all times in readiness to co-operate with our fellow-citizens in this state, Missouri and Iowa, to exterminate, utterly exterminate, the wicked and abominable 'Mormon' leaders, the authors of the troubles." All members of the Church, or sympathizers with Joseph Smith, were warned to leave these townships on pain of instant vengeance. A deputation was sent by them to the governor, stating that Joseph Smith and others had refused to obey the mandate of the writ, and with other falsehoods they attempted to prejudice him in their favor. The minutes of these unlawful and wicked proceedings were published in the *Warsaw Signal* and other papers of the state.

The Saints Threatened.—The Saints also sent messengers to the governor with full and correct accounts of the proceedings at Nauvoo, and asking for protection. In the meantime, without waiting for the governor's reply, the mob forces commenced their brutal attacks upon the Saints residing outside of Nauvoo, threatening them with destruction unless they immediately accepted one of the following propositions: Deny Joseph Smith as a Prophet of God and join the mob in securing his arrest; gather up their effects and move to Nauvoo; or give up their arms and remain quiet until the affair was over. Runners were dispatched to Missouri for aid from the mobbers there, and the whole country was inflamed by the spread of diabolical falsehoods.

Advice of Judge Thomas.—The Prophet did everything in his power to allay excitement and kept the governor posted with numerous affidavits and documents regarding the state of affairs. Judge Jesse B. Thomas, of the circuit court, advised the Prophet to go before some justice of the peace in the county and have an examination on the writ issued by Morrison, which action would take away all excuse of the mob, and then he could take steps to have them bound to keep the peace. For his pains, Judge Thomas was threatened by the mob with a coat of tar and feathers. The Prophet accepted his advice and was tried before Justice Daniel H. Wells, a non-"Mormon," and after a full investigation was discharged. His enemies knew that this trial was lawful, as the previous one had been; but they were determined not to be thwarted in their wicked purpose. They thirsted for the blood of the Prophet and were determined to drag him to Carthage, with or without process of law, there to slay him. A mass meeting was held in Nauvoo, pacific resolutions were adopted, and messengers chosen to go forth in the surrounding country to declare the truth and allay excitement; but the prejudice was too great and little was accomplished.

Nauvoo Under Martial Law.—Because of threats of mob vengeance from both Missouri and Illinois information was sent to President Tyler of the United States, acquainting him with the danger and asking for protection. Nauvoo was placed under martial law, and the legion mustered into service in self-defense. The Prophet stood before them in his uniform as lieutenant-general and addressed them at length, in defense of their liberties. In the course of his remarks he said:

"It is thought by some that our enemies would be satisfied by my destruction, but I tell you as soon as they have shed my blood, they will thirst for the blood of every man in whose heart dwells a single spark of the spirit of the fulness of the Gospel. The opposition of these men is moved by the spirit of the adversary of all righteousness. It is not only to destroy me, but every man and woman who dares believe the doctrine that God hath inspired me to teach to this generation."

Appeal to the Governor for Protection.—On June 16, Joseph wrote Governor Ford, calling his attention to the mob meetings at Carthage and Warsaw, and the threats made to exterminate the Saints. He requested the governor to come to Nauvoo to make further investigation, and to quell insurrection. Instead of going to Nauvoo, Governor Ford went to Carthage, and sent word to Nauvoo that he was there in the interest of peace, and asked that well-informed and discreet persons be sent to him. Elders John Taylor and Dr. John M. Bernhisel were immediately sent to Carthage; but to their surprise and disappointment they found the governor surrounded by some of the worst element in Illinois. The Laws, Fosters and Higbees, with Joseph H. Jackson, an adventurer and murderer, the publishers of the *Expositor,* had his ear. Elders Taylor and Bernhisel could not get an interview with the governor except in the presence of these vicious enemies who had pledged themselves to bring to pass the death of Joseph and Hyrum Smith. As they told their side of the story they were constantly interrupted by this rabble with, "that's a — — lie," and other unseemly epithets of like character. The governor treated them very rudely, showing that he was under the influence of the mob. He stated that Joseph Smith and the members of the city council should come to Carthage to be tried on the original writ as nothing short of that would satisfy the people. When the messengers protested because of the murderous spirit of the mob, the governor strenuously advised that they come without arms and pledged his faith that they should be protected. He also sent a written communication to Joseph Smith, in which he said the city council, in destroying the *Expositor* press, had committed a gross outrage upon the laws and liberty of the people. He ignored the trial before the municipal court and also that before Daniel H. Wells, justice of the peace, demanding that all who were accused should submit themselves "to be arrested by the same constable, by virtue of the same warrant, and tried before the same magistrate whose authority has heretofore been resisted. Nothing short of this can vindicate the dignity of violated law and allay the just excitement of the people." Governor Ford must have blushed with shame when he penned

Proclamation Issued by Joseph Smith

these lines, for he knew he was violating his oath of office and declaring an untruth, for the sake of finding favor with the mob. If his demand was not complied with he threatened to come with sufficient force to execute his order. "You know the excitement of the public mind," he said. "Do not tempt it too far. A very little matter may do a very great injury; and if you are disposed to continue the causes of excitement and render a force necessary to coerce submission, I would say that your city was built, as it were upon a keg of powder which a very little spark may explode." *"And I will,"* he continued, *"also guarantee the safety of all such persons as may thus be brought to this place from Nauvoo either for trial or as witnesses for the accused."*

The same day (June 22) the Prophet respectfully replied to this cravenly penned communication, defending his course and denying the false accusations contained in the governor's letter. He called attention to the promises made in Missouri, but when witnesses came they were cast into prison, and since "a burnt child dreads the fire," they were not to be blamed if they refused to place themselves in the hands of a blood-thirsty mob openly making threats to take their lives. The Prophet expressed a willingness to go before any other justice in the state, except at Carthage, or before the circuit court, but did not feel legally bound to go to Carthage to be butchered.

The governor's letter to Joseph Smith caused no small surprise among the Saints. It was evident that they could not look to him for help, for he had joined himself entirely with their enemies. He had ignored the law; refused to recognize the legality of the courts, and the right of a fair and impartial trial before an unprejudiced judge and jury.

Hyrum Refuses to Leave his Brother.—So serious had the matter become that a letter was sent to President Brigham Young and the apostles who were in the mission field, instructing them to return to Nauvoo at once. The Prophet had previously (June 20) advised his brother Hyrum to take his family and go at once by steamboat to Cincinnati. Hyrum replied: "Joseph, I can't leave you," whereupon Joseph remarked to his brethren, "I wish I could get Hyrum out of the way, so that he may live to avenge my blood, and I will stay with you and see it out."

The Proposed Journey to the West.—In the afternoon of June 22, Joseph was in consultation with Hyrum Smith, John Taylor, Willard Richards and Dr. John M. Bernhisel, when it was decided that he should go to Washington and lay the whole difficulty before President

Tyler. At dusk another consultation was held, when the Prophet called these same brethren and William W. Phelps, Abraham C. Hodge, John L. Butler, Alpheus Cutler and William Marks, to his office in his upper room. The governor's letter was read and the Prophet said, "There is no mercy—no mercy here." Hyrum said, "No; just as sure as we fall into their hands we are dead men." Joseph replied, "Yes; what shall we do, Brother Hyrum?" Hyrum replied, "I don't know." All at once the Prophet's countenance brightened up and he said, "The way is open. It is clear to my mind what to do. All they want is Hyrum and myself; then tell everybody to go about their business, and not collect in groups, but to scatter about. There is no doubt they will come here and search for us. Let them search; they will not harm you in person or property, and not even a hair of your head. We will cross the river tonight, and go away to the West." On this date Joseph wrote: "I told Stephen Markham that if Hyrum and I were ever taken again we should be massacred, or I was not a prophet of God. I want Hyrum to live to avenge my blood but he is determined not to leave me."

Between nine and ten o'clock Hyrum Smith came out of the Mansion House and gave his hand to Reynolds Cahoon, saying, "A company of men are seeking to kill my brother Joseph, and the Lord has warned him to flee to the Rocky Mountains to save his life. Good-bye, Brother Cahoon, we shall see you again." A few minutes later, as Joseph, Hyrum and Willard Richards were waiting on the river bank, William W. Phelps was instructed to take the families of the Prophet and Patriarch to Cincinnati. About midnight the three brethren were rowed across the river by Orrin P. Rockwell who returned with instructions to obtain horses and pass them over the river the next night secretly, and be ready to start for the Great Basin in the Rocky Mountains.

The Governor's Threat.—At ten o'clock on the morning of the 23rd the governor's posse arrived in Nauvoo to arrest the Prophet, but not finding him they returned, leaving one of their number to watch for him. This posse said that if Joseph and Hyrum Smith were not given up the governor was determined to send his troops into the city and guard it until they were found, if it took three years.

Joseph Smith Accused of Cowardice.—At one p.m. Emma Smith sent Orrin P. Rockwell to entreat the Prophet to come back. Reynolds Cahoon accompanied him with a letter to the same effect. Reynolds Cahoon, Lorenzo D. Wasson and Hiram Kimball accused Joseph of cowardice for wishing to leave the people, saying that their property would be destroyed, and they would be left without house or home.

Like the fable, when the wolves came the shepherds ran from the flock.

The Return to Nauvoo.—The persecutions of enemies were easy to bear, but when he was thus accused by those who should have been his dearest friends, the Prophet was stung to the quick. It was not for himself he sought safety, but for his people. If this was all they cared, he would not seek to save himself. He replied: "If my life is of no value to my friends, it is of none to myself." Turning to Rockwell he said, "What shall I do?" Rockwell answered: "You are the oldest and ought to know best; and as you make your bed, I will lie with you." Joseph then turned to Hyrum and said: "Brother Hyrum, you are the oldest, what shall we do?" Hyrum said, "Let us go back and give ourselves up, and see the thing out." The Prophet remained in deep reflection for some time, and then remarked: "If you go back I will go with you, but we shall be butchered." Hyrum said, "No, no, let us go back and put our trust in God, and we shall not be harmed. The Lord is in it. If we live or have to die, we will be reconciled to our fate."

They then returned, and the first thing the Prophet did was to notify Governor Ford, by the hands of Theodore Turley and Jedediah M. Grant, that he would be ready to go to Carthage on the morrow. The governor promised to send a posse to protect him on the way, but through the influence of the Nauvoo conspirators, he changed his mind and ordered the Prophet and Patriarch to come to Carthage without escort.

The Start for Carthage.—Early on the morning of the 24th of June, Joseph and Hyrum with the accused members of the city council and a few tried friends, left Nauvoo for Carthage. On the way the Prophet hesitated, and looked back with admiration upon the city, the temple, and his farm. "This is the loveliest place, and the best people, under the heavens;" he said, "little do they know the trials that await them!" They passed the home of Esq. Daniel H. Wells, who was unwell. The Prophet stopped and called on him, and as he parted, he said: "Squire Wells, I wish you to cherish my memory and not think me the worst man in the world either."

The Governor's Demand for Arms.—About four miles from Carthage they met Captain Dunn with a company of about sixty mounted militia, who presented the Prophet with an order from the governor for delivery of all the state arms in possession of the Nauvoo Legion, which Joseph promptly countersigned. It was not enough for the governor to demand the presence of the Prophet and Patriarch at Carthage to be murdered, but the people in Nauvoo were to be left defenseless against their enemies. This order for the delivery of the state arms was evidently intended to exasperate the Saints to commit some overt act, which might be construed as treason. Fearing that the inhabitants of Nauvoo would show resistance, Captain Dunn requested that the whole company return with him to Nauvoo, and pledged to protect them even with his life. A messenger was sent to the governor explaining the reason for the return to Nauvoo. Notwithstanding the many threats, which the governor constantly had heard against the lives of Joseph and Hyrum Smith, no action was taken to disarm the mob, who were mustered into the governor's service. It appeared very much like a repetition of the Missouri scenes, in making the Saints defenseless while in a peaceful attitude, and arming their murderous enemies with state arms.

A Lamb to the Slaughter.—When the company met Captain Dunn, the Prophet said:

"I am going like a lamb to the slaughter, but I am as calm as a summer's morning. I have a conscience void of offense toward God and toward all men. If they take my life I shall die an innocent man, and my blood shall cry from the ground for vengeance, and it shall be said of me, 'He was murdered in cold blood!'"

When the work of Captain Dunn was accomplished, he thanked the people for their peaceful compliance and promised them protection. Late that afternoon the journey to Carthage was commenced again. It was midnight when the company arrived at that town, and while passing the public square many of the troops of the Carthage Greys made murderous threats. "Stand away, you McDonough boys," they yelled, "and let us shoot the damned 'Mormons.'" "– – you, old Joe, we've got you now. Clear the way and let us have a view of Joe Smith, the prophet of God. He has seen the last of Nauvoo. We'll use him up now, and kill all the damned Mormons."

Governor Ford's Promise to the Mob-Militia.—On hearing these threats Governor Ford put his head out of a window and said, "I know your great anxiety to see Mr. Smith, which is natural enough, but it is quite too late tonight for you to have the opportunity; but I assure you, gentlemen, you shall have that privilege tomorrow morning, as I will cause him to pass before the troops upon the square, and I now wish you, with this assurance, quietly and peaceably to return to your quarters." With a faint "Hurrah for Tom Ford," they complied with his wish.

The Charge of Treason.—Early on the morning of the 25th the prisoners voluntarily surrendered themselves to Constable Bettisworth.

Shortly afterwards Joseph and Hyrum were again arrested by Bettisworth on the charge of "treason" against the state of Illinois, on complaint of Augustine Spencer and Henry O. Norton.

The Governor's Inflammatory Speech.—Shortly after eight o'clock Governor Ford called all the troops together and formed them in a hollow square. He then addressed them in a most inflammatory manner against the Prophet Joseph and the Patriarch Hyrum Smith. They needed little encouragement, as he well knew, for they even then were inflamed to a murderous degree. At the close of his speech he fulfilled his promise to the troops as they were drawn up in file, by taking Joseph and Hyrum Smith before them, and introduced them as Generals Joseph and Hyrum Smith. The Carthage Greys refused to receive them by such title, and made threats against their lives, to which the governor paid little heed.

His Lack of Sincerity.—When Joseph Smith reported to Governor Ford that he had been before Daniel H. Wells, a justice of the peace, and had been tried, the governor replied that no other justice would do to try the case but the one who had issued the writ, therefore they must be tried before Justice Morrison. His lack of sincerity is shown in the fact that they were now taken before Justice Robert F. Smith, captain of the Carthage Greys and a most bitter mobocrat. The governor's object was to drag them to Carthage to their enemies, and there was no thought of justice or right in making the demand. The accused brethren were bound over to appear at the next term of the circuit court. It was evident that the magistrate intended to place their bail at a figure which could not be met, in order to cast them into jail, but the bond was given, and Justice Smith left the court house without calling on the two prisoners, Joseph and Hyrum Smith, to answer to the charge of treason.

False Imprisonment.—About eight p.m., Constable Bettisworth appeared at their lodgings at the Hamilton House and insisted on Joseph and Hyrum going to jail. They demanded to see the copy of the mittimus, which was refused. Their counsel, Messrs. H. T. Reid and J. W. Woods, informed the constable that they were entitled to a hearing before a justice, whereupon the constable produced a mittimus which falsely stated that they had been brought before Justice Robert F. Smith and the trial had been postponed by reason of the absence of material witnesses. They vigorously protested against such false and outrageous proceedings. Justice Smith asked the governor for advice, since his mittimus was illegal, and therefore this was a false committal, when Governor Ford replied, "You have the Carthage Greys at your command!" The hint was sufficient, and

> Carthage, June 25, 1844
> 2½ O'clock P.M.
>
> Dear Emma:— I have had an interview with the Gov. Ford & he treated us honorably. Myself & Hyrum have been again arrested for Treason because we called out the Nauvoo Legion, but when the truth comes out we have nothing to fear. We all feel calm & composed.
>
> This morning Gov. Ford introduced myself & Hyrum to the Malitia, in a very appropriate manner as Gen. Joseph Smith & General Hyrum Smith. There was a little muttering among the "Carthage Greys"; but I think the Gov. has & will succeed in enforcing the laws. I do hope the people of Nauvoo will continue
>
> N. B. Governor Ford has just concluded to send some of his malitia to Nauvoo to protect the citizens, & I wish that they may be kindly treated. They will co-operate with the police to keep the peace. The Governors orders will be read in hearing of the police & officers of the Legion, as I suppose.
>
> N. B. 6 O'clock. The Governor has just agreed to march his army to Nauvoo, & I shall come along with him. The prisoners, all that can be will be admitted to bail.
>
> I am as ever
>
> Emma Smith   Joseph Smith

Letter Written in Carthage Jail by Joseph Smith

THE MARTYRDOM 313

Captain Robert F. Smith thereupon commanded his "Greys" to execute the illegal action of *Justice* Robert F. Smith, and the Prophet Joseph and Patriarch Hyrum Smith were thrust into jail in defiance of all law. Elder John Taylor protested to the governor, but was answered by that craven individual that he had no power to interfere, and the law must take its course.

The Governor's Broken Pledge.—On the morning of June 26, Joseph requested an interview with Governor Ford, which had been denied him the day before. This time it was granted and the whole cause of the trouble was reviewed, Governor Ford contemplated going to Nauvoo the following day to investigate certain charges of counterfeiting, and the Prophet said he considered himself unsafe in Carthage and requested to be taken to Nauvoo. The governor gave his word of honor that he would take him when he went, but failed to keep his promise.

The Illegal Summons.—In the afternoon, Frank Worrell appeared before the jail with the Carthage Greys and demanded that the prisoners be delivered up to the constable to be taken before Justice R. F. Smith for trial. The jailor, who had been instructed to keep them in custody "until discharged by due course of law," protested such proceedings; but by threats Worrell compelled the jailor to surrender the prisoners. They were taken before Justice Smith, where their counsel, who had been given no notice of a trial, asked for a continuance that they might obtain witnesses. A continuance was granted until noon the following day. A new mittimus was made out and the prisoners committed again to prison, and without consultation on their part the time of trial was changed until the twenty-ninth.

Threats of the Mob.—It was common conversation on the camp ground and at the hotel, in the presence of Governor Ford, that "The law is too short for these men, but they must not be suffered to go at large;" and "if the law will not reach them, powder and ball must." Previously the governor had said, in order to quiet the impatience of the Carthage Greys, that they should have "full satisfaction."

The Night in Jail.—The evening of the 26th of June was spent by the prisoners and a number of friends, viz., John Taylor, Willard Richards, John S. Fullmer, Stephen Markham and Dan Jones, in conversing on the scriptures, Hyrum Smith occupying most of the time. They all retired to bed late except Dr. Willard Richards who sat up writing until his last candle burned out. The Prophet and Patriarch occupied the bed, while the other brethren slept on a mattress on the floor. The report of a gun caused Joseph to arise from the bed, and going over to the mattress, he lay down on the floor between Dan Jones and John S. Fullmer. Stretching out his right arm he said to John S. Fullmer, "Lay your head on my arm for a pillow, Brother John." He then conversed with Brother Fullmer on many topics and gave expression to the presentiment he had from the beginning that he was to die. "I would like to see my family again," he said, and "I would to God that I could preach to the Saints in Nauvoo once more." After all was quiet he turned to Dan Jones and whispered, "Are you afraid to die?" Dan said, "Has that time come, think you? Engaged in such a cause I do not think that death would have many terrors." The Prophet replied, "You will yet see Wales and fulfill the mission appointed you before you die."

The Plotting by the Mob.—Early on the morning of the 27th, John P. Greene and William W. Phelps called at the jail, and the Prophet sent Dan Jones out to inquire what the firing of a gun in the night near the jail was for. Frank Worrell, of the Carthage Greys, and officer of the guard, replied, "We have had too much trouble to bring Old Joe here to let him ever escape alive, and unless you want to die with him you had better leave before sundown; and you are not a damned bit better than him for taking his part. And you'll see that I can prophesy better than Old Joe, for neither he nor his brother, nor anyone who will remain with them will see the sun set today." Dan Jones reported to the Prophet who directed him to go to the governor and tell him what had taken place. On his way he overheard an officer making a speech, in which he said, "Our troops will be discharged this morning in obedience to orders, and for a sham we will leave the town; but when the governor and the McDonough troops have left for Nauvoo this afternoon, we will return and kill these men, if we have to tear the jail down." This was greeted by three cheers from the troops.

The Governor Warned.—Jones immediately reported to the governor what he had heard. Governor Ford replied: "You are unnecessarily alarmed for the safety of your friends, sir, the people are not that cruel." Irritated by this remark, Jones urged the necessity of placing better men to guard the jail, and he said: "The Messrs. Smith are American citizens, and have surrendered themselves to your Excellency upon your pledging your honor for their safety; they are also Master Masons, and as such I demand of you protection of their lives."

Governor Ford's face turned pale, and Jones continued: "If you do not do this, I have but one more desire, and that is, if you leave their lives in the hands of those men to be sacrificed—"

THE MARTYRDOM 315

"What is that, sir?" Ford asked in a hurried tone.

"It is," said Jones, "that the Almighty will preserve my life to a proper time and place, that I may testify that you have been timely warned of their danger."

Jones then returned to the prison, but the guards drove him away. Going to the hotel he witnessed the discharge of the troops, as the officer had predicted, and shortly afterward Governor Ford with the McDonough militia, the most friendly to the Saints, departed for Nauvoo, leaving the Carthage Greys, the most blood-thirsty of the troops, to guard the jail. The plot was working admirably without a hitch in the proceedings.

"A Poor Wayfaring Man of Grief."—John S. Fullmer and Stephen Markham, who had gone forth on errands, were also refused admittance again to the jail, while John Taylor and Willard Richards remained with their leaders. The day passed on, the prisoners and their two friends spent the time in bearing testimony to the truth of the Gospel, the divinity of the Book of Mormon, and in writing to their friends. Almon W. Babbitt called at the jail in the forenoon with a letter from Oliver Cowdery. Shortly after three o'clock there was excitement among the guards.

At this hour Elder John Taylor sang the hymn:

"A POOR WAYFARING MAN OF GRIEF."

When he had finished, the Prophet asked him to sing it through once more, which he did. At four o'clock the guard was changed. At five o'clock the jailor, Mr. Stigall, suggested that the prisoners retire to the cell below, where they would be safer.

The Martyrdom.—Shortly after five o'clock there was a rustling at the outer door of the jail and a cry of surrender and the discharge of three or four firearms. Dr. Richards glanced out of the window and saw about one hundred armed men around the door. Many of them had their faces blackened. It is said the guard elevated their guns and boisterously threatened the mob, but took good care to fire over their heads. The mob encircled the building and some of them rushed past the guard up the flight of stairs, burst open the door and began their work of death, while others fired through the windows. Joseph, Hyrum and Elder Taylor had their coats off. The Prophet sprang for his coat to get a six barreled pistol which Cyrus Wheelock had given him, and Hyrum reached for a single barrel pistol that had been left by John S. Fullmer. They all then braced themselves against the door, Elder Taylor armed with a heavy walking stick of Elder Markham's and Dr. Richards with Elder

Taylor's cane. In an instant a ball whistled up the stairway, and Joseph Smith, John Taylor and Willard Richards sprang to the left of the door, and tried to knock aside the guns of the ruffians. Hyrum Smith retreated back and in front of the door, snapping his pistol, when a ball struck him on the left side of the nose. He fell on his back saying: "I am a dead man!" As he fell on the floor another ball from the outside entered his left side, and passed through his body with such force that it completely broke to pieces the watch he wore in his vest pocket. At the same instant another ball grazed his breast, entered his throat, and passed into his head, while another was fired into his leg. A shower of bullets was pouring into the room. Joseph reached around the door casing and discharged his six shooter into the passage, some barrels missing fire, while Elders Taylor and Richards continued to parry the muskets which were sticking through the door. When Hyrum fell, the Prophet said: "Oh, dear brother Hyrum!" Seeing there was no safety in the room, and without doubt thinking to spare his other companions, he turned calmly from the door, dropped his pistol on the floor, and sprang into the window. Two balls pierced him from the door, and one entered his right breast from without. He fell outward into the hands of his murderers, exclaiming: "O Lord, my God!" With a cry that he had jumped from the window, the assassins who were in the building rushed down the stairs. Elder Taylor was also severely wounded; four balls piercing his body, one ball struck his watch as he attempted to jump from the window, throwing him back into the room.

When the ruffians left the building, Elder Richards who had miraculously escaped, except that a ball grazed his ear, started for the door. Elder Taylor called to him; he returned and carried the wounded man upstairs into the "dungeon" and stretched him on the floor. Covering him with a bed, he said: "This is a hard case to lay you on the floor, but if your wounds are not fatal, I want you to live to tell the story." He then returned to the room below, expecting the next moment to be shot.

Terror of the Mob.—After accomplishing their deed of blood, terror seized the hearts of the assassins who fled from the scene of their diabolical crime in utmost confusion. Governor Ford, three miles out of Nauvoo, on his way to Carthage, met George D. Grant and Constable Bettisworth hastening to Nauvoo with the news of the martyrdom. With terror on his countenance, he carried them back to Carthage, that they might not spread the awful tale, until he should be at a distance beyond the vengeance which he feared.

THE MARTYRDOM

Arriving at Carthage, he advised the citizens to flee for their lives before the infuriated "Mormons" came to burn their town, and suiting action to his words he fled with his posse towards Quincy. Conscience-stricken and with the blood of prophets on his hands, he did not stop until he arrived at Augusta, eighteen miles away.

Sorrow of the Saints.—In the meantime word of the horrible tragedy was sent by Dr. Willard Richards to Nauvoo. He said he had pledged his word to the frightened citizens of Carthage, that no violence or vengeance would be attempted by the Saints, and for the Saints to keep the peace and be prepared for an attack from Missouri. Indeed, there was no thought of summary vengeance by the Saints. With heads bowed down and hearts filled with grief—for the greatest sorrow in all their history had come upon them—they silently wept and prayed, leaving vengeance to Him who said, "Vengeance is mine; I will repay!"

The Burial.—The next day, June 28, 1844, the bodies of the martyred prophets were taken to Nauvoo by Dr. Willard Richards, Samuel H. Smith and a guard of eight soldiers sent by General Deming. On the 29th, they were interred amidst the deep mourning of a stricken people.

CHAPTER 36

THE SUCCESSION OF THE TWELVE APOSTLES —PREPARATION TO LEAVE NAUVOO

1844—1846

A Crisis in the Church.—The martyrdom of Joseph and Hyrum Smith came as a terrible shock to the members of the Church. The thought that the Prophet was to be taken from them had not entered their minds, notwithstanding the many predictions he had made regarding his approaching death. He was only in his thirty-ninth year. His constitution was strong and he was possessed of exceptional vitality. The Lord had saved him so many times from perils and threatened death, that the Saints fully expected the same power to shield him always.

His death brought about a crisis in the Church, for it was the first disorganization of the presiding quorum of the Priesthood. Very little thought had been given to the subject of succession in the Presidency, even by the leading brethren, for such a contingency seemed to them to be very remote. The revelations were clear on that point, but there had been no occasion for consideration of the subject. In the revelation on Priesthood, given to the apostles in 1835 (Doc. and Cov. Sec. 107), the Lord said that the council of the apostles was equal in authority with the First Presidency, and Joseph Smith stated that its place was second only to the presidency of the Church, and where there was no First Presidency, the apostles would preside. When the Saints were left without the guiding hand of the Prophet, they were in confusion, not fully understanding this order of the Priesthood. Sidney Rigdon, first counselor to President Joseph

Smith, had lost the spirit of the work. Contrary to the direct command of the Lord in a revelation (Doc. and Cov. Sec. 124:108-9) he moved his residence to Pittsburgh, Pennsylvania, where he was of little assistance as a counselor in the presidency. For many months before his death, Joseph Smith had suspected Sidney Rigdon of being in league with his enemies. The Prophet openly accused Sidney Rigdon of being guilty of such treacherous action, from which accusation he was not entirely cleared. He had manifested much sympathy for John C. Bennett, the arch-traitor, although he denied any direct communication with him. At the October conference, 1843, the Prophet refused to sustain Sidney Rigdon as a counselor, but through the merciful pleadings of Hyrum Smith and others, he was sustained. On that occasion the Prophet said: "I have thrown him off my shoulders, and you have put him on me; you may carry him, but I will not." Amasa M. Lyman had been chosen to act as a counselor in his stead. William Law, Joseph's second counselor, had been excommunicated for apostasy, and was one of those who brought to pass the martyrdom.

Sidney Rigdon's Attempt to be "Guardian to the Church."—Most of the apostles were in the Eastern States on missions at the time of the martyrdom. Only two were at Nauvoo, and one of them seriously wounded. As soon as Sidney Rigdon heard of the death of Joseph and Hyrum Smith, he hastened to Nauvoo, where he arrived Saturday, August 3, 1844. Elders Parley P. Pratt and George A. Smith had arrived a few days before. The apostles invited Sidney Rigdon to meet with them the following morning, at eight o'clock at the home of John Taylor, where they might discuss the affairs of the Church, which Sidney Rigdon promised to do. Instead of doing so he met with William Marks and a few others, and endeavored to lay plans for the appointment of a trustee-in-trust and a "guardian" for the Church, before others of the apostles could arrive. At ten o'clock a public meeting was held and Sidney Rigdon preached declaring that a "guardian" must be appointed, "to build up the Church unto Joseph," and stating that he, Sidney, was the identical man spoken of by the ancient prophets to do the work they had spoken of in prophecy. Another meeting was held in the afternoon, at which Elder William Marks, president of the Nauvoo Stake, announced that there would be a special meeting of the Church on Thursday, August 8th, "for the purpose of choosing a guardian." Sidney Rigdon had requested that the meeting be held on the 6th, but William Marks announced it for the 8th, which was providential, for President Brigham Young and most of the other apostles arrived in Nauvoo on the evening of the 6th. The next morning the apostles held a council meeting at the home of Elder Taylor. At four o'clock the apostles met with the high council of Nauvoo and the high priests. Sidney Rigdon was invited to express his views. He spoke at some length, relating a vision he claimed to have had, and stating that there could be no successor to Joseph Smith, but that the Church must be built up to him. He, Sidney, had been called to be a spokesman to Joseph Smith, and he proposed to be a guardian to the Church, if the people would receive him.

President Young's Remarks.—President Brigham Young said he did not care who presided over the Church, but one thing he would have to know and that was what the Lord said about it. "Joseph conferred upon our heads," he said, "all the keys and powers belonging to the apostleship which he himself held before he was taken away, and no man or set of men can get between Joseph and the twelve in this world or in the world to come. How often has Joseph said to the twelve: 'I have laid the foundation and you must build thereon, for upon your shoulders the kingdom rests.'"

The Special Meeting of Thursday, the 8th of August.—Thursday, August 8, 1844, the special meeting called by William Marks in behalf of Sidney Rigdon was held at 10 o'clock. Sidney Rigdon, from a position in a wagon in front of the stand in the grove, addressed the vast assembly for about one hour and a half. He presented himself to them as a "guardian" for the Church, that it might be built up unto Joseph Smith. The longer he talked, the more the people were convinced that he was without the inspiration of the Lord, and they left the meeting feeling that his was not the voice of the true shepherd.

Brigham Young

Transfiguration of Brigham Young.—At the close of the morning meeting, President Brigham Young, made a few remarks and announced that there would be another meeting at 2 o'clock. At the appointed time a great multitude of Saints assembled. The various quorums of the Priesthood were arranged in order before the stand, and after the opening exercises President Brigham Young addressed the congregation. He spoke with great power and the people were convinced that the authority and power of presidency was with the apostles. When he first arose to speak the people were greatly astonished, for President Young stood transfigured before them and they beheld the Prophet Joseph Smith and heard his voice as naturally as ever they did when he was living. It was a manifestation to the Saints that they might recognize the correct authority. Following his remarks in the afternoon, Amasa M. Lyman, William W. Phelps and Parley P. Pratt each spoke endorsing the remarks of President Young.

The Apostles are Sustained.—After the other brethren had spoken President Young arose and was about to put the question to the assembly whether or not they wanted Sidney Rigdon for a leader and to be a "guardian" for the Church, but at the request of Elder Rigdon the question of supporting the apostles as the presiding quorum of the Church was presented first by President Young as follows:

"I will ask you as quorums: Do you want Brother Rigdon to stand forward as your leader, your guide, your spokesman? President Rigdon wants me to bring up the other question first, and that is: Does the Church want, and is it their only desire to sustain the twelve as the First Presidency of this people?

"Here are the apostles, the Bible, the Book of Mormon, the Doctrine and Covenants—they are written on the tablet of my heart. If the Church want the twelve to stand as the head, the First Presidency of the Church, and at the head of this kingdom in all the world, stand next to Joseph, walk up into their calling and hold the keys of this kingdom, every man, every woman, every quorum is now put in order and you are now the sole controllers of it.

"All that are in favor of this in all the congregation of the Saints manifest it by holding up the right hand."

There was a universal vote, after which President Young called for the negative vote as follows:

"If there are any of the contrary mind, every man and every woman who does not want the twelve to preside, lift up your hands in like manner."

There were no hands raised, and President Young then remarked that since the vote was unanimous it superseded the other question of presenting Sidney Rigdon as "guardian" and also trying the vote by quorums. In this manner the apostles, who were the rightful authorities according to the revelations of the Lord, were sustained by the vote of the people and by common consent, as the Lord had commanded that all things should be done. The matter of succession was properly and rightfully decided, and was now binding on the members of the Church. At the close of the services the Saints returned to their homes, their minds at rest, for they were, with very few exceptions, no longer in doubt regarding the authority of the Priesthood and the presidency of the Church.

Excommunication of Sidney Rigdon.—Manifesting a bitter spirit and great disappointment Sidney Rigdon returned to Pittsburgh. However, before he left Nauvoo he gave expression to his feelings declaring that the Church had not been led by the Spirit of the Lord for a long time, and he refused to sustain the apostles in their calling. A charge was made against him and his case was presented before the high council, with Bishop Newel K. Whitney presiding. After a lengthy hearing he was cut off from the Church by the unanimous vote of the council. His case was then presented to the congregation of the Saints, and they sustained the action of the high council, only ten persons voting in the negative. After his return to Pittsburgh, he organized a church with officers after the order of the Church of Jesus Christ. He published a paper and prophesied that all who followed the apostles would go with them to destruction. He gathered around him a few of the disaffected spirits from Nauvoo, but his organization did not prosper and soon came to an end.

Action Against William Marks.—At the October conference, 1844, the apostles were again sustained as the presiding quorum of the Church by a united vote of the members. When the name of William Marks, president of the Nauvoo Stake, was presented, objection was raised and he was rejected, only two persons voting to sustain him. He had favored the claim of Sidney Rigdon although he supported the apostles, but his spirit was no longer in the work and he was found in rebellion. He later left the Church and followed James J. Strang[a] and others, and was excommunicated.

---

[a]James J. Strang, a man of some ability and commanding presence, joined the Church shortly before the martydom. After the death of the Prophet and Patriarch he claimed to have been chosen and appointed by Joseph Smith as his successor. He exhibited a letter which purported to have been written by the Prophet, in which such appointment was claimed to be set forth. He gathered quite a following of the discontented element at Nauvoo and established himself on Beaver Island, in Lake Michigan, where later he was crowned "king." He was shot and killed by one of his followers, and his organization soon afterwards crumbled to pieces. Out of its fragments some years later there arose another

Trial of the Murderers of Joseph and Hyrum Smith.—In October, 1844, a grand jury selected by the Hancock County circuit court, brought into court two bills of indictment against nine individuals for the murder of Joseph and Hyrum Smith. The trial took place in May, 1845, but proved to be nothing but a farce. The sentiment throughout the country was so bitter against the Saints that no attempt was made to obtain justice, which the governor had faithfully promised them. The jurors were instructed by the court to bring in a verdict of "not guilty," which was accordingly done. Yet every man in the place, including the court and jury, knew that the defendants were among those who committed the murder. The blood of the martyrs was left unavenged to cry from the ground against their enemies, and with the blood of all the martyrs, shall continue to cry until the Son of Man shall come "red in his apparel" to take vengeance upon the ungodly.

Growth of the Work.—After the question of the presiding quorum was decided, the Saints settled down to their usual duties, and the progress of the Church continued with greater strides than ever before. At the October conference in 1844, a great deal of important business was transacted. At that time and subsequently many brethren were ordained to the ministry, a number of quorums of seventy were organized, and missionaries were called to go to various parts of the United States and abroad with the message of salvation. The building of the temple was continued with renewed diligence, and prosperity was manifest in the settlements of the Saints. On the 6th of December 1844, the last of the thirty capitals on the temple was erected, and the following April, the capstone was laid amidst solemn and enthusiastic services. Each room was dedicated separately as it was finished and ordinance work for the Saints, as well as baptisms for the dead, were performed.

Mob Activities Renewed.—The enemies of the Latter-day Saints thought that the murder of Joseph and Hyrum Smith would be the end of "Mormonism." They rejoiced in the accomplishment of their frightful deed of blood, and boasted of the downfall of the Church. To their great surprise the blood of the martyrs was the seed of the Church. The object they hoped to gain was not attained; therefore their anger was rekindled against the Church. Other leaders had arisen and the progress of the work was steady and onward. Those who had caused the death of the Prophet and Patriarch now turned their attention to the destruction of the entire "Mormon" people.

---

organization known as the "Reorganized Church of Jesus Christ of Latter-day Saints," unto which there were gathered the majority of those who had become disaffected and had been excommunicated from the Church.

Through their papers, the *Warsaw Signal, Alton Telegraph, Quincy Whig* and others, they circulated all manner of false reports. They accused the Saints of theft and every other abominable crime in order to stir up the populace against them. Schemes were launched to provoke the "Mormons" to commit some overt act that it might be seized upon as a pretext to gain the aid of the officials of the state under color of law; yet by the anti-"Mormons" the laws were constantly broken without restraint. Their malicious and murderous threats passed unnoticed so far as any check upon such actions was concerned.

Attitude of Governor Ford.—During all the trouble Governor Thomas Ford went out of his way to inform the Saints that they were bitterly hated, and that the great majority of the citizens of the state rejoiced in the death of Joseph and Hyrum Smith. Notwithstanding his bitterness, he made an investigation of the charges circulated against the Saints and reported that—

"On my late visit to Hancock County I was informed by some of their (the 'Mormons') violent enemies, that their larcenies had become unusually numerous and insufferable. They indeed admitted that but little had been done in this way in their immediate vicinity. But they insisted that sixteen horses had been stolen by the 'Mormons' in one night, near Lima, in the County of Adams. At the close of the expedition, I called at this same town of Lima, and upon inquiry, was told that no horses had been stolen in that neighborhood, but that sixteen horses had been stolen in one night in Hancock County. This last informant being told of the Hancock County story, again changed the venue to another distant settlement in the northern edge of Adams County."

In his message to the legislature he said in reference to this subject:

"Justice, however, requires me to say that I have investigated the charge of promiscuous stealing, and find it to be greatly exaggerated. I could not ascertain that there were a greater proportion of thieves in that community, than in any other of the same number of inhabitants; and perhaps if the city of Nauvoo were compared with St. Louis, or any other western city, the proportion would not be so great."

The leaven of opposition, however, was at work, and the citizens were aroused. Nothing but the departure of the "Mormon" people from the state would satisfy their unjust and iniquitous demands. They appealed to the governor to aid them in expelling the people who had done nothing to provoke opposition but who were unpopular because of their faith. While the governor informed them he could take no legal action warranting such expulsion, yet he privately advised the Saints to depart peaceably towards the West, as the Prophet Joseph Smith had contemplated doing, and there, said he, they could set up an independent government of their own. So lacking was he in the disposition to enforce the law and protect the innocent, that the enemies of the Church were encouraged in their unlawful course.

Repeal of the Nauvoo Charter.—The city charter of Nauvoo had proved a protection to the Saints, and guaranteed safety against the plottings of the wicked. It was the aim of the Nauvoo conspirators to cause its repeal. The first attempt to do this, as we have learned, failed. Now, however, the opposition had become so strong that the enemies of the Latter-day Saints accomplished their purpose. The charter was repealed by the legislature in January, 1845. Some of the murderers of Joseph and Hyrum Smith sat in that body and violently denounced the "Mormons," although it was well known that their hands were stained with innocent blood. After the repeal of the charter, and without hope of protection from the officers of the state, the Saints were at the mercy of their enemies. The prediction of the Prophet Joseph that after they had shed his blood they would seek the lives of every soul in whom was found the testimony of the Gospel, was literally fulfilled. The plots of the wicked were now turned against President Brigham Young and the leading brethren, who were forced to go into hiding from time to time.

Attacks Upon the Saints.—In September, 1845, the scattered families of Saints were sorely persecuted. Many were driven from their homes, which were burned. Sheriff J. B. Backenstos endeavored to perform his duty, and took a determined stand against mob law. For his pains he was arrested on the charge of murder, as a mobber had been killed, but violence against the "Mormons" was permitted to go unchecked. Governor Ford had promised and pledged his word that the murderers of the Prophet and Patriarch should be brought to justice. When he appealed to the citizens of Warsaw to sustain him in this pledge, they positively informed him that they would do nothing of the kind. Similar answers were given by other citizens, who not only took a stand in opposition to the trial of the murderers, but brazenly appealed to the governor to give his aid in expelling the "Mormons" from the state. That weak and pusillanimous individual, by his subsequent actions, acknowledged his defeat and the abdication of government in Illinois.

The Quincy Mass Meeting.—September 22, 1845, a mass meeting was held in Quincy to take action against the Saints. Their removal from Illinois was advocated. Those who assembled fully understood that the Prophet Joseph Smith had contemplated a removal to the West, and that plans were on foot early in 1844 to send an exploring expedition out to locate a site for a new home in the Rocky Mountains. A committee was appointed by this mass meeting to wait upon the authorities of the Church and ascertain their intentions regarding a removal from the state of Illinois, and to impress upon the brethren that such a move was determined upon by the citizens. Following the meeting the *Quincy Whig* made this statement in this boasted land of liberty:

"It is a settled thing that the public sentiment of the State is against the 'Mormons,' and it will be in vain for them to contend against it; and to prevent bloodshed, and the sacrifice of many lives on both sides, it is their duty to obey the public will and leave the State as speedily as possible. That they will do this we have a confident hope and that too, before the next extreme is resorted to —that of force."

The Reply of the Saints.—The committee appointed waited upon President Brigham Young and the apostles, and acquainted them with the action of the mass meeting and desired a reply. On the 24th, the reply was given in a written communication. The persecutions of the Saints were mentioned and the statement made that the "Mormons" had endeavored to live in peace and desired to do so with all men. In relation to their removal they answered as follows:

"We would say to the committee above mentioned and to the Governor, and all the authorities, and people of Illinois, and the surrounding states and territories, that we propose to leave this country next spring, for some point so remote that there will not need to be any difficulty with the people and ourselves, provided certain propositions necessary for the accomplishment of our removal shall be observed, as follows, to-wit:

"That the citizens of this and surrounding counties, and all men, will use their influence and exertion to help us to sell or rent our properties, so as to get means enough that we can help the widow, the fatherless and the destitute to remove with us.

"That all men will let us alone with their vexatious lawsuits so that we may have time, for we have broken no law; and help us to cash, dry goods, groceries, good oxen, beef-cattle, sheep, wagons, mules, horses, harness, etc. in exchange for our property, at a fair price, and deeds given at payment, that we may have means to accomplish a removal without the suffering of the destitute to an extent beyond the endurance of human nature.

"That all exchanges of property shall be conducted by a committee, or by committees of both parties; so that all the business may be transacted honorably and speedily.

"That we will use all lawful means, in connection with others, to preserve the public peace while we tarry; and shall expect, decidedly, that we be no more molested with house-burning, or any other depredations, to waste our property and time, and hinder our business.

"That it is a mistaken idea, that we have proposed to remove in six months, for that would be so early in the spring that grass might not grow nor water run; both of which would be necessary for our removal. But we propose to use our influence to have no more seed time and harvest among our people in this country after gathering our present crops; and that all communications to us be made in writing.

"By order of the Council,"
"BRIGHAM YOUNG,"
"President."
"W. Richards,"
"Clerk."

Decision of the Quincy Citizens.—The Quincy citizens accepted the proposition of the Church authorities to move, but very graciously declined to make any promise to buy or to assist in the purchase of the abandoned property of the Saints. Why should they put themselves out to do such a thing, when the property would naturally fall into their hands when it was abandoned?[b]

The Carthage Convention.—On the 1st and 2nd of October another convention of citizens from nine counties adjacent to Hancock, was held at Carthage. Resolutions were adopted in which the "Mormons" were accused of depredations upon the persons and property of the other citizens of Hancock County, and adjudged guilty, in spite of the personal investigation of the governor, himself unfriendly to the Latter-day Saints. Much bitterness of spirit was manifested at this meeting, which decided that it was too late to

---

[b]Dr. Conyers, in his "Hancock County Mob," makes the following comment on the action of the Quincy citizens:

"The first one [resolution] in our opinion, is unique. They accepted and recommended to the people of the surrounding counties to accept an unconditional proposition to remove. But understand, Mr. Mormon, though we accept it and recommend the surrounding counties to do so likewise, [reprobate you, unconditionally] we do not intend to bring ourselves under any obligation to purchase your property, or to furnish purchasers; but we will be very kind and obliging, and will in no way hinder or obstruct you in your efforts to sell, provided, nevertheless this shall not be so construed as to prevent us from running off the purchaser. But we expect this small favor of you, viz., that you must dispose of your property and leave at the appointed time."

settle any difficulties between the "Mormons" and the other inhabitants, and only one thing would suffice and that was the removal of the "Mormons" from the state. They declared that the "Mormons" were not being persecuted, but were suffering for their dishonest acts; at the same time they declared that from "long acquaintance with the old citizens of Hancock County," they could vouch for their "honor, integrity, and strict observance of the laws of their country," notwithstanding it was universally known that these same citizens had taken part in the assassination of Joseph and Hyrum Smith by mob force and contrary to law; moreover, that these same law-abiding citizens within the past few weeks had driven "Mormons" from their homes and burned their houses to the ground; had forced them from their fields where they had gone to gather crops; had whipped their men and stolen their cattle without any protest. It appeared that the old citizens, like the king, could do no wrong, if their depredations were committed against the Latter-day Saints. A most regrettable feature in connection with these troubles is the fact that O. H. Browning, Stephen A. Douglas and others, who had defended the Prophet Joseph Smith, now gave their influence to the mob and assisted in bringing to pass the expulsion of the "Mormon" people from Illinois. Bitter feelings against the Saints increased. Judges were intimidated, and even the officials of the state dared not raise a voice in protest above a whisper, or invoke the majesty of the law.

Duplicity of Governor Ford.—The anti-"Mormons" of Illinois became impatient for the removal of their enemies before spring arrived. Their agreements were violated, and the Saints were not permitted to dwell in peace. Vexatious lawsuits, based on falsehoods, were planted against the apostles to embarrass them and hinder the progress of their work. Even Governor Ford, fearing that the Saints would not leave the state within the stipulated time, resorted to duplicity to force them from the borders of Illinois. December 29, 1845, he wrote to Sheriff Backenstos stating that indictments in the United States Court had been found against the leading "Mormons" which would bring them for the first time in collision with the United States. "If the 'Mormons' remain in the state," he wrote, "a strong force will be ordered to Nauvoo by the Secretary of War," and he thought the government at Washington would interfere and prevent the "Mormons" from going west of the Rocky Mountains, as many intelligent persons believed that they would there join the British, and "be more trouble than ever." He thought that this consideration was likely to influence the government. He later sent word by Sheriff Backenstos that he had turned against the Saints and Major Warren was making calculations to prevent their going away. In his History of Illinois, Governor Ford admitted that he had resorted to deceit to make the "Mormons" believe that they would be prevented from going west, in order to hasten their departure.

President Young's Reply.—Commenting on the governor's letter to the sheriff, President Young remarked:

"Should Governor Ford's speculations and suppositions in relation to U. S. troops prove correct, and the government send a regular force to arrest us, we will run no risks of being murdered by them as our leaders have been; and as to fearing a trial before the courts, it is all gammon, for our danger consists only in being held still by the authorities while mobs massacre us, as Governor Ford held Joseph and Hyrum Smith, while they were butchered."

Loyalty to the Government.—Answering the charge that when they got away from the borders of the United States, the Latter-day Saints would join the forces of some other nation which might be at war with the American Government—a thought which rightfully might have been entertained after the treatment the "Mormon" people had received within the borders of that land—the high council and authorities of the Church replied:

"We also further declare for the satisfaction of some who have concluded that our grievances have alienated us from our country, that our patriotism has not been overcome by fire, by sword, by daylight nor by midnight assassinations which we have endured; neither have they alienated us from the institutions of our country.

"Should hostilities arise between the Government of the United States and any other power, in relation to the right of possessing the territory of Oregon, we are on hand to sustain the claim of the United States Government to that country. It is geographically ours, and of right; no foreign power should hold dominion there; and if our services are required to prevent it, these services will be cheerfully rendered according to our ability. We feel the injuries that we have sustained, and are not insensible of the wrongs we have suffered; still we are American."

Preparations to Leave Nauvoo.—During the fall and winter months preparations went steadily on for the removal of the entire body of the Latter-day Saints in the spring. Work on the temple continued with increased diligence, as if there were no thought of a removal, until that structure was completed. January 1, 1846, the work of finishing the assembly room for dedication was nearing completion. The general conference of the Church was held in the building in October, 1845, according to the commandment of the Lord through Joseph Smith in October, 1841. In December, the ordinance work in the temple was commenced, and thereafter the building was occupied both day and night to afford the Saints the opportunity to receive their endowments. This continued until most all of the Saints had departed on their westward journey. May 1, 1846, after the majority of the people had departed from the city, the temple was publicly dedicated in the presence of about three hundred persons.

In the meantime every available building in Nauvoo had been converted into a shop where wagons, harness and other necessary articles could be manufactured for the journey. The timber for the wagons was cut and brought to Nauvoo, where it was prepared and boiled in salt and water or kiln dried. Teams were sent to various parts of the country to procure iron; and blacksmiths, wheelwrights, carpenters and other workmen were kept busy night and day. There was very little sale of property because of the opposition of the citizens of the country, who used their influence to discourage sales by making threats against the new settlers as well as harassing the Saints.

PART FIVE

The Settlement in the Rocky Mountains

CHAPTER 37

THE EXODUS FROM NAUVOO

1846

The Abandonment of Nauvoo.—Wednesday, February 4, 1846, the first of the Saints left Nauvoo and crossed the Mississippi River on the journey to the West.[a] On the 6th of February Bishop George

---

[a]The same day two hundred and thirty-five members of the Church, from branches in the New England and the Atlantic States, under the direction of Samuel Brannan, sailed from New York for California. They had chartered the ship "Brooklyn," at twelve hundred dollars per month, the lessee to pay the port charges. They carried with them farming implements of all kinds, blacksmith carpenter and wheelwright tools and fixtures, the necessary parts for two gristmills and sawmill irons. They also carried text books on various subjects and many other volumes. The press and type on which the *Prophet*—a paper published by the Church in New York—was printed, and sufficient paper and other things as would be needed to establish a new colony in their distant home. They arrived at Yerba Buena, now San Francisco, Wednesday, July 29, 1846, having gone around Cape Horn and touched at the Hawaiian Islands. On their arrival they found the American Flag waving over the fort the guns of which had saluted them on their entrance into the bay. Three weeks earlier the United States Flag had been raised and the country occupied in the name of the government. In January, 1847, Samuel Brannan commenced publishing a newspaper at Yerba Buena called the "California Star," the first English paper published in California.

Miller and a company with six wagons crossed the river, and a few days later the work of ferrying the Saints to the Iowa side was kept up day and night. Elder Parley P. Pratt left Nauvoo on the 14th of February, and the following day President Brigham Young, Willard Richards and George A. Smith with a large company of Saints crossed the Mississippi on the ice and continued their journey about nine miles to Sugar Creek, in Lee County, where a temporary camp was formed for the exiles fleeing from Nauvoo.[b] President Young spent the 16th in organizing the camp into companies and Elder Heber C. Kimball with another company arrived on the 17th. On the 18th President Young and some of the brethren returned to Nauvoo to transact some necessary business and give instruction to those who were left there in command. Elder Joseph Young, president of the seventies, had been left at Nauvoo to preside over the Saints who still remained. The exiles tarried on Sugar Creek for some time where a number of council meetings were held and the needs of the people were duly considered.

At the October conference in 1845, the members of the Church, on suggestion of President Brigham Young, unanimously covenanted as follows: "That we take all the Saints with us, to the extent of our ability, that is, our influence and property." After the motion was

---

[b]On the first night of the encampment on Sugar Creek nine infants were born. The weather was inclement and extremely cold and the people without proper shelter. Writing of these conditions, Eliza R. Snow, the poetess, has said: "As we journeyed onward, mothers gave birth to offspring under almost every variety of circumstances imaginable except those to which they had been accustomed; some in tents, others in wagons—in rainstorms and in snowstorms. I heard of one birth which occurred under the rude shelter of a hut, the sides of which were formed of blankets fastened to poles stuck in the ground, with a bark roof through which the rain was dripping. Kind sisters stood holding dishes to catch the water as it fell, thus protecting the newcomer and its mother from a showerbath as the little innocent first entered on the stage of human life; and through faith in the Great Ruler of events, no harm resulted to either.

"Let it be remembered that the mothers of these wilderness-born babies were not savages, accustomed to roam the forest and brave the storm and tempest —those who had never known the comforts and delicacies of civilization and refinement. They were not those who, in the wilds of nature, nursed their offspring amid reeds and rushes, or in the recesses of rocky caverns; most of them were born and educated in the Eastern States—had there embraced the Gospel as taught by Jesus and his apostles, and, for the sake of their religion, had gathered with the Saints and under trying circumstances had assisted, by their faith, patience and energies, in making Nauvoo what its name indicates "the beautiful." They had lovely homes, decorated with flowers and enriched with choice fruit trees, just beginning to yield plentifully.

"To these homes, without lease or sale, they had just bade a final adieu, and with what little of their substance could be packed into one, two, and in some instances three wagons, had started out, desertward, for—where? To this question the only response at that time was God knows." (Women of Mormondom—Tullidge. Ch. 32).

carried, President Young remarked: "If you will be faithful to your covenant, I will prophesy that the Great God will shower down means upon this people to accomplish it to the very letter." The members of the Church had been constantly instructed to prepare for the journey by laying up stores of provisions for many months. It was discovered that many who had come to Sugar Creek were without supplies to last them more than a few days, and this caused serious reflection and some anxiety among the leading brethren. It was winter time and supplies could not readily be obtained in the wilderness. However, those who had, shared with those who were destitute, and the Lord blessed them in their substance.

Conspiracy in Washington.—While camped on Sugar Creek a letter was received by President Young from Samuel Brannan, in which there was presented a proposition from Amos Kendall, formerly Postmaster-General, A. G. Benson and others, to use the Church authorities as their tools to secure land in California. They represented to Brannan that there was a movement on foot to disarm the Saints and prevent their movement towards the West. However, they declared, the power was in their hands to avert the calamity, which they would do on certain terms. Their terms were that when the Saints arrived in California they would secure the lands and that every alternate section should be deeded to this combination of conspirators. They falsely represented that the President, James K. Polk, was a party to the scheme. For their service these men promised that the Saints should be permitted to travel to their destination without molestation, and with the protection of the government. With righteous indignation, President Young and the Apostles refused to make reply.

Petition to the Governor of Iowa.—On the 28th of February a petition was addressed to the governor of Iowa, imploring his protection and influence in behalf of the Saints while they passed through that territory, or remained temporarily within its borders, to raise crops and to render assistance to those who would follow after. No reply to this petition was received and the Saints continued without aid or interference.

The Journey Resumed.—March 1, 1846, camp was broken and the journey was resumed. The weather was extremely cold and stormy, and a great number of the people were without proper clothing and necessary shelter. Many of the wagons were without covers, and others had covers which would not shed the rain. Several members of the camps died from exposure and lack of proper care.

The roads were almost impassable because of the constant storms.[c] At this time there were some four hundred wagons on the road, heavily laden and without sufficient teams to permit of rapid travel. In this condition the exiles continued their toilsome journey over the plains of Iowa. By the latter part of April the great body of the Latter-day Saints had left Nauvoo and were slowly wending their way seeking a haven in the West.

Organization of the Camps.—While encamped near the Chariton River on the east fork of Shoal Creek, the organization of the camps was reduced to a more systematic order. They were divided into companies of hundreds, fifties and tens, with officers appointed to preside over each. The apostles were appointed to take charge of divisions, and the camps were divided into two grand divisions. Over one of these President Brigham Young had command. He was also sustained as "president over all the camps of Israel." Elder Heber C. Kimball was appointed to the command of the other grand division. In addition to these officers there were appointed a contracting commissary and a distributing commissary for each fifty. The duties of the former were to agree on terms, prices, etc., concerning the purchase of provisions and necessities for the camp. The latter were to distribute among the camps the grain and provisions furnished for that purpose, judiciously and with singleness of heart. This organization led to better discipline. The companies were more susceptible to advice and counsel, and the principle of obedience was more fully understood. Less selfishness was manifested among the people, and a better spirit prevailed. Of necessity the regulations in the camps were strict, yet the freedom and rightful privileges of the Saints were safely guaranteed. Much of the dross had been left behind, and the "fair weather friends," as they were called by Col. Thomas L. Kane, had forsaken the tents of Israel and had sought the

---

[c]It was not the intention of the Saints to leave Nauvoo until the springtime had fully arrived. But the human fiends, who hated the religion of the Saints and coveted their substance and property, were not willing for them to wait. What cared they for the suffering and exposure of an innocent people, driven from their homes and sheltered by the broad canopy of heaven in the midst of winter? "We could have remained sheltered in our homes," said President Brigham Young, "had it not been for the threats and hostile demonstrations of our enemies, who, notwithstanding their solemn agreements, had thrown every obstacle in our way, not respecting either life, or liberty, or property; so much so that our only means of avoiding a rupture was by starting in mid-winter. Our homes, gardens, orchards, farms, streets, bridges, mills, public halls, magnificent temple, and other public improvements we leave as a monument of our patriotism, industry, economy, uprightness of purpose, and integrity of heart; and as a living testimony of the falsehood and wickedness of those who charge us with disloyalty to the Constitution of our country, idleness and dishonesty." (Manuscript History of the Church).

tents of ease. In this manner the camps were purged of those who were not faithful enough to face the perils and deprivations of the eventful journey. Although there were difficulties and differences to be settled from time to time, President Young was led to declare that he doubted if there had ever been a body of people, since the days of Enoch, who had done so little grumbling under such unpleasant and trying circumstances.

Garden Grove.—At the beginning of the journey about one hundred men, under command of Colonel Stephen Markham, were selected as pioneers, to travel in advance of the companies to build and repair the roads; also to seek out temporary places for shelter where fields could be cultivated and homes—humble though they, of necessity, would have to be—might be provided for the exiles. The advance companies arrived at a place on the east fork of Grand River, some one hundred and forty-five miles west of Nauvoo, April 24, 1846. Here a temporary settlement was selected which they named Garden Grove. Two days later a council meeting was held and three hundred and fifty-nine laboring men were reported in the camp. From these one hundred were selected to cut trees and make rails; ten to build fences; forty-eight to build houses; twelve to dig wells and ten to build bridges. The remainder were employed in clearing land and preparing it for cultivation. Every one was busy, and in a few days a respectable village, magic-like, had risen in the wilderness. A temporary organization was effected with Samuel Bent as president, and Aaron Johnson and David Fullmer as counselors. At this point President Young addressed the Saints saying it would be necessary to leave some of their number here, because they could not continue the journey, while the main body would push on and "lengthen the cords and build a few more stakes," and so continue on until they could all gather at the place appointed, and "build the house of the Lord in the tops of the mountains."

Proposition to Explore the West.—It was the intention of President Young and the apostles to fit out a strong company of able-bodied men, unencumbered with families, and send them to the Rocky Mountains, there to build houses and plant crops, and prepare for the coming of the people as they were able to gather from year to year. "Were matters to be so conducted," he said, "none would be found crying for bread or destitute of clothing, but all would be provided for, as designed by the Almighty. But instead of taking this course the Saints have crowded on us all the while, and have completely tied our hands by importuning and saying, 'Do not leave us behind. Wherever you go, we want to go, and be with you;' and thus our hands and feet have been bound, which has caused our delay to the present time. And now hundreds at Nauvoo are continually praying and importuning with the Lord that they may overtake us, and be with us." An estimate of what would be required for a company of pioneers to take such a journey was made and the project was considered, but subsequent events prevented the undertaking until the following year.

Mount Pisgah.—On the 18th of May President Young and several of the apostles reached the middle fork of Grand River, some twenty-seven miles west of Garden Grove. Here Parley P. Pratt with a company was found encamped. He had called the place Mount Pisgah, and here it was decided to make another settlement for the Saints. Several thousand acres of land were fenced for cultivation, after the manner of the settlement at Garden Grove, and this place became a resting place for the weary exiles for several years while crossing the plains. Elder William Huntington was chosen to preside with Elders Ezra T. Benson and Charles C. Rich as counselors. The camps were now traveling through an Indian country, where there were no roads, no settlements and only Indian trails. The spring rains having ceased, however, greater progress was made although a road had to be prepared all the way, and bridges built over all the streams.

At the Missouri River.—On the 14th of June, President Young, Heber C. Kimball, Parley P. Pratt and others arrived on the banks of the Missouri, not far from Council Bluffs, with their respective companies. The next day a council meeting was held and it was decided to move back on to the bluffs where spring water could be obtained, and they would be protected from Indians. The Pottawattamie Indians were very friendly, and their chiefs showed the Saints some favor. A ferry boat was built and on the 29th the companies commenced crossing the river. About this time Elder Wilford Woodruff, who had just returned from presiding over the British Mission, and Elder Orson Hyde, who had been laboring in Nauvoo, joined the camp.

President Young was still very anxious to send an exploring company to the Rocky Mountains in advance. The camps were called together, there being about five hundred wagons on the ground and others on the way, and President Young addressed them advising them of his desire to get a company off for the Rocky Mountains. He feared, he said, that something would happen to stop the movement, and was impressed that "everything that men and hell could invent would be hatched up to prevent the camp from making any progress." He spoke plainly on the subject and said

THE EXODUS FROM NAUVOO

Council Bluffs Ferry

if the members of the Church should be blown to the four winds, and never gathered again, he wished them to remember that he had told them when and where to gather, and if they failed to do so to remember and bear him witness in the day of judgment, that they had received such information and advice.

A Call From the Government.—June 26, 1846, Captain James Allen, of the United States army, arrived at Mount Pisgah and had an interview with the brethren there. He was the bearer of a message to the "Mormon" people making a requisition on the camps for four or five companies of men, to serve as volunteers in the war with Mexico, which had recently been declared. The brethren at Mount Pisgah did not feel authorized to take any action, and therefore advised Captain Allen to visit President Young and the apostles at Council Bluffs. Captain Allen arrived at Council Bluffs on the 30th day of June, and the following day met with the Church authorities and presented his credentials for raising five hundred men. Such a demand caused some surprise and a little dismay among the camps. However, President Brigham Young declared that the volunteers would be forthcoming. It was moved by Heber C. Kimball and seconded by Willard Richards, that a battalion of five hundred men be raised, which was carried unanimously at a meeting of the brethren of the camp who were called together to consider the requisition. Consequently President Young and Elder Kimball returned to Mount Pisgah to raise volunteers, while letters were sent to Garden Grove and to Nauvoo bearing on the subject. Monday, July 13, 1846, in obedience to the call of the authorities, the camps of the Saints met on Mosquito Creek, where they were addressed by President Young, Captain Allen and Colonel Thomas L. Kane, who had arrived in camp to be of service to the people. Four companies of the battalion were raised on that and the following day, and the fifth company a few days later.

An Important Council Meeting.—July 16, a council meeting was held at the bluffs and Ezra T. Benson was ordained an apostle in the stead of John E. Page, who had been excommunicated. Elders Orson Hyde, Parley P. Pratt and John Taylor were appointed to go to England to take charge of the affairs of the Church in that land and set them in order. Reuben Hedlock and Thomas Ward, who had been in charge, had been guilty of misconduct in the use of funds and had been disfellowshiped. The same day four companies of the battalion were mustered into service by their respective captains, and on the 20th left for Fort Leavenworth in the service of the United States. The fifth company left the following day, and the entire body arrived at their destination August 1, 1846, numbering at the time five hundred and forty-nine men.

President Young's Instructions to the Battalion.—In giving instructions to the members of the battalion before their departure, President Young requested that they prove themselves to be the best soldiers in the service of the United States. He instructed the captains to be fathers to their companies, and to manage the officers and men by the power of the Priesthood. They should keep neat and clean; teach chastity, gentility, and civility. No swearing should be indulged in; no man was to be insulted, and they should avoid contentions with Missourians, or any other class of people. They were to take their Bibles and Books of Mormon with them but were not to impose their belief on others. They were advised to avoid card playing and if they had any cards with them to burn them. If they would follow the instructions given they would not be called on to shed the blood of their fellow men, and after their labors were over, they probably would be discharged within eight hundred miles of the proposed settlement of the Saints in the Great Basin, where the next temple would be built in a stronghold free from mobs.

Reasons for the Call for Troops.—January 20, 1846, while the high council of Nauvoo was considering the abandonment of that place and journeying to the Rocky Mountains, the subject of sending an advance company was discussed. There had been some talk of the government building blockhouses and forts along the road to Oregon, and the matter was then before Congress. It was decided at this meeting that "In the event of the President's recommendation to build blockhouses and stockade forts on the route to Oregon becoming a law, we have encouragement of having that work to do, and under our peculiar circumstances, we can do it with less expense to the government than any other people." Six days later Elder Jesse C. Little was appointed to preside in the Eastern States, and was furnished a letter of appointment in which the following occurs:

"If our government shall offer any facilities for emigrating to the western coast, embrace those facilities, if possible. As a wise and faithful man, take every honorable advantage of the times you can. Be thou a savior and a deliverer of that people, and let virtue, integrity and truth be your motto—salvation and glory the prize for which you contend."

Acting on this advice Elder Little wrote an appeal to President Polk in behalf of the Latter-day Saints, and afterwards called upon him and also the vice-President and members of the cabinet. At the time of his interview, June 1, 1846, word of the commencement of hostilities between Mexico and the United States had reached Washington and those governments were in a state of war. The authorities in Washington accepted the suggestion of Elder Little, thinking it might be opportune to call upon the "Mormons" for volunteers. This was a very different action than that hoped for by the authorities of the Church, as they were looking for the opportunity to labor along the road toward Oregon over which they were destined to travel. Nevertheless they had asked for aid and now they were determined to carry through the proposition of the government, hoping thereby that a blessing would be obtained and some benefit accrue to them. In complying with the order from the government over five hundred of their most vigorous young men were taken from their camps to travel westward by another route thus greatly weakening the camps.

Winter Quarters.—The call of these able-bodied men for the battalion made it impossible for the Saints in their weakened condition, to continue their journey towards the West. It became necessary, therefore, for them to seek quarters where they could prepare for the coming winter. Captain James Allen secured from the chiefs representing the Pottawattamie tribes their voluntary consent for the Saints to make the Indian lands an abiding place as long as they should remain in that country. He also wrote an open letter stating what he had done in this matter. The Indian sub-agent also endorsed the letter which Colonel Thomas L. Kane forwarded with a communication of his own, to the President of the United States. Measures were taken to gather to this place all the scattered Saints who were on the plains. Twelve men were chosen to form a high council, and a site was chosen on the west bank of the Missouri River for their settlement. A committee of twelve men was appointed to arrange the temporary city into wards, over which bishops were chosen to preside. During the summer hay was cut in sufficient quantities to provide for their stock in the winter. Every family labored diligently to construct some kind of a house in which they could find shelter, although many of these were merely dug-outs built in the side of the hill. The place was named Winter Quarters and was laid out regularly into streets. The Indians gave some trouble and it became necessary to build a stockade around the town. Through kind treatment, President Young and the Saints obtained the good will of most of the Inidans, so they lived in comparative peace.

Major Harvey's Opposition.—Major H. M. Harvey, the superintendent of Indian affairs and some others, made trouble for the Saints. Mr. Harvey called on President Young in November, and stated that he wished the Saints to move from the lands belonging to the Indians, and complained that the people were burning the Indians' wood. He said he had instructions from the government to permit no settlers on the lands without authority from Washington. President Young explained that the reason for the encampment was due to the sudden demand of the United States for troops, and if the government prevented them from continuing their journey some consideration and protection in return should be offered. Later developments indicated that the opposition was instigated by the enemies of the Saints. Through the intercession of J. K. Kane, father of Colonel Thomas L. Kane, the government gave permission for the exiles to remain where they were through the winter. Colonel Kane proved himself a faithful friend to the Latter-day Saints, and was yet to perform valiant service. He wrote to Elder Willard Richards, the camp historian, stating that he was intending to secure a lease from the government of the Omaha lands, on which some of the Saints had located. "Trust me," he said, "it is not fated that my forces shall depart before I have righted you at the seat of government, and have at least assured to you a beginning of justice besides an end of wrong."

Activities at Winter Quarters.—A gristmill was built at Winter Quarters; also a council house, where meetings could be held. This was done as much for the sake of keeping the people employed as it was for their convenience. During the winter they suffered greatly. The scurvy broke out among them and continued until potatoes were obtained from Missouri, and horse-radish was discovered in an abandoned fort near the camp. Meetings were regularly held and the spiritual as well as the temporal welfare of the refugees was not neglected. Much of the time of the leading brethren was spent in giving employment to the Saints and in devising means for the continuance of the journey when the time should come in the spring for them to move.

THE EXODUS FROM NAUVOO

Mob Uprisings at Nauvoo.—In the summer of 1846, hostilities were renewed against the members of the Church who still remained in Nauvoo. The great body of the Saints had left and only a remnant remained, composed of the poor, sick and afflicted, who had been unable to get away. They were all anxious to depart and were exerting all their energies to obtain means for that purpose. President Young and the apostles also were doing all in their power to aid them to depart. Notwithstanding their straitened circumstances and their inability to move—which was due mainly to mob violence they had suffered—their enemies became impatient at their delay and continued their vicious persecution. The new citizens, who had purchased property from the Saints, also came in for a share of the bitterness of the mob.

Major Warren's Proclamation.—Major W. B. Warren, who had been stationed in Hancock County with a small force, took up his quarters at Nauvoo by order of the governor and published a proclamation to the citizens of Hancock County attempting to quiet their opposition, in which, in part, he said:

"I have been in Nauvoo with my detachment a week, and can say to you with perfect assurance, that the demonstrations made by the 'Mormon' population, are unequivocal. They are leaving the state, and preparing to leave, with every means that God and nature has placed in their hands. Five ferry boats are running at this place night and day, and many are crossing at Nashville and Fort Madison. This ought to be satisfactory.

"The anti-'Mormons' desire the removal of the 'Mormons;' this is being effected peaceably, and with all possible dispatch. All aggressive movements, therefore, against them at this time, must be actuated by a wanton desire to shed blood, or to plunder. This course, I know, is deprecated by three-fourths of the anti-'Mormon' population, and must not be indulged in. I therefore exhort all good citizens to stay at home, with an assurance that they shall be duly advised of all movements which may take place, in which they feel interested.

"A man near sixty years of age, living about seven miles from this place, was taken from his house a few nights since stripped of his clothing, and his back cut to pieces with a whip, for no other reason than because he was a 'Mormon,' and too old to make successful resistance. Conduct of this kind would disgrace a horde of savages."

A proclamation of this kind, issued by one who was himself none too friendly to the "Mormon" people, was without effect. At the time he wrote, John McAuley and Levi Williams—the latter a Baptist preacher, and one of the mob who took part in the murder of Joseph and Hyrum Smith—with a strong force were preparing to gather under arms, contrary to the proclamation of the governor to the effect that not more than four persons with arms should assemble together, other than the state troops. Though his force was small, Major Warren notified these mobbers that he had law and moral force on his side and was able to meet successfully any mob which could assemble in that county. He advised the "Mormons" to go on with their preparations to cross the river, as speedily as they could, and leave the fighting to him; if he should be overpowered, then they could recross the river and defend themselves and property.

Kidnaping of Phineas H. Young and Others.—On the 11th day of July, eight of the citizens of Nauvoo went into the country about eleven miles from Nauvoo, to harvest wheat. While engaged in their work they were surrounded by a mob who ransacked their wagons, seized their weapons, and took them one at a time and brutally beat them with hickory goads. Several of the mobbers engaged in this were recognized, and two, John McAuley and a man named Brattle, were arrested. While they were under arrest, a second party of five "Mormons," Phineas H. Young, Brigham H. Young, Richard Ballantyne, James Standing and James Herring, were waylaid and taken prisoners. When they asked why they were treated in that manner the answer was given that they had committed no offense, but they were "Mormons," and were to be held as hostages for the safety of McAuley and Brattle. They were held by their persecutors for fourteen days, several times facing guns expecting to be shot, from which they were saved only by interposition of Divine power. Attempts were made to poison them, and they were most inhumanely treated. Finally they made their escape and returned to Nauvoo.

The "Resistance of Law."—When the two mobbers were arrested a gun was found in the possession of McAuley belonging to one of the harvesters. It was recognized and seized by William Pickett, a non-"Mormon." For this action Pickett and two others were arrested by the mobbers on a "warrant" for "stealing." Pickett had incurred the hatred of the mob, and knowing that the charge against him was only a trick to get him into their hands, he was not inclined to yield. When John Carlin came from Carthage to arrest him, Pickett asked if he would be guaranteed safety. Carlin answered no; whereupon Pickett resisted arrest. Though later he went before the magistrate at Green Plains, who issued the warrant, and was released.

The "resistance" by Pickett was the thing most desired by the mob, who only wanted a pretext to attack Nauvoo. Now there had been a defiance of law. "Nauvoo was in rebellion," and Carlin issued a proclamation calling upon the citizens to come as a *posse comitatus*, and assist him in executing the law. The citizens of Nauvoo petitioned the governor for protection, for the mob forces were collecting under command of James W. Singleton, assisted by J. B. Chittenden, N. Montgomery, James King, J. H. Sherman and Thomas S. Brockman. The governor very graciously sent Major Parker with a force of ten men, and authorized him to take command of such forces as he could raise from volunteers, and defend the city against mob attacks. There were very few members of the Church in Nauvoo at the time, less than one hundred and fifty men who were available for defense.

Counter Proclamations.—Parker issued a proclamation calling upon the mobs in the name of the state and by virtue of his authority, to disperse. Carlin and his crowd answered by a counter proclamation, stating that they would consider the government forces as a mob. Parker wrote to Singleton desiring a compromise without shedding blood. Articles of agreement requiring all the Saints to leave Nauvoo within sixty days, were drawn up and signed by Singleton and Chittenden for the mob, and Major Parker and three others for the government forces. In this manner Parker treated the mobbers as his equals and agreed to their terms.

Threats Against the Saints.—It appears that the object for which the mob forces were ostensibly raised was entirely forgotten, and no more was heard of the resistance of the officers by Pickett, but the attacking forces now determined that all the "Mormons" should go. Singleton in his communication to Parker said: "When I say to you, the 'Mormons' must go, I speak the mind of the camp and the country. They can leave without force or injury to themselves or their property, but I say to you, sir, with all candor, they shall go—they may fix the time within sixty days, or I will fix it for them."

Attack Upon Nauvoo.—These terms did not satisfy the mob. Sixty days was too long a time for them to wait for the departure of the remnant of the "Mormons" that they might plunder and rob, and besides they thirsted for blood. Singleton and Chittenden withdrew from the command of the mob forces, and wrote to Parker saying that the mob had rejected their treaty, which they considered reasonable enough. Carlin, the constable, thereupon placed Thomas S. Brockman in command, and gave orders for the mob to march. Parker also withdrew from service and Major Benjamin Clifford, Jr., took command of the government forces at Nauvoo by a commission from Governor Ford. September 10, Brockman and his mob approached Nauvoo. Many of the new citizens, seeing the danger they were in, fled from the city, leaving but a small force of volunteers to aid Major Clifford in the defense of Nauvoo. The defenders converted some steamboat shafts into canon and threw up some fortifications on the north side of Mulholland street facing the mob. This small force made a determined stand, although outnumbered two or three to one. On the 10th, 11th and 12th, there was desultory firing on both sides. On Saturday the 12th Brockman sent a communication "to the commander of the 'Mormon' forces in Nauvoo," demanding a surrender and the delivery of arms, to be returned as soon as the "Mormons" had crossed the river and were out of the state. The same day Major Clifford replied stating that there was no "commander of 'Mormon' forces" in that place; that he was there "by order of the governor and commander-in-chief of the Illinois militia to disperse your (Brockman's) forces in the name of the people of Illinois." The reply continued: "So far I have acted on the defensive, and for the sake of humanity; if for no other purpose, I hope you will at once see the propriety and justice of dispersing your forces. The armed force under your command is not necessary for any lawful purpose in this city or county."

The Battle of Nauvoo.—Upon receiving this reply, Brockman advanced upon Nauvoo, endeavoring to gain entrance at the head of Mulholland street, the main street of the city. He was driven back after a determined resistance by the defenders of the place. The cowardly mob forces were somewhat disconcerted at the sound of cannon in Nauvoo, for they thought the besieged citizens were poorly armed, and that to enter the city would be an easy thing to do. During the battle three of the defenders lost their lives, namely, Captain William Anderson, his son, August L., a lad of fifteen years of age, and David Norris. Several others were wounded. It cannot be ascertained how many were killed on the side of the mob, but a large number were wounded. The fighting continued until the 16th, and the mob was repulsed four times. On the latter day a treaty of surrender was entered into, through the agency of a committee of citizens from Quincy, who were in sympathy with the mob. This treaty which was signed by Andrew Johnson for the Quincy Committee, Thomas Brockman and John Carlin for the mob, and A. W. Babbitt, J. L. Heywood and J. S. Fullmer for the Latter-day Saints, stipulated that the city of Nauvoo should surrender September 17, at three o'clock p.m. The arms of the besieged were to be delivered up to the "Quincy Committee," to be returned at the crossing of the river. The citizens and property were to be protected from all violence. The sick and helpless were to be protected and treated with humanity, and the "Mormon" population was to leave the state as soon as they could cross the river. There were provisions of minor importance, one of which was that five men—including the trustees of the Church—were to be permitted to remain in the city to dispose of property, free from all molestation and violence. However, William Pickett, the man so much wanted according to the first reports of the mob for resisting the law, and on whose account the mob had gathered, was not to be one of this committee, nor was he to remain in the city.

Valiant Defenders.—Among those who took valiant part in the battles during the siege of Nauvoo, were the two Andersons, father and son, and David Norris, who lost their lives. They belonged to a company known as the "Spartan Band," because of the perilous situation in which they were stationed in the defense of the city. Also "Squire" Daniel H. Wells, Captain Andrew L. Lamereaux, William L. Cutler, Alexander McRae, Almon Fullmer, Benjamin Whitehead, John E. Campbell and Curtis E. Bolton. In fact the entire band of noble defenders are worthy of special mention and their names should be recorded among the true sons of liberty.[d]

Daniel H. Wells

---

[d]Daniel H. Wells, who had joined the Church August 9, 1846, after the departure of most of the members of the Church, but who had always been a true friend to the Prophet Joseph and Patriarch Hyrum Smith, addressed the remaining members of the Church, while they were in the hands of their enemies, as follows:

"There is no use in the small handful of volunteers trying to defend the city against such an overwhelming force. What interest have the Saints to expect from its defense? Our interests are not identified with it, but in getting away from it. Who could urge the propriety of exposing life to defend a place for the purpose of vacating it? I have been in the councils of Joseph and Hyrum and the twelve, and I know they were desirous that the Saints should leave the state and go westward. Have not the twelve and most of the Church

The Violation of the Treaty.—According to the agreement, the mob forces entered Nauvoo on the 17th, and in keeping with the usual mob spirit, failed to regard their agreement. Immediately they commenced to drive the Saints from the city, and treated some of the men in a most brutal manner. They commenced their diabolical deeds by searching the wagons on the bank of the river waiting to be ferried across, and ransacked their contents taking all firearms and scattering the goods over the ground. Families of the poor were ordered from the city at the point of the bayonet. The sick were sorely abused, and even those who were engaged in the burying of their dead were molested. They entered the temple, ascended the tower and rung the bell, shouting and yelling, giving vent to filthy oaths in a fiendish manner. They plundered the homes of the people, irrespective of whether they were members of the Church or not. Colonel C. M. Johnson was sentenced to death, but his persecutors could not agree on the manner of his execution and he escaped. With such inhuman treatment, the members of the Church remaining in Nauvoo, were forced across the Mississippi River in their poverty and distress. Their condition was pitiable, but it could not move the hearts of the mobs of Illinois. These outcasts camped on the bank of the river for several days, where the Lord in his mercy fed them, as he did the children of Israel, with a supply of quails, until help arrived from the camps of Israel in the wilderness. As soon as they could leave they bid farewell to the inhospitable boundaries of "civilization" and took up their journey toward the west, there to build a city of refuge, and find a haven of rest among the more tender-hearted savages of the desert.

---

gone, and is not their counsel for us to follow? Have not they told us that our safety was not in Nauvoo, but in our removal westward?

"The trustees have no means with which to carry on the defense; they are already involved. Major Parker, who was sent by the governor to aid us, when he left, promised to raise men and return immediately to our assistance, but he has forsaken us, and is it not well known that the Quincy Committee was prepared to join the mob, if a treaty was not effected? Under these circumstances, I have thrown in my influence with the trustees for the surrender of Nauvoo upon the best terms we could get, and as being the best and only wise policy left for us to pursue.

"Brethren, reflect, we have nothing to gain in defending Nauvoo, but everything to lose; not only property, but life also, is hourly in peril."

CHAPTER 38

THE MORMON BATTALION
1846–1847

Captain Allen's Circular.—When Captain James Allen arrived in the Camps of the Saints, he issued a "Circular to the 'Mormons,'" which read as follows:

"I have come among you, instructed by Colonel S. W. Kearny, of the U. S. Army, now commanding the Army of the West, to visit the 'Mormon' Camp, and accept the services for twelve months of four or five companies of 'Mormon' men who may be willing to serve their country for that period in our present war with Mexico; this force to unite with the Army of the West at Santa Fe, and be marched thence to California, where they will be discharged.

"They will receive pay and rations, and other allowances, such as other volunteers or regular soldiers receive, from the day they shall be mustered into the service, and will be entitled to all comforts and benefits of regular soldiers of the Army, and when discharged, as contemplated, at California, they will be given gratis their arms and accoutrements, with which they will be fully equipped at Fort Leavenworth. Thus is offered to the 'Mormon' people now—this year—an opportunity to send a portion of their young and intelligent men to the ultimate destination of their whole people, and entirely at the expense of the United States, and this advance party can thus pave the way and look out the land for their brethren to come after them.

"The pay of a private volunteer is seven dollars per month, and the allowance for clothing is the cost price of clothing of a regular soldier.

"Those of the 'Mormons' who are desirous of serving their country on the conditions here enumerated, are requested to meet me without delay at their principal camp at the Council Bluffs, whither I am now going to consult with their principal men, and to receive and organize the force contemplated to be raised.

"I will receive all healthy, able men of from eighteen to forty-five years of age.

"J. Allen, Captain 1st Dragoons."

"Camp of the 'Mormons,' at Mount Pisgah, one hundred and thirty miles east of Council Bluffs, June 26th, 1846."

Scarcity of Able-Bodied Men.—When this call came a great part of the young men of the ages required were scattered over the plains. Many had gone to St. Louis and other points for employment to obtain means to help them carry their families to the west. All of the Saints were poor, and some in dire want. Those who were able to travel were under the necessity of helping along the weak, the aged and infirm, who could not be left behind. Among the teamsters were found mere children, who had been forced into such service because of the limited number of men.

The Equipment of the Battalion.—At Fort Leavenworth the battalion was equipped.[a] They received one tent for every six privates and were provided with flint-lock muskets, a few cap-lock yauger rifles for sharp-shooting and hunting, and other camp accoutrements. August 5, they drew their check for clothing, forty-two dollars each, paid one year in advance. A goodly portion of this money was sent back for the support of their families and the gathering of the poor from Nauvoo. They also contributed to help Elders Orson Hyde, Parley P. Pratt and John Taylor on their way to Great Britain and Elder Jesse C. Little to return to his field in the Eastern States. The paymaster was much surprised to see every man of the battalion able to sign his name to the roll, whereas only about one out of every three of the Missouri volunteers, who previously had received their pay, could put his signature to the document.

Death of Colonel Allen.—Captain James Allen, the recruiting officer for the battalion, was selected by General Stephen W. Kearny, to take command of the "Mormon" troops, with the rank of lieutenant-colonel of volunteers. At Fort Leavenworth Colonel Allen was taken

---

[a]The five companies of the battalion were commanded respectively as follows: Company A, Jefferson Hunt; Company B., Jesse D. Hunter; Company C., James Brown; Company D., Nelson Higgins; Company E., Daniel C. Davis. Before they left Winter Quarters a farewell ball was given them in "Father Taylor's Bowery," where the afternoon was spent in dancing and such merriment as the sadness of the approaching parting would admit.

THE MORMON BATTALION

ill, and on the 12th of August, ordered the battalion to take up its march while he remained for a few days to recuperate, but on the 23rd he died. He was much lamented by the battalion members, for they had learned to love him for his kindness.

Lieutenant Smith in Command.—After the death of Colonel Allen, the command devolved upon Captain Jefferson Hunt, of Company "A." The promise had been made to President Young, by Colonel Allen, that no officers would be chosen for the battalion, except himself, outside of their ranks. On what authority the promise was made, does not appear. However, shortly afterwards Lieutenant A. J. Smith, of the regular army, was given command, contrary to the wishes of the men. With Lieutenant Smith there came Dr. George B. Sanderson, whom Colonel Allen had appointed to serve with the battalion as surgeon. According to the journals of the men, they were caused to suffer considerably because of the "arrogance, inefficiency and petty oppressions" of these two officers. Sanderson was from Missouri, and perhaps was none too friendly towards the troops; however, the enforcement of discipline, to which they were not accustomed, may have magnified the ill-treatment in their eyes to some extent. The heat of the summer was excessive, their rations were reduced, and through the drinking of brackish water, many were taken with malaria. They had already become weakened from their long marches across the plains of Iowa, in inclement weather, without proper food and shelter, so that they were more susceptible to disease. Dr. Sanderson prescribed calomel and arsenic, refusing to permit the men to resort to their own simple remedies, and evincing skepticism in the laying on of hands and their exercise of faith.

The Line of March.—Their line of march from Fort Leavenworth,

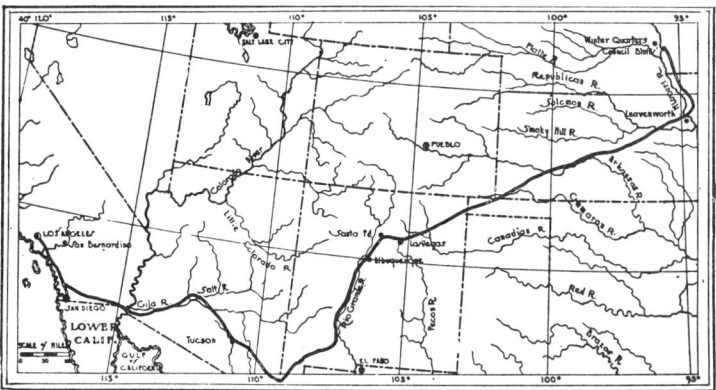

Route of the Mormon Battalion

had taken them across the Kansas River and then westward to the Arkansas, which they followed up stream for about one hundred miles. From that point they journeyed southwest to the Cimarron River and passed near what is now the junction of the states of Kansas, Colorado and Oklahoma, on a southwesterly course to the old Spanish town of Santa Fe. From Santa Fe their route was by way of the Rio Grande, southward near the present city of El Paso, and thence to the west, through the city of Tucson—which was deserted by its garrison as the battalion approached—across the Gila and Colorado to San Diego.

The Families Ordered to Pueblo.—As the battalion was leaving the Arkansas River, the commanding officer gave orders that a number of families which had accompanied the troops to that point, should be detached and sent to Pueblo, a Mexican town situated at the eastern base of the Rocky Mountains. There was some protest because it was contrary to a promise given at the beginning of the march; but it was really a necessary action. For the families of members of the battalion to travel with the companies was a hindrance to the rapid progress they were called upon to make. Captain Nelson Higgins and a guard of ten men were detailed to make the journey to Pueblo. They departed September 16, 1846, and on the way one of their number, Norman Sharp, was accidentally killed.

Colonel Cooke Takes Command.—Leaving the Arkansas the battalion resumed its journey to Santa Fe. On the 2nd of October they crossed Red River where they were divided into two divisions the following day. The strongest and most able-bodied men pushed on with all speed and arrived at Santa Fe on the 9th of that month. Here they were received with a salute of one hundred guns by Colonel Alexander Doniphan, the post commander. On October 12, the second division arrived, and immediately afterward Captain Philip St. George Cooke, an officer of dragoons, succeeded to the command with the rank of lieutenant-colonel, by appointment of General Kearny. The appointment of Col. Cooke was another disappointment to the men, who still hoped for the appointment of Captain Hunt; but they learned to respect and honor this rugged officer who was a thorough soldier and just and honorable. Lieutenant A. J. Smith remained with the battalion as acting commissary, and Dr. Sanderson continued to administer his calomel and arsenic to the men.

The Sick Sent to Pueblo.—At Santa Fe a council of officers was held with Colonels Doniphan and Cooke, and it was decided to send all the sick together with the remaining women and children in the camp, to Pueblo for the winter, with the privilege of journeying towards the main body of pioneers in the spring, at government expense. Colonel Cooke detailed Captain James Brown and Lieutenant Elam Luddington to take charge of this company on the march to Pueblo. October 18, 1846, Captain Brown left Santa Fe with nearly ninety men reported as incapable of undertaking the journey to California because of physical ailments. Accompanying them were a number of women and children. Sanderson, the physician, discharged some of these men without pay or means to procure conveyance to the states, whereupon Colonel Doniphan, in charge of the post, went to Col. Cooke and countermanded the order with the statement that General Kearny would never discharge a man under circumstances of that kind, and ordered the men with the laundresses and others, to be sent to Pueblo and to draw their pay. Their journey took them over a rough country a distance of some two hundred miles. Several died on the way and others succumbed after Pueblo was reached. They arrived November 17 and selected a place for winter quarters near the encampment of Captain Higgins and a company of Saints who had previously arrived in Pueblo from Mississippi, on their way to the Rocky Mountains. November 10, 1846, Lieutenant William W. Willis was also ordered back to Pueblo with another company of sick—fifty-six men—from a point about one hundred miles out from Santa Fe. They commenced their journey with one wagon, four yoke of oxen, and rations barely sufficient to last them five days, on a march of three hundred miles. After a most severe and toilsome journey, in which they all suffered many privations and some laid down their lives, the company arrived in Pueblo, in an emaciated condition, December 24, 1846.

The March From Santa Fe.—The march of the battalion from Santa Fe was taken up October 19, 1846. They had not traveled very far before they were reduced to the extremity of using poor oxen, which were barely skin and bones, for food. Even their raw hides were cut in small pieces and made into soup. At times they crossed deserts where water could not be found to quench their thirst, and their tongues became swollen and their lips parched until their strength failed them.

Colonel Cooke's Comment.—Writing of the condition of the battalion when he took command, Colonel Cooke made a report in the following words:

"Everything conspired to discourage the extraordinary undertaking of marching this battalion eleven hundred miles, for the much greater part through an unknown wilderness, without road or trail, and with a wagon train.

"It was enlisted too much by families; some were too old—some feeble, and some too young; it was embarrassed by many women; it was undisciplined; it was much worn by traveling on foot, and marching from Nauvoo, Illinois; their clothing was very scant; there was no money to pay them, or clothing to issue; their mules were utterly broken down; the quartermaster department was without funds, and its credit bad; mules were scarce. Those procured were very inferior, and were deterioriating every hour for lack of forage or grazing. * * *

"With every effort, the quartermaster could only undertake to furnish rations for sixty days; and, in fact, full rations, of only flour, sugar, coffee and salt; salt pork only for thirty days, and soap for twenty. To venture without pack-saddles would be grossly imprudent, and so that burden was added."[b]

A Battle With Wild Bulls.—A short distance northwest of the site of the present city of El Paso the course of the march was towards the west. On the San Pedro River they encountered herds of wild cattle, and were viciously attacked by ferocious bulls. The troops had been ordered to travel with unloaded guns, but now they were hastily forced to load without waiting the command. These vicious animals, as if resenting the encroachment on their domain, made a charge upon the camp. This constituted the only fighting the troops were called upon to do on their long and toilsome march. When the battle was over the casualties revealed a number of gored mules and overturned wagons, and among the "enemy" perhaps some sixty of the charging animals were killed. Resuming their journey they camped on the 16th of December, near the Mexican pueblo of Tucson. On their way they met three Mexican soldiers bringing a message from the governor of Tucson to Colonel Cooke, informing him that he must pass around the town, or else he would have to fight. Colonel Cooke was not to be frightened by such an order. His route would take him through the village, and hither he resumed his march. The following day he passed through Tucson without meeting opposition, as the soldiers and a great many of the citizens had fled on his approach. Before arriving at that place he instructed his men that they came not to make war on Sonora, and less still to destroy an important outpost of defense against Indians. "But," said he, "we will take the straight road before us and overcome all resistance, but shall I remind you that the American soldier ever shows justice and kindness to the unarmed and unresisting? The property of individuals you will hold sacred: the people of Sonora are not our enemies."

---

[b]"Conquest of New Mexico and California," by P. St. George Cooke, p. 91-2.

The Journey From Tucson.—Leaving Tucson, the battalion crossed an extensive desert, where, for seventy-five miles, they were without water for their mules. By hard marching they reached the Gila River and intersected General Kearny's trail, which they had left 474 miles behind in the valley of the Rio Grande. They were now in the land of the Pima and Maricopa Indians who inhabited a fertile territory. These were a superior race of Indians with peaceful tendencies, who spent their time tilling the soil, and in weaving rather than bearing arms. While passing through these villages Colonel Cooke remarked to Captain Jefferson Hunt that this might be a good place for the settlement of the "Mormon" people. Hunt proposed such a thing to the natives who received it favorably, and this may have lent its weight to the colonizing of these valleys by the Latter-day Saints in later years.

At this point they were met by pilots sent back by General Kearny to conduct them to the Pacific coast. Most of the distance on the remaining journey was over deserts with alternating stretches of deep sand and miry clay. January 9, 1847, they crossed the Colorado, near the junction of the Gila, and continued their march under great difficulties over the coast range down the Pacific slope. January 27, 1847, they passed San Luis Rey, and two days later arrived at the San Diego Mission where they located one mile below the Catholic mission, and about five miles from the seaport town of San Diego, where General Kearny had his quarters.

"Orders No. 1."—On the day after their arrival at San Diego, Colonel Cooke issued the following orders, which were read to the men:

"Headquarters 'Mormon' Battalion,
"Mission of San Diego,
"January 30, 1847."

"(Orders No. 1.)

"The Lieutenant-Colonel commanding, congratulates the battalion on their safe arrival on the shore of the Pacific Ocean, and the conclusion of their march of over two thousand miles.

"History may be searched in vain for an equal march of infantry. Half of it has been through a wilderness where nothing but savages and wild beasts are found, or deserts where, for want of water, there is no living creature. There, with almost hopeless labor, we have dug deep wells, which the future traveler will enjoy. Without a guide who had traversed them we have ventured into trackless table-lands where water was not found for several marches. With crow-bar and pick and axe in hand, we have worked our way over mountains, which seemed to defy aught save the wild goat, and hewed a passage through a chasm of living rock more narrow than our wagons. To bring these first wagons to the Pacific, we have preserved the strength of our mules by herding them over large tracts, which you have laboriously guarded without loss. The garrison of four presidios of Sonora concentrated within the walls of Tucson, gave us no pause. We drove them out, with their artillery, but our intercourse with the citizens was unmarked by a single act of injustice. Thus, marching half naked and half fed, and living upon wild animals, we have discovered and made a road of great value to our country.

"Arrived at the first settlement of California, after a single day's rest, you cheerfully turned off from the route to this point of promised repose, to enter upon a campaign, and meet, as we supposed, the approach of the enemy; and this, too, without even salt to season your sole subsistence of fresh meat.

"Lieutenants, A. J. Smith and George Stoneman, of the First Dragoons, have shared and given invaluable aid in all these labors.

"Thus, volunteers, you have exhibited some high and essential qualities of veterans. But much remains undone. Soon you will turn your attention to the drill, to system and order, to forms also, which are all necessary to the soldier.

"By order,
"Lieut. Col. P. St. George Cooke,
"P. C. Merrill, Adjutant."

Duties on the Coast.—For some time the battalion performed garrison duty at San Diego, San Luis Rey and Los Angeles. While stationed at the latter place they were called upon to guard the Cajon Pass, in the Sierra Nevada mountains, against hostile Indians. At San Diego they were employed digging wells, making brick and building houses. Their frugality and industry won the admiration of the other troops, except the Missourians of General Fremont's command, who endeavored to create prejudice against them.

The Discharge of the Battalion—Stevenson's Insult.—July 16, 1847, all of the battalion at Los Angeles were mustered out of service by Captain Smith. The time of their enlistment had expired and the prophecy of President Brigham Young that they would not be called upon to fight, had been fulfilled. Some of the men, at the request of Colonel Stevenson, of the New York Volunteers, re-enlisted for six months. Others might have done so, but he insulted them by saying: "Your patriotism and obedience to your officers have done much towards removing the prejudice of the government and the community at large, and I am satisfied that another year's service would place you on a level with other communities."

The Journey to Salt Lake Valley.—On the 20th of July most of the members of the battalion, who did not enlist, organized preparatory to going to the Rocky Mountains to the gathering place of the Saints. They went by way of Sutter's Fort and the Sacramento River, intending to follow Fremont's trail across the Sierras. Near Lake Tahoe, they met Samuel Brannan and Captain Brown of the Pueblo detachment who were on the way to California, and learned that the pioneers had entered the Salt Lake Valley. Captain Brown carried with him an epistle from the apostles advising all members of the battalion who had no means, to remain in California for the winter, and journey to the Salt Lake Valley in the spring. Acting on this advice about one half of the members obtained employment at Sutter's Fort, where they were at the time of the discovery of gold. The others pushed on to the Salt Lake Valley where they arrived October 16, 1847.

CHAPTER 39

THE PIONEERS

1847

Revelation to President Brigham Young.—January 14, 1847, the word of the Lord came to President Brigham Young, at Winter Quarters, giving instructions for the guidance of the camps of Israel on their journeyings to the west. The Saints were to be organized into companies, with captains over hundreds, fifties and tens, as the case had been while journeying across Iowa. These companies were to be presided over by a president and two counselors, under the direction of the Twelve Apostles, who were at the head of all the camps of Israel. The Saints were to enter into a covenant "to keep all the commandments and statutes of the Lord;" and each company was to bear an equal proportion of the responsibility in the care of the widows, the fatherless, and the families of those who had gone into the army. Every man was commanded to use his influence and property to remove the body of the people to the place the Lord had designated as a stake of Zion; and if they would do this they were to be blessed abundantly in their substance and in their families. Moreover, they were to prepare houses and fields for those who were to remain behind that season, that they might prepare also for the journey.

Cheerfulness Commanded.—"If thou art merry," the revelation read (Doc. and Cov. Sec. 136), "praise the Lord with singing, with music, with dancing, and with prayer of praise and thanksgiving. If thou art sorrowful, call on the Lord thy God with supplication, that your souls may be joyful." During their travels in the wilderness the exiled Saints had many hardships to endure. The lack of necessary food, of clothing and other substance, was lamentable. Yet, in the midst of poverty and distress, they were happy for they were free from enemies and the persecutions of mobs. They were going to a land of promise where they could dwell in peace, and worship the Lord without fear of men. The Lord desired that they should be cheerful and promised to bless them with his Spirit, in the hour of their sorrow, if they would call upon him. That they might be light of heart and filled with joy, the Lord commended music, singing and dancing, if done in the spirit of reverence and prayer. It was the custom, at the close of the day's journey, for the Saints to assemble in the dance, or to have an informal concert; to relate reminiscences and otherwise employ their time, that the cares and hardships of their travel might be forgotten, and their burdens lessened which they were forced to bear.[a] At the sound of the bugle, night and morning, all assembled for prayer. The Sabbath day was strictly kept, and undue levity was discountenanced in all the camps. They were commanded to be honest, sober, unselfish and to "contend not one with another," but always speak with edifying words.

The Pioneers.—It was commanded in the revelation that a company be organized to depart early in the spring, composed of a sufficient number of able-bodied and experienced men, with teams, seeds and farming utensils, to prepare for the planting of spring crops. As

---

[a]Outcasts from "civilization," with little to eat and little to wear; with few expressions of sympathy, and less help extended in their direction, it was only natural that the Saints on the plains at times would be despondent. President Young constantly labored to cheer and strengthen them. In April, 1846, shortly after the departure from Nauvoo, he requested Elder William Clayton to write something that would encourage the people. Within two hours Elder Clayton had written the following remarkable hymn, and set it to the music of "All Is Well," an old English tune:—

> Come, come, ye Saints, no toil nor labor fear,
>   But with joy wend your way;
> Though hard to you this journey may appear,
>   Grace shall be as your day.
> 'Tis better far for us to strive,
> Our useless cares from us to drive.
> Do this, and joy your hearts will swell—
> All is well! all is well!

✪ ✪ ✪

> And should we die before our journey's through,
>   Happy day! all is well!
> We then are free from toil and sorrow too;
>   With the just we shall dwell.
> But if our lives are spared again
> To see the Saints, their rest obtain,
> O, how we'll make this chorus swell—
> All is well! all is well!

spring approached preparations were under way for the departure of this pioneer band, and for other companies, as the Saints were able, to follow after. February 26, 1847, President Brigham Young met in council with the members of the twelve who were at Winter Quarters

Elkhorn River Crossing

and Bishop Newel K. Whitney, William Clayton and Jedediah M. Grant. The object of this meeting was to consider the appointment of a pioneer company and their requirements for the journey. The matter of constructing boats, the carrying of seeds, scientific investigations, the location of a site for a city, the irrigation, cultivation and seeding of the land, were all fully discussed. This is the first reference, so far as the records show, of the discussion of irrigation, which President Young and the brethren felt would be necessary for their sustenance in their new home.

The Departure for the West.—Elder Heber C. Kimball, under instructions from President Brigham Young, moved out of Winter Quarters, April 5, 1847, with six wagons, which he had equipped as a part of the pioneer company. They traveled about six miles and camped, awaiting the arrival of the rest of the company. On the 6th of April, the general conference was held in Winter Quarters, and the following day President Young, with about twenty-five wagons, traveled some ten miles and camped. From this point the company which had assembled, continued their journey to the Elkhorn River, where the information reached them that Elder Parley P. Pratt had arrived at Winter Quarters from his mission to England, and that Elder John Taylor was on the way. President Young decided to return, with other members of the twelve, to receive Elder Pratt's report of conditions in that foreign field.*b* A few days later Elder John Taylor also arrived, bringing with him two thousand dollars in gold, contributed by the Saints in Great Britain, to help the exiles on their westward journey. He also had with him a number of scientific instruments of great value, including two sextants, one circle of reflection, two artificial horizons, and a number of barometers, thermometers and telescopes.

Organization of the Pioneer Camp.—Leaving Elders Pratt and Taylor—and later Orson Hyde who joined them from England—in

Camp at Wood River

---

*b*Elders Orson Hyde, Parley P. Pratt and John Taylor had been sent to England, after the exodus from Nauvoo, to set the British Mission in order. Elders Reuben Hedlock and Thomas Ward, who were in charge, had misappropriated the funds of "The Joint Stock Company," an organization which had been formed for the purpose of assisting the Saints of the British Isles to emigrate. The three apostles took charge of affairs and soon had the mission again in a flourishing condition. Early in 1847, they again returned to the United States, Elders Pratt and Taylor preceding Elder Hyde, who remained to install Elder Orson Spencer as president of that mission. Elder Orson Spencer, a man of culture and superior education, performed an excellent work and under his ministry the mission flourished.

charge of the Saints at Winter Quarters, President Young, with the other apostles, returned to the pioneer camp, which had journeyed to a position twelve miles west of the Elkhorn, and some forty-seven miles west of Winter Quarters. President Young's departure from Winter Quarters was on the morning of April 14, 1847, and on the 16th, the pioneer camp was organized with captains of hundreds, fifties and tens, as follows:

Captains of Hundreds: Stephen Markham and Albert P. Rockwood.

Captains of Fifties: Addison Everett, Tarlton Lewis, James Case, John Pack, Shadrach Roundy.

Captains of Tens: Wilford Woodruff, Ezra T. Benson, Phineas H. Young, Luke S. Johnson,[c] Stephen G. Goddard, Charles Shumway, James Case, Seth Taft, Howard Egan, Appleton M. Harmon, John S. Higbee, Norton Jacobs, John Brown, and Joseph Matthews.

The total number of souls in the camp was one hundred and forty-eight, of whom three were women and two were children. The women were: Harriet Page Wheeler Young, wife of Lorenzo D. Young; Clarissa Decker Young, wife of Brigham Young, and Ellen Saunders Kimball, wife of Heber C. Kimball. Three of the company were colored: Hark Lay, Oscar Crosby and Green Flake, who had come west with the emigrants from Mississippi, under command of John Brown in the summer of 1846. Originally the pioneer company was composed of one hundred and forty-four men, but one, Ellis Ames, was taken sick and returned to Winter Quarters soon after the start. Two of the pioneers were not members of the Church.

Military Organization.—In addition to the organization mentioned, on April 17, they were also organized into a military camp with President Brigham Young as lieutenant-general; Stephen Markham, colonel; John Pack and Shadrach Roundy, majors; and the captains of tens, as formerly organized, to hold similar rank in the military organization. Thomas Bullock was appointed clerk of the camp, with some assistants, and Thomas Tanner, captain of the cannon, with the privilege of choosing eight men to assist him.

Division of the Watch.—The captains of tens selected forty-eight men for a constant night guard. They were divided into four watches

---

[c] Luke S. Johnson, formerly of the council of the apostles, came to Nauvoo in 1846 in a repentant spirit, and asked to be reinstated in the Church. He was baptized and was forced to leave that place with the body of the Saints. He was chosen as one of the pioneer band to come in advance to the Salt Lake Valley. In the year 1858, he settled at St. Johns, Tooele County, where he was ordained a bishop. He died in Salt Lake City, December 9, 1861.

to serve half a night at a time. President Young and others of the twelve were among the members of this guard. As there was danger of Indian raids, orders were given that every man should keep by the side of his wagon and not leave it except by permission, and he should carry a loaded gun always ready for instant use.

Regulations of the Camp.—Sunday, April 18, 1847, in the afternoon, President Young met with the captains of the camp and decided on the details for the government of the camp as follows:

"At 5 o'clock in the morning the bugle is to be sounded as a signal for every man to arise and attend prayers before he leaves his wagon. Then the people will engage in cooking, eating, feeding teams, etc., until 7 o'clock, at which time the train is to move at the sound of the bugle. Each teamster is to keep beside his team with loaded gun in hand or within easy reach, while the extra men, observing the same rule regarding their weapons, are to walk by the side of their particular wagons to which they belong; and no man may leave his post without permission of his officer. In case of an attack or any hostile demonstration by Indians, the wagons will travel in double file—the order of encampment to be in a circle, with the mouth of each wagon to the outside and the horses and cattle tied inside the circle. At 8:30 p.m., the bugles are to be sounded again, upon which signal all will hold prayers in their wagons, and be retired to rest by 9 o'clock."

The Route of Travel.—The line of travel taken by the pioneers was along the north bank of the Platte River to Fort Laramie, and from there they crossed the river, and continued over the Oregon trail up the Sweetwater and over the Continental divide through the South Pass across Green River to Fort Bridger. They then traveled to the southwest through Echo Canyon, and East Canyon over Big and Little Mountain into Emigration Canyon, and then to the valley of the Great Salt Lake.

On the south side of the Platte was the Oregon trail, but the pioneers remained on the north bank where there was not trail, for reasons expressed by Elder Wilford Woodruff as follows:

"We are convinced that it would be better for us as a company to cross the river and take the old traveled road to Laramie as there was good grass all the way on that side, while the Indians were burning it all off on the north of the river where we were traveling. But when we took into consideration the situation of the next company, and the thousands that would follow, and as we were the Pioneers and had not our wives and children with us—we thought it best to keep on the north side of the river and brave the difficulties of burning prairies to make a road that should stand as a permanent route for the Saints, independent of the then immigrant road, and let the river separate the emigrating companies that they need not quarrel for wood, grass, or water; and when our next company came along, the grass would be much better for them than it would be on the south side, as it would grow up by the time they would get along; and the vote was called and it was unanimous to go on the north side of the river; so the camp again moved on."

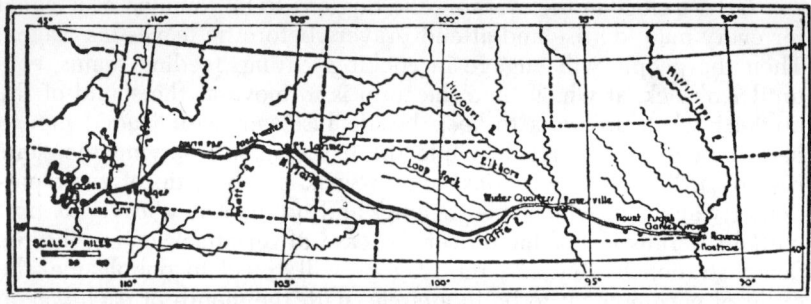

Pioneer Route

Measuring the Distance.—The pioneers were anxious to know the distance of each day's travel and the length of the entire journey. In order to obtain this information they first resorted to guess work, but this proved unsatisfactory. They then tied a piece of cloth to a wheel of one of the wagons and a man was placed on duty to count the revolutions. However, this was tedious though accurate if the count was correctly kept. April 19, William Clayton suggested to Orson Pratt that a set of wooden cog wheels might be attached to the wheel of a wagon to record the distance automatically. The result was that an odometer was constructed on "the principle of the endless screw" and was installed during the month of May, after they were well along on the journey.

Dangers on the Way.—The pioneers were under the necessity of keeping constantly on the alert to protect themselves from attacks by Indians. They had considerable anxiety while passing through the Pawnee tribes. At times the brethren were fired upon. The Indians made several attempts at night to creep into the camp, evidently to plunder and steal animals. At one time before the camp was organized for the night they were successful in stealing two of the best horses belonging to Dr. Willard Richards and Jesse C. Little. The following day, April 27, a party was sent out to search for the missing animals. They encountered a number of Indians who endeavored to decoy them to a point where the brethren would be in their power, but they were on the alert and well armed, so the Indians dared not make an attack. As the brethren prepared to return to camp the Indians fired upon them, whereupon the searching party turned upon their foe, and the Indians hastily fled.

Chimney Rock

Not all of the Indians, however, were hostile. Generally they showed a friendly spirit, but were ever ready to commit theft. The brethren at times gave them a few articles such as powder, lead, flour and salt.

Correspondence on the Plains.—On the 4th of May, after the camp had proceeded about two miles on their way, they were met by a Frenchman, Charles Beaumont, a trapper and fur trader, who was traveling eastward over the Oregon road with a camp consisting of three wagons and nine men. He crossed the river to find out who the pioneers were. During his interview he cheerfully consented to carry letters back to the Saints, so the brethren wrote some fifty or sixty letters and left them in his care. Other means of communication with the later companies on the plains were adopted. Posts were placed at prominent points along the road with writings on them and letters were placed in improvised boxes with a notice on the box. At other times they used whitened skulls of the buffalo. Over a portion of the journey, especially from Fort Laramie, the pioneers planted mile posts every ten miles as the distance was measured by their odometer.

Scientific Observations.—Astronomical observations were constantly taken. The temperature was recorded daily, also the altitude as shown by barometrical pressure. This was done under the able direction of Elder Orson Pratt, one of the great scientists of his time.

Crossing of the Platte.—At Fort Laramie the pioneers were forced to cross the Platte owing to the fact that the north side of the river was impassable. They hired a flatboat from a Frenchman, Mr. James Bordeaux, who was in charge of the post. They paid him fifteen dollars for the accommodation. Mr. Bordeaux treated the brethren very kindly, and informed them that Lilburn W. Boggs, with a company of Missourians en route to Oregon, left the fort but a short time before. These emigrants had endeavored to embitter him against the "Mormons."

Fort Laramie

The Missourians he said, were constantly quarreling and were great thieves. Bordeaux gave the pioneers information regarding the route before them and said the Crow Indians were troublesome and had lately run off all the horses and mules from the fort.

The Mississippi Emigrants.—Soon after the pioneers arrived at Fort Laramie they were joined by a company of seventeen emigrants of the Mississippi Saints who had wintered at Pueblo, where the sick detachments of the Mormon Battalion, under command of Captains Brown and Higgins, were also stationed. They had been at the fort two weeks awaiting the arrival of the pioneers. These emigrants consisted of the members of the Crow and Therlkill families, others being Archibald Little, James Chesney and Lewis B. Myers. They had five wagons, one cart, eleven horses, twenty-four oxen, twenty-two cows, three bulls and seven calves. From these Mississippi Saints the pioneers obtained their first knowledge in many months, of the battalion. Four of the pioneers, Amasa M. Lyman, Thomas Woolsey, John H. Tippits, and Roswell Stevens, were sent to Pueblo on horse-back and with mules, to take charge of the remaining body of the Mississippians and conduct them to the Salt Lake Valley.

The Ferry at the Black Hills.—From Winter Quarters to Fort Laramie the Pioneers had broken a new road over the plains, which was destined to be traveled by the emigrating Saints for many years. Subsequently the Union Pacific Railroad was built along a great portion of the trail. Continuing their journey, the pioneers arrived, Saturday, June 12, 1847, at the Black Hills, where the Oregon road crossed the Platte, some one hundred and forty-two miles from Fort Laramie. Here they overtook the Oregon emigrants, including the Missourians. The pioneers had sent an advance company three days before to prepare for the crossing of the river, with a sole-leather skiff capable of carrying eighteen hundred pounds. These brethren were employed in ferrying the emigrants over the river at the rate of $1.50 for each wagon load, receiving their pay in flour, meal and bacon, at Missouri prices. Their stock of provisions at this time was in need of replenishing, and to have the privilege of ferrying their old enemies from Missouri over the river at this price, gave them some satisfaction. "It looked as much of a miracle to me," said Elder Wilford Woodruff, "to see our flour and meal bags replenished in the Black Hills, as it did to have the children of Israel fed with manna in the wilderness. But the Lord has been truly with us on our journey, and has wonderfully blessed and preserved us." The Missourians kept on their way, quarreling, cursing and fighting among themselves, while the brethren camped, as was their custom, on the Sabbath day. Monday, June 14, they commenced crossing the river, taking their wagons on light rafts made of poles. It was concluded to leave several brethren at this ferry, to help the oncoming emigrant trains for Oregon, in the hope of earning enough to supply the pioneer company with provisions. For this purpose Thomas Grover, John S. Higbee, Luke S. Johnson, Appleton M. Harmon, Edmund Ellsworth, Francis M. Pomeroy, William Empey, James Davenport and Benjamin F. Stewart, were detailed to remain.

Discouraging Reports.—In this region of the country the pioneers were constantly meeting with trappers and traders who were familiar with the Salt Lake Valley. They all gave discouraging reports of that region and advised the Saints to locate elsewhere. They spoke more favorably of the Cache, the Bear and other valleys to the north. Among those giving this adverse advice were Major Moses Harris, Thomas L. Smith and Colonel James Bridger. The latter informed President Young that he deemed it unwise to bring a large colony into the Great Basin until it was demonstrated that it would be possible to raise grain there. He stated that he would give a thousand dollars if he knew an ear of corn could ripen in Salt Lake Valley. Undaunted by these unfavorable reports President Young with his band of pioneers pushed on with great vigor.

The Meeting with Samuel Brannan.—Wednesday, June 30, 1847, the pioneers arrived at the Green River. The water was very high, with a swift current. After dinner the brethren commenced making two rafts with which to cross the stream. While they were at work Samuel Brannan came into the camp, having come from San Francisco. He had traveled around Cape Horn from New York to California, with a company of emigrating Saints in the year 1846. Brannan and two others had braved the dangers of the mountains through deep snows to reach the camp of the pioneers, having left on the 4th of April. He brought with him several numbers of his paper, *The California Star,* and the latest news of the Mormon Battalion. He labored diligently to get President Young to continue on to California and not remain in the barren wastes of the Rocky Mountains. President Young, however, was following the inspiration of the Lord, and not the wisdom of man. The Lord had pointed out to him—as he had to the Prophet Joseph Smith in 1842—that the place of settlement for the Latter-day Saints was in the "midst of the Rocky Mountains."

An Uninviting Country.—It should be remembered that in 1847, the Salt Lake Valley was desolate and uninviting. There was little vegetation save the stubby growth of salt-grass, grease-wood and sage that covered the valley, and the few willows and cottonwood trees that stood on the banks of the canyon streams. At that time the Rocky Mountain region and a large part of the plains to the east were little known. The few emigrants who had passed through the Great Basin had made haste to get beyond and into the more inviting parts of the Pacific coast. This vast inter-mountain country was the haunt of the trapper and the hunter, to whom the possibilities and resources of the arid west were not even a dream. The valleys of the mountains had been occupied for upwards of twenty years by these nomads of the desert, who wandered from place to place hunting and trapping, content in the belief that the wild and primitive condition which then prevailed must so remain forever.

As late as 1843, two years before the exodus, the opinion held by the majority in the United States was that the whole territory of the Rocky Mountains was not worth a "pinch of snuff." Such was the expression made by Senator George H. McDuffie of South Carolina, in the senate that year. Discussing the settlement of Oregon, he said: "Who are to go there, along the line of military posts, and take possession of the only part of the territory fit to occupy—that part upon the sea coast, a strip less than one hundred miles in width. Why, sir, of what use will this be for agricultural purposes? I would not for that purpose give a pinch of snuff for the whole territory. I wish to God we did not own it."[d]

The inspiration which came to the Prophet Joseph Smith in 1842 —and even earlier and which was converted into reality by Brigham Young—shines forth with increased lustre when placed in contrast with the united opinions of all those who were familiar with the land in the year 1847.

Arrival of the Battalion Members from Pueblo.—July 1, 1847, the men commenced ferrying over Green River which was continued until Saturday the 3rd. In the evening of Saturday, the camp was called together and the men who desired to journey back to meet their families who were on the plains and supposed to be several hundred miles in the rear, were given that privilege. Five volunteered to return. President Young, Heber C. Kimball and Willard Richards accompanied the five brethren back to the ferry on Green River. Here they saw a group of thirteen men, with horses and baggage on the opposite side of the river ready to be ferried across. They were members of the Mormon Battalion journeying from Pueblo. They were given three cheers and President Young "led out in exclaiming Hosannah! Hosannah! Give glory to God and the Lamb, Amen!" These men were in pursuit of horse thieves who had stolen several of the battalion horses, of which they had recovered all but one or two. They reported to President Young that the Pueblo detachment of the battalion was within seven days march of the Green River. It was decided that as the members of the battalion had not been discharged nor had they received their pay, Samuel Brannan and Thomas S. Williams should return with them to California to

---

[d]Congressional Globe, 27th Congress, 3rd Session, pp. 198-201.

pilot them on the way. Brannan was greatly disappointed at the decision of President Young to locate in the Salt Lake Valley.

President Young and companions returned to the pioneer camp with twelve of the members of the battalion, Sunday afternoon, July 4. One of the soldiers, William Walker, had decided to accompany the five brethren back to the camps of the Saints. Sunday was spent by the pioneers in religious service under the direction of the bishops.

Orson Pratt

Orson Pratt's Vanguard.—Monday, July 5, 1847, the company took up their march and arrived at Fort Bridger on the 7th, where they camped. Here they repaired the wagons and shod their horses, preparatory for the rough mountain travel which would lead them to the end of their journey. July 9, they continued on to the head of Echo Canyon, which was reached on the 12th. At this place President Young was taken ill with mountain fever. He ordered Elder Orson Pratt to take a company and precede the main body of pioneers into the Salt Lake Valley. This advance company, consisted of twenty-five wagons and forty-two men, traveled down Echo Canyon, with instructions to look for the trail of the Reed-Donner party.[e] This they found after some difficulty, for it was almost obliterated. It was necessary for a detachment with proper tools to go on ahead

---

[e]The Reed-Donner party comprised seventy-eight men, women and children, under the direction of James F. Reed and George Donner, who left Independence in May, 1846, for California. They came *via* Fort Bridger, Echo and East Canyons through Emigration and westward through the Salt Lake and Tooele Valleys, around the south end of Salt Lake. Delayed by many misfortunes, they were caught in the snows in the Sierras in the winter of 1846, where many of them perished. Near the close of that year several of the ill-fated party put on snowshoes and crossed to the Sacramento Valley for relief. A relief expedition was sent back and found that the survivors had been living for weeks on the flesh of their dead, like cannibals. Thirty-nine of the original company had perished.

and construct a road for the wagons. From this point on to their destination, they encountered the most difficult portion of the road over which they traveled. They passed down into East Canyon and over Big and Little Mountains into Emigration Canyon, which they named "Last Creek." July 21, President Brigham Young sent Erastus Snow to meet Orson Pratt with a message for him to bear northward after entering the valley, and select the first convenient place for plowing and planting seed. The reason for this apparent haste was that the season was well advanced and every moment counted in the growing of their seed. Elder Snow overtook Orson Pratt on the afternoon of the 21st and together they entered the valley, with one horse between them. Seeing what looked like a field of waving grain to the south, they first journeyed in that direction only to find that they saw canes growing near the banks of what is known today as Mill Creek. Remembering the words of President Young, they retraced their steps and passed on to the north. When near the mouth of Emigration Canyon, Erastus Snow discovered he had lost his coat which was thrown over the saddle and he went back to find it, while Orson Pratt continued on to the north to the present site of Salt Lake City. The following day others of the advance company entered the valley.

Erastus Snow

The Land Dedicated.—July 23, they moved north and camped on what was subsequently known as the Eighth ward square, now occupied by the Salt Lake City and County Building. Orson Pratt called the camp together, dedicated the land and invoked a blessing on the seed they were about to plant. The ground was found so hard that the first attempt to plow was unsuccessful, and several plow-points were broken. By placing a dam in the stream (City Creek) they soaked the ground and in the course of a few days several acres were plowed and planted. The season being so late nothing came of their planting, save the garnering of potatoes about the size of a pea or a walnut, which served for seed the following year and produced a good crop.

"This is the Place."—On the 24th of July, 1847, President Brigham Young with the main body of the pioneers, entered the valley. He was resting in a carriage driven by Elder Wilford Woodruff and as they emerged from the canyon and pulled up onto a ridge President Young, who was ill, requested Elder Woodruff to turn his carriage around so that he could look upon the valley. This was done, and President Young gazed in silence for a few moments. Then with an expression of satisfaction, he said, "This is the place, drive on." They entered into the valley and camped with the members who had preceded them. They had found the promised land a resting place for their weary feet, where they could fulfil the predictions of the Prophet Joseph Smith, and become a mighty people in the midst of the Rocky Mountains.

CHAPTER 40

IN "THE LAND OF PROMISE"

1847

The First Sabbath in the Valley.—July 25, 1847, was the Sabbath. It was a pleasant day, and at ten o'clock the pioneers met in worship in the circle of their encampment. Elders George A. Smith, Heber C. Kimball and Ezra T. Benson were the speakers. They expressed gratitude for the blessings of the Lord during their travels to this promised land. Not a soul had died on the toilsome journey. In the afternoon another service was held and the sacrament was administered. Elders Wilford Woodruff, Orson Pratt and Willard Richards were the speakers at this service. The principal address was given by Elder Pratt who took for his text, Isaiah 52:7-8: "How beautiful upon the mountains are the feet of him that bringeth good tidings; that publisheth peace," etc. He stated that the predictions of the prophets were now being fulfilled.

President Young's Advice.—President Young was too feeble to make any extended remarks, but near the close of the services he gave some very important advice. Elder Wilford Woodruff made a synopsis of his remarks as follows; "He told the brethren that they must not work on Sunday; that they would lose five times as much as they would gain by it. None were to hunt on that day; and there should not any man dwell among us who would not observe these rules. They might go and dwell where they pleased, but should not dwell with us. He also said that no man who came here should buy any land; that he had none to sell, but every man should have his land measured out to him for city and farming purposes. He might till it as he pleased, but he must be industrious and take care of it." Later, instructions were given that there should be no private ownership of the streams, and only dead timber should be used for fuel, as trees were none too plentiful and should be conserved. These regulations were adopted by the community in justice to all, for it was expected that within a very short time the Saints who were then on the plains—the exiles from Nauvoo, some twenty thousand in number—and others coming from various states and from Europe, would be gathered to the Rocky Mountains.

Explorations of the Valley.—Naturally the pioneers were impatient to explore the surrounding country. Their first duty was to plant the seed they brought with them. Plowing began on the 23rd and continued during the 24th. Monday morning, July 26th, a number of

Salt Lake Valley in 1847

exploring companies were sent out, including the eight apostles in the camp and Elders Albert Carrington, William Clayton, John Brown and Joseph Matthews. The two latter crossed the river, which was called the Utah Outlet and later the Western Jordan, and ascended the mountains on the west of the valley. They reported, on their return, that the land on that side of the valley was not as good as the land on the east side. Some of the brethren penetrated some of the canyons where they found timber of good quality. President

Young, Wilford Woodruff and others of the brethren visited the hot and also the warm springs at the north end of the valley, and made some observations. Their explorations continued for several days. On the 27th of July, they explored the Tooele Valley. On the way they had a bath in the lake and were much surprised at the buoyancy of the water. That night they camped at Black Rock and the following day they traveled about ten miles south along the eastern base of the Oquirrh Mountains, where, in the main, they found a barren country and very little water. Orson Pratt ascended the mountain where he obtained a view of Utah Lake, which he judged to be about twenty miles away. Striking eastward across the valley they returned to camp. On this trip they saw about one hundred goats, sheep and antelope. They returned satisfied that the spot where the pioneers had camped was the best on which their city could be built.

A Place for an Ensign.—On the 26th, they also ascended the mountain above the hot springs to get a better view of the surrounding country, and by aid of their glasses were able to discern the Utah Outlet at the point of the mountain, where it enters the Salt Lake Valley on the south. A number of streams were also seen flowing from the mountains into the valley. As they stood upon the mountain President Young remarked that it would be a good place to lift up an ensign, referring to Isaiah's prophecy; so they named it "Ensign Peak," by which name it has since been known. In later years a flagstaff was placed upon it.

The Building of a City.—After returning from their explorations on the 28th, a council was held in the evening and it was decided to build a city. Some of the brethren suggested that they explore further before deciding on a site for a settlement. President Young replied that he was willing that they should explore until they were satisfied, but every time a party went out and returned he believed they would agree that this was the spot on which they should locate.

It was decided that the city should be laid out in blocks of ten acres each with streets eight rods wide running at right angles. The blocks were to be divided into lots containing one and one-quarter acres each, with exceptions in certain parts where the lay of the land would be inconvenient for such arrangement. The houses were to be of uniform distance from the street and only one house to a lot. "Upon every alternate block four houses were to be built on the east, and four on the west side of the square, but none on the north and south sides. But the blocks intervening were to have four houses on the north and four on the south, but none on the east and west sides. In this plan there will be no houses fronting each other on the opposite sides of the streets, while those on the same side will be about eight rods apart, having gardens running back twenty rods to the center of the block." Such was their description. There were to be four public squares of ten acres each in various parts of the city. "Let every man," said President Young, "cultivate his own lot and set out every kind of fruit and shade tree and beautify the city." This plan was laid before the camp and approved unanimously.

The Place for the Temple.—During the westward journey the building of a temple was a constant theme. On the evening of the 28th of July, President Young and the apostles with Thomas Bullock, the clerk, walked from their camp northward to a spot between the forks of City Creek, and there President Young designated a site for the building of a temple. Waving his hand he said: "Here is the forty acres for the temple, and the city can be laid out perfectly square north and south, east and west."

Orson Pratt's Survey.—The survey of the city was made by Orson Pratt. His line was on the southeast corner of the Temple Block. Beginning at that point the city was marked out into blocks of ten acres each. It was decided by the brethren that instead of using forty acres for the site it would be better to have that block conform in size with the others. According to Orson Pratt's calculations, the latitude of the north boundary of the Temple Block was 40 degrees, 35 minutes and 34 seconds. The longitude was 111 degrees, 26 minutes and 34 seconds west of Greenwich. The altitude was 4,300 feet above sea level. Later government observations varied from these of Elder Pratt but slightly.

Arrival of the Battalion and Mississippi Members.—In addition to the twelve members of the battalion and the advance company of Mississippi Saints who came into the valley with the pioneers,[a] the detachments of the battalion who wintered at Pueblo under the command of Captain James Brown and Nelson Higgins, together with the main body of the Mississippi Saints, entered the Salt Lake Valley, under direction of Captain James Brown, July 29, 1847. This increased the number in the camp to about four hundred souls. They

---

[a]It is quite generally understood that there were three women who entered the Salt Lake Valley with the pioneers in July, 1847. The fact had been overlooked by many that there were other noble women, besides these three who accompanied President Young across the plains, who braved the dangers and hardships of the journey to the west. Among the Mississippi Saints who met the pioneers at Fort Laramie and journeyed with them from that point into the Salt Lake Valley were the following: Elizabeth Crow, Harriet Crow, Elizabeth J. Crow, Ira Vinda Exene Crow, Irmaninda Almarene Crow and Marilla Jane Therlkill.

brought with them about sixty wagons, one hundred head of horses and mules and three hundred head of cattle.

Immediately after their arrival the battalion members built a bowery, the first structure in the valley in which public meetings could be held with some degree of comfort, and the worshipers receive protection from the excessive heat of the sun.

Renewal of Covenants.—Having been unable to live in peace in former habitations because of persecutions of wicked men, the Saints now rejoiced at the prospect before them. It was proposed by President Young and the apostles that they renew their covenants with the Lord and solemnly promise that they would henceforth keep his commandments in this land where they were free from religious persecution. In the humility and thankfulness of their hearts for their deliverance, the apostles set the example. August 6, President Young was baptized, and each of the apostles were likewise baptized in turn. This was not done as an acknowledgment that their former baptism was not efficacious, or that they had broken covenants formerly received, but as an acknowledgment before the Lord of their willingness to serve him henceforth and forever. To this proposition all the camps of Israel said Amen, and the ordinance of baptism was administered to all.

The First Births and Death in the Colony.—The first birth in the pioneer camp was that of a daughter to John and Catharine Campbell Steele, August 9, 1847. The father was a member of the battalion and he and his wife had arrived in the camp but a few days before. The child was named Young Elizabeth Steele, in honor of President Brigham Young and Queen Elizabeth. Two days later the colony was called upon to mourn because of the death of Milton H. Therlkill, three years old, and son of George W. and Jane Therlkill, of the Mississippi company. The child had wandered from the camp and was drowned in City Creek. A few days later (August 15th) a daughter was born to these same parents. This was the second birth in the colony.

The "Old Fort."—Three days after the Pioneers arrived in the valley, Indians of the Ute and Shoshone tribes commenced visiting the camp, begging and endeavoring to trade for guns and ammunition, and incidentally to steal when opportunity afforded. On one occasion a fight ensued and the Shoshones killed a Ute who had stolen one of their horses. President Young instructed the Saints that they should trade no more with the Indians, who were manifesting a spirit of jealousy because the pioneers treated one tribe the same as the other.

As a means of protection against Indian raids and thefts, it was decided to build a fort, or stockade, on one of the city ten-acre squares. The site chosen is now known as Pioneer Park, three blocks south and three west of the Temple Block. At a meeting held August 1, 1847, it was decided that the enclosure should be built of logs and sun-dried bricks (adobes). The brethren immediately went to work preparing the timbers and adobes for this purpose. August 10, work started on the stockade. The walls were twenty-seven inches thick and nine feet high on the outer side. It was built as a continua-

tion of huts joined together in rectangular form around the outside of the ten acres on which it stood. The east side was built of logs, and the three other sides of adobe walls. The roofs slanted but slightly inward, and were made of brush covered with earth. Each house had a loop-hole facing the outside and a door and windows facing the interior. The main entrances, which were on the east and west sides of the stockade, were carefully guarded by heavy gates which were locked at night. In the winter and spring months the snow and rain caused the mud to leak through the roofs, to the great discomfort of the inhabitants. Wagon covers, and other articles which would shed moisture, were utilized, to protect beds and bedding. Notwithstanding the discomforts and inconveniences of life under such conditions, the Saints spent many pleasant hours within the walls of their temporary homes. Two additional blocks were joined to the original fort, one on the north and one on the south, to accommodate later arrivals in the valley. These were designated as the North Fort and the South Fort, and were similar in construction to the first, or Old Fort, as it was called. During the first winter, schools were taught in the fort by Julian Moses and Miss Mary Ann Dillworth.

Captain Brown's Journey to the Coast.—A question had arisen regarding the Pueblo detachment of the Mormon Battalion. They were under orders to march to the Pacific coast, but the term of their enlistment had expired. Should they go to the coast to be mustered out of service, or should that duty be performed by their company officers? After some deliberation it was decided that they should be mustered out of service, and that Captain James Brown with a small company should go to California and report to the army officers there, and with a power of attorney from each of the men, draw their pay. Captain Brown, with several members of the battalion, departed for San Francisco, August 9, piloted by Samuel Brannan. Brannan returned to California greatly disappointed because President Young would not hearken to his counsel and continue on to the coast, where he thought conditions for permanent settlement were more favorable than the desolate valleys of the mountains. Captain Brown carried with him a message from President Young to the battalion members on the coast, advising all who had families to remain in California through the winter and obtain work, and in the spring come to the Salt Lake Valley with their earnings. Captain Brown's company went by way of the northern route and were accompanied as far as Fort Hall, by Jesse C. Little, Joseph Matthews, John Brown and others, who explored the Cache and Weber valleys. These brethren returned with favorable reports.

Special Conference in the Valley.—Sunday, August 22, 1847, a special conference was held in the Salt Lake Valley. It was agreed to fence the city, and such portions of adjacent lands as might be deemed proper for cultivation, thus affording protection from cattle. "By this means," said President Young, "we can raise thousands of bushels of grain next season for ourselves and also some to sustain those who shall come after us. I would rather fence a block of ten acres, and have a crop, than plant a hundred acres for the cattle to destroy."

It was decided that a presidency and a high council be appointed to preside over the Saints in the valley. Elder John Smith, uncle of the Prophet Joseph Smith, who was at the time on the plains, was chosen as president. President Young moved that "we call this place 'The Great Salt Lake City, of the Great Basin of North America.'" and that the post office be called "The Great Basin Post Office." Elder Heber C. Kimball moved that the river running west of the settlement be called "The Western Jordan." Some of the creeks were also named as follows: City Creek, Red Butte Creek, Canyon Creek (afterwards Emigration Creek) and Big Canyon Creek (Parley's Creek). Those streams farther to the south were not named at that time.

At the close of the services Elder Heber C. Kimball remarked: "This is a paradise to me, and one of the lovliest places I ever beheld. I hope none of us will be left alive to pollute this land. I would rather die than act as inconsistent as many have in times past."

The Return of the Pioneers.—President Young felt great anxiety for the companies of Saints who were on the plains wending their way to the valley. There was much to be done to care properly for those who had already arrived, protect them from hostile Indians and prepare for the coming winter season. This labor required his attention and that of the leading brethren for some days. However, it was deemed necessary that a company start back at once to meet the oncoming immigrants. Monday, August 2, 1847, it was decided in a council meeting, that Elder Ezra T. Benson with a company of horsemen should start back immediately. About noon on that day this company departed. They carried instructions from President Young to obtain the names of all who were in the several camps, together with the number of wagons, horses, oxen and other animals; also to ascertain the condition of the health and needs of the immigrants, so that assistance might be rendered where necessary. August 16 and 17, a company selected from the original pioneers and battalion started back for this purpose. This company consisted of seventy-one men, with thirty-three wagons, fourteen mules and ninety-two yoke of oxen. It was divided into two divisions with Tunis Rappleyee and Shadrach Roundy as captains. August 26, President Young and the apostles started on their return to Winter Quarters. This company consisted of one hundred and eight men, thirty-six wagons, seventy-one horses and forty-nine mules. They passed a number of trains on the way to the valley, totaling more than fifteen hundred men, women and children, with five hundred and sixty wagons and five thousand head of stock. Among these immigrants were Elders Parley P. Pratt and John Taylor of the council of the apostles, who were in charge of the companies.

President Young's Instructions and Blessing.—President Young arrived at Winter Quarters, October 31, after an eventful journey back across the plains. When the company arrived within a mile of Winter Quarters, President Young called them together and made the following remarks:

"Brethren, I will say to the pioneers, I wish you would receive my thanks for your kindness and willingness to obey orders. I am satisfied with you; you have done well. We have accomplished more than we expected. The one hundred and forty-three men who started, some of them sick, are all well. Not a man has died; and we have not lost a horse, mule or ox, except through carelessness. The blessings of the Lord have been with us. If the brethren are satisfied with me and the Twelve, please signify it with uplifted hands. (All hands were raised.) I feel to bless you in the name of the Lord God of Israel. You are dismissed to go to your homes."

The company then drove into the town of Winter Quarters in order, arriving about one hour before sunset. The streets of the town were filled with eager people and the weary pioneers rejoiced once more to behold their wives, children and friends.

Organization of a Stake of Zion.—Sunday, October 3, 1847, the Saints in the Salt Lake Valley met in conference and transacted business which had been proposed by President Young and the apostles before their departure. "Uncle" John Smith, who had been chosen before his arrival, was sustained as president of the Salt Lake Stake of Zion, with Charles C. Rich and John Young as his counselors. Members of the high council were also chosen as follows: Henry G. Sherwood, Thomas Grover, Levi Jackman, John Murdock, Daniel Spencer, Lewis Abbot, Ira Eldredge, Edson Whipple, Shadrach Roundy, John Vance, Willard Snow and Abraham O. Smoot.

Charles C. Rich was also selected as chief military commander under the direction of the stake authorities. Albert Carrington was selected to act as clerk and historian of the city, and John Van Cott as marshal.

Population at the Close of 1847.—The last company to enter the valley in 1847 arrived in October. The several companies were listed by Thomas Bullock as follows: President Young's pioneer company, 148; the Mississippi company, 47; Mormon Battalion, 210; Daniel Spencer's company, 204; Parley P. Pratt's company, 198; Abraham O. Smoot's company, 139; Charles C. Rich's company, 130; George B. Wallace's company, 198; Edward Hunter's company, 155; Joseph Horne's company, 197; Joseph B. Noble's company, 171; W. Snow's company, 148; and Jedediah M. Grant's company, the last of the season, 150. The total being 2,095 souls for the year.

CHAPTER 41

ORGANIZATION OF THE PRESIDENCY—
CHURCH ACTIVITIES

1847–1849

Activities on the Missouri.—As soon as the apostles arrived at Winter Quarters they held council meetings almost daily, which continued during the months of November and December, for there was much to be done. The Saints had been greatly blessed in their crops and a good and abundant harvest had been gathered. Instructions were given that all Church records should be gathered and prepared for removal to the Salt Lake Valley. The poor among the Saints were also to be gathered, and instructions were given to the people at Garden Grove to move to Winter Quarters in the spring. Elder Jesse C. Little was called again to preside in the Eastern States and Elder John Brown, who had led the Mississippi Saints to Pueblo, and later was one of the pioneers, was called to take charge of the work in the Southern States. November 8, it was decided to vacate Winter Quarters and move to the east bank of the Missouri, and there make a settlement for the members of the Church who were not able to continue to the west. All who could leave in the spring for the west would be called upon to do so. Elder Hyde, who had been presiding at Winter Quarters, reported that action had been taken against Bishop George Miller and James Emmett, who, contrary to counsel, had moved to Texas instead of continuing on to the Rocky Mountains. This action was approved by the council of the twelve. Elder Orson Pratt was chosen to go to England and preside in the British Mission and Elder Wilford Woodruff to Canada. Some twenty-seven elders were called to various mission fields. November 22, the brethren wrote a letter to Oliver Cowdery, whose heart had softened, exhorting him to be baptized.

Organization of the First Presidency.—From the martyrdom of the Prophet Joseph and Patriarch Hyrum Smith in 1844, until December, 1847, the Twelve Apostles, with President Brigham Young at their head, were sustained as the presiding council of the church. On the return journey to Winter Quarters from the Salt Lake Valley, the apostles conversed on the subject of reorganizing the First Presidency. December 5, 1847, they met in council at the home of Orson Hyde, on the east bank of the Missouri River, when this and other important matters were considered. Present at this meeting were: President Brigham Young, and Elders Heber C. Kimball, Orson Hyde, Orson Pratt, Willard Richards, Wilford Woodruff, George A. Smith, Amasa M. Lyman and Ezra T. Benson. Elders Parley P. Pratt and John Taylor were in the Salt Lake Valley, and Lyman Wight, who had failed to accompany the Church to the West, was in Texas. Elders Lyman and Benson had been called into the council of the twelve to succeed William Smith and John E. Page, who had been excommunicated because of insubordination and rebellion against authority. Each of the brethren present

Heber C. Kimball

expressed his views in turn in relation to the matter of the First Presirency, after which, on motion of Elder Orson Hyde, Brigham Young was unanimously sustained as President of the Church "with authority to nominate" his two counselors. He chose Elders Heber C. Kimball, as his first and Willard Richards, as his second counselor. The choosing of Heber C. Kimball, was the fulfilment of a prediction by the Patriarch Hyrum Smith. In a patriarchal blessing given to Elder Kimball March 9, 1842, Hyrum Smith said: "You shall be blessed with a fulness and shall be not one whit behind the chiefest; as an apostle you shall stand in the presence of God to judge the people; and as a prophet you shall attain to the honor of the three." The following day they selected "Uncle" John Smith to be "the Patriarch over the whole Church." Elders Orson Hyde and Ezra T. Benson were appointed to go east and Amasa M. Lyman to the north to procure means to help the Saints to emigrate the next season. The apostles also ordained Luke S. Johnson an elder.

The Sustaining Vote of the Saints.—A general conference of the Church on the Missouri was held December 24 to 27, 1847, on the Iowa side of the Missouri River. A large log tabernacle had been constructed which would seat nearly one thousand persons. On the last day of this conference the First Presidency, Brigham Young, Heber C. Kimball and Willard Richards, chosen by the apostles on the 5th of the month, were unanimously sustained by the vote of the Saints. John Smith was also sustained as the "Patriarch over all the Church." The action of this conference was subsequently ratified by the members of the Church in Iowa and in the Salt Lake Valley, at conferences held in April, 1848; and in the British Isles at a conference held in Manchester, August, 14, 1848.

Willard Richards

The day before the conference convened (Dec. 23), a general epistle was issued by the apostles to all the members of the Church, "dispersed throughout the earth." This was a very important epistle portraying the movements of the Church since the exodus from Nauvoo, and declaring the intentions and prospects of the people for the immediate future. All the members of the Church who had been driven from their homes were instructed to gather to the site selected for their settlement in the Great Basin. Others in the United States, Canada and Great Britain, were likewise counseled to gather, as circumstances would permit. They were to bring with them seeds of every kind—"everything that grows upon the face of the whole earth that will please the eye, gladden the heart, or cheer the soul of man." They were also to bring "the best stock of beasts, birds, and fowl," and tools of very kind. Advice in relation to the building of Zion; the preaching of the Gospel; the duties of parents; the building of the temple, and other matters of grave concern to the members of the Church, were also set forth, for their comfort and guidance, during those days of reconstruction and great trial.

Kanesville—Pottawattamie County.—Following the advice of President Young, the Saints residing at Winter Quarters moved across the Missouri River to the bluffs on the Iowa side. This country was called the "Pottawattamie country," because it was inhabited by a tribe of Indians by that name. These Indians had been removed by the government, a few months before, to another part, leaving the Saints in sole occupancy of the land. There were no settlements within many miles of the Latter-day Saints. President Young deemed it wise that

Kanesville

the Saints should hold these lands for some time, in the interests of immigration, and therefore many who were not prepared to go west, and some who preferred to remain, made this place their home.

The settlement established by them was in what was called "Miller's Hollow." They named it "Kanesville," in honor of Colonel Thomas L. Kane, who had been instrumental in securing for them privileges from the government, and who had shown his friendship on many occasions. Elder Orson Hyde, who was left in charge after the departure of President Young and the majority of the Saints, published a paper, the *Frontier Guardian*, which continued under his editorship for three years. When the Saints residing there were instructed to join the main body of the Latter-day Saints in the West, the paper was sold and the members of the Church left their holdings for other people.

The Iowa Legislature in 1847, provided for the counties in the Pottawattamie country, whenever the judge of that district "should decree that the public good required it." The Saints petitioned for a county organization, and learned that the judge had already taken steps in that direction. The County of Pottawattamie was therefore organized, and was officered by members of the Church. Other settlers began to arrive, after the Saints had made of the place a pleasant habitation. When the call came for the members of the Church to "arise and come home" in 1852, they deserted Kanesville and the name was soon changed to Council Bluffs, by which name it has since been known.

President Young's Second Trip Across the Plains.—During the month of May, 1848, preparations were made for the departure of the main body of the Saints on the Missouri River. On the 9th of that month the first company of twenty-two wagons departed and camped on the Elkhorn. On the 26th, President Young left Winter Quarters and took command of the camps and led them across the plains. This was to be his last trip, for his duties henceforth were to be among the settlements in the Rocky Mountains. During the month of June Presidents Young and Kimball commenced their journey at the head of camps consisting of over six hundred wagons and nearly two thousand souls, with their accompanying goods and chattels. President Willard Richards followed in the month of July with another camp of one hundred and sixty-nine wagons and over five hundred souls. These camps traveled in accordance with the regulations adopted at the beginning among the pioneers. From this time forth, for many years, companies of Latter-day Saints might be seen crossing the plains, coming from Europe and the various states of the Union. Presidents Young and Kimball arrived in the valley in September, and President Richards arrived early in October, 1848.

Plague of the Crickets.—The season was so far advanced when the pioneers arrived in the summer of 1847 that little resulted from the planting, except to obtain some seed potatoes. Their salvation depended on the success of their crops in 1848. They had built three sawmills in the mountains and one gristmill. Their planted fields consisted of five thousand one hundred and thirty-three acres, of which nearly nine hundred acres were planted in winter wheat. With the aid of irrigation all things looked favorable, and it appeared that there would be a fruitful harvest. The Saints were happy and their prospects were bright. They gave thanks to the Lord and in humility desired to serve him. In the months of May and June they were menaced by a danger as bad as the persecution of mobs. Myriads of crickets came down the mountain sides into the valley, like a vast army marshaled for battle, and began to destroy the fields. From one they would pass on to another, and in a few moments leave a field as barren as a desert waste. Something had to be done, or the inhabitants must perish. The community were aroused and every soul entered the unequal conflict. Trenches were dug around the fields and filled with water, in the hope of stopping the ravages of the pest, but without result. Fire was equally unavailing. The attempt was made to beat them back with clubs, brooms and other improvised weapons, but nothing that man could do was able to stop the steady onward march of the voracious crickets. The settlers were helpless before them.

The Miracle of the Gulls.—When all seemed lost, and the Saints were giving up in despair, the heavens became clouded with gulls, which hovered over the fields, uttering their plaintive scream. Was this a new evil come upon them? Such were the thoughts of some who expected that what the crickets left the gulls would destroy; but not so, the gulls in countless battalions descended and began to devour the crickets, waging a battle for the preservation of the crops. They ate, they gorged upon the pest, and then flying to the streams would drink and vomit and again return to the battle front. This took place day by day until the crickets were destroyed. The people gave thanks, for this was to them a miracle. Surely the Lord was merciful and had sent the gulls as angels of mercy for their salvation.[c] Since that time the gull has been looked upon by the Latter-day Saints almost as a sacred deliverer. Laws have been passed for the protection of these birds, and the wanton killing of one would be considered a crime of great magnitude.

The Feast of the Harvest.—The first harvest in the valley was none too plentiful; however, enough had been raised to tide over the season with the oncoming and constantly increasing population. It is doubtful if ever since then a harvest has filled the hearts of the people with such joy and satisfaction. With thankful hearts, August 10, 1848, a public "harvest feast" was celebrated in the valley. It had been demonstrated that abundant crops could be raised with proper care and

---

[c]September 13, 1913, a monument commemorating this event, was unveiled on the Temple Block, Salt Lake City. The "Seagull Monument," as it is called, is the work of Mahonri M. Young, grandson of President Brigham Young.

cultivation. Large sheaves of wheat, rye, barley, and other products of the soil, were placed on exhibition, and the people celebrated with music, song, speeches, prayer and thanksgiving.

The Return of Oliver Cowdery.—For some time the Spirit of the Lord had been striving with Oliver Cowdery. Finally he decided to accept the admonition of the apostles given November 22, 1847, and again unite with the Church. He came to Kanesville with his family, in October, 1848, and asked to be received as a member in the Church. He had been absent for over ten years. A special conference was held October 21, 1848, at which Oliver Cowdery arose and confessed the error of his ways and gave his testimony as follows:

"Friends and Brethren:—My name is Cowdery, Oliver Cowdery. In the early history of this Church I stood identified with her, and one in her councils. True it is that the gifts and callings of God are without repentance; not because I was better than the rest of mankind was I called; but, to fulfil the purposes of God, he called me to a high and holy calling.

"I wrote with my own pen the entire Book of Mormon (save a few pages) as it fell from the lips of the Prophet Joseph Smith, as he translated it by the gift and power of God by the means of the Urim and Thummim, or, as it is called by that book, 'holy interpreters.' I beheld with my eyes, and handled with my hands, the gold plates from which it was transcribed. I also saw with my eyes and handled with my hands the 'holy interpreters.' That book is true. Sidney Rigdon did not write it. Mr. Spaulding did not write it. I wrote it myself as it fell from the lips of the Prophet. It contains the everlasting Gospel, and came forth to the children of men in fulfilment of the revelation of John, where he says he saw an angel come with the everlasting Gospel to preach to every nation, kindred, tongue and people. It contains principles of salvation; and if you, my hearers, will walk by its light and obey its precepts, you will be saved with an everlasting salvation in the kingdom of God on high. Brother Hyde has just said that it is very important that we keep and walk in the true channel, in order to avoid the sand-bars. This is true. The channel is here. The Holy Priesthood is here.

"I was present with Joseph when an holy angel from God came down from heaven and conferred on us, or restored the lesser or Aaronic Priesthood, and said to us at the same time, that it should remain upon the earth while the earth stands.

"I was also present with Joseph when the higher or Melchizedek Priesthood was conferred by holy angels from on high. This Priesthood we then conferred on each other, by the will and commandment of God. This Priesthood, as was then declared, is also to remain upon the earth until the last remnant of time. This Holy Priesthood, or authority, we then conferred upon many, and is just as good and valid as though God had done it in person.

"I laid my hands upon that man—Yes I laid my right hand upon his head (pointing to Brother Hyde), and I conferred upon him the Priesthood, and he holds that Priesthood now. He was also called through me, by prayer of faith, an apostle of the Lord Jesus Christ."

A few days later Oliver Cowdery appeared before the high council at Kanesville and requested that he be received into the Church. His case was considered and on motion of Elder Orson Hyde, who presided at Kanesville, he was received by baptism. When Oliver appeared before the high council on this occasion he said:

"Brethren, for a number of years I have been separated from you. I now desire to come back. I wish to come humbly and to be one in your midst. I seek no station. I only wish to be identified with you. I am out of the Church. I am not a member of the Church, but I wish to come in at the door. I know the door. I have not come here to seek precedence, I come humbly, and throw myself upon the decisions of this body, knowing, as I do, that its decisions are right, and should be obeyed."

It was a sad occasion, yet a time of rejoicing to see the former "Second Elder" of the Church with a contrite spirit desiring fellowship in the Church, and the association of his former brethren. After his baptism he desired to go to the Salt Lake Valley and then take a mission to Great Britain. Before doing so he went to visit relatives in Missouri, and while there he was taken sick and died March 3, 1850. He died a happy man with the assurance that his sins had been forgiven him.

The Beginning of New Settlements.—Explorations of the surrounding valleys commenced as soon as the pioneers entered the Salt Lake Valley, for the purpose of discovering suitable sites for other gathering places. In the fall of 1847, Perrigrine Sessions, Samuel Brown and Hector C. Haight moved into the valley north (Davis County) with herds of cattle. Sessions camped near the spot where Bountiful was subsequently built, and there he lived during the winter with part of his family, first in a wagon and then in a hut. Later he built a permanent home which was the beginning of Bountiful, formerly called Sessions' Settlement. Hector C. Haight went a few miles farther north and made his camp near the present site of Farmington, on Big Creek. Later he moved about three miles north on

Haight's Creek, where he built a cabin where he lived with one of his sons during the winter of 1847-48. In 1848, Daniel Miller, Thomas Grover, Jacob F. Secrist, William Smith and many others moved to the north and became the first settlers of Bountiful, Farmington and other towns in Davis County. Early in the year 1848, Captain James Brown, who had returned from California, entered into negotiations with Miles M. Goodyear, a trapper and trader, for the purchase of lands where the present city of Ogden is built. There he located, calling the place Brownsville. John S. Higbee and others located in Utah valley in 1849. That same year John Rowberry led a company to Tooele Valley, and Isaac Morley another to Sanpete Valley. In all these places permanent settlements were established in that year. From this time on colonization continued, under the direction of President Brigham Young, and settlements began to spring up throughout the Rocky Mountains, extending for hundreds of miles. The prophecy of Joseph Smith uttered August 6, 1842, was realized.

Filling Vacancies in the Council of the Twelve.—The organization of the First Presidency and the disfellowshipment of Lyman Wight, left four vacancies in the council of the twelve. February 11, 1849, the First Presidency and apostles met in council at the home of Elder George B. Wallace to consider the filling of these vacancies. President Young nominated Elders Charles C. Rich, Lorenzo Snow, Erastus Snow and Franklin D. Richards for these positions, which nominations were approved by the apostles. The following day at the home of Elder Wallace, they were ordained.

The Salt Lake Stake.—In the fall of 1847, the Saints in the Salt Lake Valley were organized into a stake. It became necessary in 1849, to perfect that organization and make certain changes. A meeting was called, February 13, 1849, for that purpose. Elder Daniel Spencer was set apart as president of the Salt Lake Stake, succeeding Patriarch John Smith, with David Fullmer and Willard Snow as his counselors. A committee was appointed to lay the city off into ecclesiastical wards, which later reported, and at another meeting held on the 16th, the high council was organized and officers chosen for quorums of the Priesthood. The following division of the valley into wards was decided on: "South of the city and east of the Jordan River, into four wards: Canyon Creek (Sugar House) Ward, embracing the ten-acre survey and all east of it; a third ward, embracing the country between the ten-acre survey and the Cottonwood Creek; and a fourth, embracing all south of the Cottonwood. West of the Jordan: Caanan Ward; north of the city and east of the Jordan and the lake, three wards." These wards included the settlements as far north as Brownsville (Ogden). At another meeting held on the

22nd of the month the city was divided into nineteen wards of nine blocks each.

The Perpetual Emigrating Fund.—Business of great importance was considered at the October general conference of the Church in 1849. It was decided that the Church should establish a "Perpetual Emigrating Fund Company," for the gathering of the poor from the nations of the earth. The company was duly incorporated and committees were appointed for the purpose of gathering means for this fund, which were used in bringing great numbers of the Latter-day Saints to the valleys of the mountains. This continued for many years. Finally, in 1887, the Perpetual Emigrating Fund Company was disincorporated by the passage of the Edmunds-Tucker bill, and the funds escheated to the government for the benefit of the common schools of Utah. It was intended that those who were aided by this fund should pay back into it the means advanced for their transportation to the West, that others might be helped also to emigrate. In this way it would be a perpetual and self-sustaining fund. Five thousand dollars was the sum of the original contributions, and by its aid as many as five hundred wagons were furnished some seasons to help the Saints across the plains.

Increased Missionary Activity.—At this same conference missionaries were called to go to various parts of the earth as follows: Elder Charles C. Rich, to Southern California (San Bernardino) to assist Amasa M. Lyman and to succeed him in that field of labor; Addison Pratt, James Brown and Hyrum H. Blackwell, to the Society Islands; Lorenzo Snow and Joseph Toronto, to Italy; Erastus Snow and Peter O. Hansen, to Denmark; John Taylor, Curtis E. Bolton and John Pack, to France; Franklin D. Richards, Joseph W. Johnson, Joseph W. Young Job Smith, Haden W. Church, Geo. B. Wallace, John S. Higbee and Jacob Gates, to England; and John E. Forsgren, to Sweden. This was a wonderful undertaking and a remarkable trial of faith, in the days of the poverty and adversity of the people, when the help of all was needed to build up settlements and contend with the trials and hardships of pioneer life in this western country. In the evening of the 6th of October, the presidency set apart the brethren of the apostles for their fields of labor, and the apostles set apart the elders who were also called to various mission fields. In a very short time all were on their way to carry the message of salvation to the world, a duty the Lord has placed upon the elders of the Church, which is second to no other. The inspiration of these calls is seen in the fruitful harvest of souls which was gathered in England, Scandinavia and other lands.

An Unexpected Harvest.—The harvest of 1848 was hardly adequate for the needs of the Saints, for their numbers had been increased by immigration. The people therefore were under the necessity of conserving to make ends meet. They were placed on rations and were forced also to resort to the digging of sego roots, and making greens from thistles and weeds to eke out an existence. Their clothing was scant, and most of the men dressed in buckskins, and all materials were made to do extra service. During these stringent times, President Heber C. Kimball delivered a discourse in which he uttered a remarkable prophecy. He said that within a short time "states goods" would be sold in Salt Lake City cheaper than they could be purchased in St. Louis or New York, and that the people would be supplied with both food and clothing. Few, if any, who heard these remarks, believed him. Such a thing in the far west, over a thousand miles from the nearest settlements, where all goods had to be freighted by team, seemed an impossibility. Yet the prophecy was literally fulfilled.

In the summer of 1849, gold seekers on their way to California, commenced arriving in the Salt Lake Valley. Their animals were worn out by the long and strenuous journey, for in their haste for gold, these travelers had sacrificed all things, that they might make haste to their destination. Now they were anxious to obtain fresh animals for their tired ones, that they might hurry on their journey. To do this they were willing to dispose of their goods at a great sacrifice. They lightened their loads in the interest of speed and disposed of their provisions, clothing and other materials, at a price below the cost of the articles in the states at the time they started on their westward journey.

CHAPTER 42

CHURCH ACTIVITIES
1850—1857

A Provisional Government.—When the first settlers arrived in the Salt Lake Valley, they were directed exclusively by Church authority. However, the people realized that civil government must be inaugurated in their several settlements after they were founded. As early as the fall of 1847 some municipal officers were appointed, although no city government was effected at that time. Before leaving Nauvoo, the authorities of the Church had expressed the desire of organizing a civil government under the flag of the United States. While on the plains they wrote to President James K. Polk, under date of August 6, 1846, and "resolved" that as soon as they were settled in the Great Basin they would petition the United States for a territorial government, "bounded on the north by the British, and south by the Mexican dominions, and east and west by the summits of the Rocky and Cascade Mountains."

The First Political Convention.—In February, 1849, a call was issued for a political convention. The people residing within the territory bounded by the Rocky Mountains, the Republic of Mexico, the Sierra Nevada Mountains and the Territory of Oregon, were invited to assemble at Great Salt Lake City, March 5, 1849. On that date a convention was held, and Congress was petitioned to organize the Territory of Deseret.[a] A constitution was adopted and a provisional government was set up.

---

[a]Col. Thomas L. Kane advised the Saints to petition for statehood, rather than for a territorial form of government, pointing out that they would be permitted to govern themselves in a state government, but in a territory that

The Territory of Utah.—Other petitions were also sent to Washington, asking for statehood, but the government was not willing to grant all that the inhabitants of the Great Basin desired. Enemies and bitter apostates lent their aid to defeat the project. In September, 1850, Congress passed a bill for the organization of the territory of Utah, which was approved by the President. The people preferred the name "Deseret,"[b] but gladly accepted what was offered them.

Territorial Officers Appointed.—In September, 1850, President Millard Fillmore appointed the federal officers for the Territory of Utah. Brigham Young was appointed governor, a position he had held in the "Provisional State of Deseret." Broughton D. Harris, of Vermont, was appointed secretary; Joseph Buffington, of Pennsylvania, chief justice; Perry C. Brocchus, of Alabama, and Zerubbabel Snow of Ohio—the latter a member of the Church—associate justices; Seth M. Blair, attorney; and Joseph L. Heywood, United States marshal. The two latter were residents of Utah. Judge Buffington declined and Lemuel C. Brandebury, of Pennsylvania, was appointed in his stead. In addition to these officers there were three Indian agents. Four of these federal officers were members of the Church. The appointment of President Young as governor, was due to the influence of Colonel Thomas L. Kane, the staunch and faithful friend of the Latter-day Saints.

The "Run-Away Officials."—Three of these officials came to Utah filled with prejudice, and one, at least (Judge Brocchus), hoped that he might be elected to office and represent the territory in Congress. He had no desire to stay in the West. Together with Chief Justice Brandebury and Secretary Harris, he determined to leave again for the East, and preparations were made toward that end. These men complained of the smallness of their salaries, and Governor Young and other citizens petitioned Washington in their behalf. Harris declared "that he had private instructions designed for no eye but his own, to watch every movement and not pay out any funds unless

---

would likely be subject to outside politicians, who would not be in sympathy with them, and perhaps their enemies. The people took his advice, but were not successful in obtaining their desire. Even under territorial regulations they should have been granted self-government, through the appointment of officials from their own communities, but this proved to be the exception during the long history of Utah as a territory. And with a few honorable exceptions, the officers sent to them from other parts, were broken-down politicians and men to whom political office was tendered as a debt for party service. Many of them were extremely bitter against the Saints, and resorted to falsehood and misrepresentation, in order to bring the majority of the inhabitants of the territory into disrepute at Washington and throughout the nation. Under such conditions conflict was constant and inevitable.

[b]Deseret is a Book of Mormon term meaning "honeybee."

the same should be strictly legal, and according to his own judgment." When he decided to return to the East he also determined to take with him the funds which he had brought for territorial purposes. An attempt was made to prevent this action by legislative enactment, but he was sustained by the two judges, and carried the funds back to St. Louis, where he deposited them with the assistant treasurer of the United States. It was in September, 1851, when these officials left the territory.

Their Report to Washington.—The three run-away officials reported in Washington that they were compelled to leave Utah on account of the lawless acts and seditious tendencies of Brigham Young and the majority of the residents.[c] They accused Governor Young with a waste of public funds—which they had refused to let him have—and referred to the existence of "polygamy" among the "Mormons."

Governor Young's Defense.—Anticipating the accusations of these officials, because of threats made before their departure, Governor Young wrote to President Fillmore, September 29, 1851, setting forth his own course and the true condition in the territory. This letter was augmented by others from Jedediah M. Grant, mayor of Salt Lake City, who was then in the East, and Col. Thomas L. Kane.[d]

---

[c]These "lawless acts and seditious tendencies," evidently had reference to certain remarks made by President Brigham Young, in a discourse in which he said the United States looked on the scenes of mobbing, driving, and murdering of the Latter-day Saints in Missouri and Illinois, without interference, or taking steps to correct the evil, but by silence gave sanction to such proceedings. Moreover for a rebuke administered to Judge Brocchus, who at a special conference of the Church in September, 1851, was privileged to speak and accused the leaders of the Church of disloyalty, and reflected upon the virtue of the women of the Latter-day Saints.

[d]Following is a letter from Col. Thomas L. Kane to President Fillmore in defense of Governor Brigham Young:

Philadelphia, July 11, 1851.

My Dear Sir:—I have no wish to evade the responsibility of having vouched for the character of Mr. Brigham Young, of Utah, and his fitness for the station he now occupies. I reiterate without reserve, the statement of his excellent capacity, energy, and integrity, which I made you prior to his appointment. I am willing to say I volunteered to communicate to you facts by which I was convinced of his patriotism and devotion to the interest of the Union. I made no qualification when I assured you of his irreproachable moral character, because I was able to speak of this from my own intimate, personal knowledge.

If any shadow of evidence can be adduced in support of the charges of your anonymous assailant, the next mail from Utah shall bring you their complete and circumstantial refutation. Meanwhile I am ready to offer this assurance for publication in any form you care to indicate, and challenge contradiction from any respectable authority.

I am, Sir, with high respect and esteem, your most obedient servant,

THOMAS L. KANE.

The President.

Daniel Webster, secretary of state, ordered these officials to return to their posts or resign; so resign they did.

Their Places Filled.—The places of these men were later filled. Lazarus H. Reed, of New York, was appointed chief justice for Utah; Leonidas Shaver, associate justice, and Benjamin G. Ferris, secretary. Secretary Ferris did not remain in the territory very long, but the two justices were respected by the people who held them in high esteem.

The Deseret Evening News.—In each of the settlements of the Latter-day Saints, before coming to Utah, they had endeavored to publish magazines and periodicals for the benefit of the Saints. In keeping with this custom a small wrought-iron Ramage handpress, was purchased in Philadelphia and brought across the plains by one of the early companies. In 1850, this press was put to use, and the first newspaper published in the Rocky Mountains made its appearance in Salt Lake City. This was *The Deseret News*, the first number of which was published June 15, 1850, with President Willard Richards as editor. It was a small quarto, issued weekly, and has since grown into one of the influential daily papers in the intermountain country.

First Deseret News Press

Announcement of the Plural Marriage Doctrine.—August 28 and 29, 1852, a special conference was held in Salt Lake City. One hundred and six elders were called to go on missions to various fields, including the countries of Europe, Russia, India, China, South Africa, Australia, Hawaii, and other islands of the sea, as well as the states of the Union. On the second day the first public announcement of the doctrine of plural marriage was declared. The revelation given to the Prophet Joseph Smith, dealing with the new and everlasting covenant and including the doctrine of marriage for eternity and "plural wives," was read. Elder Orson Pratt delivered the first public discourse on this principle, dealing with the subject from a scriptural standpoint. He emphasized the fact that the practice of plural marriage among the Latter-day Saints was not to "gratify the carnal lusts and feelings of man," but was to be practiced in all holiness. Moreover, that there was but one who held the keys of this power, and there were "bounds and restrictions" which the Lord had set, and all who obeyed this law should be in harmony with the law, receiving the sanction of the one who held the keys. Following the discourse of Elder Orson Pratt, President Brigham Young made some remarks dealing with the history of the revelation.

Laying the Corner Stones of the Salt Lake Temple.—In February, 1853, ground was broken for the foundation of the Salt Lake Temple. Wednesday, April 6, the corner stones were laid with solemn and impressive ceremonies. This was the beginning of the most costly and imposing temple yet to be erected by the Church, and was to take forty years in the building. Other temples had been built, but the Saints had not been granted the privilege of enjoying blessings in them for any length of time. In this far western country, they hoped to build undisturbed, and have the opportunity of receiving their own blessings therein and also labor for their dead. It was at first proposed to build the temple of sandstone from Red Butte Canyon, and a wooden track was laid from the city to the canyon for the purpose of hauling the rock. It was finally decided to build of granite, which was found in abundance in Little Cottonwood Canyon, some eighteen or twenty miles southeast of the city.

A Solemn Assembly.—On the morning of April 6, 1853, thousands of Latter-day Saints assembled in conference. President Young made a few introductory remarks saying that in a few years "we may have a place sufficiently large to accommodate the Saints, although, twenty-three years ago, the Church was organized with only six members." The choir sang and prayer was offered by Elder John Taylor. The procession then formed and moved to the foundation of the temple. The general authorities of the Church and the authorities of the Salt Lake Stake, took their places around the foundation and the ceremonies of laying the corner stones proceeded.

Dedication of the Corner Stones.—The First Presidency, with John Smith the patriarch laid the first or south-east corner stone, according to the pattern given by the Prophet Joseph Smith. Following this ceremony President Young delivered an oration, and near the close he said:

"We dedicate the south-east corner stone of the temple to the Most High God. May it remain in peace till it has done its work, and until He who has inspired our hearts to fulfil the prophecies of his holy prophets, that the house of the Lord should be reared in the 'tops of the Mountains' shall be satisfied, and say it is enough."

President Kimball then offered the prayer of dedication, and the assembly gathered at the south-west corner stone, which was laid by the Presiding Bishopric, followed by an oration by Bishop Edward Hunter, and a prayer of dedication by Bishop Alfred Cordon. The north-west corner stone was laid by the presidency of the high priests, and President John Young of that quorum, delivered the oration. Elder George B. Wallace offered the prayer of dedication. The last, or north-east corner stone, was laid by the council of the twelve. Elder Parley P. Pratt delivered an oration and the prayer of dedication was offered by Elder Orson Hyde.

After benedictory remarks by President Young, the procession returned to the tabernacle and were dismissed.

President Young's Vision.—In the afternoon service of that day, President Young spoke at length in relation to temple building. In the course of his remarks he said:

"I scarcely ever say much about revelations, or visions, but suffice it to say, five years ago last July [1847], I was here and saw in the spirit the temple not ten feet from where we have laid the chief corner stone. I have not inquired what kind of a temple we should build. Why? Because it was represented before me, I never looked upon that ground, but the vision of it was there. I see it as plainly as if it was in reality before me. Wait until it is done. I will say, however, that it will have six towers, to begin with, instead of one. Now do not any of you apostatize because it will have six towers, and Joseph only built one. It is easier for us to build sixteen, than it was for him to build one. The time will come when there will be one in the center of temples we shall build, and on the top, groves and fish ponds."[e]

Success in Foreign Mission Fields.—The missionaries sent out to various parts of the earth in 1849 and succeeding years, met with varied success. The Church membership in the British Mission, before heavy emigration set in, was about twenty-eight thousand souls. Outside of Great Britain perhaps the greatest success in any foreign field fell to the lot of Erastus Snow and his companions, who introduced the Gospel in Scandinavia. Many branches were raised up, especially in Denmark, where Elders Snow, Peter O. Hansen, George P. Dykes and John E. Forsgren were laboring. Elder

---

[e]Millennial Star, 15:488.

Forsgren carried the Gospel into Sweden and, later (1851) Hans F. Petersen and Hans Peter Jensen, to Norway. In each of these countries the elders were successful, although little headway was made in Sweden until 1853, Elder Forsgren having been banished soon after his arrival there. In Denmark, persecution raged, and several of the elders were brutally treated, while in Norway they were cast into prison. Elders John Taylor and companions in France were able to make some converts, but found it to be a hard field. Elders Lorenzo Snow, Joseph Toronto and Thomas B. H. Stenhouse, in Italy, found conditions similar to those the elders encountered in France. Meeting with no success in Genoa, they moved to the Protestant valleys of Piedmont, where a few were baptized. Finally Elder Stenhouse was sent into Switzerland to open the door for the Gospel there, where many were waiting to embrace the truth. The elders in India made a number of converts, but principally among the English, and branches of the Church were organized in that land. The message of salvation was also successfully carried into Australia, by John Murdock and Charles W. Wandell; into South Africa, by Elders Jesse Haven, Leonard I. Smith and William Walker; Hawaii, by Elder George Q. Cannon and companions. In China the mission opened by Elders Hosea Stout, James Lewis and Chapman Duncan was a failure, and Elders Parley P. Pratt and Rufus Allen returned from South America, they being unable, because of political disturbances, to get a foothold there. Elders Addison Pratt, Benjamin F. Grouard, James Brown and others, were banished from the Society Islands and the native Saints were sentenced to hard labor for holding meetings. Elders Pratt and Grouard, with Noah Rogers, who died crossing the plains in 1846, had successfully introduced the Gospel in those and other islands of the Pacific in the day of the Prophet Joseph Smith.

The Foundation for Future Labors.—Those early missionaries laid the foundation for the preaching of the Gospel in many foreign lands, which has been continued since that time with wonderful results. Thousands of honest converts have gladly received the message of salvation, and with the spirit of gathering resting upon them, have come to Zion, as the prophets foretold, with songs of everlasting joy.

The Hand-Cart Immigration.—The early companies arriving in the Salt Lake Valley came with oxen, mules and horses and heavy laden wagons. The people, however, quite generally were under the necessity of walking across the plains by the sides of their wagons. It became apparent that other and cheaper methods would have to be employed to accommodate the increasing immigration. As early as 1851, the First Presidency suggested the use of hand-carts as a means of making the journey from Iowa westward. In fact, there were in the Salt Lake Valley at that time some who had crossed the plains in that manner, with comparative comfort and safety, and this had led to the suggestion of general travel in hand-cart companies. It was not until about the year 1856, however, that the idea was impressed upon the foreign Saints, and then after repeated suggestions. When they did take hold of it they entered into the spirit of hand-cart transportation with enthusiasm. Especially was this the case with the members of the Church in the British Isles. With hand-carts, the British Saints could make the journey from Liverpool to Salt Lake City for about forty-five dollars, coming by way of Boston or New York to Iowa City, where they were fitted out to cross the plains. To those who were scarcely able to raise means,

Hand-Cart Company on the Plains

or who did not care to be indebted to the Perpetual Emigrating Fund Company, this was a decided advantage.

The First Hand-Cart Companies.—The first hand-cart companies to cross the plains were led by Edmund Ellsworth and Daniel D. McArthur. Ellsworth's company, numbering 266 souls, left Iowa City, June 9, 1856. McArthur followed two days later with a company of 220. A third and smaller company of Welsh Saints, under command of Edward Bunker, left on the 23rd. The members of these three companies pushed their hand-carts containing all their worldly possessions, over the plains, the mountains, and through rivers and streams, a distance of about thirteen hundred miles. A few deaths among the aged and infirm occurred on the way, but these companies all arrived in Salt Lake City in good condition and happy to be in Zion. The companies of Ellsworth and McArthur arrived on the 26th of September, having been delayed by the breaking down of hand-carts which were built of unseasoned timber, and therefore could not stand the strain and the excessive heat of the summer sun. They were met and welcomed by the First Presidency and a large concourse of citizens, with a brass band, at the foot of Little Mountain, in Emigration Canyon, and were escorted into the city where they received a royal welcome. These two companies arrived with ninety-six hand-carts, five wagons, twenty-four oxen, four mules, and twenty-five tents. October 2, Captain Edward Bunker's company arrived without having had serious loss, and were also met with enthusiastic welcome.

The Willie and Martin Companies.—Two other companies with hand-carts were fitted out in the summer of 1856. The members of these companies were mainly from Great Britain and Scandinavia. They arrived in Iowa City, the starting point, near the end of June and in the fore part of July, where they discovered that the tents and hand-carts for their use, were not provided. Consequently they were delayed until these necessary articles could be manufactured or purchased. The delay was dangerous, for the season was advancing, and the journey across the plains should not have been undertaken as late as the middle of July, when the first company was prepared to start. This company under the command of James G. Willie, left Iowa City, July 15, and Florence [Winter Quarters], Nebraska, on the 19th of August. They were followed by the second belated company, the fifth of the season, under the command of Edward Martin, about two weeks later.

The Question of Traveling Considered.—While at Florence, the question whether they should pursue their journey from that point, or go into winter quarters, was discussed. The majority were in favor of continuing on the way, although there were dissenting voices, because of the lateness of the season and the dangers the journey entailed.*ᶠ* Nevertheless the decision was reached and they deter-

---

*ᶠ*While the consideration of this momentous question was being discussed the brethren were advised by Elder Levi Savage, who was returning from a mission to Siam and Ceylon, that such a journey so late in the season should not be undertaken, and it would be better to go into winter quarters and wait until

mined to go on rather than remain on the plains through the winter. They fully hoped to reach Salt Lake City before the chilling blasts of winter should overtake them. This was a fatal error, but one, of course, unexpected by most of the companies, for the winter season set in much earlier than usual that year, and was most severe.

The Babbitt and Margetts Tragedies.—The fore part of this handcart journey passed pleasantly enough for such a trip, except for the breaking down of carts and feelings of anxiety because of Indian raids. The Cheyennes were on the warpath and had made attacks on a number of preceding immigration trains. In September, while the handcart companies were on the Platte, Almon W. Babbitt, secretary of Utah, and a number of his camp who were in advance were killed. They were on their way to Utah from Washington, with a train of government property. A short time later Thomas Margetts and wife; James Cody, wife and child, who were on their way to England, were killed by the marauding Indians. News of these massacres did not tend to lighten the hearts of the hand-cart immigrants, but it did serve to make them more vigilant. Even then, they were deprived of many of their cattle, which were stolen by the red men.

Disasters on the Way.—Not withstanding all the difficulties and dangers in their path, these two companies pressed on with all possible speed. In the fore part of their journey, they made favorable daily progress, but as they continued, and the roads became more rough and repairs were constantly necessary, their progress was delayed. Due to the lightness of their hand-carts and the hasty manner in which they were constructed of unseasoned wood, they began to fall to pieces before the companies were well on the journey, and to repair them required time.

While they were on the Platte, in the middle of September, the first frosts of the season were encountered, which increased in severity day by day. September 30, Captain Willie's company arrived at Fort Laramie—five hundred miles east of their destination—and the next day continued on their way. From this point on they encountered

---

spring. He had been over the route and knew the dangers they would likely encounter, but he was overruled. According to the narrative of this fatal journey given by John Chislett, when Elder Savage was overruled he said: "What I have said I know to be true; but seeing you are to go forward, I will go with you; will help all I can; will work with you, will rest with you, will suffer with you, and if necessary, will die with you. May God in his mercy bless and preserve us." These were noble sentiments worthy of a place in the archives of time.

For a descriptive and comparatively full account of these journeyings of the two belated pioneer companies of hand-carts, the reader is referred to the "History of Utah," by Orson F. Whitney, Vol. 1:547.

the hardest part of their travel, and winter was fast approaching. Their rations were growing less, and restrictions were placed upon them. What was worse, due to the loss of conveyances and the heavy grades they had to climb when they reached the mountains, they had to discard a portion of their burdens. Articles of clothing and bedding had to be left on the way, that progress might be made. Improperly clad and with poor shelter, they were exposed to the piercing winds and bitter cold of the early winter storms. This caused them severe suffering, and many of the more delicate were placed in untimely graves along the way, without proper ceremony and in compelling haste. Under such adverse conditions they were forced to push on, and wait not for anything, for emergency demanded haste, lest the grim and merciless winter embrace them in the grasp of death.

The sufferings of the advance company was repeated, but with greater severity, by the one which traveled in the rear. The Martin camp was composed of a larger number of women and children, and the inclement season, augmented by the many other difficulties encountered, caused greater loss of life in their ranks.

Extreme Suffering on the Sweetwater.—On the Sweetwater, these immigrants encountered extreme winter weather and heavy snows. Death had occurred frequently during these stages of the journey. After one of these severe storms fifteen members of the camp died in one day, while others were severely injured.

A Party to the Rescue.—Through reports from returning missionaries who passed these hand-cart companies on the way, President Young learned that they were on the plains. Fearing for their safety, he organized relief parties and sent them out with provisions, clothing and bedding to help them to reach the valley. An advance guard of two young men, Joseph A. Young and Stephen Taylor, was sent in a light wagon to inform the weary and stricken travelers that relief was on the way. As these young men approached the hand-cart company led by Captain Willie, they appeared as angels of mercy. "More welcome messengers never came from the courts of glory," said John Chislett, "than these two young men were to us. They lost no time, after encouraging us all they could to press forward, but sped on further to convey their glad news to Edward Martin and the fifth hand-cart company, who had left Florence about two weeks after us, and who it was feared, were even worse off than we were. As they went from our view, many a hearty 'God bless you,' followed them."

"Martin's Ravine."—As the rescuers pressed on their way they discovered the Martin company in a ravine, between the Platte and the Sweetwater. The place has been designated "Martin's Ravine," and here the sufferers had made their camp. They had about given up all hope and were ready to succumb to the rigorous and persecuting winter, when word was received that relief was coming. The joy that filled the hearts of the survivors—for death had charged such heavy toll that the ravine was like an overcrowded tomb—is beyond the power of mortal pen to write.

The Arrival in the Valley.—With the help of the brethren, and the supplies from the valley, the survivors of these two belated trains arrived in Salt Lake City in November. Captain Willie's company entered the city on the 9th, and Captain Martin's three weeks later. Out of Captain Willie's company of between four and five hundred souls, seventy-seven had perished. Of the Martin company about one-fourth of the five hundred and seventy-six who started found graves along the way.

Later Hand-Cart Immigration.—Other companies with hand-carts crossed the plains in subsequent years. And from the Salt Lake Valley missionaries employed hand-carts to help them to their distant fields of labor. Never again, however, was a condition permitted to arise such as that which overtook the companies under Captains Willie and Martin in the fall of 1856.

The Passing of Prominent Men.—During the period covered in this chapter, several prominent elders of the Church passed away. Oliver Cowdery, who at the incipiency of the work, stood with the Prophet Joseph Smith as the second elder of the Church, and who, with the Prophet, held the keys of this dispensation, as they were received from holy angels, passed away. He died March 3, 1850, at Richmond, Missouri. Only a few months before his death [See Chap. 41] he returned to the Church after an alienation of several years. Presiding Bishop Newel K. Whitney, who was also among the first to embrace the Gospel, died in Salt Lake City, September 23, 1850. He joined the Church in Kirtland in 1831, and passed through the trying scenes of Ohio, Missouri and Illinois. He was ordained to be the second bishop of the Church, and after the death of Edward Partridge, was sustained as the presiding bishop. In 1848 he led a company of immigrants to the Salt Lake Valley. Two of his sons, Horace K. and Orson K., were members of the pioneer band, but their father remained at Winter Quarters, where his services were required during those trying times. He was succeeded as presiding bishop by Edward Hunter in 1851.

March 11, 1854, Willard Richards, second counselor to President Brigham Young, died in Salt Lake City. He was born in Massachusetts, in 1804, and was baptized by Brigham Young, December 31, 1836. The following year he accompanied Elder Heber C. Kimball and others to England and assisted in the opening of that mission. After his companions returned, he remained as one of the presidency of the British Mission, in which capacity he was laboring when the apostles went to that land. Having been called to the apostleship, he was ordained in Preston, England, by President Brigham Young and other members of the council of the apostles, April 14, 1840. He returned to the United States in 1841, and became the private secretary to the Prophet Joseph Smith, and was with him in Carthage prison at the time of the martyrdom. From 1842 until his death he was Church historian and recorder and at the reorganization of the First Presidency, was selected by President Young as his second counselor. In this position he was succeeded by Elder Jedediah M. Grant, and as historian, by Elder George A. Smith.

"Uncle" John Smith, the presiding patriarch of the Church, died in Salt Lake City, May 23, 1854. He was a man of tried integrity and had served in the councils of the Church from the time of his baptism until his death. He was among the first of the Prophet's relatives to receive the truth and through his influence others were converted. He was succeeded in the office of patriarch, by John Smith, eldest son of the Patriarch Hyrum Smith.

Elder Orson Spencer, a man of superior education, who served the Church faithfully and well as a missionary for many years, was called to the other side of the veil, October 15, 1855, while at St. Louis. He had presided in the British Mission during one of the critical periods in that land.

Jedediah M. Grant, second counselor to President Brigham Young, died in Salt Lake City, December 1, 1856, after a brief illness. He was a young man of

Jedediah M. Grant

forceful character and had been identified with the Church since 1833. He was a member of Zion's Camp in 1834; was chosen among the first seventies, and in that calling filled a number of successful missions throughout the United States. He passed through the persecutions of Missouri and Illinois, and arrived in the Salt Lake Valley, in charge of the last company to cross the plains in 1847. He was the first mayor of Salt Lake City, and when he was called to be a counselor to President Young, was serving as one of the first council of the seventies. He was succeeded as counselor in the First Presidency by Elder Daniel H. Wells.

The Assassination of Parley P. Pratt.—Another death, occurring May 13, 1857, was that of Elder Parley P. Pratt of the council of the twelve. In the autumn of 1856, Elder Pratt left Salt Lake City with a company of missionaries, and crossed the plains. That winter he labored in St. Louis, Philadelphia, New York and other cities in the East. In the spring of 1857, he was in Arkansas. While there he attempted to assist a Mrs. Hector H. McLean, who was a member of the Church, to obtain possession of her children, she having separated from her husband because of drunkenness and cruelty. McLean accused Elder Pratt of alienating the affections of his wife and attempting to abduct the children. A trial was held, and Elder Pratt was acquitted of the charge. Shortly afterwards, as he was journeying from Van Buren County where the court was held, intending to join an immigrant company for Utah, he was overtaken by McLean who plunged a bowie knife in his side. After Elder Pratt had fallen from his horse, McLean shot him with a pistol. The assassin was never punished for the foul deed. In this manner died one of the greatest expounders of the latter-day faith, a poet and writer, whose works survive and have done much to bring many to a knowledge of the Gospel. Although their author's voice has long been stilled, his work yet speaks with convincing power.

CHAPTER 43

"THE UTAH WAR"

1856–1858

Political Changes.—Chief Justice Lazarus H. Reed, after a short stay in Utah, resigned because of ill health, and returned to the East where he died in the spring of 1855. He was succeeded as chief justice by John F. Kinney, of Iowa, in 1854. After the close of the term of Judge Zerubbabel Snow, William W. Drummond, of Illinois, was appointed associate justice. Judge Leonidas Shaver died suddenly in Salt Lake City in June, 1855, due to an abscess on the brain, and he was succeeded by George P. Stiles.

Character of the Federal Judges.—Chief Justice Kinney was a gentleman, and performed his duty faithfully without partiality. The appointment of the two associate justices was a calamity. Drummond was dishonest and licentious. He left his wife and family in Illinois without means for their support, and brought with him to the territory a common courtesan, whom he introduced as his wife. This woman he honored with a place by his side while he sat in court dispensing advice to the "Mormons" on morality. Judge Stiles had been a member of the Church, but was excommunicated for immoral conduct. Like most characters of that class, he become very abusive and a bitter enemy of the Church. The corruption of Judge Drummond coming to light, that individual left the territory in disgrace.

Falsehoods of Drummond and Stiles.—March 30, 1857, Judge Drummond wrote a letter to the attorney general of the United States, making false charges against Governor Young and the "Mormon" people. He went to Carson County to hold court, and then continued on to the coast never to return to Utah. In his communication he declared that the records of the supreme court of Utah had been destroyed; that Brigham Young had given his approval of this treasonable deed, and with his knowledge it was done; that Brigham Young, as governor, had pardoned "Mormon" criminals and imprisoned innocent "Gentiles;" he had insulted federal judges; the American Government had been traduced and men "insulted, harassed and murdered for doing their duty." He accused the "Mormon" people of the murder of Almon W. Babbitt; of perpetrating the Gunnison massacre,[a] and of the death of Judge Shaver, who died a natural death. He placed the responsibility of these alleged crimes at the door of the authorities of the Church.

Judge Stiles also filed an affidavit at Washington, affirming much that Judge Drummond had said, and emphasizing the statement that the court records and papers had been destroyed. Others also added to the unrighteous accusations with the evil thought of bringing the Church into disrepute. Among them were Indian Agent Garland Hurt, and W. M. Magraw. The latter having been disappointed in losing the contract to carry mail across the plains, which contract was awarded to Hiram Kimball, a "Mormon," sought revenge by circulating falsehoods. He stated that the civil laws of the territory were "overshadowed and neutralized by the so-styled ecclesiastical organization, as despotic, dangerous and damnable" as ever existed. Other, and even more serious accusations, he forwarded in a communication to President Buchanan in October, 1856.

Denial of False Charges.—Curtis E. Bolton, deputy clerk of the supreme court of Utah made denial in his official capacity, of the Drummond charges. He stated that the records and papers of the court were all intact. This denial was speedily forwarded to the attorney general of the United States, but was ignored in the face of the various statements of the lying officials.

The Conspirators Demand Governor Young's Removal.—At the time these falsehoods were sent to Washington, Governor Brigham

---

[a]Captain John W. Gunnison, in charge of a party of topographical engineers, was murdered by Indians, with a number of his party, near Sevier Lake, in October, 1853. The massacre was in revenge for the killing of one Indian and the wounding of two others, by a company of emigrants on their way to California. According to Indian practice the next company that came along was attacked as a reprisal. At the time of this deed of blood the Indians under Chief Walker were waging war on the inhabitants of Utah, which event is known in historical annals as "The Walker War." Captain Gunnison and companions were buried at Fillmore, with respect and honor. The tragedy cast a gloom over all the "Mormon" settlements, for the leader of this company of government representatives was respected by all the people for his kindness and friendly feeling.

Young was serving his second term. At the close of his first term as governor, Col. Edward J. Steptoe of the United States Army, was appointed to that position. He declined, and with Chief Justice Kinney, headed a petition, which bore the names of the federal officials, army officers and prominent citizens in the territory, asking for the reappointment of Governor Young. The petition bore fruit and President Franklin Pierce continued Brigham Young in office. These conspirators now endeavored to have him removed, and this desire was very largely the underlying cause in their evil accusations.

"Buchanan's Blunder."—Accepting at their face value, without any investigation, the inflammatory and lying charges of the enemies of Utah, President James Buchanan determined on changing the governor, and also appointed new judges. He further directed that an army must accompany the new appointees, as a posse *comitatus*, to sustain the authority of these officers, and suppress "rebellion" among the "Mormon" people.

It was announced through the war department that the "Mormons" "implicitly obey their prophet from whose decrees there is no appeal." Moreover, that they had aimed from the beginning to secede from the Union, and had not "preserved even the semblance of obedience to authority, only as it would benefit themselves." Such was the ignorance of the authorities at Washington regarding Latter-day Saints affairs, so soon after the loyal and remarkable feat performed by the Mormon Battalion in the war which made their territory a part of the United States. Such was to be the reward of this loyal people who would sacrifice five hundred of their most capable men in the hour of their greatest distress, at the call of their country. These expressions from Washington were made in the face of the constant appeals by the "Mormon" people for a form of government under the Stars and Stripes, in spite of the evil treatment they had constantly received within the borders of the United States; and, too, after their appeal to the general government for redress of grievances was answered from Washington, that their cause was just but nothing could be done for them.

When appealing to Washington for redress, while they resided in Illinois, they were advised by governors and leading statesmen to move to Oregon, where they could set up a government of their own, free and independent of all other earthly powers. Their reply to such advice was, that they were American citizens, and where they went they would take the flag of their country with them.

It appears from this distant date, that there were other motives prompting the President of the United States in sending the flower of the army into the "Mormon" country, ostensibly to suppress a rebellion which did not exist, and aid in a rebellion soon to occur, which was destined to divide the nation asunder. Whatever the motive, the army was sent, and was kept in Utah for a number of years at the beginning of a critical period of the nation's history.

Call of the Army.—May 28, 1857, orders were issued from the war department for the assembling of an army at Fort Leavenworth, to march to Utah as soon as possible. All mail toward Utah had been stopped, and for some reason the government conducted its campaign against that territory with great secrecy. It was practically a declaration of war by the United States against one of her dependent units, without investigation or just cause—a thing without a parallel in the annals of our country. "It is probable," states Bancroft, "that no expedition was ever dispatched by the United States better equipped and provisioned than was the army of Utah, of which the portion now under orders mustered about twenty-five hundred men." Then he argues that the expedition was conducted in the interests of the contractors. The men who secured the flour contract netted in a single year the sum of one hundred and seventy thousand dollars.

How the Saints Learned of the Expedition.—While all these warlike preparations were going on, the Saints in the Rocky Mountains, dwelling in peace, were innocent of any threatened invasion. The first information of such an expedition was received by Elders Feramorz Little and Ephraim K. Hanks in February, 1857. They had just arrived at Independence with mail, where they heard from several parties who desired to secure contracts from the government for handling the supply trains, that a movement was on foot against Utah. They could hardly believe the rumors and reports that came to their ears. Later Elder Abraham O. Smoot, on his way east with mail, met Elder Little at Fort Laramie, from whom he heard the rumors. Proceeding on his way, Elder Smoot met some troops and several trains of government supplies. From his inquiries he received no satisfactory answer as to their destination, only that they were bound for a western post and that the supplies belonged to William H. Russell. At Independence he learned from Mr. Russell that the destination of the trains was Salt Lake City, and that government troops would soon follow. He was also informed that Brigham Young had been superseded as governor and that new federal officers had been appointed for Utah. Gaining all the information he could, Elder Smoot commenced his homeward journey, traveling leisurely at first, for fear of arousing suspicion, but increasing his speed as he neared his destination. A short distance east of Fort Laramie he met Orrin Porter Rockwell with the east bound mail. To him he told his story and together they, and Judson L. Stoddard, returned to the Salt Lake Valley, arriving on the evening of July 23.

The 24th of July Celebration.—When these brethren arrived they learned that President Brigham Young and about twenty-six hundred people had gone to Silver Lake, at the head of Big Cottonwood Canyon. There they expected to celebrate the twenty-fourth—the tenth anniversary of the arrival of the pioneers in Salt Lake Valley. On the morning of the 24th, Mayor Smoot of Salt Lake City, Judson L. Stoddard, Judge Elias Smith and Orrin P. Rockwell, started for the scene of the celebration. They arrived in the afternoon in the midst of the ceremonies and the first view to attract their gaze was the Stars and Stripes unfurled from two lofty peaks and some of the tallest trees. With grave countenances these messengers bearing evil tidings approached Governor Young and told their story. A council of the brethren was called and the situation discussed. That evening the assembly was informed by General Daniel H. Wells of the militia, that an army was on its way to Utah. He gave instructions as to the manner of the departure from the camp on the following morning. Early the next day (25th) the people, so happy the day before, returned to their homes with bowed heads and hearts filled with sadness.

The Decision of the Council.—Twice in Missouri and once in Illinois had the Saints been driven from their homes at the point of the bayonet, and that, too, by aid of state authority. Their Prophet and Patriarch had been foully murdered by a mob while under the pledge of protection of a governor of Illinois. The Saints had been murdered and robbed while the nation looked on without interference. And now there was coming to their distant home, a body of troops organized and equipped by the President of the United States. They were coming without warning and without valid excuse. Was it not natural under all the circumstances for this people to feel that once again they were to be butchered, robbed and driven—where, no one could tell! Naturally they were aroused. Their backs were against the wall. They must make a stand, and if to fight was the intention of the troops, then fight it should be. They were determined to maintain their inherent and constitutional rights. Conquered, they should not be; if they were driven they should leave the land as desolate as they found it. If the government of the United States desired to install new officers, they could come in peace, and welcome. Such had always been the attitude of the Latter-day Saints. They could only judge by the experiences of the past what the designs of the army might be, for no word had been sent them of its purpose. "Liars have reported that this people has committed treason, and upon their misrepresentations the President has ordered out troops to assist in officering the territory," said President Young. "We have transgressed no law, neither do we intend to do so; but as for any nation coming to destroy this people, God Almighty being my helper, it shall not be." Such was the decision of the councils of the Church. And where is the patriot whose blood would not burn within his veins; whose heart would not beat for freedom; who would not stand as this band of humble worshipers of the Lord and Savior of mankind proposed to stand, if driven to the extreme?

Captain Van Vliet.—In advance of the army there came to Utah Captain Stewart Van Vliet of the commissary department. His object was to discover if forage and fuel could be obtained for the troops while in the territory. As soon as he arrived he obtained an interview with Governor Young. He was treated with the greatest kindness and hospitality, and so he reported to his superiors. However, he was informed that no hostile force would be permitted to enter the Salt Lake Valley; there was an abundance of everything the troops would need, but not one thing would be sold to them. Federal officers could come, if they came in peace, and would be kindly and courteously received; but they could not bring an hostile army.

Captain Van Vliet's Report.—In his report Captain Van Vliet said:
"In the course of my conversation with the Governor and the influential men of the Territory, I told them plainly and frankly what I conceived would be the result of their present course. I told them that they might prevent the small military force now approaching Utah from getting through the narrow defiles and rugged passes of the mountains this year, but that next season the United States Government would send troops sufficient to overcome all opposition. The answer to this was invariably the same: 'We are aware that such will be the case; but when those troops arrive they will find Utah a desert. Every house will be burned to the ground, every tree cut down, and every field laid waste. We have three years' provisions on hand, which we will cache, and then take to the mountains and bid defiance to all the powers of the Government.'

"I attended their services on Sunday, and, in course of a sermon delivered by Elder Taylor, he referred to the approach of the troops and declared they should not enter the Territory. He then referred to the probability of an over-powering force being sent against them, and desired all present who would apply the torch to their buildings, cut down their trees, and lay waste their fields, to hold up their hands. Every hand, in an audience numbering over four thousand persons, was raised at the same moment. During my stay in the city I visited several families, and all with whom I was thrown, looked upon the present movement of the troops toward their Territory as the commencement of another religious persecution, and expressed a fixed determination to sustain Governor Young in any measure he might adopt."

Good Resulting from the Visit.—The sympathy of Captain Van Vliet was drawn out toward the people. He admired their stand although careful of his expression as he was under orders from the government. He was convinced that the people had been misrepresented and lied about, and it is said he declared that if the government made war upon the Saints, he would withdraw from the army. However, he thought the government would send to Utah an investigating committee. "I believe," said Governor Young, "God sent you here, and that good will grow out of it. I was glad when I heard you were coming. If we can keep the peace this winter, I feel sure that something will occur to prevent the shedding of blood." The captain returned to Washington and made his report to the secretary of war.

Johnston in Command.—When the army was ordered to Utah the command was given to General W. S. Harney, who was at the time in charge of Fort Leavenworth. Captain Van Vliet called on him when returning to Washington after his visit in Utah. The captain informed General Harney of the attitude of the "Mormon" people and the conditions as they existed in the Territory. The general replied: "I am ordered there, and I will winter in the valley, or in hell." Late in the summer the command was given to Colonel Albert Sidney Johnston, with the rank of brevet brigadier general.

The Start for Utah.—The vanguard of the troops, under Colonel E. B. Alexander, started from Fort Leavenworth in July, 1857. With them traveled Alfred Cumming, of Georgia, the newly appointed governor, and other federal appointees for Utah. As the troops reached the South Pass, they were met by Captain Van Vliet, who advised them not to attempt to enter the Salt Lake Valley that winter, as no arrangements could be made for supplies and they would have to fight their way through. Some of the young officers, who were in advance, ignored the warning, and expressed the thought that they were sufficiently able to force their way to Salt Lake City—"that they could whip all Utah." The second regiment he met was commanded by old officers, who considered the matter seriously and expressed the thought that it was an imposition that they should be sent out west "as a political movement to kill innocent people, or to get killed."[b]

---

[b]Colonel Alexander, the ranking officer of the advance troops, was a kindly officer inclined towards establishing peace. Captain Van Vliet had come in contact with the Latter-day Saints at Winter Quarters, when they were on the

Martial Law Proclaimed.—After the departure of Captain Van Vliet from Salt Lake City, and while the army was near the border of Utah, Governor Young proclaimed martial law throughout the territory and notified Colonel Alexander of this action. The militia was ordered to be held in readiness to repel any attempted invasion, but instructions were given that no blood should be shed, unless it was absolutely unavoidable. These instructions were carefully followed and only once during the campaign were shots fired with intent to kill, and these were fired by the government forces at a detachment under command of Major Lot Smith, who had been sent out to destroy their trains. When fired upon there was no retalliation by the members of the militia.

General Wells in Echo Canyon.—Following the proclamation of Governor Young, Lieutenant General Daniel H. Wells of the Nauvoo Legion—the name by which the militia was known—established headquarters at "The Narrows" in Echo Canyon, a defile, rugged and steep, where a few men could hold an army. To this point about twelve hundred and fifty men, from several companies of the militia, were ordered to report, and maintain the pass by force of arms against any attempted invasion.

Governor Young's Ultimatum.—Colonel Alexander continued his march, as it was fully expected that he would, and crossed the border of the territory. September 29, General Wells forwarded to Colonel Alexander copies of Governor Young's proclamation, a copy of the laws of Utah, and a letter from Governor Young addressed to "The Officer commanding the forces now invading Utah Territory." In this letter the following occurs:

"By virtue of the authority vested in me, I have issued, and forwarded you a copy of my proclamation forbidding the entrance of

---

plains. Another officer with these troops, whose sympathy and good will went out toward the "Mormons", was Colonel Philip St. George Cooke, who led the Mormon Battalion in the Mexican War. General Johnston was from the South, proud and haughty. He looked upon the "Mormons" and spoke of them as "rebels" and was inclined to treat them as such.

The spirit also prevailed among the troops that the "Mormons" were their common prey, and they constantly, while on the march, boasted with ribald jests of what they would do when they arrived in Salt Lake City. "We were well informed as to the object of the coming of the army," said Elder John Taylor to Vice-President Schuyler Colfax, in 1869. "We had men in all their camps, and knew what was intended. There was a continual boast among the men and officers, even before they left the Missouri River, of what they intended to do with the 'Mormons.' The houses were picked out that certain persons were to inhabit; farms, property, and women were to be distributed. 'Beauty and Booty' were their watchword. We were to have another grand 'Mormon' conquest, and our houses, gardens, orchards, vineyards, fields, wives and daughters were to be the spoils."

armed forces into this Territory. This you have disregarded. I now further direct that you retire forthwith from the Territory, by the same route you entered. Should you deem this impracticable, and prefer to remain until spring in the vicinity of your present encampment, Black's Fork,[c] or Green River, you can do so in peace and unmolested on condition that you deposit your arms and ammunition with Lewis Robison, quartermaster general of the Territory, and leave in the spring, as soon as the condition of the roads will permit you to march; and should you fall short of provisions, they can be furnished you, upon making the proper applications therefor. General D. H. Wells will forward this, and receive any communication you may have to make."

In forwarding these communications General Wells declared that he was determined to carry out Governor Young's instructions.

Colonel Alexander's Reply.—Colonel Alexander made the only reply possible which was to the effect that he would submit the communications to his superior officers and "in the meantime," he added "I have only to say that these troops are here by order of the President of the United States, and their future movements will depend entirely upon orders issued by competent military authority."[d]

Guerrilla Warfare.—Following this correspondence General Wells determined on carrying out his instructions. He ordered Major Joseph Taylor and others under his command to annoy the troops; stampede their cattle; set fire to their trains; burn the whole country before them and on their flanks; keep them from sleeping by night surprises; blockade the road; but must avoid strictly the taking of life. These instructions were faithfully followed and Major Lot Smith with a company of mounted rangers destroyed trains, ran off cattle and burned the grass, and otherwise inflicted damage, but no blood was shed.

Arrival of General Johnston.—Early in November, 1857, General Albert Sidney Johnston, with additional troops and supplies, overtook the main body of the army on Black's Fork. He was a capable and popular officer and soon enthused the troops who had become dispirited because of their many reverses. Their journey had not been a pleasant one, the Indians had run off many of their cattle, and the "Mormon" mountaineers had harassed them, had burned their trains

---

[c]Black's Fork and Green River mentioned here were at that time within the borders of Utah; they are now in Wyoming, the corner in which they are located having been severed from Utah in 1863 and 1868.

[d]The question might be raised as to why Brigham Young would forward a communication as governor, when another had been appointed. Governor Young had not been notified that his successor had been appointed and that successor had not qualified as governor.

of supplies, and destroyed the grass on which their teams and cattle were dependent. But their troubles were only beginning. Their haughty commander ordered a forward movement toward Fort Bridger, disdaining to turn from the direct route through the mountains.

If "the stars in their courses fought against Sisera," in the days of ancient Israel, surely the elements fought against Johnston's army in the days of modern Israel. From their camp to Fort Bridger was less than forty miles, but it was a barren desert. They found no shelter from the winter winds, there was no fuel, except the sage, and very little pasture for their animals. They broke camp on the 6th of November, and their trains, extending for many miles, were forced to face the snow and sleet of the most severe winter weather. Their teams were goaded until they dropped dead in their traces. Fifteen days they were on the journey. Their cattle died for lack of food and exposure to freezing weather. When they arrived they found that Bridger and also Fort Supply, twelve miles away, had been burned by the militia.

The Forward March Abandoned.—It became apparent that it would be impossible to reach the Salt Lake Valley before the coming spring. With great reluctance and injured pride the commander gave orders that the troops go into winter quarters on Black's Fork. During the winter months Chief Justice Eckles, who with other federal officers dwelt in the camp, organized a court, without waiting to qualify, and indicted the leading men in Utah for treason and rebellion.

Proclamation of Governor Cumming.—Governor Cumming issued a proclamation to the people of the territory in which he said: "I come among you with no prejudice or enmities, and by the exercise of a just and firm administration I hope to command your confidence. Freedom of conscience and the use of your own peculiar mode of serving God are sacred rights, the exercise of which is guaranteed by the Constitution, and with which it is not the province of the government or the disposition of its representatives in the territory to interfere." Let it be said to his credit that these sentiments were sincere, and when he was established in his office he was brave enough to execute justice as he saw it. He commanded all armed bodies in the territory to disband and return to their homes stating that disobedience would "subject the offenders to the punishment due to traitors."

There was no disposition on the part of the militia to disband. Too often had they been despoiled by mobs under guise of lawful troops. They had stood enough and were determined to defend their homes, no matter what were the accusations made against them.

"THE UTAH WAR"

The Mediation of Colonel Kane.—At the beginning of the difficulties Governor Young sent a communication to Colonel Thomas L. Kane, explaining the motives in declaring martial law in Utah, and asking him to intercede at Washington. This loyal friend of the "Mormons" did not fail. He interviewed the President and offered his services as mediator between the government and people of Utah. His services were accepted and he crossed the Isthmus of Panama, sailing from New York, and proceeded from California to Utah, where he arrived in February, 1858. At the time Congress was preparing to send reinforcements and money to carry on the "war." Colonel Kane arrived, delicate in health, and wishing to test the "Mormon" people appeared in Salt Lake City in disguise as "Dr. Osborne." He received hospitable treatment and was welcomed warmly when he became known. He reported the nature of his visit and reported that Captain Van Vliet had proved himself a friend of the "Mormons" on his return to Washington.

After a few days' rest Colonel Kane departed for the army camp on Black's Fork to interview Governor Cumming. After severe trials and adventures he arrived at the camp. Governor Cumming received him cordially and agreed to place himself under his direction and go to Salt Lake City without military air. Such a step was strongly opposed by General Johnston, who attempted to arrest Colonel Kane as a spy. Governor Cumming felt insulted at the indignity offered and demanded an explanation, which the commanding officer failed to give in a satisfactory manner. The incident almost precipitated a duel between General Johnston and Colonel Kane.

Governor Cumming Enters Salt Lake City.—His Reception.—Accompanied by Colonel Kane and two servants, Governor Cumming set out for Salt Lake City. On the way they were met by an escort of Utah cavalry. Arriving in the city he was received with a cordial reception and was conducted to the home of William C. Staines, the territorial librarian. President Young called on him and bid him welcome, saying every facility that he might require for the efficient performance of his administrative duties, would be at his command. The governor wrote to General Johnston saying: "I have been everywhere recognized as Governor of Utah; and so far from having encountered insults or indignities, I am satisfied in being able to state to you, that in passing through the settlements I have been universally greeted with respectful attentions as are due to the representative authority of the United States in the territory."

The Governor's Report to Secretary Cass.—After a thorough examination, and finding all the records of the courts in perfect order,

Governor Cumming wrote to Secretary of State Lewis M. Cass informing him of the true conditions in the territory and of the false reports which had stood as a foundation for the sending of any army.

The Exodus Toward the South.—When Governor Cumming arrived in the city he discovered that many of the inhabitants of that place and the settlements to the north, had left their homes. Others were journeying toward the south. Where they were bound he could not learn more than that they were "going south" and driving their flocks and herds before them. He expressed the belief to the government that the destiny of these people was Sonora in northern Mexico. He regretted greatly that they felt it necessary to move, but he could do nothing to persuade them to remain as long as they were menaced by an army. Their experience in the past was too bitter in this regard, and could not be forgotten.

"Our military force could overwhelm most of these poor people," wrote the governor, "involving men, women, and children in a common fate, but there are among the 'Mormons' brave men, accustomed to arms and horses; men who could fight desperately as guerrillas; and who, if the settlements are destroyed, will subject the country to an expensive and protracted war, without any compensating results. They will, I am sure, submit to 'trial by their peers,' but they will not brook the idea of trials by 'juries' composed of 'teamsters and followers of the camp.'"

The Governor's Wife Pleads for the People.—In the middle of May, Governor Cumming returned to Camp Scott where the troops were quartered. When he returned, his wife was with him. She gazed upon the deserted homes—for the people had departed, leaving only a guard to fire their property should the troops arrive in hostile attitude. The good woman wept and pleaded with her husband to do something to bring back the people. "Rest assured, madam," said he, "I shall do all I can. I only wish I could be in Washington for two hours; I am sure I could convince the government that we have no need of troops."

The Peace Commission.—Through the good services of faithful friends—among whom Colonel Thomas L. Kane stands out in bold relief—the government was persuaded to send peace commissioners to Utah. These gentlemen were Governor L. W. Powell of Kentucky and Major Ben McCullock of Texas. With them came Jacob Forney, Indian Superintendent for Utah. They met with Governor Cumming, Brigham Young and other prominent men when the whole situation was discussed. It was agreed that there should be no opposition to Johnston's army passing through the city providing they were not permitted to stop, but should pass on to make their camp at least forty miles away.

Their Epistle to Johnston.—An agreement having been reached, the commissioners addressed a communication to General Johnston advising him of what had been done and requesting him to make proclamation among his troops. The commander was surprised at the decision, stating that the army would not trespass upon the rights or property of the peaceable citizens. His men, many of them, were greatly disappointed, for they were to be denied the privilege of plunder for which they hoped and talked about as they marched upon their way.

The Arrival of the Troops.—June 26, 1858, the army under command of General Johnston, entered the Salt Lake Valley through Emigration Canyon. They passed through the city, now almost without inhabitants, and camped on the opposite side of the Jordan river. Colonel Cooke, as he rode through the streets of the city, bared his head in honor of the valiant and loyal men of the Mormon Battalion. Three days after their arrival the troops passed on to the southwest and camped in Cedar Valley where they founded Camp Floyd, named after the Secretary of War, and here was to be their scene of action for several years to come.

The President's "Pardon"—On the 6th of April, President Buchanan signed a proclamation, "offering to the inhabitants of Utah, who shall submit to the laws, a free pardon for the seditions and treasons heretofore by them committed; warning those who still persist, after notice of this proclamation in the present rebellion against the United States, that they must expect no further lenity." This document, which is quite lengthy was brought to Utah with the commissioners. The authorities of the Church denied that they had been disloyal, and disputed the statements in the President's proclamation. Nevertheless, they accepted his pardon for driving off the cattle and burning the army trains, which they stoutly maintained was done in self-defense; but the other charges they fully denied.

The fact is that President Buchanan had been roundly scored in the press, and by statesmen in our own country and abroad. The easiest way out of it, for he had committed a great blunder, was to issue a proclamation exonerating himself, and pardoning the "culprits" who dared to maintain their rights against such overwhelming odds.

CHAPTER 44

THE MOUNTAIN MEADOWS MASSACRE

1857

A Shocking Crime.—While Captain Van Vliet was interviewing President Brigham Young, there was occurring in the southwest corner of Utah—about three hundred miles from Salt Lake City—the most horrible and shocking crime ever perpetrated within the borders of the state. It was the massacre at Mountain Meadows of a company of emigrants who were journeying to southern California. This bloody and diabolical deed commenced at dawn, September 7, 1857, and continued until the 11th, when the besieged emigrants who survived the attacks, under promise of protection were foully murdered.

It was the deed of enraged Indians aided by a number of white men, who took vengeance into their hands for wrongs committed by a few of the emigrants who were pronounced enemies of both whites and Indians.

It was a crime for which there can be no apology or excuse, a thing treacherous and damnable in the extreme. But for the "Mormon" people it was most unfortunate that it should happen at this particular time. There were circulating throughout the nation many evil reports concerning the Latter-day Saints. All manner of crimes and murders occurring within a thousand miles of Utah, were charged against them. Even the executive of the nation and other high officials were countenancing these reports and aiding in their circulation. The army was on the plains making its way to Utah to suppress alleged violation of law and rebellion; and now, to add to the horror of the situation, the report went forth that the "Mormons" had attacked and killed a party of innocent people peacefully passing through their land. Thus color was given to the falsehood that life and property of "Gentiles" were unsafe within the Territory of Utah.[a]

It may be said without fear of successful contradiction, that there was less crime committed in Utah during the days of pioneer life than in any other similarly situated section of the country. California had her vigilantes who executed judgment with swift vengeance, without legal trial. Such was also the condition in other border states and territories, and woe to the individual who incurred the wrath of the powers who controlled. The "Mormon" people had been taught from the beginning: "Thou shalt not kill." Murder, according to their teaching, committed wantonly, was a sin for which there was no forgiveness in this life, neither in the life to come. Next, and like unto it stood sexual immorality. Both of these great sins were denounced by the Saints most emphatically.

Crimes Falsely Charged to the Church Authorities.—One thing most trying to the members of the Church was the attempt by their enemies to charge Brigham Young and the leaders of the Church with every wrong committed in the western country. These attempts led Jacob Forney, Indian Agent in 1859, to write to Washington saying:

"I fear, and I regret to say it, that with certain parties here there is a greater anxiety to connect Brigham Young and other Church dignitaries with every criminal offense than diligent endeavor to punish the actual perpetrators of the crime."

How the Massacre Occurred.—About the time the news arrived in Salt Lake City of the coming of an army, there was passing through the city under command of Captain Fancher, a company of emigrants from Arkansas and Missouri. This company consisted of about thirty families, numbering one hundred and thirty-seven persons. The Arkansas emigrants appeared to be respectable and well-to-do. With

---

[a]It may as well be understood at the outset that this horrible crime so often and so persistently charged upon the "Mormon" Church and its leaders, was the crime of an individual, the crime of a fanatic of the worst stamp, one who was a member of the "Mormon" Church, but of whose intentions the Church knew nothing, and whose bloody acts, the members of the Church, high and low, regard with as much abhorrence as any out of the Church. Indeed, the blow fell upon the brotherhood with threefold force and damage. There was the cruelty of it, which wrung their hearts; and there was the strength it lent their enemies further to malign and molest them. The "Mormons" denounce the Mountain Meadows Massacre, and every act connected therewith, as earnestly and honestly as any in the outside world. This is abundantly proved and may be accepted as a historical fact. (Bancroft's "History of Utah," p. 544.)

them there traveled a rough and reckless company calling themselves "Missouri Wild Cats," who conducted themselves in keeping with the name. This company was advised by Elder Charles C. Rich, one of the leaders of the Church, to take the northern route. Had they done so they would have saved their lives. They went as far as Bear River and then returned deciding to journey to the south. On their way, it is alleged, the rougher elements of the party abused the people of the southern settlements through which they passed. They tore down fences, destroyed property, insulted women, and otherwise made themselves obnoxious. It is said, on reliable authority, that at Fillmore they threatened to destroy the town, "and boasted of their participation in the murders and other outrages that were inflicted upon the 'Mormons' in Missouri and Illinois." At Corn Creek, fifteen miles farther to the south, it was reported that they poisoned the springs and also the body of an ox that had died. The carcass was eaten by a band of Piute Indians and ten of their number died. Some of the cattle of the settlers died from drinking of the poisoned springs. As the cattle were fat, the owners "tried them out" for the tallow, and a number of white persons were poisoned from the handling of the meat. These "Wild Cats" expressed their pleasure at the coming of the army, and threatened to stop at some convenient place and leave their women and children, and return to assist the troops in killing every "Mormon" there was in the mountains.

Just to what extent credence can be placed in these charges cannot be determined. The fact remains, however, that they gave expression to their hatred of the "Mormon" people, made many threats, and abused the Indians along their way.

The Purchase of Supplies.—It has been said that these emigrants could not purchase supplies in Salt Lake City and the other settlements of the Saints, and had been ordered away from Salt Lake City by President Young. This is not the fact. President Young did not know they were in the city and first heard of them after they had departed. Along the way they did obtain supplies as they desired and as the Saints were able to impart to them, as there is abundant evidence to show. They were well treated by most of the settlers, and not until their own actions brought upon them the ill will of the southern settlements was this attitude changed.

Word Sent to Brigham Young.—So intense did the feeling become on the part of both the Indians and the white population in the southern settlements that it was deemed necessary to send a messenger to Governor Brigham Young to know what should be done. Some of the people expressed the feeling that since the emigrants had declared themselves as enemies they should be treated as such, but the more sober minded maintained that they should be permitted to continue their journey to the coast unmolested. James H. Haslam carried a message from Colonel Isaac C. Haight, of the militia, to Salt Lake City to obtain advice of Governor Young. In the meantime it was agreed that every effort should be made to pacify the Indians and prevent them from making an attack. Haslam left Cedar City in the afternoon of Monday, September 7, and made all haste on horseback, arriving in Salt Lake City on the morning of the 10th. He immediately delivered his message, and Governor Young asked him if he could undertake the return journey without delay. He said he could. "Go with all speed, spare no horse flesh. The emigrants must not be meddled with, if it takes all Iron County to prevent it. They must go free and unmolested." This was the answer he received. Haslam, although he had just finished a hard journey, immediately returned arriving in Cedar City on the 13th with a written message from Governor Young to Colonel Haight.

The Answer Arrives Too Late.—The message to Colonel Haight of the militia from Governor Young was as follows:

"In regard to the emigration trains passing through our settlements, we must not interfere with them until they are first notified to keep away. You must not meddle with them. There are no other trains that I know of. If those who are there will leave, let them go in peace."

Colonel Isaac C. Haight read the letter, and shedding tears replied: "Too late, too late!" The morning (September 7) Haslam left to obtain word from Governor Young, the work of death among the unfortunate victims had commenced.

The Attack upon the Emigrant Train.—Early in September the emigrant train of the Arkansas and Missouri companies camped in the little valley known as the Mountain Meadows. There they contemplated remaining for several days. In the meantime their conduct had aroused the Indian tribes who now surrounded their camp in hostile attitude. As near as can be ascertained, on the morning of the 7th of September at the break of day, the attack upon the emigrants began. At the first volley seven men were killed and sixteen were wounded. The victims were taken unawares, but being well armed, fought bravely for their lives and were successful in repelling the attack. Several Indians were killed including two of their chiefs. The Indians sent runners throughout the surrounding country calling for reinforcements from among their tribes, and for John D. Lee, who had been in close touch with Indian affairs as their farmer, to come and lead them to victory. Lee hurried to the scene from his home in Harmony, and seemed to partake of the frenzy of the red men. Later, other white men appeared upon the scene, having been lured to the meadows, with the request that their services were needed in burying the dead. Some of them remained, willingly or by coercion, to participate in the massacre which followed.

The Surrender—Treachery of Their Captors.—During the lull following the first attack, the emigrants formed their wagons in a ring and threw up breastworks for their protection, awaiting the onslaught which they knew was sure to come. Some time was spent by the Indians and their white allies discussing the fate of the unfortunate emigrants. The victims discovered that white men were in league with the Indians, and this knowledge sealed their fate. It was determined by those making the attack that no emigrant should live who could tell the tale.

On the morning of Friday the 11th, Lee induced the emigrants to surrender under promise of protection and conveyance to a place of safety. They were led to a place where the Indians were in ambush, and at a given signal a volley of shots rang out, both Indians and white men participating in the outrage. Seventeen children of tender years—ranging in age from a few months to seven years—were all that were spared. These children were cared for by the settlers until the government by act of Congress returned them to their friends in Arkansas.

A Bloody Oath.—The white men who were engaged in this horrible slaughter entered into a league, by a strong and binding oath, that they would never reveal the part they played in this gruesome tragedy. A false report was forwarded to Governor Young. Lee also reported in person, laying the blame solely to the Indians. Governor Young wept bitterly and was horrified at the recital of the tale.

The Execution of Lee.—For several years the facts relating to the tragedy were unknown, but gradually the truth leaked out and an investigation was made of the affair. John D. Lee was excommunicated from the Church with the injunction from President Young that under no circumstances should he ever be admitted as a member again. Action was also taken against others as the truth became known. In later years Lee was convicted of the crime and paid the penalty with his life. His execution took place on the site of the horrid scene. Others who were implicated fled from the territory and died fugitives. While they thus evaded the justice which earthly tribunals might inflict, they still await the trial for their crimes before a Higher Court where justice never fails.

CHAPTER 45

THE ARMY IN UTAH

1858—1862

Demoralizing Effects of the Army's Presence.—It was the part of wisdom for President Brigham Young and his associates to insist on the camp of the army being far removed from Salt Lake City. It was with reluctance that their commander complied with the request, which was enforced by the peace commissioners. Very little good came to the people of Utah from the presence in their midst, of an armed force, with all its attendant camp followers. It is true that the people benefited in a financial way. They were able to dispose of their products for ready cash and clothing; but they could have managed to live—as they did before the army came—without these advantages, which, of course, they were ready to receive.

There was no debauchery, no immorality or fear of thieves breaking in to steal, in the communities of the Latter-day Saints, before the strangers to their faith came in. With the army all these attendant evils were introduced. The worst element with the army was, of course, the camp following—the freighters and hangers-on, who were not subject to the rigid discipline of army regulation. Yet, much of the evil which resulted, can be traced to subordinate officers and men of the ranks. With many of these, moral rectitude was a thing unknown; and woe to the foolish creatures who, like flies caught in a spider-web, were lured into camp.

To add to the difficulties, many of the enlisted men filled their term of service and were discharged. Usually they were in possession of very little means, and if a balance of pay was due them, it was soon squandered. Such characters flocked to Salt Lake City and other towns, where they became a terror to the inhabitants. Because of this, it became necessary to increase the police force of Salt Lake City, at least four fold. Appeals were made to Governor Cumming to get him to use his influence to have the discharged men marched beyond the borders of the territory. The governor took the matter up with General Johnston, with the result that the condition was relieved in this respect to some small degree. However, the situation could not fully be controlled by these officers, and as long as Camp Floyd (later Crittenden) was occupied by the troops, demoralizing agencies were at work, and the people were constantly in a state of agitation.

Governor Cumming's Report.—In reporting affairs in Utah to the Secretary of State, Governor Cumming made the following observations:

"Persons unbiased by prejudice who have visited this Territory will, I think, agree in the opinion that a community is seldom seen more marked by quiet and peaceable diligence than that of the 'Mormons.'

"After the passage of the army, hundreds of adventurers were attracted to these valleys, and met here some congenial spirits. Banded together for rapine and acts of violence, they have stolen large herds of horses and mules. Many of these men, maddened by intemperance, or rendered desperate by losses at the gambling table, or by various other causes, have shed each other's blood in frequent conflicts, and secret assassinations. These lawless and bloody deeds are committed by them almost daily with impunity, and when their atrocity and frequency shock the public mind, it has become the custom with a certain set of people to exclaim against the people of Utah; but it is an injustice to impute the acts of these desperadoes to the community in general. With an equal show of justice might they be attributed to the inhabitants of the States and Territories whence these men have so recently emigrated."

The New Federal Officers.—Chief Justice Delano R. Eckles and the new secretary of the territory, John Hartnett, arrived in Utah with the army. Jacob Forney, the superintendent of Indian affairs, arrived with the peace commissioners, and Judge Charles E. Sinclair and Attorney Alexander Wilson came near the end of July. The third judge, John Cradlebaugh, did not arrive until November. None of these officers were members of the Church.

After he had taken the oath of office, Chief Justice Eckles took up his residence at Camp Floyd and Judge Sinclair made his headquarters in Salt Lake City. Judge Cradlebaugh opened his court in Provo in March, 1859, although the seat of his district was Fillmore.

"**Progress of Civilization.**"—The majority of the government officials sent to Utah during territorial days came obsessed with the idea that the "Mormons" were an unpatriotic and ignorant class of people, bound by blind obedience to the will of a set of knaves who presided over them. When a new government appointee came to Utah, usually he felt it incumbent upon him to begin his labors with a lecture to the people on loyalty and morality, and advise them to cast off the yoke of ignorance which bound them. These would-be reformers at times gave expression to the thought that they had brought civilization among the "Mormons" and were endeavoring to reform them. At the time of the return to the east in 1858, of one official—who had been notoriously corrupt and immoral in his conduct while in Utah—a number of the civil and military officers and some non-"Mormon" merchants tendered him a dinner. In the course of their hilarity they expressed the satisfaction he would feel in joining his "family and friends in a moral and civilized community."

Such expressions as this led President Brigham Young, who was a sorrowful witness of the scenes of debauchery and crime practiced by some of these "reformers," to say to another retiring official who was about to depart: "When you get back to the states, no doubt you will be asked many questions about me. I wish you would tell them that I am here, watching the progress of civilization."

That some of these individuals were sincere, there can be no question, and they should have credit for honest conviction. However it was impossible for them to see the situation from the "Mormon" viewpoint. They came with pre-conceived ideas regarding the doctrines and practices of the Latter-day Saints, and were greatly prejudiced against them. Their prejudice stood in their own light so that they took no trouble to investigate or try to understand. In most cases it was sufficient to know that the "Mormons" were a peculiar people with a strange belief, in conflict with the doctrines of other people.

Many of these officers, however, were insincere. They were guilty of the very sins with which they accused the Latter-day Saints, and yet they brazenly sat in judgment and condemned the Saints, while they, themselves, were guilty of revolting crimes.

Attitude of the Judges.—Chief Justice Eckles was given to drunkenness and was grossly immoral; yet he felt it his duty to advise that indictments be issued against the leaders of the Church for the practice of plural marriage. He did not know just how to handle the situation, for there were no statutes either in the territory or in the United States to punish such a thing. Therefore he attempted to place the matter under the old Mexican law which had no application in United States territory.

Associate Justice Sinclair, who was usually drunk, commenced his duties on the bench by charging the grand jury of his court, to indict ex-Governor Brigham Young, General Daniel H. Wells, and other "Mormon" leaders, for treason, on the ground that President Buchanan's pardon, "while a public act in the history of the country," yet it was a thing of which his court could not "take judicial cognizance." United States Attorney Alexander Wilson took a different view and so expressed himself at length before the grand jury in open court, stating "that there are now no acts of sedition, treason, or rebellion against the government of the United States in this territory." For that reason he would not present bills or bring action against any inhabitant of the territory on such a charge.

Bitterness of Cradlebaugh.—Judge Cradlebaugh manifested a very bitter spirit against the leaders of the Church. When he opened court at Provo he made a demand on General Johnston for several companies of troops from Camp Floyd, and a detachment was furnished him. The reason the judge gave for this action was that the presence of the soldiers was necessary to preserve the peace, and take care of the prisoners because there was no jail in Provo. The real reason was a desire to insult the people of the town and to intimidate witnesses before the court. Inside of two weeks there were about one thousand men in arms surrounding the court house.

Protest of the Citizens.—Instead of keeping the peace, the presence of the troops was a menace to the peace of the town. Five hundred citizens righteously and vigorously protested against the insult in an address to the mayor and city council. They declared that their "feelings were aggrieved and outraged" by the appearance of a military force surrounding the court and infesting the halls of justice, and they considered it a "high handed outrage, a direct infringement upon the rights of American citizens and a gross violation of their liberties and municipal immunities."

The judge was informed by the mayor and city council of the petition and was asked for the immediate removal of the troops beyond the city limits. It was declared that their presence made it very difficult for the officers of the city to preserve the peace. The judge refused to listen to the appeal. Later another vigorous protest was made by the city officials, who declared that soldiers had been caught breaking into houses; they had engaged in drunken street brawls and had otherwise disturbed the peace. However, Judge Cradlebaugh turned a deaf ear to all appeals.

Governor Cumming's Proclamation.—Governor Cumming visited Provo in the month of March, and to him an appeal was made by the mayor and council. The governor could see the situation for himself, and forwarded a communication to General Johnston requesting him to withdraw the troops. General Johnston refused to hearken to the request of the governor, on the grounds that he was there to serve each of the co-ordinate branches of the territorial civil government, and was subject to the judicial as well as to the executive department. Upon this refusal of the commander of the troops, Governor Cumming issued a proclamation protesting against the presence of the military force which had been called to Provo without his sanction and contrary to the instructions given him by the government. Their presence, said the governor, had a tendency to terrify the inhabitants and disturb the peace. All future movements of the troops should be at his direction in accordance with his instructions from Washington.

Result of the Conflict.—The result of this conflict in authority was that Judge Cradlebaugh and his associate, Judge Sinclair, sent a communication to the attorney-general of the United States, Jeremiah S. Black, in relation to the matter. Other letters were sent by Judge Eckles to the secretary of state and by General Johnston to the secretary of war. The secretary of state wrote to Governor Cumming for the facts which were furnished. When the replies were received, the officious judges were rebuked and given to understand that the armed forces in the territory were subject to the command of the executive. Said the attorney general: "The governor is the supreme executive of the territory. He is responsible for the public peace. From the general law of the land, the nature of his office, and the instructions he received from the state department, it ought to have been understood that he alone had power to issue a requisition for the movement of troops from one part of the territory to another." He further stated that "the condition of things in Utah made it extremely desirable that the judges appointed for that territory should confine themselves strictly within their own official sphere," and leave accusations to the district attorney, and arrests to the marshal, who was responsible for the safe-keeping of criminals.

Attempt to Remove Governor Cumming.—The rebuke from Washington was naturally very displeasing to the judges, who were thus confined to the duties of their office. In Camp Floyd there was manifestation of displeasure. A mass meeting was held and an address was issued in which the "Mormons" were accused of disloyalty and it was set forth that a great wrong had been done in forcing the withdrawal of the troops from the protection of the courts. The wrath of the disgruntled camp was also turned against Governor Cumming, and the attempt was made to have him removed from office. This might have been accomplished through the influence of General Johnston, had not Colonel Thomas L. Kane once more come to the rescue.

Attack on President Young.—When Judge Cradlebaugh organized his court at Provo, he expressed his determination to investigate the Mountain Meadows massacre and other crimes. This action would have been commendable if it had been taken with a desire to execute justice, but it was a flagrant attempt to connect President Young and the leading Church authorities with the crime. He inferred that the guilty parties were among the leaders of the Church and should be brought to justice. Later, accompanied by a United States deputy marshal and a detachment of troops, he visited southern Utah and collected what evidence could be obtained respecting the Mountain Meadows massacre, leaving no stone unturned in the endeavor to implicate President Brigham Young and others, in which attempt he miserably failed. Nevertheless, to the grand jury he said: "The very fact of such a case as that of the Mountain Meadows shows that there was some person high in the estimation of the people, and it was done by that authority; * * * and unless you do your duty, such will be the view that will be taken of it. You can know no law but the laws of the United States and the laws you have here. No person can commit crimes and say they are authorized by higher authorities, and if they have any such notions they will have to dispel them."

Cradlebaugh's Insult to the Jury.—As the grand jury failed to act with the promptness he thought they should, the judge dismissed them "as an evidently useless appendage of a court of justice." This unjustifiable attack was resented by the grand jury in a written protest.

In a spirit of anger the judge dismissed criminals who were before his court awaiting trial on grave charges, giving for his reason the following excuse:

"When this people ['Mormons'] come to their reason, and manifest a disposition to punish their own high offenders, it will be time to enforce the laws also for their protection. If this court cannot bring you to a proper sense of your duty, it can at least turn the savages in custody loose upon you."

Attempt to Capture President Young.—Another attempt was made about this time to get President Young in the toils of the law on a groundless charge. It appears that a number of criminals at Camp Floyd plotted to rob the government. They hired a young engraver in Salt Lake City to duplicate the plate used by the quartermaster at Camp Floyd in drawing on the government at St. Louis and New York. The work was done, but the fraud was detected, and a man by the name of Brewer was arrested. He turned state's evidence and threw the responsibility for the deed upon the engraver who had been hired to do the work. As someone in the office of President Young had furnished the paper on which the counterfeit notes were printed, the army officers felt that they had a case against President Young, and manifested their great pleasure at the prospect of implicating him. The officers entered into a plot to secure his arrest. Thinking that an attempt to take him openly would meet with resistance, the army was to be ordered to Salt Lake City and the artillery was to make a breach in the wall surrounding his premises, through which they would enter to secure President Young a captive, and then carry him to Camp Floyd for trial.

Governor Cumming's Stand.—This plan was presented to Governor Cumming, who listened to the plotters and examined their papers. "They rubbed their hands," said the governor, "and were jubilant; they had got the dead wood on Brigham Young. I was indignant, sir, and told them, By ——, gentlemen, you can't do it! When you have a right to take Brigham Young, gentlemen, you shall have him without creeping through walls. You shall enter by his door with heads erect as becomes representatives of your government. But till that time, gentlemen, you can't touch Brigham Young."

The plotters were greatly disappointed and returned to Camp Floyd threatening to act in opposition to the executive. Because of these rumors, Governor Cumming ordered General Daniel H. Wells to be prepared with the militia to repel any such attack. It was a courageous thing for the governor to do in the face of the strong feeling of opposition existing at Camp Floyd against President Young.

Departure of the Army.—As long as the army remained in Utah, such conditions prevailed. In February, 1860, General Johnston departed from Camp Floyd to go to Washington. He went by way of California and the Isthmus of Panama. Shortly after, he was found leading an army of the South against an army of the North in the war of the Rebellion, endeavoring to destroy the Union. In the battle of Shiloh he was killed while commanding the Confederate forces. In 1861, Camp Floyd, then called Fort Crittenden, was abandoned.

Retirement of Governor Cumming.—Governor Cumming departed from Utah in May, 1861, a short time before his term of office expired, and returned to his old home in Georgia. His departure was much regretted, for he had served the people faithfully and well, discharging every obligation as he saw his duty, without fear or favor of men. The people certainly had good reason for regret, as his successors quite generally were men of a very different stamp.

The "Mormon" People and the Rebellion.—The loyalty of the Latter-day Saints to the United States had frequently been questioned by their enemies and those unacquainted with them. When the war of the Rebellion broke out, the Saints again manifested their loyalty to the Union. When the telegraph line across the continent was completed, in October, 1861, President Brigham Young was courteously tendered the privilege of sending the first message from Salt Lake City. It was to the president of the telegraph company, Mr. J. H. Wade, as follows:

"Sir: Permit me to congratulate you upon the completion of the Overland Telegraph Lines west to this city, to commend the energy displayed by yourself and associates in the rapid and successful prosecution of a work so beneficial; and to express the wish that its use may ever tend to promote the true interests of the dwellers upon both the Atlantic and Pacific slopes of our continent.

"Utah has not seceded, but is firm for the Constitution and laws of our once happy country, and is warmly interested in such useful enterprises as the one so far completed."

In making his reply, President Wade expressed gratitude to President Young, that his, the first message to pass over the line, "should express so unmistakably the patriotism and union-loving sentiments" of himself and people.

In April, 1862, President Lincoln requested President Brigham Young to raise a force of cavalry to guard the overland route, which was promptly done. Before the request came, the offer was made by President Young to protect that route.

Moreover, while many states were endeavoring to get out of the Union, the "Mormons" were petitioning Congress to get in. This privilege of state government was denied them. The denial was very largely due to the hostile attitude of the new officials, Governor

Stephen S. Harding, and two of the territorial judges, Charles B. Waite and Thomas J. Drake, who were decidedly unfriendly to the people of the territory.

Other reasons given were the general feeling of opposition to the faith of the Latter-day Saints—especially against the practice of plural marriage, and the belief, which still erroneously persisted, that they were disloyal. "An un-American condition of affairs was supposed to exist here," so writes Orson F. Whitney, "hostile to the Government and subversive of morality and civilization. Priestcraft, polygamy, and murder were thought to be the chief cornerstones of 'Mormonism.' A union of Church and State was alleged. It was charged that the 'Mormon' people were under the sway of an ecclesiastical despotism which overshadowed and controlled their opinions, actions, property, and lives, penetrating and supervising social and business circles, and requiring implicit obedience to the counsel of the Church, as a duty paramount to all the obligations of morality, society, allegiance and law."[a]

---

[a]Whitney's Popular "History of Utah," p. 183.

CHAPTER 46

A PERIOD OF STRIFE AND BITTERNESS
1862–1870

The "Anti-Bigamy Law."—Instead of granting statehood in answer to the petition of the people of Utah, Congress passed an "anti-bigamy law" in opposition to the practice of plural marriage. It was presented to the house of representatives by Justin R. Morrill of Vermont, but was instigated by Governor Harding and Judges Waite and Drake. The bill—the first of the kind to be placed on the statutes—was signed by President Lincoln, July 8, 1862. It defined plural marriage as bigamy, and made the contracting of such a marriage punishable by a fine of five hundred dollars and imprisonment for a term of five years. This law was considered by many leading attorneys and others not "Mormons," as being unconstitutional. It was not enforced, President Lincoln's policy being to let the "Mormons" alone. Among the features which helped to make it inoperative was the provision, aimed at the Church, forbidding religious bodies in territories to hold real estate in value to exceed fifty thousand dollars. An effort was made by Governor Harding, in 1863, to have Brigham Young punished under this law. He was taken before Judge Kinney and placed under bonds, but the grand jury failed to take action and the case was dropped.

Attempted Legislation Against the "Mormons."—The governor and two judges went even further in their desire to obtain legislation affecting the citizens of Utah. They entered into a conspiracy to have removed many powers vested in the local officers and place them under federal control. Among these changes they proposed that

Congress limit the powers of the county courts to the probating of wills, issuing titles of administration and guardianship; place in the hands of the United States marshal the power to summon jurors as he might think proper—a thing that would have proved very disadvantageous to the Saints—and give the governor full power to appoint all the officers of the militia, and designate the days when the companies should drill. When this proposed legislation was presented in Congress and it was learned who the authors were, it caused great indignation in Utah. A mass meeting was held and the guilty officials were asked to resign, which they refused to do. A petition was sent to Washington asking for their removal and for the appointment of "good men in their stead." A counter petition was sent from the companies of California volunteers, who were stationed at the time in the valley. While the people did not get all they asked for, the governor was removed and James Duane Doty, superintendent of Indian affairs in the territory, and a much better man, was chosen in his place.

The California Volunteers.—Very soon after the departure of Johnston's army, the people of Utah were inflicted with the presence of other troops. These were volunteers from California and Nevada, about seven hundred strong, who were detained in Salt Lake City, as they were on their way to the East to take part in the Civil War. They were under the command of Colonel (later General) Patrick Edward Connor, who greatly desired to take active part in the war. He was a man whose loyalty to the United States was of the highest order. When he was commanded to stay in Utah, he was exceedingly disappointed. Secretary of War Edward Stanton—who was extremely distrustful of the "Mormons"—stationed Colonel Connor at Salt Lake City ostensibly to guard the telegraph and mail route, but more particularly to watch the "Mormons." Connor established his headquarters on the foothills east of Salt Lake City, naming the place Camp Douglas, in honor of Stephen A. Douglas. He was extremely prejudiced against the Latter-day Saints, and lost no occasion to manifest his bitter feelings in public or in private, so obsessed was he that "no good thing could come out of Utah." Every word, every action of the "Mormons," was falsely interpreted; and provocation given by him to antagonize the leaders of the Church whom he considered to be disloyal.

The Union Vedette.—Under his direction an anti-"Mormon" paper edited by Captain Charles H. Hempstead was published at Camp Douglas and later in the city. It was called the *Union Vedette*, the mission of which was to fight "Mormonism." Connor also attempted to establish military rule instead of civil authority, thus depriving the citizens of their rights.

Mining in Utah.—To Patrick E. Connor is given credit for starting the mining industry in Utah. His motives, however, were not entirely commendable. If he is to be judged by his own words, his main purpose was not to "get gain" or to increase the circulation of the precious metals, but to cause an influx of "a large Gentile and loyal population sufficient by peaceful means and through the ballot-box to overwhelm the 'Mormons' by mere force of numbers, and thus wrest from the Church—disloyal and traitorous to the core—the absolute and tyrannical control of temporal and civil affairs."

He was acquainted with the fact that President Young had advised the Saints to develop the industries of agriculture and establish needful factories that they might be self-sustaining, and leave mining alone for later consideration. This advice was very wise, for in the days of pioneer life, and when the commonwealth was young, it was necessary that the people be able to support themselves. They could not live on gold and silver, but they could on the products of the soil; and they could keep warm from the spinning of wool and the manufacture of cloth out of which to make their clothing. The advice of President Young was the advice which governed the Pilgrims when they landed on the shores of America; but it seemed to be very distasteful and unpatriotic to men of little souls. All goods brought to the territory from abroad, before the advent of the railroad, had to be hauled by team upwards of a thousand miles, and with the constantly increasing population, all hands were needed to labor in producing what the people consumed. Even then, for a long time it was a difficult task, for several years were extremely lean due to the ravages of grasshoppers and crickets, and because of other obstacles unforeseen.

If the Saints had run off to develop mines, they would have sealed their own doom in the days of their pioneering. Moreover, the experience of the past, in 1849 and subsequently, when the California gold rush was on, taught them that the development of the mining industry would bring to the territory the riffraff and scum of humanity. This would mean the increase of crime and decrease of law and order.

Why the Latter-day Saints Settled in Utah.—The Latter-day Saints came to the valleys of the mountains primarily to worship the Lord and to keep his commandments; also to develop a peaceful commonwealth where others of their faith might be gathered to enjoy the fruits of their labors without molestation.

A PERIOD OF STRIFE 435

The False Attitude of General Connor.—The attitude of General Connor, and all who agreed with him, was basely false. Brigham Young was not opposed to the development of mines, but he was farsighted enough to understand—which many of his petty critics could not understand—that there were other duties more important and substantial, which held precedence, at least in the lives of the Latter-day Saints, in the development of the territory. It should be said to the credit of General Patrick E. Connor, who manifested so much bitterness in the early sixties, that after remaining in Utah for several years, his feelings towards the "Mormon" people greatly softened. When it did become possible for a ray of light and truth to penetrate his prejudice, he discovered that the Latter-day Saints were not such disloyal citizens after all.

Inspiration of Brigham Young.—President Brigham Young was a practical man by nature, but, aided by the inspiration of the Spirit of the Lord, his wisdom in the establishment of cities, villages, and industries, was far beyond his human possibilities. On many an occasion when the settlers of a selected site had chosen the low lands near the center of the valleys, he instructed them to move higher up near the foothills; and at times against their judgment settlers were advised to move to less favorable looking land than that which they had chosen. Time has proved that their leader was possessed of the inspiration which he was entitled to receive.

Home Industries.—From the very beginning of Utah's history, President Young taught the people the necessity of establishing home industries and becoming self-supporting. In these various ventures, he invariably took the lead. In the very earliest times, he advocated the cultivation of cotton in the "Dixie" land; the building of mills and factories; the harnessing of the mountain streams for power; and the development of the natural resources of the country which would be of material benefit to the people. His discourses were not confined to spiritual themes, but were ofttimes devoted to the building of roads and fences, the cultivation of the soil, the planting of vineyards and orchards, the raising of sheep and cattle, and all other useful things which would tend to encourage the members of the Church in obtaining temporal blessings, that they might live in comfort and prosperity. Had the people always followed his advice, it would have been better for them.

Plotters Against the Peace.—Due to the malicious activities of many territorial officials, and the constant desire on the part of others not of the Church who came to Utah, to "civilize" and "reform" the Latter-day Saints, feelings of unfriendliness existed between members of the Church and "outsiders." The continued attacks made by General Connor and Captain Hempstead, the editor of the *Union Vedette,* upon the Church and its authorities, had a tendency to increase this feeling. During, and after the close of the Civil War, Utah was infested with a set of characters who seemed determined to make trouble. The "Gentile" population at that time was about three hundred, the majority of whom were honorable citizens, but among them were to be found many bitter enemies of the Church, bent upon its destruction. Some of the latter had gone into business hoping to receive the patronage of the Latter-day Saints, but at the same time they were plotting against the Church, which they bitterly hated.

The Killing of Brassfield.—To add to the unfortunate condition which divided the people, there occurred in Salt Lake City, in 1866, two shocking murders. The first of these was the killing of S. Newton Brassfield, a freighter, who came to Utah from Nevada. He induced a plural wife to forsake her husband while the husband was in the mission field. Brassfield then married the woman, the ceremony being performed by Judge Solomon P. McCurdy of the supreme court of Utah. It was stated on good authority that Brassfield had deserted his wife and family before he came to Utah. This charge was denied by some of his defenders but strongly affirmed by individuals who claimed to speak from personal knowledge. One evening in April, as he was entering his boarding house, he was shot and killed by some person who made his escape in the dark and was never discovered.

The Robinson Murder.—The second killing was that of Dr. J. King Robinson, who was decoyed from his home, one night in October, under the pretext that his professional services were needed. A short distance from his home he was set upon by a band of ruffians and severely beaten and then killed. The motive for the crime remains a mystery. Dr. Robinson had been in controversy with the city corporation over property, but the matter had been settled by the supreme court of Utah in favor of the city and could not have been the basis for the murder. It is presumed by some that his assailants did not intend to take his life, but merely administer to him a severe beating for some personal or fancied wrong; but being recognized, they determined on killing him for their protection.

According to the custom of the times, the attempt was made to fasten the responsibility for these murders upon the authorities of the Church. Such accusations were openly made by prominent attorneys at the investigation of the Robinson murder. Naturally

A PERIOD OF STRIFE 437

President Young was indignant, and challenged his traducers to produce their proof. He was ready to go to court, be examined, and have the most thorough investigation made that the country could furnish. He denounced the crime as on a par with the killing of Joseph and Hyrum Smith, the Haun's Mill massacre and the tragedy at Mountain Meadows. Rewards were offered for the arrest, by the city, the county, and by private subscription, amounting to the sum of nine thousand dollars. President Young headed the list with five hundred dollars. When the effort failed to connect the authorities of the Church with the crime, the ardor of some who had been most insistent that the guilty parties be punished, cooled considerably and they lost interest in the case.

General Sherman to Brigham Young.—Following the Brassfield killing, reports were sent out through the country blaming the homicide on the "Mormon" people. General William T. Sherman, then stationed at St. Louis, wired President Brigham Young stating that "responsible officers" had informed him that four "Gentiles" had been murdered by "Mormons." As Utah was under his military jurisdiction, he declared that he was bound to give protection to all citizens and murderers must be punished and wrongs avenged, if "committed against any American citizen even in remote Utah."

President Young's Answer.—In replying to General Sherman's telegram, President Young thanked him for the opportunity of presenting the facts. He said, dispatches sent from Utah to the East were not reliable; there had been no such assassinations as the General had been led to believe. "On May 17, a soldier shot a gentleman named Mayfield, and a Mr. Brassfield came home and seduced a "Mormon's" wife, and was shot on the street by some unknown person; but neither I nor the community at large knew any more about it than an inhabitant of St. Louis. Citizens who are not of our faith do not suffer from intimidation here. In no other communities could men pursue the course many do here without experiencing the vengeance of a vigilance committee." President Young closed his telegram as follows: "There are a few speculators here who are anxious to make it appear that American citizens' lives are in danger through religious fanaticism, hoping thereby to have troops sent here to make money out of contracts. Gentiles' lives are as safe here as 'Mormons' and acts of violence occur more rarely in this city than any other of its size in any of the new States or Territories."

Citizens of Utah to General Sherman.—Another telegram was sent by prominent "Gentile" citizens of Utah, confirming the telegram of President Young. Among the signers were some of the leading business men and officers from Camp Douglas. General Sherman replied to President Young as follows: "Sir:—Your dispatch is received and I am much gratified at its substance and spirit."

A Proposed "Gentile" Exodus.—Due to the bitterness existing in Utah, President Young counseled the "Mormon" people not to patronize business institutions which were run by the enemies of the people. This was as a matter of self-defense and preservation. The result of this counsel was that a communication from "Gentile" merchants and addressed to the Church authorities, was received in which they agreed to leave the territory on certain conditions. Their conditions were as follows: The Church would guarantee the payment of their outstanding accounts owing to them by the members of the Church, and the purchase of their merchandise, chattels, houses, improvements, etc., at a cash valuation, after a deduction of twenty-five per cent had been made from the total amount. "To the fulfilment of the above," said they, "we hold ourselves ready at any time, to enter into negotiations, and on final arrangement being made and terms of sale complied with, we shall freely leave the Territory."

President Young Answers the Merchants.—In a signed communication dated Dec. 21, 1866, President Young declined to entertain their offer. He kindly pointed out to them that if they could secure such sales, they would make more money than merchants had ever made before, and perhaps "Mormon" merchants would like to sell out on the same kind of terms. They were at liberty to remain or go, just as they pleased; no intimidation or coercion had been used in the community to have them stop trading with any class, and no man had been ostracized because he was not of the "Mormon" faith. Every man who had dealt fairly and honestly, and confined his attention to his legitimate business, whatever his creed, had found friendship among the Latter-day Saints. "To be adverse to Gentiles, or Jews, because they are Jews," said President Young, "is in direct opposition to the genius of our religion. It matters not what a man's creed is * * * he will receive kindness and friendship from us, and we have not the least objection to doing business with him; if in his dealings he acts in accordance with the principles of right and deports himself as a good, law-abiding citizen should."

Attention was called to the fact that there were those doing business in the territory who for years had been the avowed enemies of the community. The disrupture and overthrow of the Church had been the object of their labors. "Missionaries of evil, there have been no arts too base, no stratagems too vile for them to use to bring about their nefarious ends," said Brigham Young. While soliciting the patronage of the people, from whom they drew their support, they had used their means thus derived "in the most shameless and abandoned manner," to destroy the very people whose favor they found it to their interest to court. They had "fostered vice and vicious institutions to oppose the unanimously expressed will of the people, to increase disorder, and to change the city from a condition of peace and quietude to lawless anarchy." The question was asked what claims such persons could have upon the patronage of the community, and what community on the earth "would be so besotted as to uphold and foster men whose aim is to destroy them." In closing his epistle, President Young declared: "It is to oppose these men whom I have described, and to these alone that I am opposed, and I am determined to use my influence to have the citizens here stop dealing with them and deal with honorable men."

Two days later in a discourse before the Saints, President Young said: "We advise you to pass by the shops and stores of your enemies and let them alone, but give your means into the hands of men who are honest men, honorable men, and upright men—men who will deal justly and truly with all. Shall we deal with the Jew? Yes. With those who call themselves Gentile? Certainly. We calculate to continue to deal with them."[a]

Building of the Tabernacle.—In 1867 the Salt Lake Tabernacle which was begun in 1863, was completed. It is one of the most remarkable buildings in the world. The building is elliptical in shape and is one hundred and fifty feet wide and two hundred and fifty feet in length. The roof is a self-supporting wooden structure, which was originally fastened together without nails, wooden pins and

---

[a]The Gentile merchants were scarcely complimentary to the intelligence of President Young when they made this proposition to withdraw from the Territory on the conditions named by them. If the Gentile claim that there was utter incompatibility between Mormon and non-Mormon in Utah could have been emphasized by a spectacular exodus of Gentile merchants from Utah, however brought about, it doubtless would have given occasion for another Utah expedition to the Territory of such other military display as would have inured to the benefit of speculators, contractors, and merchants, or to the long-hoped-for further prescription of the Latter-day Saints. Surely the Gentile merchants should have known if their action had such motive as this, that Brigham Young would have detected it; and if not, if their proposed exodus was honest and meant only that they intended to withdraw from an unpleasant situation, to end merely in their personal advantage, then they should have known that Brigham Young would know that the people of the United States would read into the facts of the exodus all the evidence they would need of the alleged incompatibility, to justify, from their viewpoint, all the coercive measures against the Mormon community for which their enemies were clamoring. Brigham Young could not fail to apprehend the danger, and accordingly avoid it. ("History of the Mormon Church," Ch. 106, p. 464, B. H. Roberts.)

rawhide being used in lieu thereof. It rests upon buttresses of red sandstone set about twelve feet apart. The acoustic powers are marvelous. The building also contains a pipe organ which was the largest in the world, when built. The organ was originally the work of Joseph Ridges, of Salt Lake City, and was made out of native timber. Since the time of its construction it has been remodeled and kept in constant repair.

The October Conference 1867.—The October Conference of the Church in 1867, was held in the new Tabernacle which was nearing completion. On this occasion one hundred and sixty-three persons were called to go and strengthen the settlements in southern Utah, and the Saints were called on to assist in the gathering of the poor from Great Britain and other foreign lands. Elder Joseph F. Smith, son of Patriarch Hyrum Smith, was called to fill a vacancy in the council of the twelve, caused by the apostasy of Amasa M. Lyman.

The Deseret Telegraph.—At a special conference of the Church held April 10, 1865, it was agreed to build a telegraph line throughout the settlements in Utah. The members of the Church were called upon to assist in this worthy undertaking. Between the years 1865 and 1867, five hundred miles of line were constructed at a cost of one hundred and fifty dollars per mile. This placed the principal settlements of the territory in ready communication with Salt Lake City. Towns in Idaho and Nevada were also reached. By means of this telegraph line, the authorities of the Church— for it was a Church enterprise—were able to facilitate their business and save many miles of weary travel and great expense, in the forwarding of instructions to the people. This line remained under the control of the Church until 1900, when it was merged into the Western Union System.

George A. Smith

Death of President Heber C. Kimball.—President Heber C. Kimball, first counselor to President Brigham Young, died in Salt Lake City, June 22, 1868. He was one of the original members called into the council of the twelve, and the "father" of the British Mission. President Kimball was greatly blessed with the spirit of prophecy; was bold and fearless, and never faltered in his integrity to the truth.

At the general conference in October, George A. Smith of the council of the twelve, and cousin of the Prophet Joseph and Patriarch Hyrum Smith, was chosen and sustained to fill the vacancy in the First Presidency. Brigham Young, Jr., was sustained as one of the apostles, succeeding Elder Smith in that body.

The Coming of the Railroad.—Another great change in Utah was brought to pass in the completion of the trans-continental railway. The railroad, together with the telegraph which spanned the country from sea to sea, brought the people of the territory in closer communication with the outside world. Isolation of the people of the Great Basin was now a thing of the past. Under the direction of President Young, much of the grading, especially from Echo Canyon to Ogden, the most difficult part of the way, was done by members of the Church. The last spike uniting the East and West with bands of steel, was driven at the junction of the two roads—the Central Pacific and the Union Pacific—at Promontory, Utah, May 10, 1869. There was assembled on that occasion a great concourse of people, numbering eleven hundred souls. The officials of both roads, and many leading men, including newspaper representatives from all parts of the country, had come by train from East and West to witness this wonderful epoch in our American history.

The Utah Local Lines.—The trans-continental railways passed through Ogden. When it was contemplated that Salt Lake City would not be on the line, President Young remarked: "If the company which first arrives should deem it to their advantage to leave us out in the cold, we will not be so far off, but we can have a branch line for the advantage of this city." The same day that the Union Pacific road finished laying rails in Ogden there was organized in Salt Lake City, the Utah Central Railway. This road and subsequently other local roads in Utah, were promoted by President Young and other members of the Church. In May, 1869, ground was broken, President Young removing the first earth, and the last spike on this road between Salt Lake City and Ogden was driven January 10, 1870. The Utah Central Railway connected Salt Lake City with the outside world, and proved to all people, that there was no desire on the part of the Latter-day Saints to be exclusive and isolated from their fellowmen. No longer were immigrants to come by handcart and ox-team.

Proposed Anti-"Mormon" Legislation.—The unfavorable attitude of certain merchants and others toward the Church naturally resulted in a movement for self-protection. The coming of the railroad was looked upon by the enemies of the Latter-day Saints as a means by which the "redemption" of the territory from "Mormon" dominion was to be brought to pass. They declared with a feeling of delight that when Utah was connected with the outside world by rail, there would come such an influx of "Gentiles" that the "Mormon" population would be overwhelmed. There were many open threats, and that too, by officials, that when that time should come there would be instituted a crusade against the members of the Church to deprive them of their liberties. The Saints were wrongfully accused of being opposed to the coming of the railroad because they feared such a result. The fact, however, was that President Young and the presiding brethren did all in their power to have the road pass through Salt Lake City rather than Ogden. Mass meetings were held and every endeavor made to accomplish this purpose, and when it failed, President Young headed a movement, as stated, to make connection by building a railroad from Salt Lake City to Ogden.

The Wade and Cragin Bills.—Nor did these individuals who opposed the Church wait for the coming of the railroad to commence their determined effort to deprive the people of their inherent rights. Appeals were made to Congress, and bills, having their origin within the territory, were presented intended to curtail the liberties of the people. In 1866 a measure was presented, known as the Wade Bill, providing for the destruction of local government in the territory. This was followed by the Cragin Bill in 1869, following the same lines, but still more drastic. The intent of these measures was to place in the hands of the governor the sole power to appoint and commission all the local officers in the territory, and remove the people from a voice in government. All juries, grand and petit, were to be selected by the United States marshal. For a "Mormon" minister to solemnize a marriage was to be a criminal act, the property of the Church, excepting twenty thousand dollars, was to be taxed, and the Church be denied from making rules and regulations respecting fellowship of its members. The governor of the territory was to become the financial head of the Church, though not a member, and the trustee-in-trust, under heavy penalty of fine and imprisonment, was required to make full and complete and annual reports to that individual accounting for "all Church properties, moneys in banks, notes, deposits with the Church," etc. All this, and more, was contemplated in free America where "life, liberty and the pursuit of happiness" are guaranteed as inalienable rights.

The Cullom Bill.—A few days later another bill just as radical in its features was presented in Congress by Shelby M. Cullom, of Illinois, and was substituted for the Cragin Bill by consent of Mr. Cragin. This measure was prepared by Robert N. Baskin of Salt Lake City, one of the most bitter and inconsiderate enemies ever arrayed against the Church. Fortunately for the Latter-day Saints, none of these measures were at the time enacted into law.

Co-operation for Defense.—The attitude of local anti-"Mormons," coupled with the proposed unfavorable and inhuman legislation, naturally drove the members of the Church closer together. It was proposed in self-protection that there be organized throughout the various settlements a chain of co-operative stores, and that the people trade with each other rather than with their enemies. And if the proposed threats were to be fulfilled, the enemies of the Church who came to Utah to do business would have to bring their customers with them, for the Saints would not patronize them. Based upon this proposition a parent institution was established in Salt Lake City, in which all the "Mormon" people were invited to take stock. This commercial house, known as Zion's Co-operative Mercantile Institution, opened its doors for business in 1869, and the following year was incorporated. In a circular announcing their intentions it was stated by the brethren that they were "convinced of the impolicy of leaving the trade and commerce of the territory to the conduct of strangers," and therefore "it was advisable that the people of Utah should become their own merchants" and "unite in a system of co-operation for the transaction of their own business." In this way there could be a consolidation of the mercantile stores in which all the people might be interested, and receive their merchandise based on a small margin of profit. Branches were established in nearly every settlement and were beneficial to the people while that condition lasted.

A Change of Feeling.—Fortunately there has been a change of feeling in the land and the necessity for such a movement has departed. However, while the full object of the co-operative movement was not accomplished it was a factor for the leveling of prices and the destruction of what has been spoken of so commonly in later years—the "profiteer." Before the advent of this great institution there were merchants in the land who endeavored from time to time to "corner the market" on certain necessities, and then charge exorbitant prices for their goods. This, of course, could not be accomplished when a large institution, established in the interests of the people, endeavored to protect their interests. The principle of co-operation, no matter where applied, is right, and should be encouraged; but many of these local institutions passed out of existence through the lack of interest on the part of many of the people who disposed of their stock to other and more enterprising individuals, until the system was destroyed.[b]

Protest of "Mormon" Women Against Legislation.—Early in January, 1870, a number of meetings were held by the women in various communities in protest against the pending legislation (the Cragin and Cullom bills) in Congress affecting "Mormonism." On the 13th of the month a mass meeting of several thousand "Mormon" women was held in the tabernacle. Great enthusiasm pervaded the gathering. While they opposed all the features of the anti-"Mormon" legislation, their action was principally in protest against the measures, and the remarks of would-be reformers, in which the women of the Church were spoken of as being "down-trodden" and "degraded" by their husband-oppressors. Sarah M. Kimball, president of the Relief Society of the Fifteenth Ward, presided at the meeting. Stating the object of the gathering she said: "We are not here to advocate woman's rights, but man's rights. The bill in question would not only deprive our fathers, husbands and brothers of the privilege bequeathed to citizens of the United States, but it would also deprive us, as women, of the privilege of selecting our husbands, and against this we unqualifiedly protest." Similar remarks of protest were made by several prominent women and a set of resolutions were unanimously and enthusiastically adopted; among them the following:

"Resolved, That we, the ladies of Salt Lake City, in mass-meeting assembled, do manifest our indignation, and protest against the bill before Congress, known as 'the Cullom Bill,' also the one known as 'the Cragin Bill,' and all similar bills, expressions and manifestoes.

"Resolved, That we consider the above named bills foul blots on our national escutcheon—absurd documents—atrocious insults to the honorable executive of the United States Government, and malicious attempts to subvert the right of civil and religious liberty. * * *

"Resolved, That we acknowledge the institutions of the Church of Jesus Christ of Latter-day Saints as the only reliable safeguard of female virtue and innocence; and the only sure protection against the fearful sin of prostitution, and its attendant evils, now prevalent

---

[b]As early as 1864 a co-operative movement was inaugurated in Brigham City by Elder Lorenzo Snow. It was attended with success and grew into a flourishing institution which existed for a number of years. Other ventures preceding the establishment of Z. C. M. I.—as the great parent institution is generally called—were established at Lehi, American Fork and other towns, in 1868.

A PERIOD OF STRIFE

abroad, and as such, we are and shall be united with our brethren in sustaining them against each and every encroachment."

Many other meetings of this nature were held in other settlements in protest against the passage of these bills, which caused great surprise and astonishment throughout the nation.

Woman Suffrage.—According to the doctrines of the Church, woman has always been granted the privilege of a voice in the affairs of the organization. All matters of importance as well as the sustaining of the various officers, are regularly presented to the membership—women and men alike—for their suffrage, or vote. The Church gave to its women the first exclusively woman's organization in all the world; and it was representatives of this organization in mass-meeting assembled who entered their vigorous protest against the pending legislation which was intended to affect them seriously in their lives.

Within about one month from the time of this meeting of protest, the legislature of Utah passed an act granting to the women of the territory the right of franchise which became a law by the approval of Acting Governor S. A. Mann. Such privileges granted to the women had previously been proposed by those opposed to "Mormonism," who thought that the women were oppressed, and this would be a means of redeeming them from "the galling yoke" under which they were "oppressed."

"The New Movement."—In the fall of 1869 a number of prominent elders were excommunicated for apostasy, by the high council of the Salt Lake Stake. Among the number were William S. Godbe, Elias L. T. Harrison, Eli B. Kelsey, and later Henry W. Lawrence, Thomas B. H. Stenhouse and others. Mr. Godbe was a merchant, and a prominent member of one of the quorums of Seventy as was also Mr. Harrison, whose business was that of an architect. Eli B. Kelsey had performed good and faithful service in the mission field abroad, until through immoral transgression he lost the spirit of the work. These men had become disaffected for various causes and now opposed many of the policies of President Young. They accused him of trying to set up in the Church a "Young dynasty," and of being guilty of "one man power," and they rebelled against his teaching regarding the opening of the mines and the establishment of mercantile institutions. Mr. Harrison, a gifted writer, had been editing the *Utah Magazine* which now became the organ of the disaffected brethren. These men still claimed to believe in much of "Mormonism" but centered their attack on President Young, publishing articles reflecting upon him by comparison and innuendo. At first they declared they would set up an organization of their own—a new church—retaining all the good features of "Mormonism" and discarding all that were bad. A presiding officer and apostles were to be chosen, and the Church was to be "redeemed" from the sad condition into which these disaffected persons claimed it had fallen. This attempt at "reformation" is known in history as "the New Movement," or the "Godbeite Movement," because of the prominent part William S. Godbe played in it; but they called it "The Church of Zion." For a time they held meetings in the Thirteenth Ward, by permission of President Young; but the organization which was without a head, and as Elder Whitney says, "with very little body," soon passed away.

Organization of the Liberal Party.—Desiring some organization in which "Mormonism" might be opposed, these excommunicated members joined with the anti-"Mormons" of the territory in the formation of a political party, the object of which was to fight the Church. "The Liberal Political Party," as it was called, was organized in February 1870. From that time forth until the organization was dissolved in the nineties, it carried on an unscrupulous warfare against the Church. Those who controlled its destiny were guilty of the most bitter and relentless actions that could be imagined. Misrepresentation, falsehood and deceit were the chief weapons of attack; and by such methods the name of the Church was maligned and its officers placed in a false light before the world. The history of this political organization is almost without a parallel, at least nothing like it has ever occurred elsewhere in free republican America; only as it has been produced by those opposed to the Church of Jesus Christ of Latter-day Saints in these valleys of the mountains. Nothing like it would be tolerated anywhere else in all the world.

The Salt Lake Tribune.—In January, 1870, the "Godbeites" commenced publishing a paper which they called the *Mormon Tribune;* it was the *Utah Magazine*, transformed, and was published in the interest of their movement. Dropping the word "Mormon" it became the organ of the Liberal Party, and the following year passed into other hands more vicious. "Its only principle, apparently, was hatred of everything Mormon," writes Historian Whitney, "in pursuance of which it spared neither age, sex nor condition; emptying the vials of its venom upon all who dared to differ from it, misrepresenting their motives, assailing their characters, and libeling and lampooning both the living and the dead. Its columns were not only filled habitually with falsehood, but often with vulgar and obscene scandals.

Many who helped to sustain the paper either from sympathy with its assaults upon Mormonism, or from fear of being abused by it and called 'Jack-Mormons' if they withheld their support, were careful to have it delivered at their down-town offices, and would not have it in their homes for their wives and daughters to read, so filthy at times were its contents. The *Nauvoo Expositor* was holy writ compared with the *Salt Lake Tribune*."[c] It had been justly said of this sheet that it was "brought into the world to lie and was true to its mission."

---

[c]History of Utah, Vol. 2:380-1.

CHAPTER 47

THE MISSION OF GOVERNOR SHAFFER AND JUDGE McKEAN
1870–1877

Governor Shaffer.—Following the removal of Governor Harding in 1863, Utah was blessed for a time with the presence of governors who were inclined to attend to the duties of their office without much interference with "Mormonism." Governors James Duane Doty and Charles Durkee had held the office and S. H. Mann, secretary of the territory, served as acting governor following the resignation of Governor Durkee in 1869, until the appointee of President Ulysses S. Grant arrived in the territory in the spring of 1870. This was J. Wilson Shaffer of Illinois, who proved to be the most bitter and bigoted anti-"Mormon" governor Utah ever had. He was in his forty-third year when he came to Utah, and was suffering from consumption, contracted while serving in the Civil War. He was a man of determined will, and evidently was sincere in his conviction that the "Mormons" were more than "rebels," who needed the drastic treatment which by some was considered proper and necessary treatment for the South, during the days of reconstruction. He came to Utah with a bias against the Latter-day Saints which nothing short of a miracle could remove. "Never after me, by ——," said he, "shall it be said Brigham Young is governor of Utah." In this expression he displayed his ignorance of the conditions in Utah—a mistake made by many others—that because the Latter-day Saints hearkened to the counsels of President Young who, as their inspired leader, directed them as members of the Church, he was usurping the prerogatives of the executive. If these men had been broad enough they might have seen that President Young respected the civil authority at all times, even when sorely abused and tried by the petty acts of presumptuous and bigoted officials, who did all in their power to annoy and humiliate him before the people.

Removal of Secretary Mann and Judge Wilson.—The anger of Governor Shaffer was kindled against Secretary Mann because he, as acting governor, signed the woman suffrage bill and endeavored to show some just consideration for the majority of the people. Likewise he displayed feelings of resentment against Chief Justice Charles A. Wilson because he would not subvert the law in favor of the anti-"Mormon" "ring" to the disadvantage of the people. Wilson was accused of exercising too much leniency towards the "Mormons," so he, like Secretary Mann, was removed through the influence of the governor.

The Coming of Judge McKean.—To succeed the deposed officials, Vernon H. Vaughan was sent to Utah as secretary of the territory and Judge James B. McKean to be chief justice. O. F. Strickland and C. M. Hawley were also appointed associate justices to fill vacancies which existed. Judge McKean, like Governor Shaffer, was a relentless anti-"Mormon," bigoted and narrow. He came to Utah with a "mission," said he, "as high above my mere duty as a judge, as the heaven is above the earth." That "mission" was the overthrow of "Mormonism." However, Judge McKean is gone, and "Mormonism" still survives and prospers.

Influence of Schuyler Colfax and Rev. Newman.—The appointment of these bigoted and narrow-souled officials was largely due to the influence of Vice-President Schuyler Colfax and Rev. John P. Newman. The former had visited Utah on two occasions; first in 1865, when he was speaker of the house of representatives, and again in 1869, when he was holding the office of vice-president in the administration of U. S. Grant. He was associated with an organized "ring" of anti-"Mormon" agitators and politicians, who were bent on the destruction of "Mormon" dominion in Utah. On each visit he had shown marked opposition to the Church. Rev. Newman was President Grant's minister, and was also chaplain of the United States Senate.

Governor Shaffer and the Militia.—By act of the Utah Legislature in 1852, the militia, under the title of the "Nauvoo Legion," met in annual muster. In keeping with the law, Lieutenant General Daniel H. Wells issued an order August 16, 1870, calling for a three days' muster, for the purpose of inspection, drill and camp duty. Governor

Shaffer was absent from the territory at the time, but as soon as he returned he issued a counter order forbidding any muster, or drill, or gathering of any military organization within the territory, except upon his orders. He also illegally appointed Patrick E. Connor major general of the militia, and William N. Johns, colonel and assistant adjutant general, and directed that all arms and munitions belonging to the territory, or to the United States, then in possession of the militia, be delivered to Colonel Johns, without delay. Through misrepresentation, the government had sent troops to Utah to act as "a moral force" in protecting Gentiles and apostates. The action of the governor practically destroyed the militia, and by aid of the government troops, he endeavored to establish a military power to intimidate the Latter-day Saints, and lessen the power of the "Mormon" leaders.

Request of General Wells.—Against this high-handed outrage, General Wells wrote, requesting the governor to suspend his order until the 20th of November to enable Adjutant General Hiram B. Clawson to make a complete report according to law, of the condition of the militia. Governor Shaffer answered General Wells, October 27, 1870, in an insulting letter denying the request. General Wells answered this attack in an open letter which was published in the *Deseret News*.

The Provo Riot.—The governor's attitude in disregarding all local civil law and authority, bore bitter fruit. The peace officers were rendered helpless in the performance of their duties, and the rabid part of the community manifested a spirit of contempt and defiance for the law. The city ordinances were broken with impunity, and the violators were protected by the governor and judges. The spirit prevailed among a certain class that the "Mormons" had ruled in Utah long enough and it was stated that the authorities at Washington were to make a change. There was to be a revolution and the minority was to assume the reins of government.

One week after the governor's proclamation disarming the militia, a mob of about forty United States soldiers, who were stationed at Fort Rawlins, near Provo, made a raid on that town. Late at night, September 22, they went to the home of Alderman William Miller, fired several shots into the building, smashed in the doors and windows, and took Miller a prisoner. Similar rioting occurred at the homes of Alderman Elijah F. Sheets and Councilor A. F. McDonald. The home of the latter was ransacked and his substance scattered in the yard and street. The doors and windows of the co-operative store, and those of the meetinghouse, were broken, and the rioters attempted to burn the latter building. Armed with needle guns they captured a number of citizens and paraded them through the streets prodding them with their bayonets. The reason for this deed was that the citizens of Provo had refused to sell liquor to the troops.

Governor Shaffer's Letter to General De Trobriand.—Several days after the riot occurred Governor Shaffer wrote to General De Trobriand, commander at Camp Douglas, censuring him for the outrage and trying to place upon his shoulders the responsibility for the raid, for which he was in no wise responsible. His command and that at Fort Rawlins, were separate and distinct units. The general answered the governor's letter—which was evidently written for political effect and to injure the commander because he had shown some kindness to the "Mormon" people--with some sharpness, showing that the governor and not the general had been derelict of duty. If the governor expected to profit by his communication, which was evidently the case for he gave it to the press before the general received it, very little benefit was derived from it.

The Rioters Punished.—The commander at Fort Rawlins, Major Osborne, as well as General De Trobriand, greatly regretted the unfortunate and unprovoked attack made by the soldiers. The matter was taken up in a proper way by the military department of the Platte, and the guilty parties were duly punished.

Death of Governor Shaffer.—Monday, October 31, 1870, Governor J. Wilson Shaffer died in Salt Lake City. He came to Utah in March and had served as governor about seven months, but during that time had shown extreme bitterness against the majority of the people in all his official acts. The day of his death a dispatch came from Washington appointing Vernon H. Vaughan, the territorial secretary, to succeed him, who in turn was succeeded by George A. Black, as secretary. Mr. Black had been Governor Shaffer's private secretary.

"The Wooden Gun Rebellion."—In November, 1870, at the regular time for the military musters, which had been prohibited by Governor Shaffer, about one hundred men assembled on the Twentieth Ward Square, many of them carrying wooden guns. Governor Vaughan was absent at the time and Secretary Black was acting governor. He had eight of the men, viz. Andrew Burt, Charles R. Savage, William G. Phillips, James Fennemore, Charles Livingston, George M. Ottinger, Archibald Livingston and John C. Graham, arrested. They were taken before Judge Hawley who bound them over to await the action of the grand jury on the ground that it appeared that probably they had committed a crime in disregarding Governor Shaffer's order. They were placed under heavy bonds, and as they refused to give bail, were given over to the military authorities at Camp Douglas.

They were kindly treated by the officers and both "Mormon" and non-"Mormon" merchants looked after their wants, furnishing them with many delicacies while they remained prisoners. The grand jury, when it met, refused to indict them, and they were released. This incident became popularly known as "The Wooden Gun Rebellion."

The Return of Martin Harris.—August 30, 1870, Martin Harris, one of the three witnesses to the Book of Mormon, arrived in Salt Lake City. He had been absent from the Church since the days of Kirtland; but had never during all those years denied his testimony. He now came back humbly to the Church, and was baptized by Elder Edward Stevenson and confirmed by Elder Orson Pratt. He died at Clarkston, Cache County, July 10, 1875, when nearly ninety-three years of age. A few hours before his death he discoursed on the Book of Mormon and reiterated the truth of the visit of the angel and bore testimony to the divine origin of the Book of Mormon.

The Pratt-Newman Discussion.—During the consideration of the Cullom Bill by Congress, Rev. John P. Newman, pastor of the Metropolitan Methodist Church in Washington, and chaplain of the senate, delivered a number of lectures trying to prove that "God's law condemns the union in marriage of more than two persons." His lectures were published in the *New York Herald*, and replies were made to them by Elder Orson Pratt. It was suggested by Edward L. Sloan, acting editor of the *Salt Lake Daily Telegraph*, a paper owned by "Gentile" interests, that the reverend gentleman was wasting his ammunition by preaching against plural marriage in Washington. It would be better for him to come to Utah where the question was a live issue, and discuss the issue with Orson Pratt, or some other "Mormon" elder. Mr. Newman, construing this as a challenge from President Brigham Young, came to Utah in the summer of 1870, armed cap-a-pie and with banners flying. He immediately informed President Young that he was here to accept his challenge to discuss the plural marriage question. President Young advised him that he had issued no such challenge. After the exchange of a number of spirited letters the reverend doctor issued a challenge to President Young to discuss the question, "Does the Bible Sanction Polygamy?"

It was evidently notoriety and worldly applause Mr. Newman was seeking, and he was quite surprised and disappointed when President Young, in accepting the challenge, appointed Orson Pratt or John Taylor, whichever Mr. Newman might prefer, to take his place in the discussion. He came to meet the chief and not a subordinate. Nevertheless, after some parleying the debate was held,

Elder Orson Pratt taking the affirmative of the question. The discussion began August 12, 1870, at 2 p.m. and continued during the two following days. Moderators were chosen, but the merits of the discussion were left to the public to decide. The press of the country took up the discussion, after the debate was over; the consensus of opinion throughout the land was that Elder Pratt had proved too skilful for Dr. Newman.

Comments of the Press.—The Washington correspondent of the New York *Sun* stated that the reverend doctor was "out of his depth" in the discussion, and that it was "plain that the apostle carried too many guns for the chaplain of the Senate." The Boston *Banner of Light* declared that "The Dr. Newman, who went forth from Washington to Salt Lake City to take Mormonism by storm by flourishing his Orthodox Bible in its face, has had to come away after a pretty severe tilt with one of the leading elders, leaving his Bible behind him. Elder Pratt took his Bible out of his hands and opened it again and again to pages that taught and upheld the polygamy doctrine, reading off whole volleys of historical texts that went to establish the leading Bible characters, esteemed Saints by Orthodoxy, as regular Mormons. Dr. Newman crawfished amazingly on this part of the argument and was at last rather glad to abandon it to his Mormon opponent." Other papers declared that force alone could settle the "Mormon Question."

Usurpation of Authority.—What the anti-"Mormon" political "ring" failed to accomplish by congressional enactment, they assumed to obtain through the actions of the governor and the judges. Judge McKean and his colleagues ignored the territorial laws enacted in 1852, which were still on the statutes, and denied to the probate courts all jurisdiction except in matters of probate. Likewise the duties of the territorial marshal and the territorial attorney general had been taken from them and placed in the hands of the United States marshal and the United States attorney. This, however, was done before the coming of McKean, but he and his associates confirmed that action. The result of these illegal proceedings was packed juries, absurd and contradictory rulings, the law becoming a mockery and justice a travesty.

The Engelbrecht Case.—August 27, 1870, three days before the arrival of Chief Justice McKean, an incident occurred in Salt Lake City which was ultimately to have much to do with the overthrow of his tyrannical and fanatical power. This was the legal abatement by the police of a liquor establishment conducted by Paul Engelbrecht, Christian Rehmke and Frederick Lutz. These men had been repeatedly fined for infraction of the law; but on each occasion had appealed their case on the ground that the city had no jurisdiction in the case. Expecting protection from the district courts, which they had ample reason to believe would be given, the firm continued to do an illegal liquor business without a city license. On the date mentioned, the police emptied all the liquor into the ditch and destroyed all the vessels that were used in its sale.

For this action suit was brought against the officers on complaint of Mr. Engelbrecht, and they were placed under bonds to await the action of the grand jury on a criminal charge.

An Illegal Jury.—Judge Strickland ordered the grand jurors for that term of court selected by the United States marshal upon a writ of open venire, when the law provided that the county clerk in the presence of other officials should select them by lot. The attorneys for the city officers challenged the proceedings and filed a motion to that effect. Judge Strickland ruled that the third district court was a United States court and subject to the acts of Congress, and not the laws of the territory, the challenge was overruled and the jurors accepted. The accused men were indicted and then convicted for "a wilful and malicious destruction of property," and were ordered to pay damages in the sum of $59,063.25, which was three times the price of the property destroyed. The supreme court of Utah affirmed the decision and an appeal was taken to the supreme court of the United States. Of this action we will speak later.

Indictment Against President Young.—When these perverters of the law had things arranged to their liking they prepared to conduct a crusade against the Church. President Young was indicted by this hand-picked grand jury for "lewd and lascivious cohabitation." He was later admitted to bail by Judge McKean in the sum of five thousand dollars.

"A System on Trial."—Arguments were made before the court to quash the indictment, which consumed several days, but Judge McKean rendered a decision in which he said:

"Let the counsel on both sides, and the court also keep constantly in mind the uncommon character of this case. The supreme court of California has well said, 'Courts are bound to take notice of the political and social conditions of the country they judicially rule.' It is therefore proper to say, that while the case at bar is called 'the People versus Brigham Young,' its other and real title is 'Federal Authority versus Polygamic Theocracy.' The government of the United States, founded upon a written Constitution, finds within its jurisdiction another government claiming to come from God—*Imperium in imperio*—whose policy and practices are, in grave particulars, at variance with its own. The one government arrests the other, in the person of its chief, and arraigns it at this bar. A system is on trial in the person of Brigham Young. Let all concerned keep this fact steadily in view; and let that government rule without a rival which shall prove to be in the right."

The motion being overruled, the defendant pleaded not guilty, and further proceedings were postponed for future action. Among the attorneys defending President Young were Thomas Fitch and Charles H. Hempstead, non-"Mormons." The latter was formerly captain of the California volunteers and editor of the *Vedette*, the first anti-"Mormon" paper in Utah. He resigned the office of United States district attorney because of the wicked and malicious methods in which the federal courts in Utah were conducted, and became legal counsel for President Young.

Throughout the entire country the attitude and remarks of Judge McKean were severely criticized for attempting to prosecute the Church in the case of Brigham Young and punish him for the alleged "evils of a system."

Unexpected Calling of the Case.—Having been given to understand that his case would not be called until the spring term of court, President Young, who was in ill-health, went to St. George to spend the winter. His leading attorney, Thomas Fitch, also departed for the East. No sooner had Judge McKean learned of the departure of President Young than he set the date for the trial for the 20th of November. Attorney Hempstead protested, and asked for further time on the ground that it was not understood that the case would be called. Mr. Baskin, the prosecutor, demanded a forfeiture of the bond because the defendant was not present, but Judge McKean granted a stay until December 4, and later to the 9th of January, 1872. It was published by the Associated Press that Brigham Young had forfeited his bond and had fled from justice, and every lie imaginable to his injury was presented to the people of the United States. Although he was sick and it was bitter winter weather, President Young, over the protest of his brethren, returned to Salt Lake City, to face trial before the unfriendly court. In the meantime, however, Mr. Baskin who had been improperly appointed district attorney, was replaced by George C. Bates.

Other Accusations.—On the statement of William A. Hickman, a self-confessed murderer, who had been excommunicated from the Church for his crimes, charges were made against Brigham Young,

Daniel H. Wells and others, as accessories to Hickman's crimes. President Young knew that he would also face this charge when he returned to Salt Lake City. Nevertheless he returned, and on the 2nd day of January, appeared in court to the astonishment of his enemies and asked to be admitted to bail. District Attorney Bates was willing that bail should be given if it should be fixed at the reasonable sum of five hundred thousand dollars, but Judge McKean refused on any terms to release the defendant. However, out of consideration for the condition of his health he permitted him to be a prisoner in his own house guarded by deputy marshals. Daniel H. Wells, who was mayor of Salt Lake City, had previously been admitted to bail in the sum of fifty thousand dollars. This was looked upon as an act of Providence—almost a miracle. A quarrel arising between the judge and the district attorney, both went to Washington and the trial of the accused brethren was postponed.

The Engelbrecht Decision.—The case never came to trial, for from the supreme court of the United States there came a decision which overturned the rulings of the tyrannical judges. It was the decision in the Engelbrecht liquor case. The dispatch announcing it, which came over the wire April 15, 1872, was as follows: "Jury unlawfully drawn: summons invalid; proceedings ordered dismissed. Decision unanimous. All indictments quashed." This decision put an end to these petty persecutions for the time, and about one hundred and twenty individuals, many of whom had been imprisoned many months, were released.

The Poland Law.—In 1874, Congress passed a measure repealing certain Utah statutes relating to the territorial marshal and attorney general, and vesting their duties in the federal officers. The probate courts were also limited in their jurisdiction to matters of estates, guardianship and divorce. This, in part, is what the anti-"Mormon" element had been contending for in Utah. While this legislation was much less radical than that previously proposed, yet it curtailed the civil and political rights of the people, which had guaranteed their protection against tyranny in the past.

The Case of Ann Eliza Webb Young.—In July, 1873, a divorce suit was filed before Judge McKean, by Ann Eliza Webb, against President Brigham Young. This woman, a plural wife, besides asking for a decree of separation also sued for alimony pending the litigation, and for permanent support for herself and two children by a former marriage. The case dragged along until February, 1875, when Judge McKean ordered the defendant to pay the plaintiff three thousand dollars attorney's fees and five hundred dollars a month for her support and the education of her children. President Young was given ten days in which to pay the fees, and twenty days to pay the alimony, which amounted for the nineteen months to nine thousand five hundred dollars.

An appeal was taken to the supreme court of the territory, but before a decision could be reached the time limit had expired, and the defendant was again dragged before the remarkable tribunal of Judge McKean to show cause why he should not be punished for contempt of court. He denied that he had any intention of showing contempt and was merely seeking the benefit of an appeal. Judge McKean held that he was guilty of contempt and sentenced him to twenty-four hours' imprisonment in the penitentiary. He was accompanied to prison by a number of friends and spent the night in comparative comfort in a room adjoining the warden's quarters.

Removal of Judge McKean.—The news of this strange trial and actions of Judge McKean spread throughout the country. There was a great deal of unfavorable comment. The San Francisco *Bulletin* said: "When Judge McKean assumes that this woman is the wife of Young, makes an interlocutory decree granting her three thousand dollars to maintain a suit for divorce, when there never was a legal marriage, and commits Young for contempt because he hesitates long enough to raise the question of the legality of the order, he burns some strange fire on the altar of justice." A Chicago paper stated: "This summary method of dealing with the Prophet looks very much like persecution, and will awaken sympathy for him instead of aiding the cause of justice." Even the President of the United States, who had stood by Judge McKean through all his dealings, when others protested and favored his removal, was forced to take some action. Five days after he sent President Young to prison, Judge McKean was removed from office for "several acts," which the dispatch stated, were deemed "ill advised and tyrannical, and in excess of his powers as a judge."

The Case of George Reynolds.—In 1874, George Reynolds, the private secretary of President Young, and a man of honor and integrity, was indicted for violation of the bigamy law of 1862. This was to be a test case. The "Mormon" people felt confident that the law was unconstitutional as it restricted them in the exercise of their religion and plural marriage had been commanded by the Lord. Elder Reynolds hearing of his indictment voluntarily appeared in court, and gave himself up for trial. He was convicted and sentenced to one year's imprisonment and to pay a fine of five hundred dollars. An appeal was taken to the supreme court of the territory, and the case was dismissed on the ground that the grand jury which found the indictment was an illegal jury.

The Second Reynolds' Trial.—A second trial was held in 1875, before Alexander White, chief justice of Utah. Judge White manifested a determination to be severe, and when a verdict of guilty was rendered, he sentenced Elder Reynolds to pay a fine of five hundred dollars and serve a term of two years in the penitentiary at hard labor. The supreme court of Utah confirmed the decree, and an appeal was taken to Washington.

Death of President George A. Smith.—September 1, 1875, President George A. Smith, first counselor to President Brigham Young, died at his residence—the Historian's Office—in Salt Lake City. He was ordained to the apostleship at the temple lot in Far West, April 26, 1838, when in his twenty-second year. He passed through the trials and vicissitudes of the Church from the days of Kirtland. He was Church historian and recorder from 1854 until the time of his death. In the fall of 1872 he took a mission to Europe and Asia, accompanied by Elder Lorenzo Snow and others, and visited the

St. George Temple

various missions and Jerusalem, where he rededicated the land for the return of the Jews. While absent he was sustained as trustee-in-trust for the Church.

Dedication of the St. George Temple.—The forty-seventh general conference of the Church was held in the St. George Temple in April, 1877. President Young, his counselors, the apostles and many leading brethren were present. The St. George Temple was dedicated on the 6th, President Daniel H. Wells offering the dedicatory prayer. This was the first temple to be erected in the Rocky Mountains, and the first which the Saints had been privileged to build without molestation by enemies. Work for both the living and dead commenced in the building following the dedication and has continued to be performed ever since.

Death of President Young.—August 29, 1877, President Brigham Young, then in his seventy-seventh year, passed away after a brief illness, at his home in Salt Lake City, surrounded by his family. On the 19th, he organized the Box Elder Stake of Zion, at Brigham City, which marked the close of his public ministry. The last words he uttered were "Joseph, Joseph, Joseph!" He was thinking of—perhaps conversing with—the Prophet Joseph Smith. September 2, the funeral services were held in the tabernacle, and there were gathered there to pay their respects and to mourn, the many thousands of modern Israel.

President Brigham Young

Brigham Young, the Prophet. —Brigham Young, the great pioneer and colonizer—but greater still the prophet of the Lord—was sincerely loved by the righteous and equally hated by the wicked. His life was one of trials and tribulations. Few were the days he spent in peace; many were the days he suffered and labored for the love of his fellowmen. He died misunderstood, save by the little band of devoted Saints who suffered with him and shared his hopes, his aspirations, and the assurance which was his of eternal life in our Father's Kingdom.

CHAPTER 48

CHURCH COLONIZATION AND PROGRESS
1847—1877

A Great People in the Mountains.—By the time President Brigham Young's administration came to a close, the Latter-day Saints had become a great people in the Rocky Mountains. They were destined still to grow in numbers, spread over greater territory, conquer more deserts, and develop spiritually and temporally in keeping with the progress of the times; but even then (1877) they had built up many settlements, spread over a vast area, and accomplished a wonderful work in the reclamation of the arid west.

The Planting of Colonies.—Before the Saints had been in the Salt Lake Valley a year many parties were sent out, principally to the north and to the south to form new settlements. Within two years from the time Salt Lake City was founded colonies had been planted in the utter-most parts of the territory. Exploring parties were sent out in advance, and when a site was selected a large company of volunteers followed to make the permanent settlement. In these colonies care was taken to have a proper representation of craftsmen, that the needs of the settlers might be supplied. Skilled carpenters, masons, millwrights, blacksmiths, cobblers, as well as tillers of the soil, went into these unbroken wastes and made them blossom by their industry. Each individual was given a specific duty to perform and did it unselfishly, according to the plan which had been arranged. Ploughs, seeds and the required animals for ploughing, ditch building and other labor, were provided, and the labor was done on the co-operative plan. All shared alike, according to their individual needs. They were happy, notwithstanding the rigorous toil required to subdue the desert places.

Unparalleled Progress.—It has been written of them, that they "made more progress and suffered less privation in reclaiming the waste lands of the wilderness than did the Spaniards in the garden spots of Mexico and Central America, or the English in the most favored region near the Atlantic seaboard." But let it be understood this was not accomplished by them without severe trial and suffering.

Their Perfect Organization.—The reason they were able to obtain such excellent results is that they had a perfect organization, and were loyal and obedient to the authority over them. This naturally resulted in complete co-operation and unity of purpose, with a minimum of individual selfishness. They had not come to the Rocky Mountains for the sake of worldly aggrandizement, but for the establishment of permanent homes, and the exercise of their religious freedom in peace according to the dictates of their conscience.

Proselytes from Europe.—Between the years 1847 and 1856, fifty-nine companies of emigrants, comprising seventeen thousand souls, sailed from European shores, bound for Utah. Five thousand others had previously emigrated, making a total of about twenty-two thousand persons from abroad, who had joined the Church through the preaching of the Gospel. They were principally from the British Isles, Scandinavia, Germany and Switzerland, with a small sprinkling from France, Italy and other nations. They came from the factories and the mines of Great Britain, the fisheries and the dairy farms of Scandinavia, the workshops of Germany, the vineyards of France and Italy—from various pursuits and occupations in which many of them were unable, in the old world, out of the scanty pittance they received as wages, to save enough to buy a passage across the sea. Of the emigration from the old country between 1850 and 1860, it was estimated that 28 per cent were common laborers; 14 per cent, miners, and about 28 per cent mechanics. From the ranks of the remaining thirty per cent there came many merchants, doctors, professors, skilled engineers, artisans, and artists.

Character of the Converts.—Occasionally there was one who had joined the Church who was in possession of an abundance of this world's goods, and big enough to share with his less fortunate neighbor, for the converts were not confined to the poor and the needy, the unlearned and the ignorant. In fact very few of the latter class received the Gospel message. The converts were gathered from all nations, but they were not the scum, the moral outcasts, the undesirable among the nations, but the very bones and sinews, the life's blood, the brawn, without which the nations would perish from the earth. This class, despised and trodden under foot from time immemorial by the haughty, the proud, the titled nobility; but upon whom, nevertheless, the aristocratic population depend for their very existence, is the salt of the earth—that class which the scriptures say, in the day of the Savior's ministry, had the Gospel preached to them and heard it gladly.

The pioneer immigrants, who established the state of Utah, belonged to the great industrial class, honest, though generally poor, which laid the foundation of our nation. Among the early members of the Church were many who fought in freedom's cause and who were descendants of the early colonial famiiles of New England and the border Atlantic States.

What the Gospel Did for Them.—"Mormonism" took hold of the dependent thousands of poor from all parts of the earth and made them virtually independent by placing them on farms, and otherwise furnishing them with remunerative employment, by which they became financially free. The year that President Young died, the population of Utah Territory was approximately one hundred and forty thousand, and of that number over forty thousand were of foreign birth. Men from the looms of England, the factories of Germany, and various other dependent vocations, in the towns and cities of Europe, were under the necessity of changing the natures of their lives. These men, unaccustomed to the severity of the labor required in farming were sent out to reclaim the desert wastes, and to till the soil in an uninviting land; yet they were successful, and were transformed into prosperous farmers, stockraisers, blacksmiths, husbandmen, and were made free landholders—a thing they never dreamed of becoming while residing in the crowded centers of Europe.

The Amalgamation of Many Peoples.—Notwithstanding they were gathered from the four quarters of the earth, with all their different customs and habits of life, their new surroundings, coupled with their unity of religious views, soon welded them together into one race and people. The Gospel as revealed through Joseph Smith teaches unity. Those who embrace it, whatever their views may have been before, soon learn to think alike; their aims are the same, their desires mutual, and all are brought to a common understanding. Such are the effects of the Gospel upon them that they forget their nationality and are absorbed by their new environment, and truly become a part of the soil on which they dwell.

Benefits from the Amalgamation.—As England was made great through the mingling of Norman, Saxon and Dane with the native tribes of Britain, so also have the "Mormon" people benefited through the amalgamation of the races. Through the preaching of the Gospel "Mormonism" has drawn on the best nations; has sifted and gathered from them their very best people, and due to the peculiar circumstances that prevail, the unity of faith and aspiration the Gospel inspires, it is moulding out a new and superior race. The "Mormon" people are strong mentally, spiritually, morally, as well as physically. Battling with the elements and contending with many difficulties have made them such. They came to the valleys of the mountains "with songs of everlasting joy" to obtain inheritances for themselves and children after them that shall endure forever, in a land of liberty, known to them as being "choice above all other lands."

Frugality and Co-operation.—The early settlers were taught to produce as far as possible, all that they consumed; to be frugal and not wasteful of their substance; to draw from the elements necessities of life and avoid all vitiated tastes which would lead them into excessive indulgence. Home industry was the watchword, and the people of necessity were called upon to be producers. Their clothing, though plain, was durable and the workmanship of their own hands. In the days of the pioneer, and until comparatively recent times, the spinning wheel and the loom were to be seen in the homes of the Saints.

Co-operation and community interests did much for the people in those early days. Houses were built, canals were dug, fields were ploughed and planted, and reservoirs were constructed on the co-operative principle for the welfare of the people. There was no money to be had, and such was the concern of the individual for the progress of the community that his time was given gratis in the making of public and civic improvements. He realized that he was bound to reap his portion of the benefits derived from his toil.[a]

---

[a]We have a marvelous combination of physiographic conditions and social organizations in the development of Utah under the guidance of Mormonism. The agriculture pursued was irrigated agriculture, which for its success is dependent upon a compact society, well knit together. Individualism was out of the question under these conditions, and in Mormonism we find precisely the cohesive strength of religion needed at that juncture to secure economic success.

Agriculture was made the foundation of the economic life, and consciously so. Brigham Young discouraged mining and adventurous pursuits, because he had a theory of socio-economic development in accordance with which agriculture should come first, manufacturing second, and mining later. It was essential that food should be produced first of all, and also there was a desire that settled habits should be acquired. Another peculiarity of the situation, namely, that the land could be made to yield a harvest only by means of irrigation, has just been mentioned, and the Mormons thus became the pioneers of modern irrigation in the United States. (Dr. Richard R. Ely, in Harper's Magazine, 1903.)

Changed Conditions of Today.—Today it is largely the case, that a man who gives his time, even though it be in some labor from which he is bound to receive his portion of the reward, feels that he must receive some monetary remuneration for the time he spends. And thus, due to the modern labor conditions and the closer contact with the outside world, with all its customs, theories and established institutions, this excellent and neighborly custom of co-operation, which existed in the days of President Brigham Young, has almost entirely passed away.

Division of Lands and Water.—President Young taught the doctrine that a man should have as much farm land as he could properly cultivate, and not more. The lands were divided among the people on that principle. From the beginning it was also established that the water from the mountain streams should belong to the people and not to private individuals. This doctrine proved extremely beneficial. Where private individuals have been permitted to file on the canyon streams, it has been a detriment to the majority of the people who are dependent upon such streams.

A Farsighted Policy.—The farsighted policy of President Young was the means of placing the people in their own homes where they could dwell "safely, every man under his vine and under his fig tree." As late as the year 1896, the year Utah was admitted into the Union, there were 19,816 farms and of that number 17,584 were free from encumbrances of mortgage and debt. Unfortunately, since the advent of the automobile and other modern conveniences and amusements, such a condition does not exist today.

The Recreation of the People.—Although the Latter-day Saints were forced to labor diligently and there was no place for idlers among them, they found time for proper recreation. President Young realized the necessity of recreation and amusement and knew their proper place. The Sabbath day was sacredly observed. There was no conflict between duty and pleasure and the labors of the people were faithfully performed. He encouraged the drama and other educational diversions in which the routine of the daily lives of the people was broken. He built the Salt Lake Theatre, which was begun in 1861 and opened to the public in March, 1862. Before that time the Social Hall, which was built in 1852, was used for such entertainment. There was much local talent among the people, which was augmented by visits to the territory of the great artists of those times. The dance—not, however, as it is conducted in these modern days—was likewise encouraged. All amusements were opened and closed with prayer; and the presence of the great Pioneer and his associates at these entertainments, not only lent encouragement to the recreation, but was an influence which established proper decorum and conduct. Their amusements were all innocent and uplifting. The main thought of President Young was to couple education with the recreation of the people, and have all entertainments controlled by the influence of the Spirit of the Lord.

Importance of Education Realized.—The education of the youth of the Church was a matter which received constant attention, nor was there anything that was considered of greater importance. The Prophet Joseph taught that "the glory of God is intelligence," and from the organization of the Church, schools have been conducted for the members who were instructed to obtain "out of the best books words of wisdom" by study and by faith.

In February, 1850, the legislature of the provisional government chartered the University of Deseret (now the University of Utah) somewhat on the lines of the charter of the University of Nauvoo. It was provided that $5000.00 be appropriated annually by the legislature for the support of the University. This was a very large sum for that day, to be provided by the handful of people for the support of such an institution. It was also provided that primary, or district schools should be supported. While this action was taken by officers of the provisional government, and later ratified by them as officers of Utah Territory, yet they were all members of the Church, with President Young taking the initiative in the educational movement.

In the spring of 1851, district school houses were built in most of the wards of Salt Lake City. These buildings were used for the general ward gatherings of the Saints, and daily schools were held in them.

The Beginning of Church Schools.—In later years, after the territory had increased in population, other schools were established. President Young founded a number of Church schools. Among these were the Brigham Young Academy (now the Brigham Young University) at Provo, one of the leading institutions of learning in the state; the Brigham Young College at Logan, and the Latter-day Saints University (later High School) at Salt Lake City. In addition to these schools the auxiliary organizations[b] also were organized for the training and education of the members of the Church and have aided materially in this direction.

---

[b]For auxiliary organizations, see appendix.

Territorial Expansion.—At the close of the first decade after the settlement of Utah, colonies of the Latter-day Saints extended from Fort Limhi on the north, to Cedar City, on the south, a distance of about five hundred miles; and from Fort Supply on the east to Carson Valley on the west, about four hundred miles. The population of this area was about fifty thousand people, nearly all members of the Church.

Fort Limhi.—In the summer of 1855, a colony was sent to the north where they founded Fort Limhi (now called Lemhi) on Salmon River. This was the most northerly settlement of the Saints, about three hundred and seventy-five miles from Salt Lake City. The settlement was continued until 1858 when it was abandoned for the reason that it was too far away and the colonists were constantly harassed by hostile Indian tribes.

On the Rio Virgin.—In 1861, a large number of Saints were called to go from the middle and central counties of Utah to settle on the Rio Virgin and Santa Clara Rivers. They located and founded the city of St. George, and other towns on the upper Rio Virgin. The following year other members of the Church were called to go to that southern country to lend strength to the settlements. That year they raised about one hundred thousand pounds of cotton in the "Dixie" of the West showing that this industry was a possibility.

San Bernardino.—At a much earlier date (1851), Elders Amasa M. Lyman and Charles C. Rich, with about five hundred souls from Utah, journeyed to southern California, where in September of that year they built the town of San Bernardino. This continued to be a flourishing settlement until 1858, when the people were called back to Utah owing to the coming of Johnston's Army, and was never again occupied as a permanent settlement by the Saints.

Bear Lake Valley.—In the fall of 1863, Bear Lake Valley was settled by a colony under the leadership of Elder Charles C. Rich, who made that country his home until his death, November 17, 1883. Cache Valley had previously been occupied and settlements founded as early as 1856.

The Muddy Mission.—Early in the year 1871, the Saints who had gone to the far south and settled on the Muddy River in 1865, abandoned their homes, due to oppressive taxation levied against them by the new state of Nevada, which had been created out of the western portion of the territory of Utah. Subsequently, however, these settlements were re-established.

In this manner were the valleys of the mountains occupied by the Latter-day Saints through the inspiration and wisdom of President Brigham Young. Many of these settlements have grown into thriving and populous centers with a future before them of still wider and greater expansion.

Organization of Stakes.—At the time of the death of President Young in 1877, there were organized in the Church twenty Stakes of Zion,[c] namely, in the order of their creation: Salt Lake, Weber, Utah, Parowan, Cache, Juab, Millard, Beaver, Bear Lake, Sevier, St. George, Kanab, Panguitch, Davis, Tooele, Morgan, Sanpete, Summit, Wasatch, and Box Elder. Two others, St. Louis and Carson Valley, had been discontinued. The wards in the Church on that date were approximately two hundred and fifty.

The Missions.—During the administration of President Young, missionary labors were performed in the various States of the Union, and in the following foreign lands: Canada, British Isles, India, Australia, Palestine, Society Islands, France, Denmark, Sweden, Norway, Hawaii, Italy, Switzerland, Iceland, Chile, Germany, Siam, Gibraltar, South Africa, Malta, West Indies, New Zealand, Holland, Austria, Finland and Mexico. In some of these fields little was accomplished; from others there have been gathered to Zion many thousands of the scattered house of Israel, and principally of the tribe of Ephraim, according to the predictions of the ancient prophets. This has been especially true of the Anglo-Saxon, Scandinavian and Teutonic races.

---

[c]For list of stakes, see appendix.

PART SIX

Recent Development

CHAPTER 49

THE SECOND PERIOD OF APOSTOLIC PRESIDENCY
1877–1879

The Apostles Again Preside.—At the death of President Brigham Young, there was rejoicing among the enemies of the Church, who thought it was due to his strong personality and force of character that "Mormonism" endured. They did not, and could not, comprehend that the Church had been restored for the last time, and was destined to endure forever with the stamp of divine approval upon it, for the Power by which it was upheld was higher and greater than the personality of any man. The Lord Jesus Christ was its founder, and he had promised to protect and watch over it unto the end.

The death of President Young again made the council of Twelve Apostles the presiding quorum of the Church, and as such they were unanimously sustained at the October conference in 1877, with President John Taylor at their head. President John Taylor was born in Milnthorpe, Westmoreland, England, November 1, 1808. About the year 1828 he left his native land and came to Canada, where he received the Gospel in 1836, through the preaching of Elder Parley P. Pratt. He was called to the apostleship in December, 1838, and was actively engaged in the ministry from that time forth. He filled numeorus missions and opened the door for the preaching of the Gospel in France in 1850. He superintended the translation of the Book of Mormon in French and German, and was engaged in literary work at home and abroad covering a period of many years. President Taylor was a man of high integrity and strong conviction. He was painfully wounded in Carthage jail—four balls entered his body—at the time of the martyrdom of the Prophet Joseph and Patriarch Hyrum Smith. Under his administration the Church grew and expanded notwithstanding the fierce and cruel persecution through which it was forced to go, when the government of the United States without mercy was arrayed against it.

President John Taylor

The Twelve Apostles continued to act as the Presidency of the Church until October, 1880, a little more than three years, when the First Presidency again was organized.

The Decision in the Reynolds Case.—The case of Elder George Reynolds, which had been appealed to the supreme court of the United States in 1875, was argued before that body in November, 1878. January 6, 1879, that court handed down a decision unanimously confirming the sentence of the courts of Utah, and also declaring the anti-bigamy law of 1862 to be constitutional. This decision was of the utmost concern to the Latter-day Saints, who were confident that the supreme court, in justice, could not give confirmation to a law which they sincerely believed to be an infringement of their religion.

President Taylor's Comment.—President John Taylor, convinced that this decision was an assault on the exercise of religion guaranteed by the Constitution, stated in an interview and in answer to questions from O. J. Hollister, United States internal revenue collector in Utah, the following:

"When the Constitution of the United States was framed and adopted, those high contracting parties did positively agree that they would not interfere with religious affairs. Now, if our marital relations are not religious, what is? This ordinance of marriage was a direct revelation to us through Joseph Smith, the Prophet. You may not know it, but I know that this is a revelation from God and a command to his people, and therefore it is my religion. I do not believe that the Supreme Court of the United States has any right to interfere with my religious views, and in doing it they are violating their most sacred obligations. * * *

"We acknowledge our children; we acknowledge our wives. we have no mistresses. We had no prostitution until it was introduced by monogamy, and I am told that these other diabolical deeds are following in its train. The courts have protected these people in their wicked practices. We repudiate all such things, and hence I consider that a system that will enable a man to carry out his professions, and that will enable him to acknowledge his wife or wives and acknowledge and provide for his children and wives, is much more honorable than that principle which violates its marital relations and, whilst hypocritically professing to be true to its pledges, recklessly violates the same and tramples upon every principle of honor, which sits down and coolly and deliberately decides how many children shall be murdered and how many shall live."

An Unjust Sentence.—The sentence including "hard labor" pronounced against Elder Reynolds, was in excess of the law. On that ground the attempt was made to have the case reopened and the proceedings quashed, but the supreme court of the United States refused to issue such an order. It did, however, remand the case to the supreme court of Utah, with instructions "to cause the sentence of the district court to be set aside, and a new one entered on the verdict in all respects like that before imposed, except so far as it requires the imprisonment to be at hard labor." A petition from over thirty thousand citizens of the territory, asking for the pardon of the defendant was forwarded to President Rutherford B. Hayes, who ignored it.

The Defendant Imprisoned.—The defendant, George Reynolds, was re-sentenced June 14, 1879, and two days later he left Salt Lake City, for Lincoln, Nebraska, in charge of George A. Black and William T. Shaughnessy, deputy marshals, to serve his sentence in the Nebraska penitentiary. He served less than a month in that prison when he was brought back to Utah and placed in the local penitentiary where he was confined until he had served out his sentence, from June, 1879 to January, 1881, receiving the remission of his fine and the reduction for good behavior of one hundred and forty-four days. While confined he taught school, his pupils being the inmates of the prison. So successful was he that the warden remarked of him: "Reynolds is worth more than all the guards in keeping order among the prisoners."

Bitter Threats Against the Church.—The bitterness of the anti-"Mormon" press of Salt Lake City, and the broadcast circulation of falsehoods by the enemies of the Church commenced an agitation throughout the nation that was to result in special legislation against the "Mormon" people intended to encompass their destruction. Ministers of the Protestant churches in the United States took up the hue and cry. Many bitter expressions were heard in condemnation of the Latter-day Saints, and threats were made against their peace and safety. A sample of the blood-thirsty utterances is that given by Rev. T. DeWitt Talmage in the Brooklyn Tabernacle, shortly after the death of President Young, as follows: "Now my friends—now, at the death of the Mormon Chieftain, is the time for the United States government to strike. They are less organized than they have been, and less than they will be. If these Mormons will not submit to authority, let so much of their rich lands be confiscated for the wants of the government as will be sufficient for their subjugation. If the government of the United States cannot stand the expense, let Salt Lake City pay for it. (Applause.) Turn their vast temple into an arsenal. Set Phil Sheridan after them. (Immense applause.) Give him enough troops and he will teach all Utah that forty wives is thirty-nine too many. I call upon the Church of Jesus Christ to pray for the overthrow of this iniquity."

Address of Anti-"Mormon" Women.—In November 1878, the Gentile women in Salt Lake City met in the Congregational Church, to the number of about two hundred, and drew up an address to the wife of the President of the United States, denouncing plural marriage and its practice in the name of religion. They called upon the "Christian women of the United States" to aid them in the arrest of "the progress of evil," and to delay the admission of Utah into statehood until this was accomplished. Congress was also memorialized and circular letters were forwarded to the clergy with the request that they be presented to their congregations for signatures and then sent to the congressmen of their respective districts.

"Mormon" Women Reply.—A counter mass meeting of the women of the Church was held November 16, 1878, in which they declared they had been misjudged and misrepresented to the nation in regard to their most sacred rights. They invited the government to make an impartial investigation of their cause.

Falsehoods of the Press.—Nearly every paper in the United States devoted space to the "Mormon" question, and almost without exception, with bitter denunciation and suggestions to Congress of the most drastic nature. The Salt Lake *Tribune* did not hesitate to circulate the most contemptible falsehoods that these fires of hate might be kept burning.

The Miles Case.—Another cause of agitation and one that went a long way towards congressional action of the severest nature against the practice of plural marriage, was the case of John H. Miles. This case ran a course of about three years, having been carried before the supreme court of the United States. Miles was arrested in October, 1878, on complaint of Caroline Owen Miles, his wife. She accused Miles of having married Emily Spencer of St. George, on the same day, and a little before her own ceremony was performed. She was not present at the ceremony, but testified that during a reception held that evening Emily Spencer was referred to as Mrs. Miles. The case was taken before Judge Emerson, in the Third district court, in April, 1879, where it was conceded that the ceremony had been performed between John H. Miles and Caroline Owen, and the defense objected to the testimony of the complaint on the ground that a wife could not testify against her husband. The marriage of Miss Spencer was not admitted. However, the evidence was taken and Miles was

"The Endowment House"

"found guilty" and sentenced to pay a fine of one hundred dollars and serve a term of five years in the penitentiary. An appeal was taken to the supreme court of Utah which affirmed the decision, and the case was then taken to the supreme court of the United States. The end of the matter came in 1881, when the supreme court handed down a decision stating that an error had been committed in the trial court by permitting Caroline Owen Miles to give evidence against Miles, since the law in Utah provided that a wife could not legally testify against her husband, or a husband against his wife. The marriage with Emily Spencer not having been admitted, and not having been proved, was the only issue in the trial. The decision was set aside and the case remanded for a new trial. The case was dropped, as the United States attorney felt that there could be no conviction. However, this case helped to stir the country to such a pitch that legislation was enacted repealing the Utah law.

Daniel H. Wells Before the Court.—While the trial of John H. Miles was before the court, Caroline Owen Miles gave a purported description of the apparel worn by those who passed through the endowment house.[a] The prosecution attempted to show that such apparel was worn by those who went there to be married. Daniel H. Wells, who had performed the ceremony for Miles and Caroline Owen, was called to the stand and questioned by Attorney Van Zile, who asked him to describe the dress worn in that building. This he declined to do. Judge Emerson decided that the question was proper, and as the witness still refused, he was placed in the custody of the marshal, with instructions that he should appear in the court the next day, to show cause why he should not be committed for contempt of court.

Imprisonment of Daniel H. Wells.—The next day, May 3, 1879, President Wells, with his attorney, appeared before Judge Emerson and stated his willingness to answer the questions, if they should be put in a proper way. The questions were put to him again, but purposely in such a way that he felt it his duty not to answer them. He declared that he was under sacred obligation to preserve what he was asked to reveal. The court insisted that he should answer, and the witness replied: "I consider a person who reveals the sacred ceremonies of the endowment house a falsifier and a perjurer; and it has been and is a principle of my life never to betray a friend, my

---

[a]The Endowment House was a comparatively small temple, erected in the northwest corner of the Temple Block to serve temporarily as a house of the Lord. It was torn down in 1889 by the order of President Wilford Woodruff.

religion, my country, or my God. It seems to me that this is sufficient reason why I should not be held in contempt."

The judge held that the witness was in contempt for not answering, and sentenced him to pay a fine of one hundred dollars and to be imprisoned for two days. President Wells was immediately placed in the hands of the United States marshal and taken to the penitentiary where he served his brief term of confinement.

A Public Protestation.—The action of Judge Emerson caused great indignation, and the Latter-day Saints were aroused. A public demonstration in protest of the action was planned, and many people gathered from the surrounding counties as far north as Bear Lake and south as far as Juab. A procession of ten thousand formed and met President Wells at the Burton Farm, three miles south of the city, and marched through the streets to the tabernacle, which was thronged with people. The presence of the released prisoner was a signal for prolonged applause. Speeches were made, interspersed with music from several bands. As the procession marched through the city they carried banners with inscriptions among which were the following:

"If courts compel men to dishonor and forswear themselves, how can they expect perjurers to give truth in evidence?"

"We honor the law and its just administration, but we despise petty tyranny."

"We will teach our children to be true to their country and their God; but to perjure themselves never! no never!"

"The rights of conscience we never submitted, we could not submit; we are answerable for them to our God."—Thomas Jefferson.

"If ever the laws of God and men are at variance, the former are to be obeyed in derogation of the latter."—Blackstone.

"God's Law."

"Thou shalt not forswear Thyself; but shall perform unto the Lord thine oaths."

"Modern Law."

"Thou shalt forswear thyself, or go to prison."

"When Free Masons, Odd Fellows and others are compelled to make their secrets public, it will be time enough to practice on Mormons; try the others first."

"We venerate the Constitution, we honor the law, we respect the Executive, Congress and the Judiciary; we bow to the righteous mandates of the law, but we despise bigots, we execrate tyranny, and protest against intolerance from any source."

Litigation over President Young's Estate.—In June, 1879, a few of the heirs of President Brigham Young, in opposition to all the rest, entered suit against the executors of the estate, claiming property held in the name of the late president as trustee-in-trust for the Church, as his personal property. The sum in litigation amounted to nearly one million dollars. Application was made for an injunction restraining the executors from further performance of their duties, and enjoining President John Taylor from disposing of any property received by him as trustee-in-trust. Judge Emerson granted the injunction and appointed William S. McCornick and United States Marshal Shaughnessy, non-"Mormons," to take charge of all the property. President Taylor asked that the injunction be dissolved, and the order appointing the receivers be revoked, on the ground that the claims against the estate were "a bona fide existing indebtedness," so recognized by the late president, who authorized in his will the settling of such claims by his executors.

Imprisonment of the Executors.—A warrant was issued by Judge Boreman, who was most bitter against the Church, for the arrest of President Taylor and the executors, George Q. Cannon, Brigham Young, Jr., and Albert Carrington. Showing that he had complied with the order of the court, President Taylor was discharged, but the executors were committed to the penitentiary, for refusing to furnish additional security, which was considered by them as nothing more or less than an attempt to levy blackmail. Their imprisonment extended from August 4 to 28, when they were released through the reversal of Judge Boreman's decision by the supreme court of the territory—Judge Boreman dissenting.

Counter Suit and Settlement.—A counter suit was brought against the heirs by the Church for the recovery of its property. The case came before Judge John A. Hunter, who had arrived in the territory the previous summer. The case was dismissed in October (1879), without coming to judgment as the parties to the suit came to a mutual agreement. The litigant heirs, according to the agreement, were paid the sum of seventy-five thousand dollars and all charges were withdrawn. The receivers were dismissed. President Taylor presented the terms of the settlement before the general conference of the Church which convened two days after the decision was made, and it was endorsed by unanimous vote.

Secretary Evarts' Circular Letter.—William M. Evarts, secretary of state, in the cabinet of President Hayes, sent out a circular letter in October, 1879, to the diplomatic officers of the United States in foreign countries, advising them that large numbers of persons from various lands were coming to the United States for the purpose of joining the "Mormons" in Utah; also that the marriage system of the "Mormons" was pronounced by the laws of the United States to be a crime against the statutes of the country. These immigrants, he said, came "to swell the numbers of the law-defying Mormons of Utah," who were endeavoring to bring persons to the United States with the intent of violating laws punishable by fine and penitentiary imprisonment. The representatives of the government abroad were instructed to "check the organization of these criminal enterprises," by calling the attention of the several governments to the situation. This was to be in the interest "not merely of a faithful execution of the laws of the United States, but of the peace, good order and morality which are cultivated and sought to be promoted by all civilized countries."

Condemnation of Evarts' Course.—It was a time when condemnation of the "Mormons" was a popular amusement in the world, but this letter of Secretary Evarts brought down on his head a storm of ridicule, even from those unfriendly to the Latter-day Saints, in this country and also in foreign lands. The London *Times* was very caustic in its treatment of the letter, and the New York *Sun* stated: "Now let Mr. Evarts instruct his diplomatic agents abroad to ask the foreign powers—as a favor and a friendly act towards the United States—to hang any of their subjects who may become murderers after their arrival in this country. The foreign powers are said to have been astonished by Mr. Evarts' circular. They had reason to be amazed."

The Murder of Joseph Standing.—The continued publication of unfavorable articles in the press of the country concerning the Latter-day Saints, and the constant repetition of falsehoods emanating from the enemies of the Church at Salt Lake City—where most all the agitation originated—caused much bitterness throughout the country. The missionaries of the Church were sorely abused, especially in the Southern States, where many of them were stripped, tied to trees and brutally beaten by mobs, until the blood ran from their wounded bodies, and when released they were ordered from that part of the country on pain of death if they remained.

On the 21st of July, 1878, Elders Joseph Standing, twenty-five years of age, and Rudger Clawson, a youth of twenty-two, were surrounded by a mob at Varnal Station, Whitefield County, Georgia, and were taken to the woods apparently for the purpose of receiving a thrashing. Elder Standing at this juncture made some show of resistance when one of the mobbers fired at him. The ball passed through his left eye and ranging upward came out of the forehead. Immediately following this deed one of the gang, pointing at Elder Clawson, said, "Shoot that man!" It was a critical moment for the young elder, who turned and cooly faced the mob with folded arms and exclaimed, —"Shoot!" His coolness seemed to unnerve the mob who lowered their guns. It was then suggested by one of the mobbers that Elder Standing had shot himself, although he was unarmed. Elder Clawson at his earnest solicitation was permitted to go after help, and while he was gone the fiends shot about twenty bullets into the body of the prostrate man, mostly into his face and neck, and so close that the wounds were powder-burned.

The Coroner's Verdict.—An inquest was held and a verdict found in which David D. Nations, Jasper N. Nations, A. S. Smith, David Smith, Benj. Clark, William Nations, Andrew Bradley, James Fawcett, Hugh Blair, Joseph Nations, Jefferson Hunter and Mack McClure, who were seen by witnesses in the mob at the time of the killing, were accused of the crime.

"Not Guilty."—The guilty parties fled from Georgia. Three of them were captured and returned to the state, but were released on furnishing bail in the sum of five thousand dollars each. The grand jury found indictments against Jasper Nations for murder, against Bradley for manslaughter, and against Blair for riot. In October, 1879, their trial was held. Elder Clawson attended as a witness, and notwithstanding the positive nature of his testimony, and that of the other eyewitnesses, all three defendants were acquitted. Elder John Morgan, who was presiding in the Southern States and who was present at the proceedings, sent a telegram to the *Deseret News* at the close of the trial of Jasper Nations, stating: "The old, old story. Verdict, not guilty!"

CHAPTER 50

THE ADMINISTRATION OF PRESIDENT JOHN TAYLOR

1880-1887

The Year of Jubilee.—April 6, 1880, was just fifty years from the day of the organization of the Church. On this date and the three succeeding days, the fiftieth annual conference of the Church was held in the tabernacle, Salt Lake City. Preliminary meetings were also held on the 4th and 5th. All the members of the Council of the apostles were present, excepting George Q. Cannon, who was in Washington representing Utah as a delegate in Congress. President John Taylor drew attention to the fact that this was the jubilee year of the Church, and referred to the custom which prevailed in old Israel, as set forth in the twenty-fifth chapter of Leviticus. It was proposed that it be made a year of jubilee and forgiveness in the Church. The Church set the example by striking off one half the indebtedness held by the Perpetual Emigrating Fund Company, against individuals classed as worthy poor, amounting to the sum of $802,000. One thousand cows and five thousand sheep were also distributed among the needy. The Saints were advised to be charitable and liberal in their dealing with one another. The sum of $75,899, in unpaid tithing, one half the amount due, was remitted against the Saints who were unable to meet their obligation. It was proposed that the Relief Society lend to the farmers, who had suffered loss because of drouth the year before, 34,761 bushels of wheat which they had on hand This was to be repaid by the farmers, without interest, at the close of the next harvest. "If you find people owing you who are distressed, if you will go to work and try to relieve them as much as you can, under the circumstances, God will relieve you when you get into difficulties," said President Taylor. "I will tell you that," he added, "in the name of the Lord. Let us act on a kind, generous, brotherly principle, doing good one to another and carrying out the principles of the everlasting Gospel in our lives."

The Pioneer Day Celebration.—The spirit of the jubilee was carried through the year, and was again made manifest in a marked manner at the celebration —on pioneer day, July 24, 1880. There was a long pageant, which paraded through the streets of Salt Lake City, and on three of the floats were natives from twenty-five countries, representing the people who had been gathered through the preaching of the Gospel. A banner was also carried upon which the inscription was written: "I will gather you out from all nations." Exercises were held in the tabernacle and patriotic speeches were made. Utah had a population at that time of 143,690, showing an increase of nearly 60,000 in the past decade. The great majority of these were members of the Church.

President Taylor's Prediction.—At this celebration President Taylor gave utterance to the following prediction: "There are events in the future, and not very far ahead, that will require all our faith, all our energy, all our confidence, all our trust in God, to enable us to withstand the influences that will be brought to bear against us. * * * We cannot trust in our intelligence; we cannot trust in our wealth; we cannot trust to any surrounding circumstances with which we are enveloped; we must trust alone in the living God to guide us, to direct us, to lead us, to teach us and to instruct us. And there never was a time when we needed to be more humble and more prayerful; there never was a time when we needed more fidelity, self-denial, and adherence to the principles of truth, than we do this day."

Re-organization of the First Presidency.—At the general semi-annual conference held in October, 1880, reports were made of the distribution of the cattle, sheep and other substance, which was voted on at the April conference. A time of great rejoicing was had and on the last day (10th) the First Presidency was again re-organized with John Taylor as President of the Church, and George Q. Cannon and Joseph F. Smith as his first and second counselor, respectively. Elders Francis M. Lyman and John Henry Smith were called to the apostleship, leaving one vacancy unfilled. The voting was done by quorums, as it was at the sustaining of President Young, beginning with the apostles; second, the patriarchs, presidents of stakes and counselors, and high councils; third, the high priests; fourth the seventies; fifth, the elders; sixth, the bishops and their counselors; seventh the lesser priesthood—priests, teachers, deacons; eighth, the presidents of various quorums, and last the whole congregation.

Death of Orson Pratt—Calling of Elders Teasdale and Grant.— Orson Pratt, the last surviving members of the original council of apostles, died in Salt Lake City, October 3, 1881. Elder Pratt possessed a remarkable analytical mind, and was one of the world's great mathematicians. His discourses and writings on the Gospel are clear and convincing. With all his learning he was humble and unassuming, having perfect assurance in the divinity of the mission of Joseph Smith.

In October, 1882, Elders George Teasdale and Heber J. Grant were called to the apostleship by revelation given through President John Taylor. Elder Seymour B. Young was also called to be one of the seven presidents of the seventies.[a] This revelation was given October 13, 1882, and the brethren were ordained three days later. The Lord, in this revelation, called upon the various quorums of the Priesthood to arise and purify themselves, and for the members to magnify their callings. The Saints were commanded to set their houses in order that they might be purged from sin. The prediction was made that eventually Zion should be established and the nations shall yet acknowledge the Lord.

George Q. Cannon

Dedication of the Logan Temple.—The Logan Temple—the second structure of the kind built in Utah—was dedicated May 17, 1884, under the direction of President John Taylor, who offered the dedi-

---

[a]For a complete list giving information regarding the apostles and other presiding brethren, see appendix.

catory prayer. The site for the temple was dedicated May 17, 1877, by Orson Pratt. The work of excavation was begun May 28, and the laying of rock in July following. September 19, 1877, the corner stones were laid, the order of temple-building being followed. The dedicatory services in 1884, which lasted three days, were very solemn and impressive, and the Saints rejoiced that another house of

Logan Temple

the Lord had been built, where work for the salvation of the living and the dead could be performed.

Anti-"Mormon" Legislation Agitated.—During the eighties there appeared to be a united effort on the part of the press and the denominational ministers to force legislation against the Latter-day Saints. The chief instigators of this campaign were anti-"Mormon" residents of Utah, with the aid of their organ, the Salt Lake *Tribune*. President Rutherford B. Hayes, who was imposed upon by this agitation, in a message to Congress in December, 1879, and again in 1880, referred to the "Mormon" question and plural marriage. President Garfield made similar reference in his inaugural address, and after the assassination of Garfield, President Arthur took the matter up in his first message to Congress.

Bitterness of "Christian" Ministers.—The bitterness of the times was expressed by the Chicago *Interior*, a Presbyterian paper, in the summer of 1881, as follows:

"Let the lands and tenements of the Mormons be thrown open to original entry by civilized settlers. * * * Let it be understood that the army will keep out of the way in Utah for four years, and that the use and occupation of Mormon property for one year is to give a preemption title. There are enough young men in the West and South, who are seeking homes, to finish up the pest, fumigate the Territory, and to establish themselves in ninety days after the word 'go' is given."

In consonance with this "Christian" spirit, the Rev. J. H. Peters, at Dayton, in October, 1881, said to his congregation: "I would that the guns of Fort Douglas were turned upon them [the 'Mormons'] and they made loyal by this means if by no other." Falsehoods of the deepest hue were also uttered. The notorious T. DeWitt Talmage, for instance, circulated the false report that the assassin of President Garfield was a "Mormon," and the Latter-day Saints were wickedly accused by this reverend, and others, of holding meetings and rejoicing because of the President's death.

The Edmunds Bill.—The result of all this agitation was the passing of a law in March, 1882, by Congress, amending the law of 1862. It was known as the Edmunds Law, because it was introduced into the senate by George F. Edmunds of Vermont. This measure not only made punishable the contracting of plural marriage, but also polygamous living, which was designated as "unlawful cohabitation." The punishment for contracting a plural marriage remained the same as in the law of 1862—a fine of five hundred dollars or imprisonment for five years, or both, in the discretion of the court.

The President of the United States was authorized to grant amnesty to those who had entered into plural marriage before the passage of this bill, under certain conditions and limitations, and their children born before January 1, 1883, were legitimated.

"No polygamist, bigamist, or any person cohabiting with more than one woman, and no woman cohabiting with any of the persons described as aforesaid * * * shall be entitled to vote at any election * * * hold any office or place of public trust, honor or emolument, in, under, or for any such Territory or place, or under the United States," was declared in this bill. Of course this was not intended to apply to "Gentiles" who "cohabited" with more than one woman, outside of the marriage relation, and such—and Utah had them—were shielded by the officers of the law. Moreover, the mere belief in the doctrine of plural marriage was sufficient to bar a person from jury service.

All registration and election offices were declared vacant, and provision was made for a commission of five persons to be appointed by the President, and with the consent of the senate, to attend to the duty of registration of voters, canvassing the returns of elections for members of the territorial legislature, and issue certificates, or other evidence of election, until otherwise provided by law. They were to be paid three thousand dollars a year and to continue in office until the legislature, elected and qualified under the Edmunds Law, should provide for filling the offices as authorized by the statute.

Self-Government Denied.—By this law, local self-government was annihilated in Utah, contrary to all the guarantees granted to free people since the days of the framing of the government of the United States, if not since the days of King John. Following in the wake of this legislation there was conducted a crusade against the "Mormon" people without a parallel in the history of the United States.

The Utah Commission.—The five commissioners appointed through the Edmunds Law, arrived in Utah, August 18, 1882. They were: Alexander Ramsey, of Minnesota, chairman; Algernon S. Paddock, of Nebraska; George L. Godfrey, of Iowa; Ambrose B. Carlton, of Indiana; and James R. Pettigrew, of Arkansas, with Arthur L. Thomas, secretary. They immediately set to work on the duties assigned them, and appointed registrars for the November election, in a manner most unjust to the "Mormon" people. Eight of the registrars out of twenty-four, were members of the Church, yet the "Mormon" population was in excess of 120,000, and the "Gentile" population—including apostates and others classed as "doubtful"—was approximately 24,000. The commissioners also published rules for the guidance of the registrars and the government of election judges, which were manifestly unfair and beyond the scope of the law, which was done to disfranchise a large portion of the "Mormon" population.

The Test Oath.—Perhaps the most abominable and shameful thing they did was to prepare the following "test oath":

Territory of Utah, } ss.
County of ....

I ...., being first duly sworn (or affirmed), depose and say that I am over twenty-one years of age, and have resided in the Territory of Utah for six months, and in the precinct of .... one month immediately preceding the date hereof, and (if a male) am a native born or naturalized (as the case may be) citizen of the United States and a taxpayer in this Territory, or (if a female), I am native born, or naturalized, or the wife, widow or daughter (as the case may be) of a native born or naturalized citizen of the United States; and I do further solemnly swear (or affirm) that I am not a bigamist or a polygamist; that I am not a violator of the laws of the United States prohibiting bigamy or polygamy; that I do not live or cohabit with more than one woman in the marriage relation, nor does any relation exist between me and any woman which has been entered into or continued in violation of the said laws of the United States prohibiting bigamy or polygamy; and (if a woman) that I am not the wife of a polygamist, nor have I entered into any relation with any man in violation of the laws of the United States concerning polygamy or bigamy.

Subscribed and sworn before me this .... day of ...., 1882.

....
Registration Officer ....Precinct.

Careful Wording of the Oath.—The expression "I do not live or cohabit with more than one woman IN THE MARRIAGE RELATION," was so placed as were other clauses to apply against the "Mormons" only. The "Mormon" press and preachers drew attention to this feature of the oath which denied to the "Mormon polygamist," but permitted the "Gentile libertine," the right to vote. The admission was commonly made that the Edmunds Law was prepared solely against the "Mormons" and did not apply to the immoralities of the "Gentiles." This led the First Presidency in an address to the Saints in August, 1882, to say that they regretted that men of high positions would take that view of the law; but they perceived "with unmixed satisfaction" the sharp distinction the oath drew between marriage and licentiousness.

The Law made Retroactive.—Another infamous ruling was that any person who had lived in the plural marriage state, but was then

ADMINISTRATION OF JOHN TAYLOR 485

not living in that relation, was denied the right of franchise; and this was interpreted to apply to those who had thus married even before the law of 1862. For instance, if a man had married two wives in 1850, before any law against plural marriage was enacted, and both wives had died before the law was passed; the commission ruled that he was a "polygamist" notwithstanding he had no wife living, and denied him the right to vote. "Once a polygamist always a polygamist," was the common expression. Other rulings and actions, contrary to the law, but intended to annoy and disfranchise the members of the Church, that the minority might rule, were attempted, among them denial to the women of their suffrage.

A Campaign of Persecution.—From this time forth until the close of President John Taylor's administration, and beyond, the government of the United States carried on a campaign of prosecution, that was relentless and even cruel, against all members of the Church who had married plural wives. Men were punished, not for contracting plural marriage since the passage of the law, but for "unlawful cohabitation;" federal officers hunted men and women and dragged them before selected grand juries, where they were shamefully insulted. Even small children did not escape, but were forced to testify and answer improper and indecent questions, with the object in view of obtaining evidence against their parents; and this was done with threats of dire punishment and contempt of court, if they refused. Such actions partook too much of the days of the Spanish Inquisition. Paid spies—men of debased character—were employed to gather evidence. Among those who sat on juries to judge the "morals" of the "Mormon" people, were those who were recreant to every law of decency. The petty officers and the judges of the courts carried on a reign of terror in their determination to stamp out the practice of plural marriage, and it appeared that the greatest crime in the world was for a man to acknowledge honestly that he was the husband of more than one wife, and that he diligently and faithfully supported them and their children; while for the libertine and the harlot there was protection by officers of the law.

President Taylor's Statement.—At the general conference of the Church in April, 1882, President John Taylor spoke of the approaching storm. "While the excitement lasts," said he, "it is useless to reason with the world; when it subsides we can talk to them." He also expressed the views of the Latter-day Saints when he said: "We do not wish to place ourselves in a state of antagonism, nor act defiantly, toward this government. We will fulfil the letter, so far as practicable, of that unjust inhuman, oppressive, and unconstitutional law. * * * But we cannot sacrifice every principle of human right. * * * While we are God-fearing and law-abiding, and respect all honorable men and officers, we are no craven serfs, and have not learned to lick the feet of oppressors, nor to bow in base submission to unreasonable clamor. We will contend, inch by inch, legally and constitutionally, for our rights as American citizens." So sore became the persecution that hundreds of homes were broken up and husbands and fathers were sent to the penitentiary for the offense of "unlawful cohabitation."

A Tribune Canard.—To add to the evil of the times the circulation of false and malicious reports increased, and the Latter-day Saints were portrayed as the vilest of the vile. The result of this was continued persecution of the elders in the mission fields.

One of these abusive and lying canards appeared in the Salt Lake *Tribune*, March 16, 1884. It purported to be the disloyal utterances of "Bishop West, of Juab." There was no Bishop West, and the falsehood was exposed. When the *Tribune* was caught red handed in its lying, it very reluctantly admitted the falsehood, but added that the report sounded like what was going on all the time. Articles of this kind were constantly appearing, and the members of the Church were repeatedly insulted and abused with the hope that some overt act might be committed through unendurable provocation, and thus occasion be made against the Church for its destruction. However, the persecuted people bore the insults without giving cause for such diabolical action.

The Canard the Cause of Murder.—The "Bishop West" hoax might have been forgotten if the falsehood had ended with the exposure of the *Tribune* story, but, unfortunately, it was circulated in Tennessee by a Reverend Vandevere, of Lewis County, who made it an occasion to attack the Saints in the South, and arouse the populace against them. He had been duly advised of the nature of the falsehood, but that made no difference; he continued to repeat the story. The result of this circulation of the *Tribune's* falsehood, was the enacting of a tragedy, at Cane Creek, Lewis County, Tennessee, of a most shocking character.

The Tennessee Massacre.—It happened Sunday, August 10, 1884, That morning a number of elders and Saints met at the home of James Condor for religious worship. While the small congregation was assembling a mob of masked ruffians invaded the premises and shot and killed Elders John H. Gibbs, of Paradise, and William S. Berry, of Kanarra, and also two young men, Martin Condor and John Riley Hudson, who were not members of the Church, but who attempted to protect the elders. Young Hudson, securing his gun, shot and killed the leader of the mob, one David Hinson, but Hinson's followers returned the fire, mortally wounding the young man who died about one hour later. Because of this retaliation the mob returned and poured a fire into the house through the windows, seriously wounding Mrs. Condor, and riddling the body of Elder Berry. They then secured the body of their leader and made off. Two other missionaries, Elders William H. Jones and Henry Thompson, escaped.

Elder Roberts Secures the Bodies of the Slain.—Elder B. H. Roberts was at Chattanooga, in charge of the mission in the absence of President John Morgan, who was in Salt Lake City. At the peril of his own life he went forth and secured the bodies of the missionaries and had them forwarded to Utah, where the "Mormon" people were in mourning. The bodies of the slain elders were interred at their home towns, but public funeral services were also held in Salt Lake City, August 24, 1884.

Governor Murray to Governor Bate.—Governor Eli H. Murray of Utah was so filled with animus against the Latter-day Saints that it was impossible for him to communicate with Governor W. B. Bate, of Tennessee, regarding the massacre, without abuse of the Latter-day Saints. Governor Bate offered a reward for the detection and arrest of the murderers. Evidently fearing that they might be caught and punished, Governor Murray, without any reason or excuse, sent a dispatch to the governor of Tennessee in which he said: "Lawlessness in Tennessee and Utah are alike reprehensible, but the murdered Mormon agents in Tennessee were sent from here as they have been for years by the representatives of organized crime, and I submit that as long as Tennessee representatives in Congress are, to say the least, indifferent to the punishment of offenders against the national law in Utah, such cowardly outrages by their constituents as the killing of emigration agents sent there from here will continue."

The Trial of Rudger Clawson.—Charles S. Zane became chief justice of Utah in 1884. He came to the territory, August 23, of that year. He was a man whose moral life was above reproach, but he was possessed of an intolerant spirit, and was determined to conduct a strict enforcement of the Edmunds Law. The first case to be tried under that law came before his court October 15, 1884. It was the case of Rudger Clawson, who was found guilty, and when asked by the court if he had any legal cause to show why judgment should not be pronounced he replied:

"Your honor, I very much regret that the laws of my country should come in conflict with the laws of God; but whenever they do, I shall invariably choose the latter. If I did not so express myself, I should feel unworthy of the cause I represent. The constitution of the United States expressly says that Congress shall make no law respecting an establishment of religion or prohibiting the free exercise thereof. (It cannot be denied I think, that marriage, when attended and sanctioned by religious rites and ceremonies, is an establishment of religion.) The law of 1862 and the Edmunds Law were expressly designed to operate against marriage as practiced and believed in by the Latter-day Saints. They are therefore unconstitutional, and of course cannot command the respect that a constitutional law would. That is all I have to say, your honor."

The speech was characteristic of the man. It was bold, sincere, but not defiant. It struck the judge with amazement and he determined on a heavy penalty. It was the third day of November when Elder Clawson was before the court. He was sentenced to pay a fine of eight hundred dollars and imprisonment for four years. Elder Clawson remained in prison until December 12, 1887—three years, one month and ten days—when he received a pardon from President Grover Cleveland.

The Segregation Ruling.—Following this trial there was inaugurated a cruel and determined persecution. Women were sent to prison for contempt because they would not testify against their husbands. The courts ruled that indictments might be found against a man guilty of cohabitation "for every day." To be seen at the home of a plural wife, or to support his plural family, was sufficient to create an offense against a man. Each "distinct and separate violation of the law," as interpreted by the judges, was a separate offense and was liable for punishment.

This order of segregation, as it was called, drove many of the leading brethren into exile, for it was virtually an announcement that the violation of the Edmunds Law could be punished by life imprisonment. Later, however, while the supreme court of the United States upheld the Edmunds Law, it condemned the action of the judges in Utah in establishing the "segregation" policy. This came in the habeas corpus case of Elder Lorenzo Snow in February, 1887. While, however, this ruling was being enforced, the First Presidency were in retirement and communicated with the Saints from time to time in general epistles.

Sincerity of the "Mormon" People.—With all the severity practiced against the "Mormon" people under the Edmunds Law, yet it did not satisfy the enemies of the Church. Without question many of the law makers had imputed to the Latter-day Saints impure motives in the practice of plural marriage. They now discovered through the prosecutions, which fell into the category of persecutions, that it was a matter of the most sincere and sacred character. Nevertheless they were determined to put an end to the practice. Heavier penalties did not seem to avail, for the members of the Church accepted plural marriage as a sacred religious rite, commanded by the Lord, and they would rather die than break their covenants. The actions of the government they looked upon as unconstitutional and an attack upon their religious duties, and while they desired to be, and were, loyal to the country, at the same time they desired to be loyal to their God.

The Edmunds-Tucker Law.—In March, 1887, Congress passed a supplemental act known as the Edmunds-Tucker Law. President Grover Cleveland neither approved nor disapproved of the act, so it became a law without his signature. Among the many features of this measure were the disincorporation of The Church of Jesus Christ of Latter-day Saints, and the dissolving of the Perpetual Emigrating Fund Company, the property of which was escheated to the government of the United States for the benefit of the common schools of Utah. Female suffrage was abolished. It was made the duty of the attorney general of the United States to proceed against the Church and wind up its affairs and the title to all property—except that "no building or grounds appurtenant thereto held and occupied exclusively for the purpose of the worship of God, or parsonage, or burial ground shall be forfeited"—be transferred and escheated to the United States.

Proceedings in Escheatment.—At the instance of the attorney general of the United States, suits were filed July 30, 1887, against the Church, and the Perpetual Emigrating Fund Company, and their property was confiscated. November 5, 1887, United States Marshal Dyer was appointed receiver, and took charge of the real and personal property of the Church to control it.

While this infamous measure was before Congress there were many brave men who stood up in the face of the popular clamor and almost united vindictiveness and hatred of the Church, and denounced the high-handed proceedings. Such also had been the case when previous legislation was enacted.

The government very graciously permitted the Church to occupy the tithing office and historian's office, at a yearly rental of $2,400; and the Gardo house at $450 a month. The Temple Block was also retained by the payment of a stipulated rent. All this happened in the

United States in the year 1887, not in Spain or Holland in the dark ages or the days of the Inquisition.

Death of President John Taylor.—Early in the year 1887, because of persecution, President John Taylor and his counselors were forced into exile. The trials and difficulties through which the Church was passing weighed heavily upon the venerable President. He did not live to see the final delivery of the Church property into the hands of a receiver. He died in exile July 25, 1887, at the home of Thomas F. Roueche, at Kaysville, Davis County, Utah, a martyr to the cause of truth which he espoused. At the time of his passing his counselors were with him. His life had been one of trial and suffering. He was a heroic character, strong in his convictions, just in his dealings, uncompromising with evil. It is proper here to quote the words of his counselors at the time of his death:

"President John Taylor has been killed by the cruelty of officials who have, in this territory, misrepresented the government of the United States. There is no room to doubt that if he had been permitted to enjoy the comforts of home, the ministrations of his family, the exercise to which he had been accustomed, but of which he was deprived, he might have lived for many years yet. His blood stains the clothes of men, who with insensate hate have offered rewards for his arrest and have hounded him to the grave. History will yet call their deeds by their right names" (*Life of John Taylor*—Roberts, p. 414).

CHAPTER 51

THE ADMINISTRATION OF PRESIDENT
WILFORD WOODRUFF

1887–1898

Changes in Leadership.—Following the death of President Taylor the duty of presidency again devolved upon the council of the apostles, Counselors Cannon and Smith resuming their places with the twelve. The apostles continued to act in that position until the April conference in 1889, when the First Presidency was again organized with Wilford Woodruff as President. He selected George Q. Cannon and Joseph F. Smith as his counselors. At the time of this organization President Woodruff was 82 years of age, but hale and vigorous. He was born in Farmington, Hartford County, Connecticut, March 1, 1807; was baptized December 31, 1833, and ordained an apostle April 26, 1839. President Woodruff was a natural missionary and accomplished a great work in England and various parts of the United States.

Wilford Woodruff

492 ESSENTIALS IN CHURCH HISTORY

The vacancies in the council of the twelve were not filled until the October conference in 1889, when Marriner W. Merrill, Anthon H. Lund and Abraham H. Cannon were called and ordained apostles.

Manti Temple

Dedication of the Manti Temple.—The temple at Manti, Sanpete County, was dedicated May 21, 1888, Elder Lorenzo Snow offering the prayer. The services were repeated the two succeeding days. This was the third temple to be dedicated in Utah. The site was chosen in June, 1875, by President Brigham Young, and the excavation was begun in April, 1877. The corner stones were laid April 14, 1879, with the usual fitting ceremonies. The building is situated on a hill north-east of the city and is an imposing structure.

The Crusade Continues.—The crusade against those who had entered plural marriage continued after the death of President Taylor, but in some respects with less severity. President Grover Cleveland pardoned a number of the imprisoned men against whom the courts had been extremely severe. These included Joseph H. Evans, a man of seventy, Charles Livingston and Rudger Clawson. From this time on there was a more tolerant attitude manifested by some of the officers. Nevertheless the government continued with unyielding determination to suppress plural marriage, and more drastic legislation was proposed by Congress.

The Crusade in Idaho.—In Idaho the anti-"Mormon" feeling was intense. One officer—who afterwards was honored with the position of United States senator from Idaho—declared that he had selected "a jury that would convict Jesus Christ." Nor was this blasphemous expression the only one uttered in that campaign. Men were hounded and treated in an inhuman manner, and the boast was that "Mormons" would be convicted with or without evidence before the courts.

The Idaho territorial legislature passed a law in 1885, containing the "Idaho test oath," which disfranchised all members of the Church. It provided that electors should swear that they were neither polygamists nor members of an organization which taught, advised or encouraged the practice of polygamy. The supreme court of the United States sustained this law in a decision given February 3, 1890. It was enough to deprive a person of the franchise simply to declare that he was a member of the Church.

The Strubble Bill.—The enemies of the Church in Utah were greatly elated over this decision of the supreme court in the "Idaho test oath" law. They knew that no legislature in Utah would pass such a measure, but they had hopes that Congress would, and thus the great majority of the people of Utah would be disfranchised and their enemies be placed in control. A bill called the Strubble Bill, following the lines of the Idaho law was presented in Congress in 1890. Robert N. Baskin, who was as bitter against the Saints as it was possible for him to be, brazenly declared the object was "to wrest from the hands of the Priesthood the political power which it had wrongfully usurped and shamefully abused." General John A. McClernand, of the Utah Commission, refused to be a party to such wickedness, and made a separate report condemning the proposed high-handed legislation. This bill never became a law for several reasons. Many of the conservative non-"Mormons" of Utah opposed the measure as being detrimental to the interests of the territory, and petitioned Congress not to pass it. Secretary of State James G. Blaine, used his influence to defeat the measure for political reasons, but insisted that the Church do something to relieve the situation.

President Woodruff's Manifesto.—While the Saints were in the midst of all these difficulties and afflictions, President Wilford Woodruff sought the Lord for relief. In answer to his earnest pleadings and constant petitions, the word of the Lord came to him in a revelation suspending the practice of plural marriage. The Latter-day Saints, with the feeling that the anti-polygamy legislation was a restriction of their religious rights, contested every move made by the government. When the supreme court sustained these laws, there was nothing left for the Church to do but submit or stand as violators of the law. They have never felt that the action of the courts was just, nor did they feel that it was within their power to suspend a commandment given to them by revelation from the Lord. The "manifesto" of President Woodruff brought relief. The people had done their duty. The Lord gave them the commandment and only he could authorize its suspension. President Woodruff, writing in his journal September 25, 1890, said:

"I have arrived at a point in the history of my life as the President of the Church of Jesus Christ of Latter-day Saints where I am under the necessity of acting for the temporal salvation of the Church. The United States government has taken a stand and passed laws to destroy the Latter-day Saints on the subject of polygamy or patriarchal marriage, and after praying to the Lord and feeling inspired, I have issued the following proclamation which is sustained by my counselors and the twelve apostles."

The same day the manifesto was published as follows:

"OFFICIAL DECLARATION"

"To Whom it May Concern:

"Press dispatches having been sent for political purposes from Salt Lake City, which have been widely published, to the effect that the Utah Commission, in their recent report to the secretary of the interior, alleged that plural marriages are still being solemnized, and that forty or more such marriages have been contracted in Utah since last June or during the past year: also that in public discourses the leaders of the Church have taught, encouraged, and urged the continuance of the practice of polygamy;

"I, therefore, as President of the Church of Jesus Christ of Latter-day Saints, do hereby, in the most solemn manner, declare that these charges are false. We are not teaching polygamy or plural marriage, nor permitting any person to enter into its practice, and I deny that either forty or any other number of plural marriages have during that period been solemnized in our temples or in any other place in the territory.

"One case has been reported in which the parties alleged that the marriage was performed in the Endowment House, in Salt Lake City, in the spring of 1889, but I have not been able to learn who performed the ceremony. Whatever was done in this matter was without my knowledge. In consequence of this alleged occurrence, the Endowment House was, by my instruction, taken down without delay.

"Inasmuch as laws have been enacted by Congress, forbidding plural marriages, which laws have been pronounced constitutional by the court of the Last Resort, I hereby declare my intention to submit to those laws, and to use my influence with the members of the Church over which I preside to have them do likewise.

"There is nothing in my teachings to the Church, or in those of my associates, during the time specified, which can be reasonably construed to inculcate or encourage polygamy, and when any elder of the Church has used language which appeared to convey any such teaching, he has been promptly reproved. And I now publicly declare that my advice to the Latter-day Saints is to refrain from contracting any marriage forbidden by the law of the land.

"Wilford Woodruff."
"President of The Church of Jesus Christ of Latter-day Saints."

The Manifesto Sustained.—At the conference of the Church held in October following, the manifesto was presented to the congregation and on motion by President Lorenzo Snow of the council of the apostles, was accepted by the Latter-day Saints by unanimous vote. Thus it became binding upon the members of the Church.

Following this action President George Q. Cannon delivered a discourse, reviewing the history of the anti-polygamy legislation and justified the action of President Woodruff on the following grounds: First, when a commandment is given to the children of men, and they are hindered by their enemies, the Lord accepts their offering. Second, the authority which gave the commandment had the right to revoke. In the course of his remarks he quoted verses 49 and 50 of section 124 in the Doctrine and Covenants.

President Woodruff followed the remarks of President Cannon and in part said:

"I want to say to all Israel that the step which I have taken in issuing this manifesto has not been done without earnest prayer before the Lord. * * * I am not ignorant of the feelings that have been engendered through the course I have pursued. But I have done my duty, and the nation of which we form a part must be responsible for that which has been done in relation to this principle.

"The Lord has required at our hands many things that we have not done, many things that we were prevented from doing. The Lord required us to build a temple in Jackson County. We were prevented by violence from doing it. * * * It is not wisdom for us to go forth and carry out this principle against the laws of the nation. * * * The Lord has given us commandments concerning many things and we have carried them out as far as we could; but when we cannot do it, we are justified. * * * The Lord will never permit me or any other man who stands as the President of this Church to lead you astray. It is not in the program. It is not in the mind of God. If I were to attempt that, the Lord would move me out of my place."

Result of the Manifesto.—Following the issuance of the manifesto the sentiment grew that those who had entered into plural marriages before that date should not be interfered with, and men were not to be compelled to desert their wives and children. In time the two political parties, the "People's Party" composed mostly of members of the Church, and the "Liberal Party" composed of the enemies of the Church, disbanded, and the people joined the two great national parties, the Democrats and Republicans, without regard to religious affiliation. However, the more rabid anti-"Mormons" held on to their animosities and organization until the opposition to them among non-"Mormons" was so great that they could resist no longer.

The Granting of Amnesty.—December 19, 1891, the First Presidency and apostles petitioned for amnesty. This petition was endorsed by the governor, Arthur L. Thomas, and Charles S. Zane, who had again become chief justice, and many leading "Gentiles." It was read before the senate committee on territories and became a part of the published record of that body. President Benjamin Harrison, who a short time before had visited Utah, on January 4, 1893, issued a proclamation of amnesty to polygamists for past offenses, limited to those who entered into that relation before November 1, 1890. The Utah commission acting on the pardon of the President, ruled that the restrictions against voters in the territory should be removed.

Laying the Capstone and Dedication of the Salt Lake Temple.— One of the great events in the history of the Latter-day Saints was the dedication of the Salt Lake Temple, April 6, 1893. As previously stated the corner stones were laid forty years before—April 6, 1853. The capstone had been laid April 6, 1892, by President Wilford Woodruff, in the presence of a vast congregation numbering about forty thousand people. After the announcement from the architect from

Salt Lake Temple

the top of the building that the capstone was ready, President Woodruff stepped before the people and said:

"Attention, all the House of Israel, and all ye nations of the earth. We will now lay the top stone of the Temple of our God, the foundation of which was laid and dedicated by the prophet, seer and revelator, Brigham Young."

He then pressed an electric button and the stone was laid. A mighty shout, of "Hosanna! Hosanna! Hosanna! to God and the Lamb! Amen! Amen! Amen!" under the direction of President Lorenzo Snow, went up from the people and was repeated three times.

The dedicatory services, which commenced April 6, 1893, continued several days, and each day the prayer was repeated, for the benefit of the great number of members of the Church who, because of the limited space, could not attend the first services in the building. The ceremonies were impressive and many of the Saints saw visions of heavenly beings and other manifestations during the dedication.

The Tabernacle Choir at the World's Fair.—At the World's Columbian Exposition, held in Chicago in 1893, the Salt Lake Tabernacle Choir entered the competition in the great choral contest which took place early in September, and were successful in winning the second prize. It was the general opinion of those who heard the contest that if it had not been for prejudice they would have received the first honors. On their way to Chicago and returning the choir gave concerts in the large cities, which was a means of allaying much prejudice against the Church.

The Church and the Parliament of Religions.—During this Exposition at Chicago, a World's Parliament of Religions was held, commencing September 11. The Church of Jesus Christ of Latter-day Saints was not invited to participate, but the Church authorities deemed it proper to seek representation and steps to that end were taken, Elder Brigham H. Roberts, of the first council of seventies, was selected to represent the Church at the parliament. When he requested the privilege of taking part and of speaking before that assembly, where Christians, Mohammedans, Jews and Pagans, had been given a public hearing, the privilege was denied him. The manifestation of bigotry was very marked, and the Church was given to understand it was "not of the world." Elder Roberts was granted the privilege of delivering a paper in one of the committee rooms which would seat about fifty persons. This privilege Elder Roberts very properly declined. The matter did not end there, however, as Elder Roberts took the matter up in the press, and the bigotry of the officials of the parliament was exposed, and the Church benefited by the advertisement thus received.

Statehood for Utah.—Delegate Joseph L. Rawlins of Utah presented a bill in the house of representatives, September 6, 1893, entitled "An Act to Enable the People of Utah to Form a Constitution and State Government and to be Admitted into the Union on an Equal Footing with the Original States." The bill met some opposition, one congressman (Morse of Massachusetts) declaring the people of Utah were "criminals and vagabonds." The bill, however, passed the house, December 13, 1893, and the senate in July, 1894, and was signed by President Grover Cleveland. Utah had made several attempts to obtain statehood and several constitutional conventions had been held, but the opposition against the "Mormon" people each time defeated the endeavor. Now both "Mormons" and non-"Mormons" supported the movement, which was successful.

The Constitutional Convention.—In the election held November 6, 1894, for delegates to the constitutional convention, the Republicans were successful. The constitutional convention met March 4, 1895, in Salt Lake City, and organized by electing John Henry Smith, a member of the council of twelve apostles, as president. "Mormons" and "Gentiles" who had opposed each other in the past sat side by side in this convention for sixty-six days, framing the constitution of the State of Utah. When it was presented to the people it was ratified by an overwhelming vote. President Cleveland issued a proclamation, January 4, 1896, and Utah entered the great Union of states. Heber M. Wells, son of Daniel H. Wells, was elected the first governor, and Charles S. Zane the first chief justice of the newly created state.

The Escheated Property Returned.—In September, 1893, Delegate Joseph L. Rawlins presented in Congress a resolution for the restoration of the personal property of the Church. The resolution was favorably acted upon by Congress and President Cleveland signed it October 25. The real estate, escheated to the government, was not returned until three years later. In the last territorial legislature, in 1894, Mr. Charles S. Varian, formerly United States attorney, presented a memorial to Congress asking for this restoration, but the matter was not decided until after Utah obtained statehood. President Cleveland, March 28, 1896, approved of a memorial to this effect presented by one of Utah's representatives in the senate and which had passed both the senate and the house of representatives.

The Pioneer Jubilee.—After Utah became a state, an era of good feeling prevailed among all the people. Governor Heber M. Wells recommended in one of his messages to the legislature, that the state hold an inter-mountain fair, or jubilee, during the month of July, 1897, it being fifty years from the entrance of the pioneers into the Salt Lake Valley. This recommendation was approved and a committee was appointed to prepare for the celebration. On the first day (July 20) of the celebration a monument which had been erected at the intersection of Main and South Temple Streets, Salt Lake City, in honor of Brigham Young and the pioneers, was unveiled and dedicated, by President Wilford Woodruff, one of the pioneers. The statue of President Young which is on a base of Utah granite, was designed by Cyrus E. Dallin, a Utah-born artist, and was presented to the state by the Brigham Young Memorial Association, the funds having been raised by popular subscription. James H. Moyle made the presentation speech, and Governor Wells the speech of acceptance. Judge Charles C. Goodwin, editor of the Salt Lake *Tribune*, delivered an oration, and remarks were made by Brigham Young, Jr., the oldest surviving son of President Young. The celebration continued until the close of Pioneer Day, with parades, speeches, music and other exercises. A badge of honor, made of gold and artistically designed, was presented to each of the surviving pioneers of 1847, who were the honored guests of the occasion.

Death of President Woodruff.—One year later, July 24, 1898, the Pioneer Square—where the stockade was built in 1847—was dedicated as a public park. President Woodruff delivered his last public address at this celebration. A few days later he departed for the Pacific coast hoping to benefit his health. He died at the home of Colonel Isaac Trumbo in San Francisco, September 2, 1898. He had been very anxious to live to see the Church out of debt, but this was not his privilege. Due to the escheatment of its property, and the persecutions during the crusade, the Church was placed in financial straits, but it was left for his successor to remedy the evil.

President Woodruff's remains were brought to Salt Lake City, where a public funeral was held in the tabernacle, September 8, and his memory was honored by all the citizens of the state. President Woodruff, at the time of his death, was in his ninety-second year. His life was one of marked simplicity and virtue. He served for many years as Church historian, and kept remarkable journals, recording in detail all important events of which he was a witness.

CHAPTER 52

THE ADMINISTRATION OF PRESIDENT LORENZO SNOW

1898—1901

The Presidency Re-organized.—Eleven days after the death of President Wilford Woodruff the apostles met in council and reorganized the First Presidency. Lorenzo Snow, then in his 85th year, was sustained as President of the Church, and selected the same counselors who had served with President Woodruff. The reason for this immediate action in reorganizing the First Presidency was a statement by President Woodruff, shortly before his death, that "it was not the will of the Lord that in the future there should be a lengthy period elapse between the death of the president and the re-organization of the First Presidency." At the October conference (1898) the usual procedure was followed in presenting the new officers of the presidency, and all the authorities of the Church were unanimously sustained. Elder Rudger Clawson,

Lorenzo Snow

president of the Box Elder Stake, was called to the apostleship and was ordained, October 10.

President Lorenzo Snow.—President Lorenzo Snow was born April 3, 1814, in Mantua, Portage County, Ohio. In June, 1836, he was baptized by John F. Boynton, and the following winter was ordained an elder. He immediately entered the ministry and was laboring in Kentucky when the Saints were expelled from Missouri. In the early forties he labored in Great Britain, his fields being Manchester, Liverpool, Birmingham and London. After the departure of most of the apostles from that mission he acted as assistant to Elder Parley P. Pratt, who presided over the British Mission. He returned to America in 1843 and made his home at Nauvoo. In 1849 he was called to the apostleship, and took a mission to Italy, where he introduced the work, but met with little success. During the anti-polygamy crusade he was sentenced by Judge Orlando W. Powers under the "segregation" ruling, to serve three terms of imprisonment of six months each, making a period of eighteen months, and to pay three fines of three hundred dollars each. The supreme court of Utah confirmed the sentence and an appeal was taken to the court of last resort. After he had served eleven months of his imprisonment the supreme court of the United States reversed the ruling made in his case, denying the right of the Utah judges to inflict punishment by "segregation," and he was released from confinement. This ruling also released others who had been illegally sentenced by the judges of the Utah courts. President Snow was sustained as the president of the Twelve Apostles when the First Presidency was re-organized in 1889, and was also called to preside in the Salt Lake Temple when that building was opened for work (1893), which position he retained until his death.

The Roberts Case.—At the general election held November 8, 1898, Brigham H. Roberts (Democrat) and a member of the presiding council of the seventies, was elected as Utah's representative in Congress, and Robert N. Baskin was elected to the Utah supreme court. During the campaign much was said by the enemies of Mr. Roberts, because he had a plural family, and the agitation became nationwide. It had been understood when Utah became a state that there should be no more plural marriages, and the Utah constitution contained a provision as follows:

"That perfect toleration of religious sentiment shall be secured and that no inhabitant of said state shall ever be molested in person or property on account of his or her mode of religious worship; provided, that polygamous or plural marriages are forever prohibited."

However it was not understood that those who had entered into that relation should be barred from political rights. President Grover Cleveland, in September, 1894, by proclamation, restored all political and civil rights to those who had been disfranchised by the anti-polygamy legislation. Similar action had previously been taken by President Benjamin Harrison. John Henry Smith, president of the constitutional convention, was a polygamist, and Brigham H. Roberts also served in that body without any question of opposition, and helped to frame the constitution which prohibited plural marriage in the state.

Opposition of the Ministers.—The opposition against Congressman Roberts was led by the Ministerial Alliance of Salt Lake City, Attorney A. T. Schroeder, and the Salt Lake *Tribune,* which at that time was the organ of the Republican party. Mr. Charles C. Goodwin, editor of the *Tribune,* had served with B. H. Roberts in the constitutional convention without a thought of opposition. It appeared now that the old question was to be revived through religious and political hate, and that the harmony which had prevailed was to come to an end. The Ministerial Alliance met December 6, 1898, and prepared an address which was signed by twenty-four "ministers of the Gospel," "most earnestly" calling upon the people of the United States to join them in a protest against the seating of Congressman-elect Roberts of Utah. They declared that the "Mormon" Church, in the election of Congressman Roberts, had broken its pledge with the government.

Statement of President Snow.—In a telegram to the New York *World,* December 29, 1898, President Snow stated, officially and emphatically, in answer to the many false reports, that plural marriages had ceased with the issuance of the manifesto by President Woodruff, and that the Church had nothing to do with the nomination and election of B. H. Roberts, that matter being entirely a secular and political affair. The record of the election showed that B. H. Roberts received greater support from the non-"Mormons" than he did from the "Mormon" people.

Declaration of Senator Rawlins.—In answer to the false accusations, Senator Joseph L. Rawlins (non-"Mormon") stated:

"That polygamists should be disqualified to vote or to hold office was no part of the compact between the state of Utah and the United States. In territorial elections polygamists were so disqualified. But Congress purposely and knowingly wiped away all such disqualifications as to the very first election to be held under the enabling act, namely, the election of delegates to the Constitutional Convention."

Congressman Roberts Excluded.—When B. H. Roberts was called to the bar of the house to be sworn in, Mr. Robert W. Tayler of Ohio arose and moved that the question of the right of the representative from Utah be referred to a committee of nine members of the house, and until such committee made report, the said B. H. Roberts should not be sworn in, or permitted to occupy a seat. The motion was carried, and after an investigation of six weeks, seven of the members of the committee reported in favor of his exclusion which should be determined by a majority vote; the other two members of the committee favored admission of the Utah member, and then expulsion afterwards. In the meantime many petitions from all parts of the United States poured into Congress asking for his expulsion. January 25, 1900, the matter came to a vote and bigotry prevailed. Congressman-elect Roberts was excluded by a vote of 244 to 50 and 36 not voting. A number of those who voted for the majority report confessed that they voted against their consciences and in favor of public clamor that their own political lives might be saved. Having been given a chance to make a defense, B. H. Roberts spoke, making a vigorous and telling protest against the bigoted action proposed against him.

The Issue of Church Bonds.—Due to the financial difficulties in which the Church was placed because of continued prosecution and persecution, it became necessary for some action to be taken. It was decided that bonds be issued, and this was done in the sum of one million dollars. The bonds were taken up by the people at home and local interests, and by this aid the Church was able to meet its many obligations and was saved from financial embarrassment.

The Law of Tithing.—The administration of President Lorenzo Snow was noted particularly for the teaching of the law of tithing, and the great reform among the members of the Church in relation to that principle. This reform was inaugurated in the spring of 1899, while the presidency were visiting the various settlements of the Church in southern Utah. On the return journey from St. George the law of tithing was made the special theme. This topic was continued in the sessions of the Mutual Improvement conference held the latter part of May, and it became the watchword, or slogan, of the various stakes. A resolution was unanimously adopted in the Mutual conference, as follows:

"*Resolved*: That we accept the doctrine of tithing, as now presented by President Snow, as the present word and will of the Lord unto us, and we do accept it with all our hearts; we will ourselves observe it, and we will do all in our power to get the Latter-day Saints to do likewise."

After a few remarks by Elder Francis M. Lyman in relation to the resolution, President Snow remarked: "Brethren, the God of our fathers Abraham, Isaac and Jacob bless you. Every man who is here, who has made this promise will be saved in the Celestial Kingdom. God bless you. Amen."

The Solemn Fast-Day.—Following the Mutual conference, a solemn assembly of all the general authorities and the officers of the various stakes, was held in the Salt Lake Temple, Sunday, July 2, 1899. The day was also observed as a general fast day according to the custom of the Church.*a* The law of tithing was discussed among other important topics, and here also a resolution was adopted by the assembled brethren, six hundred and twenty-three officers of the Church being present, that they would covenant with the Lord to observe this sacred law of tithing, and teach the Saints to do the same. From that time forth the paying of tithes and offerings on the part of the members was observed with increased interest, although there still are many who do not faithfully observe this law.

Celebration of Mission Jubilees.—The fiftieth anniversary of the introduction of the Gospel into Scandinavia was celebrated with fitting ceremonies, Thursday, June 14, 1900, in the Assembly Hall, Salt Lake City. Elder Anthon H. Lund, of the council of the apostles, presided. The festivities continued until the 17th of June.

A similar celebration was held in December, 1900, at Honolulu, Hawaii, in commemoration of the opening of the mission in the Hawaiian Islands. President George Q. Cannon, one of the first missionaries to the land, was present as the guest of honor. The Saints from the various islands assembled and engaged in a time of feasting and refreshing and were instructed by President Cannon and many others.

The Scofield Disaster.—A sad occurrence which cast a cloud of gloom over Utah, was the explosion in Mine number 4, at Winter Quarters, near Scofield, Carbon County, May 1, 1900. About two hundred miners were killed many of whom were members of the Church. Elders George Teasdale, Heber J. Grant and Reed Smoot, of the council of the twelve, attended the services which were held

---

*a*One day each month is set apart by the Church as a fast day. Before the administration of President Wilford Woodruff the first Thursday in each month was set apart for this purpose. December 6, 1896, a change in the day was made and the first Sunday of each month has been observed as a general fast day for the members of the Church since that time.

at Scofield, Sunday, May 6, 1900. Governor Heber M. Wells appealed to the public for aid for the bereaved families and the people of the state responded nobly.

The Japanese Mission.—An event of great interest which occurred near the close of the ministry of President Snow, was the opening of a mission in Japan. In keeping with the commandment to preach the Gospel in all the world, President Snow was led to send missionaries to the people of the Far East. Elder Heber J. Grant, of the council of the apostles, was chosen February 14, 1901, to open that mission. Later Elders Horace S. Ensign, Louis A. Kelsch and Alma O. Taylor, were called to assist in that labor. These brethren departed for Japan, July 24, 1901, and arrived in Yokohama, August 12. The work of teaching the natives was slow because of the many centuries of pagan teaching and the difficulty the elders had in learning the language. After the return of the other brethren, Elder Taylor remained in that land as president of the mission for nine years. Work is still being conducted among the Japanese.

Death of President Snow.—When the October conference was held in 1901, President Snow was ill and unable to attend the opening sessions. Sunday afternoon, the third and closing day (Oct. 6), he was present and, though somewhat feeble, made extended remarks. At the close of his address the general authorities were sustained. Joseph F. Smith was presented as first counselor in the First Presidency—President George Q. Cannon having died April 12, 1901, in California—and Rudger Clawson was presented as second counselor. These brethren, however, were not set apart to these positions, for President Snow returned from the conference and was confined to his room in the Bee Hive House, where, four days later (Oct. 10), he died. Funeral services were held in the tabernacle on the 13th, after which the body was taken by special train to Brigham City, President Snow's former home, and there interred, in the presence of the general authorities of the Church and a vast concourse of people.

CHAPTER 53

THE ADMINISTRATION OF PRESIDENT JOSEPH F. SMITH

1901–1918

The Presidency Re-organized.—At the regular weekly meeting of the apostles, held in the Salt Lake Temple, October 17, 1901, the First Presidency was re-organized. Joseph F. Smith, the senior apostle, was sustained as President of the Church, and he selected John R. Winder and Anthon H. Lund as his counselors. Brigham Young, Jr., was chosen president of the council of the twelve apostles. John R. Winder the first counselor in the First Presidency, was at the time of his appointment second counselor to Presiding Bishop William B. Preston. Anthon H. Lund was a member of the council of apostles. Both counselors were men of wide experience, careful and conservative, and well fitted for this new calling. One week later (Oct. 24) Hyrum Mack Smith, eldest son of President Joseph F. Smith, was called to fill the vacancy in the council of the apostles.

Joseph F. Smith

A Special Conference.—A special conference of the Church was held in the tabernacle, November 10, 1901, and the general authorities of the Church were sustained by the vote of the people. Each quorum of the Priesthood voted separately, and then the entire body of the Saints, according to the regular custom when a new First Presidency is sustained.

President Joseph F. Smith.—November 13, 1838, Joseph F. Smith was born at Far West, Missouri. A few days before his birth his father Hyrum Smith and his uncle, Joseph Smith the Prophet, and others, had been taken prisoners by the mob-militia of Missouri on the false charge of treason, and were under sentence to be shot. As a child Joseph F. Smith passed through the trying scenes of Missouri and Illinois, and in 1848 (Sept. 23) he entered the Salt Lake Valley with his mother. Although but a boy nine years of age, he drove an ox team across the plains from the Missouri River. In 1852 his mother, Mary Fielding Smith, died, and two years later, May 27, 1854, he left for a mission to the Hawaiian Islands, when but fifteen years of age. He performed active and faithful missionary service in that land and later in Great Britain and was ordained an apostle by President Brigham Young, July 1, 1866. October 8, 1867, he was chosen as one of the council of the twelve, succeeding Amasa M. Lyman. With the exception of the interim between the administration of President Taylor and that of President Woodruff, he served as a member of the First Presidency from October, 1880, until the death of President Snow.

John R. Winder

The Bureau of Information.—An important step in the missionary work of the Church was the opening of the "Bureau of Information and Church Literature," August 4, 1902, on the temple block. A small building for the entertainment of strangers and as a storehouse

ADMINISTRATION OF JOSEPH F. SMITH

for literature was erected in 1902, and the work was placed under the direction of Benjamin Goddard, Thomas Hull, Arnold H. Schulthess and Josiah Burrows. About seventy-five members of the Church were called to act as guides and entertain visitors. Literature was freely distributed and much prejudice was removed. The first year more than one hundred and fifty thousand persons visited the block, and eighteen or twenty years later over four hundred thousand people, on the average, passed through the grounds annually. In 1904 a more commodious building was erected which has been added to from time to time until now an excellent building stands upon the ground for the benefit and comfort of strangers.

Anthon H. Lund

The Reed Smoot Case.—January 20, 1903, the legislature of Utah elected Reed Smoot United States senator. He had been a candidate before, but stepped aside in favor of another. April 8, 1900, he was called to the apostleship, and the anti-"Mormon" element in Utah made this a pretext for entering a protest against his being seated. As early as November 24, 1903, when it became known that he would be a candidate, the Ministerial Alliance, an organization of Protestant ministers of Salt Lake City, adopted resolutions in protest of his candidacy. Their grounds were that he was an apostle of the "Mormon" Church, and believed in polygamy. They had been successful in eliminating B. H. Roberts from political office in 1900, and this gave them encouragement to press the matter further in their campaign to disfranchise all the elders of the Church, and if successful, eventually all members of the Church. B. H. Roberts was denied his seat on the grounds that he was a polygamist; Reed Smoot was to be eliminated because he "believed in polygamy" and was an apostle of the Church. It was commonly reported that if Reed Smoot could be denied a seat in the senate, then any member of the Church who had been through the temple could also be deprived of his franchise, and this was the aim of these reverend gentlemen and their associates.

Protest of Citizens.—January 25, 1903, nineteen citizens[a] of Salt Lake City signed and forwarded to the senate of the United States a formal protest asking for the expulsion of Reed Smoot from the senate.[b]

In substantiation of these charges the protestants quoted from various sources, including many newspaper reports utterly unreliable and false upon their very face. The Rev. John L. Leilich also made separate affidavit stating among other falsehoods that Reed Smoot was a polygamist. As this charge was untrue the reverend gentleman was unable to prove his statements.

Senator Smoot Makes Reply.—To all these charges Senator Smoot made full and complete denial in an answer in the District of Columbia, January 4, 1904. March 5, 1903, he had been sworn in as a senator and his case was referred to the committee on privileges and elections of which Julius C. Burrows of Michigan was chairman. Mr. Robert W. Tayler, of Ohio, who gained some prominence and notoriety in the case of B. H. Roberts, was the attorney for the protestants. Senator Smoot was represented by A. S. Worthington, of Washington, and Waldemar Van Cott, of Salt Lake City.

The Case Before the Senate.—The case was first considered by the committee on privileges and elections, January 16, 1904, and con-

---

[a]These nineteen were: Rev. William M. Paden, Parley L. Williams, Edward B. Critchlow, E. W. Wilson, Charles C. Goodwin, L. W. Colbath, William A. Nelden, Rev. Clarence T. Brown, Ezra Thompson, J. J. Corum, George R. Hancock, W. Mont Ferry, Rev. John L. Leilich, Harry Hill, Clarence E. Allen, George M. Scott, S. H. Lewis, H. G. McMillan and Rev. Abiel Leonard. L. W. Colbath later withdrew his name.

[b]This protest was divided under six heads as follows:

1. The Mormon Priesthood according to the doctrine of that Church, is vested with supreme authority in all things temporal and spiritual.

2. The first presidency and twelve apostles are supreme in the exercise and transmission of the mandates of this authority.

3. As this body of men has not abandoned the principles and practices of political dictation, so also it has not abandoned belief in polygamy and polygamous cohabitation.

4. That this is the attitude of the first presidency and apostolate, even since the suspensory manifesto of 1890, is evidenced by their teachings since then.

5. This body of officials, of whom Senator-elect Smoot is one, also practice or connive at and encourage the practice of polygamy and polygamous cohabitation, and those whom they have permitted to hold legislative office have, without protest or objection from them, sought to pass a law nullifying enactments against polygamous cohabitation.

6. The supreme authorities in the Church, of whom Senator-elect Reed Smoot is one, to-wit, the first presidency and twelve apostles, not only connive at violation of, but protect and honor the violators of the laws against polygamy and polygamous cohabitation.

tinued before that committee until June, 1906. The chairman, Julius C. Burrows, and other members of the committee manifested a spirit of extreme hatred in the case. It was apparent from the beginning that it was The Church of Jesus Christ of Latter-day Saints that was on trial before the nation, not Senator Reed Smoot. Many witnesses were called, including President Joseph F. Smith and other leaders of the Church, who were treated with very little consideration by the majority of the committee members. Thousands of petitions asking for Reed Smoot's expulsion poured into the senate from all over the United States, and the spirit of prejudice ran high. During the two years of the investigation the Church was thoroughly advertised before the world. The press of the country, seeking for the sensational, grasped at every item of evidence detrimental to the interest of the Church and magnified much of the testimony, coloring it with additional falsehood. Nevertheless there appeared from time to time friendly comments and articles in various quarters where men were big and broad enough to face the prejudice of the world. It can be said in perfect truth that the investigation, while carried on in the spirit of extreme hatred, resulted beneficially for the Church.

The Case Decided.—June 11, 1906, the committee made report to the senate. The majority report, which was adverse to Senator Smoot, was signed by Chairman J. C. Burrows, and supported by Senators J. P. Dolliver, Edmund W. Pettus, Fred T. Dubois, Joseph Bailey, Lee S. Overman, and William A. Clark. They stated that "the more deliberately and carefully the testimony taken in the investigation is considered, the more irresistibly it leads to the conclusion that the facts stated in the protest are true."

The minority report, signed by Senators Joseph B. Foraker, Albert J. Beveridge, William P. Dillingham, Albert J. Hopkins and Philander C. Knox, held to the opposite view.

The case was called up in the senate, December 13, 1906, and continued before that body—a large number of the senators making speeches—until February 20, 1907, when the final vote was taken. The resolution was amended so that it required the concurrence of two-thirds of the senators present. The vote stood yeas 28, nays 42, and 20 not voting; consequently the result of the vote was that the resolution was rejected and Senator Smoot retained his seat.

The "American Party."—In January 1901, Thomas Kearns, a rich mining man, was elected by the legislature to the United States senate to fill a four-year term, which had been vacant for two years because the previous legislature failed to elect a senator. Mr. Kearns was very anxious to be returned to the senate and sought the support of

President Joseph F. Smith—in other words the support of the Church—which was not given, and he was informed that the Church was not in politics. Having obtained control of the Salt Lake *Tribune* he made it his personal organ of hate against the Church in general and President Joseph F. Smith in particular. He and others of like character, in the autumn of 1904, organized the "American Party." The excuse offered for this political party was the investigation going on in the Reed Smoot case. This anti-"Mormon" political organization endured from 1904 until 1911, and during those years captured the machinery of Salt Lake City. A campaign of vindictive falsehood was conducted which was a disgrace and a foul blot on the state of Utah. During this time the *Tribune* maliciously cartooned, and wickedly vilified President Joseph F. Smith in its columns in a manner that would not have been tolerated anywhere outside of Utah. Finally, even anti-"Mormons" sickened of the condition, and the better element of the "American Party" joined with other citizens and put an end to the obnoxious condition.

President Smith's Attitude.—The only reply President Joseph F. Smith made to these vicious and daily attacks, was to express himself as follows:

"I feel in my heart to forgive all men in the broad sense that God requires of me to forgive all men, and I desire to love my neighbor as myself; and to this extent I bear no malice towards any of the children of my Father. But there are enemies to the work of the Lord, as there were enemies of the Son of God. There are those who speak only evil of the Latter-day Saints. There are those—and they abound largely in our midst—who will shut their eyes to every virtue and to every good thing connected with this latter-day work, and will pour out floods of falsehood and misrepresentation against the people of God. I forgive them for this. I leave them in the hand of the just Judge."

The Case of John W. Taylor and M. F. Cowley.—While the investigation at Washington was going on, Elders John W. Taylor and Matthias F. Cowley were requested by the senate committee as witnesses. President Smith was asked to locate them and have them go to Washington. In answer to his appeal they declined to go. It was discovered that they were out of harmony with the attitude of the Church regarding the manifesto of President Woodruff. They maintained that the manifesto applied to the United States only. However, the attitude of the Church was that it applied to the entire world.

Official Statement of President Smith.—This led to the discovery that some plural marriages had been entered into contrary to the announcement of President Woodruff, and also a statement made by President Lorenzo Snow. Therefore, President Smith, at the general conference, April 6, 1904, made the following official statement:

"Inasmuch as there are numerous reports in circulation that plural marriages have been entered into, contrary to the official declaration of President Woodruff of September 24, 1890, commonly called the manifesto, which was issued by President Woodruff, and adopted by the Church at its general conference, October 6, 1890, which forbade any marriage violative of the law of the land, I, Joseph F. Smith, President of the Church of Jesus Christ of Latter-day Saints, hereby affirm and declare that no such marriages have been solemnized with the sanction, consent, or knowledge of the Church of Jesus Christ of Latter-day Saints.

"And I hereby announce that all such marriages are prohibited, and if any officer or member of the Church shall assume to solemnize or enter into any such marriage, he will be deemed in transgression against the Church, and will be liable to be dealt with according to the rules and regulations thereof and excommunicated therefrom.

(Signed) "Joseph F. Smith."
"President of The Church of Jesus Christ of Latter-day Saints."

This statement, on motion of Francis M. Lyman, was presented to the conference and unanimously adopted. The agitation which followed led to the resignation, October 28, 1905, of Elders John W. Taylor and Matthias F. Cowley from the council of the apostles.

Dedication of the Joseph Smith Monument.—Monday, December 18, 1905, President Joseph F. Smith and about twenty-five others, including a number of the general authorities of the Church, left Salt Lake City, for Sharon, Vermont, to dedicate a monument on the farm where Joseph Smith the Prophet was born. This beautiful monument, with a polished granite shaft thirty-eight and one-half feet high—one foot for every year of the Prophet's life—had been erected under the direction of Elder Junius F. Wells. December 23, 1905, the one hundredth anniversary of the Prophet's birth, it was dedicated and unveiled, President Smith offering the prayer. A short time before this event the Mack farm, on which the monument stands, had been purchased by the Church and a cottage built on the spot where the old home stood in which the Prophet was born. Subsequently the Church purchased the Smith farm and Sacred Grove, in Manchester township, New York.

President Smith Visits Europe.—In the summer of 1906, President Joseph F. Smith and Presiding Bishop Charles W. Nibley went to Europe and spent some time in each of the missions. This was the first time a President of the Church, while holding that office, had stood on Europe's soil. It proved to be a great blessing to the Saints abroad and encouraged and built them up in the faith. An incident worthy of record which occurred on that trip was the remarkable healing of John Roothoff, a boy eleven years of age, residing in Rotterdam. The youth was blind, but learning that President Smith would be present he said to his mother: "If you will take me with you to meeting and he (President Smith) will look into my eyes, I believe they will be healed." He was permitted to accompany his mother, and at the close of the services President Smith greeted each individual and shook hands with them. As the mother presented her son, President Smith raised the bandage on his eyes, and blessed him. When he returned home the boy said: "Mamma, my eyes are well, I can't feel any more pain. I can see now, and far, too."

The Address to the World.—At the general conference of the Church in April, 1907, which was held shortly after the settlement of the case against Senator Smoot, the First Presidency of the Church issued an "Address to the World" which was read to, and adopted by the conference. It set forth clearly the attitude of the Church respecting many matters which had been discussed during the hearing at Washington, and was also a reply to numerous magazine articles which appeared about that time written expressly for the injury of the Church.

It was stated in this address, in answer to the many false accusations, that the Church had respectfully submitted to the law enacted against plural marriage. "If it is urged that there have been instances of the violation of the anti-polygamy laws," the document read, "the plain answer is that in every state and nation there are individuals who violate law in spite of all the vigilance that can be exercised; but it does not follow that the integrity of a community or a state is destroyed, because of such individual transgressions. All we ask is that the same common-sense judgment be exercised in relation to our community that is accorded to other communities." It was also declared that the Church stood for the "absolute separation of Church and State; no domination of the State by the Church; no State interference with the functions of the Church, or with the free exercise of religion; the absolute freedom of the individual from the domination of ecclesiastical authority in political affairs; the equality of all churches before the law.

"The reaffirmation of this doctrine and policy, however, is predicated upon the express understanding that politics in the States where our people reside shall be conducted as in other parts of the Union; that there shall be no interference by the State with the Church, nor with the free exercise of religion. Should political parties make war upon the Church, or menace the civil, political, or religious rights of its members as such—against a policy of that kind, by any political party or set of men whatsoever, we assert the inherent right of self-preservation for the Church, and her right to call upon all her children, and upon all who love justice, and desire the perpetuation of religious liberty, to come to her aid, to stand with her until the danger shall have passed. And this openly, submitting the justice of our cause to the enlightened judgment of our fellow men, should such an issue unhappily arise. We desire to live in peace and confidence with our fellow citizens of all political parties and of all religions."

Changes in the Presidency.—President John R. Winder, first counselor in the First Presidency, died Mar. 27, 1910. At the general conference in April following, Anthon H. Lund was advanced to the position of first counselor, and John Henry Smith was chosen as second counselor in the presidency. President John Henry Smith died October 13, 1911, and Elder Charles W. Penrose was chosen to succeed him, in the following December. The presiding patriarch, John Smith, died Nov. 6, 1911, and his grandson, Hyrum G. Smith, was sustained in that calling at the general conference of the Church, April 6, 1912.

The Saints in Mexico.—During the year 1912, on account of civil war in Mexico and the constant raid of banditti and guerrillas, the members of the Church residing in the Juarez Stake were robbed and persecuted and finally forced to seek refuge in the United States.

John Henry Smith

With the hope that they would again return to their homes most of them located near the border, but as time passed and the condition did not improve, a large number moved away and located in other stakes, abandoning their property in Mexico. Some who remained near the border returned to their homes with the hope that they would be partially reimbursed for their losses.

The World War.—In the summer of 1914, Archduke Franz Ferdinand, heir to the throne of Austria-Hungary, was murdered by a Serbian student. This event caused strained relations to exist between Austria and Serbia. Austria backed by Germany, was not willing to accept the conciliatory note of the smaller country, which did everything possible to avoid a rupture, and declared war July 28, 1914. The action was followed by a declaration of war by Germany against Russia on a pretext, August 1. Germany also made an attack on France, attempting to go through Belgium, against the wishes of that kingdom, to expedite their advancement. The invasion of Belgium brought Great Britain into the conflict, and eventually most of the countries of the earth were drawn into the war. Due to Germany's ruthless submarine campaign on the high seas, the United States was forced to declare war against that power, April 6, 1917. Those nations which were not actually aligned with one or the other hostile force, were caused to suffer great privation and hardship. The great conflict continued until November 11, 1918, when an armistice was declared, which later resulted in a treaty of peace, Germany and her Allies, Austria-Hungary and Turkey, being required to pay enormous war indemnity. Millions of lives were sacrificed and billions in property destroyed during the four years of actual conflict, and at the close the nations found themselves on the verge of bankruptcy.

Charles W. Penrose

During the first year (1917) the United States was in the war, 3,854 members of the Church were in the army; 616 in the navy; 196 in the marines and over 800 in other branches of the service, including the Red Cross and medical corps. By the early part of January, 1919, there were 14,975 members of the Church in the service. Between six and seven hundred lost their lives during the period of the war.

The Fulfilment of Prophecy.—The world war was a further fulfilment of the prophecy on war, given to Joseph Smith, Christmas day, 1832, wherein the revelation states that "the days will come that war will be poured out upon all nations." This revelation on war was partly fulfilled during the rebellion of the Southern States, which was the beginning of the end, according to the revelation. There are yet other things pertaining to war and the vexation of the nations, spoken of in that prophecy, which are to be fulfilled.

A Period of Prosperity.—The administration of President Joseph F. Smith was noted chiefly for the prosperity and advancement of the Church during the seventeen years of his presidency. The work spread abroad in the earth as well as in the stakes of Zion. Meeting houses and tabernacles, with all the modern conveniences, were erected in many stakes and wards. Even in the mission fields commodious headquarters and churches were purchased or built in various places. The Dr. Groves Latter-day Saints Hospital, one of the best in the country, was erected. Two large and important structures, the Bishop's Building and the Church Office Building, were built for the purpose of taking care of the various offices and departments of Church work. The Church school system was advanced and enlarged, and the very best facilities were obtained for the education of the youth of Zion. Two temples, one at Cardston, Canada, and one at Laie, Hawaii, were under course of erection, and the work for the salvation of the dead received an impetus which filled the present temples to overflowing. The Church was placed in a position to command the respect of all honest men. Prejudice was overcome, and the great men of our nation commenced to look upon the Latter-day Saints with more kindly feelings.

The Passing of President Smith.—In the spring of 1918, President Smith commenced to fail in health, and during the late summer and fall he attended to most of his business matters in his own room spending very little time at the office. He would generally take a short automobile ride in the afternoon, from which he received great benefit. During the October conference (1918) he was improved and presided at all the sessions. His opening address was heard in all parts of the tabernacle, but was not delivered with his usual physical vigor. After the conference he was again confined to his room the greater part of his time. October 3, 1918, the day before the conference convened, he received a remarkable manifestation in which much additional light was revealed regarding the salvation of the dead and the visit of the Savior to the world of spirits after his crucifixion. He made reference, indirectly, to this vision in his remarks at the conference, but it was not published until December, having first been submitted, October 31, to the counselors in the presidency and the apostles and patriarch and unanimously accepted by them.

Sunday, November 17, 1918, President Smith was taken with an attack of pleurisy which continued to grow in intensity, finally developing into pleuro-pneumonia, and he passed away, Tuesday morning, November 19. No public funeral could be held as the city was under quarantine because an epidemic of influenza was over all the land. Thousands of people lined the streets as the cortege passed and services in the cold open air were held at the grave, where brief remarks were made by President Heber J. Grant and Bishop Charles W. Nibley. President Anthon H. Lund had charge of the services and President Charles W. Penrose dedicated the grave.

CHAPTER 54

THE ADMINISTRATION OF PRESIDENT HEBER J. GRANT

1918–1945

President Heber J. Grant.—By virtue of his position as president of the council of apostles, Heber J. Grant became the presiding officer of the Church at the death of President Smith. Heeding the instruction of President Wilford Woodruff—which was given by revelation, and was followed by Presidents Snow and Smith—that the First Presidency should be organized without delay, the council of apostles met November 23, 1918, in the temple, and Heber J. Grant was sustained and set apart as President of the Church. He selected as his counselors Anthon H. Lund and Charles W. Penrose, who had served with President Joseph F. Smith.

President Grant was born November 22, 1856, in Salt Lake City. He was the son of Jedediah Morgan and Rachel Ridgeway Ivins Grant. He was a man of great activity and endless energy; full of sympathy for the

Heber J. Grant

520   ESSENTIALS IN CHURCH HISTORY

down-trodden and the poor. In the financial world he was recognized as a man of keen ability, yet his life was constantly devoted to the welfare and progress of the Church, his labors in the ministry dating from his early youth. In 1880 he was called to preside over the Tooele Stake of Zion, succeeding Francis M. Lyman who had been called into the council of the twelve. Two years later (October 16, 1882) he was himself ordained an apostle, having been called, with Elder George Teasdale, to that office by revelation. In 1901 he went to Japan and there opened the door for the preaching of the Gospel, and after his return he was called to preside over the European mission, where he labored for three years.

The General Conference Postponed.—Because of the influenza epidemic no meetings were held during the winter and spring of 1919. On this account, the general conference, which otherwise would have been held in April, was postponed until June 1, 1919. On that occasion the solemn assembly of the Priesthood was held, and the authorities of the Church were sustained by the usual separate vote of the quorums. That conference was devoted largely to a memorial service for President Joseph F. Smith.

Dedication of the Hawaiian Temple.—Thanksgiving day, November 27, 1919, the temple at Laie, Hawaii, was dedicated by

Hawaiian Temple

President Heber J. Grant. He was accompanied to that land by President Anthon H. Lund, Rudger Clawson, Stephen L Richards, Presiding Bishop Charles W. Nibley and Arthur Winter. The dedicatory services were repeated, five services being held to accommodate all the people—1,239 souls attending the services. This is the first temple erected outside of the continental United States, and is for the benefit of the native Saints of the islands of the Pacific. The mission in the Hawaiian Islands was opened in 1850 by George Q. Cannon and others, and thousands of the natives received the Gospel. The site for the Hawaiian temple was dedicated by President Joseph F. Smith, June 1, 1915.

Passing of President Lund—Changes in the Presidency.—After a brief illness, President Anthon H. Lund first counselor in the first presidency, passed away at his home in Salt Lake City, March 2, 1921. He served in the presidency during the entire ministry of President Joseph F. Smith, having been chosen second counselor in October, 1901. After the death of John R. Winder, the first counselor, he was advanced to that position in April, 1910. President Lund was a man without guile, faithful and true to the Gospel and to the brethren, and beloved by all the Saints.

Anthony W. Ivins

At the meeting of the council of the presiding authorities held in the Salt Lake Temple, Thursday, March 10, 1921, President Charles W. Penrose was chosen by President Heber J. Grant as his first counselor, and Elder Anthony W. Ivins as his second counselor. Rudger Clawson was at the same time set apart as president of the twelve apostles, as he became the ranking apostle after the death of President Lund.

The General Conference of April, 1920.—At the general conference of the Church held in April, 1920, the one hundredth anniversary of the Prophet's vision of the Father and the Son, was fittingly observed. Remarks by the brethren had a bearing upon the great work accomplished by the Prophet Joseph Smith, and the authenticity of his story. *The Improvement Era*, organ of the priesthood quorums and of the Young Men's Mutual Improvement Associations, devoted the April number to special articles dealing with the theme of the Vision. Other magazines did the same. A cantata by Evan Stephens, which was prepared for the occasion, was presented before a crowded house in the Tabernacle, and special topics were considered in the wards throughout the Church following the April Conference.

Progress of the Church.—Ninety years before (1830) the Church was organized with but six members. In 1920, it numbered several hundred thousands. Its property in meeting houses, tabernacles, temples and other structures, was valued at many millions of dollars. There were 83 stakes of Zion, 871 organized wards and 83 independent branches within the stakes. Missionary work had been carried to various parts of the earth, and there were 24 missions regularly established with numerous conferences (later called districts) and branches. The total number of men holding the Melchizedek Priesthood was 57,600, and the total number holding the Aaronic Priesthood was 49,780. Thousands of young people were actively engaged in the auxiliary organizations of the Church, and it was conceded by many ministers of other churches that the "Mormon" Sunday Schools were the best that could be found in all the world.[a]

Dedication of the Alberta Temple.—July 27, 1913, President Joseph F. Smith dedicated the ground for the building of a temple at Cardston, Canada. September 19, 1915, Elder David O. McKay laid the corner stone of the building, and the capstone was laid September 23, 1917. The building, one of the most elaborate and beautiful of the temples, was dedicated by President Heber J. Grant, August 26, 1923. The Services of dedication began at 10:00 a.m. August 26, and continued until the afternoon of Wednesday, August 29th, eleven sessions in all being held, most of the general authorities and many thousands of Latter-day Saints attending them.

Celebration at the Hill Cumorah and the Sacred Grove.—September 21 to 23, 1923, a solemn celebration was held at the Smith Farm, the Sacred Grove, and the Hill Cumorah, in New York State. The

---

[a]At a synod held in Salt Lake City, in September, 1921, at which the ministers of the Episcopal Church of the Fourth Province of the Pacific assembled, Rev. W. F. Buckley said: "We may learn much from the Mormon Church; it has the best Sunday School organization of any church in the world." —*Salt Lake Tribune*, September 9, 1921, p. 15.

occasion was the one hundredth anniversary of the coming of the Angel Moroni to the Prophet Joseph Smith. President Heber J. Grant and a number of the general authorities of the Church were present. Elder B. H. Roberts, who was then presiding over the Eastern States Mission, was in attendance with all his missionaries and many of the Saints were also present. Addresses were made by the leading brethren and a program of speaking, music and prayer, featured the celebration. Many strangers, as well as the members of the Church, were deeply impressed and some of the newspapers gave accurate and sympathetic accounts of the meetings and of the mission of the Prophet Joseph Smith.

Death of President Penrose—Changes in the First Presidency.— President Charles W. Penrose, first counselor to President Heber J. Grant, died May 16, 1925, in Salt Lake City. President Penrose had served as a counselor to President Joseph F. Smith from December, 1911, until the death of President Smith. He then served as second counselor to President Heber J. Grant until the death of President Anthon H. Lund, when he was advanced to the position of first counselor and Elder Anthony W. Ivins of the council of the apostles was chosen as second counselor in the First Presidency. Following the death of President Penrose, President Ivins was advanced to the position of first counselor and Charles W. Nibley, who was at the time the presiding bishop of the Church was chosen by President Grant as his second counselor. This necessitated choosing of a presiding bishop and Elder Sylvester Q. Cannon, president of the Pioneer Stake, was called and ordained to that position. Bishop Cannon selected the same counselors who had served with Bishop Nibley, namely David A. Smith and John Wells.

Dedication of the Arizona Temple.—November 28, 1921, President Heber J. Grant dedicated a site for a temple at Mesa, Arizona, in the presence of about three thousand people. The work of construction commenced shortly after on the building which was finished in due time, but was not dedicated until Sunday, October 23, 1927. On that day President Heber J. Grant offered the prayer of dedication in a solemn assembly of Saints. As was done in the dedication of other temples, several sessions were held that the multitudes of people might attend. The prayer was repeated each meeting. These meetings commenced on the morning of the 23rd of October and continued until the 27th, three sessions being held each day except on the 27th when one session was held. Most of the general authorities of the Church were in attendance and took part in the services.

Purchase of the Hill Cumorah and the Whitmer Farm.—The farm formerly owned by Peter Whitmer, Sen., in Fayette, Seneca County, New York, was purchased by the Church September 25, 1926. It was at the home of Peter Whitmer, Sen., on this farm that the Church was organized April 6, 1830, and where the latter part of the Book of Mormon was translated. In the year 1923 a portion of the Hill Cumorah on the western slope came into the possession of the Church by purchase. February 18, 1928, the Church purchased from the estate of Pliny T. Sexton of Palmyra, New York, the rest of the Hill with adjacent farm lands and in this way the full possession of this sacred spot also came into the possession of the Church. The Hill Cumorah and the Whitmer Farm are two of the outstanding landmarks of greatest interest to Latter-day Saints because of their importance in connection with the establishing of the great work of the Lord in this dispensation of the Fulness of Times.

Centennial Celebration.—The One Hundredth Annual Conference of the Church convened in the Tabernacle, Salt Lake City, Sunday, April 6, 1930, and continued until the afternoon of Wednesday, the ninth. This being the centennial anniversary of the organization of the Church, special and appropriate services were arranged for the conference. A pageant entitled, *The Message of the Ages*, was presented in the Tabernacle. The pageant commenced on the night of April 6, 1930, and continued without interruption for thirty nights. Hundreds of thousands of people attended these performances, the time being divided among the stakes. People from all parts of the earth were in attendance, and the impressions made upon them were very favorable to the Church. The Latter-day Saints who came to the conference outnumbered those present at any previous gathering. The proceedings of the sessions of the general conference were broadcast by radio over station KSL, Salt Lake City.

Repeal of the Eighteenth Amendment.—In the year 1918, the people of the United States amended the Constitution of the United States prohibiting the manufacture, possession and sale of liquor. Immediately following this action the liquor interests of the country commenced a vigorous campaign to bring about the repeal of this amendment. Propaganda was carried on vigorously through the press and the people were made to believe that the condition under prohibition was worse than before the amendment was adopted. In the general election of 1933, enough states voted for repeal to make such action effective. Utah, contrary to the wishes of the General Authorities of the Church, joined with the majority of the states in demanding repeal, and the Beehive State held the doubtful, if not

ADMINISTRATION OF HEBER J. GRANT

disgraceful, position of being the thirty-sixth state of the Union to hold a constitutional convention and thus brought about ratification of repeal. Since that action liquor has been flowing freely throughout the land, crime and drunkenness have increased and the sale of liquor and tobacco has become an outstanding menace to our youth. At this election Senator Reed Smoot, who had served in the Senate for thirty years, was defeated in a wave which swept over the country placing the opposite party into power.

Changes in the First Presidency.—President Charles W. Nibley, second counselor in the First Presidency, died Dec. 11, 1931, and at the general conference, April 6, 1933, Elder J. Reuben Clark, Jr., was sustained as second counselor to President Heber J. Grant. The delay in filling the vacancy was due to the fact that Elder Clark had been serving as Ambassador to Mexico for the United States Government until shortly before he was sustained. Sept. 23, 1934, President Anthony W. Ivins died after a brief illness, and at the general conference, October 6, 1934, J. Reuben Clark, Jr., was sustained as a member of the council of the apostles and also as first counselor to President Grant, and Elder David O. McKay, of the council of apostles, was sustained as second counselor in the First Presidency. Elder Alonzo A. Hinckley was also sustained as a member of the council of the apostles.

Other Developments.—At the beginning of the year 1935, the membership of the Church had greatly increased. There were 110 stakes of Zion, 952 wards and 82 independent branches. There were also 29 missions. The German Mission had been divided and the Swiss-German and German-Austrian Missions created in 1925. The French Mission was again opened after many years of inactivity in that land, also the Palestine-Assyrian Mission. In 1925, Elders Melvin J. Ballard of the council of the twelve, Rulon S. Wells and Rey L. Pratt of the first council of seventy, went to South America to open up a mission there. At Buenos Aires in the Argentine, December 25, 1925, Elder Ballard dedicated the land of South America for the preaching of the Gospel. The Southern States Mission was also divided and a new mission created known as the East Central States. A departure from long established custom of having an apostle preside over the British Mission and at the same time supervise the other missions in Europe, was taken, and in October, 1928, Elder August William Lund, son of President Anthon H. Lund, was chosen to preside over the British Mission, thus leaving Elder John A. Widtsoe, who was presiding over the British Mission, free to take the supervision of all the missions in Europe.

Withdrawal of the Missionaries from the Nations.—Following the armistice in November, 1918, which brought World War I to its close, the victorious nations created a number of small states in Europe and placed restriction upon the Central powers hoping that these acts would insure permanent peace for the world and make it "safe for democracy." This plan miserably failed. Following the war Germany became a republic and elected General Paul von Hindenburg president. This form of government soon came to an end and an ambitious man named Adolph Hitler rose to power from obscurity, and in the course of a very few years obtained absolute power, subjecting the German people to his rule. Men of like character also arose in Italy and Russia, and again the peace of the world was threatened. Germany regained her military strength, broke the treaties made following the war of 1914-1918, and soon subdued some of the smaller states on her border, over the protest of England and France. During the month of August, 1939, it became very evident that Germany was about to open hostilities against Poland which caused the tension in Europe to become very grave.

On August 24, 1939, it having become apparent that war was inevitable, the First Presidency sent word that all the missionaries in Germany should be transferred to neutral countries. Acting on this advice, and under the direction of Elder Joseph Fielding Smith, who was in Europe, all the missionaries of the East German Mission were directed to go to Denmark, and all those of the West German Mission to go to Holland. As Holland refused to permit the missionaries to enter her borders, the West German missionaries were also sent to Denmark, where they were permitted to enter that land. The first intention was to distribute these missionaries among the neutral nations of Scandinavia and Holland there to continue their labors. September 1, 1939, Germany invaded Poland and on the third of September England and France declared war on Germany. Following these declarations the neutral nations of Europe made it known that they desired all foreigners to leave their borders, and the missionaries were not welcome in those lands. Because of this attitude the missionaries were instructed to leave Europe and return to the United States.

There were in the European missions at the time 697 persons, of whom 611 were young men and 63 young women missionaries; the other 23 were mission presidents, their wives and children. These missionaries returned in 23 ships, mostly freight boats which had been improvised to care for the numerous passengers returning to America. The first group arrived in New York September 7, 1939, and the last, except the mission presidents in Denmark, Norway and Switzerland, their families and secretaries, arrived in New York, November 6, 1939.

Elder Joseph Fielding Smith and wife accompanied this group. The remaining presidents in Denmark and Norway arrived a few days later and Elder Thomas E. McKay with his group of four missionaries, his wife and daughter, arrived March 4, 1940. Thus all the missionaries were withdrawn from Europe, except Elder Gaston Chappuis, a native of Switzerland, who remained in France. All returned without accident of any kind knowing that the Spirit of the Lord had guided them safely to America's shores. As the greater number of the missionaries had not completed their missionary terms, they were met and cared for by Elders John H. Taylor of the first council of seventy and Frank Evans, President of the Eastern States Mission, and by them re-assigned to new fields of labor. As the war became more frightful and other peoples were involved, the Presidency later in the year 1940, withdrew the missionaries from South Africa and the missions of the Pacific, except Hawaii, a possession of the United States.

Resumption of the World War.—Friday, September 1, 1939, Germany, under the dictation of Adolph Hitler, suddenly crossed the border of Poland which brought to pass a declaration of war from England and France the following Sunday, September 3rd, against Germany. These nations were woefully unprepared for war. On the other hand Germany was, as she thought, fully equipped and ready. The results in the early months of the contest saw France subdued and forced to surrender and placed under drastic terms and heavy burdens, June 20, 1940. At this time the British soldiers in France were driven out of France, and a short time later off the European continent. On April 9, 1940, Germany, without any warning, invaded Norway, and on the 10th of May, invaded Holland with a sudden attack that left cities waste and thousands of her people murdered. Continuing this conquest, a great portion of which had previously been accomplished by threats of force in Austria, the Balkans and Slovakia, Germany took over most of France, all of Denmark, Belgium and Norway. In this dark hour, June 10, 1940, Italy, thinking the war was practically over and wishing to partake of the spoils, declared war on England and France. However, England was not defeated and continued the fight, refusing the terms offered for surrender from what was called the axis powers. September 27, 1940, Japan joined the axis powers signing a ten year tri-partite pact in Berlin.

June 22, 1941, Germany, feeling that Russia was a threat on her eastern border, and evidently feeling that in that country she could continue her easy conquest, invaded Russia and with rapid strides was soon threatening the gates of the Russian capital on the north and Stalingrad on the west, on the borders of the Black Sea, but at this point the Russians held firmly and stopped the German advance. Germany and Italy, however, had taken possession of Albania and Greece and islands in the Mediterranean and Aegean seas, and had driven the British in Africa beyond the borders of Egypt and were threatening to take possession of the Suez Canal and the passage to the East.

December 7, 1941, Japan made a sudden attack on Pearl Harbor, on the island of Oahu, Hawaii, destroying, or disabling many of the warships of the United States. The following day the Congress of the United States declared war on Japan, and on the 11th, Germany and Italy declared war on the United States, and thus, in fulfillment of the revelation on war, again war was to be poured out on all nations. Japan immediately took possession of the islands of Guam, Midway, and Wake, and after a bitter and heroic struggle drove the small American force out of the Philippines. From this time on, however, the tide began to turn. In November 1942, the American and British forces invaded North Africa, and the British forces in Egypt began to force back the opposing forces until between the army on the west and the army on the east, the German and Italian armies were driven out of Africa. Immediately the allies, as America and Britain with such help as they received were called, invaded Sicily and then Italy, making remarkable progress against Italian and German forces. On September 8, 1943, Italy was forced to surrender.

In the most bitter struggle the world has ever seen, in the midst of blood and carnage, destruction of cities and the taking of millions of lives, including innocent women and children and entire inhabitants of cities and villages, by the dropping from the air of bombs and the shooting of what have been called "robot" bombs weighing many tons, the inhabitants have been called upon to mourn. The cruelty, murders, destruction of lives and property have been too appalling to possibly describe. June 6, 1944, the American and British forces invaded Normany, and after a bitter struggle and the loss of hundreds of thousands of men, gradually forced the Germans back beyond their own borders in the West, while in the East the Russians accomplished the same result, until eventually the two forces met and the city of Berlin was in ruins. It was not until then, and when the axis powers were left powerless to continue the struggle, that the German armies were overcome and forced to grant an unconditional surrender. In the meantime the German plotters who had started the conflict either were captured, killed themselves, or went into hiding where they could not be found. May 8, 1945, the announcement was officially made that Germany had surrendered. Property estimated as worth billions had been destroyed. Millions of lives were sacrificed, the inhabitants of cities and villages ruthlessly murdered. Shipping on the seas became extremely dangerous because of the activity of German submarines, and the loss by sea became appalling. The full extent of the evil created by this conflict will never be known by mortal man. All of this destruction has come about because man has forsaken his Maker and rejected his Redeemer, and turned to his own strength aided in his selfish ambitions by the great deceiver and enemy of all righteousness.

After the surrender of Germany the struggle in the far east with Japan continued. Gradually the Allied forces made inroads into the possessions near the main islands of Japan and recaptured Manila and a large portion of the Philippines. The air force of the United States carried the warfare over the cities of Japan with devastating results. Two large cities, Hiroshima and Nagasaki were destroyed by the dropping of atomic bombs, the most horrifying and dreadful means of destruction ever witnessed in warfare. The secret formula for these bombs was prepared in the United States and released atomic energy of untold destructive power. Naturally the enthusiasm for war and conquest by the Japanese was dampened and their ardor cooled by the surrender of Germany. Moreover their supplies for carrying on war were rapidly diminishing; these together with the terrible destruction that had overtaken them and which still awaited them, caused that nation to sue for peace and Japan surrendered September 2, 1945. After more than five years of the most horrible bloodshed and destruction in which millions of lives were sacrificed and billions in value of property destroyed, the world found itself sick and feeble spiritually, mentally and morally. However the end of hostilities did not bring to the world peace. The unrest, bickerings and disagreements among the nations still go on. At the present writing delegates from the nations are in solemn conclave endeavor to work out some sort of world system of United Nations, upon which there may be universal agreement that will end war. It is very apparent that such efforts will eventually fail, for there is only one principle upon which such universal peace can come; that is an acceptance of the saving principles of the Gospel of Jesus Christ and this the world is not willing to do. When selfishness and ambition for power dominate the hearts of men and nations, there can come no permanent peace. Moreover, we know, for the Lord has revealed it, there will be no peace until the Prince of Peace comes and brings it and cleanses the earth of its iniquity.

If men would only remember their Redeemer and serve him, then he would come to their aid and fight their battles, but they have placed their strength in their own puny arms. Surely we may, and should, pray that the Prince of Peace may come speedily and hearken to the pleadings of mother earth that she be cleansed of all the filth that has gone forth upon her face that she may rest, and once again the glad tidings of the Gospel go forth to all the humble in every nation, kindred and tongue and people.

Church Progress.—In the spring of the year 1945, there were 149 stakes of Zion, 1150 wards, 128 independent branches and 35 dependent branches in the stakes. * * * There were in the stakes of Zion 89,106 men and boys enrolled in the Aaronic Priesthood and in the missions 15,547. There were also in the stakes 112,850 men enrolled in the Melchizedek Priesthood and 9,730 in the missions. The proclamation of the Gospel had been made in nearly all parts of the earth and had been brought to the attention of kings, presidents, potentates and rulers. At the close of the year 1944 there were many signs given spoken of by our Lord as presaging his second coming. The "fig trees" of prophetic warning were rapidly putting forth their leaves, showing that the summer of the Lord's coming "was nigh at hand." "For," said the Lord, "in my own due time will I come upon the earth in judgment, and my people shall be redeemed and shall reign with me on earth. For the great Millennium, of which I have spoken by the mouths of my servants, shall come. For Satan shall be bound, and when he is loosed he shall reign for a little season, and then cometh the end of the earth. And he that liveth in righteousness shall be changed in the twinkling of an eye, and the earth shall pass away so as by fire." It also appeared that the prophecy of Isaiah was about to be fulfilled:

"Go through, go through the gates; prepare ye the way of the people; * * * lift up a standard for the people.

"Behold the Lord hath proclaimed unto the end of the world, Say ye to the daughter of Zion, Behold, thy salvation cometh; behold, his reward is with him, and his work before him.

"And they shall call them, The holy people, The redeemed of the Lord; and thou shalt be called, Sought out, A city not forsaken." —Isaiah 62:10-12.

The Passing of President Heber J. Grant.—In the late afternoon, May 14, 1945, President Heber J. Grant, peacefully passed away at his residence in Salt Lake City. He had been ailing for the past five years, but his courage and determination to press on and perform his duty, never deserted him. Each day, up to a short time before his death, he was found at the office attending to duties as much as the physician permitted him to do. His life had been one of great activity. In his early years he appeared frail, was rejected for insurance, because of his physical condition, however, he had been active always, engaging in athletics, one time belonging to the champion baseball team of Utah. His energy was marvelous and his activities never ceased. There was never any compromise on his part with evil. Some of his strongest characteristics the public never realized. He had a tender, sympathetic nature, loved his friends dearly; was kind to the distressed; assisted the needy scores upon scores of times, the knowledge of which never got into any earthly record. His testimony of the Truth never wavered. His friends were legion outside of the Church, and he was dearly loved by his people.

The funeral services were held Friday, May 18th, and were attended by the greatest gathering ever assembled in Utah on any such occasion. As the cortege passed thousands stood in the streets for many blocks with bowed heads. He was honored by representatives of other Churches and the bell of the Catholic Cathedral tolled, and nurses stood at attention as the procession passed. Men of renown from distant parts came to do him honor, many of the stores in the city closed their doors and there was a general mourning because a mighty man had been taken home after a long and eventful life of more than 88 years.

CHAPTER 55

GEORGE ALBERT SMITH
EIGHTH PRESIDENT OF THE CHURCH

Organization of the First Presidency.—At the time of the death of President Heber J. Grant, President George Albert Smith of the Council of the Twelve Apostles was on his way to New York, after having attended the Chicago Stake conference. Other members of the council were also absent attending stake conferences in distant parts, and visiting missions. Telegrams were sent to each requesting him to return at once. By the day of the funeral of President Grant all of the brethren of the Council and the patriarch to the Church had returned.

Monday, May 21, 1945, a meeting of the council of the apostles and the patriarch was held in the Salt Lake Temple. The brethren assembled fasting and the day was spent in testimony bearing, at the conclusion of which, on motion of Elder George F. Richards, President George Albert Smith was sustained as President of The

George Albert Smith

Church of Jesus Christ of Latter-day Saints. On motion of Elder David O. McKay, Elder George F. Richards was also sustained as president of the council of the twelve apostles. President Smith was then ordained under the hands of all the brethren, Elder George F. Richards being voice. President Smith chose as his counselors, J. Reuben Clark, Jr., as first, and David O. McKay as second, and they were set apart under the hands of all the brethren, President Smith being voice. Elder George F. Richards was also set apart in like manner as president of the council of the twelve apostles.

President George Albert Smith, eighth president of The Church of Jesus Christ of Latter-day Saints, is the eldest son of President John Henry Smith who was called to the apostleship in the administration of President John Taylor, and who served as a counselor to President Joseph F. Smith. His grandfather, President George A. Smith after whom he was named, was called to the apostleship by the Prophet Joseph Smith, and served as a counselor to President Brigham Young. His great-grandfather, known as Father John Smith, an uncle of the Prophet Joseph Smith, was the third patriarch of the Church, and the first president of the Salt Lake Stake of Zion.

President George Albert Smith was born in Salt Lake City, April 4, 1870. He came to the presidency with a rich heritage, his ancestors were among the founders of this American commonwealth who fought for freedom and sustained the Constitution of the United States. It has been written of him:

"President George Albert Smith is possessed of a kindly, sympathetic nature. He makes friends readily. It can truthfully be said of him that he loves his fellow man and exemplifies the second great commandment in his treatment of his fellow man. His friends who are not members of the Church, scattered over all parts of the land, are legion. He has been honored by presidents of the United States, governors, and prominent men in the nation and in every walk of life. If he has enemies they must be few, and their enmity can only be based in unrighteousness. He has been extremely active in civic affairs and in the building and preservation of monuments in honor of those who blazed the trails and laid the foundations throughout the land on which others have built. He has been honored by various societies, has served as an officer in the great Boy Scout movement for many years; as an officer in the organization of the Sons of the American Revolution and other organizations. Notwithstanding all this activity he has never neglected his duty or failed in his appointments in the Church or its councils. * * *

"His life has been one of great activity and he comes to his present position ripe in experience, faithful to his trust, worthy in every respect of the great honor which has come to him, and beloved by the people."

Dedication of the Idaho Falls Temple.—The Idaho Falls Temple, one of the most beautiful of our temples, was dedicated, Sunday, September 23, 1945, President George Albert Smith officiating. It is situated near the bank of the Snake River at Idaho Falls in a most favorable setting. Three sessions were held Sunday, September 23rd, three on Monday the 24th and two on Tuesday the 25th. All of the general authorities were present and many other officers of the various organizations of the Church. Arrangements were made for all the members of the Church in the Idaho Falls district to have the privilege of attending one of the sessions of the dedication. The prayer of dedication was repeated at each session and also the hosanna shout. The Spirit of the Lord was present and a time of rejoicing was had by all who attended. This temple will serve the people in the majority of stakes in Idaho and the Big Horn and Star Valley Stakes in Wyoming. This is the eighth temple now in service in the Church where the ordinances for the salvation and exaltation for both the living and the dead are performed. Two other temples have been built, one at Kirtland where heavenly messengers came and restored keys pertaining to the salvation and exaltation of all those who are just and true who will accept and abide in the fulness of the Gospel, both the living and the dead; the other at Nauvoo which the Church was forced to abandon when it was driven from Illinois.

Destitute Condition of the Peoples of Europe.—The war with all its devastating wickedness left the peoples in Europe destitute. The supposedly neutral nations of Holland, Denmark, Norway and Belgium were overrun by the hordes of the German army. In these and other lands the people were robbed of all that they possessed. Food, clothing and every substance considered of some value to the Axis power, were carried off leaving the people destitute. Cities were left in ruins by shells and bombs dropped from the air. Men were torn from their families and carried off to labor as slaves by this power. The destructive elements of war laid waste many of the great cities of Europe. Hundreds of thousands of people were ruthlessly murdered who were not combatants in the war. Such wickedness and destruction were never known in the world before, and all of this came because mankind had rejected God and were turned from his commandments. These terrible destructions were promised to come upon the peoples of the earth if they would not repent.

In the midst of all this carnage and horrible destruction of life and property, the righteous were forced to suffer as well as the wicked. The close of hostilities found the members of the Church in the stricken countries suffering deprivations, starvation and exposure for lack of clothing, food and shelter, as well as all other peoples. Notwithstanding all of this untold suffering, they had remained loyal to the Church. The authorities of the Church took steps immediately when the way was opened to succor and alleviate the suffering of all the members of the Church. Through the Welfare organization of the Church, thousands of boxes of provisions, clothing and other necessities were sent to the Saints in Europe so that all received some relief which helped to tide them over. This same kind of help is being continued in their behalf. The government of the United States, through the Red Cross and other organizations, poured into Europe for these stricken people, food and clothing which was the means of saving many lives. It was fortunate that the Church was in a position to care for its own, and with the privileges granted by the government was able to accomplish this great work for its members.

Elder Benson's Mission to Europe.—After careful consideration of all these painful conditions among the Saints in Europe, and realizing that it was necessary that someone be sent to Europe to assist in rehabilitating the members of the Church and organizing and setting in order the missions and branches of the Church, which had suffered so greatly during the conflict at arms, the Presidency of the Church sent Elder Ezra Taft Benson to Europe. Armed with credentials from the First Presidency and aided by documents from the Government in Washington, Elder Benson departed on his mission of mercy, February 4, 1946, accompanied by Elder Frederick Wm. Babbel as secretary. He was instructed to visit all the countries in Europe which were accessible, seek out the members of the Church, administer to their wants, set in order the branches and give such encouragement as could be given to comfort and bless these stricken people. The Lord opened the way before him and in each land where he visited he was received by the members as an angel of mercy come to bring them temporal as well as spiritual salvation from a condition which the cruelties of war had imposed upon them. He was received by military officers with kindness and by them he was greatly aided in his mission of relief. He found the thousands of members of the Church loyal through all their suffering. Near the close of the year 1946, Elder Benson was released to return home having laid a foundation upon which others could build, and Elder Alma Sonne was sent to Europe to replace him and carry on this great work presiding over the missions of Europe, and this good work still goes on.

Resumption of Missionary Work.—During the years in which the nations were in open conflict, and war was raging in all parts of the earth, it became necessary, as formerly stated, to withdraw the missionaries of the Church from most of the foreign fields and thus missionary work was largely confined to the North American continent, and even there only a few missionaries were available. Nearly all of the younger men of draft age who were able-bodied were taken into the military service. This left the burden of the farms and other needed labor upon the shoulders of the fathers who were too old for military draft. Thus the work of the Lord suffered. Shortly after the surrender of the Axis powers, the young men began to be discharged from the army and navy and return home and many of them immediately volunteered for missionary labor. As rapidly as the doors were opened in foreign fields, missionaries were sent to carry on the work of the Lord in great numbers, both on the continent of America, in Europe and in the islands of the sea. By the close of the year 1946, there were over three thousand missionaries in the field and more were preparing to go. The Lord was once more granting to a perverse and wicked world the opportunity to repentance with the promise of remission of sins and a place in his kingdom.

The year 1947 commenced with great promises for the welfare and advancement of the Church. There were 164 stakes of Zion, 1230 wards and 125 branches in the stakes. The work in the mission fields throughout the world had been resumed. It was the jubilee year of the founding of Utah. July 24, 1947, was one hundred years from the time President Brigham Young led his band of 143 pioneers into the Salt Lake Valley. A celebration in every way fitting for this occasion was underway. Truly the desert has been made to blossom as the rose and great blessings await the members of the Church if they will be true to their pioneer fathers and be loyal to the principles of eternal truth for which they toiled and suffered.

President George Albert Smith was a man who loved his fellow men. He was extremely kind and considerate of the feelings of others, a friend to the poor and the distressed. He was loved by many who were not members of the Church and his acquaintance extended to the borders of the United States and beyond into many foreign countries. During his last few months his health failed him and on his eighty-first birthday anniversary, April 4, 1951, he peacefully passed away at his home in Salt Lake City, Utah.

CHAPTER 56

DAVID OMAN McKAY
NINTH PRESIDENT OF THE CHURCH

David Oman McKay.—On April 9, 1951, five days after the death of President George Albert Smith, David Oman McKay was sustained as the ninth President of the Church, in a solemn assembly in the Salt Lake Tabernacle. The date on which he was sustained was 45 years to the day since he had been ordained an apostle.

David Oman McKay was born September 8, 1873, in the town of Huntsville, Weber County, Utah, some ten miles east of Ogden in fertile Ogden Valley. He was the oldest son and third child of Bishop David McKay, who had emigrated from Scotland at the age of 12, and Jennette Evans McKay, who emigrated from Wales at the age of six. When David was seven, his father was called to return to his native Scotland as a missionary, leaving his wife and family (including a daugh-

David Oman McKay

ter who was born just a few days after his departure) to run the family farm. Young David's education began there on the farm, where he early learned to accept responsibility. His daily task instilled in him a love for all animals, and especially for horses, a love that remained with him all his life.

On his eighth birthday anniversary David Oman McKay was baptized by Elder Peter C. Geertsen. He began his formal schooling in the local school in Huntsville, after which he attended Weber Stake Academy in Ogden and later the University of Utah. He was graduated from the latter institution in 1897, having distinguished himself as a guard on the university's first football team, president of his class, and valedictorian. On August 1, 1897, he was ordained a seventy by Elder Seymour B. Young and set apart for a mission to the British Isles. There he was assigned to labor in the land of his father, the Scottish Conference (now District). Not long after his arrival he was placed in charge of that conference, serving from March 1898 to September 1899. When he returned from the mission, he became an instructor in the Weber Stake Academy, and two years later he was named superintendent of that school, a position he held until 1908. He married Emma Ray Riggs, whom he had met and courted while at the University of Utah, on January 2, 1901, and they became the parents of five sons, one of whom died in infancy, and two daughters.

President McKay's first post-mission Church assignment was in education, when he was called as second assistant superintendent of the Weber Stake Sunday School in 1899, beginning a lifetime of service to the youth of the Church.

At the general conference of the Church in 1906, David Oman McKay was called to fill one of three vacancies in the Council of the Twelve Apostles, the other two vacancies being filled by George F. Richards and Orson F. Whitney. He was ordained to the office of apostle by President Joseph F. Smith on April 9, 1906. Shortly thereafter he was called to be assistant superintendent to President Joseph F. Smith in the Deseret Sunday School Union general board, and after the death of President Smith, in 1918, he was named general superintendent, a position he held until 1934.

Throughout his life President McKay held many important positions in the field of education. In the spring of 1919, he was appointed Commissioner of Education for the Church School System, which position he held until 1921. He was appointed to the Board of Regents of the University of Utah in 1921, and a year later was awarded an honorary master of arts degree from Brigham Young University. He later served on the Board of Trustees of Utah State Agricultural

College (now Utah State University) and on the Board of Trustees of Brigham Young University. He received honorary doctorates from all three institutions as well as from Temple University in Philadelphia. He was also honored with honorary memberships in a number of educational organizations in the United States.

President McKay's interest in missionary work, which began with his call as a missionary in 1897, was recognized in 1920 when he received an assignment from President Heber J. Grant to make a general survey of the missions of the Church. Accompanied by Elder Hugh J. Cannon, president of Liberty Stake, he traveled to the nations of the Far East, the islands of the Pacific, New Zealand, Australia, and many other parts of the earth. This was the first time that any visit of this nature was ever attempted in those areas, although missionaries had gone to the islands of the Pacific before the death of the Prophet Joseph Smith and to China in 1853. Elder McKay and President Cannon visited Korea, Japan, China, Hawaii, Tahiti, Samoa, and the islands of the Polynesian group, where missions had been established by the Church. They also visited New Zealand and Australia, and on the return journey came by way of Singapore to India, then to Cairo in Egypt, and by way of the Red Sea to Palestine and Europe. In Palestine they spent some happy days visiting the sacred scenes where Israel dwelt and where the feet of our Redeemer trod. This visit to the land of Canaan left a deep impression upon them, and they prayed for the day to come when the promises and prophecies of the restoration of Israel would be fulfilled.

After visiting these sacred places, they journeyed through Europe, visiting Rome and other places in Italy, and other lands where the message of salvation has been declared. It was also their privilege to stop in England and Scotland, where President McKay visited some of the places of his first mission. During this great journey they had met with and encouraged the members of the Church in these lands wherever they could be found. Their experiences involved many outpourings of the Spirit, and they learned firsthand of the love, devotion, and brotherhood of the Saints in different lands and cultures. The entire journey covered a total of 55,896 miles.

President McKay's missionary labors continued the next year, for he had been home just a few months when he was called to preside over the British Mission and to supervise all of the European missions. In this field he accomplished a wonderful work, overcoming much prejudice, for the Church still had many enemies without any shadow of a valid cause. When his mission to Europe was completed, he returned home in 1924 and resumed his labors in the apostleship in visiting and putting in order the stakes of Zion. This labor carried him to all sections of the Church where stakes were organized, and into many of the near-by missions.

After the death of President Anthony W. Ivins, September 23, 1934, he was chosen by President Heber J. Grant to be his second counselor in the First Presidency, being set apart to this position in October 1934. Following the death of President Grant in 1945, he was chosen to serve as second counselor to President George Albert Smith, being set apart to this position May 21, 1945. He became President of the Quorum of the Twelve Apostles on September 30, 1950, following the death of President George F. Richards, and President of the Church on April 9, 1951, following the death of President George Albert Smith. From that time on the Lord blessed President McKay in a marvelous way with the vigor that enabled him to travel far and near to all parts of the earth in the performance of his duties in building up and strengthening the Church at home and abroad. During the next 19 years, until his death in January 1970, the Church experienced phenomenal growth.

Travels of President McKay.—After becoming President of the Church, President McKay traveled approximately one million miles, becoming the most widely traveled Church President in history. He visited all of the missions in South Africa, South America, the Pacific Isles, New Zealand, and Australia, and many countries where he had not traveled in his 1920-21 tour. He was the first President of the Church who had ever visited most of these areas.

While in Europe in 1952, he selected sites for temples in Switzerland, England, and other countries of Europe, and visited all of the missions in the European countries. In 1954 President and Sister McKay embarked on another historic journey, this time a 32,000-mile air trip to South Africa, South America, and Central America. Traveling by way of England and then to Lisbon and on to Dakar, on the African west coast, President McKay then made a historic visit to the South African Mission, the first time a General Authority of the Church had ever been in that land.

The most historic trip of his Presidency was taken with Sister McKay in 1955, when they toured the missions of the South Pacific, traveling more than 45,000 miles, mostly by air. During this trip he inspected the new Church school then under construction in New Zealand and also selected a site for the New Zealand Temple.

A few months after his return, he left again for Europe to dedicate the Swiss Temple and to break ground for the London Temple. In Scotland, he and Sister McKay were joined by members of the Tabernacle Choir, who were on their concert tour of Europe. He returned to New Zealand and London in 1958 to dedicate the temples in those lands. Again in 1961 he returned to England to dedicate the Hyde Park Chapel and to officiate at the organization of new stakes in Europe. In August 1962 he flew to Scotland, where he had labored as a youthful missionary, and directed the organization of the first stake in that country. The next year he flew to London and then motored to Wales, where he dedicated a chapel at Merthyr Tydfil, the birthplace of his mother.

Temples Built During His Administration.—As President of the Church, David O. McKay directed an active program of temple construction. Eight temples were built or announced during his administration, including the first ones outside North America. In earlier years he had also officiated in erecting temples, for on September 19, 1915, he laid the cornerstone for the Alberta Temple at Cardston, Alberta, and in 1940, as a counselor to President Heber J. Grant, he laid the cornerstone for the Idaho Falls Temple.

On September 22, 1951, President McKay presided and conducted at the groundbreaking for the Los Angeles Temple, and he dedicated it on March 11, 1957.

The first temple in Europe was announced in 1952, at the conclusion of President McKay's European tour. The groundbreaking, at which he officiated, was August 5, 1953; he returned to dedicate the holy structure on September 11, 1955. During that trip he also officiated at groundbreaking ceremonies for the London Temple on August 27, 1955; this temple was dedicated by him in 1958.

In February 1955 plans were completed for the erection of a temple on a site that President McKay had selected during his trip to the Pacific islands a few weeks earlier. He returned to dedicate the temple on April 20, 1958.

The Oakland Temple, for which ground was broken on May 26, 1962, was dedicated by President McKay in November 1964. In addition, three temples were announced during his administration: in Provo and Ogden, Utah, and Washington, D.C. When these temples are completed, there will be a total of 15 temples presently in use by the Church, of which eight will have been instituted under his direction. In addition, he presided at dedicatory services for additions to and remodeling of the Salt Lake Temple in 1963.

Building Programs.—During President McKay's 19-year administration, more than 3,750 Church buildings were constructed throughout the world, a number far greater than the entire number built during the first 120 years of the Church. Of these buildings, more than 2,000 were ward and branch chapels. In addition to major building programs at Brigham Young University, sixty-nine new school buildings were constructed, including elementary schools and high schools in many islands of the South Seas, Central America, South America, and Mexico. The $10-million David O. McKay Hospital in Ogden, Utah, was completed in 1969, and a subsidiary hospital for convalescent patients is being added on that hospital site. The Church Administration Building, which will become the tallest structure in the Mountain West and will house all the general Church departments and auxiliary offices, is scheduled for completion in 1972.

Missionary Activity.—Long interested in missionary work, President McKay encouraged each member of the Church to take a personal interest in telling others about the restored gospel, with the challenge: "Every member a missionary." During his administration the number of missions more than doubled, to a total of 88, and the full-time missionary force grew from about 2,000 to more than 12,000. He instituted three language training schools for missionaries, at Brigham Young University, Ricks College, and Church College of Hawaii. Seminars for newly called mission presidents were also instituted during the last week of June each year, as the new mission leaders spend several days in Salt Lake City receiving instruction and inspiration from General Authorities and heads of Church departments.

Visitors centers were established in many areas, and the Church participated with attractive pavilions at the New York World's Fair, Expo at Montreal, and Hemisfair in San Antonio, Texas. Plans were also made for the Church's participation in the first world's fair ever held in Asia, Expo '70 in Osaka, Japan. Millions of persons have heard the message of the restored gospel at these pavilions, and thousands have gone on to meet with the missionaries, receive the discussions, and be baptized.

Growth of Stakes.—During President McKay's administration, membership in the Church doubled, to nearly three million in stakes and missions on six continents and many islands of the seas. There were 184 stakes when he became President, and the 500th was created on the day of his death, January 18, 1970. The first stakes outside the United States and Canada were organized during those years, including stakes in New Zealand, Australia, Holland, England, Germany, Switzerland, Mexico, Samoa, Brazil, Argentina, Guatemala, Uruguay, and Tonga.

Education.—President McKay had a lifelong interest in education. Under his guidance, the number of seminary and institute students tripled, to more than 162,000 students. The institute program was taken to colleges throughout the United States as well as universities overseas. Seminary classes are now available for students in most areas of the world where the Church can be found. Brigham Young University, which quadrupled its enrollment, with more than 20,000 students now enrolled, was named America's largest church-affiliated university. The Church College of Hawaii, a fully accredited four-year institution, now has an enrollment of 1,200 students, primarily from Hawaii and the islands of the South Pacific, while Ricks College in Rexburg, Idaho, attracts nearly 4,000 students in a two-year junior college program. The Church College of New Zealand, a secondary school dedicated by President McKay in 1958, by 1970 had some 650 students. Other schools were established and are flourishing in American Samoa, Western Samoa, Tonga, Tahiti, Mexico, and Chile. The Latter-day Saint Student Association was also organized, to serve the needs of Latter-day Saint college students.

Priesthood Correlation.—During the early 1960s a broad program of Church correlation began under President McKay's direction to help bearers of the priesthood better fulfill their obligations and responsibilities. Four operating committees were formed to include programs of home teaching, missionary, genealogical, and welfare work. Worthy leaders of the priesthood were called to fill positions on these important general committees and to assist in preparing materials and outlines for leaders in the stakes and wards. Under the priesthood correlation program, quorums and groups were given specific leadership responsibilities. High priests were assigned genealogical work; seventies the missionary program; elders the welfare work; and all quorums the home teaching program. The former ward teaching program was greatly expanded into the new home teaching program, and those assigned as home teachers were given greater responsibilities as sipiritual advisers to a group of families.

An organized program of family home evenings was also introduced as part of the correlation program. A special manual of family lessons was published for every family in the Church, and outlines were offered on how to conduct successful family home evening instruction. Course offerings in all of the auxiliary organizations were correlated so that a unified program of gospel learning is followed in all teaching organizations of the Church.

The work of priesthood correlation and the new emphasis on family home evenings and home teaching brought a great surge of spiritual growth into the Church and marked a significant era in the Church in strengthening the homes and helping fathers and mothers take their rightful places as spiritual leaders of their children.

Coupled with the correlation program has been the creation of the body of priesthood leaders known as the Regional Representatives of the Twelve. In January 1968, 69 men were appointed to receive their counsel and instructions relative to the priesthood programs from the Council of the Twelve. These Regional Representatives, in turn, conduct leadership training of stake officers and ward bishoprics in regional meetings, while stake officers and bishoprics, in turn, train their counterparts. Since the original appointments, additional representatives have been named, and the number is now more than 75.

Honors Received.—Many honors were bestowed upon President McKay during his lifetime, on an international as well as national scale. On November 29, 1954, he received the second highest award that can be bestowed by the King of Greece, the Cross of Commander of the Royal Order of Phoenix. For his distinguished service to boyhood, he was awarded a citation and the Silver Beaver from the National Council of Boy Scouts in 1953. Other honors included honorary life membership in the Sons of Utah Pioneers, recognition from the California Legislature, honorary membership in the Brigham Young University chapter of Blue Key, life membership in the National Parent-Teacher Association, and citations from the National Retired Teachers Association and the National Dairy Council. A highlight was an unprecedented testimonial dinner on December 10, 1962, at which nearly 500 business and civic leaders of Utah, most of them nonmembers of the Church, honored him and presented to him an organ to be placed in the chapel at Merthyr Tydfil, Wales, birthplace of his mother.

Changes in the First Presidency.—When President McKay was sustained as President of the Church in April 1951, he selected as his counselors Stephen L Richards and J. Reuben Clark, Jr. President Richards died May 19, 1959, and was succeeded as First Counselor on June 12 by President Clark. Also named that day as second counselor was Henry D. Moyle. Hugh B. Brown was named a counselor in the First Presidency on June 22, 1961. After President Clark's death on October 6, 1961, President Moyle was sustained on October 12 as first counselor and President Brown as second counselor to President McKay. President Moyle died September 18, 1963, and on October 4 that year, President Brown was sustained as first counselor with Nathan Eldon Tanner as second counselor. On October 28, 1965, Joseph Fielding Smith and Thorpe B. Isaacson were named as counselors in the First Presidency. An additional counselor, Alvin R. Dyer, was sustained on April 6, 1968.

Regional Representatives of the Twelve.—On September 29, 1967 a group of 69 men were sustained, in General Conference, as Regional Representatives of the Twelve.

Death of President McKay.—David O. McKay, ninth President of the Church, died at 6 a.m. on Sunday, January 18, 1970, at his apartment home in the Hotel Utah of congestive heart failure. He was 96 years old. The body lay in state in the Church Office Building for three days, during which time tens of thousands of members and friends of the Church filed past the flower-banked bier to pay their respects to the beloved Prophet. On Thursday, January 22, a cortege of family members and General Authorities formed at the Church Office Building and moved slowly to Temple Square, where funeral services were held in the Salt Lake Tabernacle. Elder Hugh B. Brown conducted the service, with President Joseph Fielding Smith, President N. Eldon Tanner, and Elder Harold B. Lee as speakers. Music was by the Tabernacle Choir, and prayers were offered by President Alvin R. Dyer and Elder Ezra Taft Benson. Elder Richard L. Evans offered the prayer at the grave site in the Salt Lake City Cemetery.

On Saturday, November 14, 1970, Sister McKay passed away quietly at her Hotel Utah apartment. Funeral services were held on Wednesday, November 18, 1970, just ten months after the death of President McKay.

CHAPTER 57

PRESIDENT JOSEPH FIELDING SMITH
TENTH PRESIDENT OF THE CHURCH*

Joseph Fielding Smith. In the patriarchal blessing pronounced upon the head of Hyrum Smith by his father, Joseph Smith, Sr., at a special meeting on December 9, 1834 in Nauvoo, Illinois, the aged Patriarch noted: ". . . the Lord will multiply his choice blessings upon thee and thy seed after thee and thou with them, shall have an inheritance in Zion; and they shall possess it from generation to generation, and thy name shall never be blotted out from among the just; for the righteous shall rise up, and also thy children after thee, and say thy memory is just—that thou wert a just man, and perfect in thy day. . . ."

The fulfilment of these words is manifest in the perpetuation of Hyrum's lineage in the leading councils of the Church and most recently evident in the appointment of Joseph Fielding Smith as the tenth President of the Church on January 23, 1970.

Joseph Fielding Smith

---

*This biographical material on President Smith was prepared by Elder Howard W. Hunter of the Council of the Twelve, and Church Historian.

On that date he became the second descendant of Hyrum Smith to lead the Church in this dispensation.

President Smith was born on July 19, 1876 in Salt Lake City, one year before the death of Brigham Young. He is the fourth child and first son of Julina Lambson and Joseph F. Smith, both of whom crossed the plains with Mormon pioneers. President Smith's boyhood years were spent in the tasks attendant to the support and survival of a large family. At an early age he was engaged in general farm work, milking cows, chopping wood, planting, harvesting, and caring for animals. A specific task of his was to serve as stableboy for his mother, who was a licensed midwife.

During the years of his childhood between the ages of eight and fifteen, Joseph Fielding's father was forced into seclusion as a result of federal pressure against the Church on the issue of plural marriage. Between September 1884 and September 1891 his father could not move openly among the people. Part of this time he labored for the Church away from his family in Hawaii and Washington, D.C. Of this experience Joseph Fielding says, "During those days of seclusion, however, he did spend many days at home with his wives and children. On such occasions frequently family meetings were held and he spent his time instructing his children in the principles of the gospel, and they one and all rejoiced in his presence and were grateful for the wonderful words of counsel and instruction which he imparted on these occasions." It was here at the feet of loving parents that young Joseph received the groundwork instruction for his later knowledge and love for the gospel and church history. He was baptized by his father on July 19, 1884 and subsequently served in the offices of the Aaronic Priesthood.

Few men, if any, in the Church have served longer and with more diligence and integrity than has President Smith. On September 8, 1897 he was ordained an elder. He was engaged in MIA work as a young man, serving as instructor in the Sixteenth and Seventeenth Wards. In 1898-99 he served on the YMMIA Board of the Salt Lake Stake.

On May 12, 1899 he was ordained a seventy and set apart to serve in the British Mission where he labored in the Nottingham Conference. He returned home in July, 1901 after completing an honorable mission. On May 27, 1903 he was called as an aid in the general board of the MIA. He was instructor of the senior class in the Seventeenth Ward MIA from 1905-7. In 1903 he was chosen as a president of the Twenty-fourth Quorum of Seventy and served as instructor of that group until the Salt Lake Stake was divided in March 1904. At this time he was ordained a high priest and set apart as one of the high councilors of the stake. He held this position until he was ordained an apostle six years later. On January 6, 1909 he became a member of the general board of Religion Classes. Between 1901 and 1910 he served as a home missionary in the Salt Lake Stake.

President Smith's service with the Genealogical Society began in 1907. He was appointed as a director and librarian in 1908, served as secretary from 1910-1922, became vice-president in 1925, and was president from 1934 to 1963. He established the *Utah Genealogical and Historical Magazine* and was associate editor in 1910, the first year of its publication. He was instrumental in defining the objectives of the Genealogical Society. During the time that he served as one of its directors, ward and stake genealogy committees were organized throughout the Church, the Temple Index Bureau was created, and the family group sheets so widely used by genealogists were developed. Under his direction as president, the massive microfilming work of the society was begun.

On April 6, 1910, at the age of 33, President Smith was ordained an apostle and set apart as a member of the Quorum of Twelve. He filled the vacancy created when John Henry Smith was appointed a member of the First Presidency. Since that time he has visited nearly every stake in the Church in conference assignments. He was on assignment visiting missions in Europe in 1939 when hostilities leading to World War II erupted. His diligent response to a cablegram from the First Presidency resulted in the safe evacuation of all American missionaries from Europe.

During the solemn assembly that saw David O. McKay become the ninth President of the Church on April 9, 1951, President Smith was sustained as president of the Quorum of Twelve. He was appointed to assist President McKay as a counselor on October 29, 1965 where he served until his own calling as President of the Church on January 23, 1970.

Another aspect of his varied career has been his service in the Salt Lake Temple. Between 1915 and 1935 he assisted Presidents Anthon H. Lund and George F. Richards as counselor; and from 1945-1949 he served as president of that temple.

A champion of education, President Smith has been a member of the BYU Board of Trustees since 1912 and the Church Board of Education since 1917. His dedicated commitment to education in the Church was noticed on June 4, 1951 when he was awarded an honorary Doctor of Letters degree from Brigham Young University.

A characteristic of his home and family life is love and kindness. On April 26, 1898 Joseph Fielding married Louie Emyla Shurtliff who was called away by death on March 30, 1908. To this union came two daughters. On November 2, 1908 he married Ethel Georgina Reynolds, who became the mother of five sons and four daughters. On August 26, 1937 she, too, passed away. On April 12, 1938 Jessie Ella Evans, concert singer and soloist with the Salt Lake Tabernacle Choir, was married to President Smith. Of her husband, Sister Smith has noted: "He is the kindest man I have ever known. I have never heard him speak an unkind word in our home."

For length of service, Joseph Fielding Smith's sixty-nine years in the Historian's Office has no parallels in the history of the Church. His historical work began on October 1, 1901 and did not terminate until his appointment as President of the Church January 23, 1970. His talent in matters of history is indicated by his diversified activities over the years. In 1902 he traveled on special assignment to Massachusetts to gather genealogical data on the Smith family; he was engaged with Anthon H. Lund, Brigham H. Roberts, and Andrew Jenson in reading the manuscript of Joseph Smith's "History of the Church" in preparation for the publication of that work; he assisted in the compilation of evidence that was used in the Reed Smoot case before the Senate Judiciary Committee during the first decade of this century; and he personally penned the Historian's Office Daily Journal during seven years from 1903-1910. In addition, he was engaged in indexing, writing articles for publication, answering correspondence, compiling Church history, proofreading manuscripts, and serving as scribe for the First Presidency.

On April 8, 1906 President Smith was sustained as an assistant church historian to succeed Orson F. Whitney. During this time he directed the compilation of the Journal History of the Church for the post-1900 years. In 1907 he was commissioned by the Department of Commerce and Labor of the United States to collect statistics of the Church for the religious census being compiled by the government at that time.

Upon the death of Anthon H. Lund on March 2, 1921, Joseph Fielding was chosen to succeed him as church historian and recorder. Under his direction valuable historical records of the Church have been preserved through an extensive microfilming program; histories of wards and stakes of the Church have been standardized; and modern methods of cataloging, filing and preserving of historical records were inaugurated.

In addition to his many administrative assignments and responsibilities, President Smith is widely noted as an author and writer. He has written study courses for priesthood and auxiliary organizations of the Church and published numerous books and articles on church history and doctrine. For many years he has been one of the foremost expositors of historical and doctrinal matters for the Church.

Service to the Church and his fellow men has been the main concern in the life of President Smith. As a missionary, church historian, secretary, director, and president of the Genealogical Society, as a general board member, temple president, author, editor, member of the Council of Twelve Apostles, president of that Council, counselor in the First Presidency, and finally President of the Church, service has been the main concern in his life.

The crowning point of his long career came on January 23, 1970 when he was chosen to be the tenth President of the Church. He selected Harold B. Lee as his first counselor and Nathan Eldon Tanner as second. He was unanimously sustained on Monday, April 6, 1970, in solemn assembly in the Salt Lake Tabernacle. On that occasion Elder Harold B. Lee said of the newly appointed Prophet: "When you reflect that God has sent through Hyrum Smith's lineage some of the greatest men of our dispensation, you will begin to see the fulfilment of that promised blessing that his name would be had in honorable remembrance through his posterity from generation to generation, forever and forever. His son Joseph F. Smith served as the sixth president of the Church from 1901 to 1918.

"President Joseph F. Smith as a child passed through the trying scenes of Missouri and Illinois. After his father Hyrum Smith was martyred by a mob at Carthage along with his uncle, Joseph Smith, the Prophet, young Joseph, although but a boy of nine years of age, drove an ox team across the plains from the Missouri River, arriving in Salt Lake Valley in 1848. In 1852, his mother died, and two years thereafter he left for a mission to the Hawaiian Islands when but 15 years of age.

"This is the fibre of the Hyrum Smith ancestry from which our President Joseph Fielding Smith has come. I am confident that heaven is pleased today and I doubt not but during the ministry of this noble son and grandson, those who have gone on before will be permitted to draw near to their descendant, whom the Lord has now honored with this challenging responsibility, despite his great age. . . ."

In characteristic style, President Smith assumed the duties of his office with renewed vigor and added strength. He began to travel to various parts of the Church, meeting with the youth particularly, to bear witness of the truths of the gospel. In his first year as Church President, he traveled to special meetings in California, Idaho, Arizona, Mexico, and Hawaii. Also, on two separate occasions he conferred with President Richard M. Nixon who had come to Utah.

His second year as leader of the Church was even more eventful, for it saw him travel to Great Britain where he presided over the three-day area general conference of the Church in Manchester, England, an historic first for the Church. The conference was held August 27, 28, and 29, 1971, and President Smith kept a full schedule of meetings with the members in that area.

The year 1971 also marked the completion of a new visitors' center at Independence, Missouri, and President Smith flew to this historic Church site to dedicate the edifice.

As 1972 began, President Smith officiated at the dedicatory services in January and February for the new Ogden and Provo temples, and gave stirring dedicatory prayers which were an inspiration to all.

Under the presidency of President Smith the Church made rapid progress in many areas, especially in strengthening priesthood supervision and the family unit.

He chose Boyd Kenneth Packer, an assistant to the Twelve, to become a member of the Council of Twelve and named three assistants to the Twelve: Joseph Anderson, long-time secretary to the Presidency; David B. Haight of Brigham Young University; and William H. Bennett of Utah State University.

Rubie Egbert, President Smith's secretary for more than 52 years, retired in December 1971. D. Arthur Haycock became President Smith's personal secretary, assistant, and traveling companion in January 1970.

When he reluctantly relinquished his job as Church Historian and Recorder he appointed Howard W. Hunter of the Council of Twelve to succeed him. Later due to the decision to release all members of the Twelve from other specific assignments they appointed managing directors, in several different areas, from among the Assistants to the Twelve. The Historian's Office was changed to The Historical Department of The Church of Jesus Christ of Latter-day Saints and the position previously held by the Church Historian and Church Recorder was assigned to a managing director, Alvin Rulon Dyer, Assistant to the Twelve. The department was divided into three separate units: (1) Church Archivist, Earl Eidswold Olson; (2) Church Historian, Leonard James Arrington; and (3) Church Librarian, Donald Thomas Schmidt. Later Joseph Anderson was appointed assistant managing director.

The position of Church commissioner of education was reactivated with Neal Maxwell being appointed and he appointed three new college presidents: Dallin H. Oaks at BYU; Henry B. Eyring, Jr. at Ricks College; and Stephen L. Brower at Church College of Hawaii. Ernest L. Wilkinson remained at BYU to help establish a law school.

President Smith ordained several new temple presidents: Myrthus W. Evans in Los Angeles, C. Bryant Whiting in Mesa, Arizona, Fred W. Schwendiman in Salt Lake City for the New Zealand Temple, and Charles Lloyd Walch in Salt Lake City for the Hawaiian Temple, Cecil E. Hart for the Idaho Falls Temple, and Reed Whipple for the St. George Temple. He dedicated a new temple in Ogden and presided at the dedication of a new temple in Provo.

During his presidency the Church magazines were revamped with Doyle L. Green as editor-in-chief over all of them. The names, *The Improvement Era, The Instructor, The Relief Society Magazine, The Children's Friend* were dropped; also the seminary system's *Impact*. These magazines were changed into three, one for adults, one for youth, and one for children, and named respectively, *The Ensign, The New Era,* and *The Friend*. President Smith and his two counselors were listed as editors of these publications and took turns writing editorials for them. R- and X-rated movie ads were dropped from the Church's daily newspaper, the *Deseret News*.

The Deseret Sunday School Union was reorganized and renamed the Sunday School of The Church of Jesus Christ of Latter-day Saints. Upon receiving his call to preside over the Eastern States Mission, David Lawrence McKay, eldest son of President David O. McKay, was released as superintendent, and Russell M. Nelson was appointed in his place, with the new title of president. The general Sunday School board membership was considerably reduced.

The Church Social Services Department was reorganized with Marvin J. Ashton as chairman, and a church commissioner of health services, Dr. James O. Mason, was appointed. A Department of Internal Communications and a Department of External Communications were organized with J. Thomas Fyans and Wendell J. Ashton as managing directors, respectively. The Church took specific steps to aid Negroes, Indians and other minority groups, both inside and outside the Church, through various programs.

Emphasis was given to the Church's home teaching and family home evening programs, in a continuing effort to strengthen family solidarity. At October 1970 General Conference Monday night was designated to be set apart as Family Home Evening. President

Smith though in advanced age continued to set an example to the Church by meeting in family home evenings with his children and grandchildren.

A new training program for bishops was inaugurated to aid them in their duties and responsibilities. The Teacher Development Program for all prospective church teachers, inservice teachers, and their supervisors was enhanced on a church-wide basis with training for general authorities, stake, and ward priesthood leaders included.

A new program was instituted to bring the Aaronic Priesthood and MIA leaders into closer cooperation for the benefit of the growth of the Church. The Scouting program was correlated, with the Presiding Bishopric serving as the chairmen of the General Boy Scout Committee of the Church. A new Personal Achievement Program for youth was inaugurated which permits the young people to set their own goals under the supervision of leaders and ward bishops or branch presidents. Stress was placed on priesthood quorum activities, particularly the elders quorums, resulting in a more unified spirit of activity. One of the chief objectives of President Smith's was to unify the priesthood to enable its members to take their rightful place in the Church's future.

The next general area conference was announced to be held in Mexico City in August 1972.

In the two and a half years Joseph Fielding Smith served as president 14 additional missions were created, some by a division of previously existing missions, bringing the total at the time of his death to 101. During the same period an additional 82 stakes were organized, bringing the total at the time of his death to 581. Total Church membership increased from 2,930,810 in January of 1970 to 3,170,000 in July of 1972.

In June 1972, less than a week before his death, 70 new church regions were created, with mission fields as well as stakes to be included in the regions; 35 additional regional representatives were appointed, and 29 mission representatives were called to assist the general authorities in directing missionary work.

The church building program continued at a rapid pace, with hundreds of chapels, schools and other buildings being constructed. A 31-story Church office building east of the Salt Lake Temple was nearing completion at the time of his death. Its dedication had been scheduled for December 1972. Here would be housed the various church auxiliary organizations and service departments in one magnificent center.

Saddening experiences were the death of two general authorities, Thorpe B. Isaacson and Richard L. Evans and Emma Ray Riggs McKay, widow of President McKay, as well as his own wife, Jessie Evans Smith.

To the vacancy in the Council of the Twelve created by the death of Elder Evans, President Smith appointed Marvin J. Ashton, an Assistant to the Twelve and son of the late Marvin O. Ashton, who had been a counselor in the presiding bishopric years earlier.

Victor L. Brown, who had been serving as second counselor in the presiding bishopric, was appointed as presiding bishop in April 1972, with H. Burke Peterson and Vaughn J. Featherstone as his counselors. Bishop John H. Vandenberg, and his first counselor, Robert L. Simpson, were named Assistants to the Twelve.

The death of President Joseph Fielding Smith on July 2, 1972 ended a lifetime of dedicated service and counsel, which counsel recorded in his books and speeches will be a help and an encouragement to many generations to come. This was well expressed by him in a Park Stake Conference on Sept. 5, 1971: "We are under covenant to walk in virtue and holiness before the Lord; to contribute of our time and means for the building up of the Church; and to serve our fellowman with an eye single to the glory of the Lord. All those who pursue such a course shall gain peace in this life and eternal life in the world to come."

CHAPTER 58

PRESIDENT HAROLD B. LEE
ELEVENTH PRESIDENT OF THE CHURCH

In an April 1973 conference address, President Harold B. Lee said,

Harold B. Lee

"No longer might this Church be thought of as the 'Utah church,' or as an 'American church,' but the membership of the Church is now distributed over the earth in 78 countries, teaching the gospel in 17 different languages. . . . This greatly expanded church population is today our most challenging problem [and poses] some great challenges to the leadership of the Church to keep pace. . . ." Since 1941, when President Lee first became a member of the Quorum of the Twelve, the membership of the Church has grown explosively. There were just over one million members in 1948; the present population is over three million. This expansion has not only been in numbers, but in diversity. Bursts of growth through convert baptisms first in Latin America, then in the Far East, have multiplied the number of non-English speaking members. Stakes led by resident leaders have been organized in areas where previously the branches had been under the direction of mission leaders from America; three new temples have been built to serve the membership in Europe and the South Pacific; regions of the Church have been organized and leaders residing in areas away from Church headquarters have been assigned to represent the Twelve in directing the affairs of the Church in those areas. In a similar pattern, mission representatives have been called to represent the Quorum of the Twelve and the First Council of the Seventy in directing missionary work throughout the world.

Responsibility for the leadership of the mammoth organization which the Church has become rests, as it always has, with its prophet and president. Since July 7, 1972, President Harold B. Lee has held that office. His preparation for that calling is significant to the continuing direction of the Church.

President Lee was born on March 28, 1899 of parents whose history he termed "the simple annals of the poor." He was one of six children of a bishop father in the Cache Valley farming community of Clifton, Idaho. His growing-up experiences were not unlike those of his generation of Latter-day Saints. He attended the community elementary school and the Church-operated Oneida Academy, a secondary school fifteen miles away. At Albion State Normal School, at the age of seventeen, he qualified as a teacher, and was offered his first teaching post in the little one-room Silver Star School near Weston, Idaho. The salary was sixty dollars a month. The following year his school board named him principal of the four-room Oxford, Idaho, school. He was eighteen years old.

His interests expanded beyond academics into sports—he played basketball; into forensics—he participated in debate; and into music— he played piano and trombone in dance bands around the community.

Two more years Elder Lee taught, and then was called to serve as a missionary in the Western States Mission. One of his assignments was to preside over the Denver district.

Continuing in the often repeated pattern of young people maturing in the Church, he married shortly after his release from the mission. Fern Lucinda Tanner and Harold B. Lee were married in the Salt Lake Temple in 1923. Two daughters were born to them. They settled in west Salt Lake City, where Elder Lee continued his teaching, supplementing his education with courses from the University of Utah. He was named principal, first of Whittier School and later of the Woodrow Wilson School in Salt Lake County.

A summer selling job for a library service, Foundation Press, eventually involved him so completely that he left teaching to become intermountain manager for the company. Expanding his concerns still further, he was appointed in 1932 Salt Lake City commissioner for streets and public property, a post to which he was elected for a second term.

Paralleling these involvements in professional and community affairs were the Church activities which were even more profound in their impact on Elder Lee's future affairs. The Pioneer Stake in which the Lees resided called him to be superintendent of its Religion Class a forerunner of present day seminaries. He was subsequently called to be alternate member of the stake high council, counselor to the stake president, and then, in 1930 at the age of thirty-one, he was called as stake president.

The history of Pioneer Stake during the seven years of Elder Lee's presidency reflects the usual administrative concerns: building programs, stake boards, and missionary funds. In each case the history shows unusual approaches, innovations reflecting an insightful response to circumstances, some of which were particular to Pioneer Stake and some, even more demanding, particular to the economic conditions of the time. The Great Depression was creating havoc in the lives of the members of the Church in Pioneer Stake, as elsewhere.

Welfare needs of the people were crying out for solution. In 1932 the stake built and began operation of its bishop's storehouse. Relief was desperately needed to bring the stake members through the coming winter; in the spring President Lee reported to stake officers that one-third of the stake was unemployed. Under his direction Pioneer Stake took the materials from a demolished business building and constructed a stake gymnasium. From the laying of the cornerstone to the formal opening required only five months. President Lee's motto for the stake during that year was "to provide fully for the spiritual, physical, educational, and recreational needs of our people." The need for food was still a crying one in 1934 when the stake initiated negotiations with owners of orchards and farms for produce in exchange for labor. These contracts and ideas proved seminal: President Lee's experiences in the Pioneer Stake prepared him with understanding and ideas invaluable to him in his next Church assignment. He later recounted the events which culminated in the establishment of the internationally acclaimed Church Welfare Program. There came, he says,

". . . the call of the First Presidency for me to come to their office on a day that I shall never forget—April 20, 1935. I was city commissioner in Salt Lake City. I was stake president.

"We had been wrestling with this question of welfare. There were few government work programs; the finances of the Church were low; we were told that there wasn't much that could be done so far as the finances of the Church were concerned. And here we were with 4,800 of our 7,300 people who were wholly or partially dependent. We had only one place to go, and that was to apply the Lord's program as set forth in the revelations.

"It was from our humble efforts that the First Presidency, knowing that we had had some experience, called me one morning asking if I would come to their office. It was Saturday morning; there were no calls on their calendar, and for hours in that forenoon they talked with me and told me that they wanted me to resign from the city commission, and they would release me from being stake president; that they wished me now to head up the welfare movement to turn the tide from government relief, direct relief, and help to put the Church in a position where it could take care of its own needy."

Called to head the Welfare Program Churchwide, President Lee responded with what had become characteristic insight and innovation, but with a sense of dependence which he describes here:

"There I was, just a young man in my thirties. My experience had been limited. I was born in a little country town in Idaho. I had hardly been outside the boundaries of the states of Utah and Idaho. And now to put me in a position where I was to reach out to the entire membership of the Church, worldwide, was one of the most staggering contemplations that I could imagine. How could I do it with my limited understanding?

"As I kneeled down . . ."

Five years after the inauguration of the Welfare Program, Harold B. Lee was called to the apostleship, with all its accruing responsibilities. His sphere of activities widened: conferences in stakes and missions took him further throughout the Church, and administrative responsibilities in general Church departments—music, general priesthood, Relief Society and Primary general boards, publications—broadened his understanding of the demands on and responses of the growing Church.

Most particularly, though, Elder Lee responded to the problems and challenges of the young members of the Church. In 1945 Elder Lee gave a series of radio talks to youth which were compiled into a volume called *Youth and the Church,* revised and reissued in 1973 as *Decisions for Successful Living.* One of his first assignments in the Quorum of the Twelve was to head the Servicemen's Committee. World War II was being fought in Europe and the Pacific, and his concern led him on tours among the armed forces there. Later he continued his concern for the problems of military men during the Korean conflict.

Elder Lee's involvement with the educational programs of the Church, through seminaries and institutes as well as through the auxiliary programs, culminated in his assignment under direction from President David O. McKay to act as executive director of the newly conceived correlation committee. Its purpose was to examine the entire curriculum of the Church. Out of this came an exhaustive review of courses of instruction used in the teaching organizations and facilities of the Church, and under Elder Lee's direction evolved, and continues to evolve, a correlated curriculum designed to teach the gospel in its every phase to every member of the Church.

In the midst of these years of vigorous Church activity, in 1962, Elder Lee's wife Fern died. Her death was followed some four years later by that of their daughter Maurine. In 1963 Elder Lee married Freda Joan Jensen, then supervisor of elementary education in the Jordan School District and a member of the general board of the Primary Association.

Upon the death of President McKay in January of 1970, Elder Lee became first counselor to President Joseph Fielding Smith and president of the Quorum of the Twelve Apostles. With the death in July 1972 of President Smith, Harold B. Lee became President of the Church and called N. Eldon Tanner and Marion G. Romney as his counselors in the First Presidency.

At this writing President Lee has been administering the affairs of the Church for just over one year. Even in that short time he has directed among other things, the complete reorganization of the Mutual Improvement Association. His injunction to the committee assigned to that responsibility was to be "imaginative, bold, and creative" in their approach to their task. The resulting organization, announced in November 1972, called for direct priesthood responsibility for the programs, newly assigned as Aaronic Priesthood and Melchizidek Priesthood functions.

Such continuing innovation and adaptation of church programs under President Lee's administration will be required to meet the needs of a Church, the major part of whose more than three million members no longer cluster together in the intermountain west, and nearly one-third of whom live outside the United States.

The transformation of the Church from the gathering of Zion of the last century to the enlarging of her borders in this century is dramatically demonstrated in the area conferences which are becoming a practice in the Church. The first of these was held in Manchester, England, in 1971 under the direction of President Joseph Fielding

Smith. He said at that time, that "now we are coming of age as a church and as a people. We have attained the stature and strength that are enabling us to fulfill the commission given us by the Lord through the Prophet Joseph Smith that we should carry the glad tidings of the restoration to every nation and to all people."

The following year President Lee directed the second area conference in Mexico City, the largest single meeting of Mormons ever assembled. The third such conference was held for European saints in Munich, Germany, in August 1973.

The world-wide Church stood under the direction of a man who, at the beginning of his general involvement, "had hardly been outside the boundaries of Utah and Idaho." For thirty years after that Harold B. Lee prepared himself, and was prepared, by the experiences through which he passed, to carry the responsibility of the 3.5 million member organization. He became, in Joseph Smith's image, "a smooth and polished shaft in the quiver of the Almighty."

Through the fall of 1973, President Lee continued to visit and counsel the Saints throughout the Church, and during the Christmas season he spoke to numerous groups, retelling the beautiful story of the Savior's birth and inspiring the Saints to better live the teachings of the Master. On the day after Christmas, December 26, he became ill quite suddenly and in the late afternoon was admitted to the LDS Hospital in Salt Lake City for observation. There, at a few minutes before nine that evening, he passed away. Funeral services were held in the Salt Lake Tabernacle on Saturday, December 29, and interment was in the Salt Lake City Cemetery.

(This biographical material on President Harold B. Lee was prepared by Leonard J. Arrington, Church Historian.)

CHAPTER 59

PRESIDENT SPENCER WOOLLEY KIMBALL
TWELFTH PRESIDENT OF THE CHURCH

At the turn of the century in Thatcher, Arizona, a young boy sat on a short stool singing to the cows as he milked them. His father was nearby and, nodding to a friend, said, "Spencer is an exceptional boy. I have dedicated him to be one of the mouthpieces of the Lord—the Lord willing."

On December 30, 1973, Spencer Woolley Kimball was ordained twelfth President of The Church of Jesus Christ of Latter-day Saints, prophet, seer, and revelator—mouthpiece of the Lord. Since his calling to the Council of the Twelve in 1943, he has spoken "as one having authority," boldly denouncing evil and defending righteousness. With impressive frankness and power he has proclaimed against the "spiritual diseases which throttle us and plague our lives." To parents and youth confronted with an age of sexual freedom and promiscuity, he has preached fidelity and chastity; and amid

Spencer Woolley Kimball

the prosperous roar of their TV sets, cars, and boats, he has prescribed the quiet peace and strength that come with holy sabbaths and full tithes. He has pronounced the only sure cure for the world's ills to be repentance, testifying that Jesus Christ transforms lives from misery to hope.

Being mouthpiece for the Lord has not been easy, nor has Elder Kimball been unhindered in bringing forth his message. In 1957 throat cancer required surgery to remove one of his vocal cords and part of the second. But Spencer Kimball would not be left without a voice to exhort. He redeveloped his ability to speak and continued in the softer, huskier tone Saints now recognize as the voice of their prophet.

In thirty years of work with Lamanite Saints he became their teacher and foremost advocate. He admonished other members comfortable in their abundance to assist the forgotten children of Lehi. "They but wait for opportunity, encouragement, and brotherliness; and these will be redeemed, will rise and become a blessed people," he said. He has looked with an eye to the greatness of Indian and Spanish-speaking Saints, urging and encouraging bishops and stake presidents to give them the responsibilities that will enable them in turn to serve in bishoprics and in stake, mission, and temple presidencies.

Such have been the loud and powerful messages of this spokesman of the Lord, spun with a remarkable knowledge of the scriptures, woven with his own experience, and eloquently delivered. But his voice has been quieter at times, speaking to some Saints in personal interviews and to thousands more in published pamphlets and books. Occasionally while traveling, President Kimball might be seen with a small twenty-five-year-old portable typewriter, or perhaps recording thoughts and impressions in his journal, but more often composing letters of encouragement and support to particular missionaries and members. Personal thoughtfulness prompted him to jot down notes and references to give to people to help them remember his counsel. "I thought I would write a little message of encouragement and counsel. That message became twenty-three chapters in a book." So the quiet counselor reached out to the general Church membership in a classic book for Latter-day Saints, *The Miracle of Forgiveness*. After its ninth printing came a companion piece, *Faith Precedes the Miracle,* likewise offered to uplift and instruct. The message is timely.

His prophetic father was Andrew Kimball, a son of Ann Gheen and the early apostle and counselor to Brigham Young, Heber C. Kimball. For ten years Andrew Kimball served as president of the Indian Territory Mission, intermittently staying with his wife and children in Salt Lake City. He visited Salt Lake City on March 28, 1895, to witness the birth of his sixth child, Spencer Woolley Kimball, named for his mother, Olive Woolley, the strong and loyal woman who carried the responsibility for her home and family when Andrew Kimball was away. She was a daughter of Mary A. and Bishop Edwin D. Woolley, sometime business manager for Brigham Young. Spencer was only three years old when his father, six months after his release from the mission, was called to Thatcher, Arizona, and set apart as president of St. Joseph Stake. The Kimballs were received at the Thatcher train depot with showers of roses from the waiting Saints—an omen of the blossoming that would take place in the Gila Valley under the direction of Andrew Kimball. He was a cultural, intellectual, and spiritual leader of the people. He could boast a large library and was a studied scripturalist. Andrew and Olive Kimball participated in a polysophical society in Thatcher, where he often lectured and she sang. She was musically talented, so besides sewing trousers for her family, she taught them music. At fourteen, Spencer was ward chorister, choir member, and choir leader. When the family was among the first in Gila Valley to buy an organ, Olive Kimball taught her young son to play, and he played at ward services. He still plays the organ at the meetings of the First Presidency and the Quorum of the Twelve each Thursday morning in the Salt Lake Temple.

Growing up on a small farm, young Spencer worked at haying, milking, pruning orchards, and marketing fruit. Once when he was on the wagon in the field hauling hay with his brothers, he heard the meetinghouse bell signal the start of Primary. He asked his brothers if he could leave to attend the meeting. When they insisted they needed his help, he pleaded: "Father would let me go if he were here." "Father isn't here, and you are not going," replied his brothers as they covered the young boy with piles of hay. Persistent, he tramped through the hay, slid from the wagon, and ran to Primary to keep his perfect attendance record unbroken.

Childhood was not without problems for Spencer. When ten years old, he awoke one morning to find one side of his face paralyzed. The doctor could only recommend a liniment, but Spencer was healed through the power of the priesthood. A year later his mother died and Spencer felt the loss deeply. He was struck with typhoid fever in 1910 when an epidemic rush of typhoid cases hit the Thatcher area, killing many people. But again he was spared, and soon after he began work at a dairy so he could save funds for college and a mission.

On May 7, 1914, Andrew Kimball attended commencement exercises for Spencer's graduating class at the Gila Academy, now Eastern Arizona Junior College, a school to which the elder Kimball had given leadership as student body president. Spencer had also been star forward of the basketball team, and he was graduating with high honors.

Andrew Kimball noted in his diary: "I told the class . . . their president should have the privilege of travel during the interim between now and going to college." And soon Spencer W. Kimball received his mission call to the Swiss-German Mission, but with the outbreak of the first World War he was transferred to the Central States Mission. President Samuel O. Bennion recognized his capabilities and made him president of the Missouri Conference. Tracting once in St. Louis, Elder Kimball noted a new piano as a woman opened her door. "I see you have a new piano," smiled the elder. The woman beamed, "The family just bought it." "It is a Kimball, isn't it? That is my name also." The door opened wider and Elder Kimball, offering to sing and play, was invited in. He sang "O My Father" and introduced the gospel. President Kimball later called his mission a "stabilizer, an organizer, and a spiritualizer" because it provided him experience in directing and assigning and dealing with personalities and problems.

Home from his mission, Spencer Kimball enrolled at the University of Arizona and became involved in a program of military training. One week the front page of the local newspaper carried a picture of lovely Camilla Eyring, daughter of Edward Christian and Caroline Romney Eyring. Her family had fled to Arizona from the Mexican colonies as a result of that country's revolution. Having taken training at Brigham Young Academy, University of California at Berkeley, and Utah State University, she was teaching home economics at Gila Academy in Thatcher. Spencer was waiting there for his contingent to be called to the war. So in a khaki uniform he courted intelligent, blue-eyed Camilla and they were married in November 1917. The armistice was signed before Spencer's company was called.

The couple settled in Graham County, where Spencer Kimball accepted a position as a bank teller and bookkeeper and later became branch manager and assistant cashier of a chain of banks. He resigned to become part-owner and manager of the Kimball-Greenhalgh Insurance and Realty Company, where he worked until he was called to the Council of the Twelve in 1943. His involvement in Church work paralleled his professional career. Two months after his marriage, he was called to serve as stake clerk of the St. Joseph Stake, where his father still presided as president. When Andrew Kimball died in 1924, President Heber J. Grant traveled to attend the funeral and reorganize the stake. At twenty-nine, Spencer W. Kimball was set apart as second counselor in the stake presidency. After fourteen years, the stake was divided and a new stake was created in 1938, the Mt. Graham Stake, with Spencer W. Kimball named as its first president. With 250 miles between one end of the stake and the other, Mt. Graham Stake required dedicated and resourceful leadership. In 1938 the Gila River rose and flooded the streets and homes of Duncan and the surrounding farms. President Spencer Kimball rallied and coordinated forces for the relief of the members.

During this time President and Sister Kimball were living in Safford, Arizona, rearing their four children: Spencer Levan, Olive Beth, Andrew Eyring, and Edward Lawrence. In addition to his business, President Kimball had a small farm where he raised cotton and alfalfa. The Kimballs were community as well as church leaders. President Kimball was involved in the Arizona Association of Insurance Agents, State Teachers' Retirement Board, board of education of Gila Junior College, and Gila Broadcasting Company. He was governor of Rotary International for his district and appointed to two national councils of the Boy Scouts of America. Sister Kimball served as president of the Safford Women's Club and as president of the southern district of Women's Clubs for Arizona.

On July 8, 1943, Spencer W. Kimball received a phone call at his home in Safford. President J. Reuben Clark, Jr., was calling from Salt Lake City. "Spencer," he began, "the brethren have just called you to fill one of the vacancies in the Quorum of the Twelve Apostles." President Kimball later reflected that the call came like a bolt of lightning.

" 'I was dazed, almost numb with the shock; a picture of my life spread out before me,' he recalls. 'I sensed immediately my inability and limitations and I cried back, 'Not me, Brother Clark! You can't mean that!

" 'I remember reading that Jacob wrestled all night, until the breaking of day, for a blessing; and I want to tell you that for eighty-five nights I have gone through that experience, wrestling for a blessing. Eighty-five times, the breaking of the day has found me on my knees praying to the Lord to help me and strengthen me and make me equal to this great responsibility that has come to me.' "

The responsibilities were fast in coming. One of Spencer Kimball's first assignments was to work with George Albert Smith, then president of the Council of the Twelve, in reviving work with the American Indian. As an eleven-year-old boy, Spencer had been told by Patriarch Samuel Claridge that he would see Lamanites "organized and . . . prepared to stand as the bulwark 'round this people.'" Through his work on the Indian Affairs Committee, President Kimball has seen their growth and development and made a significant contribution to it through initiation of the Indian Placement Program.

He has become intimately acquainted with the missionary program of the Church, having toured hundreds of missions and stakes, dividing and reorganizing in South, Central, and North America, the South Seas, Great Britain, Europe, the Orient, South Africa, Mexico, and Canada. He helped dedicate several missions in South America, supervised missionary work there for three years, and directed work in Great Britain for two years. He was then assigned to preside over all the missions of the Church as chairman of the executive committee of the Church's Missionary Committee.

President Kimball has served in many phases of church work—as chairman of the Budget Committee, member of the Expenditure Committee and the Correlation Committee; and a member of the board of trustees of Brigham Young University and of the Board of Education of the Church schools. He extended his efforts to youth development through the Youth Rehabilitation Committee, which has since been expanded to the Church Social Services. He is president or director of a number of businesses and industries. In 1969 he was honored by Brigham Young University when an honorary doctor of laws degree was conferred on him.

His planning, traveling, and speaking were interrupted in 1971 by a condition requiring open heart surgery. The months following his phenomenal recovery found President Kimball more tireless in his work than ever. At the death of President Joseph Fielding Smith in 1972 he became President of the Council of Twelve Apostles and served in that capacity for eighteen months until the death of President Harold B. Lee, when he was ordained and set apart as President of the Church, with N. Eldon Tanner and Marion G. Romney as counselors in the First Presidency.

Spencer Woolley Kimball leads 3.3 million Latter-day Saints in seventy-eight countries throughout the world. He foresees all of those countries sending forth their own missionaries so the gospel can be preached in every land. He anticipates temples in many countries so all Saints might be strengthened through temple ordinances and the work for the dead might be expanded. He continues to call Saints to repentance that they might become the pure and perfect people he envisions.

In the news conference the morning following his ordination as President of The Church of Jesus Christ of Latter-day Saints, newsmen flooded President Kimball with questions. "What will be your message to the world?" they asked. He assured them, and through them the world, that the restored gospel holds the solution to all problems. Then he declared his message to be "what it has always been: Live the commandments of the Lord."

Appendix

THE AUXILIARY ORGANIZATIONS OF THE CHURCH

In additon to the quorums of the priesthood, there are in the Church a number of helpful organizations known as the auxiliary organizations. These are: The Relief Society of The Church of Jesus Christ of Latter-day Saints, Sunday School of The Church of Jesus Christ of Latter-day Saints, the Aaronic Priesthood Mutual Improvement Association (Young Men and Young Women), the Melchizedek Priesthood Mutual Interest Association, and the Primary Association. There are two other organizations which are not classed as auxiliaries, namely, the Church Educational System and the Genealogical Society, which is closely related in its work to the temples.

A brief statement of the organization, accomplishments and aims of these societies is here given.

THE RELIEF SOCIETY OF THE CHURCH OF JESUS CHRIST OF LATTER-DAY SAINTS

The Relief Society was organized by Joseph Smith, the Prophet, March 17, 1842, in Nauvoo. It was originally known as the Female Relief Society, but since its incorporation, October 10, 1892, it has been known as the National Women's Relief Society.* According to the minutes of the original meeting, the Prophet said the object of the society was to look after the needs of the poor, to search after objects

---

*June 27, 1945, the name was changed to Relief Society of The Church of Jesus Christ of Latter-day Saints.

of charity, and to administer to their wants; and to assist by correcting the morals and strengthening the virtues of the community. He also expressed the desire that the society should be a select company of the virtuous and those who would walk circumspectly. One feature of the work of the society, he said, should be to purge out iniquity and surmount difficulties. He also instructed the sisters that in their proceedings there must be decision of character aside from sympathy.

In the early organization in Nauvoo a committee of sixteen was appointed—four from each ward then established—to visit families regularly and to seek out suffering and those in need, in order that they might be relieved. This was the beginning of the teachers' work in the society. From an initial membership of 18, the society, in two years, increased to 1275. As of August 31, 1972, there were 715,071 members of Relief Society, which included 4,558 non-LDS members. There were 5,314 Relief Society organizations in the stakes and 1,878 in the missions for a grand total of 7,192. In 1973 new direction was given to the Relief Society, which is now responsible for all women of the Church—both married and unmarried—over 18 years of age, as well as all married women under 18. New programs have also been introduced, with greater flexibility in meeting the needs of individual members through "mini-courses" in subjects of interest to the members.

In the early years in Utah organizations were gradually effected in the wards. In 1880 a general board, with Eliza R. Snow as president, was organized to unify, co-ordinate and supervise the work throughout the Church, under the direction of the General Authorities.

The character of the organization is the same now as when organized, although the work has been enlarged. The following activities are now featured: nursing, caring for the needy, sick, aged, dependent, and the dead; and the development of a program of education for family welfare, health instruction, and household management. A special feature of the work is monthly visits by teachers to all Latter-day Saint homes. The educational and cultural activities of the society include uniform courses of study on religious and educational topics, given in regular weekly meetings.

The Woman's Exponent, established in 1872, was closely allied to the work and later became official organ of the society. In 1914 the *Relief Society Magazine* was established, it had a circulation on August 31, 1969 of approximately 281,790 in English and 6,839 in Spanish. The magazine ceased publication with the December 1970 issue.

SUNDAY SCHOOL OF THE CHURCH OF JESUS CHRIST OF LATTER-DAY SAINTS

In the fall of 1848, a little more than a year after the arrival of the pioneers, Richard Ballantyne came to the Salt Lake Valley with his family. He located in the old fort and the following spring made plans for a home. He arranged his building to provide for the holding of a Sunday School, and on Sunday, December 9, 1849, the first Sunday School in the Rocky Mountains was held at his home, Elder Ballantyne being both superintendent and teacher. His Sunday School was popular among the members of the Church and was well attended until the year 1850, when a chapel was erected in the Fourteenth Ward into which the Sunday School was transferred. Not long after this other Sunday Schools were organized in Salt Lake City and in a number of other settlements in Utah. However, there was no uniformity of method or course of study in these schools.

The possibility of the Sunday School as an agency for teaching the gospel to the youth was early recognized and the importance of uniformity and co-operation in this task was urged early in 1866. In November, 1866, as a result of the growing sentiment, a meeting was called at which a general organization was effected for the purpose of concentrating and unifying Sunday School efforts. Elder George Q. Cannon was elected president of the organization which was called the Deseret Sunday School Union. The scope of the activity of the Sunday School is Church-wide, and its purpose is to establish uniformity in Sunday School methods, to develop greater efficiency, and through co-operation to improve the quality of the work done. The *Juvenile Instructor,* first published by Elder George Q. Cannon early in 1866, was the official organ of the Deseret Sunday School Union, and a potent factor in accomplishing these results. It contained uniform lessons for each department in the Sunday Schools. Publication of the *Instructor* ceased with the December 1970 issue. Teacher-training work, as a means of developing greater teaching efficiency, was first undertaken by the Sunday Schools under the leadership of the general board. This movement has since attained Church-wide application under the leadership and direction of the priesthood. On August 10, 1971 the name of the Sunday School was changed from The Deseret Sunday School Union to SUNDAY SCHOOL OF THE CHURCH OF JESUS CHRIST OF LATTER-DAY SAINTS.

As an organization, auxiliary to the priesthood, the ultimate aim of the Sunday Schools is to teach the principles of the gospel and to stimulate the pupils to render willing obedience thereto. More specifically, the Sunday School aims so to equip its members that they will be able not only to work out their own salvation through the application of, and obedience to, the principles of the gospel which they have been taught, but also to prepare themselves for service in the priesthood, in the mission fields, and in the organizations at home, through which opportunities are afforded them to render service to others. The Sunday School recognizes no age limit, but aims to accommodate all grades of spiritual development from infancy to old age.

In recent years the programs and structure of the Sunday School have changed and have been streamlined. In June 1972 the titles of the presiding officers were changed, and the organization is now presided over by presidents and counselors, replacing the old titles of superintendents and assistants. A reduced general board now directs the program on a general level. In the stakes, the number of leadership meetings has been reduced, as has the size of the board. In the wards, study courses for the adults have been correlated with the general program of the Church. An eight-year program of scripture study has been outlined for those attending the Gospel Doctrine classes. In 1973-74 the Old Testament was the course of study; for 1974-75 it will be the New Testament.

In the mission field the Sunday School is particularly recognized as a means of arousing interest in the work of the Church and as a step toward the establishment of branches. In areas where there are few members, home Sunday Schools and dependent Sunday Schools may be organized, dependent on more fully organized branches. As the Sunday Schools increase in size and leadership, branches are then formed.

AARONIC PRIESTHOOD MIA (MUTUAL IMPROVEMENT ASSOCIATION) YOUNG MEN'S

The Young Men's Mutual Improvement Associations of The Church of Jesus Christ of Latter-day Saints were begun in the year 1875, the first organization having been effected in the Thirteenth Ward, Salt Lake City, on the 10th day of June, that year, by Junius F. Wells, under the immediate instruction and direction of President Brigham Young.

On November 9, 1972, by direction of the First Presidency, the auxiliary status of the YMMIA was changed and it became a priesthood organization known as the Aaronic Priesthood MIA—Young Men's. This organization, directed by the First Presidency and advised by members of the Council of the Twelve as to curriculum and correlation, is under the leadership of the Presiding Bishopric.

Note: At June Conference 1974 the First Presidency announced that hereafter, all activities of the former APMIA will come under the direction of the Presiding Bishopric and the Aaronic Priesthood. The name of the organization for girls was changed to Young Women.

APPENDIX

Working under the direction of the Presiding Bishopric are general president Robert L. Backman and his two counselors, LeGrand R. Curtis and Jack H. Goaslind, Jr. They direct a general board consisting of a services and activity committee and committees to plan curriculum and other class activities for youths 12 through 18 years of age. The Aaronic Priesthood for young men consists of three groups of Aaronic Priesthood boys: (1) deacons (Scouts); (2) teachers (Venturers); and (3) priests (Explorers).

In the stakes the organization is under the direction of a counselor in the stake presidency and high councilors as assigned by the stake presidency. There is a young men's presidency and small board to supervise stake activities in the three groups previously named as well as to train and assist ward leaders.

The ward organization corresponds basically to that of the stake, with the ward bishopric presiding and the ward Aaronic Priesthood MIA-YM organization consisting of presidencies and advisers for the three class groups.

Such an organization, according to the First Presidency, further coordinates, under the Presiding Bishopric, activities for youth 12 through 18. Increased emphasis is placed on service by the youth and on youth involvement in planning and directing their own activities, with the guidance of adult leaders.

The Aaronic Priesthood YMMIA provides opportunities for young men to participate in service projects and in educational, social, cultural, recreational, and religious activities designed to build religious faith, moral character, and physical fitness. All members are given the opportunity to develop their talents in dance, drama, music, speech, and recreation. The program includes the largest Church-sponsored Scouting association in the world in proportion to Church membership. Most young men of Scout age are enrolled in either the Boy Scouts of America or its counterpart in other countries.

At the organization, President Brigham Young stated the keynote of the work of these organizations to be, "the establishment in the youth of individual testimony of the truth and magnitude of the great latter-day work; the development of the gifts within them that have been bestowed upon them by the laying on of hands of the servants of God; cultivating a knowledge and an application of the eternal principles of the great science of life." This great body of young men appeals for place and opportunity to work, to offer a helping hand in building up the Church of Christ, and to lend effective service to their fellow men and in the cause of God. They stand for the mutual improvement of the youth of Zion. Their souls are thrilled with the grand vision of the future, and their hearts with the testimony of the glorious destiny of God's "marvelous work and a wonder" of the latter days. The aim of their organization is, first, to impress them and all the youth of Israel with a testimony of the gospel of Jesus Christ, as restored through Joseph the Prophet, and to this end they seek all useful knowledge by which they may be helpful in its establishment. They desire to learn to preside over public assemblies, to express themselves before the public, to study and to practice religious, civil, vocational, social and recreational, scientific and educational affairs, and to be trained in all that pertains to religious, moral, physical, and intellectual advancement. The further object of the organization is to answer every desire of the young men of our community for excellence and enjoyment, and to provide for the gratification of every legitimate ambition and impulse to excel in these fields of endeavor without having to seek opportunity elsewhere. In a world, the aim of the YMMIA is to assist every young man to "complete living on the foundation of faith in God and his great latter-day work"; or, in other words, to live in perfect harmony with the established standards of the restored gospel of Jesus Christ.

AARONIC PRIESTHOOD MIA (MUTUAL IMPROVEMENT ASSOCIATION) YOUNG WOMEN'S

On November 9, 1972, by direction of the First Presidency, the auxiliary status of the YWMIA was changed and it became a priesthood oriented organization known as the Aaronic Priesthood MIA—Young Women's. This organization, directed by the First Presidency and advised by members of the Council of the Twelve as to curriculum and correlation, is under the leadership of the Presiding Bishopric. Serving under them are a general presidency, consisting of Ruth Hardy Funk, president; Hortense H. Child and Ardeth G. Kapp, counselors, and a small general board. They are concerned with the curriculum, service projects, and activities of young girls ages 12 through 18. The girls are organized into three groups in the Aaronic Priesthood MIA: Beehive girls, for girls 12 and 13; Mia Maids, who are ages 14 and 15; and Laurels, ages 16 and 17. Special emphasis is placed on youth leadership and planning, with "shadow leadership" by adult advisers, on both ward and stake levels.

The Young Women's Mutual Improvement Association had its origin in the Retrenchment Association, organized by President Brigham Young in the Lion House on November 28, 1869. Its membership consisted entirely of his own daughters, Ella Young being president, with Emily, Zina, Maria, Carlie, Phebe, and Dora Young as associate officers. The purpose of this Retrenchment Association, as President Young expressed it, was "to retrench in dress, in speech, in everything that is bad and worthless, and to improve in everything that is good and beautiful." He also stated that he wished his daughters and the girls of the Church generally to gain for themselves a knowledge and testimony of the gospel.

Associations of other young women were soon patterned after the original one and later the name was changed to Mutual Improvement Association to harmonize with a similar organization which had been formed among the young men. In 1880 the general board was organized with Elmina S. Taylor, president; Margaret Y. Taylor, and Martha Horne Tingey as counselors.

The fundamental aim has always been to give religious and moral instruction and in addition such other lines of work as will help to prepare girls for their true position in the home and community life.

In connection with the Young Men's Association, a line of work designated as "special activities" is conducted. This comprises instruction and participation in dance, drama, music, speech, and sports. Much of the social and cultural activities of the Church is under the direction of the two associations.

The official organ of the Young Ladies Mutual Improvement Association was originally the *Young Woman's Journal,* which was merged with the *Improvement Era* in 1929. The *Era,* which was the responsibility of the MIA organizations for many years, discontinued publication in December 1970.

MELCHIZEDEK PRIESTHOOD MIA (MUTUAL INTEREST ASSOCIATION)

The Melchizedek Priesthood MIA (Mutual Interest Association) was organized in November 1972 under the direction of the First Presidency and the Council of the Twelve. Four members of the Council of the Twelve serve as advisers of this priesthood-oriented, Churchwide organization, which involves two groups:

1. *Young Adults.* Included in this group are unmarried persons who are 18 through 25 years of age. They include those who were formerly in the M Man and Gleaner program of the Church as well as members of the Latter-day Saint Student Association (LDSSA) on college campuses.

The LDSSA continues as a coordinating agency for activities involving Church members on college campuses, but the activities are part of the Young Adults program itself. In connection with institutes of religion, the program also includes gospel classes for LDS students.

2. *Special Interests.* Unmarried persons who are 26 years of age and over are included in this group. These persons are those who have never married as well as widows, widowers, and those who have been divorced.

A third group, known as Adults and comprising those 18 years of age and older who are married, including widows whose husbands were holders of the Melchizedek Priesthood, are supervised by stake Melchizedek Priesthood committees whose activities and quorum-related programs are conducted as directed by the Council of the Twelve. Henceforth there is no MIA-sponsored Young Married activities as was previously the case; these activities are now sponsored by the Melchizedek Priesthood quorums.

The Young Adults and Special Interests members may be organized on a ward, stake, or regional basis, as needed, and may also hold activities on an area basis. They are organized according to the needs and interests of the members and may plan, with approval of priesthood advisers, activities as diverse as dancing groups, gospel-related classes, bowling and other sports groups, and other activities of interest to the members. Emphasis is also placed upon service-related activities.

Giving general Church leadership, under the advisers from the Council of the Twelve, is a committee of three Assistants to the Council of the Twelve. A small general board to direct in-service projects and activities serves under this committee.

An additional organization on the general level for the Melchizedek Priesthood is a Melchizedek Priesthood Committee of the Twelve, comprised of four members of the Twelve, who direct curriculum, service projects, and activities for elders and prospective elders, seventies, and high priests.

The Melchizedek Priesthood MIA is organized in regions and stakes as follows:

1. *Region.* A Regional Representative of the Twelve serves as adviser for the Melchizedek Priesthood MIA in each region. The regional organization for Young Adults includes one stake president, called by the Council of the Twelve, who serves as the priesthood adviser. One high councilor from each stake and regional committee members may be called as needed.

For Special Interests, the regional organization is similar, with a stake president as the priesthood adviser and one high councilor from each stake and committee members as needed.

2. *Stake.* The Young Adults and Special Interests groups are supervised on a stake level by the stake presidency, high council, and stake Melchizedek Priesthood Committee. For the Young Adults, in addition to a high council adviser, officers are called by the stake president, and a council is formed consisting of stake Young Adult

APPENDIX 575

officers plus a representative from each ward and branch. The stake leadership for Special Interests is similar, with a high council adviser, officers as called by the stake president, and a representative from each ward and branch.

Churchwide athletic programs will continue on stake, regional, and area basis, but the former all-Church athletic competitions are no longer held. The athletic programs are now under the supervision of the priesthood quorums for all age groups.

THE PRIMARY ASSOCIATION

The need of child culture and special religious training for the children was the motive that prompted the organization of the Primary Association in the Church. The Lord has placed the responsibility of the training of the children of Church members on the shoulders of the parents, where it properly belongs. However, in the multitude of duties it is necessary that some help be extended to assist the parents in the important labor, and the various auxiliary organizations were given for this purpose.

The following account of the origin and aims of the Primary Association is furnished by that organization:—

"The Primary Association originated at Farmington, Davis County, Utah, where the first meeting was held on the 25th day of August, 1878.

"For some time previous, Sister Aurelia S. Rogers, the pioneer in this work, had reflected with much seriousness upon the need of a more strict guardianship over the boys and girls of Zion. She felt the necessity for more religious and moral training than they were then receiving; believed that children should be taught to beautify the home with the workmanship of their own hands, and learn to cultivate love for music, for flowers, and for the beautiful in all things.

"The matter was brought to the attention of Sister Eliza R. Snow and a consultation was held with President John Taylor, Emmeline B. Wells, and others, resulting in a decision to organize what is now known as 'The Primary Association.' It was resolved that the instruction should be of religious and moral character in all that tends toward the development of upright men and women.

"Accordingly, on the 11th of August, 1878, Aurelia S. Rogers was set apart to preside over a Primary Association in Farmington. The ward was systematically visited and the name of every child recorded. Two weeks later the children were called together, the object of the work was explained to them, and the career of the association began. In addition to the meeting where general instructions were given including lessons on obedience, faith in God, prayer (individual and in concert), punctuality, and good manners, there were program and testimony meetings. A quarterly gathering was held every three months to which the parents were invited and a special program rendered. Lessons were given on the planting of beans and corn, to be stored for times of famine, in the making of rag carpets for use in Church buildings; and much emphasis was laid on the necessity for obedience to the word of wisdom.

"Similar associations were organized in other places, and on the 19th day of June, 1880, Sister Louie B. Felt, then president of the Eleventh Ward Association in Salt Lake City, was called to preside over the Primary Associations of The Church of Jesus Christ of Latter-day Saints in all the world."

There are more than 5,000 associations in the stakes, with a total enrollment of 90,000 officers and teachers. There is an enrollment, in the stakes, of 382,305 LDS children and 20,175 non-LDS children, for a total enrollment of 420,480 children. There are 1,485 associations in the missions with a total of 9,586 officers and teachers. In the missions there is an enrollment of 42,178 LDS children and 4,980 non-LDS children for a total enrollment of 47,158 children. Three-year-olds, attending but not enrolled, in stakes and missions make a total of 29,131. This is for the year ending August 31, 1972.

CHURCH SCHOOLS

Since the first year after the Church was organized it has maintained schools in which religion has been taught. Even in their early persecutions and drivings, whenever a sufficient number of members settled in any locality long enough to justify it, some suitable person was selected to teach and a school was organized. Religion was always a prominent study in them, and the study of the Bible was common in most of the schools of the nation.

When the schools began to be maintained by the state, however, and people of all religious beliefs were obliged to pay taxes for their support, the Bible and all religious teachings were banished from the public schools because of the jealousy of the patrons over religious tenets. When this movement reached the settlements of our people in the West they yielded to it, but with deep disappointment, and to make up this loss the authorities of the Church established a system of Religion Classes to be held before or after school, and taught by volunteer teachers who served without pay.

In these Religion Classes the more practical principles of the gospel were taught, and in such a way as to induce to good and noble actions. The organization and methods of teaching resembled those of the day school whose work they were designed to supplement.

The work of the Religion Classes ultimately grew into the present-day Church Educational System. Seminary classes are held for students of grades 9 through 12, either on a release-time basis from the public schools during the day or in the early morning prior to the opening of school. Institutes are located adjacent to major college campuses. The Latter-day Saint Student Association is organized on many university campuses wherever Latter-day Saint students are found.

The 1971-1972 enrollment in Church Seminaries and Institutes was as follows: Institute enrollment 53,395; Seminary enrollment 138,069; Indian Seminary enrollment 17,013, for a total enrollment of 208,477.

The October 1972 enrollment for Brigham Young University was 24,565 daytime students and 1,703 evening students for a total of 26,268 of which 13,653 are women.

The 1972-73 school year enrollment for other Church schools: Ricks College 5,057; Church College of Hawaii 1,075; LDS Business College 901; Church College of New Zealand 521; Mapusaga High School of American Samoa 360; Tongan Schools 1,821; Western Samoa Schools 2,128; Papeete (Tahiti) Primary School 545; Mexico Schools 8,336; Suva (Fiji) Primary School 110; Chile Schools 2,454; Bolivia Schools 150; Peru Schools 156; Paraguay Schools 139.

The total enrollment in the Church Educational System was 258,498.

THE GENEALOGICAL SOCIETY

The Genealogical Society of The Church of Jesus Christ of Latter-day Saints was organized at a meeting held in the office of Franklin D. Richards, Church Historian, November 13, 1894, under the title "The Genealogical Society of Utah." It was decided by those present at this meeting to organize a society the purposes of which were "to be benevolent in collecting, compiling, establishing and maintaining a genealogical library for the use and benefit of its members and others; educational in disseminating information regarding genealogical matters; and also religious."

The original members were Wilford Woodruff, George Q. Cannon, Joseph F. Smith, Lorenzo Snow, Franklin D. Richards, John Nicholson, Amos Milton Musser, James H. Anderson, James B. Walkley, Abraham H. Cannon, George Reynolds, John Jaques, Duncan M. McAllister and Joseph Christenson.

A room in the historian's office was tendered by Elder Franklin D. Richards, for the use of the Society "until such time as circumstances required a change of location, the use of said room to be free of charge."

Franklin D. Richards was chosen as president of the society; John Nicholson, vice-president; James H. Anderson, secretary; Amos Milton Musser, treasurer; John Jaques, librarian. These, with Andrew Jenson, formed the board of directors.

At the third meeting of the society, November 20, 1894, articles of incorporation were prepared and the society was duly incorporated. The first books received by the society consisting of eleven volumes were also donated by the charter members at this meeting. This was the nucleus of a library which has become second to none in the world.

During the first 50 years of the Society's existence (1894-1944) life and annual memberships were sold to those using the library facilities. On November 20, 1944, the Genealogical Society of Utah was reincorporated as "The Genealogical Society of The Church of Jesus Christ of Latter-day Saints" and the issuance of life and annual memberships was discontinued.

In the year 1939 the Society entered the field of microfilming to secure heretofore inaccessible documents and records. The first major collection consisted of photographic reproductions of typed transcripts of most of the early county records of the State of Tennessee. Subsequently the microfilm program was expanded to include the filming of records of other southern, eastern and New England States.

Following the second world war, photographic operations were extended to Great Britain, Holland, Switzerland, certain sections of Italy, Germany, the Scandinavian countries, and Finland.

On January 1, 1942, a change was made in the process of clearing and recording of names for ordinance work in the temples with the result that the Society became a repository of all temple ordinance data.

During 1964 the Society was re-incorporated as The Genealogical Society of The Church of Jesus Christ of Latter-day Saints, Inc. Its officers consist of a board of trustees of five, with four administrative officers including a president, executive assistant, administrative office manager, and a treasurer.

As of December 1972, there were on hand at the Genealogical Society 756,062 (100 ft.) reels of microfilm: a total of 75,606,200 feet, which is the equivalent of over 3,607,002 volumes of 300 pages each. There are 114,392 printed volumes on the library stacks. The Temple Records Index Bureau contains about 30,000,000 cards. The archives contain 7,514,326 family group sheets.

The Society maintains the largest and one of the best genealogical libraries in the world. For the preservation of its records a giant series of storage vaults was carved from granite mountains some 22 miles from Salt Lake City. There are nearly 700 feet of solid granite above the six huge vaults which have been carved almost 500 feet into the heart of the granite. The natural temperature in the storage area is 57 to 58 degrees Fahrenheit the year around, and the natural humidity is always 40 to 50 per cent. These conditions are perfect for microfilm storage.

Officers of the Church and the Society believe that in the not too distant future the library will not only be the best in the world, but also will be a repository of most all other genealogical libraries.

GENERAL AUTHORITIES OF THE CHURCH

PRESIDENTS OF THE CHURCH

1. **Joseph Smith**—Born 23 Dec. 1805, at Sharon, Windsor Co., Vermont, the son of Joseph, Sr. and Lucy Mack. Received the Melchizedek Priesthood (Ordained an Apostle) from Peter, James and John in May 1829; sustained as First Elder (and Oliver Cowdery as Second Elder) of the Church 6 Apr. 1830, at the age of 24; ordained High Priest 3 June 1831, by Lyman Wight; sustained as President of the High Priesthood 25 Jan. 1832, at a conference at Amherst, Loraine Co., Ohio; martyred 27 June 1844, at Carthage Jail, Carthage, Hancock Co., Illinois.

2. **Brigham Young.**—Sustained as President of the Church 27 Dec. 1847, at the age of 46; died 29 Aug. 1877, at Salt Lake City, Salt Lake Co., Utah. (See also Apo. 3.)

3. **John Taylor.**—Sustained as President of the Church 10 Oct. 1880, at the age of 71; died 25 July 1887, at Kaysville, Davis Co., Utah. (See also Apo. 14.)

4. **Wilford Woodruff.**—Sustained as President of the Church 7 Apr. 1889, at the age of 82; died 2 Sep. 1898, at San Francisco, San Francisco Co., California. (See also Apo. 15.)

5. **Lorenzo Snow.**—Sustained as President of the Church 13 Sep. 1898, at the age of 84; died 10 Oct. 1901, at Salt Lake City, Salt Lake Co., Utah. (See also Apo. 22.)

6. **Joseph Fielding Smith.**—Sustained as President of the Church 17 Oct. 1901, at the age of 62; died 19 Nov. 1918, at Salt Lake City, Salt Lake Co., Utah. (See also 1st Coun. 6, Couns. 3 & Apo. 26.)

7. **Heber Jeddy Grant.**—Sustained as President of the Church 23 Nov. 1918, at the age of 62; died 14 May 1945, at Salt Lake City, Salt Lake Co., Utah. (See also Apo. 33.)

8. **George Albert Smith.**—Sustained as President of the Church 21 May 1945, at the age of 75; died 4 Apr. 1951, at Salt Lake City, Salt Lake Co., Utah. (See also Apo. 43.)

9. **David Oman McKay.**—Born 8 Sept. 1873, at Huntsville, Weber Co., Utah, the son of David McKay and Jennette Eveline Evans. Ordained an Apostle 9 Apr. 1906, by Joseph F. Smith; sustained as Second Counselor to President Heber J. Grant 6 Oct. 1934; sustained as Second Counselor to President George Albert Smith 21 May 1945; sustained as President of the Quorum of the Twelve Apostles 30 Sept. 1950; sustained as President of the Church 9 Apr. 1951, at the age of 77; died 18 January 1970, at Salt Lake City, Salt Lake Co., Utah, at age 96. (See also 2nd Coun. 15 & Apo. 47.)

10. **Joseph Fielding Smith.**—Born 19 July 1876, at Salt Lake City,

APPENDIX 581

Salt Lake Co., Utah, the son of Joseph Fielding Smith and Julina Lambson. Ordained an Apostle 7 April 1910, by Joseph F. Smith, at Salt Lake City, Utah; sustained as Acting President of the Quorum of the Twelve Apostles 30 Sep. 1950; sustained as President of the Quorum of Twelve Apostles 9 Apr. 1951; sustained as Counselor in the First Presidency 29 Oct. 1965; sustained as President of the Church 23 Jan. 1970, at the age of 93; died 2 July 1972, at Salt Lake City, Salt Lake Co., Utah, at the age of 95. (See also Counselors in the First Presidency 10 & Apo. 49.)

11. **Harold Bingham Lee.**—Born 28 Mar 1899, at Clifton, Oneida Co., Idaho, the son of Samuel Marion Lee and Louisa Emeline Bingham. Ordained an Apostle 10 Apr. 1941, by Heber J. Grant; sustained as President of the Quorum of the Twelve Apostles 23 Jan. 1970; sustained as First Counselor to President Joseph Fielding Smith 23 Jan. 1970, at the age of 70; sustained as President of the Church 7 July 1972, at the age of 73. Died 26 Dec. 1973, at Salt Lake City at the age of 74. (See also 1st Couns. 16 and Apo. 61.)

12. **Spencer Woolley Kimball.**—Born 28 Mar. 1895, at Salt Lake City, Utah, a son of Andrew Kimball and Olive Woolley. Ordained an Apostle 7 Oct. 1943, by Heber J. Grant, at Salt Lake City, Utah, at the age of 48; sustained as Acting President of the Quorum of the Twelve Apostles 23 Jan. 1970; sustained as President of the Quorum of the Twelve Apostles 7 July 1972; sustained as President of the Church 30 Dec. 1973, at the age of 78. (See also Apo. 62.)

ASSISTANT PRESIDENTS OF THE CHURCH

1. **Oliver Cowdery.**—Born 3 Oct. 1806, at Wells, Rutland Co., Vermont, the son of William Cowdery and Rebecca Fuller. Received the Melchizedek Priesthood (ordained an Apostle) in May 1829, by Peter, James and John (D&C 20:2-3; 27:12); sustained as Second Elder in the Church 6 Apr. 1830; ordained a High Priest 28 Aug. 1831, by Sidney Rigdon; ordained Assistant President of the High Priesthood 5 Dec. 1834, at the age of 27; to Asst. Coun. 3 Sep. 1837. (See Asst. Coun. 1.)

2. **Hyrum Smith.**—Given all the priesthood formerly held by Oliver Cowdery (including Apostle), and ordained Patriarch to the Church and Assistant President 24 Jan. 1841, by Joseph Smith, at the age of 40 (D&C 124:95, *Ess. in Ch. Hist.*, p. 255, enlarged edition); martyred 27 June 1844, at Carthage Jail, Hancock Co., Illinois. (See also 2nd Coun. 2, Pat. 2, & Asst. Coun. 3).

FIRST COUNSELORS IN THE FIRST PRESIDENCY

1. **Sidney Rigdon.**—Born 19 Feb. 1793, at Saint Clair Township,

Allegheny Co., Pennsylvania, the son of William Rigdon and Nancy .... Ordained a High Priest in June 1831, by Lyman Wight; set apart as First Counselor to President Joseph Smith by Joseph Smith 18 Mar. 1833, at the age of 40; excommunicated 8 Sep. 1844; died 14 July 1876, at Friendship, Alleghany Co., New York.

2. **Heber Chase Kimball.**—Sustained as First Counselor to President Brigham Young 27 Dec. 1847, at the age of 46; died 22 June 1868, at Salt Lake City, Salt Lake Co., Utah. (See also Apo. 4.)

3. **George Albert Smith.**—Sustained as First Counselor to President Brigham Young 6 Oct. 1868, at the age of 51; died 1 Sep. 1875, at Salt Lake City, Salt Lake Co., Utah. (See also Apo. 16.)

4. **John Willard Young.**—Sustained as First Counselor to President Brigham Young 7 Oct. 1876, at the age of 32; released at the death of President Young; sustained as a Counselor to the Twelve Apostles 6 Oct. 1877; released 6 Oct. 1891; died 11 Feb. 1924, at New York City, New York. (See also Coun. 7.)

5. **George Quayle Cannon.**—Sustained as First Counselor to President John Taylor 10 Oct. 1880, at the age of 53; released at the death of President Taylor 25 July 1887; sustained as First Counselor to President Wilford Woodruff 7 Apr. 1889; sustained as First Counselor to President Lorenzo Snow 13 Sep. 1898; died 12 Apr. 1901, at Monterey, Monterey Co., California. (See also Apo. 25.)

6. **Joseph Fielding Smith.**—Sustained as First Counselor to President Lorenzo Snow 6 Oct. 1901, at the age of 62, not set apart to this position; released at the death of President Snow 10 Oct. 1901; sustained as President 17 Oct. 1901. (See Pres. 6. See also 2nd Coun. 7 & Apo. 26.)

7. **John Rex Winder.**—Sustained as First Counselor to President Joseph Fielding Smith 17 Oct. 1901, at the age of 79; died 27 Mar. 1910, at Salt Lake City, Salt Lake Co., Utah. (See also 2nd Coun. Pres. Bp. 6.)

8. **Anthon Henrik Lund.**—Sustained as First Counselor to President Joseph Fielding Smith 7 Apr. 1910, at the age of 65; sustained as First Counselor to President Heber J. Grant 23 Nov. 1918; died 2 Mar. 1921, at Salt Lake City, Salt Lake Co., Utah. (See also 2nd Coun. 9 & Apo. 36.)

9. **Charles William Penrose.**—Sustained as First Counselor to President Heber J. Grant 10 Mar. 1921, at the age of 89; died 16 May 1925, at Salt Lake City, Salt Lake Co., Utah. (See also 2nd Coun. 11 & Apo. 44.)

10. **Anthony Woodward Ivins.**—Sustained as First Counselor to President Heber J. Grant, 28 May 1925, at the age of 72; died 23 Sep.

1934, at Salt Lake City, Salt Lake Co., Utah. (See also 2nd Coun. 12 & Apo. 48.)

11. **Joshua Reuben Clark, Jr.**—Sustained as First Counselor to President Heber J. Grant 6 Oct. 1934, at the age of 63; sustained as First Counselor to President George Albert Smith 21 May 1945; to 2nd Coun. 9 Apr. 1951. (See 1st Coun. 13, 2nd Coun. 14 & 16, Apo. 57.)

12. **Stephen Longstroth Richards.**—Sustained as First Counselor to President David O. McKay 9 Apr. 1951, at the age of 71; died 19 May 1959, at Salt Lake City, Salt Lake Co., Utah. (See also Apo. 51.)

13. **Joshua Reuben Clark, Jr.**—Sustained as First Counselor to President David O. McKay 12 June 1959, at the age of 87; died 6 Oct. 1961, at Salt Lake City, Salt Lake Co., Utah. (See also 1st Coun. 11, 2nd Coun. 14 & 16, Apo. 57.)

14. **Henry Dinwoodey Moyle.**—Sustained as First Counselor to President David O. McKay 12 Oct. 1961, at the age of 72; died 18 Sep. 1963, at Deer Park, Osceola Co., Florida. (See also 2nd Coun. 17 & Apo. 66.)

15. **Hugh Brown Brown.**—Born 24 Oct. 1883, at Granger, Salt Lake Co., Utah, the son of Homer Manly Brown and Lydia Jane Brown. Sustained as Assistant to the Quorum of the Twelve Apostles 4 Oct. 1953; ordained an Apostle 10 Apr. 1958, by David O. McKay; sustained as Counselor to President David O. McKay 22 June 1961; sustained as Second Counselor to President David O. McKay 12 Oct. 1961; sustained as First Counselor to President David O. McKay 4 Oct. 1963, at the age of 79; released at the death of President McKay 18 Jan. 1970. (See also 2nd Coun. 18; Couns. in First Presidency 9; Apo. 73; Asst. to Twelve 10.)

16. **Harold Bingham Lee.**—Born 28 Mar. 1899, at Clifton, Oneida Co., Idaho, the son of Samuel Marion Lee and Louisa Emeline Bingham. Ordained an Apostle 10 Apr. 1941, by Heber J. Grant; sustained as President of The Quorum of Twelve Apostles 23 Jan. 1970; sustained as First Counselor to President Joseph Fielding Smith 23 Jan. 1970, at the age of 70; released at the death of President Smith 2 July 1972; sustained as President of the Church, 7 July 1972. (See also Pres. 11, Apo. 61.)

17. **Nathan Eldon Tanner.**—Born 9 May 1898, at Salt Lake City, Salt Lake Co., Utah, the son of Nathan William Tanner and Sarah Edna Brown. Sustained as Assistant to the Quorum of the Twelve Apostles 8 Oct. 1960; ordained an Apostle 11 Oct. 1962, by David O. McKay; sustained as Second Counselor to President David O. McKay,

4 Oct. 1963, at the age of 65; sustained as Second Counselor to President Joseph Fielding Smith, 23 Jan. 1970; sustained as First Counselor to President Harold B. Lee, 7 July 1972, at the age of 74; sustained as First Counselor to President Spencer W. Kimball, 30 Dec. 1973, at the age of 75. (See also 2nd Couns. 19, Apo. 76, Asst. to Tw. 16.)

SECOND COUNSELORS IN THE FIRST PRESIDENCY

1. **Frederick Granger Williams.**—Born 28 Oct. 1787, at Suffield, Hartford Co., Connecticut, the son of William Wheeler Williams and Ruth Zodack. Called by revelation March 1832, to be a High Priest and Counselor to President Joseph Smith; ordained a High Priest by Miles H. Jones; set apart as Second Counselor to President Joseph Smith 18 Mar. 1833, at the age of 45; rejected 7 Nov. 1837; excommunicated 17 Mar. 1839; restored to fellowship 8 Apr. 1840; died 25 Oct. 1842, at Quincy, Adams Co., Illinois.

2. **Hyrum Smith.**—Sustained as Second Counselor to President Joseph Smith 7 Nov. 1837, at the age of 37; to Asst. Pres. 24 Jan. 1841. (See Asst. Pres. 2. See also Asst. Coun. 3.)

3. **William Law.**—Born 8 Sep. 1809. Set apart as Second Counselor to President Joseph Smith 24 Jan. 1841, at the age of 31; excommunicated 18 Apr. 1844; died 19 Jan. 1892, at Shullsburg, Lafayette Co., Wisconsin.

4. **Willard Richards.**—Sustained as Second Counselor to President Brigham Young 27 Dec. 1847, at the age of 43; died 11 Mar. 1854, at Salt Lake City, Salt Lake Co., Utah. (See also Apo. 17.)

5. **Jedediah Morgan Grant.**—Ordained an Apostle 7 Apr. 1854, by Brigham Young; sustained as Second Counselor to President Brigham Young 7 Apr. 1854, at the age of 38; died 1 Dec. 1856, at Salt Lake City, Salt Lake Co., Utah. (See also 1st Coun. of Sev. 18.)

6. **Daniel Hanmer Wells.**—Born 27 Oct. 1814, at Trenton, Oneida Co., New York, the son of Daniel Wells and Catherine Chapin. Ordained a High Priest 15 Dec. 1857, by Brigham Young; set apart as Second Counselor to President Brigham Young 4 Jan. 1857, by Brigham Young, at the age of 42; released at the death of President Young 29 Aug. 1877; sustained as a Counselor to the Twelve Apostles 6 Oct. 1877; died 24 Mar. 1891, at Salt Lake City, Salt Lake Co., Utah.

7. **Joseph Fielding Smith.**—Sustained as Second Counselor to President John Taylor 10 Oct. 1880; released with the death of President John Taylor 25 July 1887; sustained as Second Counselor to President Wilford Woodruff 7 Apr. 1889; sustained as Second Counselor to President Lorenzo Snow 13 Sep. 1898; to 1st Coun. 6 Oct. 1901. (See Pres. 6, Coun. 3, 1st Coun. 6. See also Apo. 26.)

APPENDIX   585

8. **Rudger Clawson.**—Sustained as Second Counselor to President Lorenzo Snow 6 Oct. 1901, not set apart to this position; released at the death of President Snow 10 Oct. 1901. (See also Apo. 40.)

9. **Anthon Henrik Lund.**—Sustained as Second Counselor to President Joseph Fielding Smith 17 Oct. 1901, at the age of 57; to 1st Coun. 7 Apr. 1910. (See 1st Coun. 8. See also Apo. 36.)

10. **John Henry Smith.**—Sustained as Second Counselor to President Joseph Fielding Smith 7 Apr. 1910, at the age of 61; died 13 Oct. 1911, at Salt Lake City, Salt Lake Co., Utah. (See also Apo. 31.)

11. **Charles William Penrose.**—Sustained as Second Counselor to President Joseph Fielding Smith 7 Dec. 1911, at the age of 79; sustained as Second Counselor to President Heber J. Grant 23 Nov. 1918; to 1st Coun. 10 Mar. 1921. (See 1st Coun. 9. See also Apo. 44.)

12. **Anthony Woodward Ivins.**—Sustained as Second Counselor to President Heber J. Grant 10 Mar. 1921, at the age of 68; to 1st Coun. 28 May 1925. (See 1st Coun. 10. See also Apo. 48.)

13. **Charles Wilson Nibley.**—Sustained as Second Counselor to President Heber J. Grant 28 May 1925, at the age of 76; died 11 Dec. 1931, at Salt Lake City, Salt Lake Co., Utah. (See also Pres. Bp. 5.)

14. **Joshua Reuben Clark, Jr.**—Born 1 Sep. 1871, at Grantsville, Tooele Co., Utah, the son of Joshua Reuben Clark and Mary Louise Woolley. Sustained as Second Counselor to President Heber J. Grant 6 Apr. 1933, at the age of 61; ordained a High Priest 13 Apr. 1933 by Heber J. Grant; to 1st Coun. 6 Oct. 1934. (See 1st Coun. 11.)

15. **David Oman McKay.**—Sustained as Second Counselor to President Heber J. Grant 6 Oct. 1934, at the age of 61; sustained as Second Counselor to President George Albert Smith 21 May 1945; to Pres. 9 Apr. 1951. (See Pres. 9. See also Apo. 47.)

16. **Joshua Reuben Clark, Jr.**—Sustained as Second Counselor to President David O. McKay 9 Apr. 1951, at the age of 79; to 1st Coun. 11 June 1959. (See 1st Coun. 13. See also 2nd Coun. 14.)

17. **Henry Dinwoodey Moyle.**—Sustained as Second Counselor to President David O. McKay 12 June 1959, at the age of 70; to 1st Coun. 12 Oct. 1961. (See 1st Coun. 14. See also Apo. 66.)

18. **Hugh Brown Brown.**—Sustained as Second Counselor to President David O. McKay 12 Oct. 1961, at the age of 77; sustained as First Counselor to President David O. McKay 4 Oct. 1963; released at the death of President McKay 18 Jan. 1970. (See also 1st Couns. 15; Couns. in First Presidency 9; Apo. 73; Asst. to Twelve 10.)

19. **Nathan Eldon Tanner.**—Born 9 May 1898, at Salt Lake City, Salt Lake Co., Utah, the son of Nathan William Tanner and Sarah Edna Brown. Sustained as Assistant to the Quorum of the Twelve Apostles 8 Oct. 1960; ordained an Apostle 11 Oct. 1962, by David O. McKay; sustained as Second Counselor to President David O. McKay 4 Oct. 1963, at the age of 65; sustained as Second Counselor to President Joseph Fielding Smith 23 Jan. 1970; released at the death of President Smith 2 July 1972. (See also 1st Coun. 17, Apo. 76, Asst. to Tw. 16.)

20. **Marion George Romney.**—Born 19 Sep. 1897, at Colonia Juarez, Chihuahua, Mexico, the son of George Samuel Romney and Teressa Artemesia Redd. Sustained as Assistant to the Quorum of the Twelve Apostles 6 Apr. 1941; ordained an Apostle 11 Oct. 1951, by David O. McKay; sustained as Second Counselor to President Harold B. Lee, 7 July 1972; sustained as Second Counselor to President Spencer W. Kimball, 30 Dec. 1973. (See also Apo. 68, Asst. to Tw. 1.)

COUNSELORS IN THE FIRST PRESIDENCY

1. **John Cook Bennett.**—Born 3 Aug. 1804, at Fair Haven, Bristol Co., Massachusetts, the son of J. and N. Bennett. Presented as Assistant President with the First Presidency 8 Apr. 1841; disfellowshipped 25 May 1842; excommunicated latter part of 1842; died in Polk City, Iowa.

2. **Amasa Mason Lyman.**—Appointed Counselor to the First Presidency about 4 Feb. 1843; retired from the First Presidency with the death of Joseph Smith 27 June 1844; returned to the Quorum of the Twelve Apostles 12 Aug. 1844. (See Apo. 19.)

3. **Joseph Fielding Smith.**—Ordained an Apostle and Counselor to the First Presidency 1 July 1866, by Brigham Young, at the age of 27; discontinued as Counselor to the First Presidency 8 Oct. 1867. (See Pres. 6, 1st Coun. 6 & Apo. 26.)

4. **Lorenzo Snow.**—Sustained as Counselor to President Brigham Young 8 Apr. 1873, at the age of 59; to Asst. Coun. in 1st Pres. 9 May 1874. (See Asst. Coun. 5. See also Apo. 22.)

5. **Brigham Young, Jr.**—Sustained as Counselor to President Brigham Young 8 Apr. 1873, at the age of 36; to Asst. Coun. 9 May 1874. (See Asst. Coun. 6. See also Apo. 27.)

6. **Albert Carrington.**—Sustained as Counselor to President Brigham Young 8 Apr. 1873, at the age of 60; to Asst. Coun. 9 May 1874. (See Asst. Coun. 7. See also Apo. 28.)

7. **John Willard Young.**—Born 1 Oct. 1844, at Nauvoo, Hancock

APPENDIX 587

Co., Illinois, the son of Brigham Young and Mary Ann Angell. Sustained as Counselor to President Brigham Young 8 Apr. 1873, at the age of 29; to Asst. Coun. 9 May 1874. (See Asst. Coun. 8.)

8. **George Quayle Cannon.**—Sustained as Counselor to President Brigham Young 8 Apr. 1873, at the age of 46; to Asst. Coun. 9 May 1874. (See Asst. Coun. 9. See also Apo. 25.)

9. **Hugh Brown Brown.**—Sustained as Counselor in the First Presidency 22 June 1961, at the age of 77; to 2nd Coun. 12 Oct. 1961. (See 1st Coun. 15; 2nd Coun. 18. See also Apo. 73 & Asst. to Twelve 10.)

10. **Joseph Fielding Smith.**—Sustained as Counselor in the First Presidency 28 Oct. 1965, at the age of 89; sustained as President of the Church 23 Jan. 1970. (See Pres. 10; Couns. in First Presidency 10; Apo. 49.)

11. **Henry Thorpe Beal Isaacson.**—Born 6 Sep. 1898, at Ephraim, Sanpete Co., Utah, the son of Martin Isaacson and Mary Jemima Beal. Ordained a High Priest 1 Oct. 1941, by Charles A. Callis; sustained as Second Counselor to the Presiding Bishop 12 Dec. 1946; sustained as First Counselor to the Presiding Bishop 6 Apr. 1952; sustained as Assistant to the Quorum of the Twelve Apostles 30 Sep. 1961; sustained as Counselor in the First Presidency 28 Oct. 1965, at the age of 67; released at the death of President McKay 18 Jan. 1970; resumed position as Assistant to the Quorum of the Twelve Apostles 23 Jan. 1970. Died 9 Nov. 1970, at Salt Lake City. (See Asst. to Twelve 19; 1st Couns. Pres. Bp. 8; 2nd Couns. Pres. Bp. 11.)

12. **Alvin Rulon Dyer.**—Born 1 Jan. 1903, at Salt Lake City, Salt Lake Co., Utah, the son of Alfred R. Dyer and Harriet Walsh. Sustained as Assistant to the Quorum of the Twelve Apostles 11 Oct. 1958; ordained an Apostle 5 Oct. 1967, by David O. McKay; sustained as Counselor in the First Presidency 6 Apr. 1968; released at the death of President McKay 18 Jan. 1970; resumed position as Assistant to the Quorum of the Twelve Apostles 23 Jan. 1970. (See Asst. to Twelve 15.)

ASSISTANT COUNSELORS IN THE FIRST PRESIDENCY

1. **Oliver Cowdery.**—Sustained as Assistant Counselor in the First Presidency 3 Sep. 1837, at the age of 31; excommunicated 12 Apr. 1838; baptized again 12 Nov. 1848; died 3 Mar. 1850, at Richmond, Ray Co., Missouri. (DHC 2:509.) (See also Asst. Pres. 1.)

2. **Joseph Smith, Sr.**—Sustained as Assistant Counselor to the First Presidency 3 Sep. 1837, at the age of 66; died 14 Sep. 1840, at Nauvoo, Hancock Co., Illinois. (See also Pat. 1.)

3. **Hyrum Smith.**—Born 9 Feb. 1800, at Tunbridge, Orange Co., Vermont, the son of Joseph Smith, Sr. and Lucy Mack. Ordained a High Priest in June 1831, by Joseph Smith; sustained as Assistant Counselor to the First Presidency 3 Sep. 1837, at the age of 36; to 2nd Coun. 7 Nov. 1837. (See 2nd Coun. 2.)

4. **John Smith.**—Born 16 July 1781, at Derryfield, Hillsboro Co., New Hampshire, the son of Asael Smith and Mary Duty. Ordained a High Priest 3 June 1833, by Lyman Wight; sustained as Assistant Counselor in the First Presidency 3 Sep. 1837, at the age of 56; released at the death of Joseph Smith 27 June 1844; set apart as Patriarch to the Church 1 Jan. 1849. (See also Pat. 3.)

5. **Lorenzo Snow.**—Sustained as Assistant Counselor to President Brigham Young 9 May 1874, at the age of 60; released with the death of Brigham Young 29 Aug. 1877. (See Apo. 22. See also Coun. 4.)

6. **Brigham Young, Jr.**—Sustained as Assistant Counselor to President Brigham Young 9 May 1874, at the age of 38; released with the death of Brigham Young 29 Aug. 1877. (See Apo. 27. See also Coun. 5.)

7. **Albert Carrington.**—Sustained as Assistant Counselor to President Brigham Young 9 May 1874, at the age of 61; released with the death of Brigham Young 29 Aug. 1877. (See Apo. 28. See also Coun. 6.)

8. **John Willard Young.**—Sustained as Assistant Counselor to President Brigham Young 9 May 1874, at the age of 30; to 1st Coun. 7 Oct. 1876. (See 1st Coun. 4. See also Coun. 7.)

9. **George Quayle Cannon.**—Sustained as Assistant Counselor to President Brigham Young 9 May 1874, at the age of 47; released with the death of Brigham Young 29 Aug. 1877. (See Apo. 25. See also Coun. 8.)

THE TWELVE APOSTLES OF THE CHURCH

1. **Thomas Baldwin Marsh.**—Born 1 Nov. 1799, at Acton, Middlesex Co., Massachusetts, the son of James Marsh and Molly Law. Ordained an Apostle 26 Apr. 1835, under the hands of Oliver Cowdery, David Whitmer, and Martin Harris, at Kirtland, Ohio, at the age of 35; sustained as President of the Quorum of the Twelve Apostles 2 May 1835; excommunicated for apostasy 17 Mar. 1839; baptized again in July 1857; died Jan. 1866 at Ogden, Weber Co., Utah.

2. **David Wyman Patten.**—Born 14 Nov. 1799, at Theresa, Jefferson Co., New York, the son of Benenio Patten and Abigail Cole. Ordained an Apostle 15 Feb. 1835, under the hands of Oliver Cowdery, David Whitmer, and Martin Harris, at Kirtland, Ohio, at the age of 35; killed 25 Oct. 1838, at the Battle of Crooked River, Missouri.

3. **Brigham Young.**—Born 1 June 1801, at Whittingham, Windham Co., Vermont, the son of John Young and Abigail Howe. Ordained an

APPENDIX 589

Apostle 14 Feb. 1835, under the hands of Oliver Cowdery, David Whitmer, and Martin Harris, at Kirtland, Ohio, at the age of 33; sustained as President of the Quorum of the Twelve Apostles 14 Apr. 1840. To Pres. 27 Dec. 1847. (See Pres. 2.)

4. **Heber Chase Kimball.**—Born 14 June 1801, at Sheldon, Franklin Co., Vermont, the son of Solomon Farnham Kimball and Anna Spaulding. Ordained an Apostle 14 Feb. 1835, under the hands of Oliver Cowdery, David Whitmer, and Martin Harris, at Kirtland, Ohio, at the age of 33; to 1st Coun. 27 Dec. 1847. (See 1st Coun. 2.)

5. **Orson Hyde.**—Born 8 Jan. 1805, at Oxford, New Haven Co., Connecticut, the son of Nathan Hyde and Sally Thorp. Ordained an Apostle 15 Feb. 1835, under the hands of Oliver Cowdery, David Whitmer, and Martin Harris, at Kirtland, Ohio, at the age of 30; dropped from Quorum 4 May 1839; restored to Quorum 27 June 1839; sustained as President of the Quorum of the Twelve Apostles 27 Dec. 1847; Brigham Young, on 10 Apr. 1875, took him from his original position in the Quorum and placed him in the order he would have been in when he was restored to fellowship had he come into the Quorum at the time of restoration to fellowship (following Apo. 16). (See: "Succession in the Priesthood" by John Taylor, p. 16.) Died 28 Nov. 1878, at Spring City, Sanpete Co., Utah.

6. **William E. M'Lellin.**—Born 1806, in Tennessee. Ordained an Apostle 15 Feb. 1835, under the hands of Oliver Cowdery, David Whitmer, and Martin Harris, at Kirtland, Ohio, at the age of 29; excommunicated 11 May 1838; died 24 Apr. 1883, at Independence, Jackson Co., Missouri.

7. **Parley Parker Pratt.**—Born 12 Apr. 1807, at Burlington, Otsego Co., New York, the son of Jared Pratt and Charity Dickinson. Ordained an Apostle 21 Feb. 1835, under the hands of Joseph Smith, Oliver Cowdery, and David Whitmer, at Kirtland, Ohio, at the age of 27; assassinated 13 May 1857, at Van Buren, Crawford Co., Arkansas.

8. **Luke S. Johnson.**—Born 3 Nov. 1807, at Pomfret, Windsor Co., Vermont, the son of John Johnson and Elsa Jacobs. Ordained an Apostle 15 Feb. 1835, under the hands of Oliver Cowdery, David Whitmer, and Martin Harris, at Kirtland, Ohio, at the age of 27; excommunicated 13 Apr. 1838; baptized again in 1846 in Nauvoo; died 9 Dec. 1861, at Salt Lake City, Salt Lake Co., Utah.

9. **William B. Smith.**—Born 13 Mar. 1811, at Royalton, Windsor Co., Vermont, the son of Joseph Smith, Sr. and Lucy Mack. Ordained an Apostle 15 Feb. 1835, under the hands of Oliver Cowdery, David Whitmer, and Martin Harris, at Kirtland, Ohio, at the age of 23;

dropped from the Quorum 4 May 1839; restored to Quorum 25 May 1839; dropped from the Quorum 6 Oct. 1845; excommunicated 19 Oct. 1845; died 13 Nov. 1893, at Osterdock, Clayton Co., Iowa.

10. **Orson Pratt.**—Born 19 Sep. 1811, at Hartford, Washington Co., New York, the son of Jared Pratt and Charity Dickinson. Ordained an Apostle 26 Apr. 1835, under the hands of Oliver Cowdery, David Whitmer, and Martin Harris, at Kirtland, Ohio, at the age of 23; excommunicated 20 Aug. 1842; baptized again 20 Jan. 1843 and ordained to former office in the Quorum of the Twelve Apostles; Brigham Young in 1875 took him from his original position in the Quorum and placed him in the order he would have been in when he was restored to fellowship had he come into the Quorum at the time of restoration to fellowship (following Apo. 18). (See "Succession in the Priesthood" by John Taylor, p. 16.) Died 3 Oct. 1881, at Salt Lake City, Salt Lake Co., Utah.

11. **John Farnham Boynton.**—Born 20 Sep. 1811, at Bradford, Essex Co., Massachusetts, the son of Eliphalet Boynton and Susannah Nicholas. Ordained an Apostle 15 Feb. 1835, under the hands of Oliver Cowdery, David Whitmer, and Martin Harris, at Kirtland, Ohio, at the age of 23; disfellowshipped 3 Sep. 1837; excommunicated Dec. 1837; died 20 Oct. 1890, at Syracuse, Onondago Co., New York.

12. **Lyman Eugene Johnson.**—Born 24 Oct. 1811, at Pomfret, Windsor Co., Vermont, the son of John Johnson and Elsa Jacobs. Ordained an Apostle 14 Feb. 1835, under the hands of Oliver Cowdery, David Whitmer, and Martin Harris, at Kirtland, Ohio, at the age of 23; excommunicated 13 Apr. 1838; died 20 Dec. 1856, at Prairie du Chien, Crawford Co., Wisconsin.

13. **John Edward Page.**—Born 25 Feb. 1799, at Trenton Township, Oneida Co., New York, the son of Ebenezer Page and Rachel .... Ordained an Apostle 19 Dec. 1838, under the hands of Brigham Young and Heber C. Kimball, at Far West, Missouri, at the age of 39; excommunicated 27 June 1846; died in the fall of 1867, at De Kalb Co., Illinois.

14. **John Taylor.**—Born 1 Nov. 1808, at Milnthorp, Westmoreland Co., England, the son of James Taylor and Agnes Taylor. Ordained an Apostle 19 Dec. 1838, under the hands of Brigham Young and Heber C. Kimball, at Far West, Missouri, at the age of 30; sustained as President of the Quorum of the Twelve Apostles 6 Oct. 1877. To Pres. 10 Oct. 1880. (See Pres. 3.)

15. **Wilford Woodruff.**—Born 1 Mar. 1807, at Avon (Farmington), Hartford Co., Connecticut, the son of Aphek Woodruff and Beulah Thompson. Ordained an Apostle 26 Apr. 1839, by Brigham Young,

at Far West, Missouri, at the age of 32; sustained as President of the Quorum of the Twelve Apostles 10 Oct. 1880. To Pres. 7 Apr. 1889. (See Pres. 4.)

16. **George Albert Smith.**—Born 27 June 1817, at Potsdam, Saint Lawrence Co., New York, the son of John Smith and Clarissa Lyman. Ordained an Apostle 26 Apr. 1839, by Heber C. Kimball, at Far West, Missouri, at the age of 21. To 1st Coun. 6 Oct. 1868. (See 1st Coun. 3.)

17. **Willard Richards.**—Born 24 June 1804, at Hopkinton, Middlesex Co., Massachusetts, the son of Joseph Richards and Rhoda Howe. Ordained an Apostle 14 Apr. 1840, by Brigham Young, at Preston, Lancashire, England, at the age of 35; to 2nd Coun. 27 Dec. 1847. (See 2nd Coun. 4.)

18. **Lyman Wight.**—Born 9 May 1796, at Fairfield, Herkimer Co., New York, the son of Levi Wright and Sarah Corbin. Ordained an Apostle 8 Apr. 1841, by Joseph Smith, at Nauvoo, Illinois, at the age of 44; excommunicated 3 Dec. 1848; died 31 Mar. 1858, in Mountain Valley, Texas.

19. **Amasa Mason Lyman.**—Born 30 Mar. 1813, at Lyman, Grafton Co., New Hampshire, the son of Roswell Lyman and Martha Mason. Ordained an Apostle 20 Aug. 1842, by Brigham Young, at Nauvoo, Illinois, at the age of 29; replaced in the Quorum of the Twelve Apostles 20 Jan. 1843, due to reinstatement of Orson Pratt; appointed Counselor in the First Presidency about 4 Feb. 1843; retired from the First Presidency with the death of Joseph Smith 27 June 1844; returned to the Quorum of the Twelve Apostles 12 Aug. 1844; deprived of Apostleship 6 Oct. 1867; excommunicated 12 May 1870; died 4 Feb. 1877, at Fillmore, Millard Co., Utah. (See Coun. 2.)

20. **Ezra Taft Benson.**—Born 22 Feb. 1811, at Mendon, Worcester Co., Massachusetts, the son of John Benson and Chloe Taft. Ordained an Apostle 16 July 1846, by Brigham Young, at Council Bluffs, Iowa, at the age of 35; died 3 Sep. 1869, at Ogden, Weber Co., Utah.

21. **Charles Coulson Rich.**—Born 21 Aug. 1809, at Campbell Co., Kentucky, the son of Joseph Rich and Nancy O'Neal. Ordained an Apostle 12 Feb. 1849, by Brigham Young, at Salt Lake City, Utah, at the age of 39; died 17 Nov. 1883, at Paris, Bear Lake, Idaho.

22. **Lorenzo Snow.**—Born 3 Apr. 1814, at Mantua, Portage Co., Ohio, the son of Oliver Snow and Rosetta Leonora Pettibone. Ordained an Apostle 12 Feb. 1849, by Heber C. Kimball, at Salt Lake City, Utah, at the age of 34; sustained as Counselor to President Brigham Young 8 Apr. 1873; sustained as Assistant Counselor to President Brigham Young 9 May 1874; released at the death of Brigham Young 29 Aug. 1877; sustained as President of the Quorum of the Twelve

Apostles 7 Apr. 1889. To Pres. 13 Sep. 1898. (See Coun. 4 & Pres. 5.)

23. **Erastus Snow.**—Born 9 Nov. 1818, at Saint Johnsbury, Caledonia Co., Vermont, the son of Levi Snow and Lucina Streeter. Ordained an Apostle 12 Feb. 1849, by Brigham Young, at Salt Lake City, Utah, at the age of 30; died 27 May 1888, at Salt Lake City, Salt Lake Co., Utah.

24. **Franklin Dewey Richards.**—Born 2 Apr. 1821, at Richmond, Berkshire Co., Massachusetts, the son of Phinehas Richards and Wealthy Dewey. Ordained an Apostle 12 Feb. 1849, by Heber C. Kimball, at Salt Lake City, Utah, at the age of 27; sustained as President of the Quorum of the Twelve Apostles 13 Sep. 1898; died 9 Dec. 1899, at Ogden, Weber Co., Utah.

25. **George Quayle Cannon.**—Born 11 Jan. 1827, at Liverpool, Lancashire Co., England, the son of George Cannon and Ann Quayle. Ordained an Apostle 26 Aug. 1860, by Brigham Young, at Salt Lake City, Utah, at the age of 33; sustained as Counselor to President Brigham Young 8 Apr. 1873; sustained as Assistant Counselor to President Brigham Young 9 May 1874; released at the death of President Brigham Young 29 Aug. 1877; sustained as First Counselor to President John Taylor 10 Oct. 1880; released at the death of President Taylor 25 July 1887; to 1st Coun. 7 Apr. 1889. (See Coun. 8 & 1st Coun. 5.)

26. **Joseph Fielding Smith.**—Born 13 Nov. 1838, at Far West, Caldwell Co., Missouri, the son of Hyrum Smith and Mary Fielding. Ordained an Apostle and Counselor to the First Presidency 1 July 1866, by Brigham Young; discontinued as Counselor to the First Presidency and set apart as a member of the Quorum of the Twelve Apostles 8 Oct. 1867; sustained as Second Counselor to President John Taylor 10 Oct. 1880; released at the death of President Taylor 25 July 1887; sustained as Second Counselor to President Wilford Woodruff 7 Apr. 1889. (See Pres. 6, Coun. 3 and 2nd Coun. 7.)

27. **Brigham Young, Jr.**—Born 18 Dec. 1836, at Kirtland, Geauga Co., Ohio, the son of Brigham Young and Mary Ann Angell. Ordained an Apostle 4 Feb. 1864, by Brigham Young, at Salt Lake City, Utah; set apart as a member of the Quorum of the Twelve Apostles 9 Oct. 1868, at the age of 31; sustained as Counselor to President Brigham Young 8 Apr. 1873; sustained as Assistant Counselor to President Brigham Young 9 May 1874; released at the death of President Young 29 Aug. 1877; sustained as President of the Quorum of the Twelve Apostles 17 Oct. 1901; died 11 Apr. 1903, at Salt Lake City, Salt Lake Co., Utah. (See Coun. 5.)

28. **Albert Carrington.**—Born 8 Jan. 1813, at Royalton, Windsor Co., Vermont, the son of Daniel Van Carrington and Isabella Bowman.

APPENDIX 593

Ordained an Apostle 3 July 1870, by Brigham Young, at Salt Lake City, Utah, at the age of 57; sustained as Counselor to President Brigham Young 8 Apr. 1873; sustained as Assistant Counselor to President Brigham Young 9 May 1874; released at the death of Brigham Young 29 Aug. 1877; excommunicated 7 Nov. 1885; baptized again previous to his death; died 19 Sep. 1889, at Salt Lake City, Salt Lake Co., Utah. (See also Coun. 6.)

29. **Moses Thatcher.**—Born 2 Feb. 1842, Sangamon Co., Illinois, the son of Hezekiah Thatcher and Alley Kitchen. Ordained an Apostle 9 Apr. 1879, by John Taylor, at Salt Lake City, Utah, at the age of 37; dropped from the Quorum of the Twelve Apostles, 6 Apr. 1896; died 21 Aug. 1909, at Logan, Cache Co., Utah.

30. **Francis Marion Lyman.**—Born 12 Jan. 1840, at Good Hope, McDonough Co., Illinois, the son of Amasa Mason Lyman and Maria Louisa Tanner. Ordained an Apostle 27 Oct. 1880, by John Taylor, at Salt Lake City, Utah, at the age of 40; sustained as President of the Quorum of the Twelve Apostles 6 Oct. 1903; died 18 Nov. 1916, at Salt Lake City, Salt Lake Co., Utah.

31. **John Henry Smith.**—Born 18 Sep. 1848, at Carbunca (now Council Bluffs), Pottawattamie Co., Iowa, the son of George Albert Smith and Sarah Ann Libby. Ordained an Apostle 27 Oct. 1880, by Wilford Woodruff, at Salt Lake City, Utah, at the age of 32; to 2nd Coun. 7 Apr. 1910. (See 2nd Coun. 10.)

32. **George Teasdale.**—Born 8 Dec. 1831, at London, Middlesex Co., England, the son of William Russell Teasdale and Harriett H. Tidey. Ordained an Apostle 16 Oct. 1882, by John Taylor, at Salt Lake City, Utah, at the age of 50; died 9 June 1907, at Salt Lake City, Salt Lake Co., Utah.

33. **Heber Jeddy Grant.**—Born 22 Nov. 1856, at Salt Lake City, Salt Lake Co., Utah, the son of Jedediah Morgan Grant and Rachel Ridgeway Ivins. Ordained an Apostle 16 Oct. 1882, by George Q. Cannon, at Salt Lake City, Utah, at the age of 25; sustained as President of the Quorum of the Twelve Apostles 23 Nov. 1916; to Pres. 23 Nov. 1918. (See Pres. 7.)

34. **John Whittaker Taylor.**—Born 15 May 1858, at Provo, Utah Co., Utah, the son of John Taylor and Sophia Whittaker. Ordained an Apostle 9 Apr. 1884, by John Taylor, at Salt Lake City, Utah, at the age of 25; resigned 28 Oct. 1905; excommunicated 28 Mar. 1911; died 10 Oct. 1916, at Salt Lake City, Salt Lake Co., Utah.

35. **Marriner Wood Merrill.**—Born 25 Sep. 1832, at Sackville, Westmoreland Co., New Brunswick, the son of Nathan Alexander Merrill and Sarah Ann Reynolds. Ordained an Apostle 7 Oct. 1889, by Wilford Woodruff, at Salt Lake City, Utah, at the age of 57; died 6 Feb. 1906, at Richmond, Cache Co., Utah.

36. **Anthon Henrik Lund.**—Born 15 May 1844, at Aalborg, Jutland Amt., Denmark, the son of Henrik Lund and Anne C. Andersen. Ordained an Apostle 7 Oct. 1889, by George Q. Cannon, at Salt Lake City, Utah, at the age of 45; to 2nd Coun. 17 Oct. 1901; sustained as President of the Quorum of the Twelve Apostles 23 Nov. 1918. (See 2nd Coun. 9.)

37. **Abraham Hoagland Cannon.**—Ordained an Apostle 7 Oct. 1889, by Joseph F. Smith, at Salt Lake City, Utah, at the age of 30; died 19 July 1896, at Salt Lake City, Salt Lake Co., Utah. (See also 1st Coun. of Sev. 23.)

38. **Matthias Foss Cowley.**—Born 25 Aug. 1858, at Salt Lake City, Salt Lake Co., Utah, the son of Matthias Cowley and Sarah Elizabeth Foss. Ordained an Apostle 7 Oct. 1897, by George Q. Cannon, at Salt Lake City, Utah, at the age of 39; resigned 28 Oct. 1905; disfellowshipped 11 May 1911; restored to full membership 3 Apr. 1936; died 16 June 1940, at Salt Lake City, Salt Lake Co., Utah.

39. **Abraham Owen Woodruff.**—Born 23 Nov. 1872, at Salt Lake City, Salt Lake Co., Utah, the son of Wilford Woodruff and Emma Smith. Ordained an Apostle 7 Oct. 1897, by Wilford Woodruff, at Salt Lake City, Utah, at the age of 24; died 20 June 1904, at El Paso, El Paso Co., Texas.

40. **Rudger Clawson.**—Born 12 Mar. 1857, at Salt Lake City, Salt Lake Co., Utah, the son of Hiram Bradley Clawson and Margaret Gay Judd. Ordained an Apostle 10 Oct. 1898, by Lorenzo Snow, at Salt Lake City, Utah, at the age of 41; sustained as Second Counselor to President Lorenzo Snow 6 Oct. 1901, not set apart to this position, released at the death of President Snow 10 Oct. 1901; sustained as President of the Quorum of the Twelve Apostles 17 Mar. 1921; died 21 June 1943, at Salt Lake City, Salt Lake Co., Utah. (See also 2nd Coun. 8.)

41. **Reed Smoot.**—Born 10 Jan. 1862, at Salt Lake City, Salt Lake Co., Utah, the son of Abraham Owen Smoot and Anne Kestine Morrisen. Ordained an Apostle 8 Apr. 1900, by Lorenzo Snow, at Salt Lake City, Utah, at the age of 38; died 9 Feb. 1941, at St. Petersburg, Pinellas Co., Florida.

42. **Hyrum Mack Smith.**—Born 21 Mar. 1872, at Salt Lake City, Salt Lake Co., Utah, the son of Joseph Fielding Smith and Edna Lambson. Ordained an Apostle 24 Oct. 1901, by Joseph F. Smith, at Salt Lake City, Utah, at the age of 29; died 23 Jan. 1918, at Salt Lake City, Salt Lake Co., Utah.

43. **George Albert Smith.**—Born 4 Apr. 1870, at Salt Lake City, Salt Lake Co., Utah, the son of John Henry Smith and Sarah Farr. Ordained an Apostle 8 Oct. 1903, by Joseph F. Smith, at Salt Lake City, Utah, at the age of 33; sustained as President of the Quorum of

the Twelve Apostles 1 July 1943; to Pres. 21 May 1945. (See Pres. 8.)

44. **Charles William Penrose.**—Born 4 Feb. 1832, at London, Surrey Co., England, the son of George White Penrose and Matilda Sims. Ordained an Apostle 7 July 1904, by Joseph F. Smith, at Salt Lake City, Utah, at the age of 72; to 2nd Coun. 7 Dec. 1911. (See 2nd Coun. 11.)

45. **George Franklin Richards.**—Born 23 Feb. 1861, at Farmington, Davis Co., Utah, the son of Franklin D. Richards and Nanny Longstroth. Ordained an Apostle 9 Apr. 1906, by Joseph F. Smith, at Salt Lake City, Utah, at the age of 45; sustained as President of the Quorum of the Twelve Apostles 21 May 1945; died 8 Aug. 1950, at Salt Lake City, Salt Lake Co., Utah.

46. **Orson Ferguson Whitney.**—Born 1 July 1855, at Salt Lake City, Salt Lake Co., Utah, the son of Horace Kimball Whitney and Helen Mar Kimball. Ordained an Apostle 9 Apr. 1906, by Joseph F. Smith, at Salt Lake City, Utah, at the age of 50; died 16 May 1931, at Salt Lake City, Salt Lake Co., Utah.

47. **David Oman McKay.**—Born 8 Sep. 1873, at Huntsville, Weber Co., Utah, the son of David McKay and Jennette Eveline Evans. Ordained an Apostle 9 Apr. 1906, by Joseph F. Smith, at Salt Lake City, Utah, at the age of 32; sustained as Second Counselor to President Heber J. Grant 6 Oct. 1934; sustained as President of the Quorum of the Twelve Apostles 30 Sep. 1950. (See 2nd Coun. 15 and Pres. 9.)

48. **Anthony Woodward Ivins.**—Born 16 Sep. 1852, at Toms River, Ocean Co., New Jersey, the son of Israel Ivins and Anna Lowrie. Ordained an Apostle 6 Oct. 1907, by Joseph F. Smith, at Salt Lake City, Utah, at the age of 55; to 2nd Coun. 10 Mar. 1921. (See 2nd Coun. 12.)

49. **Joseph Fielding Smith.**—Born 19 July 1876, at Salt Lake City, Salt Lake Co., Utah, the son of Joseph Fielding Smith and Julina Lambson. Ordained an Apostle 7 Apr. 1910, by Joseph F. Smith, at Salt Lake City, Utah, at the age of 33; sustained as Acting President of the Quorum of the Twelve Apostles 30 Sep. 1950; sustained as President of the Quorum of the Twelve Apostles 9 Apr. 1951; sustained as Counselor in the First Presidency 29 Oct. 1965; sustained as President of the Church 23 Jan. 1970. (See Pres. 10; Coun. 10.)

50. **James Edward Talmage.**—Born 21 Sep. 1862, at Hungerford, Berkshire Co., England, the son of James J. Talmage and Susannah Preater. Ordained an Apostle 8 Dec. 1911, by Joseph F. Smith, at Salt Lake City, Utah, at the age of 49; died 27 July 1933, at Salt Lake City, Salt Lake Co., Utah.

51. **Stephen Longstroth Richards.**—Born 18 June 1879, at Mendon, Cache Co., Utah, the son of Stephen Longstroth Richards and Emma Louise Stayner. Ordained an Apostle 18 Jan. 1917, by Joseph F. Smith,

at Salt Lake City, Utah, at the age of 37; to 1st Coun. 9 Apr. 1951. (See 1st Coun. 12.)

52. **Richard Roswell Lyman.**—Born 23 Nov. 1870, at Fillmore, Millard Co., Utah, the son of Francis Marion Lyman and Clara Caroline Callister. Ordained an Apostle 7 Apr. 1918, by Joseph F. Smith, at Salt Lake City, Utah, at the age of 47; excommunicated 12 Nov. 1943; baptized again 27 Oct. 1954; died 31 Dec. 1963, at Salt Lake City, Salt Lake Co., Utah.

53. **Melvin Joseph Ballard.**—Born 9 Feb. 1873, at Logan, Cache Co., Utah, the son of Henry Ballard and Margaret McNeil. Ordained an Apostle 7 Jan. 1919, by Heber J. Grant, at Salt Lake City, Utah, at the age of 45; died 30 July 1939, at Salt Lake City, Salt Lake Co., Utah.

54. **John Andreas Widtsoe.**—Born 31 Jan. 1872, at Daloe, Island of Froyen, Trondhjem, Norway, the son of John A. Widtsoe and Anna Karine Gaarden. Ordained an Apostle 17 Mar. 1921, by Heber J. Grant, at Salt Lake City, Utah, at the age of 49; died 29 Nov. 1952, at Salt Lake City, Salt Lake Co., Utah.

55. **Joseph Francis Merrill.**—Born 24 Aug. 1868, at Richmond, Cache Co., Utah, the son of Marriner Wood Merrill and Mariah Loenza Kingsbury. Ordained an Apostle 8 Oct. 1931, by Heber J. Grant, at Salt Lake City, Utah, at the age of 63; died 3 Feb. 1952, at Salt Lake City, Salt Lake Co., Utah.

56. **Charles Albert Callis.**—Born 4 May 1865, at Dublin, Dublin Co., Ireland, the son of John Callis and Susanna Charlotte Quilliam. Ordained an Apostle 12 Oct. 1933, by Heber J. Grant, at Salt Lake City, Utah, at the age of 68; died 21 Jan. 1947, at Jacksonville, Duval Co., Florida.

57. **Joshua Reuben Clark, Jr.**—Sustained as Second Counselor to President Heber J. Grant 6 Apr. 1933; sustained as First Counselor to President Heber J. Grant 6 Oct. 1934; ordained an Apostle 11 Oct. 1934, by Heber J. Grant, at Salt Lake City, Utah, at the age of 63; continued as 1st Coun. (See 1st Coun. 11. See also 2nd Coun. 14.)

58. **Alonzo Arza Hinckley.**—Born 23 Apr. 1870, at Cove Fort, Millard Co., Utah, the son of Ira Nathaniel Hinckley and Angeline Wilcox Noble. Ordained an Apostle 11 Oct. 1934, by Heber J. Grant, at Salt Lake City, Utah, at the age of 64; died 22 Dec. 1936, at Salt Lake City, Salt Lake Co., Utah.

59. **Albert Ernest Bowen.**—Born 31 Oct. 1875, at Henderson Creek, Oneida Co., Idaho, the son of David Bowen and Annie Schackelton. Ordained an Apostle 8 Apr. 1937, by Heber J. Grant, at Salt Lake City, Utah, at the age of 61; died 15 July 1953, at Salt Lake City, Salt Lake Co., Utah.

60. **Sylvester Quayle Cannon.**—Sustained as Associate to the Quo-

rum of the Twelve Apostles 6 Apr. 1938; ordained an Apostle 14 Apr. 1938, by Heber J. Grant, at Salt Lake City, Utah; sustained as a member of the Quorum of the Twelve Apostles 6 Oct. 1939, at the age of 62; died 29 May 1943, at Salt Lake City, Salt Lake Co., Utah. (See also Pres. Bp. 6.)

61. **Harold Bingham Lee.**—Born 28 Mar. 1899, at Clifton, Oneida Co., Idaho, the son of Samuel Marion Lee and Louisa Emeline Bingham. Ordained an Apostle 10 Apr. 1941, by Heber J. Grant, at Salt Lake City, Utah, at the age of 42; sustained as President of the Quorum of the Twelve Apostles 23 Jan. 1970; sustained as First Counselor to President Joseph Fielding Smith 23 Jan. 1970. (See also 1st Couns. 16 and President 11.)

62. **Spencer Woolley Kimball.**—Born 28 Mar. 1895, at Salt Lake City, Salt Lake Co., Utah, the son of Andrew Kimball and Olive Woolley. Ordained an Apostle 7 Oct. 1943, by Heber J. Grant, at Salt Lake City, Utah, at the age of 48; sustained as Acting President of the Quorum of the Twelve Apostles 23 Jan. 1970.

63. **Ezra Taft Benson.**—Born 4 Aug. 1899, at Whitney, Oneida Co., Idaho, the son of Samuel Marion Lee and Louisa Emeline dained an Apostle 7 Oct. 1943, by Heber J. Grant, at Salt Lake City, Utah, at the age of 44.

64. **Mark Edward Petersen.**—Born 7 Nov. 1900, at Salt Lake City, Salt Lake Co., Utah, the son of Christian Petersen and Christine M. Andersen. Ordained an Apostle 20 Apr. 1944, by Heber J. Grant. at Salt Lake City, Utah, at the age of 43.

65. **Matthew Cowley.**—Born 2 Aug. 1897, at Preston, Franklin Co., Idaho, the son of Matthias Foss Cowley and Abbie Hyde. Ordained an Apostle 11 Oct. 1945, by George Albert Smith, at Salt Lake City, Utah, at the age of 48; died 13 Dec. 1953, at Los Angeles, Los Angeles Co., California.

66. **Henry Dinwoodey Moyle.**—Born 22 Apr. 1889, at Salt Lake City, Salt Lake Co., Utah, the son of James H. Moyle and Alice E. Dinwoodey. Ordained an Apostle 10 Apr. 1947, by George Albert Smith, at Salt Lake City, Utah, at the age of 58; to 2nd Coun. 12 June 1959. (See 2nd Coun. 17.)

67. **Delbert Leon Stapley.**—Born 11 Dec. 1896, at Mesa, Maricopa Co., Arizona, the son of Orley S. Stapley and Polly M. Hunsaker. Ordained an Apostle 5 Oct. 1950, by George Albert Smith, at Salt Lake City, Utah, at the age of 53.

68. **Marion George Romney.**—Ordained an Apostle 11 Oct. 1951, by David O. McKay, at Salt Lake City, Utah, at the age of 54. (See also 2nd Coun. FP 20 & Asst. to Tw. 1.)

69. **LeGrand Richards.**—Ordained an Apostle 10 Apr. 1952, by David O. McKay, at Salt Lake City, Utah, at the age of 66. (See also Pres. Bp. 7.)

70. **Adam Samuel Bennion.**—Born 2 Dec. 1886, at Taylorsville, Salt Lake Co., Utah, the son of Joseph Bennion and Mary A. Sharp. Ordained an Apostle 9 Apr. 1953, by David O. McKay, at Salt Lake City, Utah, at the age of 66; died 11 Feb. 1958, at Salt Lake City, Salt Lake Co., Utah.

71. **Richard Louis Evans.**—Ordained an Apostle 8 Oct. 1953, by David O. McKay, at Salt Lake City, Utah, at the age of 47. Died 1 November 1971, at Salt Lake City, Salt Lake County, Utah. (See also 1st Coun. of Sev. 40.)

72. **George Quayle Morris.**—Ordained an Apostle 8 Apr. 1954, by David O. McKay, at Salt Lake City, Utah, at the age of 80; died 23 Apr. 1962, at Salt Lake City, Salt Lake Co., Utah. (See also Asst. to Twelve 6.)

73. **Hugh Brown Brown.**—Born 24 Oct. 1883, at Granger, Salt Lake Co., Utah, the son of Homer Manly Brown and Lydia Jane Brown. Sustained as Assistant to the Quorum of the Twelve Apostles 4 Oct. 1953; ordained an Apostle 10 Apr. 1958, by David O. McKay, at Salt Lake City, Utah, at the age of 74; sustained as Counselor in the First Presidency 22 June 1961; sustained as Second Counselor to President David O. McKay 12 Oct. 1961; sustained as First Counselor to President David O. McKay 4 Oct. 1963; released at the death of President McKay 18 Jan. 1970. (See also 1st Coun. 15; 2nd Coun. 18; Coun 9.)

74. **Howard William Hunter.**—Born 14 Nov. 1907, at Boise, Ada Co., Idaho, the son of John William Hunter and Nellie Rasmussen. Ordained an Apostle 15 Oct. 1959, by David O. McKay, at Salt Lake City, Utah, at the age of 51.

75. **Gordon Bitner Hinckley.**—Ordained an Apostle 5 Oct. 1961, by David O. McKay, at Salt Lake City, Utah, at the age of 51. (See also Asst. to Twelve 12.)

76. **Nathan Eldon Tanner.**—Ordained an Apostle 11 Oct. 1962, by David O. McKay, at Salt Lake City, Utah, at the age of 64; to 2nd Coun. 4 Oct. 1963. (See also 1st Coun. 17, 2nd Coun. 19, Asst. to Tw. 16.)

77. **Thomas Spencer Monson.**—Born 21 Aug. 1927, at Salt Lake City, Salt Lake Co., Utah, the son of George Spencer Monson and Gladys Condie. Ordained an Apostle 10 Oct. 1963, by Joseph Fielding Smith, at Salt Lake City, Utah, at the age of 36.

78. **Boyd Kenneth Packer.**—Born 10 Sept. 1924, at Brigham City, Box Elder Co., Utah, the son of Ira Wight Packer and Emma Jensen. Sustained as Assistant to the Quorum of the Twelve Apostles 30 Sep. 1961; ordained an Apostle 9 Apr. 1970, by Joseph Fielding Smith, at the age of 45.

APPENDIX

79. **Marvin Jeremy Ashton**—Ordained an Apostle 2 December 1971, by Harold B. Lee, at Salt Lake City, Utah, at the age of 56. (See also Asst. to Twelve 24).

80. **Bruce Redd McConkie.**—Born 29 July 1915, at Ann Arbor, Washtenaw Co., Michigan, the son of Oscar Walter McConkie and Margaret Vivian Redd. Sustained as one of the First Council of the Seventy 6 Oct. 1946; ordained an Apostle 12 Oct. 1972, by Harold B. Lee, at Salt Lake City, Utah, at the age of 57. (See also 1st Coun. of Sev. 44.)

81. **Lowell Tom Perry.**—Ordained an Apostle 11 April 1974, by President Spencer W. Kimball, at Salt Lake City, Utah, at the age of 51. (See also Asst. to Tw. 32)

PATRIARCHS TO THE CHURCH

1. **Joseph Smith, Sr.**—Born 12 July 1771, at Topsfield, Essex Co., Massachusetts, the second son of Asael Smith and Mary Duty. Ordained a High Priest 3 June 1831, by Lyman Wight; ordained Patriarch to the Church 18 Dec. 1833, by Joseph Smith, at the age of 62; also sustained as Assistant Counselor in the First Presidency 3 Sep. 1837; died 14 Sep. 1840, at Nauvoo, Hancock Co., Illinois. (See also Asst. Coun. 2.)

2. **Hyrum Smith.**—Ordained Patriarch to the Church and Assistant President 24 Jan. 1841, by Joseph Smith, at the age of 40; martyred 27 June 1844, at Carthage Jail, Hancock Co., Illinois. (See also Asst. Pres. 2.)

William B. Smith.—Ordained Patriarch to the Church 24 May 1845, by the Twelve and then gave patriarchal blessings, but was rejected by the Church membership at the conference held 6 Oct. 1845; excommunicated 19 Oct. 1845; died 13 Nov. 1893, at Osterdock, Clayton Co., Iowa. (See also Apo. 9.)

3. **John Smith.**—Ordained a Patriarch 10 Jan. 1844, by Joseph Smith; ordained as Patriarch to the Church 1 Jan. 1849, under the hands of Brigham Young and Heber C. Kimball, at the age of 67; died 23 May 1854, at Salt Lake City, Salt Lake Co., Utah. (See also Asst. Coun. 4.)

4. **John Smith.**—Born 22 Sep. 1832, at Kirtland, Geauga Co., Ohio, the oldest son of Hyrum Smith and Jerusha Barden. Ordained Patriarch to the Church 18 Feb. 1855, by Brigham Young, at the age of 22; died 6 Nov. 1911, at Salt Lake City, Salt Lake Co., Utah.

5. **Hyrum Gibbs Smith.**—Born 8 July 1879, at South Jordan, Salt Lake Co., Utah, the oldest son of Hyrum Fisher Smith and Annie Maria Gibbs. (Hyrum Fisher Smith was the oldest son of John Smith and Helen Maria Fisher. John Smith was the oldest son of Hyrum Smith and Jerusha Barden.) Ordained a High Priest and Patriarch

to the Church 9 May 1912, by Joseph F. Smith, at the age of 32; died 4 Feb. 1932, at Salt Lake City, Salt Lake Co., Utah.

From 1932 to 1937 no Patriarch to the Church was sustained. Nicholas G. Smith served as Acting Patriarch from 1932 to 1934.

George Franklin Richards.—Born 23 Feb. 1861, at Farmington, Davis Co., Utah, the son of Franklin D. Richards and Nanny Longstroth. Ordained an Apostle 9 Apr. 1906; sustained as Acting Patriarch to the Church 3 Oct. 1937; released from this position 3 Oct. 1942.

6. **Joseph F. Smith.**—Born 30 Jan. 1899, at Salt Lake City, Salt Lake Co., Utah, the oldest son of Hyrum Mack Smith and Ida E. Bowman. (Hyrum Mack Smith was the oldest son of Joseph F. Smith and Edna Lambson. Joseph F. Smith was the oldest son of Hyrum Smith and Mary Fielding.) Ordained a High Priest and Patriarch to the Church 8 Oct. 1942, by Heber J. Grant, at the age of 43; released 6 Oct. 1946, due to ill health; died 29 Aug. 1964, in Salt Lake City, Salt Lake Co., Utah.

7. **Eldred Gee Smith.**—Born 9 Jan. 1907, at Lehi, Utah Co., Utah, the oldest son of Hyrum Gibbs Smith and Martha Electa Gee. Ordained a High Priest 23 May 1938, by J. Reuben Clark, Jr.; ordained and set apart as Patriarch to the Church 10 Apr. 1947, by George Albert Smith, at the age of 40.

ASSISTANTS TO THE QUORUM OF THE TWELVE APOSTLES

1. **Marion George Romney.**—Born 19 Sep. 1897, at Colonia Juarez, Chihuahua Co., Mexico, the son of George Samuel Romney and Teressa Artemesia Redd. Ordained a High Priest 20 Apr. 1935, by Joseph Fielding Smith; sustained as Assistant to the Quorum of the Twelve Apostles 6 Apr. 1941, and set apart 23 May 1941, by Heber J. Grant, at Salt Lake City, Utah, at the age of 43; to Apostle 11 Oct. 1951. (See also 2nd Couns. 20 & Apo. 68.)

2. **Thomas Evans McKay.**—Born 29 Oct. 1875, at Huntsville, Weber Co., Utah, the son of David McKay and Jennette Eveline Evans. Ordained a High Priest 26 July 1908, by George F. Richards; sustained as Assistant to the Quorum of the Twelve Apostles 6 Apr. 1941, and set apart 23 May 1941, by Heber J. Grant, at Salt Lake City, Utah, at the age of 65; died 15 Jan. 1958, at Salt Lake City, Salt Lake Co., Utah.

3. **Clifford Earl Young.**—Born 7 Dec. 1883, at Salt Lake City, Salt Lake Co., Utah, the son of Seymour Bicknell Young and Ann Elizabeth Riter. Ordained a High Priest 1 July 1928 by Heber J. Grant; sustained as Assistant to the Quorum of the Twelve Apostles 6 Apr. 1941, and set apart 23 May 1941, by Heber J. Grant, at Salt Lake City, Utah, at the age of 57; died 21 Aug. 1958, at Salt Lake City, Salt Lake Co., Utah.

APPENDIX 601

4. **Alma Sonne.**—Born 5 Mar. 1884, at Logan, Cache Co., Utah, the son of Niels C. Sonne and Elisa Peterson. Ordained a High Priest 2 Feb. 1931, by Anthony W. Ivins; sustained as Assistant to the Quorum of the Twelve Apostles 6 Apr. 1941, and set apart 26 May 1941, by Heber J. Grant at Salt Lake City, Utah, at the age of 57.

5. **Nicholas Groesbeck Smith.**—Born 20 June 1881, at Salt Lake City, Salt Lake Co., Utah, the son of John Henry Smith and Josephine Groesbeck. Ordained a High Priest 1 Aug. 1921, by Rudger Clawson; sustained as Assistant to the Quorum of the Twelve Apostles 6 Apr. 1941, and set apart 1 Oct. 1941, by Heber J. Grant, at Salt Lake City, Utah, at the age of 60; died 27 Oct. 1945, at Salt Lake City, Salt Lake Co., Utah.

6. **George Quayle Morris.**—Born 20 Feb. 1874, at Salt Lake City, Salt Lake Co., Utah, the son of Elias Morris and Mary L. Walker. Ordained a High Priest 8 Mar. 1908, by Rudger Clawson; sustained as Assistant to the Quorum of the Twelve Apostles 6 Oct. 1951, and set apart 11 Oct. 1951, by David O. McKay, at Salt Lake City, Utah, at the age of 77; to Apostle 8 Apr. 1954. (See Apo. 72.)

7. **Stayner Richards.**—Born 20 Dec. 1885, at Salt Lake City, Salt Lake Co., Utah, the son of Stephen Longstroth Richards and Emma Louise Stayner. Ordained a High Priest 24 Feb. 1914, by George F. Richards; sustained as Assistant to the Quorum of the Twelve Apostles 6 Oct. 1951, and set apart 11 Oct. 1951, by David O. McKay at Salt Lake City, Utah, at the age of 65; died 28 May 1953, at Salt Lake City, Salt Lake Co., Utah.

8. **ElRay LaVar Christiansen.**—Born 13 July 1897, at Mayfield, Sanpete Co., Utah, the son of Parley Christiansen and Dorthe C. Jensen. Ordained a High Priest 22 Oct. 1933, by George F. Richards; sustained as Assistant to the Quorum of the Twelve Apostles 6 Oct. 1951, and set apart 11 Oct. 1951, by Stephen L Richards at Salt Lake City, Utah, at the age of 54.

9. **John Longden.**—Born 4 Nov. 1898, at Oldham, Lancashire Co., England, the son of Thomas Longden and Lizetta Taylor. Ordained a High Priest 27 Sep. 1925, by Rudger Clawson; sustained as Assistant to the Quorum of the Twelve Apostles 6 Oct. 1951, and set apart 11 Oct. 1951, by J. Reuben Clark at Salt Lake City, Utah, at the age of 52. Died 30 Aug. 1969 at Salt Lake City, Salt Lake County, Utah.

10. **Hugh Brown Brown.**—Born 24 Oct. 1883, at Granger, Salt Lake Co., Utah, the son of Homer Manly Brown and Lydia Jane Brown. Ordained a High Priest 23 May 1908, by Thomas Duce; sustained at Assistant to the Quorum of the Twelve Apostles 4 Oct. 1953, and set apart 20 Oct. 1953, by David O. McKay, at Salt Lake City, Utah, at the age of 69; to Apostle 10 Apr. 1958. (See Apo. 73.)

11. **Sterling Welling Sill.**—Born 31 Mar. 1903, at Layton, Davis Co., Utah, the son of Joseph Albert Sill and Marcetta Welling. Ordained a High Priest by Henry H. Blood, who was ordained a High Priest 25 Mar. 1906, by Hyrum M. Smith; sustained as Assistant to the Quorum of the Twelve Apostles 6 Apr. 1954, and set apart 9 Apr. 1954, by David O. McKay, at Salt Lake City, Utah, at the age of 51.

12. **Gordon Bitner Hinckley.**—Born 23 June 1910, at Salt Lake City, Salt Lake Co., Utah, the son of Bryant Stringham Hinckley and Ada Bitner. Ordained a High Priest 21 July 1946, by Charles A. Callis; sustained as Assistant to the Quorum of the Twelve Apostles 6 Apr. 1958, and set apart 10 Apr. 1958, by David O. McKay, at Salt Lake City, Utah, at the age of 43; to Apostle 5 Oct. 1961. (See Apo. 75.)

13. **Henry Dixon Taylor.**—Born 22 Nov. 1903, at Provo, Utah Co., Utah, the son of Arthur N. Taylor and Maria Dixon. Ordained a High Priest 15 Jan. 1933, by Melvin J. Ballard; sustained as Assistant to the Quorum of the Twelve Apostles 6 Apr. 1958, and set apart 10 Apr. 1958, by David O. McKay, at Salt Lake City, Utah, at the age of 54.

14. **William James Critchlow, Jr.**—Born 21 Aug. 1892, at Brigham City, Box Elder Co., Utah, the son of William James Critchlow and Anna C. Gregerson. Ordained a High Priest 16 Dec. 1934, by George F. Richards; sustained as Assistant to the Quorum of the Twelve Apostles 11 Oct. 1958, and set apart 16 Oct. 1958, by David O. McKay, at Salt Lake City, Utah, at the age of 66; died 29 August 1968, at Ogden, Weber Co., Utah.

15. **Alvin Rulon Dyer.**—Born 1 Jan. 1903, at Salt Lake City, Salt Lake Co., Utah, the son of Alfred R. Dyer and Harriet Walsh. Ordained a High Priest 2 Oct. 1927, by Joseph Fielding Smith; sustained as Assistant to the Quorum of the Twelve Apostles 11 Oct. 1958, and set apart 16 Oct. 1958, by Stephen L Richards, at Salt Lake City, Utah, at the age of 55; ordained an Apostle 5 Oct. 1967; sustained as Counselor in the First Presidency 6 Apr. 1968; released at the death of President McKay 18 Jan. 1970; resumed postion as Assistant to the Quorum of the Twelve Apostles 23 Jan. 1970. (See also Couns. 12.)

16. **Nathan Eldon Tanner.**—Born 9 May 1898, at Salt Lake City, Salt Lake Co., Utah, the son of Nathan William Tanner and Sarah Edna Brown. Ordained a High Priest 22 Aug. 1928, by Melvin J. Ballard; sustained as Assistant to the Quorum of the Twelve Apostles 8 Oct. 1960, and set apart 9 Oct. 1960, by David O. McKay, at Salt Lake City, Utah, at the age of 62; to Apostle 11 Oct. 1962. (See also 1st Coun. 17, 2nd Coun. 19, & Apo. 76.)

17. **Franklin Dewey Richards.**—Born 17 Nov. 1900, at Ogden, Weber Co., Utah, the son of Charles C. Richards and Louisa L. Peery.

Ordained a High Priest 21 Mar. 1955, by Arthur S. Woods, who was ordained a High Priest 28 July 1924, by George Albert Smith; sustained as Assistant to the Quorum of the Twelve Apostles 8 Oct. 1960, and set apart 9 Oct. 1960, by David O. McKay, at Salt Lake City, Utah, at the age of 59.

18. **Theodore Moyle Burton.**—Born 27 Mar. 1907, at Salt Lake City, Salt Lake Co., Utah, the son of Theodore T. Burton and Florence Moyle. Ordained a High Priest 27 Jan. 1945, by Marion G. Romney; sustained as Assistant to the Quorum of the Twelve Apostles 8 Oct. 1960, and set apart 9 Oct. 1960, by David O. McKay, at Salt Lake City, Utah, at the age of 53.

19. **Henry Thorpe Beal Isaacson.**—Born 6 Sep. 1898, at Ephraim, Sanpete Co., Utah, the son of Martin Isaacson and Mary Jemima Beal. Ordained a High Priest 1 Oct. 1941, by Charles A. Callis; sustained as Second Counselor to the Presiding Bishop 12 Dec. 1946; sustained as First Counselor to the Presiding Bishop 6 Apr. 1952; sustained as Assistant to the Quorum of the Twelve Apostles 30 Sep. 1961, and set apart 6 Oct. 1961, by David O. McKay, at Salt Lake City, Utah, at the age of 63; sustained as Counselor to President David O. McKay 28 Oct. 1965; released at the death of President McKay 18 Jan. 1970; resumed position as Assistant to the Quorum of the Twelve Apostles 23 Jan. 1970. Died 9 Nov. 1970, at Salt Lake City, Salt Lake Co., Utah. (See also Couns. 11; 1st Couns. Pres. Bp. 8; 2nd Couns. Pres. Bp. 11.)

20. **Boyd Kenneth Packer.**—Born 10 Sep. 1924, at Brigham City, Box Elder Co., Utah, the son of Ira Wight Packer and Emma Jensen. Ordained a High Priest 10 Dec. 1950, by Joseph F. Merrill; sustained as Assistant to the Quorum of the Twelve Apostles 30 Sep. 1961, and set apart 6 Oct. 1961, by Henry D. Moyle at Salt Lake City, Utah, at the age of 37. Ordained an Apostle 9 Apr. 1970. (See also Apo. 78.)

21. **Bernard Park Brockbank.**—Born 24 May 1909, at Salt Lake City, Salt Lake Co., Utah, the son of Taylor P. Brockbank and Sarah Le Cheminant. Ordained a High Priest 19 July 1942, by Joseph F. Merrill; sustained as Assistant to the Quorum of the Twelve Apostles 6 Oct. 1962, and set apart 10 Oct. 1962, by David O. McKay at Salt Lake City, Utah, at the age of 53.

22. **James Alfred Cullimore.**—Born 17 Jan. 1906, at Lindon, Utah Co., Utah, the son of Albert Lorenzo Cullimore and Luella Keetch. Ordained a High Priest 23 Oct. 1960, by Mark E. Petersen; sustained as Assistant to the Quorum of the Twelve Apostles 6 Apr. 1966, and set apart 8 Apr. 1966, by David O. McKay, at Salt Lake City, Utah, at the age of 60.

23. **Marion Duff Hanks.**—Sustained as Assistant to the Quorum of the Twelve Apostles 6 Apr. 1968, and set apart 8 Apr. 1968, by Alvin R. Dyer, at Salt Lake City, Utah, at the age of 46. (See also 1st Coun. of Sev. 45.)

24. **Marvin Jeremy Ashton.**—Born 6 May 1915, at Salt Lake City, Salt Lake Co., Utah, son of Marvin Owen Ashton and Rachel Grace Jeremy. Ordained a High Priest 17 May 1959, by Sanfred W. Elieson; sustained as Assistant to the Quorum of the Twelve Apostles 3 Oct. 1969, and ordained and set apart 16 Oct. 1969, by Hugh B. Brown, at the age of 54. (See also Apostle 79.)

25. **Joseph Anderson.**—Born 20 Nov. 1889, at Salt Lake City, Salt Lake Co., Utah, the son of George Anderson and Isabella Watson. Ordained a High Priest 21 Sep. 1924, by James E. Talmage; sustained as Assistant to the Quorum of the Twelve Apostles 6 Apr. 1970, and set apart 9 Apr. 1970, by Harold B. Lee.

26. **David Bruce Haight.**—Born 2 Sep. 1906, at Oakley, Idaho, the son of Hector C. Haight and Clara Tuttle. Ordained a High Priest 6 Jan. 1946, by Stephen L Richards; sustained as Assistant to the Quorum of the Twelve Apostles 6 Apr. 1970, and set apart 9 Apr. 1970, by Nathan E. Tanner.

27. **William Hunter Bennett.**—Born 5 Nov. 1910, at Taber, Alberta, Canada, the son of William Alvin Bennett and Mary Walker. Ordained a High Priest 21 Mar. 1947, by William W. Owens; sustained as Assistant to the Quorum of the Twelve Apostles 6 Apr. 1970, and set apart 9 Apr. 1970 by Joseph Fielding Smith.

28. **John Henry Vandenberg.**—Born 18 Dec. 1904, at Ogden, Weber Co., Utah, the son of Dirk Vandenberg and Maria Alkema. Ordained a High Priest 26 June 1942, by Albert E. Bowen; sustained as Presiding Bishop of the Church 30 Sep. 1951; sustained as Assistant to the Quorum of the Twelve Apostles 6 Apr. 1972, and set apart 9 Apr. 1972, by Harold B. Lee, at Salt Lake City, Utah, at the age of 67. (See also Pres. Bp. 9.)

29. **Robert Leatham Simpson.**—Born 8 Aug. 1915, at Salt Lake City, Salt Lake Co., Utah, the son of Heber Chase Simpson and Lillian Leatham. Ordained a High Priest 31 Mar. 1946, by Harold B. Lee; sustained as First Counselor to the Presiding Bishop 30 Sep. 1961; sustained as Assistant to the Quorum of the Twelve Apostles 6 Apr. 1972, and set apart 9 Apr. 1972, by Nathan Eldon Tanner, at Salt Lake City, Utah, at the age of 56. (See also 1st Coun. Pres. Bp. 9.)

30. **Oscar Leslie Stone.**—Born 28 May 1903, at Chapin, Idaho, the son of Frank J. Stone and Mabel Crandall. Ordained a High Priest 11 Oct. 1931, by Joseph Fielding Smith; sustained as Assistant to the Quorum of the Twelve Apostles 6 Oct. 1972, and set apart 8 Oct. 1972, by Harold B. Lee, at Salt Lake City, Utah, at the age of 69.

31. **James Esdras Faust.**—Born 31 July 1920, at Delta, Utah, the son of George A. Faust and Amy Finlinson. Ordained a High Priest 17 Dec. 1948, by Joseph Francis Merrill; sustained as Assistant to the Quorum of Twelve Apostles 6 Oct. 1972, and set apart 8 Oct. 1972, by Harold B. Lee, at Salt Lake City, Utah, at the age of 52.

32. **Lowell Tom Perry.**—Born 5 Aug. 1922, at Logan, Utah, the son of L. Tom Perry and Nora Sonne. Ordained a High Priest 21 June 1953, by Harold B. Lee; sustained as Assistant to the Quorum of the Twelve Apostles 6 Oct. 1972, and set apart 8 Oct. 1972, by Harold B. Lee, at Salt Lake City, Utah, at the age of 50. Ordained an Apostle 11 April 1974. (See Apostle 81)

33. **John Thomas Fyans.**—Born 17 May 1918, at Moreland, Idaho, the son of Joseph Fyans and Mary Ann Farnsworth. Ordained a High Priest 11 November 1944, by Joseph Francis Merrill; sustained as Assistant to the Quorum of the Twelve Apostles 6 April 1974, and set apart 7 April 1974, by Spencer W. Kimball, at Salt Lake City, Utah, at the age of 55.

34. **Neal Ash Maxwell.**—Born 6 July 1926, at Salt Lake City, Utah, the son of Clarence Homer Maxwell and Emma Ash. Ordained a High Priest 8 May 1957, by Henry D. Moyle; sustained as Assistant to the Quorum of the Twelve Apostles 6 April 1974, and set apart 7 April 1974, by Spencer W. Kimball, at Salt Lake City, Utah, at the age of 47.

FIRST COUNCIL OF THE SEVENTY

(FIRST SEVEN PRESIDENTS OF THE SEVENTY)

1. **Hazen Aldrich.**—Chosen and ordained one of the First Seven Presidents 28 Feb. 1835; released 6 Apr. 1837, having previously been ordained a High Priest.

2. **Joseph Young.**—Born 7 Apr. 1797, at Hopkinton, Middlesex Co., Massachusetts, the son of John Young and Abigail Howe. Ordained a Seventy 28 Feb. 1835, under the hands of Joseph Smith, Sidney Rigdon and Frederick G. Williams; chosen and ordained one of the First Seven Presidents 28 Feb. 1835, at the age of 37; died 16 July 1881, at Salt Lake City, Salt Lake Co., Utah.

3. **Levi Ward Hancock.**—Born 7 Apr. 1803, at Springfield, Hampden Co., Massachusetts, the son of Thomas Hancock and Amy Ward. Ordained a Seventy 28 Feb. 1835, under the hands of Joseph Smith, Sidney Rigdon and Frederick G. Williams; chosen and ordained one of the First Seven Presidents 28 Feb. 1835, at the age of 31; released 6 Apr. 1837, having supposedly previously been ordained a High Priest; restored to former place in First Council 3 Sep. 1837, as he had not been ordained a High Priest; died 10 June 1882, at Washington, Washington Co., Utah.

4. **Zebedee Coltrin.**—Born 7 Sep. 1804, at Ovid, Seneca Co., New York, the son of John Coltrin, Jr. and Sarah Graham. Chosen and ordained one of the First Seven Presidents 28 Feb. 1835, at the age of 30; released 6 Apr. 1837, having previously been ordained a High Priest; died 21 July 1887, at Spanish Fork, Utah Co., Utah.

5. **Leonard Rich.**—Chosen and ordained one of the First Seven Presidents 28 Feb. 1835; released 6 Apr. 1837, having previously been ordained a High Priest.

6. **Lyman Royal Sherman.**—Born 22 May 1804, at Salem, Essex Co., Massachusetts, the son of Elkanah Sherman and Asenath Hulbert. Chosen and ordained one of the First Seven Presidents 28 Feb. 1835, at the age of 30; released 6 Apr. 1837, having previously been ordained a High Priest; died 27 Jan. 1839.

7. **Sylvester Smith.**—Chosen and ordained one of the First Seven Presidents 28 Feb. 1835; released 6 Apr. 1837, having previously been ordained a High Priest.

8. **John Gould.**—Born 11 May 1808. Ordained a Seventy and set apart as one of the First Seven Presidents 6 Apr. 1837, at the age of 28; released 3 Sep. 1837, to become a High Priest.

9. **James Foster.**—Born 1 Apr. 1775, at Morgan Co., Indiana. Ordained a Seventy 6 Apr. 1837, under the hands of Sidney Rigdon and Hyrum Smith; set apart as one of the First Seven Presidents 6 Apr. 1837, at the age of 62; died 21 Dec. 1841, at Morgan Co., Illinois.

10. **Daniel Sanborn Miles.**—Born 23 July 1772, at Sanbornton, Belknap Co., New Hampshire, the son of Josiah Miles and Marah Sanborn. Ordained a Seventy 6 Apr. 1837, by Hazen Aldrich; set apart as one of the First Seven Presidents 6 Apr. 1837, at the age of 64; died in fall of 1845, at Hancock Co., Illinois.

11. **Josiah Butterfield.**—Born 13 or 18 Mar. 1795, at Saco, Maine, the son of Abel Butterfield and Mary or Mercy .... Ordained a Seventy 6 Apr. 1837, under the hands of Sidney Rigdon and Hyrum Smith; set apart as one of the First Seven Presidents 6 Apr. 1837, at the age of 42; excommunicated 7 Oct. 1844; died at Monterey Co., California, Apr. 1871.

12. **Salmon Gee.**—Born 16 Oct. 1792, at Lyme, New London Co., Connecticut, the son of Zopher Gee and Esther Beckwith. Ordained a Seventy 6 Apr. 1837, under the hands of Sidney Rigdon and Hyrum Smith; set apart as one of the First Seven Presidents 6 Apr. 1837, at the age of 44; fellowship withdrawn 6 Mar. 1838; died 13 Sep. 1845, at Ambrosia, Lee Co., Iowa.

13. **John Gaylord.**—Born 12 July 1797, at Pennsylvania, the son of Chauncey Gaylord. Ordained a Seventy 20 Dec. 1836, by Hazen Aldrich; set apart as one of the First Seven Presidents 6 Apr. 1837,

at the age of 39; excommunicated 13 Jan. 1838; rejoined the Church at Nauvoo 5 Oct. 1839; died 17 July 1878.

14. **Henry Harriman.**—Born 9 June 1804, at Rowley, Essex Co., Massachusetts, the son of Enoch Harriman and Sarah Brocklebank. Ordained a Seventy March 1835, under the hands of Joseph Smith and Sidney Rigdon; set apart as one of the First Seven Presidents 6 Feb. 1838, at the age of 33; died 17 May 1891, at Huntington, Emery Co., Utah.

15. **Zera Pulsipher.**—Born 24 June 1789, at Rockingham, Windham Co., Vermont, the son of John Pulsipher and Elizabeth Dutton. Ordained a Seventy 6 Mar. 1838, under the hands of Joseph Young and James Foster; set apart as one of the First Seven Presidents 6 Mar. 1838, at the age of 48; released 12 Apr. 1862; died 1 Jan. 1872, at Hebron, Washington Co., Utah.

Roger Orton was excommunicated 30 Nov. 1837; returned to the Church; sustained as one of the First Seven Presidents 7 Apr. 1845, but was never set apart and did not function; dropped from this position 6 Oct. 1845.

16. **Albert Perry Rockwood.**—Born 5 June 1805, at Holliston, Middlesex Co., Massachusetts, the son of Luther Rockwood and Ruth Perry. Ordained a Seventy 5 Jan. 1839, under the hands of Joseph Young, Henry Harriman and Zera Pulsipher; set apart as one of the First Seven Presidents 2 Dec. 1845, at the age of 40; died 26 Nov. 1879. at Sugar House, Salt Lake Co., Utah.

17. **Benjamin Lynn Clapp.**—Born 19 Aug. 1814, at West Huntsville, Madison Co., Alabama, the son of Ludwig Lewis Clapp and Margaret Ann Loy. Ordained a Seventy 20 Oct. 1844, under the hands of Joseph Young and Levi W. Hancock; set apart as one of the First Seven Presidents 2 Dec. 1845, at the age of 31; excommunicated 7 Apr. 1859; died in 1860 in California.

18. **Jedediah Morgan Grant.**—Born 21 Feb. 1816, at Windsor, Broome Co., New York, the son of Joshua Grant and Athalia Howard. Ordained a Seventy 28 Feb. 1835, under the hands of Joseph Smith, Sidney Rigdon and Frederick G. Williams; set apart as one of the First Seven Presidents 2 Dec. 1845, at the age of 29; to 2nd Coun. 7 Apr. 1854. (See 2nd Coun. 5.)

19. **Horace Sunderlin Eldredge.**—Born 6 Feb. 1816, at Brutus, Cayuga Co., New York, the son of Alanson Eldredge and Esther Sunderlin. Ordained a Seventy 13 Oct. 1844, by Joseph Young; sustained as one of the First Seven Presidents 7 Oct. 1854, at the age of 38; died 6 Sep. 1888, at Salt Lake City, Salt Lake Co., Utah.

20. **Jacob Gates.**—Born 9 Mar. 1811, at Saint Johnsbury, Caledonia Co., Vermont, the son of Thomas Gates and Patty Plumley.

Ordained a Seventy 19 Dec. 1838, under the hands of Joseph Smith and Sidney Rigdon; sustained as one of the First Seven Presidents 8 Oct. 1862, at the age of 51; died 14 Apr. 1892, at Provo, Utah Co., Utah.

21. **John Van Cott.**—Born 7 Sep. 1814, at Canaan, Columbia Co., New York, the son of Losee Van Cott and Lovinia Pratt. Ordained a Seventy 25 Feb. 1847, by Joseph Young; sustained as one of the First Seven Presidents 8 Oct. 1862, at the age of 48; died 18 Feb. 1883, at Salt Lake City, Salt Lake Co., Utah.

22. **William Whittaker Taylor.**—Born 11 Sep. 1853, at Salt Lake City, Salt Lake Co., Utah, the son of John Taylor and Harriet Whittaker. Ordained a Seventy 11 Oct. 1875, by Orson Pratt; sustained as one of the First Seven Presidents 7 Apr. 1880, at the age of 26; died 1 Aug. 1884, at Salt Lake City, Salt Lake Co., Utah.

23. **Abraham Hoagland Cannon.**—Born 12 Mar. 1859, at Salt Lake City, Salt Lake Co., Utah, the son of George Quayle Cannon and Elizabeth Hoagland. Ordained a Seventy 9 Oct. 1882, by George Q. Cannon; sustained as one of the First Seven Presidents 8 Oct. 1882, at the age of 23; to Apostle 7 Oct. 1889. (See Apo. 37.)

Theodore Belden Lewis.—Born 18 Nov. 1843, at St. Louis, Missouri, the son of Thomas Anderson Lewis and Martha J. O. Belden. Ordained a High Priest at Nephi, Utah (date not known); sustained as one of the First Seven Presidents 8 Oct. 1882, at the age of 38; on 9 Oct. when he appeared to be set apart he reported that he was a High Priest, and so he was not set apart and did not function in this position. (Journal of Theodore Belden Lewis)

24. **Seymour Bicknell Young.**—Born 3 Oct. 1837, at Kirtland, Geauga Co., Ohio, the son of Joseph Young and Jane Adeline Bicknell. Ordained a Seventy 18 Feb. 1857, by Edmund Ellsworth; set apart as one of the First Seven Presidents 14 Oct. 1882, at the age of 45; sustained as one of the First Seven Presidents 8 Apr. 1883; died 15 Dec. 1924, at Salt Lake City, Salt Lake Co., Utah.

25. **Christian Daniel Fjeldsted.**—Born 20 Feb. 1829, at Amagar, Sundbyvester Co., Copenhagen, Denmark, the son of Hendrik Ludvig Fjeldsted and Ann Catrine Hendriksen. Ordained a Seventy 5 Feb. 1859, by William H. Walker; sustained as one of the First Seven Presidents 6 Apr. 1884, at the age of 55; died 23 Dec. 1905, at Salt Lake City, Salt Lake Co., Utah.

26. **John Morgan.**—Born 8 Aug. 1842, at Greensburg, Decatur Co., Indiana, the son of Gerrard Morgan and Ann Eliza Hamilton. Ordained a Seventy 8 Oct. 1875, by Joseph Young; sustained as one of the First Seven Presidents 5 Oct. 1884, at the age of 42; died 14 Aug. 1894, at Preston, Franklin Co., Idaho.

APPENDIX 609

27. **Brigham Henry Roberts.**—Born 13 Mar. 1857, at Warrington, Lancashire Co., England, the son of Benjamin Roberts and Ann Everington. Ordained a Seventy 8 Mar. 1877, by Nathan T. Porter. Sustained as one of the First Seven Presidents 7 Oct. 1888, at the age of 31; died 27 Sep. 1933, at Salt Lake City, Salt Lake Co., Utah.

28. **George Reynolds.**—Born 1 Jan. 1842, at Marylebone, London Co., London, England, the son of George Reynolds and Julia Ann Tautz. Ordained a Seventy 18 Mar. 1866, by Israel Barlow; sustained as one of the First Seven Presidents 5 Apr. 1890, at the age of 48; died 9 Aug. 1909, at Salt Lake City, Salt Lake Co., Utah.

29. **Jonathan Golden Kimball.**—Born 9 June 1853, at Salt Lake City, Salt Lake Co., Utah, the son of Heber Chase Kimball and Christeen Golden. Ordained a Seventy 21 July 1886, by William M. Allred; sustained as one of the First Seven Presidents 5 Apr. 1892, at the age of 38; killed in an automobile accident 2 Sep. 1938, near Reno, Nevada.

30. **Rulon Seymour Wells.**—Born 7 July 1854, at Salt Lake City, Salt Lake Co., Utah, the son of Daniel Hanmer Wells and Louisa Free. Ordained a Seventy 22 Oct. 1875, by Brigham Young; sustained as one of the First Seven Presidents 5 Apr. 1893, at the age of 38; died 7 May 1941, at Salt Lake City, Salt Lake Co., Utah.

31. **Edward Stevenson.**—Born 1 May 1820, at Gibraltar, Spain, the son of Joseph Stevenson and Elizabeth Stevens. Ordained a Seventy 1 May 1844, by Joseph Young; sustained as one of the First Seven Presidents 7 Oct. 1894, at the age of 74; died 27 Jan. 1897, at Salt Lake City, Salt Lake Co., Utah.

32. **Joseph William McMurrin.**—Born 5 Sep. 1858, at Tooele, Tooele Co., Utah, the son of Joseph McMurrin and Margaret Leaing. Ordained a Seventy 21 Apr. 1884, by Royal Barney; sustained as one of the First Seven Presidents 5 Oct. 1897, and set apart 21 Jan. 1898, at Liverpool, England, at the age of 39; died 24 Oct. 1932, at Los Angeles, Los Angeles Co., California.

33. **Charles Henry Hart.**—Born 5 July 1866, at Bloomington, Bear Lake Co., Idaho, the son of James Henry Hart and Sabina Scheib. Ordained a Seventy 10 Aug. 1890, by John Henry Smith; sustained as one of the First Seven Presidents 9 Apr. 1906, at the age of 39; died 29 Sep. 1934, at Salt Lake City, Salt Lake Co., Utah.

34. **Levi Edgar Young.**—Born 2 Feb. 1874, at Salt Lake City, Salt Lake Co., Utah, the son of Seymour Bicknell Young and Ann Elizabeth Riter. Ordained a Seventy 18 June 1897, by Seymour B. Young; sustained as one of the First Seven Presidents 6 Oct. 1909; set apart 23 Jan. 1910, at the age of 36; died 13 Dec. 1963, at Salt Lake City, Salt Lake Co., Utah.

35. **Rey Lucero Pratt.**—Born 11 Oct. 1878, at Salt Lake City, Salt Lake Co., Utah, the son of Helaman Pratt and Emeline Victoria Billingsley. Ordained a Seventy 23 Sep. 1911, by Rulon S. Wells; sustained as one of the First Seven Presidents 29 Jan. 1925, and set apart 7 Apr. 1925, at the age of 46; died 14 Apr. 1931, at Salt Lake City, Salt Lake Co., Utah.

36. **Antoine Ridgeway Ivins.**—Born 11 May 1881, at Saint George, Washington Co., Utah, the son of Anthony Woodward Ivins and Elizabeth A. Snow. Ordained a Seventy 28 Dec. 1913, by Fred E. Barker; sustained as one of the First Seven Presidents 4 Oct. 1931, at the age of 50; ordained a High Priest 11 June 1961, by David O. McKay; died 18 Oct. 1967, at Salt Lake City, Salt Lake Co., Utah.

37. **Samuel Otis Bennion.**—Born 9 June 1874, at Taylorsville, Salt Lake Co., Utah, the son of John Rowland Bennion and Emma Jane Terry. Ordained a Seventy 14 Mar. 1904, by Samuel Gerrard; sustained as one of the First Seven Presidents 6 Apr. 1933, at the age of 58; died 8 Mar. 1945, at Salt Lake City, Salt Lake Co., Utah.

38. **John Harris Taylor.**—Born 28 June 1875, at Salt Lake City, Salt Lake Co., Utah, the son of Thomas E. Taylor and Emma L. Harris. Ordained a Seventy 24 Jan. 1896, by Heber J. Grant; sustained as one of the First Seven Presidents 6 Oct. 1933, at the age of 58; died 28 May 1946, at Salt Lake City, Salt Lake Co., Utah.

39. **Rufus Kay Hardy.**—Born 28 May 1878, at Salt Lake City, Salt Lake Co., Utah, the son of Rufus H. Hardy and Annie Kay. Ordained a Seventy 2 July 1897, by John Henry Smith; sustained as one of the First Council of the Seventy 6 Oct. 1934, and set apart 7 Feb. 1935, at the age of 56; died 7 Mar. 1945, at Salt Lake City, Salt Lake Co., Utah.

40. **Richard Louis Evans.**—Born 23 Mar. 1906, at Salt Lake City, Salt Lake Co., Utah, the son of John A. Evans and Florence Neslen. Ordained a Seventy 5 Aug. 1938, by Rulon S. Wells; sustained as one of the First Council of the Seventy 7 Oct. 1938, at the age of 32; to Apostle 8 Oct. 1953. (See Apo. 71.)

41. **Oscar Ammon Kirkham.**—Born 22 Jan. 1880, at Lehi, Utah Co., Utah, the son of James Kirkham and Martha Mercer. Ordained a Seventy 26 Feb. 1906, by Joseph W. McMurrin; sustained as one of the First Council of the Seventy 5 Oct. 1941, at the age of 61; died 10 Mar. 1958, at Salt Lake City, Salt Lake Co., Utah.

42. **Seymour Dilworth Young.**—Born 7 Sep. 1897, at Salt Lake City, Salt Lake Co., Utah, the son of Seymour Bicknell Young, Jr. and Carlie Louine Clawson. Ordained a Seventy 9 Jan. 1920, by Seymour B. Young; sustained as one of the First Council of the Seventy 6 Apr. 1945, at the age of 47; ordained a High Priest 11 June 1961, by Henry D. Moyle.

43. **Milton Reed Hunter.**—Born 25 Oct. 1902, at Holden, Millard Co., Utah, the son of John E. Hunter and Margaret Teeples. Ordained a Seventy 31 Aug. 1928, by Rulon S. Wells; sustained as one of the First Council of the Seventy 6 Apr. 1945, at the age of 42; ordained a High Priest 11 June 1961, by David O. McKay.

44. **Bruce Redd McConkie.**—Born 29 July 1915, at Ann Arbor, Washtenaw Co., Michigan, the son of Oscar Walter McConkie and Margaret Vivian Redd. Ordained a Seventy 28 Feb. 1937, by Rufus K. Hardy; sustained as one of the First Council of the Seventy 6 Oct. 1946, at the age of 31; ordained a High Priest 11 June 1961, by Henry D. Moyle; ordained an Apostle 12 Oct. 1972, by Harold B. Lee. (See Apo. 80.)

45. **Marion Duff Hanks.**—Born 13 Oct. 1921, at Salt Lake City, Salt Lake Co., Utah, the son of Stanley Alonzo Hanks and Maude Frame. Ordained a Seventy 5 May 1944, by Antoine R. Ivins; sustained as one of the First Council of the Seventy 4 Oct. 1953, at the age of 32; ordained a High Priest 27 July 1961, by David O. McKay; to Asst. to Twelve Apostles 6 Apr. 1968. (See Asst. to Twelve 23.)

46. **Albert Theodore Tuttle.**—Born 2 Mar. 1919, at Manti, Sanpete Co., Utah, the son of Albert M. Tuttle and Clarice Beal. Ordained a Seventy 25 Sep. 1939, by Rulon S. Wells; sustained as one of the First Council of the Seventy 6 Apr. 1958, at the age of 39; ordained a High Priest 27 July 1961, by Henry D. Moyle.

47. **Paul Harold Dunn.**—Born 24 Apr. 1924, at Provo, Utah Co., Utah, the son of Joshua Harold Dunn and Geneve Roberts. Ordained a Seventy 15 Oct. 1950, by Levi Edgar Young; sustained as one of the First Council of the Seventy 6 Apr. 1964, at the age of 40; ordained a High Priest 9 Apr. 1964, by David O. McKay.

48. **Hartman Rector, Jr.**—Born 20 Aug. 1924, at Moberly, Randolph Co., Missouri, the son of Hartman Rector and Vivian Fay Garvin. Ordained a Seventy 19 May 1956, by George Q. Morris; sustained as one of the First Council of the Seventy 6 Apr. 1968, at the age of 43; ordained a High Priest 8 Apr. 1968, by Nathan Eldon Tanner.

49. **Loren Charles Dunn.**—Born 12 June 1930, at Tooele, Tooele Co., Utah, the son of Alex F. Dunn and Carol Horsfall. Ordained a Seventy 23 Aug. 1965, by John Longden; sustained as one of the First Council of the Seventy 6 Apr. 1968, at the age of 37; ordained a High Priest 8 Apr. 1968, by S. Dilworth Young.

50. **Rex Dee Pinegar.**—Born 18 Sep. 1931, at Orem, Utah, the son of John F. Pinegar and Grace Murl Ellis. Ordained a Seventy 28 Apr. 1957, by Marion D. Hanks; sustained as one of the First Council of the Seventy 6 Oct. 1972, at the age of 41.

PRESIDING BISHOPS

1. **Edward Partridge.**—Born 27 Aug. 1793, at Pittsfield, Berkshire

Co., Massachusetts, the son of William Partridge and Jemima Bidwell. Ordained a High Priest 6 June 1831, by Lyman Wight; called by revelation to be the First Bishop of the Church 4 Feb. 1831, at the age of 38; died 27 May 1840, at Nauvoo, Hancock Co., Illinois.

2. **Newel Kimball Whitney.**—Born 5 Feb. 1795, at Marlborough, Windham Co., Vermont, the son of Samuel Whitney and Susanna Kimball. Called by revelation to be the First Bishop of Kirtland; sustained as First Bishop in the Church 7 Oct. 1844, at the age of 49; sustained as Presiding Bishop of the Church 6 Apr. 1847; died 23 Sep. 1850, at Salt Lake City, Salt Lake Co., Utah.

George Miller.—Born 25 Nov. 1794, at County of Orange, Virginia, the son of John Miller and Margaret Pfeiffer. Sustained as Second Bishop of the Church 7 Oct. 1844, at the age of 49; dropped prior to 1847; disfellowshipped 20 Oct. 1848.

3. **Edward Hunter.**—Born 22 June 1793, at Newton, Delaware Co., Pennsylvania, the son of Edward Hunter and Hannah Maris. Ordained a High Priest 23 Nov. 1844, by Brigham Young; sustained as Presiding Bishop of the Church 7 Apr. 1851, at the age of 58; died 16 Oct. 1883, at Salt Lake City, Salt Lake Co., Utah.

4. **William Bowker Preston.**—Born 24 Nov. 1830, at Halifax, Franklin Co., Virginia, the son of Christopher Preston and Martha Mitchell Clayton. Ordained a High Priest 14 Nov. 1859, by Orson Hyde; sustained and set apart as Presiding Bishop of the Church 6 Apr. 1884, at the age of 53; released due to ill health 4 Dec. 1907; died 2 Aug. 1908, at Salt Lake City, Salt Lake Co., Utah.

5. **Charles Wilson Nibley.**—Born 5 Feb. 1849, at Hunterfield, Midlothian Co., Scotland, the son of James Nibley and Jane Wilson. Ordained a High Priest 9 June 1901, by Joseph F. Smith; sustained as Presiding Bishop of the Church 4 Dec. 1907 and ordained and set apart 11 Dec. 1907, at the age of 58, to 2nd Coun. to President Heber J. Grant 28 May 1925. (See 2nd Coun. 13.)

6. **Sylvester Quayle Cannon.**—Born 10 June 1877, at Salt Lake City, Salt Lake Co., Utah, the son of George Quayle Cannon and Martha Hoagland. Ordained a High Priest 24 Mar. 1904, by Rudger Clawson; sustained as Presiding Bishop of the Church 6 Oct. 1925, at the age of 48; sustained as Associate to the Quorum of the Twelve Apostles 6 Apr. 1938. (See Apo. 60.)

7. **LeGrand Richards.**—Born 6 Feb. 1886, at Farmington, Davis Co., Utah, the son of George Franklin Richards and Alice Almira Robinson. Ordained a High Priest 29 June 1919, by Charles W. Penrose; sustained as Presiding Bishop of the Church 6 Apr. 1938, at the age of 52; to Apostle 10 Apr. 1952. (See Apo. 69.)

APPENDIX 613

8. **Joseph Leopold Wirthlin.**—Sustained as Presiding Bishop of the Church 6 Apr. 1952, at the age of 58; released 30 Sep. 1961; died 25 Jan. 1963, at Salt Lake City, Salt Lake Co., Utah. (See also 1st Coun. Pres. Bp. 7, & 2nd Coun. Pres. Bp. 10.)

9. **John Henry Vandenberg.**—Born 18 Dec. 1904, at Ogden, Weber Co., Utah, the son of Dirk Vandenberg and Maria Alkema. Ordained a High Priest 26 June 1942, by Albert E. Bowen; sustained as Presiding Bishop of the Church 30 Sep. 1961, at the age of 56; sustained as Assistant to the Quorum of Twelve Apostles 6 Apr. 1972. (See also Asst. to Tw. 28.)

10. **Victor Lee Brown.**—Born 31 July 1914, at Cardston, Alberta, Canada, the son of Gerald Stephen Brown and Maggie Calder Lee. Ordained a High Priest 17 Jan. 1953, by ElRay L. Christiansen; sustained as Second Counselor to the Presiding Bishop 30 Sep. 1961; sustained as Presiding Bishop 6 Apr. 1972, at the age of 57. (See also 2nd Coun. Pres. Bp. 13.)

FIRST COUNSELORS TO PRESIDING BISHOPS

1. **Isaac Morley.**—Born 11 Mar. 1786, at Montague, Hampshire Co., Massachusetts, the son of Thomas Morley and Editha Marsh. Ordained a High Priest 3 June 1831, by Lyman Wight; set apart as First Counselor to the Presiding Bishop 6 June 1831, at the age of 45; released at the death of Bishop Edward Partridge 27 May 1840; died 24 June 1865, at Fairview, Utah.

2. **Leonard Wilford Hardy.**—Born 31 Dec. 1805, at Bradford, Essex Co., Massachusetts, the son of Simon Hardy and Rhoda Hardy. Ordained a High Priest 6 Apr. 1856, by John Taylor; sustained as First Counselor to the Presiding Bishop 6 Oct. 1856, at the age of 50; died 31 July 1884, at Salt Lake City, Salt Lake Co., Utah.

3. **Robert Taylor Burton.**—Sustained as First Counselor to the Presiding Bishop 5 Oct. 1884, at the age of 62; died 11 Nov. 1907, at Salt Lake City, Salt Lake Co., Utah. (See also 2nd Coun. Pres. Bp. 4.)

4. **Orrin Porter Miller.**—Sustained as First Counselor to the Presiding Bishop 4 Dec. 1907, at the age of 49; died 7 July 1918, at Salt Lake City, Salt Lake Co., Utah. (See also 2nd Coun. Pres. Bp. 7.)

5. **David Asael Smith**—Sustained as First Counselor to the Presiding Bishop 18 July 1918, at the age of 39; released 6 Apr. 1938; died 6 Apr. 1952, at Salt Lake City, Salt Lake Co., Utah. (See also 2nd Coun. Pres. Bp. 8.)

6. **Marvin Owen Ashton.**—Born 8 Apr. 1883, at Salt Lake City, Salt Lake Co., Utah, the son of Edward T. Ashton and Effie W. Morris. Ordained a High Priest 22 June 1917, by Heber J. Grant; sustained as First Counselor to the Presiding Bishop 6 Apr. 1938, at the age of 55; died 7 Oct. 1946, at Salt Lake City, Salt Lake Co., Utah.

7. **Joseph Leopold Wirthlin.**—Sustained as First Counselor to the Presiding Bishop 12 Dec. 1946, at the age of 53; to Pres. Bp. 6 Apr. 1952. (See Pres. Bp. 8. See also 2nd Coun. Pres. Bp. 10.)

8. **Henry Thorpe Beal Isaacson.**—Sustained as First Counselor to the Presiding Bishop 6 Apr. 1952, at the age of 53; to Asst. to Twelve 30 Sept. 1961. See Couns. 11; Asst. to Twelve 19; 2nd Coun. Pres. Bp. 11.)

9. **Robert Leatham Simpson.**—Born 8 Aug. 1915, at Salt Lake City, Salt Lake Co., Utah, the son of Heber Chase Simpson and Lillian Leatham. Ordained a High Priest 31 Mar. 1946, by Harold B. Lee; sustained as First Counselor to the Presiding Bishop 30 Sep. 1961, at the age of 46; sustained as Assistant to the Quorum of Twelve Apostles, 6 Apr. 1972. (See also Asst. to Tw. 29.)

10. **Harold Burke Peterson.**—Born 19 Sep. 1923, at Salt Lake City, Salt Lake Co., Utah, the son of Harold A. Peterson and Juna Tye. Ordained a High Priest 1 Dec. 1947, by Delbert L. Stapley; sustained as First Counselor to the Presiding Bishop 6 Apr. 1972, at the age of 48.

SECOND COUNSELORS TO PRESIDING BISHOPS

1. **John Corrill.**—Born 17 Sep. 1794, at Worcester Co., Mass. Ordained a High Priest 6 June 1831, by Edward Partridge; set apart as Second Counselor to the Presiding Bishop 6 June 1831, at the age of 36; released 1 Aug. 1837; excommunicated 17 Mar. 1839.

2. **Titus Billings.**—Born 25 Mar. 1793, at Greenfield, Franklin Co., Mass., the son of Ebenezer Billings and Esther Joyce. Ordained a High Priest 1 Aug. 1837, by Edward Partridge; set apart as Second Counselor to the Presiding Bishop 1 Aug. 1837, at the age of 44; released at the death of Bishop Edward Partridge 27 May 1840; died 6 Feb. 1866, at Provo, Utah Co., Utah.

3. **Jesse Carter Little.**—Born 26 Sep. 1815, at Belmont, Waldo Co., Maine, the son of Thomas Little and Relief White. Ordained a High Priest 17 Apr. 1845, by Parley P. Pratt; sustained as Second Counselor to the Presiding Bishop 6 Oct. 1856, at the age of 41; resigned summer of 1874; died 26 Dec. 1893, at Salt Lake City, Salt Lake Co., Utah.

4. **Robert Taylor Burton.**—Born 25 Oct. 1821, at Amherstburg, Essex Co., Ontario, Canada, the son of Samuel Burton and Hannah Shipley. Ordained a High Priest 2 Sep. 1875, by Edward Hunter; sustained as Second Counselor to the Presiding Bishop 9 Oct. 1874, at the age of 52; to 1st Coun. to Pres. Bp. 5 Oct. 1884. (See 1st Coun. Pres. Bp. 3.)

5. **John Quayle Cannon.**—Born 19 Apr. 1857, at San Francisco, San Francisco Co., California, the son of George Quayle Cannon and Elizabeth Hoagland. Ordained a High Priest October 1884, by John

APPENDIX

Taylor; sustained as Second Counselor to the Presiding Bishop 5 Oct. 1884, at the age of 27; excommunicated 5 Sep. 1886; died 14 Jan. 1931, at Salt Lake City, Salt Lake Co., Utah.

6. **John Rex Winder.**—Born 11 Dec. 1821, at Biddenden, Kent Co., England, the son of Richard Winder and Sophia Collins. Ordained a High Priest 4 Mar. 1872, by Edward Hunter; sustained as Second Counselor to the Presiding Bishop 8 Apr. 1887, at the age of 66; to 1st Coun. to President Joseph F. Smith 17 Oct. 1901. (See 1st Coun. 7.)

7. **Orrin Porter Miller.**—Born 11 Sep. 1858, at Mill Creek, Salt Lake Co., Utah, the son of Reuben G. Miller and Ann Craynor. Ordained a High Priest 8 Aug. 1886, by Angus M. Cannon; sustained as Second Counselor to the Presiding Bishop 24 Oct. 1901, at the age of 43; to 1st Coun. Pres. Bp. 4 Dec. 1907. (See 1st Coun. Pres. Bp. 4.)

8. **David Asael Smith.**—Born 24 May 1879, at Salt Lake City, Salt Lake Co., Utah, the son of Joseph Fielding Smith and Julina Lambson. Ordained a High Priest 11 Dec. 1907, by Anthon H. Lund; sustained as Second Counselor to the Presiding Bishop 4 Dec. 1907, at the age of 28; to 1st Coun. Pres. Bp. 18 July 1918. (See 1st Coun. Pres. Bp. 5.)

9. **John Wells.**—Born 16 Sep. 1864, at Carlton, Nottinghamshire, England, the son of Thomas Potter Wells and Sarah Cook. Ordained a High Priest 12 Feb. 1911, by Richard W. Young; sustained as Second Counselor to the Presiding Bishop 18 July 1918, at the age of 53; released 6 Apr. 1938; died 18 Apr. 1941, at Salt Lake City, Salt Lake Co., Utah.

10. **Joseph Leopold Wirthlin.**—Born 14 Aug. 1893, at Salt Lake City, Salt Lake Co., Utah, the son of Joseph Wirthlin and Emma Hillstead. Ordained a High Priest 24 Feb. 1926, by Charles W. Nibley; sustained as Second Counselor to the Presiding Bishop 6 Apr. 1938, at the age of 44; to 1st Coun. to the Pres. Bp. 12 Dec. 1943. (See 1st Coun. Pres. Bp. 7.)

11. **Henry Thorpe Beal Isaacson.**—Born 6 Sep. 1898, at Ephraim, Sanpete Co., Utah, the son of Martin Isaacson and Mary Jemima Beal. Ordained a High Priest 1 Oct. 1941, by Charles A. Callis; sustained as Second Counselor to the Presiding Bishop 12 Dec. 1946, at the age of 48; to 1st Coun. to the Pres. Bp. 6 Apr. 1952. (See Couns. 11; Asst. to Twelve 19; 1st Coun. Pres. Bp. 8.)

12. **Carl William Buehner.**—Born 27 Dec. 1898, at Stuttgart, Wuertemberg, Germany, the son of Carl F. Buehner and Anna B. Geigle. Ordained a High Priest 9 Dec. 1935, by Richard R. Lyman; sustained as Second Counselor to the Presiding Bishop 6 Apr. 1952, at the age of 54; released 30 Sep. 1961.

13. **Victor Lee Brown.**—Born 31 July 1914, at Cardston, Alberta,

Canada, the son of Gerald Stephen Brown and Maggie Calder Lee. Ordained a High Priest 17 Jan. 1953, by ElRay L. Christiansen; sustained as Second Counselor to the Presiding Bishop 30 Sep. 1961, at the age of 47; sustained as Presiding Bishop 6 Apr. 1972. (See also Pres. Bp. 10.)

14. **Vaughn J. Featherstone.**—Born 26 Mar. 1931, at Stockton, Utah, the son of Stephen E. Featherstone and Emma M. Johnson. Ordained a High Priest 27 Aug. 1961, by Joseph L. Wirthlin; sustained as Second Counselor to the Presiding Bishop 6 Apr. 1972, at the age of 41.

CHURCH RECORDERS AND HISTORIANS

1. **Oliver Cowdery.**—Sustained as Second Elder in the Church and as Church Recorder 6 Apr. 1830, at the age of 23; released 8 Mar. 1831, having been called to other duties. (See Asst. Pres. 1.)

2. **John Whitmer.**—Born 27 Aug. 1802, at Fayette, Seneca Co., New York, the son of Peter Whitmer and Mary Musselman. Called by revelation to be Church Recorder 8 Mar. 1831, at the age of 28; released 14 Sep. 1835, as he had removed to Missouri; excommunicated 10 Mar. 1838; died 11 July 1878, at Far West, Caldwell Co., Missouri.

3. **Oliver Cowdery.**—Appointed Church Recorder 14 Sep. 1835, at the age of 28; released as Church Recorder 17 Sep. 1837, as he had removed to Missouri. (See Asst. Pres. 1.)

4. **George W. Robinson.**—Born 14 May 1814, at Pawlet, Rutland Co., Vermont, the son of Ephraim Robinson and Mary Upham. Sustained as General Church Recorder 17 Sep. 1837, at the age of 23; released 3 Oct. 1840, as he intended to remove to Iowa.

5. **John Corrill.**—Sustained as Church Historian 6 Apr. 1838, at the age of 43, together with Elias Higbee; excommunicated 17 Mar. 1839. (See also 2nd Coun. Pres. Bp. 1.)

6. **Elias Higbee.**—Born 23 Oct. 1795, at Falloway, Gloucester Co., New Jersey, the son of Isaac Higbee and Sophia Somers. Sustained as Church Historian 6 Apr. 1838, at the age of 42, together with John Corrill; died 8 June 1843, at Nauvoo, Hancock Co., Illinois.

7. **Robert Blashel Thompson.**—Born 1 Oct. 1811, at Great Driffield, Yorkshire Co., England. Sustained as General Church Clerk 3 Oct. 1840, at the age of 29; died 27 Aug. 1841, at Nauvoo, Hancock Co., Illinois.

8. **James Sloan.**—Born 28 Oct. 1792, at Donighmore, Tyrone Co., Ireland, the son of Alexander Sloan and Anna .... Sustained as General Church Clerk 2 Oct. 1841, at the age of 49; released 30 July 1843, as he had left Nauvoo on a mission to Ireland.

9. **Willard Richards.**—Appointed Church Historian 21 Dec. 1842, by Joseph Smith, at the age of 38; sustained as General Church Recorder 30 July 1843, at the age of 39; sustained as Church Historian

APPENDIX

and General Church Recorder 6 Oct. 1845, at the age of 41; died 11 Mar. 1854, at Salt Lake City, Salt Lake Co., Utah. (See also Apo. 17.)

10. **George Albert Smith.**—Sustained as Church Historian and General Church Recorder 7 Apr. 1854, at the age of 37; released as Church Historian and General Church Recorder 8 Oct. 1870. (See also Apo. 16.)

11. **Albert Carrington.**—Sustained as Church Historian and General Church Recorder 8 Oct. 1870, at the age of 58; released as Church Historian and General Church Recorder 9 May 1874. (See also Apo. 28.)

12. **Orson Pratt.**—Sustained as Church Historian and General Church Recorder 9 May 1874, at the age of 63; died 3 Oct. 1881, at Salt Lake City, Salt Lake Co., Utah. (See also Apo. 10.)

13. **Wilford Woodruff.**—Sustained as Assistant Church Historian 6 Oct. 1856; sustained as Church Historian and General Church Recorder 7 Oct. 1883, at the age of 76; released 7 Apr. 1889, having been chosen President of the Church. (See also Apo. 15.)

14. **Franklin D. Richards.**—Sustained as Assistant Church Historian 6 Apr. 1884; sustained as Church Historian and General Church Recorder 7 Apr. 1889, at the age of 68; died 9 Dec. 1899, at Ogden, Weber Co., Utah. (See also Apo. 24.)

15. **Anthon Henrik Lund.**—Sustained as Church Historian and General Church Recorder 26 July 1900, at the age of 56; died Mar. 1921, at Salt Lake City, Salt Lake Co., Utah. (See also Apo. 36.)

16. **Joseph Fielding Smith.**—Born 19 July 1876, at Salt Lake City, Salt Lake Co., Utah, the son of Joseph Fielding Smith and Julina Lambson. Sustained as Assistant Church Historian 8 Apr. 1906; ordained an Apostle 7 April 1910, by Joseph F. Smith; sustained as Church Historian and General Church Recorder 17 Mar. 1921, at the age of 44; sustained as Counselor in the First Presidency 29 Oct. 1965; released 11 Feb. 1970, having been chosen President of the Church. (See also Pres. 10; Couns. 10; Apo. 49.)
age of 62. (See also Apo. 74.)

17. **Howard William Hunter.**—Born 14 Nov. 1907, at Boise, Ada Co., Idaho, the son of John William Hunter and Nellie Rasmussen. Ordained an Apostle 15 Oct. 1959, by David O. McKay; sustained as Church Historian and General Church Recorder 11 Feb. 1970, at the age of 62. Released 14 Jan. 1972. (See also Apo. 74.)

HISTORICAL DEPARTMENT OF THE CHURCH OF JESUS CHRIST
OF LATTER-DAY SAINTS

On January 14, 1972 the First Presidency announced the reorganization and change of name of the Church Historian's Office.

The name was changed to the Historical Department of The Church of Jesus Christ of Latter-day Saints. The organizational setup was changed and the position formerly held by the Church Historian and General Recorder was assigned to a Managing Director. The organization was broken down into three departments: (1) Church Archivist, (2) Church Historian, and (3) Church Librarian. On December 15, 1972 an assistant managing director was appointed.

MANAGING DIRECTOR:

Alvin Rulon Dyer.—Born 1 January 1903, at Salt Lake City, Salt Lake Co., Utah, the son of Alfred R. Dyer and Harriet Walsh. Appointed 14 January 1972 as Managing Director.

ASSOCIATE MANAGING DIRECTOR:

Joseph Anderson.—Born 20 November 1889, at Salt Lake City, Salt Lake Co., Utah, the son of George Anderson and Isabella Watson. Appointed 15 December 1972 as assistant managing director. Appointed Associate Managing Director 8 March 1974.

ASSISTANT MANAGING DIRECTOR:

Earl Eidswold Olson.—Born 17 May 1916, at Salt Lake City, Salt Lake Co., Utah, the son of Alvin Edward Olson and Eva Howell Jenson. Appointed Church Archivist 14 January 1972. Appointed Assistant Managing Director 8 March 1974.

CHURCH HISTORIAN:

Leonard James Arrington.—Born 2 July 1917, at Twin Falls, Idaho, the son of Noah Wesley Arrington and Edna Grace Corn. Appointed Church Historian on 14 January 1972.

CHURCH LIBRARIAN-ARCHIVIST:

Donald Thomas Schmidt.—Born 13 September 1919, at Brighton, Macoupin Co., Illinois, the son of Harvey Newton Schmidt and Helen Elizabeth Jacoby. Appointed Church Librarian 10 March 1972. Appointed Church Librarian-Archivist 8 March 1974.

STAKES OF ZION**
(In Chronological Order)

	NAME	ORGANIZED	PRESIDENT
1	Kirtland		
	*by 1838	Feb. 17, 1834	Joseph Smith, Jr.
2	Clay-Caldwell		
	*by 1846	July 3, 1834	David Whitmer
2	Adam-ondi-Ahman		
	*May 24, 1841	June 28, 1838	John Smith
3	Nauvoo		
	*by 1846	Oct. 5, 1839	William Marks
4	Iowa (Zarahemla)		
	*Jan. 6, 1842	Oct. 5, 1839	John Smith
5	Crooked Creek (Ramus)		
	*Dec. 4, 1841	4 July, 1840	
6	Lima		
	*by 1846	Oct. 22, 1840	Isaac Morley
7	Quincy		
	*by 1846	Oct. 25, 1840	Daniel Stanton
8	Mount Hope		
	*May 24, 1841	Oct. 27, 1840	Abel Lamb
9	Freedom		
	*by 1846	Oct. 27, 1840	Henry W. Miller
10	Geneva		
	*by 1846	Nov. 1, 1840	William Bosley
11	Springfield		
	*by 1846	Nov. 5, 1840	Edwin P. Merriam
1	Salt Lake	Oct. 3, 1847	John Smith
2	Weber	Jan. 26, 1851	Lorin Farr
3	Provo		
	(ch to Utah 1855)	Mar. 19, 1851	Isaac Higbee
4	San Bernardino		
	*by 1857	July 6, 1851	David Seely
5	Parowan	May 1852	John Calvin L. Smith
6	St. Louis		
	*by 1858	Nov. 4, 1854	Milo Andrus
7	Carson Valley		
	*by 1858	Oct. 4, 1856	Orson Hyde
5	Nephi		
	(ch to Juab 1871)	Sept. 20, 1868	Jacob G. Bigler
6	Millard	Mar. 9, 1869	Thomas Callister

*Discontinued
**Stakes are listed here by names under which they were created, for historic purposes. See page 641 for listing of name changes put into effect February 1, 1974.

NAME		ORGANIZED	PRESIDENT
7	Beaver	Mar. 12, 1869	John Murdock
8	Bear Lake	June 20, 1869	David P. Kimball
9	St. George	Nov. 7, 1869	Joseph W. Young
10	Sevier	May 24, 1874	Joseph A. Young
11	Kanab	April 18, 1877	L. John Nuttal
12	Panguitch	April 23, 1877	James Henrie
13	Cache	May 21, 1877	Moses Thatcher
14	Davis *June 20, 1915	June 17, 1877	William R. Smith
15	Tooele	June 24, 1877	Francis M. Lyman
16	Morgan	July 1, 1877	Willard G. Smith
17	Sanpete *Dec. 9, 1900	July 4, 1877	Canute Peterson
18	Summit	July 9, 1877	William W. Cluff
19	Wasatch	July 15, 1877	Abram Hatch
20	Box Elder *Nov. 12, 1944	Aug. 19, 1877	Oliver G. Snow
21	Little Colorado *Dec. 18, 1887	Jan. 27, 1878	Lot Smith
22	Eastern Arizona *Dec. 18, 1887	June 29, 1879	Jesse N. Smith
23	Emery	Aug. 1880	Christen D. Larsen
24	Maricopa	Dec. 10, 1882	Alex F. McDonald
25	St. Joseph	Feb. 25, 1883	Christopher Layton
26	San Luis	June 10, 1883	Silas S. Smith
27	San Juan	Sept. 23, 1883	Platte D. Lyman
28	Bannock (ch to Fremont Aug. 6, 1898; ch to Rexburg June 23, 1935)	Feb. 4, 1884	Thomas E. Ricks
29	Oneida	June 1, 1884	William D. Henricks
30	Uintah	July 11, 1886	Samuel R. Bennion
31	St. Johns	July 23, 1887	David K. Udall
32	Cassia	Nov. 19, 1887	Horton D. Haight
31	Snowflake	Dec. 18, 1887	Jesse N. Smith
32	Malad	Feb. 12, 1888	Oliver C. Hoskins
33	Star-Valley	Aug. 14, 1892	George Osmond
34	Wayne	May 27, 1893	Willis E. Robison
35	Alberta	June 9, 1895	Charles O. Card

*Discontinued

APPENDIX 621

	NAME	ORGANIZED	PRESIDENT
36	Bingham (ch to Idaho Falls Aug. 16, 1925)	June 9, 1895	James E. Steele
37	Juarez	Dec. 9, 1895	Anthony W. Ivins
38	Woodruff	June 5, 1898	John M. Baxter
39	Bannock (new)	July 25, 1898	Lewis S. Pond
40	Pocatello (ch to East Pocatello April 19, 1959) (ch to Pocatello East 29 May 1970)	Aug. 7, 1898	William C. Parkinson
41	Jordan *May 8, 1927	Jan. 21, 1900	Orrin P. Miller
42	Granite	Jan. 17, 1900	Frank Y. Taylor
	*Sanpete 9 Dec, 1900		
42	North Sanpete (ch to Sanpete North 29 May 1970)	Dec. 9, 1900	Christian N. Lund
43	South Sanpete (ch to Sanpete South 29 May 1970)	Dec. 9, 1900	Canute Peterson
44	Alpine	Jan. 13, 1901	Stephen L. Chipman
45	Nebo	Jan. 13, 1901	Jonathan S. Page, Jr.
46	Hyrum	April 30, 1901	William C. Parkinson
47	Benson	May 1, 1901	William H. Lewis
48	Big Horn	May 26, 1901	Byron Sessions
49	Union	June 9, 1901	Franklin S. Bramwell
50	Teton	Sept. 2, 1901	Don Carlos Driggs
51	Taylor	Aug. 30, 1903	Heber S. Allen
52	Blackfoot	Jan. 31, 1904	Elias S. Kimball
53	Liberty	Feb. 26, 1904	Hugh J. Cannon
54	Pioneer	Mar. 24, 1904	William McLachlin
55	Ensign	April 1, 1904	Richard W. Young
56	Rigby	Feb. 3, 1908	Don C. Walker
57	Ogden	July 26, 1908	Thomas B. Evans
58	North Weber (ch to Weber North 29 May 1970)	Aug. 2, 1908	James Wotherspoon
59	Bear River	Oct. 11, 1908	Milton H. Welling
60	Yellowstone	Jan. 10, 1909	Daniel G. Miller
61	Carbon	May 8, 1910	Gustave A. Iverson
62	Duchesne	Sept. 14, 1910	William H. Smart

*Discontinued

NAME	ORGANIZED	PRESIDENT
63 Young	May 21, 1912	David Halls
64 Moapa	June 9, 1912	Willard L. Jones
65 Deseret	Aug. 11, 1912	Alonzo A. Hinckley
66 Boise	Nov. 3, 1913	Heber Q. Hale
67 Shelley	Aug. 16, 1914	Joseph H. Dye
68 Cottonwood (ch to Mill Creek Feb. 11, 1951)	Nov. 29, 1914	Uriah G. Miller
69 Raft River (ch to Cassia East 15 Jun. 1969)	April 27, 1915	John A. Elison
70 Curlew *Feb. 11, 1940 *Davis June 1915	May 17, 1915	Jonathan C. Cutler
70 North Davis (ch to Davis North 29 May 1970)	June 20, 1915	Henry H. Blood
71 South Davis (ch to Davis South 29 May 1970)	June 20, 1915	James H. Robinson
72 Portneuf	Aug. 14, 1915	George T. Hyde
73 Idaho	Nov. 19, 1916	Nelson J. Hogan
74 Tintic (ch to Santaquin-Tintic April 2, 1939)	April 22, 1917	E. Franklin Birch
75 Montpelier	Dec. 23, 1917	Edward C. Rich
76 Twin Falls	July 26, 1919	L. G. Kirkman
77 Burley	July 27, 1919	David R. Langlois
78 Blaine	Aug. 3, 1919	William Lenox Adams
79 Lost River	Aug. 18, 1919	William N. Patten
80 Logan	June 4, 1920	Oliver H. Budge
81 Franklin	June 6, 1920	Samuel W. Parkinson
82 Roosevelt	June 26, 1920	William H. Smart
83 Garfield	Aug. 29, 1920	Charles E. Rowan, Jr.
84 North Sevier (ch to Sevier North 29 May 1970)	Jan. 30, 1921	Moroni Lazenby
85 South Sevier (ch to Sevier South 29 May 1970)	Jan. 30, 1921	John E. Magleby

*Discontinued

NAME	ORGANIZED	PRESIDENT
86 Lethbridge (ch to Calgary Nov. 15, 1953)	Nov. 10, 1921	Hugh B. Brown
87 Mount Ogden	May 21, 1922	Robert I. Burton
88 Los Angeles (ch to South Los Angeles 19 Nov. 1939; ch to Los Angeles South 29 May 1970) *Aug. 12, 1973	Jan. 21, 1923	George W. McCune
89 Gunnison	May 6, 1923	Allen E. Park
90 Oquirrh	June 3, 1923	George A. Little
91 Minidoka	May 11, 1924	Richard C. May
92 Grant	May 25, 1924	Joseph J. Daynes
93 Kolob	Nov. 23, 1924	George R. Maycock
94 Palmyra	Nov. 23, 1924	Henry A. Gardner
95 Lyman	July 18, 1926	H. Melvin Rollins
96 Nevada *Jordan 8 May 1927	Sept. 19, 1926	Carl K. Conrad
96 East Jordan (ch to Jordan East 29 May 1970; to Fort Union June 17, 1973)	May 8, 1927	Heber J. Burgon
97 West Jordan	May 8, 1927	Joseph M. Holt
98 Hollywood (ch to Los Angeles Nov. 19, 1939)	May 22, 1927	George W. McCune
99 San Francisco	July 10, 1927	W. Aird Macdonald
100 Lehi	July 1, 1928	Anchor C. Schow
101 Timpanogos	July 1, 1928	Wilford W. Warnick
102 Moroni	June 16, 1929	James Louis Nielsen
103 Sharon	Sept. 15, 1929	Arthur V. Watkins
104 Zion Park	Dec. 8, 1929	Claudius Hirschi
105 Wells	Dec. 31, 1933	Thomas E. Towler
106 South Summit (ch to Summit South 29 May 1970)	July 8, 1934	Zach J. Oblad
107 Gridley	Nov. 4, 1934	John C. Todd
108 Sacramento	Nov. 4, 1934	Mark W. Cram
109 Oakland *Aug. 26, 1956	Dec. 2, 1934	W. Aird Macdonald
110 New York	Dec. 9, 1934	Fred G. Taylor

*Discontinued

	NAME	ORGANIZED	PRESIDENT
111	San Bernardino (new)	Feb. 3, 1935	A. Lyndon Larson
112	North Idaho Falls (ch to Idaho Falls North 29 May 1970)	May 12, 1935	David Smith
113	Oahu	June 30, 1935	Ralph E. Woolley
114	Highland	Sept. 8, 1935	Marvin O. Ashton
115	Bonneville	Oct. 27, 1935	Joseph L. Wirthlin
116	Pasadena (ch to San Fernando Oct. 15, 1939)	April 19, 1936	Wilford G. Edling
117	Long Beach	May 3, 1936	John W. Jones
118	Chicago	Nov. 29, 1936	William A. Matheson
119	Smithfield	Jan. 9, 1938	Alfred W. Chambers
120	Mount Graham	Feb. 20, 1938	Spencer W. Kimball
121	Phoenix	Feb. 27, 1938	James Robert Price
122	Moon Lake *Nov. 10, 1957	April 24, 1938	Edwin L. Murphy
123	Portland	June 26, 1938	Monte L. Bean
124	Seattle	July 31, 1938	Alex Brown
125	Nampa	Nov. 27, 1938	Peter E. Johnson
126	Weiser	Nov. 27, 1938	Scott B. Brown
127	Provo	Feb. 19, 1939	Charles E. Rowan, Jr.
128	Pasadena (new)	Oct. 1, 1939	Bertram M. Jones
129	Inglewood *Curlew 11 Feb. 1940	Nov. 26, 1939	Alfred E. Rohner
129	Emigration	Mar. 10, 1940	George A. Christensen
130	Riverside	Mar. 24, 1940	John B. Matheson
131	Washington	June 30, 1940	Ezra T. Benson
132	Denver	June 30, 1940	Douglas M. Todd, Jr.
133	Big Cottonwood (ch to Cottonwood Feb. 11, 1951)	Oct. 20, 1940	Irvin T. Nelson
134	Uvada	Dec. 15, 1940	David J. Ronnow
135	Reno	Feb. 9, 1941	Nathan T. Hurst
136	San Diego	Feb. 9, 1941	Wallace W. Johnson
137	Southern Arizona (ch to Arizona South 29 May 1970)	Mar. 2, 1941	A. B. Ballantyne
138	South Salt Lake	Sept. 2, 1941	Axel J. Andresen
139	South Ogden	Dec. 7, 1941	William J. Critchlow, Jr.

*Discontinued.

APPENDIX

	NAME	ORGANIZED	PRESIDENT
140	Farr West	Jan. 18, 1942	Wilmer J. Maw
141	Lakeview	Mar. 22, 1942	John Child
142	Mount Jordan	May 3, 1942	Stanley A. Rasmussen
143	Humboldt	May 31, 1942	Rodney S. Williams
144	Sugarhouse	May 16, 1943	Thomas M. Wheeler
145	Park	Oct. 24, 1943	J. Percy Goddard
146	Ben Lomond	Nov. 21, 1943	William Arthur Budge
147	Grantsville *Box Elder 12 Nov. 1944	Jan. 16, 1944	Paul E. Wrathall
147	North Box Elder (ch to Box Elder North 29 May 1970)	Nov. 12, 1944	John P. Lillywhite
148	South Box Elder (ch to Box Elder Aug. 30, 1959)	Nov. 12, 1944	Abel S. Rich
149	West Pocatello (ch to Pocatello West 29 May 1970)	May 6, 1945	Twayne Austin
150	East Mill Creek	June 17, 1945	L. B. Gunderson
151	North Carbon (ch to Carbon North 29 May 1970)	June 24, 1945	Cecil Broadbent
152	Davis (new)	Oct. 14, 1945	Leroy H. Duncan
153	North Rexburg (ch to Rexburg North 29 May 1970)	Oct. 28, 1945	Orval O. Mortensen
154	Hillside	Jan. 13, 1946	Casper Hugh Parker
155	Temple (ch to Temple View April 14, 1946)	Jan. 13, 1946	Adiel F. Stewart
156	Palo Alto	June 23, 1946	Claude B. Petersen
157	South Idaho Falls (ch to Idaho Falls South 29 May 1970)	June 30, 1946	Cecil E. Hart
158	East Rigby (ch to Rigby East 29 May 1970)	July 7, 1946	James E. Ririe
159	Berkeley *Aug. 26, 1956	Oct. 13, 1946	W. Glenn Harmon

*Discontinued.

NAME	ORGANIZED	PRESIDENT
160 Mount Logan	Nov. 17, 1946	A. George Raymond
161 Mesa	Dec. 8, 1946	L. M. Mecham, Jr.
162 North Jordan (ch to Jordan North 29 May 1970)	Jan. 12, 1947	John B. Hill
163 Florida	Jan. 19, 1947	Alvin C. Chace
164 East Cache (ch to Cache East 29 May 1970)	Feb. 2, 1947	J. Howard Maughan
165 East Provo (ch to Provo East 29 May 1970)	April 13, 1947	Charles E. Rowan
166 Orem	April 13, 1947	Walter R. Holdaway
167 West Utah (ch to Utah West 29 May 1970)	May 4, 1947	J. Earl Lewis
168 Spokane	June 29, 1947	Albert I. Morgan
169 South Carolina	Oct. 19, 1947	W. Wallace McBride
170 American Falls	Feb. 1, 1948	George R. Woolley
171 San Joaquin	April 25, 1948	Wendell B. Mendenhall
172 Cedar	May 2, 1948	David L. Sargent
173 South Bear River (ch to Bear River South 29 May 1970)	May 1, 1949	Clifton G. M. Kerr
174 East Riverside *Oct. 9, 1955	May 22, 1949	Thaddeus M. Evans
175 Glendale	Dec. 4, 1949	Edwin Smith Dibble
176 Nyssa	Jan. 8, 1950	Arvel L. Child
177 East Long Beach (ch to Long Beach East 29 May 1970)	Feb. 12, 1950	John C. Dalton
178 University (ch to University 1st April 30, 1967)	Feb. 12, 1950	J. Quayle Ward
179 East Los Angeles (ch to Los Angeles East 29 May 1970)	Feb. 26, 1950	Fauntleroy Hunsaker
180 Richland	June 25, 1950	James V. Thompson
181 Santa Rosa	Jan. 7, 1951	J. LeRoy Murdock

*Discontinued

APPENDIX

	NAME	ORGANIZED	PRESIDENT
182	Wilford	Feb. 11, 1951	George Z. Aposhian
183	Murray	Feb. 11, 1951	Oral J. Wilkinson
184	Santa Barbara	Mar. 18, 1951	Arthur J. Godfrey
185	Fresno	May 20, 1951	Alwyn C. Sessions
186	Bakersfield	May 27, 1951	E. Alan Pettit
187	Monument Park	June 24, 1951	George L. Nelson
188	Santa Monica	July 1, 1951	E. Garrett Barlow
189	East Lethbridge (ch to Lethbridge Nov. 15, 1953)	Oct. 28, 1951	Grant Goddard Woolley
190	Columbia River	Dec. 2, 1951	Royal Spencer Papworth
191	Willamette	Dec. 2, 1951	Ralph B. Lake
192	Gooding	Mar. 9, 1952	Ross C. Lee
193	Bountiful	Mar. 23, 1952	Thomas Amby Briggs
194	El Paso	Sept. 21, 1952	Edward V. Turley, Sr.
195	Tacoma	Sept. 28, 1952	Elvin E. Evans
196	Mount Rubidoux	Oct. 26, 1952	Vern Robert Peel
197	Detroit	Nov. 9, 1952	George W. Romney
198	Lorin Farr	Nov. 16, 1952	Elton William Wardle
199	East Sharon (ch to Sharon East 29 May 1970)	Nov. 23, 1952	Henry D. Taylor
200	East Ogden (ch to Ogden East 29 May 1970)	Nov. 23, 1952	Scott B. Price
201	Riverdale	Nov. 30, 1952	Rudolph L. Van Kampen
202	San Jose	Nov. 30, 1952	Vernard L. Beckstrand
203	Layton	Jan. 25, 1953	I. Haven Barlow
204	Cannon	Mar. 1, 1953	Fred H. Peck
205	Klamath	Mar. 22, 1953	Carroll William Smith
206	North Tooele (ch to Tooele North 29 May 1970)	Mar. 29, 1953	Orland Tolman Barrus
207	North Pocatello (ch to Pocatello North 29 May 1970)	June 21, 1953	Jared O. Anderson
208	Butte	June 28, 1953	Edgar T. Henderson
209	Houston	Oct. 11, 1953	Jack Byron Trunnell
210	Dallas	Oct. 18, 1953	Ervin W. Atkerson

	NAME	ORGANIZED	PRESIDENT
211	Salmon River	Oct. 18, 1953	Earl Stokes
212	East Phoenix (ch to Phoenix East 29 May 1970)	Feb. 28, 1954	Junius E. Driggs
213	Grand Coulee	April 18, 1954	Elmo J. Bergeson
214	South Blackfoot (ch to Blackfoot South 1 Mar 1970)	June 20, 1954	Lawrence T. Lambert
215	Orange County (ch to Fullerton Mar. 14, 1965)	June 27, 1954	John C. Dalton
216	Las Vegas	Oct. 10, 1954	Thomas Gay Meyers
217	Taylorsville	Oct. 10, 1954	Wayne Charles Player
218	West Boise (ch to Boise West 29 May 1970)	Nov. 7, 1954	David Keith Ricks
219	North Sacramento (ch. to Sacramento North 30 Sept. 1969)	Dec. 12, 1954	Austin G. Hunt
220	Redondo	May 29, 1955	Leslie Lloyd Prestwich
221	New Orleans	June 19, 1955	Clive M. Larson
222	Honolulu °East Riverside 9 Oct. 1955	Aug. 28, 1955	J. A. Quealy, Jr.
222	Rose Park	Oct. 9, 1955	Joseph F. Steenblik
223	Grand Junction	Oct. 16, 1955	Loyal B. Cook
224	East Mesa (ch to Mesa East 29 May 1970)	Nov. 20, 1955	Donald Ellsworth
225	Brigham Young University	Jan. 8, 1956	Antone K. Romney
226	Covina	Feb. 26, 1956	Elden L. Ord
227	Holladay	Mar. 18, 1956	G. Carlos Smith, Jr.
228	Lake Mead	Aug. 19, 1956	James I. Gibson
227	Oakland-Berkeley	Aug. 26, 1956	O. Leslie Stone
228	Hayward °Berkeley 26 Aug. 1956 °Oakland 26 Aug. 1956	Aug. 26, 1956	Milton P. Ream
229	Walnut Creek	Aug. 26, 1956	Emery R. Ranker

APPENDIX

	NAME	ORGANIZED	PRESIDENT
230	Reseda	Sept. 16, 1956	Hugh C. Smith
231	Burbank	Sept. 16, 1956	James D. Pratt
232	Flagstaff	Sept. 23, 1956	Burton R. Smith
233	Spanish Fork	Sept. 30, 1956	Joseph Y. Toronto
234	Kansas City	Oct. 21, 1956	Martin V. Witbeck
235	Springville	Oct. 21, 1956	Leo A. Crandall
236	Valley View	Oct. 28, 1956	Lamont B. Gundersen
237	Canyon Rim	Oct. 28, 1956	Verl F. Scott
238	Tucson	Dec. 2, 1956	Leslie O. Brewer
239	Ashley	Dec. 2, 1956	William Budge Wallis
240	Murray South	April 28, 1957	Donald William Challis
241	Atlanta	May 5, 1957	William L. Nicholls
242	North Seattle (ch to Seattle North 29 May 1970)	May 19, 1957	Wilford H. Payne
243	Missoula	June 16, 1957	Grant K. Patten
244	Great Falls	June 16, 1957	Victor Bowen
245	Virginia	June 30, 1957	Cashell Donahoe, Sr.
246	Midvale	June 30, 1957	Reed H. Beckstead
247	San Mateo	Sept. 15, 1957	Melvin P. Pickering
248	San Luis Obispo	Sept. 22, 1957	Arthur J. Godfrey
249	Monument Park West	Sept. 29, 1957	Frank Carl Berg
250	Albuquerque	Oct. 27, 1957	William J. Wilson
251	Orem West *Moon Lake 10 Nov. 1957	Nov. 3, 1957	Edward Carlyle Bunker
251	Santa Ana	Dec. 8, 1957	Karl C. Durham
252	San Antonio	Jan. 19, 1958	Roland C. Bremer
253	Phoenix North	Jan. 19, 1958	Rudger G. Smith
254	Shreveport	Jan. 26, 1958	J. Milton Belisle
255	Kearns	Feb. 2, 1958	Merrill A. Nelson
256	Kearns North	Feb. 2, 1958	Volma W. Heaton
257	Orlando	Feb. 23, 1958	W. Leonard Duggar
258	Monterey Bay	Mar. 2, 1958	James N. Wallace, Jr.
259	Utah State University	April 13, 1958	Reed Bullen
260	Bountiful North	April 20, 1958	Henry E. Peterson
261	San Diego East	April 20, 1958	Cecil I. Burningham
262	Bountiful South	April 20, 1958	Ward C. Holbrook
263	Yuma	April 27, 1958	Marion Turley
264	Auckland	May 18, 1958	George R. Biesinger
265	St. Louis (new)	June 1, 1958	Roy N. Oscarson

	NAME	ORGANIZED	PRESIDENT
266	Granger	June 8, 1958	William Grant Bangerter
267	Olympus	June 29, 1958	Heber E. Peterson
268	Lewiston	Oct. 19, 1958	Golden Romney
269	Norwalk	Oct. 26, 1958	Lewis Milton Jones
270	Cincinnati	Nov. 23, 1958	Thomas Blair Evans
271	West Sharon (ch to Sharon West 29 May 1970)	Nov. 30, 1958	Clyde M. Lunceford
272	Weber Heights	Nov. 30, 1958	Keith W. Wilcox
273	Parleys	Dec. 7, 1958	Walter J. Eldredge, Jr.
274	Winder	Jan. 25, 1959	M. Elmer Christensen
275	Granite Park	Feb. 22, 1959	Rolf Christiansen
276	Sandy	April 12, 1959	Stanley A. Rasmussen
277	Clearfield	April 12, 1959	George Smith Haslam
278	Pocatello (new)	April 19, 1959	Roland K. Hart
279	Huntington Park	April 19, 1959	Clifford B. Wright
280	Whittier	April 26, 1959	John Collings
281	West Covina	May 3, 1959	Mark W. Smith
282	Torrance	May 3, 1959	Roland Earl Gagon
283	Indianapolis	May 17, 1959	Phillip F. Low
284	Yakima	May 24, 1959	F. Edgar Johnson
285	East Idaho Falls (ch to Idaho Falls East 29 May 1970)	June 7, 1959	Charles P. Birzee
286	Cheyenne	June 21, 1959	Archie R. Boyack
287	Denver West	June 21, 1959	Thomas L. Kimball
288	Mojave	Aug. 16, 1959	Sterling Arthur Johnson
289	Tampa	Oct. 25, 1959	Edwin H. White
290	American River	Dec. 6, 1959	Austin G. Hunt
291	University West	Feb. 7, 1960	Lemonte Peterson
292	New Jersey	Feb. 28, 1960	George H. Mortimer
293	Sydney	Mar. 27, 1960	Dell C. Hunt
294	Manchester	Mar. 27, 1960	Robert G. Larson
295	Brigham Young University 2nd	April 17, 1960	Bryan W. Belnap
296	Brigham Young University 3rd	April 17, 1960	William Noble Waite
297	Napa	April 17, 1960	Harry S. Cargun
298	Tulsa	May 1, 1960	Robert N. Sears

APPENDIX

	NAME	ORGANIZED	PRESIDENT
299	Puget Sound	June 19, 1960	Herbert S. Anderson
300	Toronto	Aug. 14, 1960	William M. Davies
301	Pikes Peak	Sept. 11, 1960	Ralph M. Gardner
302	Taber	Sept. 11, 1960	Ray B. Evenson
303	Riverton	Sept. 18, 1960	J. Harold Berrett
304	Philadelphia	Oct. 16, 1960	Bryant F. West
305	Oklahoma	Oct. 23, 1960	James A. Cullimore
306	Brisbane	Oct. 23, 1960	William E. Waters
307	Melbourne	Oct. 30, 1960	Boyd C. Bott
308	Las Vegas North	Nov. 6, 1960	William L. Taylor
309	Palomar	Nov. 6, 1960	Wallace F. Gray
310	Hamilton	Nov. 13, 1960	Wendell H. Wiser
311	Miami	Nov. 13, 1960	Paul R. Chessman
312	Edmonton	Nov. 15, 1960	Leroy Rollins
313	Hawkes Bay	Nov. 20, 1960	Joseph Alvin Higbee
314	Ben Lomond South	Nov. 20, 1960	Robert Milton Yorgason
315	Vancouver	Nov. 21, 1960	Ernest E. Jensen
316	Cedar West	Nov. 27, 1960	Franklin D. Day
317	Minnesota	Nov. 29, 1960	Delbert F. Wright
318	Winter Quarters	Dec. 11, 1960	William D. Hardy
319	Redding	Dec. 13, 1960	Albert C. Peterson
320	Craig	Jan. 15, 1961	Loyal B. Cook
321	Salem	Jan. 22, 1961	Hugh F. Webb
322	St. George East	Feb. 5, 1961	Rudger C. Atkin
323	London	Feb. 26, 1961	Donald W. Hemingway
324	Granger North	Feb. 26, 1961	Franklin J. Kennard
325	Leicester	Mar. 5, 1961	Derek Alfred Cuthbert
326	Holland	Mar. 12, 1961	Johan Paul Jongkees
327	Leeds	Mar. 19, 1961	Dennis Liversey
328	Roy	Mar. 26, 1961	Henry Adolph Matis
329	San Leandro	May 21, 1961	Milton R. Ream
330	Garden Grove	June 25, 1961	James Malan Hobbs
331	Alaska	Aug. 13, 1961	Orson P. Millet
332	North Carolina	Aug. 27, 1961	Cecil E. Reese
333	Beaumont	Sept. 3, 1961	Alden S. Stout
334	Berlin	Sept. 10, 1961	Rudi Seehagen
335	Greensboro	Sept. 13, 1961	Eugene A. Gulledge
336	Cleveland	Sept. 20, 1961	E. Doyle Robison
337	Canoga Park	Oct. 8, 1961	Collins E. Jones

	NAME	ORGANIZED	PRESIDENT
338	Reno North	Oct. 22, 1961	Vern Waldo
339	Redwood	Oct. 22, 1961	David DeBar Felshaw
340	Stuttgart	Oct. 26, 1961	Hermann Moessner
341	Swiss	Oct. 28, 1961	Wilhelm Friedrich Lauener
342	Hamburg	Nov. 12, 1961	Michael Panitsch
343	Ammon	Nov. 26, 1961	Harold W. Davis
344	Mexico	Dec. 3, 1961	Harold Brown
345	South Cottonwood	Dec. 10, 1961	James S. McCloy
346	Cumorah	Jan. 21, 1962	Bryant W. Rossiter
347	Pomona	Jan. 21, 1962	Vern R. Peel
348	Pearl Harbor	Feb. 4, 1962	George Q. Cannon
349	Lansing	Feb. 18, 1962	Sylvan H. Wittwer
350	Kaysville	Feb. 18, 1962	Alan B. Blood
351	Columbus	Feb. 25, 1962	James L. Mortensen
352	Fort Wayne	Mar. 4, 1962	Howard W. Thompson
353	Apia	Mar. 18, 1962	Percy John Rivers
354	Boston	May 20, 1962	Wilbur W. Cox
355	Wichita	June 24, 1962	Lee R. Meador
356	Glasgow	Aug. 26, 1962	Archibald R. Richardson
357	Casper	Oct. 14, 1962	W. Reed Green
358	Wind River	Oct. 14, 1962	J. Rex Kocherhans
359	Coeur d'Alene	Oct. 14, 1962	Gerald E. Browning
360	San Diego South	Oct. 21, 1962	Cecil Ivan Burningham
361	Butler	Nov. 18, 1962	James C. Taylor
362	Mesa South	Nov. 18, 1962	Stanley F. Turley
363	Raleigh	Dec. 9, 1962	William Victor Bartholomew
364	Scottsdale	Dec. 9, 1962	Junius E. Driggs
365	Sandy East	Jan. 13, 1963	Orren J. Greenwood
366	South Carolina West (ch to Greenville 19 Nov. 1972)	Jan. 27, 1963	Ivan A. Larsen
367	Milwaukee	Feb. 3, 1963	DeWitt C. Smith
368	Chicago South	Feb. 3, 1963	Lysle R. Cahoon
369	Billings	Feb. 10, 1963	Howard C. Anderson
370	Illinois	Feb. 17, 1963	Ross A. Kelley
371	Washington Terrace	Feb. 24, 1963	Ernest B. Wheeler
372	Potomac	Mar. 3, 1963	Miller F. Shurtleff
373	Macon	Mar. 10, 1963	Rayford L. Henderson
374	Sunderland	Mar. 17, 1963	Fred W. Oates

APPENDIX

	NAME	ORGANIZED	PRESIDENT
375	South Box Elder (ch to Box Elder South 29 May 1970)	April 28, 1963	LeGrande Tea
376	American Fork	May 12, 1963	Stanley D. Roberts
377	Alameda	May 12, 1963	Homer S. Satterfield
378	Concord	June 23, 1963	Ted Eugene Madsen
379	Cascade	June 30, 1963	Robert E. Jones
380	Phoenix West	Sept. 1, 1963	Keith W. Hubbard
381	Fresno East	Sept. 15, 1963	Melvin P. Leavitt
382	Brigham City	Sept. 22, 1963	Lawrence C. Taylor
383	Bountiful East	Sept. 29, 1963	Rendell N. Mabey
384	Santa Maria	Oct. 20, 1963	Clayton K. Call
385	Corvallis	Nov. 3, 1963	Hugh F. Webb
386	Portland West	Nov. 10, 1963	C. Carlile Carlson
387	San Jose West	Nov. 10, 1963	Louis W. Latimer
388	Seattle East	Dec. 1, 1963	Raymond W. Eldredge
389	North Columbia River (ch to Columbia River North 29 May 1970)	Dec. 1, 1963	Wallace V. Teuscher
390	Hunter	Jan. 5, 1964	Eldon Verne Breeze
391	Tempe	Feb. 2, 1964	George Isaac Dana
392	Norfolk	April 12, 1964	Walter H. Hick
393	Mt. Olympus	April 12, 1964	Orin R. Woodbury
394	Denver South	April 19, 1964	R. Raymond Barnes
395	Brigham Young University 4th	May 3, 1964	William R. Siddoway
396	Brigham Young University 5th	May 3, 1964	A. Harold Goodman
397	Brigham Young University 6th	May 3, 1964	Wayne B. Hales
398	Corpus Christi	May 31, 1964	Clarence Cottam
399	Modesto	June 7, 1964	Clifton A. Rooker
400	Medford	Aug. 23, 1964	Dennis R. Hassell
401	Las Vegas East	Jan. 24, 1965	Rulon A. Earl
402	Anaheim	Mar. 14, 1965	Max V. Eliason
403	Memphis	April 18, 1965	Richard Stoddard
404	Jackson	May 2, 1965	Neil J. Ferrell
405	Ricks College Stake (ch to Ricks College 1st 1 Jun. 1969)	May 7, 1965	J. Wendell Stucki

	NAME	ORGANIZED	PRESIDENT
406	Idaho State University	May 9, 1965	Robert E. Thompson
407	Wellington	May 12, 1965	Keith A. Harrison
408	Hattiesburg	June 27, 1965	Edwin White
409	North Boise (ch to Boise North Jan. 1966)	Sept. 26, 1965	L. Alden Porter
410	Oquirrh East	Oct. 17, 1965	William B. Martin
411	Taylorsville West	Oct. 31, 1965	Richard A. Barker
412	Rose Park North	Nov. 28, 1965	Joseph L. Lundstrom
413	College of Southern Utah (ch to Southern Utah State College Sep. 1969)	Jan. 6, 1966	Robert Burton White, Jr.
414	Adelaide	Feb. 23, 1966	Dudley Russell Tredrea
415	Rialto	Mar. 20, 1966	Wayne A. Reeves
416	Calgary North	April 17, 1966	Gerald E. Melchin
417	Sao Paulo	May 1, 1966	Walter Spat
418	Butler West	May 8, 1966	Sherman M. Crump
419	Cedar Rapids	May 29, 1966	Richard F. Hagland
420	Huntington Beach	June 5, 1966	Conway W. Nielsen
421	Hartford	Sept. 18, 1966	Hugh S. West
422	Albuquerque East	Sept. 25, 1966	George Van Lemmon
423	Buenos Aires	Nov. 20, 1966	Angel Abrea
424	Sunset	Dec. 11, 1966	John L. Nicholas
425	Fremont (new)	Dec. 11, 1966	Francis B. Winkel
426	Grand Coulee North	Jan. 29, 1967	Leslie H. Boyce
427	Utah State University II	Feb. 12, 1967	Reynold K. Watkins
428	Fair Oaks	Feb. 12, 1967	Harvey Stansell Greer
429	New Jersey Central	Mar. 26, 1967	Robert H. Daines
430	Arlington	April 23, 1967	Clarence Leon Sirrine
431	Brigham Young University 7th	April 30, 1967	Dean A. Peterson
432	Brigham Young University 8th	April 30, 1967	David H. Yarn
433	University 2nd	April 30, 1967	Oscar W. McConkie Jr.
434	Mexico City North	May 7, 1967	Agricol Lozano
435	Sydney South	May 14, 1967	John Daniel Parker
436	Guatemala City	May 21, 1967	Udine Falabella
437	Pasco	May 21, 1967	David K. Barber

	NAME	ORGANIZED	PRESIDENT
438	Roy North	June 11, 1967	Walter D. Bingham
439	Long Island	Aug. 20, 1967	Gordon E. Crandall
440	Olympia	Aug. 27, 1967	Herbert Springer Anderson
441	Palm Springs	Aug. 27, 1967	Quinten Hunsaker
442	El Monte	Sept. 17, 1967	James Cyril Brown
443	Fort Worth	Sept. 24, 1967	John Kelly, Jr.
444	Montevideo	Nov. 12, 1967	Vicente C. Rubio
445	Hamilton South	Nov. 19, 1967	Harry S. Peckham
446	Texas North	Nov. 26, 1967	Franklin Spencer Gonzalez
447	Perth	Nov. 28, 1967	Donald W. Cummings
448	Simi	Dec. 10, 1967	John Lyman Ballif III
449	Layton East	Feb. 4, 1968	Robert F. Bitner
450	San Jose South	Feb. 11, 1968	DeBoyd L. Smith
451	Las Vegas Central	Feb. 18, 1968	Samuel M. Davis
452	Alabama	Mar. 3, 1968	Raymond D. McCurdy
453	Newport Beach	Mar. 31, 1968	Ferren L. Christensen
454	South Carolina East	April 21, 1968	Clyde Elmer Black, Sr.
455	Auckland South	May 5, 1968	Geoffrey Richard Garlick
456	Houston East	May 5, 1968	Martell A. Belnap
457	East Midvale (ch to Midvale East 29 May 1970)	May 5, 1968	R. Kent King
458	Weber State College	May 12, 1968	E. LaMar Buckner
459	Antelope Valley	May 12, 1968	Sterling A. Johnson
460	Holladay South	June 16, 1968	Marvin L. Pugh
461	Maine	June 23, 1968	Olie W. Ross
462	Marin	June 23, 1968	Weston L. Roe
463	Nuku'alofa	Sept. 5, 1968	Orson Hyde White
464	Helena	Sept. 8, 1968	Ronald Rex Dalley
465	Jacksonville	Sept. 15, 1968	Louis Blaine Vorwaller
466	Servicemen's Stake Europe	Oct. 30, 1968	Herbert B. Spencer
467	Sao Paulo East	Nov. 24, 1968	Helio da Rocha Camargo
468	Murray West	Nov. 24, 1968	Robert Harmon McLloyd Killpack
469	Mid-Michigan	Dec. 1, 1968	E. Richmond Packham
470	Fort Collins	Dec. 1, 1968	Raymond Price

	NAME	ORGANIZED	PRESIDENT
471	Texas West	Dec. 15, 1968	Roland Lamar Hamblin
472	Bend	Dec. 15, 1968	Norman K. Whitney
473	Hilo	Dec. 15, 1968	Rex Alton Cheney
474	Dearborn	Jan. 12, 1969	Carl S. Hawkins
475	New Zealand North	Jan. 19, 1969	Stanley J. Hay
476	Baton Rouge	Jan. 26, 1969	Clive M. Larson
477	Tucson North	Feb. 2, 1969	Don Hakan Peterson
478	Brigham Young University 9th	Apr. 27, 1969	Carl D. Jones
479	Brigham Young University 10th	Apr. 27, 1969	Ivan J. Barrett
480	Ricks College 2nd	Apr. 27, 1969	Loren Homer Grover
481	Pittsburgh	May 11, 1969	William Preston Cook
482	South Jordan (ch to Jordan South 29 May 1970; ch to So. Jordan 30 Nov. 1970)	May 18, 1969	Theron Bird Hutchings
483	Susquehanna	May 25, 1969	Harold R. Capener
484	Arkansas	June 1, 1969	Deon C. Andrew
485	Hudson River	June 8, 1969	Thomas Lorin Hicken
486	Pensacola	June 15, 1969	Stanford Leroy Stapleton
487	Sacramento South	June 15, 1969	John Henry Huber
488	Pago Pago	June 15, 1969	Patrick Peters
489	San Diego North	June 22, 1969	Ray Michael Brown
490	Twin Falls West	Aug. 17, 1969	Joel A. Tate
491	Granger East	Aug. 24, 1969	David D. Lingard
492	Visalia	Aug. 24, 1969	Alva D. Blackburn
493	Oregon West	Sept. 12, 1969	Edward Harold Sypher
494	Birmingham	Sept. 14, 1969	Derek Alfred Cuthbert
495	Parramatta	Nov. 2, 1969	Stanley Owen Gray
496	Texas East	Nov. 9, 1969	Gerald Christian Franklin Knackstedt
497	Granger West	Jan. 4, 1970	Dwayne T. Johnson
498	Woods Cross	Jan. 4, 1970	D. Hatch Howard
499	Roanoke	Jan. 11, 1970	Russell Brown Maddock
500	Fallon	Jan. 18, 1970	G. Verl Hendrix
501	Val Verda	Jan. 25, 1970	Milton W. Russon
502	Anaheim West	Feb. 15, 1970	Hugh J. Sorensen
503	Lima	Feb. 22, 1970	Roberto Vidal
504	Blackfoot West	Mar. 1, 1970	Allan Franklin Larsen
505	Tokyo	Mar. 15, 1970	Kenji Tanaka

NAME		ORGANIZED	PRESIDENT
506	Transvaal	Mar. 22, 1970	Louis P. Hefer
507	Merrimack	Mar. 22, 1970	William Albert Fresh
508	Monterrey	Mar. 22, 1970	Guillermo Gonzalez Garza
509	Las Vegas South	Mar. 29, 1970	Erval LeGrande Bindrup
510	Gettysburg	Apr. 19, 1970	Laurence L. Yager
511	Columbia	Apr. 19, 1970	Samuel D. Richards
512	Mt. Vernon	Apr. 26, 1970	Allen Claire Rozsa
513	Apia West	Apr. 26, 1970	Percy J. Rivers
514	Renton	May 3, 1970	Harris Arbor Mortensen
515	Roseville	May 17, 1970	S. Lloyd Hamilton
516	Dayton	May 24, 1970	Joseph M. McPhie
517	Prescott	June 7, 1970	Edward A. Dalton
518	La Canada	June 7, 1970	Robert C. Seamons
519	Nuku'alofa South	July 26, 1970	Tevita F. Mahuinga
520	Nuku'alofa West	July 26, 1970	Orson H. White
521	Mt. Whitney	Aug. 16, 1970	AlDean Washburn
522	West Virginia	Aug. 23, 1970	David L. Atkinson
523	Sao Paulo South	Sept. 6, 1970	Saul M. de Oliveira
524	Niagara	Sept. 6, 1970	Elden C. Olsen
525	Des Moines	Sept. 6, 1970	Donald G. Woolley
526	Chesapeake	Sept. 13, 1970	June B. Thayn
527	London North	Sept. 20, 1970	Thomas Hill
528	Cache North	Oct. 11, 1970	Charles L. Hyde
529	Pleasant Grove	Oct. 11, 1970	Leon R. Walker
530	Ft. Lauderdale	Oct. 18, 1970	Stanley C. Johnson
531	Oklahoma South	Oct. 18, 1970	H. Aldridge Gillespie
532	Cascade South	Oct. 25, 1970	Wesley K. Duce
533	Orem North	Nov. 1, 1970	Eli Karl Clayson
534	Mexico City East	Nov. 15, 1970	Agricol Lozano
535	Holbrook	Nov. 22, 1970	Jay Barder Williams
536	Nashville	Dec. 6, 1970	Robert N. Brady
537	Kalispell	Dec. 20, 1970	Roy K. Deming
538	Savai'i	Jan. 8, 1971	Amuia W. Hunt
539	Bountiful Center	Jan. 10, 1971	Steven S. Davis
540	Louisville	Jan. 17, 1971	Henry H. Griffith
541	Edgemont	Jan. 17, 1971	Richard A. Call
542	Mt. Ranier	Jan. 17, 1971	Owen H. Dickson
543	Little Cottonwood	Feb. 21, 1971	James S. McCloy
544	Independence	Mar. 25, 1971	Melvin James Bennion
545	Upolu West	Apr. 25, 1971	Tua'ifaiva O. Aiono

	NAME	ORGANIZED	PRESIDENT
546	Bountiful Heights	May 16, 1971	Jesse Earl Godfrey
547	Provo North	May 30, 1971	Wayne Alvin Mineer
548	Ventura	May 30, 1971	Joseph F. Chapman
549	East Anglia	June 20, 1971	Dennis Raymond Reeves
550	Nuku'alofa East	July 21, 1971	Viliami Pele Folau
551	Melbourne South	Aug. 22, 1971	Bruce James Opie
552	Curitiba	Sept. 12, 1971	Jason Garcia Souza
553	Moab	Sept. 19, 1971	Leland D. Teeples
554	Orem South	Sept. 19, 1971	Richard Phil Shumway
555	Mesa West	Oct. 10, 1971	Weymouth D. Pew
556	Spokane East	Oct. 17, 1971	James B. Cox
557	Mesa Verde	Nov. 7, 1971	Del A. Talley, Sr.
558	Maricopa North	Nov. 7, 1971	Raymond Louis Russell
559	Ben Lomond West	Nov. 21, 1971	Jay Herbert Rhees
560	Kaneohe	Nov. 21, 1971	Robert H. Finlayson
561	Providence	Dec. 12, 1971	Asa L. Beecher
562	Tempe University	Dec. 12, 1971	Leo Rae Huish
563	Oregon City	Jan. 16, 1972	James Hayward Bean
564	Caldwell	Jan. 30, 1972	Talmage C. Blacker
565	Chico	Feb. 6, 1972	Lloyd Johnson Cope
566	Pearl Harbor West	Feb. 20, 1972	William Erich Fuhrmann
567	Tampico	Feb. 27, 1972	Guillermo Garmendia
568	Kaysville East	Feb. 27, 1972	Lawrence E. Welling
569	Cordoba	Feb. 28, 1972	Arturo Palmieri
570	Mendoza	Mar. 1, 1972	Mario Armando Rastelli
571	Lexington	Apr. 23, 1972	Philip Maughan Moody
572	Monterrey East	May 7, 1972	Jose Humberto Gonzalez
573	Tahiti	May 14, 1972	Raituia Tehina Tapu
574	Wilmington	May 21, 1972	Dean Bevin Powell, Jr.
575	Centerville	May 21, 1972	Joseph A. Kjar
576	Big Cottonwood	May 28, 1972	Robert Barlow Barker
577	Dusseldorf	June 4, 1972	Kaus Fritz Karl Hasse
578	Bountiful West	June 11, 1972	Clarence D. Samuelson
579	Sandy West	June 11, 1972	Reed Neff Brown
580	Meridian	June 11, 1972	J. Richard Clarke
581	Knoxville	June 25, 1972	Eugene H. Perkins
582	Hunter West	Aug. 13, 1972	Evans Thomas Doxey
583	Upland	Aug. 13, 1972	Frank E. Finlayson
584	Charleston	Aug. 20, 1972	Fred Ittner Harley
585	San Jose North	Aug. 20, 1972	Lloyd M. Gustaveson
586	Osaka	Sept. 12, 1972	Noboru Kamio
587	Minidoka West	Sept. 24, 1972	Keith C. Merrill

APPENDIX

	NAME	ORGANIZED	PRESIDENT
588	Escondido	Sept. 24, 1972	Donald R. McArthur
589	Rio de Janeiro	Oct. 22, 1972	Valdemar Cury
590	Santiago	Nov. 19, 1972	Carlos Antonio Cifuentes
591	Charlotte	Nov. 19, 1972	Byron Cole Williams
592	Rapid City	Dec. 10, 1972	Briant LeRoy Davis
593	Cody	Jan. 7, 1973	Parley Livingston
594	Tallahassee	Jan. 21, 1973	Jay Nichols Lybbert
595	Boulder	Jan. 28, 1973	C. Rodney Claridge
596	Denver North	Jan. 28, 1973	Gus F. Ranzenberger
597	Nottingham	Feb. 4, 1973	Ernest Hewitt
598	Taylorsville Central	Feb. 4, 1973	Richard A. Barker
599	Columbia River West	Feb. 4, 1973	Walter Lee Robinson
600	Southampton	Feb. 11, 1973	Reginald V. Littlecott
601	Porto Alegre	Feb. 13, 1973	Miguel Sorrentino III
602	Idaho Falls West	Mar. 4, 1973	Terry Lavelie Crapo
603	Butler South	Mar. 4, 1973	Alvin Donald Nydegger
604	Seoul	Mar. 8, 1973	Ho Nam Rhee
605	Lake Mead West	Mar. 11, 1973	Joseph Dee Reese
606	Jefferson	Mar. 25, 1973	Edwin Cutler Adamson
607	Iona	Apr. 15, 1973	Joseph Dudley Tucker
608	Hull	Apr. 26, 1973	Ian David Swanney
609	Bristol	Apr. 29, 1973	Donald Victor Norris
610	Ozark	Apr. 29, 1973	Carroll S. Claybrook
611	Sandy North	Apr. 29, 1973	Eugene Delbert Tenney
612	Glendale (Arizona)	May 6, 1973	Melvin Lee Huber
613	Manila	May 20, 1973	Augusto Alandy Lim
614	Jordan River	May 20, 1973	Max Curtis Jewkes
615	Thames Valley	May 24, 1973	Peter Charles Brighty
616	Dallas North	May 27, 1973	Ivan Leslie Hobson, Jr.
617	Mexico City-Aragon	May 27, 1973	Agricol Lozano Herrera
618	San Salvador	June 3, 1973	Mario Edmundo Scheel
619	Savai'i West	June 3, 1973	Fa'afoi Tuitama
620	Santos	June 8, 1973	Jose Gonzales Lopez
621	Campinas	June 9, 1973	Nelson de Genaro
622	Sao Paulo West	June 10, 1973	Jose Benjamin Puerta
623	Willow Creek	June 17, 1973	Wayne E. Saunders
624	American Fork North	June 17, 1973	Leland Forbes Priday
	*Los Angeles South August 12, 1973		
624	Indianapolis Indiana North	Aug. 19, 1973	David Val Glover
625	Littleton Colorado	Sept. 2, 1973	Clinton L. Cutler
626	Austin Texas	Oct. 14, 1973	Amos Luther Wright

NAME		ORGANIZED	PRESIDENT
627	Crescent Utah	Oct. 21, 1973	Allen Eugene Hilton
628	Valle Hermosa Mexico	Oct. 28, 1973	Benjamin Morales
629	Taylorsville Utah North	Oct. 28, 1973	LeVere Elihu Brady
630	Auckland N.Z. Harbour	Nov. 4, 1973	Kenneth M. Palmer
631	Montevideo Uruguay East	Feb. 17, 1974	Ariel A. Fedrigotti
632	Pueblo Colorado	Mar. 3, 1974	Louis Edward Butler
633	Page Arizona	Mar. 10, 1974	J. Ballard Washburn
634	Payson Utah East	Mar. 24, 1974	David R. Mangelson
635	Reno Nevada North	Mar. 24, 1974	Wilford Darrell Foote
636	Salt Lake Granger Central	Mar. 31, 1974	Norman H. Bangerter

Note: The following pages give the name changes for stakes as effected on February 1, 1974.

APPENDIX 641

STAKES OF ZION—NEW NAMES
(In Alphabetical Order)

Former Stake Names	New Names
Adelaide	Adelaide Australia Stake
Alabama	Huntsville Alabama Stake
Alameda	Pocatello Idaho Alameda Stake
Alaska	Anchorage Alaska Stake
Alberta	Cardston Alberta Stake
Albuquerque	Albuquerque New Mexico Stake
Albuquerque East	Albuquerque New Mexico East Stake
Alpine	Alpine Utah Stake
American Falls	American Falls Idaho Stake
American Fork	American Fork Utah Stake
American Fork North	American Fork Utah North Stake
American River	Sacramento California East Stake
Ammon	Idaho Falls Idaho Ammon Stake
Anaheim	Anaheim California Stake
Anaheim West	Cypress California Stake
Antelope Valley	Palmdale California Stake
Apia	Apia Samoa Stake
Apia West	Apia Samoa West Stake
Arizona South	St. David Arizona Stake
Arkansas	Little Rock Arkansas Stake
Arlington	Riverside California West Stake
Ashley	Vernal Utah Ashley Stake
Atlanta	Atlanta Georgia Stake
Auckland	Auckland New Zealand Mt. Roskill Stake
Auckland South	Auckland New Zealand Manurewa Stake
Bakersfield	Bakersfield California Stake
Bannock	Grace Idaho Stake
Baton Rouge	Baton Rouge Louisiana Stake
Bear Lake	Paris Idaho Stake
Bear River	Garland Utah Stake
Bear River South	Tremonton Utah Stake
Beaumont	Beaumont Texas Stake
Beaver	Beaver Utah Stake
Ben Lomond	Ogden Utah Ben Lomond Stake
Ben Lomond South	Ogden Utah North
Ben Lomond West	Ogden Utah Stake Pleasant View Utah Stake
Bend	Bend Oregon Stake
Benson	Richmond Utah Stake
Berlin	Berlin Germany Stake
Big Cottonwood	Salt Lake Big Cottonwood Stake
Big Horn	Lovell Wyoming Stake
Billings	Billings Montana Stake
Birmingham	Birmingham England Stake
Blackfoot	Blackfoot Idaho Stake
Blackfoot South	Blackfoot Idaho South Stake
Blackfoot West	Blackfoot Idaho West Stake
Blaine	Richfield Idaho Stake
Boise	Boise Idaho Stake
Boise North	Boise Idaho North Stake
Boise West	Boise Idaho West Stake
Bonneville	Salt Lake Bonneville Stake
Boston	Boston Massachusetts Stake
Boulder	Boulder Colorado Stake
Bountiful	Bountiful Utah Stake
Bountiful Center	Bountiful Utah Central Stake
Bountiful East	Bountiful Utah East Stake
Bountiful Heights	Bountiful Utah Heights Stake
Bountiful North	Bountiful Utah North Stake
Bountiful South	Bountiful Utah South Stake
Bountiful West	Bountiful Utah West Stake
Box Elder	Brigham City Utah Box Elder Stake
Box Elder North	Brigham City Utah North Stake
Box Elder South	Brigham City Utah South Stake
Brigham City	Brigham City Utah Stake

Former Stake Names	New Names	Former Stake Names	New Names
Brigham Young University	Brigham Young University 1st Stake	Chesapeake	Silver Spring Maryland Stake
Brigham Young University 2nd	Brigham Young University 2nd Stake (All other BYU stakes retain former names)	Cheyenne	Cheyenne Wyoming Stake
		Chicago	Wilmette Illinois Stake
		Chicago South	Naperville Illinois Stake
		Chico	Chico California Stake
Brisbane	Brisbane Australia Stake	Cincinnati	Cincinnati Ohio Stake
Bristol	Bristol England Stake	Clearfield	Clearfield Utah Stake
Buenos Aires	Buenos Aires Argentina Stake	Cleveland	Cleveland Ohio Stake
		Cody	Cody Wyoming Stake
Burbank	Los Angeles California North Hollywood Stake	Coeur D'Alene	Coeur D'Alene Idaho Stake
Burley	Burley Idaho Stake	Columbia	Columbia Missouri Stake
Butler	Salt Lake Butler Stake	Columbia River	Portland Oregon East Stake
Butler South	Salt Lake Brighton Stake		
Butler West	Salt Lake Butler West Stake	Columbia River North	Vancouver Washington Stake
Butte	Butte Montana Stake	Columbia River West	Longview Washington Stake
Cache	Logan Utah Cache Stake		
Cache East	Logan Utah East Stake	Columbus	Columbus Ohio Stake
Cache North	North Logan Utah State	Concord	Concord California Stake
Caldwell	Caldwell Idaho Stake	Cordoba	Cordoba Argentina Stake
Calgary	Calgary Alberta Stake	Corpus Christi	Corpus Christi Texas Stake
Calgary North	Calgary Alberta North Stake	Corvallis	Corvallis Oregon Stake
		Cottonwood	Salt Lake Cottonwood Stake
Campinas	Campinas Brazil Stake		
Cannon	Salt Lake Cannon Stake	Covina	Covina California Stake
Canoga Park	Los Angeles California Canoga Park Stake	Craig	Meeker Colorado Stake
		Crescent Utah	Sandy Utah Crescent Stake
Canyon Rim	Salt Lake Canyon Rim Stake		
Carbon	Price Utah Stake	Cumorah	Rochester New York Stake
Carbon North	Price Utah North Stake	Curitiba	Curitiba Brazil Stake
Cascade	Mount Vernon Washington Stake	Dallas	Dallas Texas Stake
		Dallas North	Dallas Texas North Stake
Cascade South	Everett Washington Stake	Davis	Farmington Utah Stake
		Davis North	Syracuse Utah Stake
Casper	Casper Wyoming Stake	Davis South	Bountiful Utah Orchard Stake
Cassia	Oakley Idaho Stake		
Cassia East	Declo Idaho Stake	Dayton	Dayton Ohio Stake
Cedar	Cedar City Utah Stake	Dearborn	Dearborn Michigan Stake
Cedar Rapids	Cedar Rapids Iowa Stake	Denver	Denver Colorado Stake
		Denver North	Denver Colorado North Stake
Cedar West	Cedar City Utah West Stake		
		Denver South	Lakewood Colorado Stake
Centerville	Centerville Utah Stake		
Charleston	Charleston South Carolina Stake	Denver West	Arvada Colorado Stake
		Des Moines	Des Moines Iowa Stake
Charlotte	Charlotte North Carolina Stake	Deseret	Delta Utah Stake
		Detroit	Bloomfield Hills Michigan Stake

APPENDIX 643

Former Stake Names	New Names
Duchesne	Duchesne Utah Stake
Duesseldorf	Duesseldorf Germany Stake
East Anglia	Ipswich England Stake
East Mill Creek	Salt Lake East Millcreek Stake
Edgemont	Provo Utah Edgemont Stake
Edmonton	Edmonton Alberta Stake
El Monte	El Monte California Stake
El Paso	El Paso Texas Stake
Emery	Castle Dale Utah Stake
Emigration	Salt Lake Emigration Utah
Ensign	Salt Lake Ensign Stake
Escondido	Escondido California Stake
Fair Oaks	Fair Oaks California Stake
Fallon	Fallon Nevada Stake
Farr West	Ogden Utah Farr West Stake
Flagstaff	Flagstaff Arizona Stake
Florida	Jacksonville Florida West Stake
Franklin	Preston Idaho South Stake
Fremont	Fremont California Stake
Fresno	Fresno California Stake
Fresno East	Fresno California East Stake
Ft Collins	Fort Collins Colorado Stake
Ft Lauderdale	Fort Lauderdale Florida Stake
Ft Wayne	Fort Wayne Indiana Stake
Ft Worth	Fort Worth Texas Stake
Fullerton	Placentia California Stake
Garden Grove	Garden Grove California Stake
Garfield	Escalante Utah Stake
Gettysburg	Gettysburg Pennsylvania Stake
Glasgow	Glasgow Scotland Stake
Glendale	Glendale Arizona Stake
Glendale	Glendale California Stake
Gooding	Jerome Idaho Stake
Grand Coulee	Moses Lake Washington Stake
Grand Coulee North	Quincy Washington Stake
Grand Junction	Grand Junction Colorado Stake
Granger	Salt Lake Granger Stake
Granger East	Salt Lake Granger East Stake
Granger North	Salt Lake Granger North Stake

Former Stake Names	New Names
Granger West	Salt Lake Granger West Stake
Granite	Salt Lake Granite Stake
Granite Park	Salt Lake Granite Park Stake
Grant	Salt Lake Grant Stake
Grantsville	Grantsville Utah Stake
Great Falls	Great Falls Montana Stake
Greensboro	Greensboro North Carolina Stake
Greenville	Greenville South Carolina Stake
Gridley	Gridley California Stake
Guatemala City	Guatemala City Guatemala Stake
Gunnison	Gunnison Utah Stake
Hamburg	Hamburg Germany Stake
Hamilton	Hamilton New Zealand Stake
Hamilton South	Temple View New Zealand Stake
Hartford	Hartford Connecticut Stake
Hattiesburg	Hattiesburg Mississippi Stake
Hawkes Bay	Hastings New Zealand Stake
Hayward	Hayward California Stake
Helena	Helena Montana Stake
Highland	Salt Lake Highland Stake
Hillside	Salt Lake Hillside Stake
Hilo	Hilo Hawaii Stake
Holbrook	Holbrook Arizona Stake
Holladay	Salt Lake Holladay Stake
Holladay South	Salt Lake Holladay South Stake
Holland	The Hague Holland Stake
Honolulu	Honolulu Hawaii Stake
Houston	Houston Texas Stake
Houston East	Houston Texas East Stake
Hudson River	Albany New York Stake
Hull	Hull England Stake
Humboldt	Elko Nevada Stake
Hunter	Salt Lake Hunter Stake
Hunter West	Salt Lake Hunter West Stake
Huntington Beach	Huntington Beach California Stake
Huntington Park	Huntington Park California Stake
Hyrum	Hyrum Utah Stake
Idaho	Soda Springs Idaho Stake

Former Stake Names	New Names	Former Stake Names	New Names
Idaho Falls	Idaho Falls Idaho Stake	Las Vegas Central	Las Vegas Nevada Central Stake
Idaho Falls East	Idaho Falls Idaho East Stake	Las Vegas East	Las Vegas Nevada East Stake
Idaho Falls North	Idaho Falls Idaho North Stake	Las Vegas North	Las Vegas Nevada North Stake
Idaho Falls South	Idaho Falls Idaho South Stake	Las Vegas South	Las Vegas Nevada South Stake
Idaho Falls West	Idaho Falls Idaho West Stake	Layton	Layton Utah Stake
Idaho State University	Pocatello Idaho University Stake	Layton East	Layton Utah East Stake
		Leeds	Huddersfield England Stake
Illinois	Champaign Illinois Stake	Lehi	Lehi Utah Stake
Indianapolis	Indianapolis Indiana Stake	Leicester	Leicester England Stake
Indianapolis North	Indianapolis Indiana North Stake	Lethbridge	Lethbridge Alberta Stake
		Lewiston	Lewiston Idaho Stake
Inglewood	Los Angeles California Inglewood Stake	Lexington	Lexington Kentucky Stake
		Liberty	Salt Lake Liberty Stake
Iona	Iona Idaho Stake	Lima	Lima Peru Stake
Jackson	Jackson Mississippi Stake	Little Cottonwood	Murray Utah East Stake
Jacksonville	Jacksonville Florida East Stake	Littleton	Littleton Colorado Stake
Jefferson	Roberts Idaho Stake	Logan	Logan Utah Stake
Jordan East	Midvale Utah Fort Union Stake	London	London England Stake
		London North	London England North Stake
Jordan North	Salt Lake Jordan North Stake	Long Beach	Long Beach California Stake
Jordan River	West Jordan Utah South Stake	Long Beach East	Long Beach California East Stake
Juab	Nephi Utah Stake	Long Island	Plainview New York Stake
Juarez	Colonia Juarez Mexico Stake	Lorin Farr	Ogden Utah Lorin Farr Stake
Kalispell	Kalispell Montana Stake		
Kanab	Kanab Utah Stake	Los Angeles	Los Angeles California Stake
Kaneohe	Kaneohe Hawaii Stake		
Kansas City	Kansas City Missouri Stake	Los Angeles East	Los Angeles California East Stake
Kaysville	Kaysville Utah Stake		
Kaysville East	Kaysville Utah East Stake	Lost River	Moore Idaho Stake
		Louisville	Louisville Kentucky Stake
Kearns	Kearns Utah Stake	Lyman	Rock Springs Wyoming Stake
Kearns North	Kearns Utah North Stake	Macon	Macon Georgia Stake
Klamath	Klamath Falls Oregon Stake	Maine	Augusta Maine Stake
Knoxville	Knoxville Tennessee Stake	Malad	Malad Idaho Stake
Kolob	Springville Utah Kolob Stake	Manchester	Manchester England Stake
La Canada	La Crescenta California Stake	Manila	Manila Philippines Stake
		Maricopa	Mesa Arizona Maricopa Stake
Lake Mead	Henderson Nevada Stake	Maricopa North	Mesa Arizona Maricopa North Stake
Lake Mead West	Henderson Nevada West Stake		
		Marin	San Rafael California Stake
Lake View	Hooper Utah Stake	Medford	Medford Oregon Stake
Lansing	Lansing Michigan Stake		
Las Vegas	Las Vegas Nevada Stake		

APPENDIX 645

Former Stake Names	New Names
Melbourne	Melbourne Australia Fairfield Stake
Melbourne South	Melbourne Australia Moorabbin Stake
Memphis	Memphis Tennessee Stake
Mendoza	Mendoza Argentina Stake
Meridian	Meridian Idaho Stake
Merrimack	Manchester New Hampshire Stake
Mesa	Mesa Arizona Stake
Mesa East	Mesa Arizona East Stake
Mesa South	Mesa Arizona South Stake
Mesa Verde	Durango Colorado Stake
Mesa West	Mesa Arizona West Stake
Mexico City	Mexico City Mexico Stake
Mexico City Aragon	Mexico City Mexico Aragon Stake
Mexico City East	Mexico City Mexico East Stake
Mexico City North	Mexico City Mexico North Stake
Miami	Miami Florida Stake
Mid-Michigan	Midland Michigan Stake
Midvale	Midvale Utah Stake
Midvale East	Midvale Utah East Stake
Millard	Fillmore Utah Stake
Millcreek	Salt Lake Millcreek Stake
Milwaukee	Milwaukee Wisconsin Stake
Minidoka	Rupert Idaho Stake
Minidoka East	Paul Idaho Stake
Minnesota	Minneapolis Minnesota Stake
Missoula	Missoula Montana Stake
Moab	Moab Utah Stake
Moapa	Logandale Nevada Stake
Modesto	Modesto California Stake
Mojave	Barstow California Stake
Monterrey Bay	Monterrey California Stake
Monterrey	Monterrey Mexico Stake
Monterrey East	Monterrey Mexico East Stake
Montevideo	Montevideo Uruguay Stake
Montpelier	Montpelier Idaho Stake
Monument Park	Salt Lake Monument Park Stake
Monument Park West	Salt Lake Foothill Stake
Morgan	Morgan Utah Stake
Moroni	Moroni Utah Stake
Mt. Graham	Safford Arizona Stake

Former Stake Names	New Names
Mt. Jordan	Draper Utah Stake
Mt. Logan	Logan Utah Mt. Logan Stake
Mt. Ogden	Ogden Utah Mt. Ogden Stake
Mt. Olympus	Salt Lake Mt. Olympus Stake
Mt. Rainier	Puyallup Washington Stake
Mt. Rubidoux	Riverside California Stake
Mt. Vernon	Annandale Virginia Stake
Mt. Whitney	Ridgecrest California Stake
Murray	Murray Utah Stake
Murray South	Murray Utah South Stake
Murray West	Murray Utah West Stake
Nampa	Nampa Idaho Stake
Napa	Napa California Stake
Nashville	Nashville Tennessee Stake
Nebo	Payson Utah Stake
Nevada	Ely Nevada Stake
New Stake	Austin Texas Stake
New Stake	Taylorsville Utah North Stake
New Stake	Auckland New Zealand Harbour Stake
New Jersey	Caldwell New Jersey Stake
New Jersey Central	East Brunswick New Jersey Stake
New Orleans	New Orleans Louisiana Stake
New York	New York Stake
New Zealand North	Kaikohe New Zealand Stake
Newport Beach	Newport Beach California Stake
Niagara	Hamilton Ontario Stake
Norfolk	Norfolk Virginia Stake
North Carolina	Kinston North Carolina Stake
Norwalk	Cerritos California Stake
Nottingham	Nottingham England Stake
Nuku'alofa	Nuku'alofa Tonga Stake
Nuku'alofa East	Nuku'alofa Tonga East Stake
Nuku'alofa South	Nuku'alofa Tonga South Stake
Nuku'alofa West	Nuku'alofa Tonga West Stake

Former Stake Names	New Names	Former Stake Names	New Names
Nyssa	Nyssa Oregon Stake	Phoenix West	Phoenix Arizona West Stake
Oahu	Laie Hawaii Stake		
Oakland Berkeley	Oakland California Stake	Pikes Peak	Colorado Springs Colorado Stake
Ogden	Ogden Utah Stake	Pioneer	Salt Lake Pioneer Stake
Ogden East	Ogden Utah East Stake	Pittsburgh	Pittsburgh Pennsylvania Stake
Oklahoma	Oklahoma City Oklahoma Stake	Pleasant Grove	Pleasant Grove Utah Stake
Oklahoma South	Norman Oklahoma Stake	Pocatello	Pocatello Idaho Stake
Olympia	Olympia Washington Stake	Pocatello East	Pocatello Idaho East Stake
Olympus	Salt Lake Olympus Stake		
Oneida	Preston Idaho North Stake	Pocatello North	Pocatello Idaho North Stake
Oquirrh	Magna Utah Stake		
Oquirrh East	Magna Utah East Stake	Pocatello West	Pocatello Idaho West Stake
Oregon City	Oregon City Oregon Stake		
Oregon West	Coos Bay Oregon Stake	Pomona	LaVerne California Stake
Orem	Orem Utah Stake	Portland	Portland Oregon Stake
Orem North	Orem Utah North Stake	Portland West	Beaverton Oregon Stake
Orem South	Orem Utah South Stake	Portneuf	Arimo Idaho Stake
Orem West	Orem Utah West Stake	Porto Alegre	Porto Alegre Brazil Stake
Orlando	Orlando Florida Stake	Potomac	Oakton Virginia Stake
Osaka	Osaka Japan Stake	Prescott	Prescott Arizona Stake
Ozark	Springfield Missouri Stake	Providence	Providence Utah Stake
Pago Pago	Pago Pago Samoa Stake	Provo	Provo Utah Stake
Palm Springs	Palm Springs California Stake	Provo East	Provo Utah East Stake
		Provo North	Provo Utah North Stake
Palmyra	Spanish Fork Utah Palmyra Stake	Puget Sound	Bremerton Washington Stake
Palo Alto	Menlo Park California Stake	Raleigh	Raleigh North Carolina Stake
Palomar	Carlsbad California Stake	Rapid City	Rapid City South Dakota Stake
Panguitch	Panguitch Utah Stake		
Park	Salt Lake Park Stake	Redding	Redding California Stake
Parleys	Salt Lake Parleys Stake	Redondo	Torrance California Stake
Parowan	Parowan Utah Stake	Redwood	Eureka California Stake
Parramatta	Parramatta Australia Stake	Reno	Reno Nevada Stake
Pasadena	Pasadena California Stake	Reno North	Sparks Nevada Stake
Pasco	Pasco Washington Stake	Renton	Renton Washington Stake
Pearl Harbor	Honolulu Hawaii West Stake	Reseda	Los Angeles California Chatsworth Stake
Pearl Harbor West	Waipahu Hawaii Stake	Rexburg	Rexburg Idaho Stake
		Rexburg North	Rexburg Idaho North Stake
Pensacola	Pensacola Florida Stake		
Perth	Perth Australia Stake	Rialto	Rialto California Stake
Philadelphia	Philadelphia Pennsylvania Stake	Richland	Richland Washington Stake
		Ricks College 1st	Rexburg Idaho College 1st Stake
Phoenix	Phoenix Arizona Stake		
Phoenix East	Phoenix Arizona East Stake	Ricks College 2nd	Rexburg Idaho College 2nd Stake
		Rigby	Rigby Idaho Stake
Phoenix North	Phoenix Arizona North Stake	Rigby East	Rigby Idaho East Stake

APPENDIX 647

Former Stake Names	New Names	Former Stake Names	New Names
Rio de Janeiro	Rio de Janeiro Brazil Stake	San Salvador	San Salvador El Salvador Stake
Riverdale	Ogden Utah Riverdale Stake	Sandy	Sandy Utah Stake
Riverside	Salt Lake Riverside Stake	Sandy East	Sandy Utah East Stake
Riverton	Riverton Utah Stake	Sandy North	Sandy Utah North Stake
Roanoke	Roanoke Virginia Stake	Sandy West	Sandy Utah West Stake
Roosevelt	Roosevelt Utah Stake	Sanpete North	Mount Pleasant Utah Stake
Rose Park	Salt Lake Rose Park Stake	Sanpete South	Manti Utah Stake
Rose Park North	Salt Lake Rose Park North Stake	Santa Ana	Orange California Stake
Roseville	Roseville California Stake	Santa Barbara	Santa Barbara California Stake
Roy	Roy Utah Stake	Santa Maria	Santa Maria California Stake
Roy North	Roy Utah North Stake	Santa Monica	Los Angeles California Santa Monica Stake
Sacramento	Sacramento California Stake	Santa Rosa	Santa Rosa California Stake
Sacramento North	Sacramento California North Stake	Santaquin Tintic	Santaquin Utah Stake
Sacramento South	Sacramento California South Stake	Santiago	Santiago Chile Stake
Salem	Salem Oregon Stake	Santos	Santos Brazil Stake
Salmon River	Salmon Idaho Stake	Sao Paulo	Sao Paulo Brazil Stake
Salt Lake	Salt Lake Stake	Sao Paulo East	Sao Paulo Brazil East Stake
San Antonio	San Antonio Texas Stake	Sao Paulo South	Sao Paulo Brazil South Stake
San Bernardino	San Bernardino California Stake	Sao Paulo West	Sao Paulo Brazil West Stake
San Diego	San Diego California Stake	Savai'i	Savai'i Samoa Stake
San Diego East	San Diego California El Cajon Stake	Savai'i West	Savai'i Samoa West Stake
San Diego North	San Diego California North Stake	Scottsdale	Scottsdale Arizona Stake
San Diego South	San Diego California South Stake	Seattle	Seattle Washington Stake
San Fernando	Los Angeles California Van Nuys Stake	Seattle East	Bellevue Washington Stake
San Francisco	San Francisco California Stake	Seattle North	Seattle Washington North Stake
San Joaquin	Stockton California Stake	Seoul	Seoul Korea Stake
San Jose	San Jose California Stake	Servicemen's Europe	Kaiserslautern Germany Servicemen Stake
San Jose North	Santa Clara California Stake	Sevier	Richfield Utah Stake
San Jose South	San Jose California South Stake	Sevier North	Salina Utah Stake
San Jose West	Saratoga California Stake	Sevier South	Monroe Utah Stake
San Juan	Monticello Utah Stake	Sharon	Orem Utah Sharon Stake
San Leandro	San Leandro California Stake	Sharon East	Provo Utah Sharon East Stake
San Luis	Lajara Colorado Stake	Sharon West	Orem Utah Sharon West Stake
San Luis Obispo	San Luis Obispo California Stake	Shelley	Shelley Idaho Stake
San Mateo	Pacific California Stake	Shreveport	Shreveport Louisiana Stake
		Simi	Simi Valley California Stake
		Smithfield	Smithfield Utah Stake
		Snowflake	Snowflake Arizona Stake

Former Stake Names	New Names	Former Stake Names	New Names
South Carolina	Columbia South Carolina Stake	Tempe University	Tempe Arizona University Stake
South Carolina East	Columbia South Carolina East Stake	Temple View	Salt Lake Temple View Stake
South Cottonwood	Salt Lake South Cottonwood Stake	Teton	Driggs Idaho Stake
South Jordan	South Jordan Utah Stake	Texas East	Longview Texas Stake
South Ogden	Ogden Utah South Stake	Texas North	Lubbock Texas Stake
South Salt Lake	Salt Lake South Stake	Texas West	Odessa Texas Stake
Southampton	Southampton England Stake	Thames Valley	Reading England Stake
		Timpanogos	Pleasant Grove Utah Timpanogos Stake
Southern Utah State College	Cedar City Utah College Stake	Tokyo	Tokyo Japan Stake
Spanish Fork	Spanish Fork Utah Stake	Tooele	Tooele Utah Stake
Spokane	Spokane Washington Stake	Tooele North	Tooele Utah North Stake
Spokane East	Spokane Washington East Stake	Toronto	Toronto Ontario Stake
		Torrance	Torrance California Stake
		Transvaal	Johannesburg South Africa Stake
Springville	Springville Utah Stake		
St. George	St. George Utah Stake	Tucson	Tucson Arizona Stake
St. George East	St. George Utah East Stake	Tucson North	Tucson Arizona North Stake
St. Johns	St. Johns Arizona Stake	Tulsa	Tulsa Oklahoma Stake
St. Joseph	Thatcher Arizona Stake	Twin Falls	Twin Falls Idaho Stake
St. Louis	St. Louis Missouri Stake	Twin Falls West	Twin Falls Idaho West Stake
Star Valley	Afton Wyoming Stake		
Stuttgart	Stuttgart Germany Stake	Uintah	Vernal Utah Stake
Sugar House	Salt Lake Sugar House Stake	Union	La Grande Oregon Stake
		University West	Salt Lake Central Stake
Summit	Coalville Utah Stake	University 1st	Salt Lake University 1st Stake
Summit South	Kamas Utah Stake		
Sunderland	Sunderland England Stake	University 2nd	Salt Lake University 2nd Stake
Sunset	Sunset Utah Stake		
Susquehanna	Ithaca New York Stake	Upland	Upland California Stake
Swiss	Zurich Switzerland Stake	Upolu West	Upolu Samoa West Stake
Sydney	Sydney Australia Greenwich Stake	Utah	Provo Utah Central Stake
		Utah State University	Logan Utah University 1st Stake
Sydney South	Sydney Australia South Stake	Utah State University 2nd	Logan Utah University 2nd Stake
Taber	Taber Alberta Stake		
Tacoma	Tacoma Washington Stake	Utah West	Provo Utah West Stake
Tahiti	Papeete Tahiti Stake	Uvada	Enterprise Utah Stake
Tallahassee	Tallahassee Florida Stake	Val Verda	Bountiful Utah Val Verda Stake
Tampa	Tampa Florida Stake		
Tampico	Tampico Mexico Stake	Valle Hermosa	Valle Hermosa Mexico Stake
Taylor	Raymond Alberta Stake		
Taylorsville	Taylorsville Utah Stake	Valley View	Salt Lake Valley View Stake
Taylorsville Central	Taylorsville Utah Central Stake	Vancouver	Vancouver British Columbia Stake
Taylorsville West	Taylorsville Utah West Stake	Ventura	Ventura California Stake
Tempe	Tempe Arizona Stake	Virginia	Richmond Virginia Stake

APPENDIX

Former Stake Names	New Names	Former Stake Names	New Names
Visalia	Visalia California Stake	Whittier	Whittier California Stake
Walnut Creek	Walnut Creek California Stake	Wichita	Wichita Kansas Stake
Wasatch	Heber City Utah Stake	Wilford	Salt Lake Wilford Stake
Washington	Washington D.C. Stake	Willamette	Eugene Oregon Stake
Washington Terrace	Washington Terrace Utah Stake	Willow Creek	Sandy Utah Willow Creek Stake
Wayne	Loa Utah Stake	Wilmington	Wilmington North Carolina Stake
Weber	Ogden Utah Weber Stake	Wind River	Riverton Wyoming Stake
Weber State College	Ogden Utah College Stake	Winder	Salt Lake Winder Stake
Weiser	Weiser Idaho Stake	Winter Quarters	Omaha Nebraska Stake
Wellington	Wellington New Zealand Stake	Woodruff	Evanston Wyoming Stake
		Woods Cross	Woods Cross Utah Stake
Wells	Salt Lake Wells Stake	Yakima	Yakima Washington Stake
West Covina	La Puente California Stake	Yellowstone	St. Anthony Idaho Stake
West Jordan	West Jordan Utah Stake	Young	Farmington New Mexico Stake
West Virginia	Charleston West Virginia Stake	Yuma	Zuma Arizona Stake
		Zion Park	Hurricane Utah Stake

MISSIONS
(In Chronological Order)

	NAME	ORGANIZED	PRESIDENT
1	British (ch to England East June 10, 1970)	July 20, 1837	Heber C. Kimball
2	Eastern States*	May 6, 1839	John P. Green
3	Society Islands*	April 30, 1844	Noah Rogers
4	Welsh* (Combined with British Mission 26 March 1864)	Dec. 15, 1845	Dan Jones
5	California*	July 31, 1846	Samuel Brannan
6	French* (Eastern States disc April 1850)	June 18, 1849	John Taylor
6	Scandinavian*	May 11, 1850	Erastus Snow
7	Italian*	Nov. 1, 1850	Lorenzo Snow
8	Swiss*	Nov. 24, 1850	Thomas B. H. Stenhouse
9	Sandwich Islands*	Dec. 12, 1850	Hiram Clark
10	Australasian*	Oct. 30, 1851	John Murdock
11	East Indian*	1851	Lorenzo Snow
12	Malta*	Feb. 26, 1852	Lorenzo Snow
13	Gibraltar*	Mar. 7, 1852	Edward Stevenson & Nathan T. Porter
14	German* (Society Islands disc May 16, 1852)	April 3, 1852	Daniel P. Garn
14	South African* (Welsh disc 1854) (Italian disc Jan. 1, 1854) (Swiss disc Jan. 1, 1854)	April 19, 1853	Jesse Haven
12	Swiss and Italian*	Jan. 1, 1854	Thomas B. H. Stenhouse
13	Siam*	April 6, 1854	Elam Luddington
14	European* (Administrative) (Gibraltar disc about July 5, 1854) (Siam disc Aug. 12, 1854)	June 28, 1854	Franklin D. Richards
13	Eastern States*	1854	John Taylor
14	Indian Territory* (Malta disc about 1856) (East Indian disc May 2, 1856) (Eastern States disc 1858) (California disc 1858) (Sandwich Islands disc May 1, 1858) (Indian Territory disc 1860) (German disc Jan. 1, 1861)	June 26, 1855	Henry W. Miller

*Discontinued

APPENDIX

	NAME	ORGANIZED	PRESIDENT
7	(Swiss & Italian disc Jan. 1, 1861) Swiss, Italian & German (Ch to Swiss & German Jan. 1, 1868) (French disc 1864)	Jan. 1, 1861	Jabez Woodard
7	Sandwich Islands (Ch to Hawaiian before 1900. Ch to Hawaii April 1, 1950)	Mar. 27, 1864	Joseph F. Smith
8	Netherlands (Ch to Netherlands-Belgium Jan. 31, 1891) (Ch to Netherlands May 15, 1914) (South African disc April 12, 1865)	Nov. 1, 1864	Joseph Weiler
8	Eastern States* (Eastern States disc 1869)	1865	William H. Miles
8	Southern States	Oct. 9, 1876	Henry G. Boyle
9	Indian Territory* (Indian Territory disc Sept. 12, 1877)	Mar. 1877	Matthew W. Dalton
9	Northwestern States (Ch to Northern States July 20, 1889)	May 6, 1878	Cyrus H. Wheelock
10	Mexican*	Nov. 15, 1879	Moses Thatcher
11	Indian Territory (Ch to Southwestern States Mar. 29, 1898) (Ch to Central States Apr. 4, 1904) (Ch to Kansas-Missouri June 10, 1970)	April 20, 1883	George Teasdale
12	East Indian*	Aug. 1, 1884	William Willes
13	Turkish* (East Indian disc June 10, 1885)	Dec. 31, 1884	Jacob Spori
13	Samoan (Ch to Samoa June 10, 1970) (Mexican disc 1889)	June 17, 1888	Joseph H. Dean
13	Society Islands (Ch to Tahitian 1907) (Ch to French-Polynesian Nov. 25, 1959) (Ch to French-Polynesia June 10, 1970)	April 29, 1892	Joseph W. Damron
14	California	Aug. 23, 1892	John L. Dalton
15	Eastern States	Jan. 1893	Job Pingree
16	Montana*	Sept. 10, 1896	Phineus Tempest
17	Colorado (Ch to Western States Apr. 1, 1907)	Dec. 15, 1896	John W. Taylor

*Discontinued

	NAME	ORGANIZED	PRESIDENT
	(Ch to Colorado-New Mexico June 10, 1970)		
18	Northwestern States (new)	July 26, 1897	George C. Parkinson
	(Ch to Oregon June 10, 1970)		
	(Swiss & German disc Jan. 1, 1898)		
	(Australasian disc Jan. 1, 1898)		
17	Swiss°	Jan. 1, 1898	Henry E. Bowman
18	German°	Jan. 1, 1898	Peter Loutensock
19	Australian	Jan. 1, 1898	Andrew Smith
	(Ch to Australia East June 10, 1970)		
20	New Zealand	Jan. 1, 1898	Ezra F. Richards
	(Ch to New Zealand North June 10, 1970)		
	(Montana disc June 12, 1898)		
20	Mexican	June 8, 1901	Moses Thatcher
	(Ch to Mexico June 10, 1970)		
21	Japan°	Aug. 12, 1901	Heber J. Grant
22	Middle States°	June 28, 1902	Ben E. Rich
23	South African	July 25, 1903	Warren H. Lyon
	(Ch to South Africa June 10, 1970)		
	(Middle States disc Aug. 7, 1903)		
	(Swiss disc May 22, 1904)		
	(German disc May 22, 1904)		
21	Swiss & German°	May 22, 1904	Hugh J. Cannon
	(Scandinavian disc July 1, 1905)		
21	Swedish (Ch to Sweden June 10, 1970)	July 1, 1905	Peter Mattson
22	Danish-Norwegian°	July 1, 1905	Jens M. Christensen
	(Turkish disc Oct. 1, 1909)		
22	French°	Oct. 15, 1912	Edgar B. Brossard
	(French disc Sept. 18, 1914)		
22	Tongan (Ch to Tonga June 10, 1970)	July 8, 1916	Willard L. Smith
23	Canadian	July 1, 1919	Nephi Jensen
	(Ch to Ontario-Quebec June 10, 1970)		
	(Danish-Norwegian disc Apr. 1, 1920)		
23	Danish	April 1, 1920	Carl E. Peterson
	(Ch to Denmark June 10, 1970)		

°Discontinued

APPENDIX

	NAME	ORGANIZED	PRESIDENT
24	Norwegian (Ch to Norway June 10, 1970)	April 1, 1920	Andrew S. Schow
25	Armenian* (Ch to Palestine-Syrian Aug. 12, 1933)	Nov. 6, 1921	Joseph Wilford Booth
26	French (Ch to France June 10, 1970) (Japan disc July 31, 1924)	Aug. 20, 1923	Russell H. Blood
26	German-Austrian*	Aug. 23, 1925	Fred Tadje
27	North Central States (Ch to Manitoba- Minnesota June 10, 1970)	July 12, 1925	John G. Allred
28	South American*	Dec. 6, 1925	Melvin J. Ballard
29	East Central States (Ch to Kentucky- Tennessee June 10, 1970)	Dec. 9, 1928	Miles L. Jones
30	Czechoslovak*	July 24, 1929	Arthur Gaeth
31	Texas (Ch to Texas-Louisiana May 1945) (Ch to Gulf States June 19, 1955) (South American disc May 25, 1935)	Jan. 11, 1931	Charles Elliott Rowan, Jr.
31	Brazilian (Ch to Brazil Central June 10, 1970)	May 25, 1935	Rulon S. Howells
32	Argentine (Ch to Argentine South June 10, 1970)	Aug. 14, 1935	W. Ernest Young
33	Spanish-American*	June 28, 1936	Orlando C. Williams
34	Japanese* (Ch to Central Pacific May 14, 1944)	Feb. 24, 1937	Hilton A. Robertson
35	New England (Swiss & German disc Jan. 1, 1938) (German-Austrian disc Jan. 1, 1938)	Sept. 24, 1937	Carl Eyring
34	Swiss-Austrian* (Ch to Swiss Nov. 21, 1938) (Ch to Swiss-Austrian Mar. 17, 1946)	Jan. 1, 1938	Thomas E. McKay
35	West German (Ch to Germany West June 10, 1970)	Jan. 1, 1938	Philemon M. Kelly
36	East German (Ch to North German Sept. 12, 1957)	Jan. 1, 1938	Joseph Weiler

*Discontinued

	NAME	ORGANIZED	PRESIDENT
	(Ch to Germany North June 10, 1970)		
	(Palestine-Syrian disc 1939)		
36	Western Canadian	Sept. 15, 1941	Walter Miller
	(Ch to Alberta-Saskatchewan June 10, 1970)		
37	Northern California	Jan. 2, 1942	German E. Ellsworth
	(Ch to California North July 15, 1966)		
38	Navajo-Zuni	Mar. 7, 1943	Ralph William Evans
	(Ch to Southwest Indian Jan. 1, 1949)		
39	Pacific*	Dec. 7, 1946	Matthew Cowley
	(Administrative)		
40	Uruguay	Aug. 31, 1947	Fred S. Williams
	(Ch to Uruguay-Paraguay June 10, 1970)		
41	Finnish	Sept. 1, 1947	Henry A. Matis
	(Ch to Finland June 10, 1970)		
42	Central Atl. States	Oct. 26, 1947	Robert J. Price
	(Ch to North Carolina-Virginia June 10, 1970)		
43	Palestine-Syrian*	Nov. 8, 1947	Badwagon Piranian
	(Ch to Near East Jan. 25, 1950)		
44	Japanese*	Mar. 6, 1948	Edward L. Clissold
45	Chinese*	July 10, 1949	Hilton A. Robertson
46	Great Lakes	Oct. 14, 1949	Carl C. Burton
	(Ch to Indiana-Michigan June 10, 1970)		
	(Pacific disc Nov. 27, 1949)		
	(European disc Feb. 14, 1950)		
	(Central Pacific disc April 1, 1950)		
	(Czechoslovak disc April 6, 1950)		
43	West Central States	Nov. 11, 1950	Sylvester Broadbent
	(Ch to Montana-Wyoming June 10, 1970)		
	(Near East disc Jan. 1951)		
43	Central American	Nov. 16, 1952	Gordon M. Romney
	(Ch to Central America June 10, 1970)		
	(Chinese disc Feb. 9, 1953)		
43	South Australian	July 3, 1955	Thomas S. Bingham
	(Ch to Southern Australian Nov. 1958)		

*Discontinued

APPENDIX 655

	NAME	ORGANIZED	PRESIDENT
	(Ch to Australia South Aug. 1, 1968)		
	(Japanese disc July 28, 1955)		
43	Northern Far East*	July 28, 1955	Hilton A. Robertson
44	Southern Far East	Aug. 17, 1955	Herald Grant Heaton
45	Northern Mexican	June 10, 1956	Joseph Taylor Bentley
	(Ch to Mexico North June 10, 1970)		
46	West Spanish-American	Mar. 8, 1958	Leland M. Perry
	(Ch to West Spanish America June 10, 1970)		
47	New Zealand South	Sept. 1, 1958	Alexander P. Anderson
48	Brazilian South	Sept. 20, 1959	Asael T. Sorensen
	(Ch to Brazil South June 10, 1970)		
49	South German	Oct. 4, 1959	John A. Beuhner
	(Ch to Germany South June 10, 1970)		
50	Andes	Nov. 1, 1959	J. Vernon Sharp
	(Ch to Peru-Ecuador June 10, 1970)		
51	European* (Administrative)	Jan. 17, 1960	Alvin R. Dyer
52	North British	Mar. 27, 1960	Bernard P. Brockbank
	(Ch to England North June 10, 1970)		
	(Swiss-Austrian disc Sept. 18, 1960)		
52	Swiss	Sept. 18, 1960	William S. Erekson
	(Ch to Switzerland June 10, 1970)		
53	Austrian	Sept. 18, 1960	Winslow W. Smith
	(Ch to Austria June 10, 1970)		
54	Eastern Atlantic States	Oct. 16, 1960	George R. Hill
	(Ch to Delaware-Maryland June 10, 1970)		
55	Florida	Nov. 1, 1960	Karl R. Lyman
56	West Mexican	Nov. 1, 1960	Harold E. Turley
	(Ch to Mexico West June 10, 1970)		
57	Rarotonga*	Nov. 20, 1960	Joseph R. Reeder
58	Alaskan-Canadian	Nov. 21, 1960	Milton L. Weilenman
	(Ch to Alaska-British Columbia June 10, 1970)		
59	French East	Jan. 19, 1961	Henry D. Moyle, Jr.
	(Ch to France-Switzerland June 10, 1970)		
60	Texas (New)	Feb. 16, 1961	Ralph J. Hill
	(Ch to Texas North June 10, 1970)		

*Discontinued

NAME	ORGANIZED	PRESIDENT
61 Scottish-Irish (Ch to Scottish July 8, 1962)	Feb. 28, 1961	Bernard P. Brockbank
62 Central British (Ch to England Central June 10, 1970)	Mar. 6, 1961	James A. Cullimore
63 Central German (Ch to Germany Central June 10, 1970)	Mar. 15, 1961	Stephen C. Richards
64 West European* (Administrative)	April 30, 1961	Nathan E. Tanner
65 Berlin*	July 14, 1961	Percy K. Fetzer
66 South American* (Administrative)	Aug. 25, 1961	A. Theodore Tuttle
67 Chilean (Ch to Chile June 10, 1970)	Oct. 8, 1961	A. Delbert Palmer
68 Southwest British (Ch to England Southwest June 10, 1970)	Feb. 1, 1962	A. Ray Curtis
69 Bavarian*	Mar. 4, 1962	Owen Spencer Jacobs
70 Irish (Ch to Ireland June 10, 1970)	July 8, 1962	Stephen R. Covey
71 Korean (Ch to Korea June 10, 1970)	July 8, 1962	Gail Edward Carr
72 Northeast British*	Sept. 1, 1962	Grant S. Thorn
73 North Argentine (Ch to Argentina North June 10, 1970)	Sept. 16, 1962	Ronald V. Stone
74 North Scottish*	Nov. 24, 1962	William Noble Waite
75 Southeast Mexican (Ch to Mexico Southeast June 10, 1970)	Mar. 27, 1963	Carl J. Beecroft
76 Franco-Belgian (Ch to France-Belgium June 10, 1970)	Oct. 1, 1963	Joseph T. Edmunds
77 Cumorah	Dec. 6, 1963	N. Lester Petersen
78 Northern Indian	April 8, 1964	Grant Roper Farmer
79 British South (Ch to England South June 10, 1970) (Northeast British disc May 1965) (North Scottish disc May 31, 1965) (Bavarian disc June 10, 1965) (South American disc July 17, 1965)	Dec. 27, 1964	Don K. Archer
76 Guatemala-El Salvador (European disc Sept. 14, 1965)	Aug. 1, 1965	Terrance L. Hansen

*Discontinued

APPENDIX

	NAME	ORGANIZED	PRESIDENT
	(West European disc Sept. 14, 1965)		
	(Rarotonga disc April 15, 1966)		
	(Berlin disc May 31, 1966)		
73	California South	July 10, 1966	D. Crawford Houston
74	Italian	Aug. 2, 1966	John Duns, Jr.
	(Ch to Italy June 10, 1970)		
75	Andes South	Nov. 14, 1966	Franklin Kay Gibson
	(Ch to Bolivia 1969)		
76	Philippine	June 28, 1967	Paul S. Rose
	(Ch to Philippines June 10, 1970)		
77	Ohio	June 29, 1967	E. Garrett Barlow
	(Spanish-American disc Dec. 10, 1967)		
77	Texas South	Dec. 10, 1967	Dean Larson
78	Pacific Northwest	Jan. 1, 1968	Joe E. Whitesides
	(Ch to Washington June 10, 1970)		
79	Brazilian North	May 26, 1968	Hal Roscoe Johnson
	(Ch to Brazil North June 10, 1970)		
80	Colombia-Venezuela	July 1, 1968	Stephen L. Brower
81	Australian West	Aug. 1, 1968	Milton J. Hess
	(Ch to Australia West June 10, 1970)		
82	Mexico North Central	Aug. 5, 1968	Arturo R. Martinez
	(Northern Far East disc Aug. 31, 1968)		
82	Japan	Sept. 1, 1968	Walter R. Bills
83	Japan-Okinawa	Sept. 1, 1968	Edward Y. Okazaki
	(Ch to Japan Central Mar. 16, 1970)		
84	Dresden	June 14, 1969	Johannes Henry Burkhardt
85	California Central	July 1, 1969	Wilbur Wallace Cox
86	California East	July 7, 1969	William L. Nicholls
87	Arizona	Aug. 1, 1969	Clark M. Wood
88	South Central States	Aug. 4, 1969	Albert B. Crandall
	(Ch to Oklahoma June 10, 1970)		
89	Southeast Asia	Nov. 1, 1969	G. Carlos Smith
90	Japan East	Mar. 16, 1970	Russell N. Horiuchi
91	Japan West	Mar. 18, 1970	Ken Watanabe
	(West Spanish-America disc. 1 July 1970)		
91	Spain	July 1, 1970	R. Raymond Barnes
92	Pennsylvania	July 15, 1970	George M. Baker
93	Ecuador	Aug. 1, 1970	Louis W. Latimer
94	Taiwan	Jan. 11, 1971	Maylin R. Jackson
95	Italy North	July 1, 1971	Dan Charles Jorgenson
96	Venezuela	July 1, 1971	Clark D. Webb
97	Alabama-Florida	July 1, 1971	Hartman Rector
98	Nauvoo	July 1, 1971	J. LeRoy Kimball

	NAME	ORGANIZED	PRESIDENT
99	Fiji	July 23, 1971	A. Sherman Lindholm
100	Quebec	July 1, 1972	John K. M. Olsen
101	Argentina East (Brazil Central disc. 1 July 1972)	July 1, 1972	Joseph T. Bentley
101	International	Nov. 9, 1972	Bernard P. Brockbank
102	Brazil North Central	July 1, 1972	Leroy Alfred Drechsel
103	Brazil South Central	July 1, 1972	Owen Nelson Baker
104	Australia Northeast	July 1, 1973	Jay Martell Bird
105	Canada-Maritimes	July 1, 1973	Thurn J. Baker
106	Japan-Naguya	July 1, 1973	Satoru Sato
107	Michigan	July 1, 1973	C. Russell Hansen
108	North Carolina	July 1, 1973	Charles M. Alexander
109	Thailand	July 1, 1973	Paul D. Morris

APPENDIX

CHURCH PUBLICATIONS
(Chronologically arranged with date and place of issue.)

BOOK OF MORMON

LANGUAGE	PLACE	YEAR
English	Palmyra, New York,	1830
Danish	Copenhagen, Denmark,	1851
German	Hamburg, Germany,	1852
French	Paris, France,	1852
Italian	London, England,	1852
Welsh	Merthyr Tydfil, Wales,	1852
Hawaiian	San Francisco, California,	1855
Swedish	Copenhagen, Denmark,	1878
Spanish	Salt Lake City, Utah,	1886
Maori	Auckland, New Zealand,	1889
Dutch	Amsterdam, Holland,	1890
Samoan	Salt Lake City, Utah,	1903
Tahitian	Salt Lake City, Utah,	1904
Turkish	New York City, New York,	1906
Japanese	Tokyo, Japan,	1909
Czechoslovak	Prague, Czechoslovakia,	1933
Armenian	Los Angeles, California,	1937
Portuguese	Sao Paulo, Brazil,	1939
Tongan	Salt Lake City, Utah,	1946
Norwegian	Oslo, Norway,	1950
Finnish	Helsinki, Finland,	1954
Rarotongan	Salt Lake City, Utah,	1965
Chinese	Hong Kong, China,	1965
Korean	Seoul, Korea,	1967
Afrikaans	Salt Lake City, Utah	1972

The Book of Mormon was published in the Deseret Alphabet in New York City, in 1869, and in Braille in 1936 at Louisville, Ky. It has also been translated into Hindostani, Greek, Bulgarian, Russian, Hungarian, Hebrew (Yiddish), Serbo-Croatian (Yugoslavia), Rumanian, Filipino (Ilicano) and Arabic, but not published in these languages. In some of these languages listed here the Book of Mormon has been republished in many editions; the total number of copies published is not known because no systematic record has been kept of the several editions, many of which were reprinted from plates.

Book of Commandments, 1833, Independence, Missouri.

Doctrine and Covenants, 1835, Kirtland, Ohio.
    Welsh, 1851, Merthyr Tydfil, Wales.

Danish, 1852, Copenhagen, Denmark.
German, 1876, Bern, Switzerland.
Swedish, 1888, Salt Lake City, Utah.
Dutch, 1908, Rotterdam, Holland.
Hawaiian, 1914, Honolulu, Hawaii.
Maori, 1919, Auckland, New Zealand.
Armenian, 1941, Los Angeles, California.
Spanish, 1948, Salt Lake City, Utah.
Braille, 1948, Louisville, Kentucky.
Portuguese, 1950, Sao Paulo, Brazil.
Finnish, 1955, Helsinki, Finland.
Japanese, 1957, Tokyo, Japan.
Norwegian, 1957, Jonkoping, Sweden.
French, 1958, Paris, France.
Tongan, 1959, Salt Lake City, Utah.
Samoan, 1963, Salt Lake City, Utah.
Italian, 1965, Salt Lake City, Utah.
Tahitian, 1965, Salt Lake City, Utah.
Korean, 1968, Seoul, Korea.

Translated but not published: Bulgarian, Chinese, and Icelandic.

Hymnbook, 1835, Kirtland, Ohio.

Pearl of Great Price, 1851. Liverpool, England.
Welsh, 1852, Merthyr Tydfil, Wales.
German, 1882, Bern, Switzerland.
Danish, 1883, Salt Lake City, Utah.
Dutch, 1911, Rotterdam, Holland.
Hawaiian, 1914, Honolulu, Hawaii.
Maori, 1919, Auckland, New Zealand.
Swedish, 1927, Salt Lake City, Utah.
Czechoslovak, 1939, Prague, Czechoslovakia.
Armenian, 1941, Los Angeles, California.
Samoan, 1944, Salt Lake City, Utah.
Spanish, 1948, Salt Lake City, Utah.
Portuguese, 1952, Sao Paulo, Brazil.
Braille, 1952, Louisville, Kentucky.
Tahitian, 1952, Papeete, Tahiti.
Norwegian, 1955, Jonkoping, Sweden.
Finnish, 1957, Helsinki, Finland.
Japanese, 1957, Tokyo, Japan.
French, 1958, Paris, France.
Tongan, 1959, Salt Lake City, Utah.
Italian, 1965, Salt Lake City, Utah.
Korean, 1968, Seoul, Korea
Translated but not published: Bulgarian.

APPENDIX

CHURCH PERIODICALS

(Chronologically arranged by place and date of issue)

(*discontinued).

*The Evening and Morning Star, Independence, Missouri and Kirtland, Ohio, 1832-1834.
*Upper Missouri Advertiser, Independence, Missouri, 1832-1833.
*L. D. S. Messenger and Advocate, Kirtland, Ohio, 1834-1837.
*Northern Times, Kirtland, Ohio, 1835.
*The Elder's Journal, Kirtland, Ohio and Far West, Missouri, 1837-1838.
*Times and Seasons, Commerce (Nauvoo), Illinois, 1839-1846.
The Millennial Star, Manchester, Liverpool and London, England, 1840-1970.
*The Gospel Reflector, Philadelphia, Pennsylvania, 1841.
*The Wasp, Nauvoo, Illinois, 1842-1843.
*The Nauvoo Neighbor, Nauvoo, Illinois, 1843-1845.
*The Prophet, New York City, New York, 1844-1845.
*The New York Messenger, New York City, New York, 1845.
*Prophetic Almanac, New York City, New York, 1845-1865.
*Prophwyd y Jubili new Seren y Saint (Welsh), Merthyr Tydfil, Wales, 1846-1848.
*The California Star, Yerba Buena (San Francisco), California, 1847-1848.
*Udgorn Seion new Seren y Saint (Welsh), Merthyr Tydfil, Wales, 1849-1858.
*The Frontier Guardian, Kanesville (Council Bluffs), Iowa, 1849-1853.
The Deseret News, Salt Lake City, Utah, 1850-
*Skandinavians Stjerne (Danish), Copenhagen, Denmark, 1851-1956. (See: Den Danske Stjerne, 1956-   )
*Zion's Panier (German), Hamburg, Germany, 1851-1852.
*Etoile Du Deseret (French), Paris, France and Liverpool, England, 1851-1852.
*Western Bugle, Kanesville, Iowa, 1852.
*Zion's Watchman, Sydney, New South Wales, 1853-1855.
*Le Reflecteur (French), Geneva, Switzerland, 1853.
*The Seer, Washington, D.C., 1853-1854.
*Journal of Discourses, Liverpool, England, 1854-1886.
*L. D. S. Millennial Star and Monthly Visitor, Madras, India, 1854.
*St. Louis Luminary, St. Louis, Missouri, 1854-1855.
*The Mormon, New York City, New York, 1855-1857.
*Der Darsteller (German), Geneva, Switzerland, 1855-1857.

*The Western Standard, San Francisco, California, 1856-1857.
*Pony Dispatch, Salt Lake City, Utah, 1861.
*Die Reform (German), Geneva, Switzerland, 1862-1863.
*Juvenile Instructor, Salt Lake City, Utah, 1866-1929. (Changed to The Instructor; 1930-1970.)
Der Stern (German), Zurich, Switzerland, 1869-
*The Women's Exponent, Salt Lake City, Utah, 1872-1914.
*Utah Posten (Danish and Norwegian), Salt Lake City, Utah, 1873-1874.
*Bikuben (Danish and Norwegian), Salt Lake City, Utah, 1876-1935.
Nordstjernan (Swedish), Goteborg, Sweden, 1877-
*The Contributor, Salt Lake City, Utah, 1879-1896.
*Ungdommens Raadgiver (Danish and Norwegian), Copenhagen, Denmark, 1880-1887.
*Morgenstjernen (Danish and Norwegian), Salt Lake City, Utah, 1882-1885.
*Svenska Harolden (Swedish), Salt Lake City, Utah, 1885-1892.
*Historical Record, Salt Lake City, Utah, 1886-1890.
*Young Woman's Journal, Salt Lake City, Utah, 1889-1929.
*Salt Lake City Beobachter (German), Salt Lake City, Utah, 1890-1935.
*De Ster (Dutch), Rotterdam, Holland, 1896-
*Mutual Messenger, Salt Lake City, Utah, 1897.
*Mutual Improvement Messenger, Salt Lake City, Utah, 1897-1931.
*Improvement Era, Salt Lake City, Utah, 1897-1970.
*L.D.S. Southern Star, Chattanooga, Tennessee, 1898-1900.
*Truth's Reflex, St. John, Kansas, 1899-1901.
*Utah Posten (Swedish), Salt Lake City, Utah, 1900-1935.
*Children's Friend, Salt Lake City, Utah, 1902-1970.
*The Elder's Journal, Atlanta, Georgia and Chattanooga, Tennessee, 1903-1907.
*Elders' Messenger, Auckland, New Zealand, 1907.
  (See: The Messenger, 1907-   ).
*The Messenger, Auckland, New Zealand, 1907-1915.
*Liahona, Independence, Missouri, 1907.
*Liahona, The Elders' Journal, Chattanooga, Tennessee and Independence, Missouri, 1907-1945.
*Te Heheuraa Api (Tahitian), Papeete, Tahiti, 1907-1961.
*Ka Elele Oiaio (Hawaiian), Honolulu, Hawaii, 1908-1911.
*Utah Genealogical and Historical Magazine, Salt Lake City, Utah, 1910-1940.
*Messenger to the Sightless (Braille), Provo, Utah, 1912-1953.
  (See: The New Messenger, 1953-   )

*The Relief Society Magazine, Salt Lake City, Utah, 1915-1970.
*Morgenstjernen (Norwegian), Christiana, Norway, 1922-1925.
*Genealogical and Historical Magazine of Arizona Temple District, Mesa, Arizona, 1924-1947.
*Der Wegweiser (German), Basel, Switzerland, 1927-1936.
*Cumorah Monthly Bulletin, Mowbray, South Africa, 1927-1929.
  (See: Cumorah's Southern Cross, 1929-1933).
L'Etoile (French), Geneva, Switzerland, 1928-
*Hvezdika (English-Czechoslovakian), Prague, Czechoslovakia, 1929-1939.
*The Instructor (was Juvenile Instructor to 1929), Salt Lake City, Utah, 1930-1970.
*Cumorah's Southern Cross, Mowbray, South Africa, 1929-1933.
  (See: Cumorah's Southern Messenger, 1933-   )
*Austral Star, Sydney, Australia, 1929-1958.
Cumorah's Southern Messenger, Mowbray, South Africa, 1933-
*El Atalaya (Spanish), Mexico, 1937-1944.
  (See also: In Yaotlapixqui, 1937-1940).
*Week-day Religious Education, Salt Lake City, Utah, 1937-1940.
*El Mensajero Deseret (Spanish), Buenos Aires, Argentina, 1937-1955.
Lys Over Norge (Norwegian), Oslo, Norway, 1937-
*Progress of the Church, Salt Lake City, Utah, 1938-1943.
*The Church News, L.D.S. Servicemen's Edition, Salt Lake City, Utah, 1944-1948.
*A Gaivota (Portuguese), Sao Paulo, Brazil, 1948-1950.
  (See: A Liahona, 1951-   ).
Valkeus (Finnish), Helsinki, Finland, 1950-
A Liahona (Portuguese), Sao Paulo, Brazil, 1951-
  (See: A Gaivota, 1948-1950).
LDS Messenger (Japanese), Tokyo, Japan, 1952-
The New Messenger (Braille), Louisville, Kentucky, 1953-
Liahona (Spanish), Mexico, 1955-
*The Messenger, Salt Lake City, Utah, 1956-64.
Den Danske Stjerne (Danish), Copenhagen, Denmark, 1957-
  (See: Skandinavians Stjerne, 1851-1956).
The Priesthood Bulletin, Salt Lake City, Utah, 1965-

The Ensign of The Church of Jesus Christ of Latter-day Saints, 1971-
The New Era, 1971-
The Friend, 1971-

In 1967 the Church began the Unified Magazine. Magazines that were already in publication continued on with the same name but with the Unified Magazine plan. Others have been added since 1967.

The languages and magazines are as follows:

Published in March 1967: DANISH: Den Danske Stjerne; DUTCH: De Ster; FINNISH: Valkeus; FRENCH: l'Etoile; GERMAN: Der Stern; NORWEGIAN: Lys Over Norge; SPANISH: Liahona; SWEDISH: Nordstjarnan; & Indian Liahona in English (discontinued October 1971). CHINESE: (*Shengtao che sheng*) The Voice of the Saints; ITALIAN: La Stella; JAPANESE: (*Seito No Michi*) The Way of the Saints; KOREAN: (*Songdo Wi Bot*) The Friend of the Saints; PORTUGUESE: A Liahona; SAMOAN: O Le Liahona; and TONGAN: Ko E Tuhulu.

Published August 1968 and discontinued November 1970: TAHITIAN: Te Tiarama.

INDEX

— A —

Aaronic Priesthood-MIA-YM, 570-572
Aaronic Priesthood-MIA-YW, 572-573
"A Lamb to the Slaughter," 310
Abbott, Hiram, killed at Haun's Mill, 196
"Abominable Church," to be destroyed, 125
Abraham, pays tithes, 3; receives priesthood, 3
Adam, transgression of, 2; baptized and ordained, 2; to be at the head, 177; to hold council before Christ comes, 228
Adam-ondi-Ahman, 176, 177
"Address to the World," 514-515
Alberta Temple, site and building dedicated, 522
Aldrich, Hazen, 152; first seven presidents of seventy, 605
Alexander, Col. E. B., 411, 412, 413
Allen, Charles, abused by mob, 134
Allen, Felatiah (mobber), 122
Allen, Capt. James, 337, 347, 348
Allred, James, kidnapped by Missourians, 247-248
America, a land of freedom, 18
American Party, the, 511-512
Amnesty, granted to the Saints, 496
Amos, prophecy of, 6
Ancient of Days, coming of, 7
Anderson, August L., death of, 344
Anderson, Capt. William, death of, 344
Anderson, Joseph, assistant to council of twelve, 551, 604; associate managing director of Historical Department, 618
Angels, residence of, 277
Anti-Bigamy law, 432
Anti-"Mormon" mass meeting, 325-326, 327; legislation, 442, 481
Anthon, Prof. Charles, 54, 55
Apostasy, commenced in days of apostles, 7; in the Church, 166
Apostles, in Meridian of Time, 3; commission of, 4; call of, by revelation, 72; choosing of the twelve, 151-152; testimony of, 155; go to England, 179; foreign mission of, 227; epistle of the, 229; return of, from England, 235-236; meeting of, with high council in Nauvoo, 319-320; sustained as presiding council, 321-322; reply to anti-"Mormon" mass meeting, 326-327; vacancies in council of, filled, 388, 468-469, 588-599

Appeal to Washington, 238-239, 242
Archbishop Arundel, denounces scripture reading, 14-15
Archivist, 551
Area General Conference, 551, 553, 560
Arizona Temple, site and building dedicated, 523
Army in Utah, 408, 417, 423, 429
Arrington, Leonard J., church historian, 551, 618
Articles of Faith, 261-262
Ashton, Marvin J., assistant to council of twelve, 604; apostle, 599; director of social services, 552
Ashton, Marvin O., first counselor to presiding bishop, 613
Ashton, Wendell J., external communications, 552
Atchison, David R., counsel for the Saints, 137; takes witnesses to Independence, 140; report of, to Gov. Boggs, 190; false report of, 191-192; dismounted, 192; presents petition to legislature, 208
Austin, Dr., raises mob, 184; lays siege to Diahman, 184; lays siege to De Witt, 184-185
Auxiliary organizations of the Church, 567-579
Avard, Sampson, 206
Avery, Daniel, 293, 296
Avery, Philander, 293

— B —

Babbitt, Almon W., 315, 344, 400; death of, 400
Babylon to fall, 20
Backenstos, Sheriff J. B., 325, 328
Backman, Robert L., 570
Baldwin, Caleb, in Liberty prison, 207, 213
Ballantyne, Richard, 342, 569
Ballard, Melvin J., apostle, 525, 596
Baptism, how performed, 75; in the temple, 256
Baptism for the dead, doctrine of, first taught, 252; declared to the apostles, 252; performed in the river, 253, 256
Barber, Andrew, death of, 138
Baskin, Robert N., 493, 502
Bates, George C., 455
Battalion, the Mormon, 337; Pres. Young's instruction to, 338; reason for call of, 338; call of, 347
Battle of the Blue, 137-138
Bear Lake Valley, settled, 466

INDEX

Benbow, John, 233-234
Benner, Elias, killed at Haun's Mill, 196
Bennett, John C., mayor of Nauvoo, 226, 264; major general of legion, 264-265; immorality of, exposed, 265; resigns as mayor, 265; joins with Missourians, 266; writes to Sidney Rigdon and Orson Pratt, 273, 283; flight to Missouri, 283; counselor in first presidency, 586
Bennett, William Hunter, assistant to council of twelve, 551, 604
Bennion, Adam S., apostle, 598
Bennion, Samuel O., first seven presidents of seventy, 610
Benson, A. G., 333
Benson, Ezra T., apostle, 338, 591; journey of, back to the Missouri River, 378; preaches at first meeting in Salt Lake Valley, 371
Benson, Ezra Taft, mission of mercy, 535; apostle, 597
Bent, Samuel, 296, appointed to preside at Garden Grove, 335
Bernhisel, John, 307; sent to Carthage to see Gov. Ford, 305
Berry, William S., murder of, 486-487
Bettisworth, Constable David, 303, 310-311, 316
Bible, early translations of, 14; revision of, 116-117
Billings, Titus, second counselor to presiding bishop, 614
Birch, Judge, 200, 212
Birth, the first, in Salt Lake Valley, 375
Black, Adam, 182, 183, 205
Black, George A., 451, 470
Black, Jeremiah S., 427
Blair, Seth M., 392
Bogart, Rev. Samuel (mobber), 187, 188, 197, 200, 206, 216
Boggs, Gov. Lilburn W., 136; issues order to B. M. Lisle, 183; proclamation of, 183-184; accepts evil report, 190-191; orders of, to Gen. Clark, 192; order of extermination, 192-193, and note, 193; orders military court in Daviess County, 205; shooting of, 266; makes accusation against Joseph Smith and O. P. Rockwell, 266; removal of, to Oregon, 364
Bolton, Curtis E., 345, 406
Bonds, Church, issued, 504
Book of Abraham, 154; translation of, 157, 261
Book of Commandments, 118, 123, 659
Book of Mormon, revealed, 44; printed, 68-69; copyright of, 70; contains fulness of gospel, 74; copy to Greene and to P. H. Young, 88-89; the record of a fallen people, 74; British copyright of, 232-233; languages, 659
Booth, Ezra, apostasy of, 116, 120
Bordeaux, Mr., 364
Bowen, Albert E., apostle, 596
Boyce, Benjamin, kidnapped by Missourians, 247-248
Boyington, Dr., incites mob, 88
Boynton, John F., apostle, 152, 590; apostasy of, 167
Brandebury, Lemuel C., 392
Brannan, Samuel, 331, 333, 355, 366, 367
Brassfield, S. Newton, 436
Brazeale, Hugh L. (mobber), 138
Bridger, Col. James, 366
Bridger, Fort, 414
British Mission, 168; separate president placed over, 525
Brocchus, Judge Perry C., 392
Brockbank, Bernard Park, assistant to council of twelve, 603
Brockman, Thomas S. (mobber), 343, 344
Brower, Stephen L., College of Hawaii, 552
Brown, Alanson, kidnapped by Missourians, 247-248
Brown, Hugh B., first counselor in first presidency, 583; second counselor in first presidency, 585; counselor in first presidency, 587; apostle, 598; assistant to council of twelve, 601
Brown, Capt. James, 351, 355, 374, 376-377, 388
Brown, John, 380
Brown, Samuel, 387
Brown, Victor, second counselor to presiding bishop, 615-616; presiding bishop, 613
Browning, O. H., defends Joseph Smith, 249; aid of, to anti-"Mormons," 328
Brunson, Seymour, 174, 246, 252
Buchanan, James, 407, 417
Buckley, Rev. W. F., Mormons have best Sunday School in world, 522
Buehner, Carl W., second counselor to presiding bishop, 615
Bullock, Thomas, clerk of pioneer camp, 360
Buffington, Joseph, 392
Bulls, battle with wild, 352
Bunker, Edward, 399
Burton, Robert Taylor, first counselor to presiding bishop, 613; second counselor to presiding bishop, 614
Burton, Theodore M., assistant to council of twelve, 603

INDEX 667

Butler, John L., opposes mob at Gallatin, 182, 183, 308
Butterfield, Josiah, first seven presidents of seventy, 606
Butterfield, Justin, 270-271, 272
Bureau of Information, 508-509
Byers, John, killed at Haun's Mill, 196

— C —

Cahoon, Reynolds, 106, 129, 250; accuses the Prophet of fleeing from the flock, 308
Caldwell County, organization of, 164-165
Calhoun, John C., 242, 294
California Star, The, 366
California Volunteers, 433
Callis, Charles A., apostle, 596
Campbell, Alexander, 97; killed at Haun's Mill, 196
Campbell, John E., defends Nauvoo, 345
Campbell, Sheriff, 285, 286
Campbellites, *see* Disciples
Canada, work in, 168-169
Cannon, Abraham H., apostle, 492, 594; first seven presidents of seventy, 608
Cannon, George Q., mission of, to Hawaii, 397; imprisoned by Judge Emerson, 479; first counselor to Pres. John Taylor, 479, 582; first counselor to Pres. Wilford Woodruff, 491, 582; guest of honor at Hawaii mission jubilee, 505; president of Sunday Schools, 569; death of, 506; apostle, 592; counselor in first presidency, 587; assistant counselor in first presidency, 588
Cannon, John Quayle, second counselor to presiding bishop, 614-615
Cannon, Sylvester Q., presiding bishop, 523, 612; apostle, 596-597
Carlin, John (mobber), 342-344
Carlin, Gov. Thomas, memorial to, 248; acknowledges requisition from Missouri, 248-249; offers reward for capture of Joseph Smith, 270
Carrington, Albert, apostle, 592-593; counselor in first presidency, 586; assistant counselor in first presidency, 588; Church historian, 617
Carter, Gideon, 188
Carter, Jared, 142
Carter, Simeon, 98, 235
Carthage Convention, 327-328
Case, James, 360
Catholic Church, *see* Rome, Church of
Caton, Judge J. D., 285

Celestial kingdom, 129, vision of, 157-158
Centennial celebration, 524
Central Pacific Railroad, 441
Chandler, Michael H., 154
Chase, Darwin, 207, 214, 217
Child, Hortense H., 572
Children to be taught, 109, 119
Chislett, John, 401
Chittenden, J. B. (mobber), 343
Cholera, in Zion's Camp, 148
Christ, chosen before foundations of the world, 1; came to fulfill law, 3; second advent of, 7, 18, 20; church of, not established by reformers, 16; building up of church of, 72; is the light of truth, 126
Christiansen, ElRay L., assistant to council of twelve, 601
Church Archivist, 551, 618
Church Correlation Committee, 566
Church developments, other, 525
Church Historian, 551, 616-617
Church Librarian, 551, 618
Church of Jesus Christ, Joseph Smith called to restore, 20-21, 78; organized, 78-79
Church progress, 522, 530
Church government, revelation on, 74
Church of England, established, 17
Church Office Building, 553
Church publications and periodicals, 659-664
Church schools, beginning of, 465, 576-577
Church social services department, 552, 566
Clapp, Benjamin L., first seven presidents of seventy, 607
Clark, Gen., 194; harangue of, 204-205; makes false charges against prisoners, 206
Clark, Hiram, 230, 233, 257, 278
Clark, J. Reuben, Jr., second counselor in first presidency, 525, 585; first counselor in first presidency, 525, 533, 583; apostle, 596
Clawson, Hiram B., 450
Clawson, Rudger, present at death of Joseph Standing, 476; trial of, 487; comments of, before the court, 488; apostle, 501, 594; president of twelve apostles, 521, 594; second counselor in first presidency, 585
Clay, Henry, 294
Clayton, William, in presidency of British Mission, 176, 358; warns Joseph Smith at Dixon, 284; carries message to Nauvoo, 286

Cleminson, John, 197
Cleveland, Grover, 488, 492, 499
Clifford, Benjamin, Jr., 343, 344
Coe, Joseph, 107, 128, 142, 167
Cole, printer of *The Reflector*, 70
Colesville Branch, 81, 84; removes to Ohio, 101, 106; arrival of, in Missouri, 108
Colfax, Schuyler, 449
Colonies, organizations of, 460-467
Coltrin, Zebedee, first seven presidents of seventy, 152, 606
Columbus, guided by spirit of the Lord, 16
Commandments, to be kept, 113, 115; to be punished, 118; dedication of, 120
Committee to locate lands, 220
Comstock, Nehemiah, 194
Condor, Martin, murder of, 486-487
Conference, the first, 82; the second, 95-96; important, 106; first in Zion, 113; special, held in November, 1831, 118; the Amherst, 120; at Far West, 174; special, held in Salt Lake Valley, 377; first, in Tabernacle, 440; general, in April, 1919, postponed, 520; general, of April, 1920, 521
Congress, answer of, to appeal for redress, 242-243; memorial of Joseph Smith to, 296
Connor, Patrick E., 433, 434, 435, 450
Consecration, Zion, to be built by, 131
Constantine, Christianity made state religion by, 9
Constitution, guarantees of, 238
Constitutional Convention, the, 499
Convention, first political, in Salt Lake Valley, 391
Cooke, Col. Philip St. George, 350-354
Co-operation, for defense, 443; and frugality, 463
Cordon, Alfred, 396
Corrill, John, ordained a high priest, 106; offers himself as ransom, 135; comment on injustice received, 137; replies to Judge Ryland, 146; presents petition to legislature, 208; historian, 174, 616; disaffection of, 198; second counselor to presiding bishop, 614
Council meeting, at Council Bluffs, 338
Covenant, everlasting, 6; the new, 279-280; renewal of, in Salt Lake Valley, 375
Cowdery, Marcellus F., 174
Cowdery, Oliver, writes for Joseph Smith, 57; goes to Harmony, 56-57; receives Aaronic Priesthood, 57; baptized, 57-58; ordained second elder, 58, 83; receives Melchizedek Priesthood, 58; transcribes the manuscript, 70; at organization of Church, 79; preaches first discourse, 81; to keep the record (historian), 83, 616; threatened by mob, 87; error of, 91; commands Joseph, 92; to print textbooks, 109; ordained a high priest, 115; goes to Kirtland to report, 136; member of high council, 142; covenants to pay tithing, 150, 178; called to be assistant president, 150-151, 581; presides at general assembly, 154-155; excommunicated, 174-175; blessing of, given to Hyrum Smith, 254-255; return of, to the Church, 386; death of, 387, 402; assistant counselor in first presidency, 587
Cowles, Austin, 300
Cowley, Matthew, apostle, 597
Cowley, Matthias F., 512; apostle, 594
Cox, Simeon, killed at Haun's Mill, 196
Cradlebaugh, John, 424-428
Cragin Bill, the, 442
Crickets, plague of, 384-385
Crisis in the Church, 318
Critchlow, William James, Jr., assistant to the council of twelve, 602
Crooked River, battle of, 187-188
Crusade against the Church, 492, 493
Cullimore, James Alfred, assistant to council of twelve, 603
Cullom Bill, the, 443
Cumming, Gov. Alfred, 411, 414, 415; letters of, to Gen. Johnston and Sec. Cass, 415-416; wife of, pleads for people, 416; report of, 424; proclamation of, 427; attempt made to remove, 427; opposition of, to plotters, 429; departure of, 430
Curtis, John, 23
Curtis, LeGrand R., 570
Cutler, William L., defends Nauvoo, 345

— D —

Dallin, Cyrus E., 500
Daniel, prophecy of, 7, 20, 207
"Danites," 189, and note, 190
Dark Ages, 13
Davidson, James, defends Joseph Smith, 85, 86
Deacons, duties of, 76
Death, the first, in Salt Lake Valley, 375
Delaware Indians, gospel preached to, 99

INDEX 669

Democratic Association of Quincy, 219
Denunciation of false doctrines, 42
"Deseret," 392
Deseret News, The, 394
Deseret Sunday School Union, 552, 568-570; change in name, 569
Deseret Telegraph, 440
De Trobriand, Gen., 451
Developments, other Church, 525
De Witt, siege of, 184-185; defense of, 185; Prophet visits, 185-186
Dibble, Philo, miraculously healed, 138
Dickson, Joseph, false report of, 191
Dillworth, Mary Ann, 376
"Disciples" (Campbellites), 96, 97
Dispensation, of the Meridian of Time, 4; of the Fulness of Times, 17
Doctrine and Covenants, 154-155; 643-644
Dogberry, Obediah, pseudonym for Cole, 70
Doniphan, Alexander W., counsel for the Saints, 137; defends the Saints, 147; at siege of Far West, 196-197; refuses to obey order to shoot Joseph Smith, 201; greets battalion, 350
Douglas, Stephen A., 249, 264, 286, 328, 433
Drake, Thomas J., 431, 432
Drummond, William W., 405
Duncan, Chapman, 397
Dunham, Jonathan, 296
Dunklin, Gov., replies to petition, 136; futility of his advice, 136-137; petitioned by the Saints, 144; his reply, 144-145; dishonorable action, 162
Dunn, Loren Charles, first seven presidents of seventy, 611
Dunn, Paul Harold, first seven presidents of seventy, 611
Duty, Mary, grandmother of Joseph Smith, 23, 25
Dyer, Alvin Rulon, counselor in first presidency, 587; assistant to council of twelve, 602; managing director of Historical Department, 618
Dykes, George P., 396

— E —

Earth, to be a celestial body, 125; to be a Urim and Thummim, 277
East Central States Mission, organized, 525
Eaton, M. G., affidavit of, 300
Echo Canyon, 412
Eckles, Delano R., 414, 424, 425
Edmunds Bill, the, 482
Edmunds-Tucker Law, 489
Education, 465, 576-577

Egbert, Rubie, 551
Eighteenth Amendment, repeal of, 524-525
Elders, duties of, 75
Eldredge, Horace S., first seven presidents of seventy, 607
Elias, appears in Kirtland Temple, 159
Elijah, coming of, spoken of by Moroni, 45; appears in Kirtland Temple, 159; keys of sealing held by, 280-281
Ellsworth, Edmund, 398
Emigration to U. S., first, 235
Emmett, James, 296
Endowments, inauguration of, 263
Englebrecht Case, 453, 456
Ensign, a place for an, 373
Ensign, Horace S., 506
Ensign, The, 552, 663
Epistles, from Liberty prison, 210-211
Erasmus, New Testament translation of, 14
Escheatment of Church property, 489; property returned, 499
Ether, prophecy of, concerning Zion (New Jerusalem), note, 112
Evans, David, at Haun's Mill Massacre, 195
Evans, Myrthus W., Los Angeles temple, 552
Evans, Richard L., apostle, 598; first seven presidents of seventy, 610
Evarts, Sec. William M., 475, 476
Eve, teaches gospel to children, 2
Everett, Addison, 360
Ewing, Rev. Finis, incites mob, 132
Exodus, from Nauvoo, 331; of Saints to southern Utah, 416
Exploration, proposition of pioneers, 335, 336; of Salt Lake Valley, 372-373
Expulsion of Saints from Missouri, 214-215
External communications, Wendell J. Ashton, 552
Eyring, Henry B. Jr., Ricks College, 552

— F —

Fall, all men subject to the, 2
Family home evening, Monday, 552
Fancher, Capt., 419
Far West, a gathering place, 176; temple to be built at, 176, 178; siege of, 196-197
Fast Day, changed from Thursday to Sunday, (note), 505; solemn, 505
Faust, James Esdras, assistant to council of twelve, 605
Feast of the harvest, 385

670 INDEX

Featherstone, Vaughn G., second counselor in presiding bishopric, 616
Feeling, change of, 443
Ferris, Benjamin G., 394
Fielding, Rev. James, 169
Fielding, Joseph, 168, 169, 176, 233
First Council of Seventy, 605-611
First Presidency, organization of, 127, 142, 380, 381; changes in, 479, 491, 507, 515, 521, 523, 525; "Address to the World," 514-515; first counselors in, 581-584; second counselors in, 584-586; counselors in, 586-587; assistant counselors in, 587-588
First Seven Presidents of Seventy, 605-611
Fitch, Thomas, 455
Fjeldsted, C. D., first seven presidents of seventy, 608
Flournoy, J. H., 132, 136
Floyd, Camp, 417
Follett, King, imprisonment and release, 214
Ford, Gov. Thomas, Joseph Smith appeals to, 305; demand of, that Joseph Smith should go to Carthage, 305; threat of, 310; promise of, to the mob militia, 310; inflammatory speech of, 311; lack of sincerity of, 311; terror of, 316; flees to Quincy, 317; broken pledge of, 319; attitude of, towards the Saints, 324; report of, to legislature, 324; duplicity of, 328
Fordham, Elijah, healing of, 223-224
Foreign Mission Labors, 227, 396-397
Forney, Jacob, 416, 419, 424
Forsgren, John E., 389, 396
Fort, *see* specific name
Foster, Charles A., 300
Foster, James, first seven presidents of seventy, 606
Foster, Robert D., accompanies Joseph Smith on way to Washington, 239, 293; in league with apostates, 300
French Mission reopened, 525
Friend, The, 552
Frontier Guardian, 384
Fuller, Josiah, killed at Haun's Mill, 196
Fullmer, Almon, defends Nauvoo, 345
Fullmer, David, 296, 335
Fullmer, John S., 313-314
Funk, Ruth Hardy, 572
Fyans, J. Thomas, internal communications, 552; assistant to council of the twelve, 604

— G —

Galland, Dr. Isaac, 220, 248
Garden Grove, 335
Garden of Eden, 2
Gates, Jacob, first seven presidents of seventy, 607-608
Gates, Lydia, grandmother of Joseph Smith, 26
Gathering, doctrine of, revealed, 94-95
Gause, Jesse, 122
Gaylord, John, first seven presidents of seventy, 606-607
Gee, Salmon, first seven presidents of seventy, 606
Genealogical Society, 577-579
General Area Conference, England, 551; Mexico, 553; Germany, 560
General Authorities of the Church, 580-617
Gentiles, times of, soon to come in, 45; Book of Mormon to go to the, 50; gospel to be declared to, 73; Oliver Cowdery first preacher to, 79
Gentile exodus, proposed, 438
German-Austrian Mission, organized, 525
Gibbs, John H., murder of, 485-486
Gibbs, Luman, in Richmond prison, 207, 214
Gifford, Alpheus, 126
Gilbert, Algernon S., 107; agent to receive money, 109; offers himself as ransom, 135; replies to Judge Ryland, 146
Gilliam, Cornelius (mobber), 186, 197
Goaslind, Jack H., Jr., 570
Godbe, William S., 445
Godbeite Movement, 445
Godhead, doctrine of, changed, 9
Goodson, John, British missionary, 168-169
Goodyear, Miles M., 388
Gospel, older than the Law of Moses, 1; rejected in days of Noah, 2; fulness of, 3, 4; preached to Abraham, 3; preached to the children of Israel, 3; perverted, 8-9; everlasting, 20, 44
Gould, John, 136; first seven presidents of seventy, 606
Graham, Gen., at siege of Far West, 196
Grandin, Egbert B., prints Book of Mormon, 70
Grant, Heber J., apostle, 480, 593; opens Japanese Mission, 506; president of Church, 519, 580; dedicates Hawaiian Temple, 520-521; dedicates Alberta Temple, 522; dedicates Arizona Temple, 523; passing of, 530-531
Grant, Jedediah M., carries message to Gov. Ford, 309; leads company of

INDEX 671

pioneers, 379; letter of, sent to Washington, 393; death of, 403; second counselor in presidency, 584; first seven presidents of seventy, 607
Grant, Ulysses S., 448
Green, Doyle L., editor-in-chief, 552
Greene, John P., 88, 126, 225, 301, 314
Grouard, Benjamin F., 278, 397
Grover, Thomas, 388
Guerrilla warfare, 413
Gulls, miracle of the, 385
Gunnison, John W., 406 and note

— H —

Hadley, Samuel, 212
Haight, David Bruce, assistant to council of twelve, 604
Haight, Hector C., 387-388
Haight, Isaac, 421
Hale, Alva, 52
Hale, Emma, becomes wife of Joseph Smith; see also Smith, Emma
Hale, Isaac, 50, 52, 59, 93
Hammer, Austin, killed at Haun's Mill, 196
Hancock, Levi W., first seven presidents of seventy, 152, 605
Handcart immigration, 397-402
Hanks, Ephraim K., 408
Hanks, Knowlton F., 278
Hanks, Marion Duff, assistant to council of twelve, 604; first seven presidents of seventy, 611
Hansen, Peter O., 396
Harding, Stephen S., 431, 432
Hardy, Leonard W., first counselor to presiding bishop, 613
Hardy, Rufus K., first seven presidents of seventy, 610
Harney, W. S., 411
Harriman, Henry, first seven presidents of seventy, 607
Harris, Broughton D., 392
Harris, Denison L., 298-300
Harris, Emer, 298
Harris, Martin, 52; revelation to, 73; baptized, 80; ordained a priest, 83; goes to Missouri, 107; disaffection of, 173; dropped from high council, 173; return of, to the Church, 452
Harris, Major Moses, discouraging report of, 366
Harrison, Benjamin, 496
Harrison, E. L. T., 445
Hart, Cecil E., Idaho Falls temple, 552
Hart, Charles H., first seven presidents of seventy, 608
Hartnett, John, 424
Harvey, Major H. M., 340

Haslam, James H., 421
Haun's Mill massacre, 194-196
Haven, Jesse, 397
Hawaiian Temple, dedication of, 520-521
Hawley, C. M., 449
Haycock, D. Arthur, 551
Hayes, Rutherford B., 470, 481
Health Services, Church, 552
Hebrew, taught in Kirtland, 157
Hempstead, Charles H., 433, 436, 455
Henry VIII, Bible reading prohibited in reign of, 15; revolt of, from Rome, 17
Herring, James, 342
Heywood, J. L., 344, 392
Hibbard, David, 222
Higbee, Chauncey L., excommunication of, 265; in league with apostates, 300
Higbee, Elias, Church historian, 174, 616; goes to Washington, 239
Higbee, Francis M., complaint of, against Joseph Smith, 303
Higgins, Capt. Nelson, 351, 367
High Council, organization of first, 142; organization of, in Missouri, 149
High Priests, first ordained, 106
Hill Cumorah, 47, 57; celebration held at, 522; purchased, 524
Hinckley, Alonzo A., apostle, 525, 596
Hinckley, Gordon B., apostle, 598; assistant to council of twelve, 602
Hinkle, George M., commands force at DeWitt, 185; treachery of, 198, 200; at court martial, 200; testifies against prisoners, 206
Historians, 616-617
Historical department, 551, 616-617; managing director, 618; assistant managing director, 618
Holy Ghost, sign of, 276
Home industries, 435
Horne, Joseph, 379
Hotchkiss, Horace R., 222
Hubble, Mrs., spurious revelations of, 103-104
Hudson, John R., murder of, 486
Hunt, Capt. Jefferson, 349
Huntington, William, 215, 336
Hunter, Edward, 379, 396; presiding bishop, 612
Hunter, Howard William, apostle, 598; church historian, 617
Hunter, Milton Reed, first seven presidents of seventy, 611
Huntly, Aaron, 26
Hurlburt, Philastus, apostate, 129; note, 129-130
Hurt, Garland, 406

INDEX

Hyde, Orson, sent to Jefferson City with petition, 136; member of high council, 142; delegate sent to see Gov. Dunklin, 145; apostle, 152, 589; set apart for British Mission, 168; returns from England, 176; false affidavit of, 188, 189; return of, to the Church, 189; set apart for mission to Palestine, 230, 258; departure of, for Palestine, 235; dedicates Palestine, 258, 259; sent to Washington, 296; arrival of, at pioneer camp, 336; return of, from England, 359; presides at Kanesville, 383, 387
Hymnbook, 660

– I –

Immigrants, characteristics of, 461-462
Improvement Era, 573, 662
Indians, Catteraugus, gospel preached to, 96, 99; Wyandots, 96, 98
Indulgences, sale of, 11
Iniquity, mystery of, 8
Inquisition, the, 15
Institutes, 576-577
Instructor, The, 569, 663
Internal Communications Department, 552
Isaacson, Thorpe B., counselor to first presidency, 587; assistant to council of twelve, 603; first counselor to presiding bishop, 614; second counselor to presiding bishop, 615
Isaiah, prophecy of, 6, 45, 111; fulfilled, 54
Israel, children of, Book of Mormon to go to, 50
Israelites, subject to Law of Moses, 1, 3
Intelligence, glory of God is, 125
Ivins, Anthony W., first counselor in presidency, 523, 582-583; second counselor in presidency, 521, 585; apostle, 595
Ivins, Antoine R., first seven presidents of seventy, 610

– J –

Jacobs, Henry, 188, 189
James, promise of, tested, 37
Japanese Mission, 506
Jerusalem, New, *see* Zion
Jennings, Col. William O., 194, 195, 197
Jews, attitude of, toward Christ, note, 260-261
Joel, quoted by Moroni, 45
John the Baptist, ordains Joseph and Oliver, 58; preaching of, 276

John the Revelator, vision of, 20; mission of, 106
Johns, William N., 450
Johnson, Andrew, 344
Johnson, John, conference at home of, 119; member of high council, 142
Johnson, Luke S., member of high council, 142; apostasy of, 167; reinstated, note, 360; apostle, 589
Johnson, Lyman E., apostle, 152, 590; excommunication, 175
Johnston, Albert Sidney, 411, 413, 417, 427, 429
Jones, Dan, 278; goes to rescue of Joseph Smith, 287; in Carthage jail, 313; interview with Gov. Ford, 314
Jubilee, the Pioneer, 499-500
Juvenile Instructor, The, see Instructor

– K –

Kane, J. K., 340, 415
Kane, Col. Thomas L., 334, 337, 339, 340, 383, 392, 393; mediation of, 415, 428
Kapp, Ardeth G., 572
Kearns, Thomas, 511
Kearny, Col. S. W., 347, 348
Kelsch, Louis A., 506
Kelsey, Eli B., 445
Kendell, Amos, 333
Keys of Kingdom, 127
Kimball, Andrew, 562
Kimball, Camilla Eyring, 564
Kimball, Heber C., visits Joseph Smith, 126; apostle, 152, 589; loyalty of, 167; called to open British Mission, 168; returns from England, 176; petitions Missouri Legislature, 208; goes to Jefferson City, 212; assists Saints to leave Missouri, 215; fulfills prophecy at Far West, 215-216; departs for England, 230; departure for the West, 332; in command of division of exiles, 334; preaches at first meeting in Salt Lake Valley, 371; first counselor in presidency, 381, 582; at laying of cornerstones of Salt Lake Temple, 396; death of, 440
Kimball, Hiram, 222, 308, 406
Kimball, J. Golden, first seven presidents of seventy, 609
Kimball, Spencer W., biography of, 561-566; twelfth president of Church, 566, 581; apostle, 565, 597; acting president of the council of the twelve, 597; president of the council of the twelve, 566, 581

King, Austin A., 182, 183, 200, 206, 212
King Charles V, 10; introduced Inquisition, 15
King, James (mobber), 343
Kingdom of God, 276
Kinney, John F., 405
Kirkham, Oscar A., first seven presidents of seventy, 604
Kirtland Camp (Seventies), 179-180
Kirtland Safety Society, 165; failure of, 166
Kirtland Temple, 128; blessings in, 157; dedication of, 159
Kneighton, Henry, denounces scripture reading, 14
Knight, Joseph, Jr., baptized, 85
Knight, Joseph, Sr., 59, 85, 87
Knight, Newel, 81; miraculously healed, 82; baptized, 82; vision of, 84

— L —

Laban, sword of, 62
Lamanites, mission to, 94; programs for, 562, 565-566
Lamborn, Josiah, 272
Lamereaux, Andrew L., defends Nauvoo, 345
Land, division of, 464
Law, carnal, *see* Moses, Law of
Law, given to govern Church, 103; Saints to keep, 109-110
Law, William, 297, 298, 300; second counselor in first presidency, 584
Law, Wilson, 225, 297
Lawrence, Henry W., 445
Learning, revival of, 13
Lee, Harold B., first counselor in first presidency, 583; apostle, 597; biographical sketch, 555-560; president, 581
Lee, John, killed at Haun's Mill, 196
Lee, John D., 421, 422
Legislation against the "Mormons," 432-433, 444, 481-482
Lewis, Benjamin, killed at Haun's Mill, 196
Lewis, James, 397
Lewis, Joshua, conference held at home of, 113
Lewis, Tarlton, 360
Lewis, Theodore B., 608
Liberal Party, 446, 496
Liberty Prison, 207, 210
Limhi, Fort, settled, 466
Lincoln, Abraham, message of, to Pres. Young, 430
Linville, Thomas (mobber), 138
Little, Feramorz, 408

Little, Jesse C., 339, 380; second counselor to presiding bishop, 614
Logan Temple, dedication of, 480-481
Longden, John, assistant to council of twelve, 601
Loyalty of Saints to government, 329
Lucas, Robert, gov. of Iowa, 214, 220
Lucas, Samuel D., secretary of mob gathering, 132; threats of, against the Saints, 190; false report of, 192; in command of troops, 196; order of, to Doniphan to shoot prisoners, 201
Lund, Anthon H., apostle, 505, 594; first counselor in first presidency, 515, 519, 582; second counselor in first presidency, 507, 585; death of 521; historian, 617
Luther, Martin, 12, 16-17
Lyman, Amasa M., 200, 321, 440; counselor in first presidency, 586; apostle, 591
Lyman, Francis M., 479, 513; apostle, 593
Lyman, Richard R., apostle, 596

— M —

Mack, Ebenezer, 26
Mack family of Connecticut, 26, 28
Mack, Jason, 27
Mack, John, ancestor of Joseph Smith, 26
Mack, Solomon, 26, 28; patriotic services of, 27
Mack, Stephen, 27, 28
Magraw, W. M., 406
Malachi, quoted by Moroni, 44-45
Manifesto, the 493-495; "Official Declaration" of, 494-495; sustained, 495-496; result of, 496
Mann, S. A., 445, 448, 449
Manti Temple, 492
Manuscript lost by Martin Harris, 55-56
Margetts, Thomas, 400
Markham, Stephen, warns Joseph Smith at Dixon, 284; in Carthage jail, 313; in command of company to build roads, 335
Marks, William, 222, 225; calls special meeting, 320; rejection of, 322
Marriage, eternity of, 278-279; plural, revealed, 281-282; announcement made, 394
Marsh, Thomas B., apostle, 152, 588; apostasy of, 188; affidavit of, 189; return of, to the Church (note), 190
Martyrdom, the, 315-316
Martin, Edward, 399
Marvelous work and a wonder, 19
Mason, Dr. James O., 552

Mass meeting, anti-"Mormon," held at Quincy, 325-326
Massacre, Mountain Meadows, 418-422
Massacre, the Tennessee, 486-487
Maxwell, Neal A., Commissioner of Education, 552; assistant to the council of twelve, 605
McArthur, Daniel, 398
McAuley, John (mobber), 342
McBride, Thomas, killed at Haun's Mill, 196
McClernand, Gen. John A., 493
McClentic, Mr. (mobber), 122
McConkie, Bruce Redd, apostle, 599; first seven presidents of seventy, 611
McCullock, Ben, 416
McCurdy, Solomon P., 436
McDonald, A. F., 450
McDuffie, Sen. George H., remarks of, concerning Rocky Mountains, 367
McIlwaine's Bend, revelation given at, 113
McKay, David Lawrence, 552
McKay, David O., second counselor in first presidency, 525, 533, 540, 585; childhood of, 537-538; mission of, 538; instructor and principal at Weber Stake Academy, 538; superintendent of Weber Stake Sunday Schools, 538; marriage of, 538; apostle, 538, 595; assistant superintendent and then superintendent of Deseret Sunday School Union, 538; commissioner of education in Church School System, 538; world tour of missions with Hugh J. Cannon, 539; supervisor of all European Missions, 539; president of Church, 540, 580; established missions in Far East, 540; traveled world-wide, 540; dedicated Swiss Temple, 540; dedicated Los Angeles Temple, 541; dedicated New Zealand Temple, 541; dedicated London Temple, 541; dedicated Oakland Temple, 541; temples built during administration, 541; building programs under, 541-542; missionary activity under, 542; growth of stakes under, 542; education program under, 542-543; priesthood correlation under, 543-544; honors received by, 544; first presidency changes under, 544; death of, 544-545; death of wife, Emma Ray, 545
McKay, Emma Ray Riggs, death, 554
McKay, Thomas E., assistant to council of twelve, 600
McKean, James B., 449, 453, 455, 457
McLellin, William E., 118, folly of, 119; apostle, 152, 589; excommunicated, 175
McMaster, Cyrus, incites mob, 88
McMurrin, Joseph W., first seven presidents of seventy, 609
McRae, Alexander, in Liberty prison, 207; escapes from Missouri, 213; defends Nauvoo, 345
Melchizedek, King of Salem, 2
Melchizedek Priesthood MIA, 573-575
Melling, Peter, 233
Members, duties of Church, 76
Merrick, Charles, killed at Haun's Mill, 196
Merrick, Levi N., killed at Haun's Mill, 196
Merrill, Joseph F., apostle, 596
Merrill, Marriner W., 492; apostle, 593
Merrill, Philemon C., 354
Message of the Ages, 524
Mexico, the Saints in, 515
Miles Case, the, 472-473
Miles, Daniel S., first seven presidents of seventy, 606
Miller, Daniel, 388
Miller, Eleazer, 126
Miller, Bishop George, 248, 332, 380, 612
Miller, Orrin Porter, first counselor to presiding bishop, 613; second counselor to presiding bishop, 615
Miller, William, 450
Millennial Star, first issued, 232
Mining in Utah, 434
Ministerial Alliance, 503
Ministers, opposition of, 471, 482, 503
Miracle, the first, 82
Miraculous healing, 223-224
Mission Representatives, 553
Missionaries, withdrawal of, from nations, 526; return of, to nations, 536
Missions, 467, 650-658
Mitchell, Dr. Samuel L., 54
Mob, Joseph Smith threatened by, 87; violence of, in Hiram, 122; in Zion, 128; council of, 132; declaration of, 133; demands of, 134; report of, committee, 134; vengeance of, 134; second gathering of, in Zion, 135; threatens to kill all members of the Church, 135; forces the Saints to agree to leave Jackson County, 135; breaks contract, 135-136; makes raids, 137; makes threats against Zion's Camp, 145; dispersed by a storm, 145-146; makes proposition to buy or sell lands, 146-147; unfairness of the proposition of, 147; kidnap-

ping of Alanson Brown and others by, 247-248; threats of vengeance by, 269; gathering of, at Carthage, 302; threats of, 303-304; threats of, at Carthage, 313; plotting of, at Carthage, 314; terror of, 316; activities of, renewed, 323-324; uprising of, at Nauvoo, 341; attack by, on Nauvoo, 343; violation of treaty of Nauvoo by, 346
Montgomery, N. (mobber), 343
Morgan, John, first seven presidents of seventy, 608
Morley, Isaac, joins the Church, 98; offers himself as a ransom, 135; first counselor to presiding bishop, 613
Mormon Battalion, equipment of, 348; line of march of the, 349-350; discharged, 354; arrival of members of, from Pueblo, 367; arrival of members of, in Salt Lake Valley, 374-375
Monson, Thomas S., apostle, 598
Moroni, Angel, appearance of, to Joseph Smith, 44, 46-47; gives plates to Joseph Smith, 51
Morrill, Justin R., 432
Morris, George Q., apostle 598; assistant to council of twelve, 601
Moses, appears in Kirtland Temple, 159
Moses, Book of, 89, 101, 261
Moses, Julian, 376
Moses, Law of, 1, 3, 6; annulled, 3
Moses, words of, revealed, 89
Motley, John Lathrop, quoted, 10, 11, 12, 15
Mountain Meadows, massacre at, 418, 421
Mountfort, Henry de, 11
Mount Pisgah, 336
Moyle, Henry D., first counselor in first presidency, 583; second counselor in the first presidency, 585; apostle, 597
Muddy Mission, 466
Mulholland, James, 246
Murderers, trial of the, of Joseph and Hyrum Smith, 323
Murdock, John, joins the Church, 98, mission of, 397
Murray, Gov. Eli, 487
Mysteries to be revealed to the faithful, 115

— N —

Napier, William, killed at Haun's Mill, 196
Nations, withdrawal of missionaries from, 526; return of missionaries to, 536

Nauvoo, founding of, 221; meaning of, 221; charter of, 224; University of, 225; Legion, 225; attempt to repeal charter of, 277-278; growth of, 291; under martial law, 304-305; repeal of charter of, 325; preparation of Saints to leave, 329-330; abandonment of, 331; attack upon, by mob, 343; battle of, 344
Nauvoo House, 253
Nauvoo *Expositor*, 301, declared a nuisance, 301-302
Nelson, Russell M., Sunday School president, 552
Netherlands, indulgences in the, 11-12, 15, 16
New Era, The, 552, 663
New Jerusalem, *see* Zion
Newman, Rev. J. P., 449, 452
"New Movement," the, 445
Nibley, Charles W., 513; second counselor in first presidency, 523, 585; death of, 525; presiding bishop, 612
Nixon, Richard M., president, 551
Noble, Joseph B., leads company of pioneers, 379
Norris, David, death of, 344, 345

— O —

Oakland Temple, dedication of, 541
Oaks, Dallin H., BYU president, 552
O'Banion, Patrick, death of, 187-188
Ogden Temple, 551-552
Old Fort, the, 375, 376
"Olive Leaf," the (Sec. 88), 125
Olson, Earl E., archivist, 551; assistant managing director of Historical Department, 618
"One Mighty and Strong," 125
Only Begotten of the Father, 2
Orton, Roger, 607
Owens, Samuel C. (mobber), 136, 146, 283

— P —

Packer, Boyd K., apostle, 598; assistant to council of twelve, 603
Page, Hiram, witness of Book of Mormon, 66; ordained a teacher, 83; spurious revelations of, 94; apostasy of, 175
Page, John E., apostle, 179, 216, 590; set apart for mission to Palestine, 230, 258; sent to Washington, 296; excommunication of, 381
Palestine, Orson Hyde's mission to, 235; dedication of, 258
Palestine-Assyrian Mission, organized, 525

Parker, Major, 343
Parks, Gen., at siege of Far West, 196
Parliament of Religion, 498
Parrish, Warren, 154; sees vision, 158; apostasy of, 167
Partridge, Edward, joins the Church, 98, 100-101; visits Joseph Smith, 100; presiding bishop, 103, 611-612; goes to Missouri, 107; to be Bishop in Zion, 109; abused by mob, 134; offers himself as ransom, 135; lays cornerstone of temple at Far West, 178; death of, 246, 402
Patriarchs, 599-600
Patrick, Shepherd G., 285, 288
Patten, David W., apostle, 152, 588; death of, 187-188
Paul, apostasy predicted by, 7, 8, 40
Peace Commission, the, 416-417; epistle to Gen. Johnston, 417
Pearl of Great Price, 660
Peniston, William P. (mobber), 182, 183, 187
Penrose, Charles W., second counselor in first presidency, 515, 585; first counselor in first presidency, 519, 520, 582; death of, 523; apostle, 595
Peoples, amalgamation of many, 462; of Europe, destitute condition of, 534-535
People's Party, 496
Periodicals, Church, 661-664
Perpetual Emigrating Company, 389, 489
Perry, Lowell Tom, assistant to council of twelve, 605; apostle, 599
Persecution, campaign of, 485
Peter, prophecy of, 8
Peters, Rev. J. H., 482
Petersen, Mark Edward, apostle, 597
Peterson, Harold Burke, first counselor to presiding bishopric, 614
Peterson, Ziba, 96
Phelps, Morris, in Richmond prison, 207, 214
Phelps, William W., goes to Missouri, 107; preaches in Jackson County, 108; appointed to assist Oliver Cowdery in printing, 108-109; vision of, at McIlwaine's Bend, 113; offers himself as ransom, 135; sent to Jefferson City with petition, 136; makes comments on attitude of state officials, 140; rejected by the Saints, 173; excommunicated, 174; meets with Lucas and his aides, 198; gives testimony against prisoners, 206; return of, to the Church, 245
Pickett, William, 342, 343, 345

Pierce, Pres. Franklin, 407
Pinegar, Rex Dee, first seven presidents of seventy, 611
Pioneer Day Celebration, 409, 479
Pioneer Monument, 500
Pioneers, departure of, for the West, 358, 359; organization of camp of, 359-360; regulation in camp of the, 360; route of travel of the, 361; met by the, on the way, 362-363; scientific observations of the, 364; crossing the Platte, 364; joined by Mississippi emigrants, 365; ferry at the Black Hills, 365; meet with Samuel Brannan, 366; arrive in Salt Lake Valley, 370
Pitcher, Col. Thomas, 136, 138, 139
Pixley, Rev., incites mob, 132
Plural Marriage, official statement of first presidency, 394
Poland Law, the, 456
Pope, Judge, 272
Pope, temporal power of, 10
Powell, L. W., 416
Pratt, Addison, 278, 397
Pratt, Orson, called on mission, 100-101, 168; apostle, 152, 590; gives letter to Joseph Smith, 273; sent to Washington, 296; observations made by, 364; leads vanguard into Salt Lake Valley, 368-369; remarks of, at first meeting in Salt Lake City, 374; called to preside in Great Britain, 380; discussion of, with J. P. Newman, 452; death of, 480; Church historian, 617
Pratt, Parley P., baptized, 96; mission to Lamanites, 96; returns to Ohio, 98; ordained a high priest, 106; delegate sent to see Gov. Dunklin, 145; apostle, 152, 589; taken prisoner at Far West, 198, 200; relates story of Prophet's rebuke at Richmond prison, 203-204; in Richmond prison, 207; escape of, 214; departure of, for the West, 332; at Mt. Pisgah, 336; arrival of, from England, 359; leads company of pioneers, 378, 379; at laying of cornerstones of S. L. Temple, 395; death of, 404
Pratt, Rey L., 525; first seven presidents of seventy, 610
Presidency, First, organized, 142
Presidents of Church, 580-581; assistant presidents, 581
Presiding Bishops, 611-613; first counselors to, 613-614; second counselors to, 614-616
Press, falsehoods of, 472

INDEX

Preston, William B., presiding bishop, 612
Priesthood, after the order of the Son of God, 2; given to Adam and patriarchs, 3; Higher, taken from Israel, 3; Lesser, holds keys of preparatory Gospel, 3; Aaronic, restored, 57; Melchizedek, held by Peter, James, and John, 57; Melchizedek restored, 58; ordinations to the, 82; Patriarchal, conferred, 141; revelation of (Sec. 84), 124; great revelation on, 153; items on, 228; fulness of, 251
Priests, duties of, 76
Primary Association, 575-576
Printing Press, to be purchased, 116; paper purchased for, 122
Progress of the Church, 522, 530
Prophecy, fulfilment of, 148, 215-216; on removal of Saints to Rocky Mountains, 276; on war, 517
Prophets, School of, (see School of Prophets)
Prosperity, period of, 517
Protest of citizens against Reed Smoot, 510
Protest of women against legislation, 444
Protestant Revolution, a preparatory work, 17
Provisional government, organization of, 391
Provo temple, 551, 552
Pulsipher, Zera, first seven presidents of seventy, 607
Punishment, eternal, explained, 73-74

– Q –

Quincy Committee, 344

– R –

Railroad, transcontinental, 441
Rawlins, Fort, 451
Rawlins, Joseph L., 498, 499, 503
Record, Oliver Cowdery to keep, 83
Records to be kept, 79
Recreation of the Latter-day Saints, 464-465
Rector, Hartman, Jr., first seven presidents of seventy, 611
Redeemer, provided in the beginning, 2
Reed-Donner Party, 368
Reed, Lazarus H., 394, 405
Reese, Amos, counsel for Saints, 137; false report of, 191
Reflector, The, Palmyra paper, 70; part of Book of Mormon, 70
Reformation, 14, 16

Regional Representative of Twelve, 544, 553
Reid, H. T. (attorney), 311
Reid, John, defends Joseph Smith, 185; statement of, 86-87
Relief Society, organization of, 262-263; 567-568
Relief Society Magazine, 552, 568
Restoration, the time of the, 19; reasonable to expect, 19
Requisition by Missouri, for Joseph Smith and others, 248-259
Retrenchment Association, 572
Revelations, came to an end, 8; to be published, 118; endorsement of, 118; criticism of, 118-119; arrangement of, 119; dedication of, 120; of things kept from the world, 253
Reynolds, George, 457-458, 469, 470; first seven presidents of seventy, 609
Reynolds, J. H., under arrest, 285-286, 287-288
Reynolds, Gov. Thomas, offers reward for capture of Joseph Smith, 270; requisition issued by, for Joseph Smith, 284
Rich, Charles C., seeks interview with Doniphan, 197; leads company of pioneers, 379; apostle, 388, 591; settles San Bernardino, 466; death of, 466
Rich, Leonard, first seven presidents of seventy, 152, 606
Richards, Franklin D., apostle, 388, 592; historian, 617
Richards, Franklin Dewey, assistant to the council of twelve, 602-603
Richards, George F., apostle, 533, 595; acting patriarch, 600
Richards, George S., killed at Haun's Mill, 196
Richards, LeGrand, apostle, 597; presiding bishop, 612
Richards, Stayner, assistant to council of twelve, 601
Richards, Stephen L, first counselor in first presidency, 583; apostle, 595-596
Richards, Willard, loyalty of, 167; in presidency of British Mission, 176; apostle, 179, 215, 232, 591; in Carthage jail, 313; escapes injury, 316; departure for the West, 332; remarks of, at first meeting in Salt Lake Valley, 371; second counselor in first presidency, 381-382, 584; editor of *Deseret News,* 394; death of, 403; church historian, 616-617
Richmond Prison, 202, 204, 207, 211

INDEX

Ridges, Joseph, 440
Rigdon, Sidney, joins the Church, 97, 98; writes for Joseph, 101; ordained a high priest, 106; goes to Missouri, 107; dedicates land of Zion, 110-111; exhorts Saints in Zion, 111; writes for Joseph Smith, 116; commanded to labor with Joseph Smith, 120; beaten by mob in Hiram, 122; first counselor in first presidency, 127, 581-582; presides at general assembly, 154-155; orator at Independence Day celebration, 178; taken prisoner at Far West, 198, 200; released from prison, 211-212; elected a member of Nauvoo City Council, 225; at Quincy, 238; appointed to take grievances to Washington, 239; receives a letter from J. C. Bennett, 273; assists in selecting brethren to go to the West, 296; attempt of, to be guardian, 319; claims of, presented to the Saints, 320; rejection of, 321; excommunication of, 322, 582
Riley, Rev., (mobber), 146
Rio Virgin, settlements made on, 466
Roberts, B. H., secures bodies of Elders Gibbs and Berry, 487; at Parliament of Religions, 498; case before Congress, 502; excluded from Congress, 504; first seven presidents of seventy, 609
Robinson, George W., appointed Church recorder, 174, 616; taken prisoner at Far West, 198, 200
Robinson, Dr. J. King, 436-437
Rockwell, Orrin P., baptized, 80; arrested on Missouri charges, 268; release of, from Missouri, 289-290; story of, 290; accompanies Joseph Smith across the Mississippi River, 308; on mail route, 408
Rockwood, Albert P., 265, 360; first seven presidents of seventy, 607
Rogers, Mr., murderer at Haun's Mill, 195
Rogers, David W., 220
Rogers, Noah, kidnapped by Missourians, 247-248, 278
Roman Empire, 7
Rome, Church of, 9, 11, 141
Romney, Marion George, 16, 17; apostle, 597; assistant to council of twelve, 600; second counselor in first presidency, 566, 586
Roundy, Shadrach, 215, 360
Russell, Isaac, 169
Russell, William H., 408
Ryder, Simonds (apostate), 122
Ryland, Judge, makes proposition to the Saints, 146

– S –

Sabbath Day, to be kept, 119
Sacrament, corrupted, revelation on, 92-93
Sacred Grove, celebration held at, 522-523
Saints, to be gathered, 94-95; commanded to go to Ohio, 101; remove from New York, 103; employ counsel, 137; driven from Jackson County, 139; seek redress, 139; instructed to importune for redress, 143; make counter proposition to buy lands of mobbers, 147; rejected by citizens of Clay County, 162-163; reply to citizens of Clay County, 164; sorrow of, 317; attack upon the, 325; threats against, by mob, 343; attitude of, towards the rebellion, 430; gathering of, 460; progress of, 461
Salt Lake City, founding of, 373-374; survey of, 374
Salt Lake Tribune, 446-447
Salt Lake Valley, uninviting country, 366-367; dedication of, 369; arrival of pioneers in the, 370; first Sabbath in the, 371; explorations of, 372
Salvation, individual, 2; taught to Adam, 2
San Bernardino, established 1851, 466
Sanderson, Dr. George B., 349
Satan, the prince of darkness, 49
Schmidt, Donald Thomas, Church librarian-archivist, 618
School of the Elders, commenced, 151, 157
School of Prophets, 125-126, 127
Schwendiman, Fred W., New Zealand Temple, 552
Scofield disaster, 505
Sconce, Colonel, 146
Scott, Robert, 298-300
Scouting in Church, 570-571
Second counselors to the president, 584-586
Secrist, Jacob F., 388
Seebohm, Frederick (quoted), 10
Segregation ruling, 488
Seizas, Professor, teaches Hebrew, 157
Self-government of Saints, denied, 483
Seminary classes, 558-559
Sessions, Perrigrine, 387
Settlements, beginning of, in Utah, 387-388
Seventies in Meridian of Time, 4

Seventy, organization of first quorum, 152
Sexton, Pliny T., 524
Shaffer, J. Wilson, 448, 450, 451
Shaver, Leonidas, 394, 406
Shearer, Rev., opposes the work, 84, 88
Shearer, Norman, in Richmond prison, 207, 214, 217
Sherman, J. H. (mobber), 343
Sherman, Lyman, first seven presidents of seventy, 152, 606
Sherman, William T., 437
Sheets, Elijah F., 450
Sill, Sterling W., assistant to the council of twelve, 602
Simpson, Richard, chairman of mob gathering, 132
Simpson, Robert L., assistant to council of twelve, 604; first counselor to presiding bishop, 614
Sinclair, Charles E., 424, 426, 427
Singleton, James W. (mobber), 343
Sloan, James, 225, 278; Church historian, 616
Smith, Lieutenant A. J., 349, 350
Smith, Agnes, forced to wade Grand River, 186
Smith, Alma, wounded at Haun's Mill, 196
Smith, Alvin, death of, 34, 50; in celestial kingdom, 129
Smith, Asael, 23-24; accepts gospel, 89
Smith, David A., 523; first counselor to presiding bishop, 613; second counselor to presiding bishop, 615
Smith, Don Carlos, visits Stockholm, N. Y., 25; baptized, 84; to be remembered by bishop of Zion, 120; assists Saints to leave Missouri, 215; death of, 257
Smith, Eldred Gee, patriarch, 600
Smith, Elias, 409
Smith, Emma, to select hymns, 91, 123; appeal of, to the Prophet, 269, 308
Smith, George A., baptized, 126; hauls first stone for Kirtland Temple, 129; apostle, 215, 591; departs for England, 230; departure of, for the West, 332; preaches at first meeting in Salt Lake Valley, 371; Church historian, 403, 617; first counselor in the first presidency, 441, 582
Smith, George Albert, president of the Church, 532, 580; dedicated Idaho Falls Temple, 534; died, 536; apostle, 594
Smith, Hyrum, attends school at Hanover, 29; tenderness of, 29; assistance rendered by, 30; joins Presbyterian Church, 37; baptized, 60; witness of Book of Mormon, 66; at organization of Church, 79; ordained a high priest, 83; to be remembered by bishop of Zion, 120; digs trench for Kirtland Temple, 129; second counselor to Joseph Smith, 170, 584; supervises constitution of Kirtland Camp, 179-180; condemned to be shot, 200; taken to Independence, 201; taken to Liberty, 207; escapes from Missouri, 213; elected a member of Nauvoo City Council, 225; patriarch, 253-254, 599; assists in selecting brethren to go West, 296; in consultation with brethren, 307-308; refusal of, to leave his brother, 307; leaves Nauvoo for the West, 308; return of, to Nauvoo, 309; departure of, for Carthage, 309; arrival at Carthage, 310; charged with treason, 310-311; false imprisonment of, 311, 313; martyrdom of, 315-316; assistant president of Church, 581; assistant counselor in first presidency, 588
Smith, Hyrum G., patriarch, 599-600
Smith, Hyrum M., apostle, 594
Smith, Jessie Evans, death, 554
Smith, John, 164; member of high council, 142; chosen to preside in Salt Lake Valley, 377, 379; patriarch, 382, 599; death of, 403; assistant counselor in first presidency, 588
Smith, John (Patriarch), death of, 515; patriarch, 599
Smith, John Henry, apostle, 479, 593; in constitutional convention, 499; second counselor in first presidency, 515, 585; death of, 515
Smith, Joseph the Prophet, divinely called, 20-21, 78; ancestry of, 22; birth of, 22, 28; affliction of, 29-30; removal of, to New York, 33; story of, 36; vision of the Father and the Son, 38-39; reflection of, 40; vision of, rejected by the world, 41; is visited by Moroni, 44, 46; visits the Hill Cumorah, 47-48; is tempted, 48; receives the record, 51; importunes the Lord, is rebuked, 55; forbidden to translate, 56; translates, 57; receives Aaronic Priesthood, 57; baptized, 57; ordained first elder, 57, 83; receives Melchizedek Priesthood, 58; removes to Fayette, 59; to be called a seer, 79; visits Colesville, 81; is arrested, 85; trial, at S. Bainbridge, 85; second arrest, 86; taken to Colesville, 86; trial, 86; threatened by mob, 87; re-

ceives words of Moses, 89; corrects Oliver Cowdery's error, 92; corrects Hiram Page, 94; moves to Kirtland, 102; ordained a high priest, 106; goes to Missouri, 107; dedicates temple site in Zion, 112; returns to Kirtland, 113; commenced revision of the Bible, 116-117; reviews commandments, 118; commanded to labor among enemies, 120; views on the vision of the glories, 121; beaten by mob in Hiram, 122; second visit of, to Missouri, 123; returns to Kirtland, 123; revises the scriptures, 121; finishes the New Testament, 126-127; president of Church, 127, 567; warns the Saints in Zion, 131; gives patriarchal blessings, 141; disbands Zion's Camp in Missouri, 148; covenants to pay tithing, 150, 178; translates Book of Abraham, 154, 157; sees vision of Celestial Kingdom, 157-158; receives keys from Moses, Elias and Elijah, 159-161; endorses action of Saints in Clay County, 164; withdraws from Safety Society, 165; goes to Missouri, 167; holds council, 167; accused by false brethren, 167; flees from Kirtland, 172; arrested on Peniston charges, 183; tried before Judge King, 183; visits De Witt, 185-186; at funeral of David W. Patten, 188; taken prisoner at Far West, 198, 200; condemned to be shot, 200; taken to Independence, 201; in Richmond prison, 202; rebukes the guards, 203-204; taken to Liberty, 207; escapes from Missouri, 213; moves to Commerce, 221; heals the sick at Montrose, 223; elected a member of Nauvoo council, 225; instructs the apostles, 227; discourses on priesthood, 228; comment of, on the mission of the apostles, 236-237; appointed to importune at Washington for redress, 238; appeal of, to the people, 239; interview of, with President Van Buren, 240, 242; interview with John C. Calhoun, 242; return of, from Washington, 243; released on habeas corpus by Stephen A. Douglas, 249; writes to John Wentworth, 261-262; teaches temple ordinances, 263; at sham battle at Nauvoo, 264; John C. Bennett's treachery shown to, 265; chosen mayor of Nauvoo, 265; accused as an accessory to the assault on L. W. Boggs, 266; prophesies that Saints would be driven to Rocky Mountains, 267; arrested on Missouri charges, 268; arrested on charge of being accessory, 268; goes into retirement, 268; writes to Wilson Law, 269; surrenders for trial, 272; discharged by Judge Pope, 272; entertains his friends, 273-274; intimation of his death, 276; instructs the Saints in doctrine, 276-277; prophecy of, to Stephen A. Douglas, 282; fulfillment of, (note) 282; conspiracy of J. C. Bennett and others against, 283; departure of, for Dixon, 285; preaches at Pawpaw Grove, 286; arrives in Nauvoo, 287; address of, to the Saints, 288; trial of, before Municipal court, 287; candidacy of, for president, 293-294; views of, on government, 294-295; memorial of, to Congress, 296; discourse on plottings of traitors, 297; indictment of, for polygamy, 300; appeal of, to Gov. Ford, 305; receives command from Gov. Ford to go to Carthage, with pledge of protection, 306-307; reply of, to Gov. Ford, 307; departure of, for the West, 308; decision of, to go to the West, 307-308; prophecy of, to Stephen Markham, 308; accused by false brethren, 308-309; preparation of, to go to Carthage, 309; departure of, for Carthage, 309; remarks to Daniel H. Wells, 309; return of, to Nauvoo with Capt. Dunn, 310; charged with treason, 310-311; false imprisonment of, 311, 313; illegal summons of, for trial, 313; martyrdom of, 315-316; first president of Church, 580; apostle, 580

Smith, Joseph, Sr., witness of Book of Mormon, 66; baptized, 80; ordained a high priest, 106; ordained patriarch, 142, 599; member of high council, 142; death of, 246-247; assistant counselor in first presidency, 587

Smith, Joseph F., apostle, 440, 592; second counselor in presidency to John Taylor and Wilford Woodruff, 479, 491, 584; president of Church, 507, 580; attitude of, toward traducers, 512; official statement of, on plural marriages, 512-513; dedicates Joseph Smith Monument, 513; visits Europe, 513; address to the world, 514; manifestation given to, 518; death of, 518; first counselor in first presidency, 582; counselor in first presidency, 586

Smith, Joseph F., patriarch, 600

INDEX

Smith, Joseph Fielding, life and administration of, 546-551; tenth president of the church, 546, 580-581; counselor in first presidency, 587; apostle, 595; Church historian, 617; wife, Jessie E. Evans, dies, 549; death of, 554
Smith, Leonard I., 397
Smith, Lot, 413
Smith, Lucy Mack, mother of the Prophet, 22, 28, 37; baptized, 80
Smith, Nicholas G., acting patriarch, 600; assistant to council of twelve, 601
Smith, Robert F., (justice of peace), 311, 313
Smith, Samuel, fought in Revolutionary War, 23
Smith, Samuel Harrison, joins Presbyterian Church, 37; baptism of, 60; one of the eight witnesses, 66; at organization of Church, 79; ordained an elder, 83; takes missionary journey, 88; member of high council, 142
Smith, Sardius, killed at Haun's Mill, 196
Smith, Silas, 25
Smith, Sylvester, member of high council, 142; chosen a seventy, 152; clerk of general assembly, 154; apostasy of, 167; first seven presidents of seventy, 606
Smith, Thomas L., discouraging report of, 366
Smith, Warren, killed at Haun's Mill, 196
Smith, William, baptized, 84; apostle, 152, 589-590; excommunication of, 381, 590; ordained patriarch, 599
Smoot, Abraham O., leads company of pioneers, 379, 408, 409
Smoot, Reed, case of, before the Senate, 509; reply of, to charges, 510; the case of, decided, 511; defeated for Senate, 525; apostle, 594
Snow, Eliza R., 568
Snow, Erastus, accompanies Orson Pratt to Salt Lake Valley, 369; apostle, 388, 592; mission of, to Scandinavia, 396
Snow, Lorenzo, apostle, 388, 591-592; mission of, to Italy, 389; president of Church, 501, 580; statement of, on Roberts' case, 503; holds solemn assembly, 505; issues bonds, 504; teaches tithing, 504; death of, 506; counselor in first presidency, 586; assistant counselor in first presidency, 588

Snow, Zerubbabel, 392, 405
Snyder, John, 169
Solemn assembly in Kirtland Temple, 158-159; at site of Salt Lake Temple, 395
Sonne, Alma, 535; assistant to the council of twelve, 601
Southwick, Edward, 285, 288
Spencer, Daniel, 296; leads company of pioneers, 379; calling of, to preside, 388
Spencer, Orson, 403
Spiritual gifts, decline of, 8; ceased in the primitive church, 8
Sprinkling, doctrine of, denies mercies of Christ, 9
Staines, William C., 415
Stakes of Zion, to be appointed in Missouri, 176, 177-178; organized in Illinois and Iowa, 222; organization of, in Salt Lake Valley, 379, 467; list of, 619-640; new names of, 641-649
Standing, James, 342
Standing, Joseph, murder of, 476-477
Stanton, Edward, 433
Stapley, Delbert L., apostle, 597
Statehood for Utah, 498-499
Steadwell, Mary, wounded at Haun's Mill, 195
Steele, John, 375
Steele, Young Elizabeth, 375
Stenhouse, T. B. H., 397, 445
Steptoe, Col. Edward J., 407
Stevenson, Edward, first seven presidents of seventy, 609
Stiles, Judge, 406
Stoddard, Judson L., 409
Stone, Oscar Leslie, assistant to council of twelve, 604
Stowel, Josiah, 50; testifies for Joseph Smith, 85-86
Strang, James J., 322 and note, 322
Strickland, O. F., 449, 454
Stringham, William, baptized, 85
Strong, Elial, 126
Strubble Bill, the, 493
Stout, Hosea, 397
Sugar Creek, 331
Sunday School, Mormons have best in world, 569-570; name change, 552, 569

— T —

Tabernacle, 439-440
Tabernacle Choir, at World's Fair, 498
Talmage, Rev. T. De Witt, 471, 482
Talmage, James E., apostle, 595

Tanner, Nathan Eldon, second counselor in first presidency, 586; apostle, 598; assistant to council of twelve, 602; first counselor in first presidency, 583-584
Tanner, Thomas, 360
Tarbill, Squire, 50
Taylor, Alma O., 506
Taylor, Elmina S., 543
Taylor, Henry D., assistant to council of twelve, 602
Taylor, John, loyalty of, 167; petitions Missouri legislature, 208; assists Saints to leave Missouri, 215; apostle, 179, 215, 590; sent to Carthage to see Gov. Ford, 305; in Carthage jail, 313; wounding of, 316; arrival of, from England, 359; mission of, to France, 397; remarks of, on approach of army, 410; character and labors of, 468; comment on Reynolds' case, 469-470; enjoined by the court as trustee-in-trust, 475; remarks of, at jubilee celebration, 478, 479; president of the Church, 479, 580; prediction of an approaching storm, 485; death of, 490
Taylor, John H., first seven presidents of seventy, 610
Taylor, John W., case of, 512; resignation of, 513; apostle, 593
Taylor, Margaret Y., 573
Taylor, Stephen, 401
Taylor, William W., first seven presidents of seventy, 608
Teachers, duties of, 76
Teasdale, George, apostle, 480, 593; attended services for victims of Scofield mine disaster, 505
Telegraph completed, 430
Temples, dedication of site in Zion, 112; at Kirtland, 128; blessings in Kirtland, 157; dedication of Kirtland, 159; revelation on the Nauvoo, 250-251; order of building, 256; laying cornerstones of Nauvoo, 255; dedication of font in Nauvoo, 256; first baptism in Nauvoo, 259; sealing blessings obtained in the, 281; ordinance work in Nauvoo, 330; dedication of Nauvoo, 330; site chosen for Salt Lake, 374; laying cornerstones of Salt Lake, 395-396; dedication of St. George, 459; dedication of Logan, 480-481; dedication of Manti, 492; dedication of Salt Lake, 496; dedication of Hawaiian, 520-521; dedication of Alberta, 522; dedication of Arizona, 523; dedication of Idaho Falls, 534; dedication of Swiss, 540; dedication of Los Angeles, 541; dedication of New Zealand, 541; dedication of London, 541; dedication of Oakland, 541
Tennessee Massacre, 486-487
Territorial Expansion, 466
Test Oath, the, 484
Thatcher, Moses, apostle, 593
Therlkill, George W., 375
Therlkill, Milton H., 375
"This Is the Place," 370
Thomas, Judge Jesse B., 304
Thompson, Robert B., 225, 248, 257; Church historian, 616
Tillery, Samuel (jailer), 212, 213
Times and Seasons, 257, 261
Tingey, Martha Horne, 573
Tithing, 150; law of, 178-179, 504-506
Tomlinson, Bro., assists Joseph Smith, 172
Toronto, Joseph, 397
Town, David, 286
Transubstantiation, doctrine of Catholics, 9
Tribulations to come before blessings, 110
Turley, Theodore, 212, 215, 233, 309
Turnham, Judge, 146, 211
Tuttle, Albert Theodore, first seven presidents of seventy, 611
Twelve Apostles, 73, 151, 155, 179, 318, 468-469, 588-599; assistants to, 600-605; Regional Representatives, 544

– U –

Unified Magazine, 663-664
Union Pacific Railroad, 441
Union Vedette, 433, 436
Urim and Thummim, deposited with the plates, 45, 48, 49; not to be shown, 45; delivered to Joseph Smith, 51; used in the translation of the plates, 53; revelation given through, 55; taken from Joseph Smith and restored again, 56; should be shown to three witnesses, 62
Utah Central Railroad, 441
Utah Commission, the, 483; test oath of, 484
Utah Magazine, 445
Utah, territory of, created, 392
Utah War, 405

– V –

Valdez, Jean, 10
Van Buren, Martin, answer of, to Joseph Smith, 240, 242

INDEX

Van Cott, John, first seven presidents of seventy, 608
Van Vliet, Capt. Stewart, 410-411
Vandenberg, John H., assistant to council of twelve, 604; presiding bishop, 613
Varian, Charles S., 499
Vaughan, Vernon H., 449, 451
Vedette, see Union Vedette
Venable, Dr. Samuel (mobber), 187
Vicar of Croyden, denounces printing, 14-15
Vision of Joseph Smith, 35, 38-39, 41; rejected, 41; of the Celestial Kingdom, 129; of the glories, 121

— W —

Wade Bill, the, 442
Wade, J. H., 430
Waite, Charles B. (judge), 431, 432
Walch, Charles Lloyd, Hawaiian temple, 552
Walker, Cyrus, 285, 288, 293
Walker, William, 397
Wall, Gen., 243
Wallace, George B., leads company of pioneers, 379; dedication prayer of, 396
Wandell, Charles W., 397
Ward, Thomas, 278
Warren, Maj. W. B., 329, 341-342
Washington, conspiracy in, 333
Wasson, Lorenzo D., accuses the Prophet of fleeing from the flock, 308
Water rights established, 464
Waters, dangers on the, 113
Watt, George D., 296
Webster, Daniel, 394
Wells, Daniel H., sells land to Church, 222; elected alderman of Nauvoo, 225; carries message to governor, 248; trial of Joseph Smith before, 304; defends Nauvoo, 345; second counselor in first presidency, 404, 584; at Silver Lake, 409; in Echo Canyon, 412; request of, to Gov. Shaffer, denied, 449-450; falsely accused of crime, 456; testimony of, in Miles case, 473; imprisonment of, 473-474; demonstration in honor of, 474
Wells, Heber M., 499
Wells, John, 523; second counselor to presiding bishop, 615
Wells, Junius F., 570
Wells, R. W., 139-140
Wells, Rulon S., 525; first seven presidents of seventy, 609
Wentworth, John, letter to, 261-262

West, contemplated expedition to the, 295-296; departure for the, 358-359
Weston, Samuel, justice of the peace, 136, 266
Whipple, Reed, St. George Temple, 552
Whitehead, Benjamin, defends Nauvoo, 345
Whiting, C. Bryant, Mesa Temple, 552
Whiting, Colonel, 26
Whitmer, Christian, witness of Book of Mormon, 66; to be remembered by bishop of Zion, 120; death of, 157
Whitmer, David, meets the Prophet, 59-60; baptized, 60; testimony of, 65; at organization of Church, 79; to be remembered by bishop of Zion, 120; rejected by the Saints, 173; excommunicated, 174-175
Whitmer, Jacob, witness of Book of Mormon, 66; excommunicated, 175
Whitmer, John, 60; witness of Book of Mormon, 66; Church historian, 104, 616; offers himself as ransom, 135; rejected by the Saints, 173; excommunicated, 174; withholds church record, 174; testifies to truth of Book of Mormon, 216
Whitmer, Peter, Jr., zeal of, 60; baptized, 60; witness of Book of Mormon, 66; at organization of Church, 79; mission to Lamanites, 96
Whitmer, Peter, Sen., receives the Prophet, 60; Church organized at home of, 78; Church buys farm of, 524
Whitney, Newel K., 122, 322, 358; death of, 402; presiding bishop, 612
Whitney, Orson F., 431; apostle, 596
Widtsoe, John A., supervises all missions, 525; apostle, 596
Wight, Lyman, joins the Church, 98; ordained high priest, 106; arrested on Peniston charge, 183; tried before Judge King, 183; aids in defense of Far West, 197; taken prisoner at Far West, 198, 200; in Liberty Prison, 210; escapes from Missouri, 213; disfellowshipped, 388; apostle, 591
Wilkinson, Ernest L., BYU Law School, 552
Williams, Abiathar B., affidavit of, 300
Williams, Frederick G., joins the Church, 98; on mission to Lamanites, 99; second counselor in first presidency, 127, 584; rejected as counselor in first presidency, 170, 584; return of, to the Church, 245, 584
Williams, Thomas S., 367

684   INDEX

Williams, Wiley C. (mobber), 191
Willie, James G., 399, 402
Willis, Lieut. Williams W., 351
Wilson, Alex, 424, 426
Wilson, Charles A., 449
Wilson, Harmon T., under arrest, 284, 285-286, 289, 293
Wilson, Gen. Moses, 196, 202, 205
Winder, John R., first counselor in first presidency, 507, 582; death of, 515, 582; second counselor to presiding bishop, 615
Winter Quarters, 339, 340, 356, 360, 380
Wirthlin, Joseph L., presiding bishop, 613; first counselor to presiding bishop, 614; second counselor to presiding bishop, 615
Witnesses, the Three Special, 61; revelation to, 62; behold the plates, 63-64; their testimony, 65-66; the Eight, behold the plates, 65; their testimony, 66; impossibility of collusion of, 68
Woman Suffrage, 445
Woman's Exponent, 568
Women protest against legislation, 444; anti-"Mormon," 471
Wood, William T., 137
Wooden Gun Rebellion, 451
Woodruff, Abraham O., apostle, 594
Woodruff, Wilford, loyalty of, 167; apostle, 215, 590-591; gives account of miraculous healing at Montrose, 223, 224; departs for England, 229, 231; labors of, in Herefordshire, 233; return of, from England, 235-236; preaches at first meeting in Salt Lake Valley, 371; called on mission to Canada, 380; sustained as President, 491, 580; issues the manifesto, 493; unveils the Pioneer Monument, 500; death of, 500; Church historian, 617
Woods, J. W. (attorney), 311
Woods, Rev. Sashiel (mobber), 186, 191, 200
"Word of Wisdom," 125; revelation on, 142; action of high council, 142
World War I, 516
World War II, 527-530
Worrell, Frank, 313, 314
Wycliff's Bible, 14

— Y —

YMMIA, 570-572
YWMIA, (YLMIA) 572-573
Yearsley, David D., 296
York, John, killed at Haun's Mill, 196
Young, Ann Eliza, 456

Young, Alphonzo, 296
Young, Brigham, Book of Mormon from Phineas H. Young, 88-89; visits Joseph Smith, 126; speaks in tongues, 126; apostle, 152, 588-589; loyalty of, 167; flees from Kirtland, 171; petitions Missouri Legislature, 208; assists Saints to leave Missouri, 214-215; fulfills prophecy at Far West, 215-216; departs for England with other apostles, 229; arrives in England with other apostles, 231; arrival of, in Nauvoo, 236, 319; remarks of, at special meeting of August 8, 320; transfiguration of, 320-321; loyal expression of, 329; reply of, to Gov. Ford, 329; departure of, for the West, 332; organization of pioneer camp by, 332, 334; sustained president over all the camps, 334; arrival of, at Missouri River, 336-337; revelation to, 356; in council with apostles, 358; return of, to Winter Quarters, 359; meeting of, with Battalion members from Pueblo, 367; arrival in Salt Lake Valley, 370; advice of, to pioneers in Salt Lake Valley, 371-372; exploration by, 372-373; selects site for temple, 374; instruction of, 375; return of, to Winter Quarters, 378; instructions and blessing of, for pioneers, 378; sustained as president of the Church, 381-382, 580; departure of, for the Salt Lake Valley, 384; arrival of, in Salt Lake Valley, (1848), 384; appointment of, as governor, 392; accused by territorial officials of lawlessness, 393; denies charges of federal officers, 393; at laying of cornerstones of Salt Lake Temple, 395; vision of, 396; second term of, as governor, 406-407; at celebration of Silver Lake, 409; proclamation of, 412; ultimatum of, 412-413; welcome of, to Governor Alfred Cumming, 415; attitude of, towards Arkansas emigrants, 420-421; comment of, on "Civilization," 425; accused by Cradlebaugh of Mountain Meadows crime, 428; enemies of, attempt to capture, 429; sends message over telegraph, 430; inspiration of, 435; communication of, with Gen. Sherman, 437; answer of, to the merchants, 438; advice of, to L.D.S., 439; respect of, for civil authority, 448; on trial, 454, 456; indictments against, 455; falsely accused of crime, 455; present at dedication of St. George Temple,

INDEX

459; death of, 459; the administration of, 460; president of Church, 580
Young, Brigham, Jr., apostle, 441; 592; imprisoned by Judge Emerson, 479; counselor in first presidency, 580; assistant counselor in first presidency, 588; president of quorum of twelve, 589
Young, Brigham H., kidnaping of, 342
Young, Clifford E., assistant to the council of twelve, 600
Young, Ella, 572
Young, John, death of, 246
Young, John W., first counselor in first presidency, 582; counselor in first presidency, 586-587; assistant counselor in first presidency, 588
Young, Joseph, first seven presidents of seventy, 126, 605
Young, Levi Edgar, first seven presidents of seventy, 609
Young, Phineas H., 296; Book of Mormon, 88-89; kidnapping of, 342
Young, Richard W., 219, 241
Young, Seymour B., first seven presidents of seventy, 608
Young, Seymour Dilworth, first seven presidents of seventy, 610
Young Woman's Journal, 573, 632

— Z —

Z.C.M.I., beginning of, 443
Zane, Charles S., 499
Zelph, white Lamanite, 144
Zion, days of rejoicing of, 79; a place of refuge, 104; the New Jerusalem, 104; to be built in Missouri, 107; location of, revealed, 109; dedication of land of, 110; glory of, 110, 111; object of mission to, 111; first conference in, 113; to be obtained by purchase, 116; stakes of, 123; stake of, at Kirtland, 127-128; to be built by law of consecration, 128; not to be removed, 142; to be built upon celestial law 148
Zion's camp, 143; journeys of, 143-144; threatened by the mob, 145; cholera in camp, 148; camp disbands, 148; accomplishment of, 149

ANNOUNCEMENTS

Please note - there are items in the lost and found that need to be picked up. Please check the shelf and hangers at the South East corner exit way. Thank you.

Cub Scout Pack Meeting on April 29th at the Stake Center at 7:00 pm. There will be a film on Ecology and all ward members are invited. Especially the Cub Scout's family.

A family in our ward is in need of the following pieces of furniture:
- a single bed frame and chest of drawers
- a couch that will sleep one and
- a living room chair (matched if possible)

call Edith Russell with info. 761-3755

For those of you who know Sister Gwendolyn Smith 1400 So. Ash, we are sorry to announce that her husband passed away recently. His services were Monday, April 12. Our sincere sympathy to Sister Smith and her family.

Sister Betty Tanner is home and we wish her many happy, carefree days ahead.

Primary welcomes as a new worker, Sister Terri Decker. She will teach CTR B.

*Relief Society Sisters to play tennis at 10:00 am at Floyd and Williams.

Don't forget to bring sacks for the Bishop's storehouse and toys for the nursery.

> If we lack confidence in each other, and be jealous of each other, our peace will be destroyed. If we cultivate the principles of unshaken confidence in each other, our joy will be full.
> — Brigham Young

Call 761-3755 before Tuesday evening and place your announcements and new items in the bulletin - each week.

Thank you,
Edith Russell, Editor

THE INCREDIBLE Mr. Limpet

April 23, 1976
7:00 PM
$5.00 family
$1.00 single
Refreshments

Children under 12 years - .50

Easter Sunday

Priesthood...	8:00 am
Senior Sunday School...	9:45 am

Prelude...Sister Vivian Fitzpatrick
Music Director...Sister Jan Mason
Opening Hymn #9 "In Hymns of Praise"
Invocation...Mike Allen
Special Music Number by Pat and Evan Thorley
    "Oh, Love, That Glorifies Thy Son"
Worship through music..."Resurrection"
    #4 "All Creatures of Our God and King"
    #61 "He Is Risen"
    #10 "Christ The Lord Is Risen Today"
2½ minute inspirational talks...
    Danny Jackson
    Timothy Ethington
Special musical number by Brother Jerry Gray
    "The Holy City"
Talk...Brother Mark Mason
Sacrament Hymn #201 "There is A Green Hill"
Sacrament Gem...Lee Russell
    Jesus said:...If ye love me, keep my
    commandments.
Administration of Sacrament...
Dismissal for classes...
    Benediction in class.

Junior Sunday School...	9:45 am

Coordinator...Sister Judy Campbell
Organist...Sister Deane Davis
Music Director...Sister Pat Schweighofer
Prayer...Kimberly Jackson
Sacrament Gem...Bruce Riter
    Jesus said:...If ye love me, keep my
    commandments.
2½ minute talk...
    Melenda Patterson
Dismissal for classes.

Choir...(with nursery)...	1:30 pm
Sacrament Worship Service...	2:30 pm
Special Interest Group Fireside...	8:00 pm
7th and Pearl	

Those who were at the Special Interest Group Annual Spring Banquet - enjoyed a beautiful evening.

Monday, April 19...
    Relief Society Recreation Program 10:00 am *
    Family Home Evening

Tuesday, April 20...
Primary...	4:30 pm
Webeloes...	7:00 pm
Relief Society...	7:00 pm

      Social Relations # 7
      Sister Helen Robinson

Wednesday, April 21...
Relief Society...	9:30 am

      Social Relations # 7
      Sister Edith Hall
         and
      Mother Training # 7
      Sister Jeannie Groberg

Cub Scouts...	7:00 pm
AP & YW...	7:15 pm

Thursday, April 22...

Friday, April 23...
    Special Interest Group Dinner - Tri-Stake
    Dinner Dance at Regency Inn   call 424-2353

Saturday, April 24...
    SIG cook-out....bring your lunch, drinks
    furnished. Ellsworth Park on Lookout
    Mountain. 3 pm til sundown. 424-2353.

Sunday, April 25...
Priesthood...	8:00 am
Sunday School...	9:45 am
Choir...	1:30 pm
Sacrament Worship Service...	2:30 pm
SIG Bi-Regional Fireside...	8:00 pm
7th and Pearl	

    Recognizing that the family is the basic unit of both the Church and society generally, we call upon Latter-Day Saints everywhere this year to strengthen and beautify the home with renewed effort in these specific areas:
    1. Food production, preservation and
       storage
    2. Production and storage of non-food
       items
    3. Fixup and cleanup of homes and
       surroundings.
                    President Kimball

THE CHURCH OF JESUS CHRIST OF LATTER-DAY SAINTS

DENVER 10TH WARD

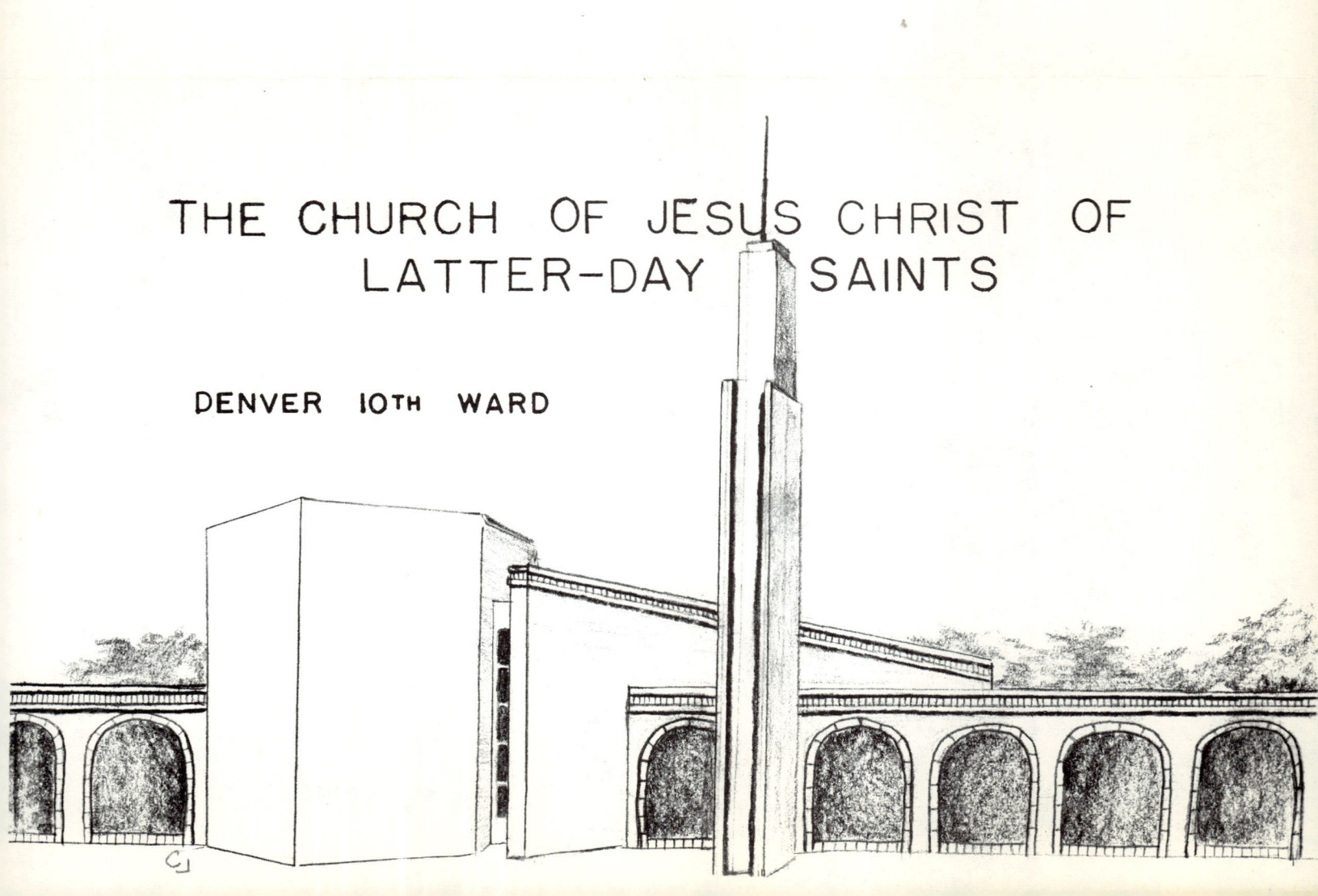